the backpacker's HANDBOOK

the backpacker's
HANDBOOK

fourth edition

CHRIS TOWNSEND

New York Chicago San Francisco Lisbon London Madrid Mexico City
Milan New Delhi San Juan Seoul Singapore Sydney Toronto

Copyright © 2012 by Chris Townsend. All rights reserved. Printed in the United States of America. Except as permitted under the United States Copyright Act of 1976, no part of this publication may be reproduced or distributed in any form or by any means, or stored in a database or retrieval system, without the prior written permission of the publisher.

2 3 4 5 6 7 8 9 10 11 12 13 14 15   DOC/DOC   1 9 8 7 6 5 4 3 2

ISBN   978-0-07-175489-7
MHID   0-07-175489-X

e-ISBN   978-0-07-175959-5
e-MHID   0-07-175959-X

Library of Congress Cataloging-in-Publication Data

Townsend, Chris, 1949-
    The backpacker's handbook / Chris Townsend. — 4th ed.
        p.   cm.
    Includes index.
    ISBN-13: 978-0-07-175489-7 (alk. paper)
    ISBN-10: 0-07-175489-X (alk. paper)
    1. Backpacking—Handbooks, manuals, etc.   I. Title.

    GV199.6.T69   2011
    796.51—dc23   2011028816

McGraw-Hill books are available at special quantity discounts to use as premiums and sales promotions or for use in corporate training programs. To contact a representative, please e-mail us at bulksales@mcgraw-hill.com.

To Denise Thorn for her patience, love, and companionship.

All drawings by Elara Tanguy unless otherwise noted. All photographs by the author unless otherwise noted. Bootprint courtesy arttoday.com.

Page	Credit
16	Map courtesy Natural Resources Conservation Service/USDA, from Hall: *The Essential Backpacker*
51	Christopher Hoyt drawing from Kestenbaum: *The Ultralight Backpacker*
75	Annie Getchell drawing from Getchell and Getchell: *The Essential Outdoor Gear Manual*
77	Christopher Hoyt drawing from Townsend: *Backpacker's Pocket Guide*
93	Ice ax courtesy Black Diamond Equipment, Ltd.
155	Mike Walsh drawings from Townsend: *The Backpacker's Handbook*, second edition
190	Christopher Hoyt drawing from Townsend: *Backpacker's Pocket Guide*
196	Christopher Hoyt drawing from Kestenbaum: *The Ultralight Backpacker*
197	Mike Walsh drawing from Townsend: *The Backpacker's Handbook*, second edition
205	Christopher Hoyt drawing from Townsend and Aggens: *Encyclopedia of Outdoor & Wilderness Skills*
274	Christopher Hoyt drawing from Townsend: *Backpacker's Pocket Guide*
275	Christopher Hoyt drawing from Townsend: *Backpacker's Pocket Guide*
282	Christopher Hoyt drawing from Townsend and Aggens: *Encyclopedia of Outdoor & Wilderness Skills*
284	Christopher Hoyt drawing from Townsend: *Backpacker's Pocket Guide*
295	Christopher Hoyt drawing from Townsend and Aggens: *Encyclopedia of Outdoor & Wilderness Skills*
305	Christopher Hoyt drawing from Townsend: *Backpacker's Pocket Guide*
360	Christopher Hoyt drawings from Townsend: *Backpacker's Pocket Guide*
361	Christopher Hoyt drawing from Townsend: *Backpacker's Pocket Guide*
369	Christopher Dowling drawing from Johnson: *The Ultimate Desert Handbook*
387	*Left:* Mike Walsh drawing from Townsend: *The Backpacker's Handbook*, second edition. *Right:* Christine Erikson drawing from Seidman: *The Essential Wilderness Navigator*
388	Christine Erikson drawing from Seidman: *The Essential Wilderness Navigator*
393	Mike Walsh drawing from Townsend: *The Backpacker's Handbook*, second edition
394	Mike Walsh drawing from Townsend: *The Backpacker's Handbook*, second edition
395	Mike Walsh drawing from Townsend: *The Backpacker's Handbook*, second edition
402	Christine Erikson drawing from Seidman: *The Essential Wilderness Navigator*
413	Christopher Hoyt drawing from Townsend and Aggens: *Encyclopedia of Outdoor & Wilderness Skills*
421	*Bottom two:* William Hamilton drawing from Hall: *The Essential Backpacker*
422	Christopher Hoyt drawing from Townsend: *Backpacker's Pocket Guide*
423	Christopher Hoyt drawing from Townsend and Aggens: *Encyclopedia of Outdoor & Wilderness Skills*

CONTENTS

PREFACE
to the fourth edition

Since the last edition of this book, seven years have gone by. During that time, I've spent time in the deep cold of winter in the Rockies, hiked the Pacific Northwest Trail, and further expanded my backpacking and wilderness experience on many other trips. I've learned new techniques, gained some new ideas, revived some old ones, and generally tried to enhance my skills and knowledge so my trips are more enjoyable and comfortable. In terms of equipment, there have been many changes, especially in the electronics field with mapping GPS, signalling devices, smartphones, e-book readers, digital cameras, and other devices becoming popular for backpacking. The lightweight-backpacking movement has spread into the mainstream to some extent, and lighter loads are now more possible than ever. New materials like Cuben Fiber have appeared, while titanium, merino wool, and silnylon have become more standard. Heat-exchanger and wood-burning stoves—old and new technology—have increased in number and popularity. All this and more is covered in this updated edition. And as always, the opinions and thoughts are mine. This is a subjective book based on what has worked for me in many thousands of miles of backpacking.

Backpacking as an activity hasn't changed, of course. Going out into the wilderness to experience nature, whether on a quiet walk in the summer woods, an exciting scramble high in the mountains, a long-distance trail hike, or a journey in the snow and cold of winter, doesn't change because of new fabrics or means of communication. As I wrote in the preface to the third edition, my memories of trips aren't about gear or the weight of my load but about the experience of being out there. The summer before writing this edition, I hiked the Pacific Northwest Trail. Thinking about that long hike, I recall the jagged peaks of the Rockies; the steep, lonely forests of the Selkirk and Purcell Mountains; waking to look over calm lakes shining in the dawn; walking through majestic old-growth forests that felt timeless and eternal; watching the sun set over glacier-clad mountains; bald eagles swooping past out of the mist; a mother bear leading two cubs into a meadow to feed; and the joy in being in the natural world for week after week. That's what backpacking is about.

ACKNOWLEDGMENTS

Far too many people have added to my store of knowledge and assisted on my walks to thank them all individually here, but some I must single out. As each edition of this book appears, the numbers grow. Although I travel solo more often than not, I've shared trails and campsites with many companions over the years, and I have many valued memories of these times. I've also spent many hours discussing backpacking with individuals and at hikers' gatherings. Many readers have written to me by e-mail and letter—a great encouragement—and I've had many discussions with other outdoor writers.

I can't mention everybody I've hiked with, talked to, or corresponded with, but I would like to thank Chris and Janet Ainsworth; Brad Allen; Judy Armstrong; Colin Baxter; Kieran Baxter; Karen Berger; Li Brannfors; Brad, Karen, and Mark Buckhout; Georgina Collins; Carey Davies; Alan Dixon; Mark Edgington; Ron Ellis; Lou Ann Fellows; Wayne Fuiten; Mick Furey; Franjo Goluza; Kris Gravette; Leanne Gravette; Rick Hagar; Brice Hammack; Sam Haraldson; Andrew Helliwell; Ed Huesers, Dave Hewitt; Pete Hickey; Andy Hicks; the late John Hinde; Tony Hobbs; Andy Howell; Graham Huntington; Colin Ibbotson; Andy Ince; Ray and Jenny Jardine; Jörgen Johansson; Ryan Jordan; Alain Kahan; Dave Key; David Knight; Larry Lake; Alex Lawrence; Rowena Lawrence-Thorn; Paul Leech; Peter and Pat Lennon; David Lynch; Duncan MacDonald; John Manning; Michael Martin; Cameron McNeish; the late Al Micklethwaite; Colin Mortlock; Eugene Miya; Tony Morfe; Joris Naiman; Steve Nelson; Tom Phillips; Dave Rehbehn; Will Rietveld; Emily Rodway; Jake Schas; Gary D. Schwartz; Todd Seniff; Pat Silver; Jane and Andy Smith; Clyde Soles; Alastair Soutar; Wallace Spaulding; Scott Steiner; Douglas K. Stream; Ron Strickland; Lesya Struz; Graham Thompson; Denise Thorn; Hazel Thorn; Dave Toms; the late Fran Townsend; John Traynor; Ronald Turnbull; Steve Twaites; Roy Wagner; Stan Walker; Bill Watson; Scott Williamson; Simon Willis; and Shirley Worrall.

I'd also like to thank all those I've met at the annual gatherings of the American Long Distance Hiking Association–West and the Appalachian Long Distance Hikers Association and at meetings of the Backpackers Club (UK), plus all those I've guided on wilderness ski tours. I've had much-appreciated help and assistance from the Appalachian Mountain Club, the Arizona Trail Association, the Pacific Northwest Trail Association, and the staffs of many national parks and national forests, especially Yosemite National Park.

Many equipment makers and designers have been generous with information and equipment. My thanks in particular to George Andrews of AntiGravity Gear; the late Chris Brasher of Brasher Boots; Nick Brown of Nikwax and Páramo; Rab Carrington of Rab; Gordon Conyers of Tor Outdoor Products; Demetri "Coup" and Kim Coupounas of GoLite; Coral Darby; Andrew Denton; Brian Frankle; Gordon Fraser of Anatom; Jeff Gray of Superfeet; Bo and Rolf Hilleberg and Peter Carati of Hilleberg; Ed Hueser of Grand Shelters (IceBox); Steve Laycock; Rand Linsly of Trail Designs; Phil Oren; Barry Robertson; Staffan Ronn of Optimus; Bob Rose, boot expert; Aaron Rosenbloom of Brasslite stoves; Christer Svensson of Silva Sweden; Aarn Tate of Aarn Designs; Glen Van Peski of Gossamer Gear.

The views expressed in this book are my own, of course. None of those mentioned above are assumed to agree with any of them.

Many thanks, too, to Molly Mulhern at International Marine.

Finally, I would like to thank my family, Denise and Hazel Thorn, for their love and their patience in listening to me rambling on about bootfitting, GPS, and more. Denise also read through the manuscript and made many valuable suggestions. Both of them posed for photographs and Hazel also took some of the photos of me.

the backpacker's
HANDBOOK

into the wilderness

> KEEP CLOSE TO NATURE'S HEART . . . AND
> BREAK CLEAR AWAY, ONCE IN AWHILE, AND
> CLIMB A MOUNTAIN OR SPEND A WEEK IN
> THE WOODS. WASH YOUR SPIRIT CLEAN.
> —*John Muir*

This is a how-to book, an instructional manual on how to hike and camp in wild country safely and in comfort. Much of the book concerns techniques and equipment—factual stuff leavened with a little bias and opinion, but down to earth and functional nonetheless. The scope, theoretically, is worldwide, though you won't find much about tropical travel; my own experience has been mostly in the wild areas of North America and Western Europe, ranging from the hot deserts of the Southwest to the Arctic wastes of Greenland.

Over the years I have made several hikes lasting many months, the sort that refine your techniques and show you what equipment works. These include through-hikes of the Pacific Crest and Continental Divide Trails; 1,600 miles along the length of the Canadian Rockies; 1,000 miles south to north through Canada's Yukon Territory; 1,300 miles through the mountains of Norway and Sweden; 1,250 miles from Land's End to John o'Groat's in Britain; 1,600 miles over the 517

summits of 3,000 feet in the Scottish Highlands; the 800-mile Arizona Trail; and the 1,200-mile Pacific Northwest Trail. These experiences, along with many shorter trips—more than thirty years of backpacking at least 25,000 miles—constitute my credentials for presuming to offer advice. Along the way I've made many mistakes; these are related for entertainment and with the hope that you can learn from them without having to experience them firsthand.

But my highest qualification is my enjoyment of backpacking, and the fact that, for me, it is a way of life, a reason for existing. I want to share that by pointing others in the same direction. The result is this book—an attempt to mesh the reasons for backpacking with the ways to do it.

Capturing the essence of backpacking in words —the joy of walking through the ever-changing, ever-constant natural world, the magic of waking to sunlight glinting on a mist-wreathed lake, the excitement of striding through a mountain

I

At the start of the Pacific Northwest Trail in Glacier National Park.

storm—is difficult. At heart I suspect it is impossible to describe this experience to those not disposed to listen. How can one convey to a skeptic the liberating sense of living in the moment, free of thinking about tomorrow; the painful delight in the exquisite beauty of a fleeting cloud, a tiny flower in an ocean of rock, a butterfly's wing; the awe engendered by a mountain vista stretching unbroken beyond the power of sight; the fragile moment of identity when you stare deeply into a wild animal's eyes and just for a second connect? But then, it's not for skeptics that this book was written. If you are interested in my thoughts on backpacking, you are already responsive to the real world outside our technological shells.

Why backpack? Why forgo the comforts of home or hotel for a night under the stars or sheltered by a flimsy nylon sheet? Many people hike in the wilds but return to civilization at night. This is experiencing only part of what the wilderness has to offer; it's like dipping your toe in the water instead of taking an invigorating swim. Only by living in the wilderness twenty-four hours a day, day after day, do you gain that indefinable feeling of rightness, of being *with* instead of *against* the earth, that gives the deepest contentment I have found.

I'm aware that this sounds mystical, but I make no apology. We are too prone to value only what can be defined in logical terms or assigned a cash value. Yet the natural, self-regulating earth cannot be quantified, calculated, and summed up—every attempt uncovers another mystery just beyond our grasp. And this pleases me. I'm content not to fully comprehend the joy I find in the wilderness; to try would be a fruitless task, like chasing the end of a rainbow; and the goal, if ever realized, would only disappoint.

The heart of backpacking lies in the concept of the journey itself, a true odyssey, a desire to explore a world beyond our everyday lives, and in doing so to explore ourselves. Not so long ago, all journeys were like this, because the known world extended little beyond one's hometown. Now, with modern communications and mass transportation, most "journeys" consist of nothing more than the mechanized moving of bodies from one place to another, a process so sanitized, safe, controlled, and so insulated from its surroundings that it precludes any sense of freedom, adventure, or personal involvement. Only when I shoulder my pack and set out into the wilderness do I feel a journey is really beginning, even though I may have traveled halfway around the world to take that first step.

A journey requires a beginning and an end, though what it is really about lies between those two points. Many journeys are circles, starting and finishing at the same place; others are point-to-point, linear hikes that finish far from where they start; and still others are there-and-back-again routes where you retrace your outbound steps. All three are appealing, but I especially like circles, routes that take you through new country every day yet return you to your starting point. A circle emphasizes the primacy of the experience rather than the conclusion. Closing the circle finishes the journey, returning you to the same place, enriched by the wilderness you have hiked through.

Though being in the wilderness is what matters, and the real goal of any hike is to experience nature, a more specific purpose gives shape to a trip and provides an incentive to keep moving. Thus I always set a goal, even on day hikes—a summit, a lake, a distance to cover, a crag to visit, a vista to see. Once I'm under way, the overall goal is subordinated to the day-by-day, minute-by-minute events and impressions that are my reason for hiking.

Walking is the only way to really see a place, to really grasp what it's like, to experience all its aspects. This is true even for cities but applies much, much more to mountains and deserts, forests and meadows. Seen from a car, a train, or even a "scenic viewpoint," these are only pretty pictures, postcard images for the surface of the mind, quickly forgotten. By walking through a landscape, you enter into it, experience it with every one of your senses, learn how it works and why it's as it is. You become, for a time, a part of it. And once you stay out overnight and entrust your sleeping self to its care, a deeper bond is forged and, fleetingly and at the edge of your mind, you begin to grasp that we are not apart from but part of the earth.

This process of exploring the relationship between the self and the natural world grows and expands as you become more experienced and confident in wilderness wandering. It does not, I suspect, have limits. Perhaps it reflects a need to return to or at least acknowledge our primordial roots, to recall the time, the vast time that covers most of human existence, when humans were nomadic hunter-gatherers.

I would not contemplate returning to such a state, even if it were possible. Civilization has good points as well as bad ones, but I do think we have gone too far toward a belief that we are superior to and separate from nature, that it exists for us to tame, control, and exploit. And in taming and controlling nature we tame and control ourselves, losing our freedom and the ability to live in and be part of the wilderness.

If backpacking has any validity apart from being an enriching personal experience (good enough in itself, of course), it lies in this. At a time when the balance of nature itself is threatened, backpackers in particular should understand that we have to change our ways, to acknowledge that our interests coincide with nature's. By experiencing the wilderness directly, by being in touch with the land, we can learn how valuable—how essential—it is, and that we must try to preserve and restore our still-beautiful world.

But what do we mean by *wilderness*, a magic word, redolent of mountain and forest, untamed nature and wild beauty? As defined by the Wilderness Act of 1964, wilderness is "an area where the earth and its community of life are untrammeled by man, where man himself is a visitor who does not remain." To be viable as a complete ecosystem, a wilderness needs to be large—huge, even—providing space for wildlife to survive and live free and for the landscape to be complete from valley bottom to mountaintop, from foothills to highest peaks. These vast, pristine areas are the prime places for backpacking, places of dreams

The Rocky Mountains in Glacier National Park.

and adventures. However, many areas backpackers hike are neither this size nor untouched. In Europe in particular, wilderness areas are small and, if defined in terms of never having been touched by human hand, virtually nonexistent. I think that wilderness is as much an idea, a concept, as a physical reality. If there is enough land to walk into, enough room to set up a camp and then walk on with that freedom that comes when you escape the constraints of modern living, then it is wilderness, in spirit if not by definition.

All wilderness areas need defending, from the vast expanse of Antarctica to the small pockets that still exist even in heavily industrialized countries. That there are places you can reach only on foot, requiring effort and commitment to visit, is vital. It will be a sad day when the last such spot succumbs to the paved road and the hollow stares of detached tourists.

Ironically, wilderness also needs defending from those who love it. Damaging practices and an increasing number of hikers are turning many popular areas into worn-out remnants. Wilderness travelers traditionally lived off the land for shelter as well as for food; they built lean-tos and tepees, cut boughs for mattresses and logs for tables and chairs. Today this is irresponsible—and often illegal—in most wilderness areas. There is too little wilderness left, and every scar diminishes what remains.

Even with modern equipment, backpackers have more impact on the land than dayhikers and therefore have more responsibilities. No-trace, low-impact camping must be the norm if the wilderness is to stay intact. This book emphasizes these techniques, because there are only two solutions to the problem of hikers' damaging the wilderness: self-regulation and the practice of minimum-impact techniques by all, or bureaucratic regulation, which already is the norm in many parks worldwide. In some areas wilderness camping is allowed only on specified sites. In a few places in the Alps and elsewhere, wild camping is forbidden altogether, and people are required to use campgrounds or stay in mountain huts. Such restrictions are anathema to the spirit of freedom inherent in backpacking, but they will become common unless backpackers learn to respect the wilderness.

preparing for the trail

FAREWELL WE CALL TO HEARTH AND HALL!
THOUGH WIND MAY BLOW AND RAIN MAY FALL,
WE MUST AWAY ERE BREAK OF DAY
FAR OVER WOOD AND MOUNTAIN TALL.
—*J. R. R. Tolkien*, The Lord of the Rings

Backpacking isn't difficult, but it does require both physical and mental preparation. Every year, first-time hikers set off along the trail unfit, ill equipped, and with unrealistic expectations. Many of them never venture into the wilderness again. The better your planning, the more enjoyable your trip will be. You need not know exactly how far you'll walk each day, or precisely where you'll camp each night (though such detailed planning is useful for beginners), but you should know your capabilities and desires well enough to tailor your trip to them. Setting out to carry 65 pounds twenty-five miles a day through steep, mountainous terrain just about guarantees exhaustion, frustration, and disappointment unless you are extremely fit and know beforehand that you can do it.

FITNESS

Backpacking requires fitness. You need aerobic, or cardiovascular, fitness to walk and climb all day without having your heart pound and your lungs gasp for air. Without muscular fitness, particularly of the legs, you'll be stiff and aching all over on the second day out. Also, if you set out unfit, you're much more susceptible to strains and muscle tears.

Getting fit takes time. I know people who claim they'll get fit over the first few days of an annual backpacking trip. They usually suffer for most of the walk; yet with a little preparation, they could enjoy every day.

The best way to train for carrying heavy loads over rough terrain is to carry heavy loads over rough terrain—what sports trainers call *specific training*. Although this isn't always practical, you'd be surprised what you can do if you really want to, even if you live and work in a city. In *Journey Through Britain*, John Hillaby wrote that he trained for his 1,100-mile, end-to-end walk across Britain by spending the three months before the trip walking the six miles "from Hamp-

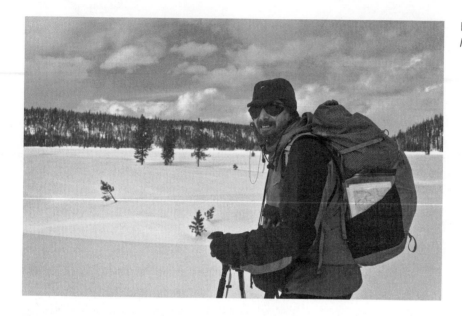

*Winter in Yellowstone
National Park.*

stead to the City [London] each day and farther at the weekends. On these jaunts I carried weight lifters' weights sewn high up in a flat rucksack that didn't look too odd among people making their way to the office in the morning."

At the very least, spend a few weekends getting used to walking with a load before setting off on a longer trip. Walk as much as you can during the week—including up and down stairs. Brisk strolls or runs in the evening help too, especially if there are hills. In fact, trail running in hilly country is probably the best way to improve both your aerobic fitness and your leg power in a short time.

I trained at a fitness center once, before a through-hike of the Canadian Rockies. For six months I did hour-long circuit sessions on the weight machines three times a week and hour-long runs on the days between, with one day off a week. It helped, but probably no more than if I'd hiked regularly with a pack and exercised in the woods and fields, which I prefer. I haven't followed an exercise program since. Good advice on training is contained in Courtney and Doug Schurman's *The Outdoor Athlete*. The main thing I learned from fitness center training was that you need rest from strenuous exercise and that you need to pace yourself. I'd never heard of overtraining before, having never regarded backpacking or hiking as a "sport." But once I discovered that pushing yourself too hard results, unsurprisingly, in excess stress to the body and reduced performance, I understood why, after hiking all day every day for two weeks or more, I often felt tired and run-down instead of superfit. Now on walks longer than two weeks I aim to take a rest day every week to twelve days. I don't stick to a rigid timetable—a day off every week, say—but rather pay attention to my body and my mind. If I feel lethargic or uninterested, develop aches and pains, or find myself being clumsy and careless, I know I need to rest. Resting while training is important—if you force yourself to train hard every day because you've got a big trip coming up, you may burn out before the hike starts.

After my brief bout with the fitness center, I abandoned formal training and returned to short, brisk hikes in the local woods and fields, the occasional 5- to 10-mile cycle ride, and as an aim if not in reality, at least one full day a week walking or skiing in the mountains. This is apart from the two- to three-day backpacking trips I try to take once a month or so between longer walks.

If you haven't exercised for some time, return to it gradually, especially if you're over thirty-five. Preparing for a walk takes time anyway. You can't go from being unfit to toting a heavy load all day in a week or even a month.

THE ART OF WALKING

While the simple act of putting one foot in front of the other seems to require no instruction or comment, there are, in fact, good and bad ways to walk, and good and bad walkers. Good walkers can walk effortlessly all day, while bad ones may be exhausted after a few hours.

To make walking seem effortless, walk slowly and steadily, finding a *rhythm* that lets you glide along and a *pace* you can keep up for hours. Without a comfortable rhythm, every step seems tiring, which is one reason that crossing boulder fields, brush-choked forest, and other broken terrain is so exhausting. Inexperienced walkers often start off at a rapid pace, leaving the experienced plodding slowly behind. As in Aesop's ancient fable of the tortoise and the hare, slower walkers often pass exhausted novices long before a day's walk is complete.

The ability to maintain a steady pace hour after hour has to be developed. If you need a rest, take one; otherwise you'll wear yourself out.

The difference between novices and experts was graphically demonstrated to me when I was leading backpacking treks for an Outward Bound school in the Scottish Highlands. I let the students set their own pace, often following them or tra-

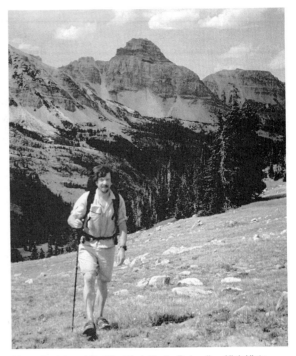

Mount Beulah and the West Fork Blacks Fork valley, High Uinta Wilderness, Utah.

versing at a higher level than the group. But one day the course supervisor, an experienced mountaineer, turned up and said he'd lead the day's walk—and he meant *lead*. Off he tramped, the group following in his footsteps, while I brought up the rear. Initially, we followed a flat river valley, and soon the students were muttering impatiently about the supervisor's slow pace. The faint trail began to climb after a while, and on we went at the same slow pace, with some of the students close to rebellion. Eventually we came to the base of a steep, grassy slope with no trail. The supervisor didn't pause—he just headed up as if the terrain hadn't altered. After a few hundred yards, the tenor of the students' response changed. "Isn't he ever going to stop?" they complained. One or two fell behind. Intercepting a trail, we turned up it, switchbacking steadily to a high pass. By now some of the students seemed in danger of collapse, so I hurried ahead to the supervisor and said they needed a rest. He seemed surprised. "I'll see you later then," he said, and started down, his pace unaltered, leaving the students slumping in relief.

This story also reveals one of the problems of walking in a group: each person has his or her own pace. The best way to deal with this is not to walk as a large group but to establish pairs or small groups of walkers with similar abilities, so people can proceed at their own pace, meeting up at rest stops and in camp. If a large group must stay together, perhaps because of bad weather or difficult route finding, let the slowest member set the pace, perhaps leading at least some of the time. It is neither fair nor safe to let the slowest member fall far behind the group, and if this happens to you, you should object.

The ability to walk economically, using the least energy, comes only with experience. If a rhythm doesn't develop naturally, it may help to try to create one in your head. I sometimes do this on long climbs if the right pace is hard to find and I'm constantly stopping to catch my breath. I often chant rhythmically any words that come to mind. When I can remember them, I find the poems of Robert Service or Longfellow are good. I need to repeat only a few lines: "There are strange things done in the midnight sun / By the men who moil for gold; / The Arctic Trails have their secret tales / That would make your blood run cold" (from Service's "The Cremation of Sam McGee"). If I begin to speed up, I chant out loud, which slows me down. It is of course impossible to walk for a long time at a faster-than-normal pace, but walking too slow is surprisingly tiring, since it is hard to establish a rhythm.

Once in a while all the aspects of walking come together, and then I have an hour or a day when I simply glide along, seemingly expending no energy. When this happens, distance melts under my feet, and I feel I could stride on forever. I can't force such moments, and I don't know where they come from, but the more I walk, the more often they happen. Not surprisingly, they occur most often on really long treks. On such days, I'll walk for five hours and more without a break, yet with such little effort that I don't realize how long and far I've traveled until I finally stop. Rather than hiking, I feel as though I'm flowing through the landscape. I never feel any effects afterward, except perhaps greater contentment.

Distance

How far can I walk in a day? This is a perennial question asked by walkers and nonwalkers alike. The answer depends on your fitness, the length of your stride, how many hours you walk, the weight you're carrying, and the terrain. There are formulas for making calculations, including a good one proposed in the late nineteenth century by William W. Naismith, a luminary of the Scottish Mountaineering Club. Naismith's formula allows one hour for every 3 miles, plus an extra half hour for every 1,000 feet of ascent. I've used this as a guide for years, and it seems to work; a 15-mile day with 4,000 feet of ascent takes me, on average, eight hours including stops. Of course, 15 miles on a map will be longer on the ground, since map miles are flat miles, unlike most terrain. As slopes steepen, the distance increases.

The time I spend between leaving one camp and setting up the next is usually eight to ten hours, not all of it spent walking. I once measured my pace against distance posts on a flat, paved road in the Great Divide Basin during a Conti-

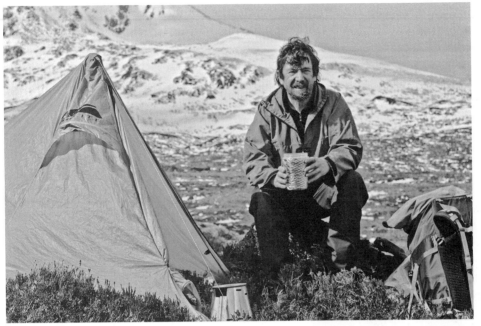

A spring camp in the
Scottish Highlands.

nental Divide hike. While carrying a 55-pound pack, I went about 3¾ miles an hour. At that rate I would cover 37 miles in ten hours if I did nothing but walk (and the terrain was smooth and flat). In practice, however, I probably spend no more than seven hours of a ten-hour day walking, averaging about 2½ miles an hour if the terrain isn't too rugged. That speed, for me, is fast enough. Backpacking is about living in the wilderness, not racing through it. I cover distance most quickly on roads—whether tarmac, gravel, or dirt—because I always want to leave them behind as soon as possible.

How far you can push yourself to walk in a day is less important than how far you are happy walking in a day. This distance can be worked out if you keep records of your trips. I plan walks based on 15 miles a day on trails and over easy terrain. For difficult cross-country travel, I estimate 12 miles a day.

ADDITIONAL DISTANCE HIKED FOR SLOPES OF DIFFERENT ANGLES OVER ONE MILE ON THE MAP

Slope Angle	Height Gained	Additional Distance Traveled
10°	930 feet	1.5%/80 feet
20°	1,920 feet	6.5%/340 feet
30°	3,050 feet	15.5%/815 feet
40°	4,435 feet	31.0%/1,615 feet
45°	5,280 feet (1 mile)	41.0%/2,186 feet
50°	6,295 feet	56.0%/2,936 feet
60°	9,146 feet	100%/5,289 feet (1 mile)

When planning treks, it also helps to know how far you can walk over a complete trip. You can get an idea by analyzing your previous walks. For example, I averaged 16 miles a day on the 2,600-mile Pacific Crest Trail (PCT), a 1,600-mile Canadian Rockies walk, a 1,300-mile Scandinavian mountains walk, and an 800-mile Arizona Trail hike and 16¾ miles a day on the 3,000-mile Continental Divide, which seems amazingly consistent. A closer look, however, reveals that daily distances varied from 6 to 30 miles, and the time between camps varied from three to fifteen hours. All these walks were mainly on trails. My 1,000-mile Yukon walk was mostly cross-country, and on that my average dropped to 12½ miles a day.

Backpackers at a remote overlook.

One problem with a two-week summer backpacking trip is that many people spend the first week struggling to get fit and the second week turning the first week's efforts into hard muscle and greater lung power. By the time they're ready to go home, they're at peak fitness. The solution is to temper your desires. It's easy in winter to make ambitious plans for the next summer's hikes that fall apart the first day out as you struggle to carry your pack half the distance you intended. On all walks, I take it easy until I feel comfortable being on the move again. This breaking-in period may last only a few hours on a weekend trip or a couple of weeks on a long summer trek. On two-week trips, it's a good idea to take it easy the first two or three days by walking less distance than you hope to cover later in the trip, especially if you're not as fit as you intended to be.

GOING ALONE

It's customary to advise hikers never to go alone, but I can hardly do that since I travel solo more often than not—I feel it's the best way to experience the wilderness. Only when I go alone do I achieve the feeling of blending in with the natural world and being part of it. The heightened awareness that comes with solo walking is always absent when I'm with others. Solitude is immeasurably rewarding. Going alone also gives me the freedom of self-determination. I can choose to walk twelve hours one day but only three the next, or to spend half a day watching otters or lying in the tent wondering if the rain will ever stop without having to consult anyone else. This is more than just freedom or what might seem self-indulgence, though. At a deeper level it's about finding your natural rhythm, the one where your body and mind work best and which is unique to you, and attuning it to the rhythms of nature. Your rhythm is most obvious when you're walking, but it is there when you eat, sleep, and rest. You can slip into this rhythm much more easily alone than with others, when it may not even be possible.

Of course, solo walking has its dangers, and it's up to you to calculate what risks you're prepared to take. When crossing steep boulder fields or fording streams, I'm always aware that if I slip there's no one to go for help. The solo walker must weigh every action carefully and assess every risk. In the foothills of the Canadian Rockies I once spent eight days struggling cross-country through rugged terrain. I was constantly aware that even a minor accident could have serious consequences, especially since I was also way off the trail. Such situations demand greater care than trail travel, where a twisted ankle may mean no more than a painful limp out to the road and potential rescuers may not be too far away.

The wilderness is far safer than civilization. Having a car accident on your way to the wilderness is more likely than getting injured while you're there.

Leaving Word

You always should leave word with somebody about where you are going and when you'll be back, especially if you're going out alone. The route details you leave may be precise or vague—but you must leave some indication of your plans with a responsible person. If you're leaving a car anywhere, you should tell someone when you'll be back for it. This isn't a problem in places where you must register a trail permit, but elsewhere a parked car could cause concern or even lead to an unnecessary rescue attempt if it's there for many days. Unfortunately, leaving a note on your car is an invitation to thieves.

Whenever you've said you'll let someone know you're safe, you *must* do so. Rescue teams have spent too many hours searching for hikers who were back home or relaxing in a café because someone expecting word didn't receive it.

SLACKPACKING AND FASTPACKING

Different hiking styles produce different outlooks —philosophies, even, if that's not too grand a word for a simple pleasure. Some hikers stride along the trail, aiming for the maximum mileage per hour, day, or week. Others dash up and down the peaks, bagging as many summits as possible. The more contemplative meander through forests and meadows, studying flowers, watching clouds, or simply staring into the distance when the spirit moves them.

The term *slackpacker* was first coined to describe Appalachian Trail (AT) hikers who, while intent on walking the entire 2,150 miles, nevertheless planned on doing it as casually as possible. Now it's often used to mean hiking without a heavy pack, which is accomplished by having gear and supplies transported to road crossings along the route. In this book I use the original meaning.

One of the walkers the description was first applied to holds the record for the slowest continuous Appalachian Trail walk: o.d. coyote (his "trail" name—an AT tradition—which has become his real name) took 263 days for his hike, an average of 8 miles a day.

In the September–October 1994 issue of *Appalachian Trailway News*, the journal of the Appalachian Trail Conference, o.d. coyote described slackpacking as an "attempt to backpack in a manner that is never trying, difficult, or tense, but in a slowly free-flowing way that drifts with whatever currents of interest, attraction, or stimulation are blowing at that moment" and wrote that slackpacking means escaping from "our culture's slavish devotion to efficiency" and banishing "the gnawing rat of goal-orientation" by relearning how to play.

The opposite of slackpacking is *fastpacking*, or *powerhiking*, which maximizes daily mileage by walking for long hours with only a few short stops. It can mean speed hiking, too, where you hike as fast as possible, but speed isn't the main aim—distance is. Fastpackers usually travel ultralight so they don't need to rest often. They can cover more miles and therefore see more in a weekend or hike long trails in half the normal time. Ultimately fastpacking merges into *trail running*, so I was interested but not surprised to hear from one fastpacker that he'd run sections of the Appalachian Trail while through-hiking. Fastpacking and trail running may sound like tough, painful work, but for devotees there are many rewards. Hearken to the words of long-distance runner John Annerino, who has run the length of the Grand Canyon on both the north and south sides of the Colorado River: "And so I run, run like the wind, the wind pushing me across a rainbow of joy that now extends from one end of the Grand Canyon to the other. The running is a fantasy come alive; there is no effort, nor is there the faintest hint of pain. It is pure flight" *(Running Wild)*. And British long-distance wilderness runner Mike Cudahy, who has run the 270-mile Pennine Way in England in under three days, offers this explanation for the "indescribable joy" that can occur on a long, hard run: "Perhaps the artificiality of a conventional and sophisticated society is stripped away and the simple, ingenuous nature of a creature of the earth is laid bare."

Fastpacking and slackpacking are extremes. Most backpackers do neither, but everyone tends toward one or the other. Is one better? No. Different approaches are right for different people. There's nothing wrong with walking the Appalachian Trail at 8 miles a day or running the length of the Grand Canyon in a week—as long as it satisfies and rejuvenates you and you respect nature and the land you are moving through. There's no need for hikers to criticize each other for being too fast or too slow, for bagging peaks or collecting miles, for going alone or in large groups, for sticking to trails or not sticking to trails—for being, in fact, different from the critic.

I've tried most forms of wilderness walking and running, including attempting 100 miles in forty-eight hours and more than one two-day mountain marathon race. I've also wandered mountains slowly, averaging maybe 10 miles a day. Overall, I prefer the latter approach, but I wouldn't call it superior. At times during long runs I've felt flashes of what Annerino describes, but these moments have never made up for my exhaustion and aching limbs. I gain the greatest fulfillment on backpacking trips lasting weeks at a time. How far I walk on such trips doesn't seem to matter. It's living in the wilds twenty-four hours a day, day after day, that's important to me. I still enjoy walking fast and am quite happy doing 25 to 30 miles a day in easy terrain with a light load, but I don't like *having* to do so. I like to know I can stop whenever I want, for as long as I want.

There are practical reasons for being able to cover long distances at times, though. Being able to travel fast if necessary can be important for safety. Having that ability in reserve means you are always hiking within your capabilities, so if a storm arises or you find your planned campsite a morass, you'll have the extra energy and strength to keep going. And if the weather or unforeseen hazards—difficult river crossings, blocked trails—slow you down, being able to hike fast for a day or two can mean finishing the trip when you intended without arriving exhausted and footsore.

To experience all that walking has to offer, it's worth trying different approaches. If you generally amble along, stopping frequently, try pushing yourself occasionally to see what it feels like. If you always zoom over the hills, eating up the miles, then slow down once in a while, take long rest stops, look around.

PLANNING

In its simplest form, planning means packing your gear and setting off with no prescribed route or goal in mind. This is what I sometimes do in areas I know well, especially when the weather might affect any route plans I did make. I've even done it in areas I've never visited before so that I could go wherever seemed interesting. Once, owing to an eleventh-hour assignment to attend and write about a mountain race, I found myself in the Colorado Rockies with ten days to spare and no plans. Having no route, no clear destination, worried me at first. Where would I go, and why? But there was freedom in not knowing. I didn't have to walk a certain distance each day. There were no deadlines, no food drops, no campsites to book in advance. I could wander at will. Or not wander. The Colorado Rockies are ideal for such an apparently aimless venture, because their small pockets of wilderness are easy to escape when you need to resupply or want a day or two in town.

Usually, though, a little more planning is required. Guidebooks, maps, Web sites, DVDs, CD-ROMs, and magazine articles can all provide information on where to go. A Web search with Google is a good place to start. Once you've selected an area, you can obtain up-to-date information from the land managers—the National Park Service, the Forest Service, the Bureau of Land Management, or state forest or park services.

There is no such thing as too much information. The problem is sorting out what is useful from what is irrelevant. Information on water

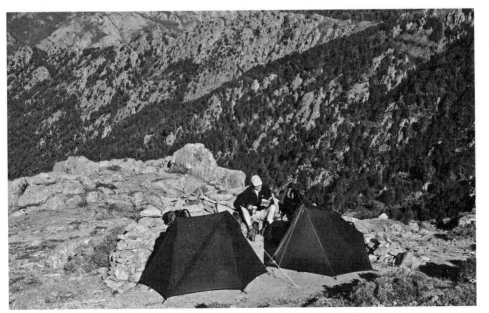

A high camp on the GR20 long-distance trail on the island of Corsica.

Squaw Lake,
John Muir
Wilderness,
High Sierra.

sources may be unnecessary in wet coastal mountains, but it's critical in the desert. The Internet can quickly overwhelm you with masses of information. Start to sift through it though, and you'll find that much is not of value for your hike. Consider whom the site is aimed at; often it's not hikers. Many Web sites are updated regularly, some daily. Up-to-date local knowledge is still important, however. Nothing beats talking to someone who hiked over that ridge last week or drank from that spring yesterday. In really remote areas like the Yukon, local knowledge is invaluable. On my walk through that area, I changed my route several times based on information from locals.

For the initial route planning I use small-scale (1:250,000) maps covering large areas before purchasing the appropriate topographic maps and working out a more detailed line. DeLorme's Atlas and Gazetteer volumes—one for each state of the United States—and similar volumes are excellent for an overview of an area. Mapping software can be used too, though I find it easier to plan routes on a large paper map than on a screen, probably because I've had years of practice. When planning I'm always aware, however, that cross-country routes may be impassable or that a far more obvious way may show itself, so I don't stick rigidly to my prehike plans. It's easy to draw bold lines across a paper map, carried away by the excitement of anticipation, without considering the reality of trying to walk the route.

One of the big problems with planning a hike of more than a few days is resupplying. For popular trails like the Appalachian and the John Muir, there are regularly updated lists of facilities like post offices and grocery stores. There are even companies that will ship food parcels to you. Hikers may be rare or even unheard of in other places, however, so it's always best to write and ask about amenities.

Permits

Most areas don't require permits, but many national parks and some wilderness areas with easy access do. The number of permits issued may be severely restricted in the most popular places, making it essential to apply long before your trip. If you want to backpack popular trails in national parks like Grand Canyon or Yosemite, you need to apply for a permit many months in advance and must be flexible about your route. Whatever you think about limiting numbers by permit (I would rather see access made more difficult by long walk-ins in place of entry roads and back-country parking lots), it means that even in popular areas, you won't meet too many people. There remain vast areas of less-frequented wilderness where permits aren't needed, and even the trails most crowded in summer are usually quiet out of season, making permits much easier to obtain. On a two-week ski-backpacking trip through the

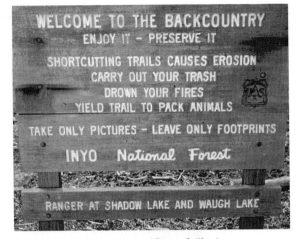

Backcountry advice, Inyo National Forest, California.

High Sierra in May, my group encountered only two other parties, both on the same day. Where good campsites are rare, such as the Grand Canyon, you can camp only in certain spots and must have a permit for each site in the most visited areas, though wild camping is allowed elsewhere in the park. It's best to check whether permits are needed before making firm plans for an area.

Long-Distance Trails

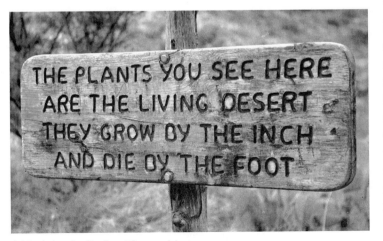

Advice to tread softly, Grand Canyon, Arizona.

Many backpackers dream of hiking a long-distance trail in one continuous journey. The big three National Scenic Trails, known as the Triple Crown, are the 2,100-mile Appalachian Trail, the 2,600-mile Pacific Crest Trail, and the 3,100-mile Continental Divide Trail (CDT). Hiking such mammoth distances is a major undertaking. A few people have set off on one of these with no more than a hazy idea of the route or what to expect yet have completed the whole trail. But far more give up within the first few days or weeks—and this includes those who do some planning. The numbers succeeding have increased since the previous edition of this book, however. Then, just 15 to 20 percent of PCT through-hikers completed the trail. Now, of the three hundred or so who set off each year, some 60 percent finish (information from the Pacific Crest Trail Association). Figures for the much more popular Appalachian Trail aren't so good. Of the two thousand or so through-hikers each year, only 20–30 percent reach the end (information from the Appalachian Trail Conference).

There are various reasons for failure. Heavy packs, sore feet, exhaustion, overly ambitious mileage goals, unexpected weather, terrain, and trail conditions are the most common. Detailed planning is advisable for a long-distance hike, especially one that will take several months. A surprising number of hikers set off each spring for Mount Katahdin, Maine (the northernmost point of the AT), having done no more than a few weekend hikes, if that. This in itself ensures a high failure rate. A gradual progression—an apprenticeship, in fact—should precede a multimonth trip. Before attempting one of the big three, try hiking a shorter but still challenging trail, such as the 211-mile John Muir Trail in California, the 471-mile Colorado Trail, or the 265-mile Long Trail in Vermont. My first solo distance hike, a seventeen-day,

The U.S. offers many backpacking opportunities.

270-mile trip along Britain's Pennine Way, followed several years of two- to five-day trips. Two years later, I made a 1,250-mile Britain end-to-end hike. Then, after another three years of shorter trips, I set out on the Pacific Crest Trail. I still made lots of mistakes, but I had enough knowledge and determination to finish the walk. If it had been my first distance hike, I doubt I would have managed more than a few hundred miles.

Preparation for a long trek doesn't mean just dealing with logistics—knowing where to send food supplies, where stores and post offices are, how far you can realistically walk per day—it also means accepting that at times you will be wet, cold, or hungry and the trail will be hard to follow. Adventures are unpredictable by definition. Every long walk I've done included moments when I felt like quitting, but I've always continued, knowing the moment would pass. If the time ever comes when the moment doesn't pass, I'll stop. If backpacking isn't enjoyable, it's pointless. Completing the trail doesn't matter—it's what happens along the way that's significant.

For me, the ultimate backpacking experience is to spend weeks or months in wilderness areas without long-distance trails, or sometimes without any trails at all. Walking a route of my own is more exciting and satisfying than following a route someone else has planned.

Planning such a walk can be difficult, however. Compiling information takes time, and there are always gaps. The easiest approach is to link shorter trails, as I did for the southern half of my walk the length of the Canadian Rockies. Even there, though, I had to travel cross-country on one trailless section.

First, of course, you have to decide where you want to start and finish. This inspiration can come from the nature of the land, from the writings of others, and occasionally from photographs. My first long-distance walk from Land's End to John o'Groat's was inspired by John Hillaby's *Journey Through Britain*. Soon after that walk I read *Hamish's Mountain Walk*, by Hamish Brown, about the first continuous round of the Munros, Scottish mountains over 3,000 feet high. Brown's walk inspired a couple of 500-mile walks in the Scottish Highlands, but the idea of a *really* long walk there was put aside in favor of other ventures. A PCT walk was inspired by a slide show of the Yosemite backcountry and by Colin Fletcher's *The Thousand-Mile Summer*. On the PCT, I learned of the CDT, so it was that trail I hiked next. On a ski-backpacking trip in the Canadian Rockies I came upon Ben Gadd's *Handbook of the Canadian Rockies* and read that no one had hiked the length of the range. Another dream was born. A later Yukon trip was, in a sense, a continuation of this walk into an area I'd read about in the writings of Jack London and Robert Service.

I always thought that one day I would hike all the Munros in one go. The spur that turned a vague thought into a concrete plan came from another book, Andrew Dempster's fascinating *The Munro Phenomenon*, a sentence of which flew off the page: "It is interesting and almost strange that no one has yet attempted all the Munros and Tops in a single expedition." I knew instantly that I wanted to try this—a round of all 517 of Scotland's 3,000-foot summits. A year later I set off. (For the story of this walk, see my book *The Munros and Tops*.)

The thought of being the first to do something lends excitement and adventure to an expedition. Yes, the heart of any backpacking trip is spending weeks at a time living in wild country, and it is the great pleasure and satisfaction of doing this that sends me back again and again. But a goal gives a walk focus—a shape, a beginning, and an end.

The initial buzz of excitement eventually gives way to a sober assessment of what is involved. This is the point at which ventures come closest to being abandoned. The planning often seems more daunting than the walk itself, but once begun, it's usually enjoyable.

The Scottish summits walk and the one that preceded it, a 1,300-mile traverse of the mountains of Norway and Sweden, both took place in mostly wet and windy weather. In between them I had spent two weeks hiking in the Grand Canyon. Having had enough of dampness and mist and loving the sharp clarity and burning sunshine of the Southwest, I decided my next long hike

would be the 800-mile Arizona Trail, a route still incomplete in many places. On the Scottish and Scandinavian hikes I never carried more than a pint of water, and mostly I carried none. In Arizona I often carried a gallon and sometimes three gallons. (The story of that hike is told in *Crossing Arizona.*) Water went from being an insignificant concern during the planning stages to the most important factor. Most recently, I hiked the 1,200-mile Pacific Northwest Trail, a tough trail still in its infancy with much rugged terrain, many barely visible trails, and some hard bushwhacking. On this trail, I hiked both sections where a shortage of water sources meant I had to carry a gallon or

Spring backpacking by the Dubh Lochain, Beinn A'Bhuird, Cairngorm National Park, Scotland.

more and sections where heavy rain meant there was too much water, making stream fords dangerous and difficult.

Planning a hike, whether for a weekend or a summer, takes time and energy, and the adventure itself can vanish in a welter of lists, logistics, maps, and food. This is only temporary, of course. When you take that first step, all the organization fades into the background. Then it's just you and the wilderness.

Moose, Kidney Lake, High Uinta Wilderness, Utah.

chapter two

the load on your back

Backpacking is about enjoying nature, about experiencing the wilderness—not about suffering. But many people are put off by the prospect of carrying on their backs everything they need for days, maybe even weeks. To the uninitiated the load looks backbreaking, a burden that will take all the joy out of walking, all the pleasure from a day in the mountains. For the uninformed novice, this may be true. It certainly was for me when I began. I am not a masochist, however; I don't like aching shoulders, sore hips, and trail-pounded, blistered feet. Nor do I like being wet or cold. After suffering all those conditions in my first attempts at backpacking, I developed a keen interest in techniques and equipment and learned that backpacking can be pleasurable and pain-free.

While experience and skill play a large part, no amount of technique will allow a poorly designed pack to carry 50 pounds comfortably or make a leaking rain jacket waterproof. Experienced backpackers are able to avoid such problems, however. The right equipment can make the difference between a trip you want to repeat and a nightmare that will make you shudder every time you see a pack. I've met walkers who recoil at the mere mention of backpacking, muttering about their one attempt on the Appalachian Trail—how their backs ached, their knees gave way, their tents leaked, and they suffered for weeks afterward. It doesn't have to be like that.

My interest in equipment was born from a couple of day hikes on which I got soaked (inadequate rain gear) and then lost (no compass), resulting in difficult night descents (no flashlight on the first occasion, dead batteries and no spares on the second) and near hypothermia. On my first camping trips I lugged a heavy canvas tent that leaked at the merest hint of rain in a pack that resembled a medieval torture rack. Not that I ever carried the tent into the wilderness—reaching a valley campground from a bus stop was exhausting enough. I used this equipment through ignorance; I didn't know anything better existed.

Two long-ago experiences showed me what was possible. Once, another hiker was horrified at the sight of my huge pack frame. "No hipbelt?" he exclaimed. "What's a hipbelt?" I replied. He handed me his pack, an even bigger one than mine. I put it on and tightened the hipbelt. The weight of the pack seemed to melt away. Ever since, I've viewed a hipbelt as the key feature of any pack designed for heavy loads. The other occasion was at a roadside campground when I was using a very heavy wooden-poled canvas tent. Sitting outside this monstrosity, I watched a walker with a moderate-size pack come down from the mountains and pitch a tiny green nylon tent. The next morning he packed everything up, shouldered his modest load, and headed—effortlessly it seemed—back into the wilderness. The realization that it was possible to backpack

in comfort led me to visit outdoor shops, write away for equipment catalogs, and read everything I could find about backpacking.

Later I worked in an equipment shop and started writing reviews of gear for outdoor magazines. I've been doing this since the 1970s and have acquired a fairly detailed knowledge of what to look for in equipment. It's important, though, not to assign gear a greater value than it deserves—it's only a tool. Backpacking is not about having the latest tent or trying out the new clothing system "guaranteed to keep you comfortable in all

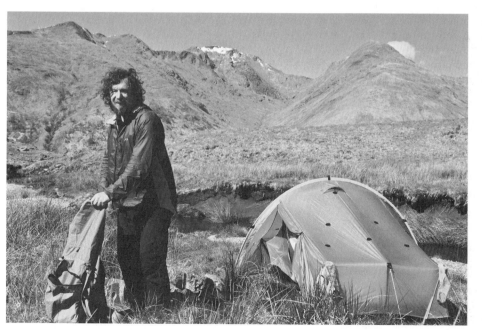

A wild camp in the Scottish Highlands.

weather." If you know enough about equipment to select what really works, you won't need to think about your gear when you're in the wilderness. You can get on with what you're really there for—experiencing the natural world. Worrying about getting wet because you don't trust your rain jacket to keep you dry, or shivering through the night in your threadbare sleeping bag will come between you and the environment and may even dominate your walk. In extreme circumstances, inadequate gear could even be life-threatening. So it's worth

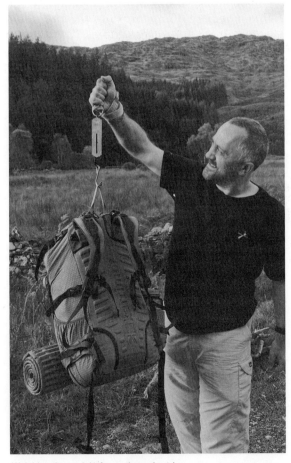

Weighing the pack before a three-day trip.

taking your time when choosing equipment. It will be with you for many miles and many nights. Don't forget, though, that you also need the skills to use it properly. No gear is magic, despite what many advertisements imply. Just having the latest jacket doesn't mean you can cope with a mountain storm, nor does having the fastest-boiling stove on the market necessarily mean you can produce anything edible.

WEIGHT

Three major factors govern choice of gear: *performance*, *durability*, and *weight*. The first is simple—an item must do what's required of it. Rain gear must keep out the rain; a stove must boil water. How long it goes on doing so efficiently is a measure of its durability. It's easy to make items that perform well and last for ages, but the backpacker's (and equipment designer's) problem is the weight of such gear. Backpackers probably spend more time trying to reduce the weight of their gear than on all other aspects of trip planning. Such time is well spent. Saving 2 pounds means you can carry another day's food; the difference between a 25-pound pack and a 35-pound pack is considerable, especially near the end of a long, hard day. Although your pack is supported by your shoulders and hips, it's your legs that carry the weight and will feel most tired with a heavy load. The heavier your load, the more often you need to stop and rest, the slower you walk, especially uphill, and the sooner you are likely to stop and make camp. Even if you aren't planning on high-mileage days or thousands of feet of ascent, the lighter your pack, the more comfortable you'll feel.

The total weight carried includes *everything*: everything you wear, everything hung round your neck, everything carried in your hands, and everything in your pockets as well as what's in your pack. Actual pack weight varies according to how much food, fuel, and water you're carrying, how much clothing you're wearing, and what's in your hands or pockets. In the following discussion the weights mentioned are for all nonvariable gear, not just what's in your pack. To this must be added approximately 2 pounds a day for food and fuel plus a pound for each pint of water carried.

Equipment used to fall into two rough categories: *standard* and *lightweight*. There is now a third: *ultralight*. With standard equipment compromises are made between weight and durability; it is reasonably light but strong enough to withstand years of average use or the rigors of a multimonth expedition. With standard equipment, a load for a summer solo trip is likely to weigh about 25 to 35 pounds. If you're traveling with a group, sharing camping and cooking equipment will reduce this a little; specialized and warmer gear for winter conditions will add to it. With lightweight gear the weight can be reduced to 20 to 25 pounds; with the latest ultralight gear and a severe look at every item, 10 pounds or less is possible. Ultralight gear usually won't be as tough as standard gear (though there are exceptions), but the best is surprisingly durable.

To some extent, the way weight feels is subjective. If you set out deep into the wilderness with two weeks' supplies and a total pack weight of 70 pounds, the 40-pound load you emerge with feels amazingly light. But set off cold with 40 pounds for a weekend, and the burden can seem unbearable. There are limits, of course. Once, when I was young and foolish, I carried more than 110 pounds (including snowshoes, ice ax, crampons, and twenty-three days' food) through the snowbound High Sierra. I couldn't lift my pack; I had to sit down, slide my arms through the shoulder

The finish of the Pacific Northwest Trail at Capa Alava.

straps, then roll forward onto all fours before slowly standing up. Carrying this much weight was not fun, and I was exhausted by the end of every 12-mile day. I wouldn't do it again, though the hike through the Sierra was marvelous despite the load. Since then, I have started sections of long treks in remote wilderness with 80 pounds in my pack and found that too much. Only after the first week do such loads slim down to a bearable weight. I now try never to carry more than 50 pounds on any trip. Sometimes I have to break that intention—I had to carry three gallons of water and six days' food on one section of the Arizona Trail, pushing my pack weight up to 70 pounds—but the exceptions are rare. I find 50 pounds manageable as long as my pack can support the load and I'm not planning to cover more than 12 to 15 miles a day or climb thousands of feet. If I want to cover more distance or ascent, 30 pounds is my target pack weight, since I've found this to be the weight at which the load starts to slow me down noticeably. On one- or two-night trips, the average weight, including food and fuel, is now 20 to 25 pounds, a good 10 pounds less than when I started backpacking. The weight goes

GEAR FOR A 75-DAY THROUGH-HIKE ON THE 1,200-MILE PACIFIC NORTHWEST TRAIL

My 1,200-mile Pacific Northwest Trail hike took me from the Rocky Mountains through the dry, hot Purcell, Selkirk, and Kettle River mountain ranges to the wet and humid Cascade and Olympic Mountains. During the trip, I had to deal with thunderstorms, heat waves, and many days of low-cloud conditions and rain. In the first forty-nine days, there was only significant rain on six days and a little drizzle on a few others. In the last twenty-six days, there was rain on nineteen days, often heavy. And in those first forty-nine days, the humidity level was usually quite low, with any rain quickly followed by dry, sunny conditions. Every morning I recorded the relative humidity, and it only reached 100 percent eight times in the first period and sometimes dropped as low as 50 percent. In the last twenty-six days, relative humidity was 100 percent every day but one—when it was 99.4 percent. Often I camped and hiked in wet mist even when it wasn't raining. Temperatures were mild and only fell below zero twice the whole trip and then only slightly, with the lowest temperature being 28°F (-2.2°C). During the first part of the walk, daytime temperatures were often in the 80s Fahrenheit (30s Celsius), and staying cool and hydrated was the main problem. For the last month, the temperatures were 60°F (20°C) and below, and the rain and high humidity meant it felt chilly much of the time. The terrain varied enormously from paved roads to pathless dense vegetation. Mostly I was on trails or disused dirt roads, both often overgrown with bushes that reached shoulder high. When wet, these could soak me far faster than any rain. This was nothing, though, compared to the bushwhacking through dense, tangled vegetation, which was some of the toughest walking I've ever done. A mile an hour was good progress.

Gear	Weight in Ounces
PACK[*]	
4,392 cu. in. frameless, first half of walk	33.0
4,392 cu. in. internal frame, second half of walk	49.0
SHELTER	
ridge tent with mesh inner erected with trekking poles	34.0
three-season 800-fill-power down quilt	25.0
insulated air bed	11.0
KITCHEN	
alcohol/wood stove with windscreen	8.0
plastic fuel bottle	0.9
0.9 qt. titanium pot	5.0
1 pt. titanium pot/mug	3.0
hard-anodized aluminum spoon	0.3
long-handled titanium spoon	0.6
pot scrubber	0.5
firesteel	0.9
two 2 qt. collapsible water bottles	2.5
widemouthed 1.5 pt. water bottle	2.75
UV light water purifier	3.5

up for longer trips only because of extra food and fuel, not because I carry more equipment.

If the total weight seems excessive, I look for any item I can replace with a lighter option or even leave out—a lighter fleece jacket, say, or no extra socks. (It's a bit late to decide you could do with a lighter tent or sleeping bag when you're packing for a trip, though, which is the reason your original gear choices are so important.) When the only difference between two items is weight, I go for the lighter one every time. The big items—tent, sleeping bag, pack, stove—add weight most rapidly, but it all has to be carried.

I like to know the weight of *everything* I carry, down to the smallest item. I use a digital scale that measures to the nearest tenth of an ounce. If you can't decide between two items and the store where you're shopping doesn't have a scale, you might want to take yours along. Manufacturer's advertised weights are often inaccurate, and

FOOTWEAR

trail shoes	24.5
sandals	24.25

CLOTHING

two pairs merino wool socks	6.5
nylon trail pants	11.0
nylon running shorts	4.5
polypro briefs	1.75
merino wool T-shirt	5.75
polyester hiking shirt	7.25
nylon hooded windshirt	5.0
microfleece sweater	8.0
down jacket	7.5
waterproof-breathable rain smock	10.0
waterproof-breathable rain pants	3.75
merino wool beanie hat	2.0
cotton sun hat	5.5
polypro liner gloves	1.5
two cotton bandannas	2.0

ACCESSORIES

trekking poles	18.5
three waterproof stuff sacks	7.25
three clear, waterproof zipped bags	1.5
LED headlamp	2.75
compass	0.8
safety whistle	0.5
sunglasses	0.5
notebook, wallet, documents, pens	0.5
paperback book	0.6
reading glasses	5.0

maps	3.5
guidebook sections	1.75
first aid and repair	5.5
cell phone/GPS	5.5
altimeter/watch	2.5
weather recorder	3.75
solar charger	1.75
mini multitool	1.5
wash/teeth kit	3.5
mini binoculars	5.25

PHOTOGRAPHY

DSLR camera and 18 to 55 mm lens in padded case	27.75
memory cards, spare batteries, filters	17.0
tripod	21.0

The total weight of all my gear was approximately 28 pounds (including about 4 pounds of camera gear). I usually wore or carried separately around 8 pounds, so my pack's base weight—without food, fuel, or water—was about 20 pounds.

The most food I carried was for 10 days, making a pack weight of 40 pounds. With water and fuel as well, my heaviest pack weight was around 45 to 50 pounds.

* Note: I had problems with the frameless pack after the first few weeks, so I swapped it for an internal-frame model, which, although heavier, was more comfortable.

descriptions such as "lightweight" often bear little connection to reality. I also find that it helps to set maximum target weights and to disregard all heavier items.

As an exercise, I once compiled two lists of gear from a mail-order catalog. The first consisted of standard items, chosen regardless of weight; the second contained the lightest gear in each category. The difference between items was small, often no more than a few ounces, yet the overall weights were 25 pounds for the lightweight gear and 35 for the standard.

I conducted a second exercise for a magazine feature on a spring weekend in wet coastal mountains with two hikers, one carrying his standard load, one an ultralight load that he was testing for a forthcoming Pacific Crest Trail through-hike (which he successfully completed). John Manning, the standard hiker, started with 33.5 pounds of gear and provisions, including clothes and

GEAR FOR A NINE-DAY SUMMER TRIP IN HIGH MOUNTAINS

This hike took place mostly at or above timberline—10,500 to more than 11,000 feet. I expected hot, sunny weather with occasional afternoon thunderstorms and cool but not cold nights. As it turned out, the lowest overnight temperature was 36°F (2°C), and most nights were in the upper 30s and lower 40s. The daytime temperatures were in the 60s and 70s, so I mostly hiked in a trail shirt, shorts, and sandals. I wore the trail shoes on the one rainy day; otherwise the sandals sufficed. A pair of waterproof-breathable socks instead of the trail shoes would have meant less weight and bulk to carry and would have kept my feet drier in the rain. On the wet day I found the EPIC jacket and my wide-brimmed sun hat were enough to keep me dry. I never wore the rain jacket and pants. I wore the two wicking base-layer tops in camp, but they weren't really necessary. The synthetic sleeping bag was a test item. It kept me warm and comfortable, but a lighter, more compressible down bag would still be my first choice. There were no opportunities to resupply, so I carried all my supplies. The two fuel cartridges lasted the trip. There was just enough fuel left to make a hot drink and some soup while waiting for my ride at the end of the hike.

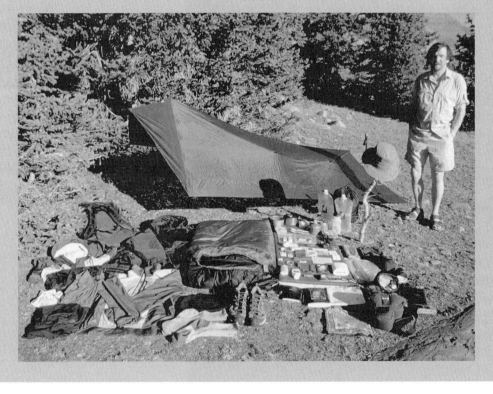

The author with gear for a nine-day hike in the Uinta Mountains, Utah.

footwear worn and two days' food; Simon Willis, the ultralight hiker, carried 19.5 pounds. They started out on a cool, breezy day, wearing a fair amount of clothing and with packs weighing 26 and 12 pounds, respectively. That's a huge gap. The packs themselves accounted for much of the difference: the ultralight pack weighed 14 ounces, the standard one 76 ounces, a difference of 3

Gear	Weight in Ounces
PACK	
4,500 cu. in. frameless	35.0
SHELTER	
7 ft. by 11 ft. silnylon (silicone nylon) tarp with stakes and cord	17.0
Polarguard sleeping bag	54.0
three-quarter-length self-inflating pad	17.0
KITCHEN	
cartridge stove	3.0
foil windscreen	1.0
2 8 oz. gas cartridges	28.0
0.9 qt. titanium pan	5.0
1.1 pt. titanium pan—doubles as mug	3.0
2 Lexan plastic spoons	1.0
dishcloth	0.5
matches/lighter	1.0
1 pt. water bottle	2.0
2 2.5 qt. collapsible water containers	2.75
FOOTWEAR	
trail shoes	36.0
hiking sandals	27.0
CLOTHING	
2 pairs midweight merino wool socks	5.0
nylon shorts	4.0
ripstop nylon trail pants	8.0
2 pairs polyester underpants	4.0
C-Thru polyester wicking T-shirt	3.0
C-Thru long-sleeved wicking polyester top	5.0
Supplex nylon trail shirt	9.5
Nextec EPIC wind shell with fleece lining in front	12.0
Polarguard 3D insulated jacket	18.0
rain jacket	13.0
rain pants	5.5
fleece hat	2.0
cotton sun hat	5.75
cotton bandanna	1.0
ACCESSORIES	
trekking poles	20.5
LED headlamp	2.5
compass	1.0
safety whistle	1.0
map	2.0
first-aid kit	4.0
repair kit	4.0
altimeter-watch	2.0
knife	2.0
8x21 binoculars	5.5
wash kit	1.0
sunscreen	2.0
insect repellent	2.0
toilet paper	2.0
toilet trowel	2.0
notebook and pens	4.0
paperback	8.0
TOTAL	**24.2 POUNDS**

To this must be added 5.75 pounds of camera gear and, at the outset, 18 pounds of food, giving an initial total weight of 48 pounds. Since I wore or carried at least 4 pounds of the basic load plus 3 pounds of cameras, my pack weighed about 41 pounds at the outset and 23 pounds at the finish. The ultralight pack had no padding in the hipbelt and was not comfortable with loads of more than 30 pounds. I reduced the discomfort considerably by threading a padded lens case and a padded compact camera case onto the hipbelt. When I got home I secured foam pads to the belt with duct tape.

pounds, 14 ounces. Shelter was significant too. The ultralight hiker had a tarp weighing 30 ounces including stakes and groundsheet, the standard hiker a tent weighing 68 ounces. That's another 2 pounds, 6 ounces. The variation in clothing was also startling. Leaving out clothing worn all the time (boots, socks, long pants, base layer), there was a difference in weight of 2 pounds, 4 ounces, with the standard load including 5 pounds, 6 ounces of clothing, the lightweight one 3 pounds, 2 ounces. Together, pack, shelter, and clothing constituted two-thirds of the difference between the two loads. After the weekend the standard hiker became interested in reducing the weight of his load, feeling he could do so without affecting his comfort, while the ultralighter felt he couldn't reduce his load any more without compromising comfort too much.

Five years later, I made another two-night trip in similar wet coastal mountains with the same two hikers, both of whom had through-hiked the Pacific Crest Trail since our first trip. In the intervening years, both had reduced the weight of their gear, but unsurprisingly, it was John, who had had the heavy load on the first trip, who had made big changes. John's total weight, including clothing and footwear, was down to 22 pounds, a saving of a third. John made savings across almost all his gear. The biggest ones were changing a 5.75-pound internal-frame pack for a 1.75-pound frameless pack; a 4.25-pound double-skin tent for a 2-pound single-skin tent; 4.5-pound boots for 2.5-pound trail shoes; a 1.5-pound self-inflating mat for a 0.65-pound closed-cell foam pad; and a 19-ounce stainless steel cookset for a 7-ounce titanium mug. Simon's total weight dropped to 15 pounds, mainly due to changing from 4.75-pound boots to 1.6-pound trail shoes, though some of his gear was actually heavier: he changed his 1.9-pound tarp (including stakes and groundsheet) for a 2.6-pound single-skin tent, as he wanted a sewn-in groundsheet for bug protection, and his 14-ounce pack for a 22-ounce one, as he wanted a hipbelt.

Overall, Simon modified his gear a little but basically stayed with the same ultralight approach, while John abandoned his traditional gear and went for lightweight gear in every area, a major change in outlook.

The Ultralight Approach

In the past twenty years ultralight hiking has boomed, though it's still a minority pursuit among most backpackers. A wealth of ultralight gear, books, and Web sites has aided its spread. As the name suggests, it involves using the lightest gear possible and carrying the absolute minimum. If you leave an item at home, you've cut its weight completely. Ultralight hikers modify gear too, shaving away every possible fraction of an ounce. Straps are trimmed and labels and even toothbrush handles are removed. When your total gear weighs only 10 pounds, removing ounces makes a difference. When it weighs 30 pounds, a few ounces here and there aren't so significant. Hiking styles go in cycles, and ultralight hiking has boomed before. Usually it's received with great enthusiasm; then, as the reality of hiking with minimum gear, especially in wet and cold weather, sets in, pack weights start to rise again. Gear designers can't help tinkering, either, adding extras here and there until their ultralight gear no longer merits the name, though it might be more comfortable or functional.

There's always been an interest in how little you need to carry, going right back to the early days of recreational backpacking. John Muir famously traveled with very little equipment or food. In the early twentieth century, Horace Kephart described in *Camping and Woodcraft* a summer load weighing 18 pounds, 3 ounces without food and a "featherweight" one of just 10 pounds including pack, tent, down sleeping bag, and spirit stove. And in 1976, Hamish Brown traveled very light on his 1,600-mile, 112-day round of the Scottish 3,000-foot summits. He reckoned his total pack weight, including food, averaged 23 pounds and only twice went above 30 pounds. This is impressive for a time before titanium, silnylon, Cuben Fiber, and other lightweight materials. Some of Brown's gear and his attitude sound remarkably similar to that of ultralight backpackers today. His pack had no frame, padding, hipbelt, or pockets. His tent was single-skin with a tray groundsheet attached by elastic loops. It weighed just over 3 pounds. He didn't use an insulating mat, saying one was only needed on snow. Instead of a hat, he used his rain jacket hood, and instead of gloves, he used his shirt sleeves, which were long enough to cover his hands. He didn't bother with a knife, sharpening the edge of his spoon so it would cut. For one section, he used a solid-fuel stove, though mostly he used a canister stove.

The current surge in popularity can be traced back to 1992 and the publication of Ray Jardine's *The Pacific Crest Trail Hiker's Handbook*. Ray and his wife, Jenny, hiked the PCT with packs averaging an astonishing 8.5 pounds without food, and Ray described how he did this in that book and later in his influential and provocative *Beyond Backpacking* and *Trail Life* books. There have been several books on lightweight and ultralight backpacking since Jardine's. One of the most interesting is Jörgen Johansson's *Smarter Backpacking*, which is about applying lightweight and ultralight techniques. Jörgen is from Sweden, and his approach shows that lightweight backpacking can work in wet or cold northern climes. His book is also interesting because it "is a living book with one leg on the Internet" that's linked to a Web site at http://smarterbackpacking.com. Also good is Mike Clelland's *Ultralight Backpackin' Tips*, which is full of useful ideas and features the author's excellent and amusing illustrations. So new I haven't seen it yet is *A Walker's Complete Guide to Backpacking & Hiking Gear* by Andrew Skurka, whose long-distance journeys using ultralight gear are phenomenal, especially his 4,700-mile, six-month Alaska-Yukon expedition. (See his Web site at http://andrewskurka.com.)

Lightweight hiking shades into ultralight hiking instead of being clearly separate. Arguably a pack weight below 20 pounds, including food and water, defines the ultralight hiker. Ultralight hiking works best in summer conditions on good trails in places with generally benign climates and is best suited to those who like to keep moving and spend as little time as possible resting or in camp. It also requires expertise and fitness—there's no backup gear to get you out of trouble. I've tried the ultralight approach on weekends when I wanted to cover high mileage, managing to get my total load down to 16° pounds including food for two days (see sidebar, page 30). I enjoyed the light weight, but I worried that any extended period of stormy weather would be unpleasant. I wouldn't want to travel with such minimal gear for long, but if you're interested in high daily mileage and stoic enough to endure minimal comfort in camp in bad weather, this could be the way to go.

Even though I don't try to reduce my pack weight to the absolute minimum—I like a pack with a hipbelt, a roomy shelter, enough warm clothing to sit outside in comfort, a proper stove, a paperback book, and more—my overall pack weight has come down because I've incorporated some ultralight items and because there's been a general reduction in weight of much standard gear. These days my average loads are a good 10 pounds lighter than those from several years ago; the ultralight movement has certainly benefited me and, I think, all backpackers.

SUGGESTED TARGET WEIGHTS

Gear	Weight in Ounces
FOOTWEAR*	
hiking sandals	25
running shoes	25
trail shoes	32
hiking boots	44
SHELTER	
groundsheet	8
bivy bag	20
tarp, solo	20
tarp, duo	32
tent, solo	56
tent, duo	88
sleeping bag (summer)	25
sleeping bag (three-season)	48
sleeping bag (winter)	56
closed-cell foam mat	9
self-inflating mat	21
COOKING GEAR	
stove (cartridge)	4
stove (multifuel/white gas)	16
stove (alcohol)	8
liter pot with lid	8
CLOTHING	
Summer	
wool or synthetic base layer	6
synthetic hiking shirt	10
fleece top	12

Gear	Weight in Ounces
shorts	6
trail pants	12
base-layer long pants	4
windshirt	8
rain jacket	20
rain pants	8
warm hat	2
sun hat	6
Winter	
zip-neck shirt base layer	10
fleece top	12
synthetic fill top (for wet cold)	20
down top (for dry cold)	20
base-layer/fleece pants	8
long pants	24
rain jacket	32
rain pants	21
warm hat	4
windproof, pile-lined cap	4
liner gloves	2
fleece/wool/synthetic gloves/mitts	6
shell gloves/mitts	5
PACK	
loads up to 20 lbs.	30
loads up to 30 lbs.	40
loads up to 45 lbs.	60
heavy loads	125

* Note: these weights are for a pair of men's size 10; scale up or down for different sizes.

Green Gear

Given our interest in unspoiled wilderness, it's not surprising that many backpackers and hikers are deeply concerned about the environment and involved with conservation groups. This concern spills over into outdoor equipment companies, and many of them are also involved in the environmental movement in various ways, usually by making cash donations. Companies often list the campaigns and organizations they support in catalogs and on Web sites. Some have environmental audits and do their best to minimize their impact on the environment. Many use recycled materials in both products and packaging. Whatever the companies' motivations (and the more cynical—or realistic—may have doubts about some of them), using recycled materials does less damage to the environment than using virgin materials and is therefore recommended. Patagonia was first on the market with recycled fleece garments way back in 1993, and it still makes these along with other environmentally friendly stuff. It also promotes various environmental and conservation causes through its catalog and Web site (patagonia.com) rather more strongly than most companies. Even some huge corporations pay attention to the environment these days. Nike, for example, has a Reuse-a-Shoe program whereby you can return old sports shoes (any make, not just Nike) for recycling. The rubber from old shoes, called Nike Grind, can be found on several of the brand's hiking shoes (see nikereusea shoe.com).

Using gear made from recycled materials is only a first step, of course. What happens when you've finished with it? Donating it to a worthy cause, selling it, or passing it along to friends is preferable to sending it to a landfill.

Buying quality gear in the first place is a good idea too. Top-quality items usually last longest, covering the high initial cost, and perform best, making it less likely you'll want to replace them. Equipment lasts longer with proper maintenance, too. Annie and David R. Getchell's *The Essential Outdoor Gear Manual* covers repair and care of everything from packs to kayaks and is highly recommended. Repair centers exist, but unless you live near one or near an outdoor store that will forward gear, you will have to mail your gear to them, so they're worth using only for major problems you can't fix yourself.

CHECKLISTS

For any walk you have to decide exactly what to take. Here I find a checklist essential (see Appendix 1). No two hikes are the same, and I doubt I've ever taken exactly the same gear twice. When, where, and for how long you go will determine what you carry. You need to know about the weather, the terrain, and the environment. I work from a complete list of all my gear, then distill a shorter list for the walk at hand. Because I know what each item weighs, I can work out how much gear I'll be carrying. Adding about 2 pounds of food per day, plus the weight of my camera gear, tells me what the total load will be. At that point I review the list to see if anything can be left out or replaced with a lighter alternative. For a major trip that will last many weeks, I repeat this process obsessively, though this rarely makes much difference. With experience, you'll probably find that your first list needs only a little tinkering.

I keep a list of all my gear on my computer. Before each trip I make up a specific checklist, print it out, then check off each item as I pack it—and not before. (It's all too easy to remember that an item is hanging up drying somewhere, check it off, and then forget to go and get it. I know. I've done it.) You can list the gear on a database that adds up the weights for you. There's even a little online program that does this, which I've used for a number of years now: the Backpacking Gear Weight Calculator, developed by hiker Chris Ibbeson. You add your gear in various categories along with the weights and any notes you want to remember. For each trip you check the items you want to take and the program computes the total weight. You can get further details at www.chrisibbeson.com.

CHOOSING AND BUYING

The highly competitive nature of the outdoor equipment market means that styles and names

ULTRALIGHT OVERNIGHT SUMMER TRIP IN COASTAL MOUNTAINS

One purpose of this trip was to try a pack with no frame or hipbelt and an ultralight load. I covered 30 miles and 8,600 feet of ascent, mostly cross-country in rough, rocky terrain, and the light load made the trip seem like a day hike. The temperature was in the 60s during the day and the 40s at night with no rain and only light winds.

Gear	Weight in Ounces
PACK	
3,100 cu. in. frameless, no back padding, no hipbelt	14.25
SHELTER	
7 ft. by 11 ft. silnylon tarp with stakes	17.0
14 oz. 800-fill-power down sleeping bag	17.5
three-quarter-length foam pad	9.0
KITCHEN	
cartridge stove	3.0
foil windscreen	1.0
1 half-full 8 oz. gas cartridge	10.0
0.9 qt. titanium pan	5.0
1.1 pt. titanium pan—doubles as mug	3.0
2 Lexan plastic spoons	1.0
dishcloth	0.5
matches/lighter	1.0
1 pt. water bottle	2.0
2.5 qt. collapsible water containers	1.5
FOOTWEAR	
trail shoes	33.0
CLOTHING	
merino wool socks	2.5
running shorts—doubled as underpants	3.0
nylon trail pants	8.0
polyester long-sleeved top	4.0
Silmond polyester wind shell	7.5
Polartec 100 microfleece sweater	13.5
rain jacket	9.5
rain pants	5.5
fleece hat	2.0
cotton bandanna	1.0
ACCESSORIES	
trekking poles	18.0
LED headlamp	2.5
compass	1.0
whistle	1.0
map	2.0
first-aid kit	2.5
repair kit	2.0
altimeter-watch	2.0
Windwatch (see Chapter 9)	1.75
knife	2.0
wash kit	1.0
sunscreen	2.0
dark glasses	2.5
insect repellent	3.0
toilet paper	2.0
toilet trowel	2.0
binoculars	5.5
notebook and pens	4.0
paperback	5.0
TOTAL	**16.25 POUNDS**

I wore or held 4 pounds of the items above, so my basic pack weight was 12.25 pounds. My camera gear weighed 3.25 pounds, but this was all carried in a padded case slung across my body. I had 3 pounds of food at the outset, making a pack weight of 15.25 pounds and a total weight of 22.5 pounds.

change rapidly—companies come and go, brand names are taken over, new materials emerge. While many changes are cosmetic and have more to do with fashion than function, some do involve new designs and practical improvements. There are basically four sources for the latest information on equipment: specialty stores, mail-order companies, manufacturers and importers, and outdoor magazines (see Appendix 3). All of these have Web sites, of course.

If you can find a good store with staff members who use the equipment they sell and know what they're talking about, give it your support. The employees in such a store can keep you well informed and advised. Popping in to chat and look at the latest gear can be enjoyable, too. Being able to handle gear and see it in three dimensions and talk face to face with real human beings beats cyberspace any day, in my opinion.

Paper catalogs still exist, of course, if you prefer them; however, Web sites are now the norm and arguably the best way to access information. If you don't have a good store nearby, buying through the Web is a good alternative. Equipment Web sites—from companies like Campmor, REI, Backcountry.com, and Mountain Gear—often feature equipment comparison charts and may have "house brand" items not available elsewhere. Many small specialty manufacturers whose products you may never find in a store have Web sites. Indeed, the Web has provided the opportunity for these companies to market their gear much more easily.

Gear manufacturers and retailers can hardly be expected to be objective about the gear they make their living from; for that you need to consult outdoor magazines and the plethora of hiking Web sites. Most test and review gear, often in great detail. They also carry news of the latest items and developments. (See Appendix 3.)

The leading U.S. backpacking specialty magazine for many decades has been *Backpacker*, which publishes gear tests in every issue. In the spring, *Backpacker* publishes an annual gear guide listing specifications for thousands of items along with the editor's choice of new gear. In the United Kingdom, *TGO* magazine publishes gear tests in every issue—many written by me! *Outside* and

Canada's *Explore* cover a much wider field of activities but often have features of interest to backpackers.

Of the many backpacking Web sites, one stands out for its rigorous and authoritative gear reviews—Backpacking Light (http://backpackinglight.com). To see much of the content, a subscription is needed, and the emphasis, as the name suggests, is very much on lightweight and ultralight gear. BackpackGearTest.org offers masses of detailed reviews by readers on all weights of equipment. Many backpacking blogs also carry useful and informative gear reviews (see Appendix 3).

Many companies, Web sites, and blogs can now be found on social networking sites like Facebook and Twitter. These social-networking sites are a quick way to get news and up-to-date information. Often posts and messages contain links to sites where more details can be found.

The Rise of the Cottage Manufacturers

A new development for the twenty-first century is the rise of small cottage manufacturers making innovative specialist outdoor gear and selling it through the Internet. Often based on the work of just one or two people, the products are mostly, though not exclusively, on the ultralight and lightweight side. While you can't usually see this gear in any store, the companies generally offer a personal service and are very involved in the backpacking community, as the designers are usually active hikers themselves. It's not unusual to see notices on Web sites saying that the business is closed for a few months while the owner is away on a long-distance trail. Such small specialist companies have always been around, of course—Stephenson's Warmlite, which makes tents and sleeping systems, being a good example, having begun in the 1950s—but, until recently, there had never been many of them. Now there are well over fifty, with new ones appearing all the time. The line between cottage manufacturers and mainstream companies is blurred, and as the former become more successful, they often expand, contract out manufacturing, and move into the second category. Quite a few of the big, well-known outdoor companies started with one person, a good idea, and a sewing machine. Online reviews and comments in backpacking forums make it easy to find opinions on their products, and the owners and designers are usually very approachable and often get involved in online discussions. Their designs are exciting and imaginative and have had a positive effect on backpacking equipment with many bigger mainstream companies copying and adapting them. I've used products from AntiGravity Gear (alcohol stoves, pans), Brasslite (alcohol stoves), Bushbuddy (wood stove), Gossamer Gear (packs, shelters, sleeping pads), Pacerpole (trekking poles), PHD (down sleeping bags, clothing), Tarptent (tents), Titanium Goat (stoves), Trail Designs (stoves), Ultralight Adventure Equipment (packs), Ursack (animal-resistant stuff sacks), Vargo Outdoors (titanium stoves, stakes, pots), Tramplite (packs), the Boilerwerks (chimney kettle), and Warmlite (tents) and found all of them excellent and the companies helpful, friendly, and approachable. I haven't tried products from Jacks 'R' Better (quilts, hammocks), McHale (packs), Mountain Laurel Designs (shelters), Nunatak (down quilts, clothing), RBH Designs (vapor-barrier clothing), enLIGHTened equipment (quilts), Suluk 46° (bivy bags, ice axes, crampons, more), Hyperlite Mountain Gear (tents, tarps, packs), or Six Moon Designs (shelters, packs), though they have all been highly recommended by knowledgeable and experienced hiking friends and contacts.

Quality

Today, outdoor companies are international. Globalization is the name of the game. Much high-quality equipment from reputable companies is made in the Far East, a region once known only for budget items. You may want to buy gear made at home for patriotic or environmental reasons, but you don't need to do so to ensure that you're getting good quality.

It's wise to check carefully and thoroughly every bit of gear you buy. However reputable the company, and however good the quality control, a faulty item occasionally slips through. It is better to discover that your tent door zipper jams or that the snaps fall off your jacket when you're home rather than when you're out in a raging blizzard. Check that stitching is neat and unbroken and that seam ends are finished properly. (With filled garments and sleeping bags, you can't see the interior work, but if the shell is put together well, chances are the insides are too.) All waterproof-breathable garments should have taped seams; check that the tapes are flat and run in straight lines. The same applies to tents with pretaped seams. You should be able to spot any gross manufacturing defects before they cause problems in the field.

Cost

Buy the best you can afford. During a mountaintop blizzard, a few dollars saved on a cheap jacket are meaningless. This doesn't mean you need to buy the most expensive items or that you can't go hiking if you can't afford top-of-the-line gear.

There are huge price ranges—especially in clothing, where high prices often just mean the latest style, color, or fabric rather than better performance. Indeed, the most expensive gear is often too complex and heavy for backpacking. The simplest, lightest designs—not the most costly—are best. If you don't want the latest colors or styles (and why does this matter in the wilderness?), last year's models can often be had at knockdown prices. Cosmetic "seconds" can be good value too. Before I started testing gear for magazines, and therefore had an endless supply of the stuff pouring through the door, I looked for gear at sales and in surplus stores. My first down sleeping bag had a patch on the inside where it was torn in the factory. This didn't affect the performance, but the cost was half that of a perfect bag. I used to wear army surplus wool shirts—itchy next to the skin but fine if worn over another layer. I enjoyed sorting through piles of gloves, socks, hats, and other items in surplus stores—a sort of treasure hunt where I never knew just what wonderful bit of gear would turn up. I still occasionally go through the bargain bins in outdoor stores and have to remind myself that I really don't need another hat, however inexpensive. Web sites like eBay can provide bargains too, though I have never bought anything on them. Thrift shops may have hiking gear too, especially clothing. With care you can put together a top-quality backpacking outfit for very little money from sales, seconds, and secondhand stores. Doing this is certainly better than buying brand-new budget gear that probably won't last long.

Depending on where and when you plan to go, there are critical items for which money should be no object, but other items need not be expensive or even cost anything at all. You probably have clothing in your closet that will do for most hiking. Remember, too, that good gear isn't a substitute for skill. Equipment is no use if you don't know what to do with it. An experienced backpacker can function more efficiently and safely with a minimum of basic gear than a novice can with the latest high-tech designs. Many of us learned with gear that seems primitive now, but it let us get into the wilderness and survive there. Don't let a lack of gear keep you from getting out there. Just be careful to tailor what you do to your skill level and the gear you have.

Making Your Own

One way to cut costs is to make your own gear. This is also a way to design items the way you want. I've never made my own gear, but I've hiked with people who have and I greatly admire them. I can see that using an item you've made gives it a value and personal meaning that a store-bought item just cannot have.

Making complex items like geodesic dome tents is of course way beyond most people's skills, so home gear making tends to be the province of ultralight hikers who want very simple, basic gear. Ray and Jenny Jardine made their own gear for their ultralight long-distance hikes because they couldn't find what they wanted commercially. There are details of how to do this at www .rayjardine.com. There also are many Web sites about making your own gear, especially alcohol and solid fuel tablet stoves made from soda cans. Backpacking.net has a whole section on making gear, with instructions for everything from packs and shelters to stoves and headlamps. Trail Quest has a fair amount of information on making gear too, though it is scattered among the other topics.

GEAR FOR A TWO-MONTH ARIZONA TRAIL THROUGH-HIKE IN SPRING

Although this trip lasted two months, the same gear would be suitable for much shorter desert trips in spring or autumn. I took the large, heavy pack because I knew I would have to carry a great deal of water. I carried a gallon for a few hours most days, and three gallons on a few occasions. I took eight small water containers rather than a couple of large ones so that if any of them sprang a leak, most would still be OK. The rigid water container was for filling from trickles and shallow pools. The plastic coffee filter was for filtering visible dirt. Because I was resupplying in small towns along the way, I took a multifuel stove. Automotive gas was always available. Most nights were above freezing, but some were below, and the lowest overnight temperature was 21°F (–6°C).

Gear	Weight in Ounces
PACK	
5,550 cu. in. internal frame	109.0
SHELTER	
9.8 ft. by 9.8 ft. silnylon tarp	27.9
silnylon ground cloth	7.25
stakes and guylines	7.5
14 oz. 750+-fill-power down sleeping bag	31.5
three-quarter-length foam pad	9.0

KITCHEN	
multifuel stove and windscreen	17.75
2 20 fl. oz. fuel bottles	8.75
0.9 qt. titanium pan	5.0
1 pt. stainless steel cup—doubles as second pan	4.0
2 Lexan plastic spoons	1.0
dishcloth	1.0
matches/lighter	2.0
1 qt. water bottle	5.0
4 1 qt. collapsible water containers	4.0
2 2.5 qt. collapsible water containers	2.75
4 qt. water bag	3.0
chlorine dioxide water purification treatment	2.75
plastic coffee filter and filter papers	2.75
food stuff sack	3.5
FOOTWEAR	
ultralight leather boots	38.0
hiking sandals	23.0
CLOTHING	
2 pairs CoolMax liner socks	3.25
CoolMax midweight socks	3.5
Pertex nylon zip-off leg pants	8.75
polypro long johns	3.0
Capilene polyester underpants	1.5
DriClime polyester long-sleeved base layer	5.0

Color

When I began backpacking, most items were green, brown, or blue, with an occasional splash of orange. However, the past two decades have seen an explosion of brilliant colors and multi-hued equipment that shows no sign of abating, to the point where some dully clad hikers—who don't go to the wilderness to see bright displays of nylon—mutter about "visual pollution."

Overall, I'm with the "dull crowd" rather than the peacocks. I prefer being inconspicuous when outdoors, blending in with my surroundings without broadcasting my presence like a neon sign. For a while, I was concerned I might be mistaken for someone using the outdoors as a backdrop for pseudomilitary games. At least one bright item of gear ensured this was unlikely (as would a Sierra Club or Greenpeace badge on my pack). Now, however, the outdoors is also used as a backdrop for "adrenaline sports," which seem to require tight, shiny, and very bright clothing. I don't like the idea of nature's being a backdrop to anything, but I no longer worry about being mistaken for

nylon trail shirt	12.0	toilet paper	1.0
Pertex wind shell	6.25	toilet trowel	2.25
Polartec 100 microfleece sweater	13.5	umbrella	9.5
down vest	14.5	notebook and pens	7.5
Gore-Tex Paclite II rain jacket	16.0	paperback	8.0
polyurethane-coated rain pants	4.4		
polypro liner gloves	1.0	**TOTAL**	**32.5 POUNDS**
fleece hat	2.0		
cotton sun hat	5.75		
cotton bandanna	1.0		

ACCESSORIES

trekking poles	20.5
headlamp and spare AA batteries	9.5
2 candles	3.75
compass	1.4
safety whistle	0.5
maps	8.75
first-aid kit	2.5
repair kit	7.5
altimeter-watch	2.0
Windwatch (see Chapter 9)	1.75
knife	3.0
8x21 binoculars	5.5
wash kit	3.0
sunscreen	3.5
dark glasses and case	2.5

Of this total, 5 pounds were worn or carried every day, leaving a basic pack weight of 27 pounds. I also had 6.25 pounds of camera gear; 3.75 pounds of it were normally in a case slung across my body. The remaining camera gear upped the basic pack weight to 29.5 pounds. The pack never actually weighed this little, however, since I always had food, fuel, and water as well. At one point I carried six days' food (12 pounds) and three gallons of water (24 pounds), which, with stove fuel and extra items like camera film and paperback books, made for a total pack weight of 70 pounds.

The basic pack weight was on the high side for a desert hike. On future trips in similar conditions I would take a smaller tarp, an LED headlamp (not available at the time of the hike), and a much lighter rain jacket. I wore the rain jacket for only a few hours. I would also take a pack weighing about 4 pounds or less rather than 6.8 pounds.

those who use it as an adventure playground or a mock battlefield. If I'm going to worry at all, I'll worry about the future of wilderness.

A different visual issue is photography. When I hiked the Pacific Crest Trail, I wore dark blue and green clothing and used a sludge-brown tent. In the photographs, I look like a black smudge, and the tent blends neatly into the background. A brightly colored garment, especially a red one, can give a splash of color that makes a visually striking photograph, assuming the wearer is meant to be prominent.

Why object to bright colors? There are many vivid hues in nature, but there's a difference between a field of flowers and a sheet of red nylon. I remember reaching a mountain pass and staring down on a beautiful green bowl dotted with green groves and blue pools and having my eye drawn instantly to a searing yellow tent pitched in the center of a meadow. On another occasion a line of orange- and red-clad hikers dominated a distant ridge, destroying any feeling of wildness and solitude. These are aesthetic reasons, but I think they're important, especially in popular backcountry areas where blending in helps make the place seem less crowded. Of course if the background is colorful, bright gear may not stand out. A red tent can disappear into the fall colors of a huckleberry-covered mountainside.

I don't stick strictly to my inconspicuous dogma. Sometimes I have bright items to test (sometimes I'm so embarrassed by them that I try them only in really remote or little-visited areas or, with clothing, when cycling on a road—highways are one place I really want to be noticeable). And in winter all colors tend to look black at a distance except for very pale ones. Against snow, green is just as conspicuous as blaze orange.

Testing

Many companies spend a great deal of time and money conducting laboratory tests on equipment and fabrics, and the results often appear prominently in their catalogs, Web sites, and advertisements. There are tests for everything from water-proofness to wind resistance, from heat output to tear strength. Test methods vary, however, so comparing results can be difficult, and each company seems to find a method that shows its products are better than its competitors'. Moreover, although these tests can *suggest* how a garment might work in the outdoors, they don't guarantee performance—and performance is often a subjective judgment anyway. This applies especially to warm clothing and sleeping bags—what keeps one person cozy may not stop some-

one else from shivering. Read and note laboratory test results by all means, but don't assume an item that works perfectly in a lab will perform perfectly in the real world.

FINAL THOUGHTS

The chapters that follow cover the intricacies of equipment and techniques. Technical details on gear and descriptions of techniques are interwoven because, as I've said, no equipment, however good, is of any value if you don't know how to use it.

The views here are my own, and experienced backpackers will undoubtedly find much to disagree with, which I hope will amuse and entertain them. Those who don't have enough experience to have strong views of their own should note that many of the techniques and items of equipment I describe are those that have worked well for me. No one can try out even a fraction of what's available, and there's plenty of undoubtedly excellent gear I've never tried. I've named names only to make it easier to illustrate details. So take the things I say as guides, not rules. I make no claim to objectivity. In putting my thoughts on paper, I've reappraised my views about gear and techniques. The general outline holds true even if the gear I describe changes form or name or even ceases to exist, as is bound to happen with some items. The reason for describing specific items is to illustrate types of gear and basic principles, not to say that a particular item is the only one to use.

chapter three

footwear and wilderness travel

IT ISN'T THE MOUNTAIN AHEAD THAT
WEARS YOU OUT—IT'S THE GRAIN OF
SAND IN YOUR SHOE.
—*Robert Service*

Feet are marvelously complex, both flexible and tough, but if they are to carry you and your load mile after mile through the wilderness in comfort, they need care and protection. More backpacking trips are ruined by sore feet than by all other causes combined. Pounded by the ground and bearing the weight of you and your pack, your feet receive harsher treatment than any other part of your body.

Feet come in different shapes as well as sizes.

This chapter covers the generic styles of hiking boots and shoes, the critical process of fitting footwear, how and of what materials footwear is constructed, and finally models and brands. (A note on terminology: by shoes, I mean footwear that does not cover the ankles; anything that does is a boot.)

A variety of accessories can make walking easier and safer—from staffs to socks and, for snow travel, ice axes, crampons, snowshoes, and skis. Though snowshoes and skis aren't walking accessories per se, they make travel in deep snow much easier, especially with a heavy pack. The end of this chapter covers all these accessories.

ABOUT FOOTWEAR

The main purposes of backpacking footwear are to protect your feet against bruising and abrasion from rough wilderness terrain, to cushion your soles from the constant hammering of miles of walking, and to provide good traction on slippery, steep, and wet terrain.

Protection for the sole of the foot comes from layers of cushioning; these layers must be thick enough to prevent stones from bruising the feet but flexible enough to allow natural heel-to-toe movement. Thick soles also insulate against snow and cold ground and the heat of desert sand and rock. The tread of the outer sole offers grip; the best soles not only give security on rough terrain but also minimize damage to the ground.

Footwear should also support your foot and ankle, though this is less important than some people think. Support comes from a fit snug enough to keep the foot from slipping around inside the shoe but not so tight that it won't allow the foot to swell. The ankle is supported by a stiff lower heel counter, or heel cup (see Heel Counters and Toe Boxes and the illustrations later in this chapter), and not simply by a high-cut boot; some running shoes give more ankle support than some boots do.

Keeping your feet dry isn't a major purpose of footwear. Top-quality leather is fairly water resistant, but only boots with waterproof-breathable membrane linings can be considered waterproof. How long they stay so is open to question, however, and they have other disadvantages. Plastic and rubber boots are waterproof, of course, but they make your feet hot and sweaty except in snow.

Light versus Heavy Footwear

Once upon a time, virtually all boots were what we now call heavyweight—with leather inners and outers, leather midsoles, steel shanks, and heavily lugged rubber soles. A typical pair of size 9s weighed at least 4 pounds, and it took dozens, if not hundreds, of miles of walking to break them in. A few lighter boots were available, but they were neither very supportive nor very durable.

Lightweight boots mean less weight to lift with each step.

The introduction of lightweight leathers, synthetic fabrics, and running shoe features in the early 1980s revolutionized hiking footwear. Most backpackers were won over, though some stayed—and still stay—loyal to the old heavyweights, and the lightweight versus heavyweight debate has rumbled on ever since. I am firmly on the side of lightweight footwear. My conversion came during a Pacific Crest Trail through-hike in 1982. I set off from the Mexican border in heavy traditional boots that soon gave me hot, sore feet. After just a few days, I ended up carrying them and wearing running shoes (brought along for campwear) much of the time. The heavy boots were more comfortable on my back than on my feet. Only in the snow of the High Sierra did I need them. After 1,500 miles, when the running shoes were just about worn out, I replaced both boots and shoes with a pair of the then-new fabric-suede hiking shoes, Asolo Approaches. These weighed less than half as much as my boots. The staff in the store where I bought the shoes were horrified to hear that I intended to backpack more than a thousand miles in them. But my feet rejoiced at being released from their stiff leather prisons, and my daily mileage went up. Although they were full of holes by the end of the trip, the shoes gave me all the support and grip of my old boots and vastly increased my comfort. I have never since worn heavy traditional footwear for summer backpacking.

That lighter footwear is less tiring seems indisputable. The general estimate is that every pound on your feet equals 5 pounds on your back. If that's correct, and it certainly feels like it, then wearing 2-pound rather than 4-pound boots is like removing 10 pounds from your pack. Boots weighing more than 3 pounds make my feet ache after about twelve miles, and after fifteen miles all

WALKING STYLE

Heavy boots are bulldozers on the trail. Their rigidity forces a walker to stumble along, kicking rocks and gouging chunks out of the path.

Lightweight, flexible footwear encourages a better walking style. You can move faster and more gently, with less effort; you can step around and over rocks instead of banging into them. Gliding instead of trudging, you can cover more miles with the same effort simply because you are lifting less weight with each step.

I want to do is stop. Yet in shoes that weigh half as much, I can cover twice that distance before my feet complain. This isn't surprising when you consider that I lift my feet about 2,500 times a mile (my hiking stride is about two feet long). That means I'm lifting 7,500 pounds per mile when I wear 3-pound boots but only 3,750 pounds when I wear shoes that weigh a pound and a half. Over fifteen miles that's 112,500 pounds lifted with the boots versus 56,250 pounds with the shoes, an enormous difference.

Proponents of heavy boots sometimes argue vociferously that lightweight footwear is not a good idea for most hikers. However, my personal experience and that of many other backpackers regarding the advantages of lighter footwear has been backed up by several scientific studies. One study of ten hikers walking on a treadmill, carried out by the TNO Institute for Perception's Thermal Physiology Research Group in the Netherlands, concluded that "the mass of footwear resulted in an increase in the energy expenditure which was a factor 1.9–4.7 times greater than that of a kilogram of body mass, depending on sex and walking speed." (For a summary of this study, visit http://ncbi.nlm.nih.gov/pubmed/1396635.) The results of a separate study at London University indicated that "it was 6.4 times more expensive to carry weight on the feet as compared to the back." (The study results are available online at http://informaworld.com/smpp/content~content=a779402900~db=all.)

Another study, at the U.S. Army Research Institute of Environmental Medicine, Natick, Massachusetts, concluded "that the . . . energy cost for wearing a weight on your feet was 4.7–6.3 (depending on speed) times as big as carrying the same weight on your torso. This means that for trained and untrained persons walking and running in boots mean a considerable increase in energy expenditure compared to the same activities in running shoes." (This study results are available online at http://informaworld.com/smpp/content~db=all~content=a779187451~frm=abslink.) The last two studies suggest that the claim that a pound on your foot equals five on your back might actually be an underestimate.

Heavier boots usually also mean thicker materials and more padding. In all but winter conditions this can give you hot, sweaty feet, which swell and ache and are more apt to blister.

The ultimate in weight saving is to wear no shoes at all. This might seem like a good way to hurt your feet, but in warm weather walking barefoot is perfectly feasible. I occasionally walk short distances barefoot when my feet feel hot and sweaty in my shoes, and I often wander around camp barefoot. Wearing sandals (as I do for most summer hiking) is close to going barefoot. In fact, there is much evidence that going barefoot is better for the feet and the limbs than wearing shoes, and some footwear companies are taking this into account. Inov-8, which makes ultralight off-road running and hiking footwear, says that all its footwear is designed to allow the foot to move naturally and that "the inov-8 range of off-road shoes

follows the precision shape of the foot, providing the wearer with a secure and intimate fit that's almost like running bare foot." I've worn Inov-8 shoes on multiweek backpacking trips without problems and found them very comfortable. Even more minimalist are Vibram Five-Fingers—thin, stretchy footwear with separate compartments for each toe. Really all these do is protect your feet against dirt and sharp stones. Otherwise, wearing them really is like going barefoot. If you're interested in this idea, Richard Frazine's *The Barefoot Hiker* is worth reading (see also barefoot ers.org/hikers).

The Ankle-Support Myth

One of the main arguments for heavy, stiff footwear is that you need it for ankle support when carrying a heavy pack or hiking on rough terrain. This is not true.

To begin with, most walking boots offer little ankle support, since their soft cuffs give easily under pressure. (Try standing on the outer edge of the sole of a standard walking boot and you'll feel the strain on your ankle.) Only boots with high, stiffened cuffs give real ankle support. My plastic telemark ski boots give good ankle support; I can balance on the edges without strain and traverse steep, icy slopes on my skis without my ankles' aching. But the stiff ankle support restricts foot movement so much that when I walk in these boots I loosen the clips to let my ankles flex fairly normally. Stiff-ankled boots and natural foot movement do not go together.

What actually holds your ankle in place over the sole of a shoe is a rigid heel counter, or heel cup, found in good-quality running shoes as well as most hiking footwear (see Heel Counters and Toe Boxes later in this chapter). I once tested a pair of high-top leather boots without heel cups.

On rough terrain they were worse than useless— my foot constantly slid off the insole, and my ankle kept twisting sideways. I ended up using them only on good paths between campsites. For mountain ascents, I wore the running shoes I'd brought along as campwear—their heel cups made them more stable than the boots.

Some of the greatest strain on your ankles occurs when you run over steep, rough ground. Yet mountain runners, who do this regularly (sometimes for days on end), never wear boots. Try running in boots and you'll see why. For traversing steep, rugged terrain, you need strong, flexible ankles and lightweight, flexible footwear. Doing exercises to strengthen your ankles is better than splinting them in heavy, rigid boots.

The Stiffness Myth

The other argument in favor of heavy boots is that stiff soles protect your feet from rough terrain and help support heavy loads. I disagree. In my experience, restricting normal foot movement with stiff soles makes me feel unstable and insecure. Lateral stiffness—from side to side—is fine, though not required on most trails, since this stops the footwear from twisting under your feet when you traverse steep terrain. Heel-to-toe stiffness is what restricts natural foot movement.

Stiff soles can't flex enough to accommodate to the terrain. I find they prevent me from placing my feet naturally, leading to a slow and clumsy gait, which could lead to injury, since your feet are repeatedly forced into the same unnatural position. Also, straining against the stiffness requires energy and is tiring.

What really protects against rough terrain is footwear that cushions your feet and stops stones and rocks from bruising them. The best way to do this is with a hard but flexible thin synthetic midsole plus a shock-absorbing layer. Most lightweight boots and shoes have soles like this.

In flexible footwear you can place your whole sole in contact with the ground, even on steep terrain, rather than digging in your heels or boot edges, which jars your legs, can make you unstable, and often gouges holes in the hillside.

Sole stiffness is required only on steep, hard-packed snow. Then a bit of stiffness makes it easier to kick the boot toes and edges into the snow.

FOOTWEAR TYPES

Boots and shoes are complex constructions, and there are many ways of making them, using many different materials. You can buy and use footwear happily without knowing whether it has a "graded flex nylon midsole" or "EVA wedges" or is "Blake sewn." (I'll explore the more relevant terms in the Footwear Materials and Construction section later in this chapter.) What may be more important to you is whether the boots contain any recycled materials (many now do). The selection is enormous (one gear guide lists forty-two hiking footwear companies and more than four hundred models, and this isn't comprehensive). Choosing footwear can be daunting. But if you go to a store that has a good selection and a knowledgeable, helpful staff trained to fit boots, you can't go far wrong. Those who want to know more will find information about materials and construction below.

Running and Trail Shoes

Shoes designed for trail running and adventure racing make ideal lightweight backpacking footwear, as do the hiking shoes made by many boot companies, often described as cross-trainers, trail shoes, or multisport shoes, suggesting that

Inov-8 Terroc trail shoe.

the makers are not sure what they're actually for or whom to aim the marketing toward. Construction usually features suede-synthetic fabric uppers, often with large mesh areas for breathability, shock-absorbing midsoles, and strong heel counters. Because these shoes are not very warm, I wouldn't recommend them for snow or very cold weather, but for summer trails, dry or wet, they're a good choice. I wear them anytime I think sandals might be too cold or not quite protective enough.

Some trail shoes incorporate toe boxes, graded (for flex) nylon midsoles, and even half-length metal shanks (for explanations, see Footwear Materials and Construction later in this chapter). These weigh more than simpler designs but also give a little more protection.

Shoes weigh from 7 to 12 ounces a pair for the lightest running shoes to 40 ounces or so for the heaviest trail shoes. (Be wary of look-alike street shoes, which probably won't stand up to backcountry use for long, and of road-running shoes without enough tread for good grip on rough, wet ground. To avoid these, buy from a reputable backpacking gear retailer.)

Trail shoes are usually designated as suitable for easy to moderate trails with light loads. I think this does them a disservice. I've carried heavy loads—50 to 60 pounds—over rugged mountain terrain in trail shoes without trouble.

Lightweight Boots

This is the most popular footwear category and has many names, including trekking, trail, off-trail, long-distance hiking, lightweight, and more. The designers hope one of these descriptions will catch your attention. Lightweight boots weigh between 1 and 3 pounds, the lighter end shading into the higher-cut trail shoes, the heavier end into midweight boots suitable for occasional crampon and snow use. The category includes most synthetic-suede boots and quite a few leather ones. The advantages of lightweights are comfort and weight. However, they are not usually waterproof because of the thin materials (except, for a while when new, those with waterproof-breathable linings), and some have many vulnerable seams. Lightweight boots reach the ankle or higher and have protective rands, or bumpers (either full or just at the toe and heel), cushioned linings, sewn-in tongues, graded flexible midsoles, and on some models, half-length shanks. When I wear boots they are usually light ones. They can cope with most terrain except steep, hard snow and ice. I wore a pair of 34-ounce leather lightweights for most of the Arizona Trail with a pack that weighed 70 pounds at one point (six days' food and three gallons of water). They lasted the 800-mile hike and were very comfortable except on the hottest days, when I wore sandals.

Medium-Weight Boots

Weighing from 3 to 4 pounds, medium-weight boots are good for mountain and winter backpacking where cold, wet weather is expected and crampons may be needed. The best models combine the durability and support of traditional boots with the comfort of lightweight designs. Although most have one-piece leather construction, a few models are fabric-leather combinations. Most medium-weight boots incorporate a sole stiffener—either stiff nylon midsoles or half-length shanks or both—and can be fitted with crampons for hard snow and ice. Generally these boots are designed to cope with rugged, off-trail terrain in any weather. The best ones are made on curved lasts and feature one-piece top-grain leather, padded sewn-in tongues, heel counters, toe boxes, and shock-absorbing midsoles or dual-density outsoles. Many also include waterproof-breathable sock liners.

The proper fitting of medium-weight boots is critical, and a short break-in period is advisable.

Heavyweight Boots

Heavy boots (4 pounds and up) are, in my opinion, too stiff and heavy for most backpacking, though some traditionalists prefer them. But they are good for *easy mountaineering*—trips that combine hiking with scrambling, easy rock climbing, or long periods of crampon use—the type carried out on easy alpine snow ascents in summer. Light- and medium-weight footwear may be too soft and flexible for these activities, especially crampon use. Heavyweight designs have modern features, though, with synthetic cushioning midsoles, graded nylon midsoles, footbeds, synthetic linings, curved soles, and shock-absorbing heel inserts.

Heavyweights can require considerable breaking in. I find them uncomfortable and tiring to walk in and wear them rarely—only when prolonged crampon use and step kicking in snow are likely. I can accomplish most of the very easy snow and ice climbing I do when backpacking using medium-weight boots that accept flexible crampons and are far more comfortable on easier terrain; on steep, rocky terrain where scrambling and easy climbing may be required, I find lightweight footwear perfectly adequate. The latest heavy boots are more comfortable than traditional models, though, because of rocker soles and carefully shaped uppers.

Insulated Boots

Lightweight and midweight boots and trail shoes with thick socks can keep your feet warm in spring and autumn and in mild winter weather. But when the temperature drops tens of degrees below freezing and the snow is deep, such footwear is likely to prove inadequate. Insulated boots, which may be single boots with synthetic insulation linings or double boots, can make backpacking in severe cold far more enjoyable. Most have higher tops than noninsulated boots, though gaiters may still be needed in deep snow. Soles should be thick to provide insulation from the snow or frozen ground. Insulated boots are bulky and can feel a little clumsy, but in the conditions for which they are designed, warmth is the most important factor. These are generally not mountain boots designed for steep slopes and crampons use, though flexible crampons can be worn with them, but boots for forests, rolling hills, and tundra. Modern materials and construction methods mean weights don't have to be high, with some models weighing as little as 40 ounces. These are specialist boots, and most backpackers won't need them, but if you spend much time in temperatures below around 10°F (-12°C), they are worth considering.

Sandals

Hiking sandals are my favorite footwear for hot weather. Sometimes I use them in cooler conditions with waterproof-breathable or wool socks, too. I long ago overcame my first reaction: that they might be fine for leaping out of rafts in the Colorado River but that their only use to the backpacker was as campwear and for river crossings. Once I tried a pair, I quickly became a convert. Not just any old sandals excel for hiking, of course. To be suitable for walking any distance, they have to support the feet, cushion against hard, rough, and hot surfaces, and grip adequately. The best of them do all of this very well.

Essential features are thick, shock-absorbing soles with a shaped platform that supports the foot; a deep tread for grip; and a strapping system that holds the heel and forefoot firmly. Straps may be leather, synthetic leather, or nylon webbing. The last two materials absorb little moisture and dry quickly and would be my first choice for wet-weather use. They are usually fastened by hook-and-loop (e.g., Velcro) fabric, though some models use clip buckles.

A broad and fairly rigid heel strap is needed to keep the heel centered over the sole. Some models have instep straps that run over the foot, through the sole, and back over the foot. With these it's easy to get a very snug fit. I also look for curved or rimmed edges that protect the feet—especially the toes—from bumping against rocks and stones.

Like other footwear, sandals need to fit properly. Your foot shouldn't hang over the sole at the sides or at the toe or heel, and the straps should hold the foot snugly in place without rubbing. Try sandals on and walk around the store to see if they rub anywhere, just as you would with boots. If you're going to wear them without socks, you may need a size smaller than your boot size. Stabilizing footbeds like Superfeet won't stay put in most sandals, so if you need these, sandals may seem a poor choice. However, many sandals have firm, shaped soles that mimic the effects of footbeds.

Although I haven't had any problems with sandals, they obviously have limitations. They're fine on trails and most rocky terrain but not so good in spiky vegetation. In deserts you need to take great care to avoid cacti; in forests, thorn bushes can be a problem. Though clearly best suited to warm or dry conditions, they can be worn with wool socks when it's cool and dry and waterproof-breathable socks when it's wet. I first learned just how superior sports sandals are to other footwear in hot weather on a trek in the Himalaya, when I wore a pair for more than 75 miles on rugged, steep, stony trails. My feet stayed dry and cool and never felt sore or swollen, nor did I suffer any blisters. Sweaty socks weren't a problem—I wore socks only when it was cold and in camp. When streams crossed the trail, I sloshed straight through, unlike the others in the party, who had to stop to remove their boots and socks. Wearing sandals toughens your feet, too, as I found at the end of a Nepal trek, when I did a 2,000-foot scree run in them.

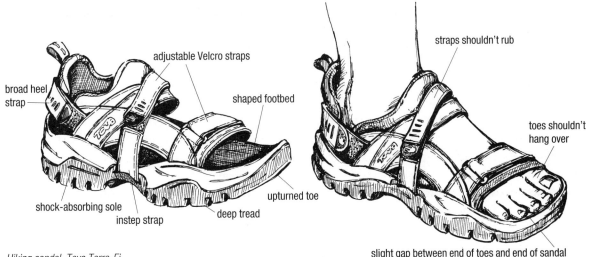

broad heel
strap

adjustable Velcro straps

shaped footbed

shock-absorbing sole

instep strap

deep tread

upturned toe

Hiking sandal. Teva Terra-Fi.

straps shouldn't rub

toes shouldn't
hang over

slight gap between end of toes and end of sandal

The stones that slid between my feet and the sandals were irritating, but they didn't bruise or cut my feet. Really sharp tiny stones, like the pumice found in the Devils Postpile region of the High Sierra, are quite painful, but they would be if they got in your boots, too. An advantage of sandals is that usually you just need to tap the toe on the ground to shake out debris—much quicker than removing boots or shoes.

Since that Nepal trek, I've worn sandals for a 500-mile, five-week hike in the High Sierra; on a through-hike of the 212-mile Southern Upland Way in Scotland; two-week trips in the Colorado Rockies, the Grand Canyon, and the High Uinta Mountains in Utah; and innumerable day and weekend hikes. Whereas sandals used to be my backup footwear, now I sometimes carry lightweight shoes for cool evenings in camp or the occasional cold, stormy day. Mostly, though, I make do with socks.

Five weeks is my longest hike in sandals. Others have gone much farther. Scott Williamson walked the Florida Trail and the Appalachian Trail in sandals, plus the country in between, and Hamish

Brown hiked the 900-mile crest of the Atlas Mountains in Morocco in sandals. Ray and Jenny Jardine wore sandals over a significant portion of the Pacific Crest Trail, though Ray reported that the soles of his feet dried out on this trip and developed painful, deep cracks that took a long time to heal. On my 500-mile High Sierra hike, I had the same problem, with splits appearing in the tips of my big toes. Sunscreen kept the cracks moist and helped them heal, but one got so bad I ended up covering it with 2nd Skin gel, taped

Teva Terra Fi hiking sandal.

into place. Under this dressing it healed in about a week. It's wise to apply sunscreen to bare feet anyway. They don't usually see much sunlight. In sandals they are exposed and, just like any other part of your body, can get burned. Straps can rub, too. If they do, you need a patch of moleskin, Compeed, 2nd Skin, or other hot-spot treatment, just as with boots.

Hiking sandals weigh from 20 to 35 ounces, comparable to hiking shoes. If you just want a pair for campwear, simpler sandals like flip-flops are much lighter.

FITTING BOOTS AND SHOES

Take your time when choosing footwear—if the fit isn't right, you'll suffer. Nothing is worse than footwear that hurts. You need to consider the types of boots and shoes available, construction methods, and materials, but the most modern, high-tech, waterproof, breathable, expensive boots are worse than useless if they don't fit. Given the bewildering variety of foot shapes, good fit entails more than finding the right size. It's unwise to set your heart on a particular model of boot or shoe before you go shopping, however seductive the advertising or the recommendation from a famous hiker, mountaineer, or even backpacking author. Since trying on footwear is essential, this is one item I wouldn't buy on the Internet or from a mail-order catalog.

All footwear is built around a *last*, a rough approximation of the human foot that varies in shape according to the bootmaker's view of what a foot looks like. Lasts sometimes are designated "American," "European," or "British," but these descriptions don't mean much in the real world and can be ignored.

Since women's feet are generally narrower and lower volume (less volume relative to the length and width) than men's, women's boots are made on different-sized lasts. Men with small, narrow feet may find that women's boots fit them best, just as women with larger, wider feet may prefer men's boots.

Curved lasts, which produce a boot with a "rocker" sole, make a big difference, especially in stiff-soled, heavy boots. The curve of the sole rolls with your foot, mimicking the flex of the forefoot and allowing a more natural gait.

Allow several hours for buying footwear, and try to visit a store at a quiet time, not on a busy Saturday afternoon. Feet swell during the day, so it's best to try on new footwear later in the day. Take your hiking socks with you, but if you forget them, most stores provide suitable socks to wear while trying on footwear. Use your normal shoe size only as a starting point; sizes vary from maker to maker and, just to make matters more confusing, there are different sizing systems. A store may stock footwear made in the United States, Italy, Austria, South Korea, and more, so you can't expect consistency.

USA Men's	3.5	4	4.5	5	5.5	6	6.5	7	7.5	8	8.5	9	9.5	10	10.5	11	11.5	12	13	14	15	16
USA Women's	5	5.5	6	6.5	7	7.5	8	8.5	9	9.5	10	10.5	11									
European	35	35.5	36	37	37.5	38	38.5	39.5	40	40.5	41.5	42	42.5	43	44	44.5	45	45.5	47	48	49	50
British	2.5	3	3.5	4	4.5	5	5.5	6	6.5	7	7.5	8	8.5	9	9.5	10	10.5	11	12	13	14	15
Japanese	21.5	22	22.5	23	23.5	23.5	24	24.5	25	25.5	26	26	26.5	27	27.5	28	28.5	29	29.5	30	31	31

Boot size comparison chart.

Phil Oren checking the fit on an incline board.

Phil Oren checking heel fit on an incline board.

Make sure you try on both shoes. One of your feet is almost certainly larger than the other, perhaps by as much as half a size. *Make sure the larger foot has the best fit.* An extra sock or a volume adjuster can pad a boot that's slightly too large, but nothing can be done for one that's too small.

Lightweight boots and shoes are fairly easy to fit because they are soft and mold to the feet quickly. Medium- and heavy-weight boots tend to be uncomfortable at first, which makes finding a good fit in the store more difficult. But because they are so unforgiving, a good fit is essential, even though they should eventually stretch a little (in width, not length) and adapt to your feet. Even more care is needed when fitting traditional heavy leather boots.

I used to recommend the standard fitting method—put your finger down the back with the boots unlaced, wiggle your toes, lace the boots, walk around the store, kick something. It was, I thought, good advice. It is in fact totally inadequate. However just like everyone else, I didn't know any better. I do now. I know that with proper fitting you can get footwear that doesn't hurt your feet. If you're one of those lucky people—those lucky few—whose feet and legs don't hurt, whose boots don't rub, who don't get blisters, then you can ignore the next section. For those whose feet may give the occasional twinge, to those for whom blisters and aching feet are major problems, the next few paragraphs could be the most important part of this book.

Proper fitting begins with the feet, not the footwear. The system that has revolutionized boot fitting was developed by Phil Oren after he had problems finding footwear that fit properly for a 750-mile hike on the Pacific Crest Trail. His feet had been damaged by ill-fitting footwear in the past, so standard boots wouldn't fit him. After having his boots modified at a ski shop, he successfully completed his hike. Along the way he met many hikers with foot problems traceable to poorly fitting footwear, and he started searching for a better way to fit hiking footwear. The result was a sophisticated fitting system that really does work. Phil has now retired, but there are still boot fitters who were trained by him and his staff, and companies like Superfeet train fitters in similar methods. I had footwear fitted by Phil and took training in his FitSystem. I'm convinced it's the best way to fit footwear.

Everyone's feet are different, so it's hardly a surprise that mass-produced footwear is unlikely to fit well without modification. I certainly had problems finding footwear that fit well until I used the FitSystem. These problems increased over the years as my feet appeared to get bigger. I was faced with a choice between footwear that hurt my toes, especially when hiking downhill, and larger sizes that allowed my toes room but didn't support my ankles or hold my heels in position, resulting in holes in the linings and in the heels of my socks. I went for the larger size, since this was less painful over a day's hiking, but it certainly wasn't ideal. Since having a proper fitting, I've gone back to my original size without sore toes, and I don't wear holes in the linings or my socks. I suggest asking store staff if they are trained in footwear fitting and seeing if they follow the procedure I outline next, which is based on Phil Oren's FitSystem.

Foot Examination

A boot fitter should examine and measure your feet before you try on any footwear in order to find out whether you have any fitting problems and which footwear is likely to fit. Information from the examination should be entered on a foot chart, which you can do while being examined. This can be unnerving, as I discovered when Phil examined my feet and informed me I had (slight) hammertoes, Morton's toe, chubby toe, toe drift, calluses, and the beginnings of bunions. Ouch! Would I ever walk again?

Next comes the toe test, which is done standing, so the feet are bearing weight. The fitter tries to lift your big toe off the ground with a finger placed under its tip. If your feet are aligned properly, the toe should move easily. If, like mine, it seems glued to the ground, your foot is overpronated. To check this, the fitter twists your knee outward, putting the foot into the neutral position. The big toe should now be flexible.

The biomechanics of walking explains what the toe test tells us. As you walk, the shape of your foot changes constantly. All footwear interferes with this. When your foot is in midstride, with no weight on it, it's in the neutral position. When your heel hits the ground, your foot rolls to the inside and the arch flattens slightly. This *pronation* allows the foot to adapt to rough, uneven surfaces; remember that our feet were designed for

CUSTOM-MADE FOOTWEAR

Several companies offer a made-to-measure service for those who can't find a suitable pair of boots off the shelf. I once had the Swedish bootmakers Lundhags make boots for me by mail order (not something I recommend). Working from a sketched outline of my feet, they produced a well-fitting pair of their 3-pound Mountaineer boots, which I immediately wore on a two-week walk in the Pyrenees. They proved very comfortable. I had no problems with sore spots or blisters, though the lack of a heel counter made them unsuitable for off-trail travel. Peter Limmer of New Hampshire (limmer boot.com)

is the best-known maker of custom boots. I know people who rave about theirs. It's not surprising that the wait for a pair can be long. Other makers include Van Gorkom Custom Hiking Boots of British Columbia (www.hikingbootshandcrafted.com), Altberg the Yorkshire Bootmakers of Richmond, England (www. altberg.co.uk), and Esatto (esatto.biz), which offers a kit for measuring your feet at home. Your local outdoor store may know of more.

If you have to order boots by mail, most companies have clear instructions for obtaining the right size. But nothing beats trying on boots in a store.

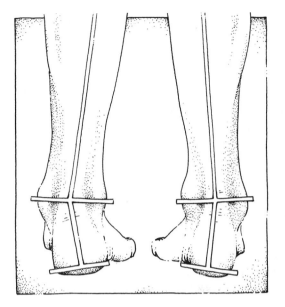

Overpronation (left) and oversupination (right).

walking on soil, grass, stone, sand, and other natural terrain, not flat, smooth, man-made surfaces. As your foot flattens against the ground, it should go into neutral and stiffen for stability and forward movement. As your heel lifts off the ground, your foot becomes a rigid lever with a high arch and instep so you can spring forward off your big toe. This is called *supination* (oversupination can occur but is very rare). After years of wearing unsupportive footwear and walking on pavements and floors, instead of going into neutral and then becoming slightly supinated, the foot often just flattens out (overpronation). In this position your foot is locked to the ground with no spring in the toes (hence the toe test). To take your next step, you have to move from the inside of your foot rather than from your toes. When you do this the foot tends to turn slightly outward, which distorts the skeletal structure, twisting the ankle, knee, and hip when they should be aligned. This unstable posture can lead to joint problems. When your foot overpronates it also elongates, which

makes boot fitting very difficult. Do you fit to the shorter, neutral position or the longer, overpronated one? That was my problem. This elongation can be shown by drawing around the foot while it is weighted and unweighted and comparing the two outlines. It's then easy to see that the same boot can't fit both shapes. Phil Oren's data show that overpronation affects about 80 percent of us, so it's a major boot-fitting issue.

Foot Measurement

The toe test shows whether you overpronate. But that in itself doesn't help much with boot fitting. Next you need to know what size your feet are and what difference overpronation makes. Each foot should be measured with the Brannock Device (an instrument for measuring foot length and width) for overall length (heel to toe) and for heel-to-ball length, which is important because boots should flex where your foot does. The measurements should be taken with the foot weighted and again with it unweighted and in the neutral position. The width of your feet should be measured too. Each of my feet varied by one size in total length and one and a half to two sizes from heel to ball. That explained why my feet appeared to be getting bigger. They weren't; they were overpronating and elongating when weighted.

Foot volume is important too, but this has to be estimated; the Brannock Device cannot measure volume. My feet are low volume, and I have narrow heels and very narrow Achilles tendons. However, my feet are also quite wide, so I need footwear that is wide across the metatarsals (the base of the toes) but low in volume and narrow at the heel.

Stabilization and Footbeds

If your feet overpronate, and chances are they do, they need stabilizing if your footwear is to fit properly. This can be done with footbeds that support the foot and hold it in position, which means junking the soft foam inserts found in most boots and shoes. These "footbeds" provide no support and don't stabilize the feet. Just try pushing your finger against the sides of the heel section while holding the center down with the other hand. With virtually all inserts that come in footwear, the sides collapse easily. They'll do the same under your foot. (Montrail and Haglöfs do both provide moldable footbeds with some of their footwear.)

There are several types of stabilizing footbeds (Conform'able and Sole Custom are two) as well as prescription orthotics. The ones I use are Superfeet footbeds. They have a hard plastic and cork rear and midsection that holds the heel in place, minimizing foot movement and overpronation. There are two types: off-the-shelf footbeds, called Trim to Fit, and Custom Fit. Trim to Fit footbeds can stabilize the foot 40 to 75 percent, and Custom Fit ones stabilize it up to 95 percent. Due to my level of overpronation, I wear Custom Fit Superfeet. To make these, the fitter holds the foot in the neutral position (footbeds made with the feet weighted will fit the overpronated foot, which you don't want). The footbeds, which are partially shaped already, are heated and then held under your feet in plastic bags. All the air is then sucked out of the bags—a slightly peculiar sensation—while the footbeds mold to your feet.

Since your feet are so firmly supported and no longer move in your footwear, stabilizing footbeds can feel strange and even uncomfortable at first. It may be a good idea to wear them for just a few hours at a time until you adjust, though I could wear them all day immediately. Once the footbeds are fitted they can be transferred from one pair of shoes or boots to another, and I now put them in all my footwear. I now take a smaller

BREAKING IN

Gone, thankfully, are the days when you had to wear boots for many short, gentle strolls before you dared subject your feet to them on a real walk. Today you can set off on a fifteen-mile walk the same day you buy a pair of lightweight boots and suffer not a blister; for medium-weight models a short break-in period is advisable, though not essential. Only if you have particularly tender feet or heavyweight boots (which I don't recommend) will you need to wear your boots for a long time before setting off on a major trek. Old-fashioned remedies like soaking your boots and then walking them dry or filling them with hot water were designed for old-fashioned stiff leather. This brutal treatment probably didn't do boots much good in the old days, and it would certainly harm modern boots.

size because my feet no longer elongate much when weighted. I can stride off my toes too, rather than the insides of my feet, so I've lost that slightly splayed duck-footed walk I had. My feet ache less because the footbeds prevent the cushioning fat pad under the heel from flattening and spreading sideways when weighted, and my knees ache less on long descents because my ankles, knees, and hips are properly aligned.

To test your alignment, stand with your feet slightly apart and your hands held out in front of you, one over the other. Have a friend slowly press down on your hands. If you overpronate you'll lose your balance quickly and feel very unstable.

Next stand on a pair of stabilizing footbeds and repeat the test. With your joints properly aligned, you should be able to resist the downward pressure without much effort.

To demonstrate the fat pads, get a friend to push her fingers against the base of your unsupported heel. She should be able to feel the heel bone easily. Then have her squeeze the sides of the heel together with the other hand and press with her fingers again. This time the fat pad will prevent her from feeling the bone. Stabilizing footbeds do the same. If your feet don't overpronate, these tests won't show much difference, and you won't need stabilizing footbeds.

stand arm's-length apart, feet slightly apart

apply pressure downward

Testing proper alignment.

Volume Adjusters and Tongue Depressors

Stabilizing footbeds will have an effect only if your footwear fit properly. If they are too roomy, the footbeds alone won't stop your feet from moving in them. For that you'll need to reduce the boots' volume by wearing thicker socks; by putting a solid, noncompressible flat piece of neoprene, called a volume adjuster, under the footbed; or by placing a piece of soft rubber under the laces to push the tongue down on the foot when the laces are tightened (a tongue depressor). These methods can make boots and shoes with too high a volume fit better, but it's best to have a good fit to start with. Luckily that is easier than it used to be. Since Phil Oren's FitSystem came to prominence, some bootmakers have altered the shape of their lasts and reduced the volume of their footwear so they are more like most people's feet. Certainly I more often find footwear that fits well.

The Right Fit

Once your feet have been inspected and measured and the fitter has decided whether you need stabilizing footbeds or other accessories, it's finally time to try on some footwear. It's best to wear your hiking socks for this. Don't, even now, expect to find a perfect fit: as close as possible is what you're looking for, meaning a boot that approximates the shape of your foot in volume and width as well as length. Beware of boots that are too big. These tend to feel comfortable because they don't press anywhere on your feet, but in use they'll rub and be unsupportive. Boots should fit snugly around the heel, ankle, and instep but have room for you to wiggle your toes. They should flex at the same point as your feet do

so you don't have to fight them every time you take a step, which is tiring and may make your feet slip inside your footwear.

Incline Board

Once you've found a rough fit, you need to try the boots on a 20-degree ramp known as an incline board. Lace the boots firmly, then stand facing up the board while the fitter checks that the boot heels fit properly and sees whether there is any space or loose fabric around the instep and ankle, showing that the boot has too much volume. The fitter should also mark on the boots with chalk or a piece of tape the points where they flex and, by feeling for the first metatarsal head at the base of your toes, check whether your feet flex in the same place. Once this is done, you face down the incline board and jump up and down before the fitter again checks to see if your feet have moved much in the boots. If they have, the boots have too much volume. This can be solved as described earlier, but it is preferable to try lower-volume footwear instead.

Modification

The footwear that fits your feet best is still unlikely to fit exactly. A good fitter should be able to modify footwear to achieve a custom fit. Pressure points, often around the flex point, are the main problem. Boots can be stretched to remove them, using the blunt end of a bent metal *rubbing bar* to gradually ease out the leather or fabric. Just a tiny modification can have quite an effect on the fit. Since I test boots for a hiking magazine, I have my own rubbing bar at home so I can stretch boots that are too narrow for me. This has let me test many boots that would otherwise have hurt

Right: Adjusting a boot-stretching device to the correct foot shape. Below: Jeff Gray of Superfeet placing a boot (without the footbed) in hot water to soften it for modification. Bottom: Jeff Gray stretching a boot.

my feet. Occasionally there may be tiny bumps inside footwear due to manufacturing anomalies. With the boot on the rubbing bar, these can be flattened with a convex hammer.

Although leather can be stretched on the rubbing bar, you can't stretch hard, synthetic toe boxes and heel counters or rubber rands (see the next section, Footwear Materials and Construction) without heating them first to soften the material. This can be done by sealing the boots in a plastic bag and dunking them in a large pot of boiling water. Various hydraulic devices can then be used along with the rubbing bar to stretch the boots.

For the fit that is closest to perfect, you can have casts made of the front or rear of your foot and then inserted into footwear to stretch it to the exact shape of your feet. Although initially expensive, the casts can be used for all your footwear.

A good boot fitter should make any required modifications when you buy footwear. If you already have footwear that doesn't fit properly,

Making a foot cast.

Foot casts can be used to ensure that footwear fits properly.

you can take it to a store to be modified. Phil Oren believes that most footwear needs modification of some sort to get the best fit.

I suggest going through the fitting process every time you buy new hiking footwear even if it is the same model. Manufacturing processes can change, and new lasts may be used. I've found that models that once fitted me well didn't do so a few years later. I discovered that a different factory was producing them and that the fit had indeed changed slightly. If you keep the details of your foot examination and measurements, this process doesn't need to be done every time, though it's worth an occasional check to see if anything has changed, especially if you have any foot problems. It's advisable to always fit footwear using any accessories you expect to use with them, such as stabilizing footbeds.

When you get your new footwear home, wear them inside for a few hours or even a few days just to check that they really do fit. A store should exchange footwear that haven't been worn outside. Once they're muddy and scuffed, they're yours.

FOOTWEAR MATERIALS AND CONSTRUCTION

There are two basic parts to a boot or shoe: the *uppers*, which are flexible and mold around the foot; and the *sole*, which is more rigid and lies under the foot. The sole is usually made up of a number of layers. The *insole* lies under the footbed and is usually quite thin. The *midsole* lies between the insole and the outsole and may itself consist of several layers of shock-absorbing and stiffening materials. The *outsole* contacts the ground and has a tread cut into it. The uppers and the sole are made separately and then attached via the construction method.

Uppers

Leather

Leather is still the main material for uppers, though synthetics now dominate midsoles and linings and fabric-leather combinations are standard for running and trail shoes and common in the lightest boots. Leather lasts longer than other upper materials, keeps your feet dry longer, and absorbs and then disperses moisture (sweat) quickly and efficiently. It is also flexible and comfortable.

Although fancy names abound, there are two basic types of leather: *top-grain* and *split-grain*. Top-grain leather, made from the outer layer of the cow's hide, is tougher and thicker and holds water-repellent treatment and its shape better than split-grain leather, which is the inner layer of the hide. Split-grain leather is often coated with polyurethane or polyvinyl chloride (PVC) to make it more water resistant and attractive. However this shiny layer soon cracks and allows the leather to soak up water like a sponge, while the remaining coating impedes drying. Full-grain leather is the full thickness of the hide. It's very tough and water resistant but also thick and heavy, so it's rarely used in boots, although the term is often used for top-grain leather. Nubuck (also spelled *nubuc* and *nubuk*) is top-grain leather that has been sanded and polished to give it a smooth finish somewhat similar to suede. It's much tougher and more water resistant than suede, which is split leather with the inner surface turned outward and brushed. Nubuck is popular with bootmakers because it shows scuffs and scratches less than smooth leathers do and has a sensuous feel. Some top-grain leather boots

have the rough inner surface of the leather facing out, though this is less common now that nubuck is available. Rough-out and nubuck leathers are easily distinguished from suede by their thickness and solidity. Suede is often used to strengthen the wear points of fabric footwear. Although it is not as durable, supportive, or water resistant as top-grain leather or the best split leathers, good-quality suede is still worth considering for lightweight footwear.

Leather comes in various thicknesses, always measured in millimeters—inches just aren't precise enough. Heavyweight mountaineering boots usually have 3-millimeter leather, light hikers 2-millimeter or less.

To make it usable in footwear, all leather has to be tanned—treated with chemicals or oils. With some leathers a water-repellent substance—usually silicone—is chemically bonded to the fibers during tanning. This leather goes by various names, such as HS12, Prime WeatherTuff, and Pittards WR100. I've found that this leather performs as advertised, especially when new, and is nearly waterproof. In time, though, the waterproofing breaks down and waxing (for more on this, see Waterproofing and Sealing later in this chapter) is required.

A new and potentially exciting way to waterproof boots is ion-mask technology from P2i. This is a treatment in which "every single fiber is given a layer of water-repellent polymer only molecules thick." It's applied to the whole of the footwear, inside and out, and is claimed to make leather waterproof and nonabsorbent while remaining breathable. The treatment also repels oil and dirt, so the boots should remain cleaner longer. Being nonabsorbent means that they should not take up much weight when wet and should dry very quickly. And because it's chemically bonded to every fiber, the treatment cannot wear off. The

WET FEET/DRY FEET

One reason many people wear leather boots is to keep their feet dry. On weekend hikes, many boots will indeed do this, at least when they're fairly new. But on longer trips it becomes more difficult; on walks of several weeks it's impossible if the rain lasts many days. This is because leather boots need to be fully dried and then treated with a waterproofing compound after a few wet days if they are to keep your feet dry. Boots with waterproof linings need less care, but they have other disadvantages (see Linings and Padding, later in this chapter).

On a long walk in wet weather, completely drying any kind of boot material is very difficult. I walked 1,300 miles up the length of Norway and Sweden during a very wet summer. Because much of the route was over rough terrain, I wore lightweight leather boots. For most of the walk they were sodden, which doubled their weight, reduced the breathability, and softened the leather so it gave less support. I would have been far better off with fabric-leather shoes, which wouldn't have gained as much weight when wet, would have been much more breathable, and would have dried more quickly when

it wasn't raining. My feet would still have been wet, but they'd have been much more comfortable. I'd rather have cool, wet feet than hot, sweaty feet.

In warm weather, wet feet aren't a problem—as long as you can keep them dry overnight. When it's cold, the answer is thick socks, preferably with a high wool content, changed regularly. During a forty-day walk through wet, thawing spring snow in the High Sierra, my heavy leather boots were soaked most of the time. (If I did that trip again, I'd ski and wear plastic boots.) By the end of each day, my wool socks were soaked. To keep my feet as warm and dry as possible, I alternated two pairs of thick wool socks, hanging the previous day's wet socks on the back of my pack to dry each morning and wearing the pair I'd dried the day before. I kept a third dry pair for wearing in the tent. It worked— I had no blisters or other foot problems during the walk. An alternative for wet weather is a pair of waterproof-breathable socks (see Waterproof Socks, later in this chapter). These will keep your feet dry and are, in my opinion, a far better choice than footwear with waterproof-breathable linings.

treatment is applied by placing boots in a vacuum chamber in which plasma is generated followed by the injection of a fluorocarbon, which penetrates every fiber of the shoe. Next, a polymer is introduced that is only nanometers thick (1,000 times thinner than a human hair) to "enhance" the surface of the shoe. The process is more environmentally friendly than alternatives, as only tiny quantities of chemicals are needed, and it takes place at room temperature. Potentially it could render waterproof-breathable membranes in boots unnecessary and would solve the problem of such membranes reducing breathability and increasing warmth (not a problem in cold weather, of course). Ion-mask footwear should be comfortable year-round. Hi-Tec was the first out-

door company to use this technology. I've been using ion-mask Hi-Tec boots, and they've lived up to the claims made.

Fabric-Leather

Many lightweight boots and trail shoes copy the nylon-suede design of the running shoes they were based on. This works well in all but the coldest, snowiest conditions. Uppers are mostly fabric, often nylon mesh in shoes but usually textured nylon in boots (though sometimes polyester), reinforced with leather, suede, or synthetic leather. This design requires many seams, which are vulnerable to abrasion and thus may not be durable in rough, rocky terrain, where boot uppers take a hammering. (I found this out the hard way many years ago while scrambling and walking on the incredibly rough and sharp gabbroic rock of the Cuillin Ridge on Scotland's Isle of Skye. After two weeks, my nylon-suede boots were in shreds, and virtually every seam had ripped open.)

Waterproofness is not a strong point of fabric-leather footwear either, unless they are lined with a waterproof-breathable membrane. This is again mostly because of the seams but also comes from the thinness of the materials. Grit and dirt can penetrate nylon much more easily than leather, however, so such membranes do not last as long in synthetic boots as in leather boots, whether they are lightweight nylon or the much tougher Cordura. I like synthetic leather for trail shoes, but for lightweight boots I prefer all leather since I wear boots only in terrain I feel is too rugged for shoes.

So why consider fabric-leather footwear at all? Because it's cool in warm weather (as long as there's no membrane), it needs little or no breaking in, it's comfortable, and it dries more quickly than heavier footwear. It's also used on many of the lightest, most flexible shoes.

Synthetic Leather

Many sandals, some shoes, and a very few boots (such as the Garmont Kiowa Vegan) use synthetic leather for the uppers, often in combination with nylon. Synthetic leather is flexible and mimics fairly well the performance of split-grain leather, though not top-grain. It has the advantage of being nonabsorbent and therefore quick drying, but it's not very breathable.

Plastic

Plastic is now the dominant material for mountaineering boots, alpine ski boots, and telemark ski boots because it's better than leather at provid-ing the rigidity, waterproofness, and warmth such pursuits require. But hiking boots need to be flexible and permeable to moisture so that sweat can escape. I've hiked in plastic telemark and climbing boots, and I've never had such sore and blistered heels or such aching feet. With their rigid soles and outer shells, such boots work against your feet rather than with them. Now when I hike to the snow in my plastic telemark boots, I undo the clips on the uppers to allow my feet to flex. This isn't very stable, but it's less painful than keeping the boots done up. Plastic hiking boots have appeared in the past but soon vanished, since they were too hot and sweaty.

Heel Counters and Toe Boxes

Heels need to be held in place and prevented from twisting, and toes need room to move and protection from rocks and other natural protuberances. *Heel counters*, or heel cups, are stiff pieces of material—usually synthetic, though sometimes leather—built into the rear of boots or shoes to cup the heels and hold them in place. You usually can't see them, although some makers put them on the outside of some footwear, but you can feel them under the leather of the heel. Heel counters are essential. A soft, sloppy heel without a counter won't support your ankle, no matter how high the upper.

Toe boxes are usually made from similar material inserted in the front of a boot; some boots dispense with this construction in favor of a thick rubber rand around the boot toe.

Linings and Padding

Traditionally, linings were made from soft leather —as they still are in some boots—but lighter, less-absorbent, harder-wearing, quicker-drying, moisture-wicking, nonrotting synthetics are taking over. The main one is Cambrelle. I find these new linings superior to their leather counterparts (unless the boots have waterproof-breathable membrane linings, as discussed below, in which case leather protects the membrane better). Some wearers have found an odor problem with synthetic linings, but that hasn't occurred in the footwear I've used.

Many boots have a thin layer of foam padding between the lining and the outside, usually around the ankle and the upper tongue, but occasionally throughout the boot. Such padding does provide more cushioning for the foot, but it also makes boots warmer, something to be avoided in hot weather. Foam also absorbs water and dries slowly. I prefer boots with minimum padding; I rely on socks for warmth.

Many boots now feature linings, sometimes called *booties*, made from vapor-permeable waterproof membranes such as Gore-Tex and eVent. These certainly make the boots waterproof when they are new, but once the membrane is torn or punctured, it will leak. How long they keep water out varies. The membrane itself is fragile, and if your feet move in your boots, the membranes can wear out very quickly. Some people swear by them, others swear at them. My experience suggests that such linings last longest and perform best in boots that have few seams and are made from leather rather than nylon and suede. Membranes laminated to leather are less likely to be cut by tiny specks of sharp grit than those laminated to more open-weave synthetic fabrics. The first membranes leaked fairly quickly, sometimes after only a few weeks' use, but newer ones do last longer. I have a pair of trail shoes several years old that have had months of use and are still waterproof. Even so, good-quality footwear should long outlast a membrane lining.

Waterproof-breathable membranes have another big disadvantage. Although they let some water vapor out, they are far less breathable than footwear without them. Thus they are hot and sweaty in warm weather, especially if the uppers get saturated—which is why water-repellent leathers are best for the outside. And if you do get them wet inside (say, by stepping in a deep pool or creek), they are slow to dry, because although vapor can pass through the membrane, liquid cannot. There are better ways to keep your feet dry (see Waterproof Socks, later in this chapter).

A few boots have nonbreathable waterproof liners. These are suitable only for cold, wet conditions, and even then your feet can get quite wet from sweat. I'd avoid these boots.

The Tongue

Sewn-in, gusseted tongues with light padding inside are the most comfortable and water resistant, and they're found on most footwear; the only disadvantage of gusseted tongues is that if you're not wearing gaiters, snow can collect in the gussets and soak into the boots. *Oxford construction* is a better design for snow: two flaps of leather (basically extensions of the upper) fold over the inner tongue, which may or may not be sewn in, often held in place by small hook-and-loop tabs. Some heavier boots achieve the same purpose by a gusseted tongue with another tongue behind it, sewn in only at the base. On high-ankle and stiff leather boots, the tongue may be hinged so it flexes easily.

Lacing

Boots may be laced up using D-rings, hooks, eyelets, webbing, miniature pulleys, and speed lacing (tiny metal tunnels through which the laces can be pulled quickly). D-rings may be plastic

KEY FEATURES: THREE-SEASON BOOTS AND SHOES

- A good fit. This is more important than anything else. Regardless of the quality, badly fitting footwear means blisters and sore feet.
- Light weight. One pound on your feet equals five pounds on your back.
- Deep lugs for good grip on rough ground.
- A torsionally stiff insole that flexes at the right point.

- Shock-absorbing midsoles for cushioning and comfort.
- A solid heel counter to center your foot over the sole.
- A soft cuff to minimize rubbing (in boots).
- Speed hooks or pulleys for quick lacing.
- A sewn-in tongue to keep water out.

pull-on finger tab

tall foam-padded, sewn-in, gusseted tongue

combination of D-rings and speed hooks to adjust laces and fine-tune fit

foam padding around ankle support

combination of nylon and leather for light weight and breathability

A lightweight hiker (see details, left).

stabilizing footbed for fine-tuning fit

heel cup (heel counter) for support and stability

protective toe rand

nylon lasting board (insole) for torsional support

above-the-ankle height for support

minimal seams for minimal leakage

fully gusseted tongue to keep water out

deep-lugged outsole for good traction

welt to accept clip-on crampons

locking hook

A heavy-duty mountain boot.

molded polyurethane/EVA midsole for shock absorption

high-rubber-content lugged outsole for good traction

synthetic and suede for light weight and breathability

An approach shoe.

Cross section through a three-season boot.

and sewn to the upper (the norm on shoes and ultralight boots) or metal and attached to a swivel clip riveted to the upper. The easiest system to use combines two or three rows of D-rings at the bottom of the laces with several rows of hooks or speed lacing at the top. With this system you can open the boot fully at the top yet tighten the laces quickly. This advantage is not trivial when you're trying to don a stiff, half-frozen boot in a small tent while wearing gloves, with a blizzard outside. Boots with D-rings alone involve far more fiddling with the laces and are harder to tighten precisely. Some boots use tiny pulleys instead of D-rings. These make it very easy to adjust the fit evenly across the foot. Whatever the type of lacing, many boots have a locking hook offset at the ankle that holds the lace in place even when it's undone. The offset position allows you to tighten the boot around the instep to stop your foot from slipping.

Old-style eyelets are rare on boots now, though they are still found on some shoes. Although they are the most awkward system to use, eyelets are the least susceptible to breakage. Shoes often have webbing loops for laces, and these are starting to appear on boots.

My current winter boots (5-pound high-topped leather monsters, but good with crampons) have four rows of speed lacing, one set of metal D-rings, one set of offset webbing loops, and two rows of hooks. My lightweight hikers (2 pounds, 2 ounces, leather) have two rows of speed lacing, offset locking hooks, and two rows of hooks. And my trail shoes (1 pound, 8.5 ounces, mostly mesh with webbing and synthetic leather reinforcements) have four sets of webbing loops and two sets of eyelets. All these lacing methods work well, enabling me to lace the boots quickly and adjust the tension so the footwear fits snugly.

Laces are usually made from braided nylon, which rarely breaks, though it may wear through from abrasion after much use. Round laces seem to last longer than flat ones, though not by much. I used to carry spare laces, but I gave it up long ago; it's been years since I had a lace snap, even on long walks. If one ever does, I'll replace it with a length of the nylon cord I always carry.

Whatever the type of lacing system, footwear must be laced properly if it is to support your feet. The laces should hold the footwear snugly around the forefoot but not be too tight across the instep, which can hinder the forward flex of the ankle. Loose laces allow the feet to move in the footwear; too-tight laces are painful.

Scree Collars

Many boots have one or more rolls of synthetic material or foam-padded soft leather at the cuff to keep out stones, grass seeds, mud, and other debris, but for this to work well the boots have to be laced up so tightly that they restrict ankle movement. The collars themselves don't seem to cause any problems, so their presence or absence can be ignored when choosing a boot.

Seams

Conventional wisdom says the fewer seams, the better, because seams may admit water and can abrade, allowing the boot to disintegrate; thus one-piece leather boots with seams only at the heel and around the tongue should prove the most durable and water resistant.

I agree. Having used quite a few pairs of shoes and boots made from several pieces of stitched fabric and leather, I've found their life expectancy limited by how long the seams remained intact. Side seams usually split first. (This can be postponed, but not prevented, by coating them heavily with a seam sealer or quick-setting flexible epoxy, which also decreases the likelihood of leaks.)

I don't rely solely on one-piece leather construction for footwear, however, as it's usually found only in medium to heavy footwear. But for long treks in cold, wet conditions, I still prefer one-piece leather boots. It's a difficult trade-off. I learned this the hard way. Walking the length of the Canadian Rockies, I used two pairs of sectional leather boots from different makers; they both split at the side seams after about 750 miles. I guessed that only a one-piece leather boot would have lasted the whole walk, so two years later, when I set off on a thousand-mile walk across the Yukon Territory, I wore one-piece boots. They lasted the whole trip.

However, it's debatable whether you should wear just one pair of boots or shoes for an entire long-distance hike. I now think you should change footwear after a while because the internal structure can begin to break down and the cushioning in the sole can compact. This is especially so with midsoles made from Evazote (EVA), a closed-cell foam, and similar materials. Heavier boots are generally more durable, but even they will change shape eventually and may no longer fit so well.

Removable Inserts

Most boots and shoes have a removable foam insert, sometimes incorrectly called a footbed or an insole. Some are made from dual-density foam or have pads of shock-absorbing material built into the heel and forefoot for cushioning. Thicker inserts made from shock-absorbing materials such as Sorbothane are said to improve cushioning. Some of these inserts are relatively heavy, adding up to 5 ounces to the weight of footwear, and they may also be hot in warm weather. I used to use such inserts but found they didn't last. Since they don't support your foot, the cushioning they give is mostly illusory, as your foot can still flatten out and overpronate. For real support, you need a stabilizing footbed (see Stabilization and Footbeds, previously in this chapter).

If your feet tend to swell a lot (as is likely on long-distance walks and in hot weather), removing the inserts will make your footwear roomier. I've often done this toward the end of a long day. Inserts and footbeds get damp from sweat during the day, and moisture can accumulate beneath them, so taking them out each evening to let them and the boots dry is a good idea. Don't put them near a fire or other heat source, though—they melt very easily.

Insoles, Midsoles, and Lasting

The boot sole must support the foot, protect it from shock, and be flexible enough to allow a natural gait, but it doesn't need to be stiff. Extensive hiking over rugged terrain in sandals and flexible trail shoes has convinced me that flexibility is more important.

The upper layer of the sole is the insole, or lasting board, a flat, foot-shaped piece of material. Shoes with this layer are described as being board-lasted because the board is fixed to the last and the shoe built around it. The stiffness of a shoe or boot is in part due to the material the board is made from. A flexible fiberboard insole (which may be made from pressed wood pulp or may be synthetic) is common in running and trail shoes and the lightest boots. In inexpensive footwear, the insoles may be cardboard. (There are reports of cardboard insoles breaking up when wet, though this hasn't happened to any I've used.) Much hiking footwear now has torsionally stiff plastic or nylon insoles graded for flex according to the size of the boot. This means that small boots have the same relative flex as larger boots (other stiffening materials can make small boots too stiff and large ones too bendy). Many manufacturers vary the stiffness of the different insoles—the stiffest material is reserved for mountaineering boots, and the most flexible for what is usually described as "easy trail use" with a light load. You can judge flex by bending the boot: a stiff, hard-to-bend shoe is fine for kicking steps in snow but is tiring for most walking. A flexible shoe makes for easy hiking.

The lightest, most flexible shoes and boots may not have a lasting board at all. Instead, when the insole is removed, a line of stitching will be seen running round the edge of the sole or down the middle. This is known as *sliplasting*, in which the upper is sewn into a sock shape and then slipped onto the last. I prefer this construction for lightweight footwear, since it conforms to the natural shape of the foot and is very flexible. Sliplasted shoes are not usually as stiff as board-lasted ones, though there may be a flexible plate similar to a lasting board between the cushioning midsole and the outsole. Some shoes have *combination lasting* —the front is sliplasted, but there is a half-board in the heel. This gives a flexible forefoot but a more rigid heel.

The traditional sole stiffener is a half- or three-quarter-length steel shank, only half an inch or so wide, placed forward from the heel to give solidity to the rear of the foot as well as lateral stability and support to the arch while allowing the front of the foot to flex when walking. Full-length shanks are for rigid mountaineering boots, not for walking. Some boots combine a steel shank with a graded nylon insole.

Many boots incorporate a midsole of a shock-absorbing material. This is usually EVA in lightweight footwear and heavier but much harder-wearing polyurethane or microporous rubber in heavier boots. These midsoles are often tapered wedges, thickest under the heel. They absorb shock well, and I wouldn't consider footwear without them—the difference they make in how your feet feel at the end of a long day is startling. They are designed to protect against the shock of heel strike—the impact when your heel hits the ground—which jars the knees and lower back as well as the feet. Cushioning also is needed at the ball of the foot, and the best shock-absorbing wedges are quite thick under the forefoot as well as the heel.

Some boots also have a stiffening and supportive synthetic plate under the cushioning midsole—

this is a way to give some stiffness to a sliplasted shoe. Sometimes this plate—which is usually latticelike rather than solid—combines with the shock-absorbing midsole and the rand, cradling the foot and providing cushioning as well as good side-to-side support and stability. Even the heel counter and the toe box may be incorporated into these units.

Outsoles

This is the bit of the boot that determines whether you stay upright or skid all over the place. Once there were only a few outsole patterns, with the Vibram carbon-rubber Roccia and Montagna lug outsoles as the standard tread; now they are legion. Vibram has become a whole extended family of sole patterns in itself, and there are many others (Skywalk is one of the most common). Having tried a wide variety of these, I've concluded that any pattern of studs, bars, or other shapes seems to grip well on most terrain. The key is a pattern that bites into soft ground so that the shoe doesn't slip and a sole made from soft enough rubber that when pressure is applied it grips rock and smooth surfaces by friction. I've had shoes with shiny outsoles that were just too hard to provide much friction; they were dangerous on wet pavement. Once the surface of the lugs had worn away, they gripped better. Note that no rubber sole, whatever the pattern or stickiness of the rubber, will grip on hard snow or ice. For that you need metal.

Some footwear uses the "sticky rubber" that revolutionized rock-climbing footwear. Soles with this material are ideal for scrambling and difficult rocky terrain, but the sticky, soft rubber that grips well on rock and other hard, fairly smooth surfaces doesn't bite into soft ground so well. It's

also not very durable. Harder rubbers grip better on mud and wet vegetation and also last longer, so these are used for most boot soles. Some treads combine soft and hard rubber so that the edges grip well on soft ground while the center has good friction. Others are designed with different patterns and rubber densities for downhill braking and traction and uphill traction and push-off. I can't say I can tell any difference between these and traditional soles, but they sound good.

The type of sole footwear has depends on its purpose. Soles with the deepest lugs are found on mountaineering boots, those with the shallowest on sandals and trail running shoes—though some sandals now have surprisingly deep lugs.

There has been some concern about the damage that heavily lugged soles do to soft ground, and some manufacturers have designed soles said to minimize this damage by not collecting debris in the tread. Studded soles seem to work best in this respect, but unless all your walking will be done on gentle trails, grip is the most important quality of outsoles. Grip should not be compromised, especially if you're walking on steep, rugged terrain. Modern soles aren't quite as damaging as traditional ones, since they tend not to have the 90-degree angles at the edges and heels that cut into the ground so deeply. Instead, the edges are rounded and canted.

Many soles are made from a dual-density rubber—a soft upper layer for shock absorption and a hard outer layer for durability—and combine grip with cushioning.

Heavier outsoles with deeper treads should outlast lighter soles, though it's hard to predict tread life. Wear depends on the ground surface—pavement wears out soles fastest, followed by rocks and scree. On soft forest duff, soles last forever. I have found that on long walks, lightweight soles last

Boot heel designs. Rounded (left) and right-angled (right).

In stiff-soled boots you have to come down steep slopes on your heels, so square-cut heels are best. In flexible footwear you can put your feet flat on the ground so rounded heels are fine.

square heels, stiff boots

round heels, flexible footwear

800 to 1,000 miles, while the traditional Vibram Montagna lasts at least 1,250 miles. However, soft EVA midsoles last only about 500 miles (polyurethane lasts longer), so the life of the sole depends on more than the wear of the lugs.

There is little controversy over outsole patterns, but the shape of the heel has generated heated discussions. Indeed, some designs have been blamed for fatal accidents. The debate is over the lack of a *forward heel bar* under the instep, together with a *rounded heel* (derived from running shoe outsoles) and how these features perform when descending steep slopes, especially wet, grassy ones. Traditional soles have a deep bar at the front of the heel and a right-angled rear edge, which their proponents say make descents safe. Rounded heel designs, they say, don't allow you to dig in the back of the heel for grip or use the front bar to halt slips; instead, the sloping heel

makes slipping more likely. To overcome these criticisms, some soles have deep serrations on the sloping heels and forward edges.

After experimenting with different outsoles and observing other hikers, I've concluded that it all depends on how you walk downhill. If you use the back or sides of the heel for support, you're more likely to slip in a boot with a smooth, sloping heel than in one with a serrated or square-cut edge. If you descend as I do, however, with your feet flat on the ground, pointing downhill, and your weight over your feet, heel design is irrelevant. I've descended long, steep slopes covered with slippery vegetation in smooth, sloping-heel footwear without slipping or feeling insecure. I've noticed too that many people who slip while descending steep slopes keep their boots angled *across* the slope and descend using the edges of the sole, without much contact with the ground.

For this a stiff boot with a right-angled heel works best. Of course, if you descend hills flat-footed, you need fairly flexible footwear.

Rounded heels are said to minimize heel strike, because they allow a gradual roll from the heel to the sole instead of the jarring impact when the edge of a square-cut heel hits the ground, but I haven't noticed any difference in practice. A shock-absorbing midsole seems far more important for reducing heel-strike injury.

Rands

The most likely place for water to penetrate a boot is where the sole and the upper meet. Some boots have a rubber *rand* running around this joint, while others have just toe or toe and heel rands, or bumpers. Rands seal the joint against water and also protect the lower edge of the uppers from scuffs and scratches.

Stitching vs. Bonding

Joining the soles to the uppers is a critical part of footwear manufacture. If that connection fails, the shoe or boot will fall apart. Stitching used to be the only way of holding footwear together but is now used mainly in leather boots made for mountaineering or Nordic ski touring rather than for walking. The most common stitched construction is the *Norwegian welt*, sometimes called *stitchdown construction*, in which the upper is turned out from the boot, then sewn to a leather midsole with two or three rows of stitching. These stitches are visible and exposed, but they can be protected by daubing them with sealant.

Currently, on most footwear the uppers are *heat bonded* (glued at high temperatures) or cemented to the sole. (Some are also *Blake* or *Littleway stitched*, which means the uppers are turned in and stitched to a midsole, to which the outsole is cemented.) Unlike the Norwegian welt, the quality of these construction methods cannot be checked. A bonded sole has failed me only once, many years ago. On that occasion, the sole started to peel away from the boot at the toe after only 250 miles. I was on a long trek and far from a repair shop, so I patched the boots with glue from my repair kit almost every night and nursed them through another 500 miles. I wouldn't like to repeat the experience.

FOOTWEAR MODELS AND CHOICES

Because fit is so crucial, I'm reluctant to recommend any specific models. I'm often asked to do so, though, so here are some hints. Over the years I've happily worn footwear from Adidas, Asolo, Bite, Brasher, Chaco, Five Ten, Garmont, Hi-Tec, Inov-8, Keen, Kayland, Lowa, Merrell, Montrail, Nike ACG, Raichle, Rockport, Salomon, Scarpa, Teva, The North Face, Timberland, Vasque, and Zamberlan. That's a lot of boots, shoes, and sandals. Most of the specific models I've used are no longer available. Well-recommended brands I've never tried include Alico, Birkenstock, Boreal, Danner, Dunham, Gronell, La Sportiva, Limmer, Technica.

Of the footwear I've tried most recently and that therefore hadn't disappeared when I wrote this, here are my current favorites, described as examples rather than recommendations. Remember: my ideal shoe might be your worst nightmare.

Sandals

Sandals come in two basic types: open and closed toe. The latter give more protection to the feet—

indeed, some are more like trail shoes with air gaps than sandals. However, while I find them fine for casual wear, I don't like them for hiking, as grit and dirt can easily get inside and then can't be kicked out, as can be done with open-toed sandals. If you find the idea of unprotected toes alarming, they are worth considering, though. Keen pioneered this design and makes several good models.

Teva created the sport sandals genre, and for several years, my favorite sandals have been the different versions of its Terra Fi sandals, which have proven comfortable and durable. They have open toes and webbing straps closed by three long Velcro strips, so there is good adjustability. The straps are padded on the underside, where they press down on the feet. There are rigid plastic supports either side of the ankle that help hold the feet in place. With the straps tightened, I find them very secure. There's also a raised edge to the heel that provides support and protection. The outside edge of the sole is also raised a little, and the sole curves up to the toe. Shock absorption is excellent, especially in the heel, where there is a thick soft insert. Grip is excellent too, the sticky rubber working well on wet rocks, and the deep tread on other terrain. The sole is quite stiff side to side but flexes well at the forefoot. My size 10s weigh 23 ounces. I've also hiked successfully in sandals from Merrell and Hi-Tec.

Trail Shoes

In the 2000s, the trail-running and hiking-shoe field was revolutionized by British company Inov-8, which produces ultralight yet still functional shoes. Of its extensive range, I've found the Terroc 330 the best for hiking. Indeed, it has become my favorite backpacking footwear. The Terrocs are mesh shoes with webbing and synthetic leather reinforcements that weigh just

24.5 ounces in a size 10. I've worn Terrocs on a through-hike of the Pacific Northwest Trail and two TGO Challenge coast-to-coast crossings of the Scottish Highlands (a noncompetitive backpacking event organized every May by *TGO* magazine), as well as many shorter trips. Terrocs flex easily at the forefoot but are laterally quite stiff at the rear, which helps stop the ankle twisting out of the shoe on rough terrain. This is helped by the lacing, which is attached to strips of material running down to the sole, so that when tightened, it pulls the shoe in firmly around the foot. There's a hard toe bumper to protect the toes and strips of synthetic leather between the mesh and the sole that give some abrasion protection. The sole unit is low profile and fairly thin but still provides reasonable cushioning and good grip. It also gives a feeling of being in contact with the ground, which I like, as it's good for stability and free movement. Drying time is good as long as there's some dry weather—on a constantly wet nine-day section of the Pacific Northwest Trail, they were soaked the whole time. Durability is better than I initially expected, and I get 500 to 600 miles out of a pair, which is better than with some lightweight boots. The seams are vulnerable, and I've found that coating them with epoxy is worthwhile.

A heavier trail shoe I've often worn in cold, wet weather as it has a waterproof-breathable membrane is the Keen Targhee II. When the snow wasn't deep, I found these excellent as long as I could keep the water out. Breathability has been adequate in cool weather, but in temperatures above 50°F (10°C), my feet get sweaty quite quickly, so these are not summer shoes. There is a version without the membrane called the Voyager, but it's quite a bit heavier than the Inov-8 Terrocs, so I'd rather have those when it's warm. The Targhee shoes weigh 33 ounces (in men's size 10) and are made from leather and mesh. They

Keen Targhee II trail shoe.

have wide toes and quite a high volume, which means I can wear them with thick socks, unlike many shoes, including the Terrocs. They are reasonably flexible at the forefoot and laterally quite stiff. The lacing, which runs through webbing loops, is effective at pulling the shoes in around the feet and preventing heel lift. The heel cup is firm and supportive, and the toe bumper hard and protective. Cushioning and grip are both good. On ice and hard snow, the shoes can be fitted with flexible crampons.

Lightweight and Midweight Boots

I mostly wear boots from October through April, as I find dealing with snow and cold, wet conditions easier with a high ankle. I used to choose midweight boots for this, but the improvements in lightweight ones have meant I don't see the need for boots weighing more than 3 pounds except for technical mountaineering. Some boots are ultralight. Inov-8's Roclite 400 GTX leather boots weigh 28 ounces, less than many shoes. I haven't tried these, but I have used the Roclite 390

GTX synthetic boots, which weigh just an ounce more. These are basically a trail shoe with a high ankle. They are well cushioned for Inov-8 while still keeping to the company's principle of keeping the foot close to the ground. They don't cushion quite as well as boots with thicker midsoles, however. The studded sole grips well on a variety of terrain. There's a supportive heel and a hard band around the forefoot and toe. The lacing by four sets of fabric loops and two sets of eyelets isn't quite as easy to use as on Inov-8 shoes due to the high ankle. A thick piece of material connects the top lacing to the ankle, so when the laces are tightened, the boot is pulled in firmly round the ankle. They have a Gore-Tex membrane and so are waterproof. The thin mesh outer part of the uppers helps keep them reasonably cool. With midweight socks, I've found them just warm enough in temperatures around freezing as long as I keep moving.

My favorite boots are quite a bit heavier, though. These are Hi-Tecs clumsily named V-Lite Altitude Ultra WPi, which weigh 41 ounces. I like them because of the ion-mask technology, which makes them waterproof while retaining breath-

Hi-Tec V-Lite Altitude Ultra WPi with ion-mask technology.

ability, and because they are warm enough to wear in snow and can be used with flexible crampons. To see just how breathable they are, I did try them on hot summer days, when my feet usually overheat badly in boots with membranes, and was surprised that my feet only felt slightly warm. I also thoroughly tested the waterproof claims, paddling through streams, sloshing through bogs, and tramping through wet grass (usually a good way to remove wax and soak boots). To test the durability of the treatment, which is meant to be permanent, I didn't clean the boots, and they were soon scuffed and scratched, with most of the color gone from the toes. The leather remained waterproof. Initially, water beads up and runs off the leather, leaving it instantly dry. This doesn't last, and after prolonged immersion, the boots do end up with a film of moisture covering the leather. When they were soaked, through water getting in at the top, the boots dried fairly quickly, certainly faster than leather boots usually take to dry and much faster than boots with membranes.

Most of the water uptake was in the synthetic linings rather than the leather outers. Apart from the ion-mask technology, these are good leather boots with excellent cushioning and grip, a flexible forefoot, and lateral stiffness.

Heavyweight Boots

This is my least favorite category; I rarely wear boots this stiff and heavy. But I have been pleasantly surprised by the relative comfort of Scarpa Mantas. These 4-pound, 6-ounce rigid-soled boots have a rocker sole, a rigid nylon midsole with a steel insert, polyurethane cushioning, speed lacing, and a well-fitting, padded upper that makes them quite bearable, though I wouldn't want to do a long trail hike in them. However, on steep slopes if there's much hard snow and ice around and crampons are needed most of the time, they're my first choice. The uppers are made from rough-out water-resistant leather, and the sole is a deep-cleated Vibram Jorasses with

A winter-weight boot (Garmont Pinnacle).

grooves at the toe and heel so clip crampons can be fitted. The polyurethane cushioning takes some of the sting out of rocks and hard surfaces, and the slight rocker in the sole makes walking on the flat easier than with a flat-soled boot. Although the ankles are held firmly in place, they can flex forward thanks to a cutaway section below the top two lace clips, which also makes walking on the flat relatively comfortable. The overall quality of the boots is superb.

Insulated Boots

I first became interested in insulated boots after a winter ski tour in Yellowstone National Park during which temperatures fell to -31°F (-35°C) and were usually far below freezing. My plastic ski boots were just warm enough while moving, but in camp and when building igloos, my feet became unpleasantly cold. Soon afterward, I was offered some Baffin Mountain Boots to test. These high-topped double boots are claimed to be warm

down to -60°F (-51°C). The outer boots are made from silicone-treated, full-grain leather, and the inner boots from a composite of an aluminum membrane, a wicking synthetic, hollow fiber, and open-cell foam with a wicking lining. There's a wide rubber band around the thick sole and a toe bumper. The soles have deep cleats that bite into snow. The silvery inner boots look space-age, and the outer boots look like traditional loggers' or trappers' boots. Although they are bulky and heavy-looking, the weight is actually a reasonable 4 pounds, 6 ounces. In deep snow and temperatures well below freezing, they've been warm and comfortable. I took them on ski tours in Yellowstone and the Wind River Range to wear when I wasn't skiing and felt they were worth the extra weight. The name is a misnomer, though, as these are not mountain boots, in that they are quite soft and flexible and also somewhat clumsy due to the bulk. I've worn them for walking in woods and

Insulated Baffin Mountain Boot.

fields and on moors but not on steep or rocky mountains. They've just kept my feet warm at -25°F (-31°C), so at -60°F (-51°C), they might be a little chilly.

In milder winter weather—down to 5°F (-15°C)—I've also had success with the Keen Growler (replaced by the similar Delta) and the Hi-Tec Whistler insulated boots. Looking much more like conventional hiking boots than the Baffin boots, these boots have linings made of synthetic insulation like Primaloft and Thinsulate plus waterproof-breathable membranes. They're still quite chunky with wide, thick soles and rubberized protection on the leather and fabric uppers. Weights are reasonable at 44 ounces for the Growler or Delta and 52 ounces for the higher-topped Whistler. I wouldn't choose either of these for extreme cold, but for hiking in much cold snowy weather, they are fine.

CARE OF FOOTWEAR

Waterproofing and Sealing

Although most footwear is fairly tough, it needs proper care to ensure a long life and good performance. This care can start before you wear the boots. Sealing any exposed stitching to protect it from abrasion will increase durability and make the seams waterproof. Urethane sealers like McNett Seam Grip work well, as do products specially designed for this use, like Aquaseal Stitch Guard. Some sealants come with an applicator; others are best applied with a syringe. Stitching should be sealed *before* you wear or wax the footwear so that the sealant has a clean, dry surface to stick to. I always used to seal the welts of my leather Nordic ski boots so that water didn't wick in through the stitching when the boots flexed.

My plastic telemark boots don't have stitching. I've also sealed the seams on Inov-8 Terroc trail shoes, which definitely prolongs their life.

Muddy, dirty boots need washing; if mud dries on the uppers, especially if they're leather, they can harden and crack. A soft brush (I use an old toothbrush) helps remove mud from seams, stitching, and tongue gussets, though you should be careful not to scratch leather. I find cold tap water adequate for cleaning hiking footwear, and I don't use soap. I'm not bothered if footwear is stained or discolored; indeed, this can add character. But if ingrained dirt is particularly stubborn or you want to remove any stains, there are specific cleaning products—Nikwax Cleaning Gel, Aquaseal All-Purpose Footwear Cleaner, Granger's G-MAX Footwear Cleaner, and ReviveX Boot Cleaner Concentrate. The first two have easy-to-use sponge applicators. You just rub them over the boots, then rinse off the foam, scrubbing with a soft nylon brush if necessary. A sink is the best place to do this.

The insides of boots can get dirty too, making them smelly and less breathable, so sweaty socks are more likely. In boots with waterproof membranes, tiny specks of grit may work their way through the lining and cut the membrane so it leaks. Just a wipe with a clean, damp cloth may be enough cleaning—it's all I ever do. However, Nikwax suggests filling boots with water and leaving them to soak overnight before emptying them out and rinsing them.

Excessive heat is very likely to make leather harden and split and may melt the glues that hold footwear together. Wet footwear should never be dried in a hot place such as next to a car heater, a house radiator, or a campfire. Leather should never become too hot to touch. Even midday sunshine can be too warm, and if you stay in a mountain hut or hostel with a drying room, you should keep your footwear out of there. Footwear should be left in a cool, dry place to dry slowly, with the insoles removed and the tongues fully open. If shoes are really soaked, stuffing them with newspaper will help them dry. Replace the paper when it gets really wet. Fabric-leather shoes without internal padding dry quickly, but foam-lined leather boots can take a long time—at least several days for medium-weight ones.

Drying footwear can be a problem on long hikes, when it is tempting to dry sodden boots by a fire. I'm occasionally guilty of this. The second half of a Canadian Rockies walk was mostly cross-country in wet terrain, and my lightweight leather boots were soaked by the end of most days. I often helped them dry out by standing them a little too close to my campfire. I had to wear boots with cracked uppers and peeling soles for the last few snowy weeks of the hike.

When wet footwear has dried, it needs to be treated to restore suppleness and water repellency. Bootmakers recommend various products for this, sometimes proprietary ones. It isn't necessary to stick to the treatment specified. All footwear can be treated, including that with waterproof-breathable linings. Indeed, because such linings work well only if the outer of the boot is breathable, it is important that the water repellency of the outer is maintained. If it fails and the outer soaks up moisture, breathability will be impaired. Remove the laces and open the tongue fully so you don't miss any areas. The base of the tongue is a key leak point, so make sure you treat this area.

Once it's no longer part of a living animal, leather isn't waterproof. It's treated with waterproofing compounds during tanning, but this treatment will wear off after a few hikes, especially in wet conditions. Proper treatment increases water repellency and prolongs life by keeping leather footwear supple. What constitutes proper treatment depends in part on the type of leather. Virtually all leathers are now chemically treated rather than oil tanned, and they must be dressed with wax or the new water-based treatments rather than oil. Traditional dressings like neat's-foot oil (made by boiling down cattle feet and shinbones) or mink oil can oversoften leather; I'd use them only for leather that has dried out and hardened. Even then I'd rather use a modern softening product like Nikwax Conditioner for Leather. Makers sometimes suggest not treating specially tanned waterproof leathers until they are scuffed, since they won't absorb proofing before then. Others say all leather should be treated before the first use. I have found that new boots won't absorb much treatment, so I don't bother applying any until the leather loses the initial sheen or water starts to soak into it rather than bead up.

The traditional way to proof leather boots is to apply a soft wax with a cloth or your fingers. Granger's G-Wax, Sno-Seal, and Biwell Classic are made from beeswax, while Aquaseal Leather Waterproofing is silicone based. These waxes work best when applied to warm, dry leather and

Footwear can get extremely dirty after a few miles of muddy forest trail.

left to soak in overnight. Any residue visible on the surface should be wiped off. Several thin coats are more effective than one thick one. Too much can soften the leather anyway, so it's best not to slop the stuff on in dollops. Also, a thick layer of wax can prevent your boots from breathing and lead to sweaty feet. There is a trade-off between the amount of wax you apply, the degree of water resistance obtained, and the breathability of your boots. Several layers of wax will mean better and longer-lasting water resistance but less breathability. In hot weather I'd go easy on the wax, or your feet will get wetter from sweat than from the occasional summer shower. Even for desert hiking I still treat leather, though, to prevent it from drying out and cracking.

There's something sensuous about applying wax to warm leather with your fingers (I prefer fingers to a cloth because their heat helps soften the wax), but I rarely do this anymore because there are much better water-based products. It may seem odd that a waterproofing product's main ingredient is water, but it does work. Water-based treatments were first developed by Nikwax, which makes the widest range, and you can now get them from Granger's (G-MAX Universal Footwear Proofer) and Aquaseal (Liquid Aquaseal). Nikwax water-based treatments consist of polymers made from EVA (the same material used for cushioning midsoles) and mineral wax. The active ingredients take the form of an emulsion—droplets of oil suspended in water. Nikwax treatments coat the fibers of leather and fabric with flexible water-repellent molecules. These molecules will stick only to fibers that aren't already water repellent, so you can't apply too much. The water soaks into areas that aren't water repellent, taking the active ingredients with it. Water-based treatments can be applied to wet leather; indeed, Nikwax says it's best to do so, since the active ingredients are then drawn into those areas that need them most. It's certainly convenient not to have to dry footwear before treating it. Water-based treatments don't block the spaces between the fibers, so footwear remains breathable. And because they can flex, they don't wear off quickly. Water-based products have other advantages. Nikwax says its products can deliver up to five times as many active ingredients per fluid ounce as solvent-based treatments. Water-based products are also environmentally friendly; they contain no petroleum solvents or propellant gases, which contribute to global warming and to the thinning of the ozone layer. The absence of solvents also means water-based products are nonflammable and don't give off noxious fumes, so they are safe to use indoors.

Nikwax Waterproofing Wax for Leather, designed for use on smooth leather, has been my first choice for leather footwear for many years. It lasts longer than other treatments, doesn't soften leather, and is quick and easy to use. The treatment comes in black and brown as well as neutral if you want to restore color to your scuffed boot toes. This wax will work on nubuck or suede, but these will look like smooth leather afterward. If you want to keep the rough texture, use Nikwax Nubuck and Suede Proof. Or you can use a brush to raise the surface of the leather and return it to its original look, though I've never done this.

Fabric-leather footwear has poor water resistance unless there is a waterproof-breathable lining. It can be treated to keep the material supple and to prevent it from soaking up too much moisture, but no amount of proofing will make such footwear waterproof. The best treatment I've found is Nikwax Fabric and Leather Footwear Proof, another water-based product. Another option is the silicone-based Biwell Trekking, which comes in a tube and can be applied with fingers or a cloth. On long walks I don't treat such footwear and have found it dries fairly quickly in warm weather, even when it hasn't been treated for weeks.

Most water-based treatments come with easy-to-use sponge applicators. They're also fine to use on footwear with waterproof-breathable linings.

There are also spray products like Granger's G-MAX Universal Footwear Proofer, ReviveX Leather Spray Water Repellent, and Tectron Footwear Water Repellent. I prefer water-based, rub-on treatments. Too much of the spray can miss the footwear!

Whatever treatment you use, polishing or buffing the leather produces a hard finish or shine that is more water repellent than a matte finish.

Repair

On lightweight boots the uppers often wear out at about the same time as the soles, so resoling is hardly worthwhile. Top-quality lightweights in good condition can be worth repairing, however; I have had trail shoes successfully resoled. Medium-weight boots should last the life of at least two soles, heavyweights even more (I had a pair that were on their fourth soles when I retired them). The key is to have boots resoled before the midsole needs replacing, which can be very expensive. However, EVA midsoles usually need replacing along with the soles, since they compress rather quickly (after 500 miles or so in my experience). For your own safety, don't let outsoles wear down too much.

Many outdoor stores accept boots for repair and send them to either a local cobbler or a national repair store. If you can't find a repair service, ask the manufacturer for advice.

REGLUING A SOLE AT HOME

- Regluing any major boot part is essentially a surgical procedure—cleaning and preparing are key. Wash the boot with soap and water. Once it is thoroughly dry, lightly sand the gluing surfaces. Wipe down the clean, dry boot thoroughly with denatured alcohol before gluing.
- Stuff the boot with paper to provide structure.
- Use contact cement (Barge brand is the most popular footwear adhesive.) Spread a thin layer of adhesive on each prepared surface and let them rest until almost dry.
- Align and mate the parts carefully—you only get *one* chance with contact cement.
- Clamp the parts together with a C-clamp or wrap tightly with strong tape, and let dry. Secure clamping is important to the success and life of your repair.
- Finally, seal the joint with seam sealer.

glue toe and heel bumpers or sole, then clamp and tape

Small holes or severe abrasions can be patched with a urethane seam sealant or a product like McNett Freesole Urethane Formula Shoe Repair. The latter can also be used for reattaching soles that are peeling away, as can Barge Cement. In the backcountry this is not easy to do, since you need some way of holding the sole and boot tightly together while the adhesive dries. Wrapping them with duct tape is probably the easiest way to do this. Don't expect such a repair to last long—just hope it gets you to the nearest trailhead. Duct tape and adhesive can also be used to patch torn seams, though again, such repairs don't usually last long.

FOOT CARE

Keeping your feet in good condition is a prerequisite to pain-free hiking. Toenails should be cut short and square; long nails can bruise, cut into the toes on either side, and inflict pain during descents. When possible, dry wet feet to avoid softening the skin too much. Some people try to harden their skin both before and during a trip with rubbing alcohol. I've never tried this, but I do go barefoot around the house and outside whenever I can. By going barefoot and wearing sandals as often as possible, I usually manage to keep my feet reasonably tough.

Blisters are the bane of many hikers, but too few take preventive measures. The moment you feel a hot or sore spot, stop and attend to it, covering the affected area with a dressing to prevent further rubbing. This may prevent a blister from appearing. This is easy to preach but hard to practice. All too often I ignore warning signs, telling myself that I'll have a look when I next stop. When I do, I invariably find a plump blister.

Blister remedies are legion. What is common to all is that the blister must be covered to prevent infection and cushioned against further rubbing. You can cover a blister with ordinary adhesive tape, moleskin, micropore tape, or even duct tape, but I have found the most effective to be cushioning and friction-resistant dressings such as Spenco 2nd Skin Blister Pads, Spyroflex, and Compeed. These are easier to use than the original 2nd Skin, which had to be taped in place; they come with a thin sticky backing and border and so can be applied just like an ordinary Band-Aid. I carry up to half a dozen of these dressings, depending on the length of the hike.

Some experts advise against lancing a blister before covering it, but if you continue to walk after a blister forms, as you probably will, you need to remove the fluid built up inside to minimize the pain. To do this I sterilize a needle in a match flame, pierce the blister at one edge, then roll the needle over the blister until all the fluid drains out. A piece of toilet tissue can be used to absorb the fluid and wipe the area dry. Large blisters may need several holes to expel all the fluid. I know from painful experience that, however long it takes, the blister must be fully drained before being dressed, or your first steps will hurt so much you'll have to stop again. Antiseptic wipes can be used to clean the area, though gel dressings do this quite well.

Friction causes blisters, so try to find and remove the cause, which may be a tiny speck of grit, a rough sock seam, or more commonly, your foot moving in the boot and rubbing against it. Sometimes the cause isn't obvious, and you just have to hope that covering the blister will solve the problem. Mysteriously, footwear that has never given problems before can cause a blister one day yet be fine again on future trips. However, I would suspect footwear that repeatedly causes sore spots. Either it doesn't fit properly or something inside needs smoothing.

I like to remove my footwear and socks several times during the day, weather permitting, to let my feet cool down and air. Pouring cold water over them provides even more relief on really hot

Treating blisters. Wash the area and treat it with antiseptic (1). Insert a sterile needle into the base or side of the blister (2). (If you don't have a sterile needle in your first-aid kit, you can sterilize a sewing needle by holding it in a match or lighter flame.) Roll the needle over the blister so all the liquid is squeezed out, wiping it up with a piece of tissue (3). (Squeeze out every drop, or the blister will be very painful when you start walking again.) If the blister is very large or under hard skin, you might need several needle holes. Once you've drained the blister, treat it with antiseptic (4), being careful not to break or move the loose skin covering it, as this protects the area while new skin forms. Cover the blister with a gel that will cushion and help heal the blister, such as 2nd Skin Blister Pads or Compeed (5).

days. Some people also apply foot powder to help keep their feet dry, but I've never found that powder makes a difference.

SOCKS

Buying whatever socks the store has on hand or making do with whatever is in your sock drawer is not the best way to treat your feet. I used to do that until I realized that socks do affect how your feet feel and deserve more careful consideration. Socks cushion feet, reduce abrasion from your footwear, wick away moisture, and keep feet at the right temperature. Good socks should fit snugly and stay in place. Poorly fitting socks, or socks with rough seams, can rub and cause blisters. Socks that are too thick can make your feet sweat; socks that are too thin let them get cold. People are different. Some have cold, clammy feet that need plenty of insulation even in warm weather. Others, like me, have warm feet that overheat easily.

On a backpacking trip you may not be able to wash your socks every day (or want to even if you can); you may end up wearing one pair of socks for days, even weeks, at a time, with just an occasional quick rinse in cold water to freshen them up. After a few days' constant wear, many socks mat down into a hard, sweaty mass, and rinsing them out in cold water doesn't do much to restore their fluffiness. Even repeated machine washings won't revive some types. Such socks provide little insulation or comfort underfoot—I relegate them to the spares box, which is crammed with dozens of pairs of test socks that may have had only two weeks or less of use.

For many years I wore traditional flat-knit ragg socks (ragg is a three-ply wool yarn); I found them vastly superior to the first terry-loop socks, which matted down very quickly. The more open structure of the ragg socks resisted matting better; when rinsed in cold water, they're almost as good as new. However, new construction methods and improved materials mean that the best terry-loop socks don't mat down fast and do fluff up when rinsed. Since they're far more comfortable than ragg socks, they're now my first choice. Ragg socks are very durable, though, and last longer than all but the best terry-loop socks. Companies like Fox River still make ragg wool socks.

Materials

Wool became the standard material for socks because wool socks cushion your feet, keep them warm in winter yet cool in summer, absorb and wick away sweat, and retain warmth when wet. Wool isn't very abrasion-resistant, however, so nylon is often added as reinforcement at the heel and toe. Wool has a natural crimp that makes it very springy, trapping air in its millions of tiny coils, so it's a good insulator. Because these coils stretch out when wool is stretched but spring back into shape once the pressure is off, wool holds its shape well.

Feet can give off a great deal of moisture, up to a pint in twelve hours when you're hiking.

This liquid has to go somewhere, and only some of it can escape through your footwear. Wool socks will absorb this moisture until it can pass through your footwear or go out at the ankles. Good-quality wool also keeps its shape when damp. Socks that sag and wrinkle when wet feel uncomfortable and can cause blisters.

Synthetic socks, made from acrylic (Lumiza, Duraspun, Ginny Microfiber), polyester (Cool-Max, Capilene, Hollofil, Dacron, Thermolite), polypropylene, and nylon are supposed to wick moisture faster than wool and dry more quickly. Certainly if you take a synthetic sock and drip water on it, the water will rapidly pass through the fabric whereas wool would absorb it. This property is fine when the socks are worn with sandals or very breathable shoes, but with most footwear the moisture still can't escape, so it stays on the sock's surface, making it feel clammy and sticky. Whereas wool can absorb up to 30 percent of its own weight in moisture and still feel dry and warm, nonabsorbent synthetics feel damp when only a small amount of moisture is present. I find synthetic socks don't feel as warm as wool when damp or keep my feet as comfortable over a wide range of temperatures. Synthetics mat down more quickly than wool, too, and don't wash as well in cold water. They also stink quickly, though silver fibers like X-Static, found in many socks, do reduce this noticeably. Wool is naturally odor resistant. After a week or so of wear there is a faint smell of wet sheep, but that's about it. I used to wear thin synthetic socks in hot weather because they seemed drier and cooler than thicker wool ones even though they needed rinsing out just about every day. But now I wear wool year-round—lighter socks in summer, heavier ones in winter.

The quality of the wool makes a huge difference, and the best is merino wool, used by just about all the major wool sock makers in their top-end models. Merino has longer, softer, and finer fibers than other wool, making it more comfortable and more durable. Wool with thicker and coarser fibers can feel prickly or itchy next to the skin; merino wool just feels luxurious. It also fluffs up well when washed in cold water and holds its shape longer than other wool. Its durability is good too. And finally, merino wool socks smell less than any other wool socks I've tried, something I first discovered when a companion threw a pair he'd been wearing for a week at me saying, "Smell those!" I did, and they didn't, at least not much. Most merino wool comes from Australia, Argentina, and New Zealand, where merino sheep were brought from Spain in the late eighteenth century.

Blends of wool and various synthetics such as Isolwool, a fifty-fifty merino wool–polypropylene mix used by Fox River, are common and can work well. I find ones with at least 50 percent wool best. A few cold-weather socks are made with Outlast, an unusual material containing a substance that is supposed to regulate the temperature of your feet by absorbing heat when you are working hard and producing lots of it, then releasing it when you start to cool down. The theory sounds great, but I've tried socks with Outlast, and I can't tell any difference from socks without it. To test this I several times wore an Outlast sock on one foot and an ordinary sock on the other. By the end of a hike I couldn't tell which was which. However, others have reported that Outlast works for them.

Avoid cotton in socks; it soaks up sweat and then feels cold and clammy and takes a long time to dry. When wet it loses its shape and easily wrinkles and bunches up under the foot, which is uncomfortable and can cause blisters. Silk is a different matter. It absorbs moisture while staying warm and holds its shape pretty well. It's found in thin liner socks and as a component of cold-weather socks.

Whatever the material, sweat-soaked socks should be changed for dry ones or your feet will soften and are more likely to blister. If you have very sweaty feet you may need to change your socks once or twice a day, especially in hot weather. You can hang damp socks on your pack to dry.

Construction

How socks are made affects their comfort, performance, and durability. Densely knitted socks, with a high number of stitches per square inch, cushion better, feel more comfortable against the skin, and resist matting better than socks with fewer stitches per inch, which can feel rough against the skin. Terry loops on the inside, especially underfoot, are warmer and more comfortable than flat knits. The density of the terry loops makes a difference. Low-density loops will quickly collapse and become matted; high-density loops resist crushing, cushion more, and hold their shape better. For cold weather, terry loops throughout are worth having. In warmer weather, a flat knit over the foot and rib knit on the legs is cooler, with terry loops underfoot for cushioning. Some socks have different densities of material at different points for more cushioning or warmth. These look very complex and high-tech, but I haven't found that they feel any different from socks without them. Some socks have an elasticized section over the instep, which helps with the fit, though it isn't essential. Elastic fibers in the leg or at the top of the sock are more important, since they keep the legs from sagging and slipping down. Ribbed legs, with alternating thin and thick sections, also help socks stay up. Good socks are shaped at the heel for a good fit with no loose fabric. The best have stitching here in the shape of a Y rather than in a straight line, to conform better to the shape of your heel. Tube socks tend to have loose material around the heel that can slip and bunch up under your foot. They're best avoided.

Rough and bulky seams can rub, especially at the toe. The seam should be flat and smooth and set back from the toes, making it more comfortable and more durable. When buying new socks, you can turn them inside out to check the seams. You can also wear them that way if a seam does rub.

For a while I was impressed with double-layer socks. These usually are made from synthetics, though some have a wool content. They're actually two thin socks attached at the toe and ankle and can be awkward to put on if the layers become twisted, but once on they are comfortable, warm, and quick drying. I used to wear them in shoes and lightweight boots when it was too cool for really thin socks. They weigh about 2.5 ounces a pair. But I found that they didn't remain as soft as terry-loop wool socks after repeated washings. Now that you can get lightweight terry-loop socks suitable for warm weather, I wear these rather than double-layer socks.

Choices

Thick wool socks go with boots and cool, wet weather. When wearing shoes rather than boots in warm weather, I prefer lighter, thinner, cooler socks, though still made from wool. Of the many socks I've tried over the years, two brands have become favorites: SmartWool and Teko, whose merino wool socks I find very comfortable even after many days of wear. In fairly warm weather—expected daytime temperatures above 50°F (10°C)—with light trail shoes or lightweight boots, I like the Teko Summit Series Light Hik-

ing (71 percent organic merino wool, 28 percent nylon, 1 percent Lycra) and the SmartWool Hiking Light Crew (76 percent merino wool, 23 percent nylon, 1 percent elastic), both of which have medium-density terry-loop soles, flat-knit uppers with stretch over the arch, rib-knit legs, and weights of 3 ounces in the large size. I wore Teko Light Hiking socks on the Pacific Northwest Trail and found that a pair lasted about 500 miles before holes appeared. In cooler weather—30 to 50°F (-1 to 10°C)—Teko Mid Hiking (74 percent organic merino wool, 25 percent nylon, 1 percent Lycra) and SmartWool Hiking Medium Crew (74 percent merino wool, 25 percent nylon, 1 percent elastic) are warmer, as they have terry loops all around the foot. A large pair of either weighs 3.5 ounces. I wear these socks in early autumn and late spring and sometimes carry them on long trips when cold weather is possible.

In below freezing temperatures and when snow is on the ground, I like thick Teko Expedition (85 percent organic merino wool, 12 percent nylon, 2 percent polyester, 1 percent Lycra) and Smart-Wool Trekking Heavy Crew (80 percent merino wool, 19 percent nylon, 1 percent elastic) socks. These have thick terry loops on the foot and the leg and are very warm. If it's much above freezing, I find them too hot. These socks weigh 5.7 ounces for a size large.

I don't wear liners with any of these socks. It seems a waste to me to put a barrier between the soft terry loops and my skin. I've also found that liners need rinsing every day if they are to stay comfortable—particularly synthetic liners. Silk is better and wool is best, but no liners can be worn for many days without being washed. The theory is that liners help reduce friction and remove sweat quickly, but I haven't found any increase in comfort over a single pair of socks, probably

inside of hiking sock with terry toops

elasticized ankle

cushioned heels

Y-heel gore

toe seam

inside of flat-knit sock

toe seam

Terry-loop sock (left) and flat-knit sock (right).

because modern socks are soft next to the skin and are efficient at wicking moisture. When socks were made from rough, scratchy wool, liners may have been more necessary. I sometimes carry liners, which weigh 1 to 2 ounces a pair, to wear with sandals if it's cool. More often I carry the lightweight wool socks. All these socks are crew (mid-calf) height. Longer socks are hard to find, as are the knickers they were meant to reach. Socks that reach to or just above the ankle, designed to be worn with sandals or low-cut shoes, are becoming more common. I've tried them but returned to higher ones, because I can turn the cuffs down when they're not needed and pull them up if it gets chilly. They ensure a good overlap between long pants and sock tops, too, cutting out drafts around the ankles.

Although I prefer SmartWool and Teko, these companies don't have an exclusive on good-quality socks. There are many excellent socks today. Other brands I've tried and liked are Bridgedale, Wigwam, Fox River, Thorlo, Rohner, Patagonia, Dahlgren, Extremities, Brasher, 1,000 Mile, and X-Socks.

Fit

Whatever type of socks you choose, make sure they fit well. This is difficult to determine in the store because most socks come prepackaged and can't be tried on. Sock sizes bear no relation to shoe sizes, so you'll need to check the chart on the package to find the size that should fit. Nor are sizes standardized between makes—a good reason for sticking to the same brand once you've found some you like that fit well. Sock sizes often cover three or four shoe sizes, so you may find yourself at the junction of two sizes. Most socks, particularly wool ones, tend to stretch over time, so the smaller size is usually the better choice. There are women's socks, with narrower heels, slimmer ankles, and narrower feet than men's or unisex socks, but don't assume they'll fit just because you're female. My partner, Denise Thorn, found one brand's women's socks to be so broad at the toes that they bunched up uncomfortably inside her boots. Other women's socks fit her well, however, though her favorite socks are unisex merino wool.

Before you wear the socks it's worthwhile to check for loose threads, knots, harsh stitching, or bulky seams that might cause blisters and sore spots.

When putting on socks, make sure the heel pocket is in the right place and that the fabric is smooth and not too tight over the toes. There should be no loose fabric anywhere. If there is, the socks don't fit properly. Socks need to fit your footwear as well as your feet. Cramming thick socks into close-fitting boots won't make your feet warmer; they'll just be uncomfortable. Since the insulation will be crushed, your feet could end up colder. Thin socks in a roomy boot will let your feet slide around. When you fit your footwear, you should be wearing the thickness of socks you will always wear with it.

Waterproof Socks

Wet feet aren't a problem when wearing sandals or for short periods in boots and shoes. Lightweight shoes and boots without waterproof-breathable linings dry quickly when wet as long as the air is dry. However, in prolonged wet weather and in damp areas, your footwear can stay wet for days on end. This is unpleasant, especially when it's cold, and can lead to blisters and sore spots as the skin of your feet gets softer and softer. Boots and shoes with waterproof-breathable linings are one answer to this. I've already explained why I don't think it's a good one (see Wet Feet/Dry Feet, earlier in this chapter). Plastic bags are an emergency solution. I've used these at times, pulling one bag over my bare foot or a liner sock to act as a vapor barrier, then another over a thick sock. It works after a fashion, though it's not particularly comfortable, your feet can get sweaty, and the bags don't last long. Companies like Integral Designs, Stephenson's Warmlite, and RBH Designs sell vapor-barrier socks that should last far longer, but except in extreme cold, these can be very hot and sweaty.

Waterproof-breathable socks are much better than waterproof lined boots because you need wear them only when it's wet. They give more protection than boots because they are much higher, some reaching to just below the knee. They're not sweaty either, except in warm weather.

Most companies that have made waterproof-breathable socks have dropped them, leaving just SealSkinz, which has its own proprietary membrane.

Years ago I tried some of the early Gore-Tex socks and wasn't impressed with any of them, since they lasted only a couple of weeks and weren't very comfortable. The Rocky socks are an advance on these and should last longer, though I haven't used them myself. I was more impressed with the first SealSkinz socks. There are three styles, all with nylon-Lycra outers and CoolMax inners. The All Season Socks and Over-the-Calf Socks are the same except for the height—11

On a walk through boggy terrain, one hiker wore waterproof shoes and wool socks (left) and had wet feet after a few hours. Another hiker wore non-waterproof shoes and waterproof socks (right) and had dry feet for three days.

inches for the first, 15 inches for the second. The Waterblocker Socks have a close-fitting seal at the top so, the maker claims, water won't enter even when you wade a stream. The socks are stretchy and quite comfortable against the skin. They're not as soft as wool socks and haven't got the same temperature range, though they are quite breathable. Although I mostly wear them for only a few hours at a time, I did once wear a pair for four days on a cold, wet fall hike in the White Mountains of New Hampshire. I was wearing trail shoes that were soaked the whole time, and I was in snow at higher elevations, but the SealSkinz kept my feet warm and dry. They work better than waterproof linings too, since they're closer to the skin, which keeps them warmer, so they transport moisture more efficiently. And if you don't need the socks or your feet start to overheat, you can swap them for an ordinary pair.

Although in the right conditions—wet, cold around freezing—waterproof socks can work well, and I was quite keen on them for a while, I've stopped using them much, as I've found the comfort range too limited. Just a few degrees rise in temperature can lead to hot, sweaty feet. When wet, they are slow-drying, too (turning them inside out helps), and durability isn't very good, especially when they are worn with mesh trail shoes or sandals. When I expect cold, wet conditions, I do sometimes still carry a pair, but often I only wear them in camp.

Caring for Socks

On most trips I carry two or three pairs of socks. Usually I change them every couple of days, though on long trips I have worn a pair for as long as ten days. I like to keep one pair dry for campwear unless I'm carrying booties or fleece socks for that. Clean socks are warmer and more comfortable and wick moisture better than dirty ones. Whenever possible, I rinse socks in water taken from a stream or lake, using a cooking pot as a washbowl (and making sure to rinse it out well afterward). If using a cooking pot doesn't seem attractive, you can put socks in a plastic bag full of water and wash them by shaking the bag. Turning them inside out helps ensure that sweat is removed from the inside so the socks can fluff up again. I don't use soap for washing socks in the backcountry. If you do, make sure you dump the dirty water well away from water sources and rinse the socks well. Washed socks can be hung on a line in camp or just draped over a rock or branch to dry (don't forget them when you break camp, though—something I've done more than once). Thick wool socks take time to dry, so you often need to hang them on the back of your pack the next day to finish drying.

At home, socks should be either hand washed or put through the washing machine's delicate cycle (inside out), then line-dried. Pure soap and plant-based washing products such as those from Ecover, Nikwax Tech Wash, and Gaiam's Seventh Generation Laundry Liquid are less harsh on fabrics than soaps derived from petrochemicals. They're also kinder to the environment. Fabric softeners are good for synthetic socks—you want them as soft as possible. I use them on wool only if the socks have become very matted and don't fluff up after washing. However, the wicking properties of some socks can be affected by fabric softeners, so check the washing instructions before you throw the packaging away. Too much heat can cause socks to shrink, especially those containing polypropylene. Most socks shouldn't be tumble-dried on a hot setting or draped over a hot radiator or near a fire—again, check the instructions.

GAITERS

In deep snow, neither waterproof-breathable lined boots nor waterproof-breathable socks will keep your boots and feet dry and, most important, warm for long. The waterproof socks may keep your feet dry, but your boots will fill with snow and your feet will be cold. Gaiters are a necessity. Some people like them for keeping out mud, water, dust, and dirt as well. The lightest and simplest of these coverings for the lower leg are short (6 to 8 inches high) and are sometimes called stop tous (stop everything) or *anklets*. These are fine for keeping stones and bits of grass out of your boots and for snow that's only a few inches deep. I've tried a few pairs over the years but have always found even the ones made from uncoated fabric too warm.

Gaiters that come to just below the knee are the best choice for deep snow. They come in two types: those that cover only the upper part of the boot, and *supergaiters* that cover the entire boot. Supergaiters are usually made from waterproof-breathable fabrics like Gore-Tex. Gaiters may have zippers on the back, side, or front. Those with front zippers are easier to put on and let you adjust your laces without removing the gaiters. Those with zippers at the back are hardest to use—I avoid these. Zippers aren't waterproof, so a hook-and-loop (Velcro) flap is needed to keep out moisture. Some models dispense with the zipper and just use Velcro, which makes them very easy to get on and off as long as the Velcro doesn't become clogged with ice or mud. The lower edge of a gaiter may be elasticized or randed so it grips the boot. There may also be an elasticized section around the ankle. A drawcord tightens the gaiter below the knee.

In spite of their benefits, I don't like gaiters and wear them only when the alternative is wet, cold feet, which I like even less. However, when the snow lies deep, I often wear gaiters all day. I used to prefer supergaiters, which grip the lower edge of the boot with a tight-fitting rubber rand, sealing out snow and water. They keep boots dry and unscuffed for days on end. No other gaiters come close in terms of performance. They seem to be disappearing, though, probably because they are heavy and hard to fit and the rands are fragile and expensive to replace. The rise of plastic ski touring and mountaineering boots has probably hastened their demise. Without any conscious decision, I stopped wearing supergaiters and went back to lighter, easier-to-fit standard gaiters, and I guess many others did the same. The supergaiters that do remain tend to be insulated ones designed for extreme cold, like Mountain Tools Thinsulate Insulated Supergaiters, which weigh 23 ounces a pair. Climb High does make the uninsulated Glacier supergaiters, which weigh 20 ounces.

Standard gaiters are available in waterproof-breathable and uncoated fabrics. They have an adjustable cord, strap, or wire that fits under the instep. These straps fray and eventually break, so gaiters with attachment points for replacements are best. I'd avoid gaiters with fancy buckles that work only with the original straps. Gaiters range from 5 to 12 ounces a pair. The heaviest ones, made from fabrics such as Cordura, are the most durable. Since I abandoned supergaiters I've used Páramo gaiters, which are made from lined polyester and are extremely breathable (see Chapter 5 for fabric details). They have a front zipper, a stud-closed flap, a replaceable underfoot strap, and a front hook (which fastens to the boot laces to hold the gaiters down) that can be folded out of the way if not needed. I find them very comfortable and warm. They weigh 12 ounces a pair. There are plenty of other good gaiters available from companies like Outdoor Research and Black Diamond.

OVERBOOTS

Overboots are an alternative to gaiters if you want total protection for your boots and shoes. Basically they are gaiters with lug soles. Most overboots are insulated and are designed for high-altitude mountaineering and polar expeditions (see www.40below.com for a good range of these), but NEOS makes a few uninsulated pairs that are useful for backpackers. I have a pair, which are knee high and have a thick sole with a good grip. They're made from nylon with a front zipper and a strap over the instep. You can wear them over running shoes and tramp around in snow without getting wet or cold feet. They're quite bulky and heavy, though, at 2.6 pounds, so I wouldn't want to carry them in my pack. The sole is soft, too, and wide and bulky to accommodate boots, so they're not very stable or precise on steep or rough terrain. I mostly use them for short hikes around home, but they could be an alternative to mukluks for long trips in the snow or mud.

CAMPWEAR

On most trips I don't bother with spare footwear. In the long-ago days when I hiked in heavy boots, I always carried spare footwear to relieve my hot, sore feet in camp. My morale got such a boost when I donned light, cool sandals or running shoes after a long day that it was well worth the weight of the spare footwear. However, I'm happy to forgo that pleasure in return for not having the initial pain that the heavy boots caused. Now I carry spare footwear only occasionally, usually on trips longer than a few weeks, when a change of hiking footwear can ease leg or foot pains. Light sandals or running shoes make good spare footwear for both hiking and camp use. If you do carry spare footwear for campwear in warm weather, simple sandals are the lightest choice. Basic flip-flops—no more than a slab of foam and a thin strap—weigh only about 3 or 4 ounces. You can make even lighter ones from pieces of closed-cell foam or old footbeds and bits of cord. It's easy;

even I can do this. There's a description of how to make a pair on the Trail Quest Web site (trailquest.net), where they are called one ounce camp sandals or, more interesting, gram weenie sandals.

If the weather during a trip is apt to be very cold and snowy and I'm with a group and don't want to spend all evening in the tent, or if I plan to use huts or shelters, I carry insulated *booties*. These are very warm, and the mere thought of them is comforting when your feet are cold and wet, but many are useless on anything except flat ground because of their smooth soles—climbing down a bank to fetch water can seem like a major expedition. Booties come with down and synthetic fill and fleece linings. Although the synthetic and fleece ones are slightly heavier, I prefer them, since I don't have to worry about getting them wet in the snow. There isn't a wide selection, but features vary. If you're going to wander around camp, your booties need a closed-cell foam insole, preferably sewn in, to insulate your feet from the ground. For many years I've used REI Polarguard Booties, which weigh 11.25 ounces in the large size and have pack-cloth soles, closed-cell insoles, nylon outers, a warm polyester-cotton-nylon lining, and a front drawcord. These have been unavailable for quite a few years, but there are several similar ones, such as Integral Designs Hot Socks with 4 ounces Primaloft Sport insulation, Pertex microfiber shell, and Cordura soles, weighing 4.7 ounces (medium size); Forty Below Camp Booties with continuous-filament synthetic insulation, nylon shells, closed-cell foam footbeds, and rubber-dot soles, weighing 10 ounces; and Mountain Hardwear's Compressor Booties with synthetic insulation, closed-cell foam footbeds, Cordura/polyester shells, and antislip soles, weighing 10 ounces.

Down-filled booties include Sierra Designs Pull-On Down Booties with a nonslip sole and a weight of 12 ounces, Western Mountaineering Down Booties with either Windstopper or nylon shell, a nonslip sole, and a weight of 6 to 8 ounces, and Feathered Friends Down Booties (9 ounces), which have removable EPIC shell booties, removable foam insoles, and 4 ounces of 800-fill-power down. I particularly like the idea of the last ones, since you could wear them outdoors, then remove the shells and the insoles and wear them in a tent and in your sleeping bag. The shells could be used just over socks too.

On solo cold-weather trips when I'm likely to spend most if not all of my camp time in the tent (probably in a sleeping bag), I often carry pile or fleece socks, since they're much warmer for their weight than wool socks. For years I've used Helly Hansen fiber-pile boot liners, which just reach my ankle and weigh 3.5 ounces. The name suggests they could be worn in boots, but I wouldn't do this except around camp, because pile and fleece are nonabsorbent and don't wick moisture quickly, so they get sticky with sweat quite quickly, though you could wear them with sandals. They are, however, wonderful to pull on over cold, wet feet at the end of the day; great for sleeping in; and nice for wearing in the tent when you aren't in the sleeping bag. My Helly socks are no longer sold, but there are plenty of similar socks, usually made from 200-weight fleece and often promoted for wearing with sports sandals. Wyoming Wear is a major brand.

TREKKING POLES AND STAFFS

When I started hiking, it never occurred to me to use a staff or trekking pole, and these aids were rarely used by anyone else. Using two poles was unheard of. When I started Nordic skiing, however, I discovered that when I had to carry the skis on my pack, using the poles improved my balance. After a while, I realized I didn't need skis on my pack for a staff to be useful, and I began picking up stout sticks to help me on steep slopes and when fording streams. Staff in hand, I found I could negotiate steep scree slopes, boulder fields, and tussocky tundra with much more confidence and less worry that my unwieldy burden would tip me over.

I soon found that a staff has even more uses. On level ground and good trails, it helps me maintain a walking rhythm. When crossing soft boggy ground or snow, it can probe for hidden rocks and deep spots as well as provide support. It can hold back bushes, barbed wire, stinging plants, and other trail obstructions and even fend off aggressive dogs. Perhaps most important, it takes some weight off my feet, particularly when I lean heavily on it as I climb steep slopes. Experts claim that using trekking poles can take between 10 and 18 pounds off the lower body with each stride, which adds up to a lot of weight over a day. Of course it's not a free ride—the strain is just moved to your arms and upper body, and you have to carry the weight of the poles. But sharing the effort does mean that my legs get less tired while my upper body and arms maintain their strength between ski seasons.

Most experts recommend using two poles, and this is what I now mostly do. All the advantages of a staff are more than doubled when you use two. Walking with two poles uses the upper body muscles and takes much of the strain off the legs and hips. Using one pole takes the strain off only some of the time and can make you feel unbalanced. If I don't swap the pole from hand to hand occasionally, I find that my shoulder starts to ache.

On steep terrain, especially direct descents, you can always have three points of contact with the ground if you carry two poles, which gives much greater stability. When using two poles I can walk faster and farther before I begin to feel tired, and I no longer have aching knees at the end of days with long, steep descents. On long ascents, I can go faster with poles.

My poles have other uses. During rest stops, they turn my pack into a backrest. In camp they can turn a fly-sheet door into an awning, support a wash line or tarp, and retrieve bear-bagged food. Some tents can be pitched with trekking poles, too.

When I began using a pole, it made me an oddity and other hikers used to stare at me; when I began using two, some people avoided me altogether and others asked where my skis were. Now poles are more common, and you get fewer strange looks and odd comments. Some people really dislike them, though, and can get quite worked up about them, which baffles me, since they hardly intrude on anyone else. For most hikers they're not essential, but if you suffer from sore knees, hips, or back, they can make a huge difference. They can also be useful if you hike infrequently. Demetri "Coup" Coupounas, president of GoLite, says, "[I find] dual poles *very* useful in allowing me to take on big-mileage days and weekends when I hike infrequently—the poles add so much stability in motion that I am not restricted to short, easy hikes when my ankles are not strengthened from frequent hiking on rough trails—i.e., gym fitness translates into trail fitness much more readily with dual poles than with none."

I also think a pole is a useful emergency item. If you injure a foot or leg, having a pole could make the difference between limping out of the backcountry and having to be rescued. And of course, having a pole makes injuries less likely anyway, since it can prevent stumbles from turning into falls. There are a few disadvantages to poles; for instance, your hands aren't free. But it's easy to dangle the poles from your wrists by their straps if necessary.

Materials and Designs

The obvious material for a staff is wood, and it's easy to find a suitable piece in any forest. As long as it's reasonably straight, solid, and at least elbow height (so you can hold it with the lower arm at a right angle to the body, the most comfortable position), any strong stick will do. Many tourist stores in popular mountain areas sell wooden staffs, usually inexpensive. But you can't always buy or find a staff when you reach an area, and wooden staffs aren't easy to transport. You can't put them in your pack, and they're awkward to take on trains, buses, and planes.

The answer to this problem is the *adjustable metal staff*. Derived from (and sometimes identical to) adjustable ski touring poles, these staffs are lighter than wooden sticks yet stronger and can be carried in or on a pack when not in use. Many alpine ski pole manufacturers began to make them once they noted that mountaineers and hikers in the Alps often used ski poles. Indeed, a ski pole makes a perfectly functional staff if you don't need an adjustable one, and old ones are usually easy to find at any ski resort. Most poles are made from light aluminum; the lightest (and most expensive) are carbon fiber.

Trekking poles, designed to be used in pairs, are far more common than staffs meant to be used singly. One of the few staff makers is Tracks (part of Cascade Designs, more noted for its sleeping mats), which makes several models. I've used its Sherlock staff for many years. This two-piece staff adjusts from 42.5 to 57.5 inches by means of a locking button that clips into holes in the shaft. The upper shaft is covered with soft foam topped by a wooden knob that you can remove to reveal a camera monopod mount. Rather than a sharp carbide tip, the Sherlock has a blunter steel point. It comes with a removable rubber tip too. Mine weighs 17.5 ounces; current models are 16.5 ounces. The Sherlite staff is the same model without the foam sheath, which cuts the weight to 15 ounces. I find the sheath, which is warm and soft, well worth 1.5 ounces.

The Sherlock is fine when I use a staff, as I sometimes do with light loads and on day hikes, and when I don't expect to have to carry it on my pack, as it's a bit long for that. With heavier loads I usually use two trekking poles. These come in many models, and having tested quite a few, I can say confidently that there's not much difference between most of them. Leki, Masters, Komperdell, Life-Link, Black Diamond, Garmont, Gabel, Tracks, MSR, and more all make a wide range of good models, and there are store-brand poles from places like REI, often made by Komperdell. Weights range from 6 to 32 ounces for a pair. Packed lengths range from 20 to 30 inches. The differences lie mostly in the handles and grips and the locking mechanisms. There are two-piece poles, but the packed length is quite long, so I prefer three-section ones, of which there are far more. Of course the more sections, the weaker the pole, at least in theory, but I've never broken a three-section pole.

What can fail, though, is the locking mechanism. Most poles have a twist-lock adjustment with an internal adjustable, expanding section that locks and unlocks depending on the direction you twist the shaft. This is fine when it works, but it can slip or jam. To help minimize the chance of its happening, dismantle the poles after use and make sure they are dry before you reassemble them to prevent corrosion. Some expanders are all plastic, some are plastic and metal. The expanding section can be replaced if it starts to slip repeatedly, as can happen. I haven't had serious failures with any of the poles I've used, but the most secure and strongest expanders look to be those from Masters and Leki. Most poles are circular. Life-Link poles, however, have oval sections, which are said to be more secure, since an oval can't twist inside another oval the way two circles can. I use Life-Link Variant Carbon Fiber ski touring poles and have found them very secure. There are two alternatives to internal expanders. As I described previously, Tracks poles have locking buttons that can't slip. Black Diamond poles have external adjustable cam locks called Flicklocks that have large levers that are easy to use when wearing gloves. All of these methods work, and I haven't found any one to be superior to the others.

For grips, cork, soft foam, or soft rubber is more comfortable than hard rubber or plastic, though there's not a huge difference. I like poles with a long foam grip that I can hold lower down when I want a shorter length. I also like poles with a camera mount under a knob on the top, since poles make excellent monopods. Some poles have forward-angled grips that are meant to give a more relaxed wrist position.

This design is taken to radical extremes in British-made Pacerpoles, which have molded thermoplastic-rubber grips, acutely angled, that are shaped for each hand. These enable you to transmit far more power through the poles, since the angle is "calculated for optimum range of arm leverage." The grips are very comfortable,

and the poles are a leap forward in design. I now use Pacerpoles almost exclusively; they really are more efficient, which makes it easier to transmit power through them and to take the weight off my legs, especially on long climbs. They have only a short piece of cord as a security loop rather than a proper strap, which isn't needed—you hold the poles loosely in your hands rather than letting the loops take the weight. The poles come in three sections with an internal locking mechanism. There is a soft neoprene sleeve on the upper section. There is a camera mount that slots into the handle, which I'vd found very useful. Three-section Pacerpoles (two-section ones are available) come in aluminum at 23 ounces and carbon fiber at 18.5 ounces. I used the carbon-fiber ones on the Pacific Northwest Trail, where they doubled as tent poles, and they were excellent. For more information, see pacerpoles.com.

I don't consider the weight of trekking poles very significant. I've never had tired arms after long days with standard-weight poles. However, for ultralight backpackers for whom every fraction of an ounce counts, there are ultralight poles available. Ones that are highly regarded are Gossamer Gear's carbon-fiber Lightrek poles, which come in fixed and adjustable lengths with weights of 5.4 to 5.8 (depending on length) and 7.2 ounces, and Titanium Goat aluminum or carbon-fiber Adjustable Goat Poles, which weigh 7 ounces.

Many poles have an antishock device, a spring built into the handle or the shaft that gives slightly when weight is applied. Antishock mechanisms add weight, increase packed length, and raise the price, all to no advantage in my experience. I've tried hiking with an antishock pole in one hand and a regular pole in the other, and I've noticed no difference. Antishock is supposed to absorb

The unique Pacerpoles handles.

the shock of pole placements so your arm doesn't feel them, but my arms don't ache or feel any more tired whether I use them or not. On many poles, antishock can be turned off. I'd rather not have it at all.

Most poles come with small solid baskets. These are a hangover from skiing origins and aren't really necessary. If you're going to use your poles on snow, whether skiing or not, you do need to be able to fit large baskets to stop the poles from sinking in. Tip shafts are often synthetic and designed to break before the main shaft if they get caught in rocks, since they are cheaper and easier to replace. Some poles have blunt steel or alloy points, which are fine on everything except ice, but most have sharp carbide points. Poles can poke holes in trails and scratch rocks. I don't

think this is a big problem, but you can put rubber or plastic covers over the tips. These covers are quite durable; one set lasted me for a five-week hike on the hard, rocky terrain of the High Sierra.

Using Poles

To gain the most benefit from hiking poles, you need to use them properly. I've seen many people letting poles dangle limply from their hands, ineffectually waving them around, rendering them just about useless, or else gripping them tightly and stabbing the ground, which is a good way to tire your arms and doesn't reap much benefit from the poles. Except with Pacerpoles, the straps should be used to support your hands and take the weight. To use the straps, put your hand up through the strap from below, then bring it down so the strap runs between the thumb and fingers and over the back of the hand. With the poles held like this, you can flick them back and forth without having to jerk your arms around or grasp them tightly. Place the poles by swinging one in front, placing the tip on the ground, pressing down on it, then walking past it while swinging the other pole forward. On even terrain you can get a good rhythm. You should feel the poles pushing you forward as you push down on them. On ascents you won't get as much of a forward swing, but you can really push down on the poles to help propel you upward.

To get the maximum benefit from poles, they need to be the right length. Many people use a pole that's too long, which requires more effort and can make your arms and shoulders ache. For hiking on the flat and gentle slopes, the longest poles should be is when they touch the ground when held pointing straight down with your elbow bent at a right angle. On steep ascents a shorter pole is better. You can slip your hands out of the loops and grasp the shaft lower down or adjust the poles to a shorter length. When descending steep ground, you can plant a longer pole below you for greater support. On long descents, adjusting the pole length might be worthwhile; otherwise you can lengthen a pole by placing your hand over the top of the grip. When traversing steep slopes, you can slip your hand out of the strap on the upper pole and grasp it lower down on the shaft so it doesn't push you away from the slope. To make changing pole length quicker, you can adjust the lower section to its full length and then just alter the middle section when you want to change the length. Overall, though, it's better to alter each section by the same amount, so that one section isn't overloaded.

ICE AXES

Whenever you're likely to encounter slopes of hard snow and ice, you need an *ice ax*. Winter might seem the obvious time to expect such terrain, but the snow then is often deep and soft. It's

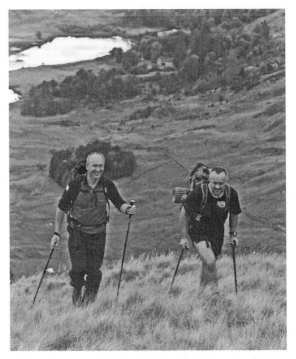

Hiking poles are particularly useful on rough and steep terrain.

normal grip

pole shortened

pole lengthened

Holding the pole.

in spring and early summer, after the surface of the snow has melted and refrozen, perhaps several times, that ice axes are most often needed. An ax may be needed well into July for hikes above the timberline in some areas, and I've had to seek out an alternative route as late as September when a steel-hard bank of old snow blocked the trail to a high pass.

A trekking pole, very useful for balance in soft snow, is inadequate when crossing steep, hard-packed snow or ice. On such surfaces, a slip can easily become a rapidly accelerating slide. The only way to stop such a fall is by a method known as *self-arrest*, which requires an ice ax. For instruction, take a course in snow and ice skills at an outdoor center or learn from a competent friend. *Mountaineering: The Freedom of the Hills*, edited by Ronald C. Eng, is a useful source for all aspects of snow travel other than skiing, but I'm not convinced that self-arrest can be learned from a written description. Practice is essential; in a real fall you have to react immediately and automatically, and you must be able to stop yourself whether you fall on your front or your back and with your head uphill or downhill. On slopes where you may have to self-arrest, carry your ice ax with the pick pointing backward so it's in position. On easier slopes I prefer to walk with the pick pointing forward so that if I stumble I won't impale myself.

Ice axes also can be used to cut steps in ice and snow too hard to kick your boots into (though wearing crampons makes this unnecessary) and can replace a staff for balance on snow. If you do slip, thrusting the ax shaft into the snow will often prevent you from sliding down the slope. Other things I've found an ice ax useful for include pull-

BUT IT'S STILL SUMMER

An unexpected early September blizzard had blanketed the mountains with fresh snow—deep, soft, and wet. I struggled up to the 11,900-foot Farview Pass in the Never Summer range in the Colorado Rockies with the aid of a thick stick I'd picked up in the forest below. I had no ice ax, and this was in the days before I carried a staff or hiking poles. It was also in the days before I discovered waterproof socks, and my feet, in running shoes, were quickly sodden and chilled. At the pass, where the view was all of 50 yards, I wiped the snow off a trail sign, then followed the directions down into the Parika Lake basin, where I camped in the slight shelter of some stunted spruce. Once in the tent, I stripped off my wet shoes and socks, pulled dry wool socks over my frozen feet, and slid into my sleeping bag. After several hot drinks and a steaming bowl of curry, my feet began to warm up. The temperature in the tent was a damp 40°F (5°C). Thankfully, the next day arrived with sunshine and a clear sky, and my feet felt only slightly cool as I followed the Continental Divide Trail across the snowy slopes of the White Cloud Peaks and into Rocky Mountain National Park.

With the rest of Colorado to cross in the next few weeks, however, I needed more than running shoes and a stick. In the little mountain resort of Grand Lake, I did a round of the stores. But it was still summer, and no one stocked gaiters or ice axes. (Outside, the mountains shone white with new snow.) They had boots, of course, and I continued my walk in a sturdy pair of midweight leather Pivettas, good for stomping steps in snow. But it was nineteen days and 320 miles of snowy trails later before I finally managed to find gaiters and an ice ax in the town of Creede—just in time to deal with a blizzard in the San Juans. The lesson from this is to have items I might need mailed ahead just in case. I can always send them on if they aren't required.

Using ice axes to safeguard a steep descent on hard snow.

pick

adze

shaft

spike

ing stakes out of frozen ground or hard-packed snow, chopping holes in frozen streams or ponds to get water, chipping ice off rocks so you can stand on them without slipping when fording streams, and digging toilet holes.

Ice axes come in many complicated and even bizarre styles; most are specialty designs for climbing frozen waterfalls and iced-up vertical cliffs. All a backpacker needs is a simple, traditional ice ax, usually described as a "walking" or "general mountaineering" ax. The head should have a wide adze, useful for cutting steps and possibly for self-arrest in soft snow, and a gently curved pick with a few teeth at the end. Two-piece heads are perfectly adequate for walking use. They may be made from steel (strong but quite heavy), titanium (strong and light but expensive), or aluminum (light but not so strong and easily blunted). Shafts are normally aluminum, which is strong enough for most uses. Titanium shafts, found on a few axes, are stronger but expensive.

An ice ax. Always carry an ice ax and crampons if you're likely to encounter steep, snowy areas or ice.

Metal shafts are cold to touch and slippery when damp. Some form of tape or a rubberized sheath makes the shaft warmer and gives you a better grip. It shouldn't be very thick, though, or it can impede the shaft when you thrust it into the snow. A wrist loop is useful and worth attaching if your ax doesn't come with one. Length is a matter of debate; I like an ax whose spike is a half-inch or so off the ground when I hold the ax by my side with my arm hanging down. An ax this length will touch the snow on gentle slopes, which is good for security. On steeper slopes the shaft can be pushed into the snow, also good for security. On descents, it's easier to place a longer ax down the slope ahead of you without crouching or leaning forward. Climbers, who are used to being on very steep, icy slopes, often prefer shorter axes.

Axes weigh from 5 to 28 ounces. The lightest models are adequate for backpacking. Makes to look for include Cassin, Salewa, Stubai, SMC, Petzl Moser, Omega Pacific, Stanley Alpine, Grivel, DMM, C.A.M.P., Ushba, and Black Diamond. Since I don't do any alpine mountaineering or technical climbing, I don't need an ax designed for these pursuits; and since my ax spends most of its time strapped to my pack, weight is more important than technical design. For many years I used a 70-centimeter C.A.M.P. HL250 ax that weighs just 12 ounces. It has a head made from alloy rather than steel and isn't suitable for serious climbing—it even has "not for ice climbing" stamped on the pick—but for backpacking it's fine.

The HL250 has been replaced by the even lighter alloy Corsa and the Corsa Nanotech, which has a steel end to the alloy pick. I have a 60-centimeter Corsa, which weighs just 8.7 ounces and is now my choice over the HL250. Even lighter is the interesting (and expensive) TiCa

Ice Tool R2 from Suluk 46°, which weighs 5.22 ounces in the 60-centimeter length and has a titanium head and spike and carbon-fiber shaft. The maker says "this tool is to be used specifically in situations where one's life or safety will not be at risk," which applies to the Corsa too, which C.A.M.P. says is "not suitable for ice climbing or mixed terrain" but "absolutely perfect for low-angle glacier travel, ski mountaineering, and adventure racing." When I'm visiting steep mountains where I'm likely to be using my ice ax most of the time, I prefer a heavier ax with a steel head. Mine is the Grivel Air Tech Racing, which is still light for this type of ax at 16 ounces in the 66-centimeter length.

Ice axes are potentially dangerous implements and require care both in use and when being carried. Rubber head and spike protectors are useful when transporting the ax to and from the mountains—a wine bottle cork will do to cover the spike, and cardboard or foam can be wrapped around the head if necessary. On planes, trains, and buses I pack the ax inside my pack or duffel bag with the head and spike covered (on planes, the ax must be in your checked baggage).

CRAMPONS

If conditions warrant carrying an ice ax, *crampons* will probably be useful as well. These metal spikes strap or clamp onto the soles of your boots so you can cross ice and hard snow without slipping. I rarely use them, but when I do they are essential, so I carry them on any trips where ice or hard snow is likely. Flexible crampons—ones with a hinge or a sprung bar in the middle—can be fitted to most hiking boots, and some will fit trail shoes. Rigid crampons are strictly for climbers and rigid-soled boots.

The number of points on a crampon doesn't matter much for walkers; there are eight-, nine-, ten-, and twelve-point models. Points that angle out from the front of the boot are useful for climbing steep slopes because you can use your boot toes.

Crampons are usually made from steel, which is strong and stays sharp, though the lightest models are made from an aluminum alloy, which blunts quickly but is all right for occasional hiking use, and titanium, which holds an edge better but is expensive. For most backpacking use, aluminum is fine. Weights for crampons range from 16 ounces to more than 2 pounds.

Fitting crampons to boots is a complicated business the first time, and finding the right size can be difficult. First-time buyers should take their boots to the store and have the salesperson demonstrate how to fit them. A properly fitted crampon shouldn't fall off when you pick up the boot and shake it with the crampon straps unfastened.

Crampons attach to boots by various methods; some are much easier to use than others, especially with cold fingers. Awkward systems may mean you don't bother to put the crampons on when you should or that you don't fit them properly, both of which can be dangerous. Practice attaching crampons until you can do it quickly. A blizzard isn't the place to work out what goes where.

The easiest system is the step-in with a wire bail at the front and a heel lever at the back. Unfortunately, these require boots with a pronounced lip at the heel and toe, which few hiking boots have anymore. Old-fashioned leather boots with external stitched seams and modern plastic climbing boots will take these crampons. To minimize the chance of the front bail's coming off, these crampons should have a strap linking the toe and heel pieces.

Kahtoola aluminum crampons fitted to lightweight boots.

Almost as easy to fit are crampons with flexible plastic cradles at the front and back that wrap around the boot when tensioned with a single strap that runs from the heel to the front cradle and then back to a buckle at the rear. This is the system I prefer, since it will fit most hiking boots. Traditional systems use sets of straps. There are many variations of these. A common one has an O-ring linked by straps to the front of the crampons and a long strap at the heel that runs through this ring and then back to the heel. There are also mixtures of systems with O-rings and straps at the front and heel levers or cradles at the back.

The companies that make ice axes usually make crampons as well. For several years, when I've expected to need crampons for long periods I've used Grivel G10s, flexible ten-point steel crampons with plastic cradles that make them easy to attach to hiking boots. They're somewhat heavy at 29 ounces, though (all weights are per pair). Grivel also makes a much-lighter-alloy twelve-point crampon, the Air Tech Light, at 21.3 ounces, which I've used successfully with lightweight, flexible footwear. Both the Grivel crampons have front points, which aren't needed and indeed serve no purpose on gentle terrain with no steep slopes. Then I use alloy Kahtoola KTS Crampons, which have ten vertical points, weigh

19 ounces, and have a strapping system that is easier than most to use. They pack up compactly, too, and fit well on lightweight footwear. Kahtoola also makes a similar steel crampon weighing 23.3 ounces that would stay sharper for longer when used on mixed snow and rock terrain. The lightest full-length crampons I am aware of are the Hillsound Trail Crampons, which weigh 16.2 ounces in the medium size and have an interesting-looking stretch harness attached to the crampons with chains. These are steel crampons with eleven vertical points and could be the best model for backpackers not intending on doing any mountaineering that requires front points. For those times when crampons are not really needed but icy trails and patches of hard snow may be encountered, simpler devices such as the Kahtoola MICROspikes are all that's needed. These have a stretch harness with chains similar to the Hillsound crampons that attaches to seven short steel spikes. MICROspikes can be fitted to any-

thing, including running shoes, and work well on frozen trails. The weight is low, just 12.7 ounces in the medium size. I carry MICROspikes when I might encounter the odd stretch of ice but don't expect to need full crampons. Much lighter at 5.7 ounces are the titanium TW Crampons from Suluk 46°. These are short-instep crampons that don't run the whole length of the boots and so are only suitable for fairly flat terrain. The weight is tempting, but they cost nearly four times as much as the MICROspikes, and titanium will blunt more quickly than steel.

Like ice axes, crampons can be dangerous, so if you strap them to the outside of your pack, you should cover the spikes with rubber protectors. The tangled rubber strands of these protectors can be a big nuisance, however; I long ago abandoned them and instead carry crampons inside the pack in a tough Cordura nylon pouch. The pouch I use hasn't been sold for years, but Lowe Alpine makes a very similar one, the 7-ounce Crampon Bag

A ten-point flexible crampon.

flexible plastic cradles

single strap

flexible bar

II, which can be attached to the pack or carried inside. You can also wrap crampons in a length of tough cloth such as heavy-duty canvas, neoprene, or PVC. Some packs come with a pocket on the front designed to hold crampons.

Walking in crampons involves a change in gait and special techniques on steep slopes. You must take care not to catch the points on your pants or gaiters or the other crampon, so you need to spread your legs slightly wider than usual. On gentle slopes you need to keep your feet flat on the snow or ice so that all the points bite. On steep slopes you can kick just the front points into the snow and walk up on your toes, though this is tiring and difficult in flexible boots. I find the least tiring way to climb moderately steep ground is to front-point with one foot while keeping the other flat on the ground, alternating feet as they start to ache. If you're going to venture onto really steep terrain, I suggest you take a mountaineering course.

SKIS AND SNOWSHOES

Walking through snow more than ankle deep can be very difficult; once you sink up to your shins and deeper, it becomes an exhausting and slow process, aptly known as *postholing*. The Scandinavians answered the problem some four thousand years ago: strap something to your feet that spreads your weight and allows you to ride on the snow's surface. After years of slogging through soft, wet snow, I discovered this for myself when I traveled with three hikers who used snowshoes in the San Bernardino Mountains on the Pacific Crest Trail in California. I bought a pair to use in the snowbound High Sierra, but then I watched enviously as two in our party swapped snowshoes for Nordic skis, swooped down snowfields, and slid through the forest, leaving the two of us on snowshoes to plod along in their wake. I became determined to learn to ski.

Snowshoes have their uses, though. They are more maneuverable than skis in thick forest, and the largest ones will keep you on the surface of deep, powdery snow, which the widest skis will sink into. You also can use them with ordinary walking boots. And it's much easier to learn to snowshoe than to ski. You can still get traditional wooden snowshoes, but they're heavy and need careful maintenance. Better and far more common are the more durable aluminum-framed ones with synthetic decking and pivoting bindings. The ones I used in the Sierra were Sherpa Featherweight Sno-Claw models that weighed a little more than 3 pounds with straps. Since I learned to ski a year later, I didn't use snowshoes again for many years. However, a few years ago I did get a new pair, which I've been using in the local woods where skis would be awkward to handle. My current shoes are the Baldas Matterhorn Treks, which have a metal frame with polypropylene decking, a pivoting binding with spikes, and an optional extension called a spatula. They measure 9 by 20.5 inches, weigh 4.5 pounds, and are designed to support more than 240 pounds. I've used them in moderate terrain with light loads, and for this they are fine. If I'd had them instead of the Sherpas for the hike through the High Sierra, I imagine they would have performed just as well.

Walking in snowshoes is slow work compared with skiing but far easier than walking in deep snow without them. Snowshoes have become popular for winter recreation, and there are now several good models with weights from 2 pounds upward. Sherpa snowshoes are no more but besides Baldas, well-regarded brands include Atlas, Tubbs, Northern Lites, Redfeather, and MSR. There are many books on snowshoeing, such as *The Essential Snowshoer: A Step-by-Step Guide* by Marianne Zwosta, *Snowshoeing: From Novice to Master* by Gene Prater and Dave Felkley, and *The Snowshoe Experience: Gear Up & Discover the Wonders of Winter on Snowshoes* by Claire Walter.

I abandoned snowshoes for many years because skiing looked like more fun. Snowshoeing seemed functional but tedious by comparison. Crossing the High Sierra in May with a 100-pound pack was not the time to learn to ski, however. The next winter I took a Nordic ski course and have since been on ski backpacking trips most years in places as far afield as the High Sierra, Greenland, Spitsbergen (which lies in the Arctic Ocean north of Norway), the Yukon, the Alps, Lapland (in Arctic Scandinavia), the Norwegian mountains, Yellowstone, and the Canadian Rockies. For nine seasons I worked as a ski touring leader, based in Norway.

Skiing is a complex subject. Alpine (downhill) skis are strictly for lift-served skiing and ultrasteep mountain descents. Although alpine ski mountaineering gear has become much lighter in recent years, progress on flat and undulating terrain is still slow as the skis don't slide much. These skis are worth considering only if your aim is a long, steep descent. For most snow backpacking, they are unsuitable. The same applies to the heaviest telemark gear, which is again designed for resort skiing and steep descents. The lightest telemark gear is suitable for touring, however, especially in mountainous terrain. At the other extreme, light, skinny cross-country skis are designed for cut tracks and don't have much flotation or stability in untracked snow.

The best skis for ski backpacking are variously called *Nordic*, *backcountry*, or *mountain touring* skis. For carrying a heavy load and breaking trail in snow that ranges from deep powder to breakable crust, skis with metal edges are best. All skis are narrower at the waist than at the tip and tail. The difference between the waist and the tip is called the *sidecut*. More sidecut means a ski that is easier to turn going downhill, which is good for mountain skiing. I used to look for about 8 to 10 millimeters of sidecut, but this is now very little, since there has been a revolution in ski design and there are now many wide touring skis with plenty of sidecut. My current mountain touring skis, Tua Hydrogens, now discontinued, as is the company, have 30 millimeters of sidecut and measure 102-72-92 millimeters, tip to tail yet, at 5.5 pounds, weigh no more than my old narrow skis, which measured 62-54-58 millimeters. The advantage of wide skis is in soft snow, where they have better flotation than narrow ones. Makers of quality touring skis include Fischer, Madshus, K2, Hagan, Black Diamond, and Salomon.

Whatever the skis, you need strong bindings, either cables, strong clip-in systems bindings like the Rottefella BC, or bindings with three pins that fit into the toe of your boots, since they'll have to undergo the stress caused by your body weight plus a heavy pack. Touring bindings haven't changed much over the past few decades; they've just become stronger. Boots have changed, however, and plastic has taken over. At first this was just for lift telemark skiing and steep mountain descents, and the boots were too stiff and heavy for ski backpacking, but now you can get excellent plastic touring boots from Scarpa, Garmont, and Crispi for three-pin and cable bindings and in plastic/fabric/leather combinations from Alpine and Salomon for backcountry bindings. I use Garmont Xcursions, which weigh 6 pounds. The plastic shell keeps my feet dry in wet spring snow while the inners make good hut and tent boots.

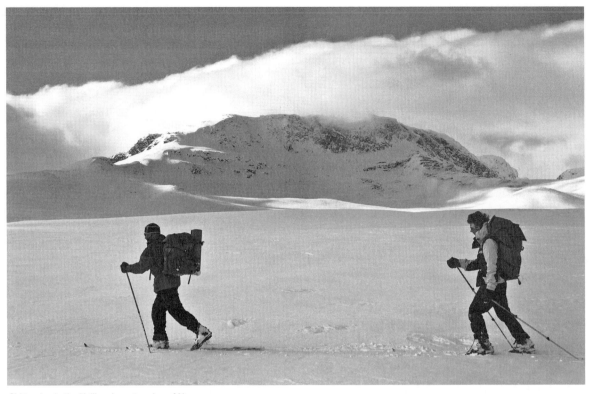

Ski touring in the Hallingskarvet region of Norway.

Poles are essential with skis (and a great help with snowshoes). Since lightweight fiberglass poles break easily (my first pair of poles shattered within a week), I use a metal pair. I like adjustable ones (long for the flat, shorter for uphill, shortest for downhill). There are many models—see the discussion of hiking poles earlier in this chapter. I use two-section Pacerpoles for skiing, finding the shaped handles are more comfortable than straight ones.

Climbing skins are long strips of "grippy" fabric that attach to the bottom of your skis. They make ascents much easier and are a worthwhile investment for mountain ski tours.

You need only moderate skill to travel the wilderness on skis, and the enjoyment of ski touring far outweighs the effort required. Beginners will benefit from a course at a ski school; I did. For more specifics on wilderness touring there are several good books, including Allen O'Bannon and Mike Clelland's entertaining *Allen and Mike's Really Cool Backcountry Ski Book* and also their *Really Cool Telemark Tips*. The classic book on skills is Paul Parker's superb *Free-Heel Skiing*.

chapter four

carrying the load

the pack

> THINK POSITIVE; LIKE SO MANY ACTIVI-
> TIES THAT SEEM PURELY PHYSICAL,
> PACKING A HEAVY LOAD IS 75 PER-
> CENT MENTAL.
>
> —*Laura and Guy Waterman,*
> Backwoods Ethics

The heart of the backpacker's equipment is the pack. Tents, boots, stoves, and rain gear may be unnecessary at some times and places, but your pack is always with you. It must hold everything you need for many days' wilderness travel yet still be as small a burden as possible.

Ever since aluminum frames and hipbelts were introduced in the 1940s and 1950s, designers have tried to make carrying loads as comfortable as possible. Internal and external frames, adjustable back systems, sternum straps, load-lifter straps, side ten-sion straps, triple-density padded hipbelts, lumbar pads—the modern pack suspension is a complex structure that requires careful fitting. Only your footwear is as important to your comfort as your pack, so take the time to find a pack that fits.

The last decade of the twentieth century saw a huge change in pack design—a revolution even, though I'm wary of that word—with the advent of lightweight and ultralight packs weighing a small fraction of the weight of earlier packs. This shook up the pack world, and established makers scram-

WALKING BEFORE DAWN

Under a soft gray light, mountaintops lie black and brooding, draped in pale, wraithlike clouds. The last stars still shine in a dark sky, though far to the east a faint tinge of pink spreads along the horizon. As the light strengthens, the dark lines of peaks beyond the flat lake stand out as if etched onto the sky. The pink intensifies into red and orange, then a spot on the horizon darkens and flares; a shaft of light rushes from it, cutting the air. The spot becomes an arc, a bright curve that slowly edges above the horizon, turning into a hot white orb, the sun. The reeds on the tiny islet out in the lake are transformed from black shadows to green life. I must turn my eyes from the brightness.

bled to produce their own lightweight designs. Except for long cold-weather trips, there's now no need to carry a pack weighing even half what standard packs used to weigh. An added bonus is that these lightweight packs are usually less expensive than heavier ones.

TYPES OF PACKS

Walk into any outdoor equipment store and you'll be confronted by a vast array of packs. Any could be used for backpacking; the problem is to determine which are right for your kind of backpacking. Many people use one pack for all their hiking. If you do, then you need a pack with enough capacity for the bulkiest loads you're likely to carry. Overstuffing a too-small pack is not the way to achieve a comfortable carry. If you go on trips year-round, you may be better off with more than one pack, so you can tailor the load to their capacity and weight. I now regularly use three packs: a 32-ounce, 3,050-cubic-inch frameless pack for loads less than 30 pounds; a more supportive 32-ounce, 4,400-cubic-inch frameless pack for loads between 30 and 40 pounds; and a 58-ounce, 5,800-cubic-inch internal-frame pack for loads much over 40 pounds. A pack designed to carry 60 pounds comfortably will be fine with 30 pounds, but the converse is not usually true. If I could keep only two packs, I'd drop the lightest one. If I could keep only one, it would be the heaviest. But if you do only short three-season hikes with light loads, then you'll need only a light, relatively inexpensive pack. You can always add a larger, heavier pack if you decide on longer or colder-weather hikes and an even bigger one for extended cold-weather trips.

Before I go into the details of pack design and construction, here's a brief overview of types of packs.

Ultralight Packs

The new ultralight packs weigh about a pound and are designed for loads up to 20 pounds. These packs have minimal features, with no frames and often no back padding or hipbelts. Once you'd probably have had to make such a pack yourself, but now several are sold by companies like Gossamer Gear, Six Moon Designs, LWGear, ZPacks, and ULA. The pack that started this revolution was the GoLite Breeze, designed by Ray Jardine based on the one he uses on his long-distance hikes. The Breeze is as simple as can be—just a large nylon bag made from tough Dyneema gridstop nylon with padded shoulder straps, mesh side and rear pockets, and a rollover closure. The medium size holds 2,900 cubic inches, plus another 850 if you use the

roll top

padded shoulder strap

mesh pockets

An ultralight pack. GoLite Breeze.

CLOCKWISE FROM TOP LEFT: *(1)* Lightweight pack with internal framesheet and padded hipbelt for loads up to 30 pounds (Granite Gear Vapor Trail). *(2)* Lightweight pack made from Dyneema with padded back and hipbelt for loads up to 30 pounds (GoLite Jam). *(3)* GoLite Jam back system showing foam padding and hipbelt with pockets. *(4)* Lightweight pack made from Dyneema with internal frame for loads up to 40 pounds (ULA Catalyst). *(5)* Lightweight pack with internal frame and thick padded hipbelt for loads up to 50 pounds (GoLite Odyssey).

extension, and weighs 14 ounces. The Breeze is no longer available but Ray Jardine sells a kit for making a similar pack on his website (www.rayjardine .com). I've tried the Breeze and a few other similar packs, and although they're OK with loads under 15 to 20 pounds, they're a little too minimalist for me. Using them reminded me why padded backs, frames, and hipbelts were developed. It's interesting to see that some of the early makers of ultralight packs have now incorporated these features in many of their packs. Some are still ultralight, such as the 3,600-cubic-inch Gossamer Gear Mariposa Plus at 21.3 ounces, but they are more comfortable than packs with no support system other than shoulder straps.

An interesting new range of ultralight packs designed for ultralight backpacking comes from a U.K. company so new that production is not under way at the time of writing. Tramplite packs, designed by ultralight hiker Colin Ibbotson, are modular with interchangeable hipbelts, pack bags (known as *skins*), and carbon-fiber frames plus ventilated backs, rain covers, pack liners, and more. Fabrics are Dyneema or Cuben Fiber, and weights for a 2,500- to 3,000-cubic-inch pack are around 7 ounces for the lightest version to 21 ounces for a fully featured Dyneema one. These weights are astonishing. Colin reckons the packs should be fine with 25 pounds, and ones with the beefier hipbelts and frame maybe up to 35 pounds and more. I've used a prototype 3,000-cubic-inch Dyneema Tramplite pack with a 26-pound load and it was comfortable and stable. (Colin has many other ideas for gear to watch out for in the future. I did an overnight trip with him on which he used one of his tarp designs; it stood up to a gusty wind and was less noisy than the semi-geodesic tent I was testing.)

Add a little more weight and a few more features, and there are plenty of day packs in the 1,800- to 2,500-cubic-inch range weighing 1 to 2 pounds that could do for ultralight backpacking.

Lightweight Packs

Not many people get their total loads (including food and water) below 20 pounds, but plenty carry no more than 25 to 45 pounds. For these weights you don't need a fully specified heavy, traditional backpacking sack, but you do need more support than you get from an ultralight pack with no frame or hipbelt. Lightweight packs weigh from 1 to 4 pounds and have capacities from 2,500 to 5,000 cubic inches. The most basic have padded backs but no frames and simple unpadded hipbelts. Thirty pounds is usually the comfort limit for these. Add an internal frame and a padded belt, and that limit goes up to as much as 50 pounds. Until the first ultralight packs appeared, lightweight packs were hard to find. At first I couldn't find one I liked; now the problem is deciding which one to choose. In the previous edition, I listed packs in this weight range. There are now so many of them, including many from established pack makers, that such a list is no longer needed. Makes include GoLite, Granite Gear, Gossamer Gear, Gregory, McHale, ULA, Osprey, Lowe Alpine, Lightwave, OMM, Aarn, The North Face, Mystery Ranch, and Mountain Hardwear. Capable of carrying loads up to 40 to 45 pounds, these are the ideal packs for most backpackers in my opinion.

Standard Packs

Despite the lightweight revolution, most packs still fall into the standard pack category, and there

framesheet

padded adjustable
straps

mesh
pockets

padded back

mesh pocket

*A lightweight
pack. ULA P-2.
(Padded hipbelt
not shown.)*

mesh pocket

are dozens of models. I now use a standard pack only for loads of more than 45 pounds. I no longer carry that much very often, but when I do I still appreciate the comfort. These packs are sophisticated, complex, expensive, and marvelous. Without them, carrying heavy loads would be much more arduous. This category subdivides into two suspension systems based on frame type. Each system has its dedicated, vocal proponents.

First came the *external frame* of welded, tubular aluminum alloy; its ladderlike appearance was common on trails worldwide in the 1950s, 1960s, and 1970s. It's a simple, strong, and functional design, good for carrying heavy loads along smooth trails but unstable in rougher, steeper terrain. It's easy to lash extra items to the frame, making capacities enormous.

Although external frames have been to the summit of Everest, mountaineers found them unstable for climbing, generally preferring frameless "alpine" packs that hugged the back closely. However, these were uncomfortable with heavy loads. To combine stability with comfort, flat, flexible metal bars were added to the backs of the alpine packs, stiffening them and making it easier to transfer the weight to the hips. Thus, in the late 1960s the *internal-frame* pack was born. The design developed rapidly, and today most backpackers choose internal-frame packs. Ranging in capacity from 3,000 to a frightening 9,000 cubic inches, they serve just about any sort of backpacking, from summer weekend strolls to six-month expeditions. Internal-frame packs require careful fitting and adjustment, but if you're prepared to take the time for a proper fit, they're an excellent choice.

Although much less popular than a few decades ago, external-frame packs are still available from

KEY FEATURES: PACKS FOR LOADS OVER 30 POUNDS

- A good fit. A poorly fitted pack can give you sore shoulders and hips and an aching back and is also unstable.
- A well-designed hipbelt. A good hipbelt should support 90 percent or more of the load without rubbing or making your hips sore.
- Curved, padded shoulder straps with top tension/load-lifter straps to take pressure off the top of your shoulders.
- A frame or framesheet to help transfer weight to your hips and prevent lumpy gear from poking you in the back.
- A capacity and design suitable for the gear to be carried. A pack for summer trails doesn't need ice-ax loops, ski slots, or room for a four-season sleeping bag—a pack for a winter ski-backpacking trip does.
- Light weight. The pack should be as light as possible for the weight to be carried—10 percent of the total load weight at most.

An external-frame pack.

front

back

area for stuff sack
lash-down points
aluminum frame
sternum strap
back band
lumbar pad
padded hipbelt

lash strap
external pockets

cinch straps

area for sleeping bag stuff sack

An internal-frame pack.

front

removable top lid
extendable cowl
support framesheet
with aluminum stays
lash-down points
cinch straps

back

top pocket
load-lifter straps
padded mesh back pad
compression straps
sternum straps

lumbar pad
padded hipbelt

Bulky winter loads require big packs like the 5,490-cubic-inch GoLite Odyssey.

companies like Kelty, JanSport, Mountainsmith, ALPS Mountaineering, and Coleman.

Travel Packs

Travel packs are derived from internal-frame packs and have similar suspension systems and capacities. The frame and harness can be covered by a zippered panel when they're not needed (or when you don't want to risk the suspicion that packs engender in some officials and in some countries) and to protect them from airport baggage handlers. With the harness hidden, travel packs look like soft luggage, with handles, zip-

around compartments, and front pockets, and they can be used like suitcases when packing and unpacking. My limited usage of one Lowe Alpine model suggests that they're all right for the occasional overnight trip but don't compare with real internal-frame packs for comfort, which seems to be the general consensus. The larger ones with internal frames are probably adequate for moderate loads (40 pounds or so) as long as you don't mind the panel zippers.

SUSPENSION SYSTEMS

The suspension system is the most important feature to consider when choosing a pack; it supports the load, and it's the part of the pack that comes in contact with your body. A top-quality, properly fitted suspension system will let you carry loads comfortably and in balance. An inadequate or poorly fitted one can cause great pain. As with boots, it takes time to fit a pack properly. This applies even to frameless packs—they still need to be the right length for your back.

Frames

To hold the load steady and help transfer the weight from the shoulders to the hips, the back of the pack needs some form of stiffening. For loads less than 30 pounds, simple foam padding is adequate, but once the weight exceeds 30 pounds, a more rigid system is needed.

As I said earlier, there are two frame types: external, with the packbag hung on a frame by straps or clips or clevis pins, and internal, which fits inside the fabric of the pack, often completely integrated into it and hidden. The debate centers on which frame best supports a heavy load and which is more stable on rough ground; the answer used to be external for the first and internal for the second. Today, however, the best designs and materials have made the distinction less clear-cut.

For many years my choice has been internal-frame packs. It's a couple of decades since I last used an external frame. Internals are more stable than all but a few externals, easier to carry around when you're not on the trail, and less prone to damage. Some are comfortable with any weight you're likely to carry. That said, I have a friend who has used a Kelty Tioga external-frame pack for decades and finds it just about perfect. His only complaint is that he can't replace it with an identical model. Since his stomping grounds are the Colorado Rockies and the Wind River Range and he likes challenging off-trail hikes above the timberline, he's clearly adapted to the rigidity of the frame.

THE LIMITS OF EXTERNAL FRAMES

The trail was steep and rough, a direct line up the rocky mountainside. Just below the summit were two bands of rock I had to surmount. Climbing them wasn't difficult—just easy scrambling—but for a few yards the broken rock was very steep and I needed to steady myself with my hands. The only problem was that the tubes of my external-frame pack towered above my head and pushed my face forward into the slope so I couldn't look up to see where the trail went. The rigid frame made balancing difficult, too, and I lurched sideways when I took high steps. The situation wasn't dangerous, just awkward, but the experience was one of the main reasons I soon changed to an internal-frame pack, a design I've preferred ever since.

External Frames

The traditional external frame is made of tubular aluminum alloy and consists of two curved vertical bars to which a number of crossbars are welded. Kelty introduced such frames back in the 1950s and still makes them in barely altered form for their Yukon and Trekker packs. Variations have appeared over the years, such as hourglass-shaped frames and frames made from flexible synthetic materials. External frames are usually not adjustable, though some have frame extensions for carrying larger loads while others telescope and come in different back lengths. Suspension systems are similar to those found on internals. With externals the weight transfers directly through the rigid frame to your hips, so they will handle very heavy loads comfortably as long as the hipbelt is well padded and supportive enough. Because of their rigidity, it's easy to keep the weight high up and close to your center of gravity, enabling you to walk upright. Also, because the packbag is held away from the back, they allow sweat to dissipate, unlike internal-frame packs, which hug the body. Even so I've always found that when I work hard carrying a heavy load, I end up with a sweaty back whatever the type of frame.

The disadvantages of external frames are balance and stability. External frames do not move with you; on steep descents and when crossing rough ground, they can be unstable and may make walking difficult or even unsafe. They also tend to be bulkier than internal-frame packs, making them awkward for plane, car, and bus travel and difficult to stow in small tents. Their rigidity also makes them more vulnerable to damage, especially on airplanes. My last external frame cracked during airplane baggage handling.

Externals are generally less expensive than internals, though, and some are lighter for similar capacity and load-carrying comfort.

Internal Frames

The basic internal frame consists of two flat aluminum alloy stays running vertically down the pack's back. This original design, introduced in the late 1960s by Lowe Alpine, addressed the instability of external-frame packs on rugged terrain and the difficulty of designing a frameless pack to carry a heavy load comfortably. The bars, or stays, are usually parallel, though in some designs they form an upright or inverted V and in others an X.

Many internal frames now have flexible plastic *framesheets* in addition to or instead of stays to give extra rigidity to the pack and prevent hard bits of gear from poking you in the back. There are many variations on the framesheet/parallel stays theme, using aluminum, carbon fiber, polycarbonate, thermoplastic, Evazote, and polyethylene. Some packs have single stays down the center of the framesheet, and some have Delrin or titanium rods running down the sides to help transfer the weight to the hipbelt. One (McHale Bayonet) even has a two-part frame—remove the top for a smaller pack. Each pack maker has its own type of internal frame; all, of course, claim theirs can carry heavy loads more comfortably than anything else. The ones I've tested over the years—Aarn, Arc'teryx, Berghaus, GoLite, Granite Gear, Gregory, Dana Design (now reincarnated as Mystery Ranch), Lowe Alpine, The North Face, Osprey, PODsacs, ULA, Vaude, and Jack Wolfskin—all did a pretty good job with moderately heavy loads (45 to 55 pounds). Some—Dana Design/Mystery Ranch, Arc'teryx, Gregory—will handle 60 pounds or more while some lightweight models (ULA P-2) will handle up to 40 pounds.

Whatever the style, internal frames are flexible and with use conform to the shape of the wearer's back, allowing a body-hugging fit that gives excellent stability.

Because internal frames move with your body and let you pack the weight lower and closer to your back, they are excellent where balance is important, such as when rock scrambling, skiing, and hiking over rough, steep terrain. A disadvantage of this is that you tend to lean forward to counterbalance the low weight. Careful packing with heavy items high up and close to the back is a partial answer when you are walking on a good trail but is no panacea if the pack is poorly designed (see Packing later in this chapter).

On many packs, the stays are removable; this is one way to lighten the pack for a side trip or an ultralight trip. In snow, the stays could be used as tent stakes or even an emergency snow saw.

Crude internal frames for frameless packs can be created with a foam pad by folding it to fit down the back of the pack or rolling it up, placing it in the pack, and allowing it to unroll. Pads take up a fair amount of room, however, and can still distort under heavy loads; I think 30 pounds is the upper limit. Some packs are designed with sleeves in the back to use foam pads as frames; the pad takes up no room inside the pack.

The Hipbelt

Your back and shoulders are not designed for bearing heavy loads. In fact, the human spine easily compresses under a heavy weight—one reason back injuries are so prevalent. Furthermore, when you carry a load on your shoulders, you bend forward to counterbalance the backward pull of the load. This is uncomfortable and bad for your back, and the pressure on sensitive muscles and nerves can make your shoulders ache and go numb.

The solution is to lower the load to the hips, a far stronger part of the body. The *hipbelt* is by far the most important part of any pack suspension system designed for carrying loads of more than 20 to 25 pounds. It's the part of the pack I always examine first. A well-fitting, well-padded hipbelt transfers most of the pack weight from the shoulders onto the hips, allowing the backpacker to stand upright and carry a properly balanced load in comfort for hours. Some ultralight packs don't have hipbelts—indeed, some ultralight hikers seem to regard hipbelts as demonic symbols of submission to advertising hype. They argue that they are unnecessary with ultralight loads and restrict freedom of movement. Having tried hiking with the GoLite Breeze, which doesn't have a hipbelt, I can't agree. Even with less than 20 pounds in the pack, my shoulders could feel the weight by the end of the day, and I found not having a belt restrictive. Stability was poorer, too. Even with very light loads I like a hipbelt, though for loads under 30 pounds it doesn't need to be big and bulky or even have any padding at all.

The first hipbelts were unpadded webbing. On some ultralight packs they still are, but most of today's hipbelts are complex, multilayered creations of nylon, foam, plastic, and even graphite. A good hipbelt should be well padded with soft, thick foam that molds around your hips. Those designed for loads of more than 40 pounds should also have some form of stiffening to prevent twisting when loaded. This may be an outer layer of firm foam or stiff but flexible polypropylene or polyethylene plates. Many belts are made from thermal-molded foam that forms a belt with a firm conical shape that hugs the body without sagging.

As always, somebody disagrees with the prevailing wisdom. McHale, a custom pack maker in Seattle, claims stiff belts are uncomfortable and unnecessary; its soft belts, McHale says, made from Evazote foam with double buckles, wrap round the hips so well that they create their own firm structure. They are continuous, attached to the pack only at the bottom edge, and run outside the lumbar pad so they wrap around the body and mold to your shape. I haven't used a McHale hipbelt, but they look interesting. I haven't found any problems with conventional, stiffened belts, though.

In addition to being thickly padded, a hipbelt should be at least 4 inches wide where it passes over the hips, narrowing toward the buckle. Conical or cupped belts are less likely than straight-cut ones to slip down over the hips (though most belts eventually slip with ridiculously heavy loads, whatever the shape); most belts on top-quality packs designed for heavy loads are shaped. For the heaviest loads, continuous wraparound belts perform better than those sewn to the side of the pack; again, most top models have these. To support the small of your back, the lower section of the pack should be well padded. This can be a continuation of the hipbelt (as in most external-frame packs), a special lumbar pad (as in most internal frames), or part of a completely padded back. The lumbar pad is important for supporting the load and spreading the weight over your lower back and hips. A too-stiff or too-soft lumbar pad can lead to pressure points and sore spots. Continuous hipbelts run behind the lumbar pad and may be attached to it with Velcro.

Belts that are attached to the frame or the lumbar pad only at or near the small of the back need side stabilizer or side tension straps (also called hip tension straps) to prevent the pack from swaying. These straps pull the edges of the pack in around the hips, which increases stability. Most internal-frame packs have them. A few models also have diagonal compression straps, which run downward across the side of the pack to the hipbelt and help pull the load onto the hipbelt. These work well.

Many hipbelts are nylon-covered inside and out. Although adequate, a smooth covering like this can make the belt slip when it's worn over smooth synthetic clothing, a problem that worsens as the load increases. Cordura or other texturized nylon is better; some companies use special high-friction fabrics. These may cover the whole inside of the belt or just the center of the lumbar pad.

Most hipbelt buckles are the three-pronged Fastex type or something similar. These are tough and easy to use, but they can break if you step on them, so be careful when the pack is on the ground. Carrying a spare on long trips, or putting one in a supply box, is a good idea. I had a buckle break at the start of a two-week winter trip. How, I'm not sure, though I suspect baggage handlers even though the pack was in a duffel bag. I didn't have a spare, and I was very glad that the mountain hut where I spent the first night sold them. Otherwise I'd have had to go out to a town to get one, since carrying a heavy winter load without a hipbelt was unthinkable. There are a few other buckle types around, such as the cam-lock buckles McHale uses.

Hipbelt size is important. The padded part of the belt should extend at least 2.5 inches in front of the hipbone, and after you tighten the belt there should be enough webbing left on either side of the buckle to allow for weight loss on a long hike and for adjustment over different thicknesses of clothing. Some packs come with permanent hipbelts, so you have to check the size when you buy. Packs that come in two or three sizes often have belts sized to the frame length (e.g., medium frame, medium belt), which is fine unless you are tall and thin or short and stout. Companies that make packs with removable belts often offer a choice of belt sizes. Such modular systems are the best way to achieve the optimum fit, especially if

you're not an "average" size. Gregory, for example, makes hipbelts in four sizes—small, 22 to 28 inches; medium, 28 to 34 inches; large, 34 to 40 inches; and extra large, 40+ inches. My waist (measured around the top of the iliac crest, not the stomach) averages 34 inches (occasionally less, sometimes more), so I have a medium belt on my Gregory Shasta. There are different hipbelts for men and women, too, though since everyone is a different shape, it may be that one labeled for the opposite sex fits best. Keep an open mind! Rather than have belts for each gender, some makers, such as Gregory, have belts whose angle over the hips can be altered so it follows your shape.

How big a belt you need depends on the weight you intend to carry. The basic principle is simple: big loads need big belts. I've found that moderately padded belts handle loads up to 45 pounds adequately. Heavier loads, however, cause these belts to compress and press painfully on the hipbones or else twist out of shape, making it difficult to put most of the load on the hips. For heavy loads, wide hipbelts with thick layers of padding and stiffened flexible reinforcements on the outside are best. My favorite for many years has been the one found on the biggest Dana Gleason–designed packs, once Dana Design now Mystery Ranch, which is massive and thick. I've carried loads of 60 pounds or more for weeks at a time using this belt and never had bruised or sore hips. I'm also impressed with the Arc'teryx Bora hipbelt, made from four layers of laminated, thermoformed foam in a curved, cupped shape that fits neatly around my hips.

Finally, consider what you wear *under* a hipbelt as well, because this will be pressed against your skin. Pants with thick side seams, belt loops, rivets, and zippered pockets can rub painfully. Wide, elasticized waistbands or bib styles are better. If you do find a sore point under a hipbelt, check to see if it's caused by your clothing before you curse the pack.

Shoulder Straps

Most of the time, shoulder straps do little more than stop the pack from falling off your back. But because there are times when you have to carry all or some of the weight on your shoulders (for example, river crossings when you've undone the hipbelt for safety and rock scrambles and down-hill ski runs where for balance you've fully tightened all the straps to split the weight between shoulders and hips), these straps need to be foam-filled and tapered to keep the padding from slipping. This design is now standard on most good packs. Many straps are also curved so they run neatly under the arms without twisting. The key to a good fit is the distance between the shoulder straps at the top. Some straps are adjustable here so they will fit both broad and narrow shoulders. A few, like those on Gregory packs, adjust automatically. There are different shoulder straps for men and women, too. As with hipbelts, this isn't a strict division, however. Shoulder straps also come in different lengths—Gregory offers three for men and three for women, for example. Usually the length that corresponds to the frame length will fit, but if it doesn't you can change it for a different one.

Load-Lifter Straps

Packs designed for moderate to heavy loads (30 pounds and up) should have load-lifter straps (sometimes called top tension, load-balancing, or shoulder stabilizer straps) running from the top of the shoulder straps to the pack. These straps pull the load in over your shoulders to increase stability; they also stop you from feeling that the pack is falling backward and lift the shoulder straps off the sensitive nerves on top of the shoulders, transferring the weight to the collarbone. By loosening or tightening the straps, which you can do while walking, you can shift the weight of the pack between the hips and the shoulders to find the most comfortable position for the terrain you're on. Take a little time to adjust both the shoulder and load-lifter straps until the pack feels comfortable and stable. To work well, the straps need to rise off the front of the shoulders at about 45 degrees.

On most packs, the load-lifter straps are sewn to the shoulder straps, which means that altering the tension of one changes the other; so when you tighten the load-lifter straps for better stability, you also pull the shoulder straps down onto your shoulders. If they then feel too tight, you slacken them off, which also loosens the load-lifter straps and causes the pack to fall backward. To maintain stability, you tighten the load-lifter straps again. Repeating the cycle over and over can mean that by the end of the day the top tension straps are at their minimum length and therefore not as effective as they should be, while the shoulder straps have crept down your back and their buckles are pinching your armpits. I always try to get the adjustment about right at the start of the day and keep any alterations to a minimum. Even so, I end some days with a pack that is very badly adjusted. Though I haven't tried it, McHale seems to have found a simple solution with the Bypass shoulder system, in which the stabilizer straps aren't sewn to the shoulder straps. This means that the shoulder straps can slide along the stabilizers when they're adjusted without the latter's moving at all. The Bypass shoulder system has been around for a while, and I fully expected other makers to come up with their own versions. They haven't, however, presumably because they believe the conventional one works.

Sternum Straps

Sternum straps are found on most packs, attached to buckles or webbing on the shoulder straps. They pull the shoulder straps in toward the chest and help stabilize the pack. I don't use them much of the time, since they feel restrictive, but they can be helpful for stability when skiing or scrambling and for varying the pressure points of a heavy load during a long ascent. Most are simple webbing straps, but some have stretch sections that prevent overtightening. Fully elasticized straps can't be tightened at all and are useless. The position of sternum straps is important. They should sit high up, just below your neck, to reduce pressure on your chest.

Back Bands and Padding

In addition to a padded hipbelt and lumbar pad, most internal-frame packs have padded backs, some of them cushy panels of thermo-molded foam. If the entire back isn't padded, then the padding on the shoulder straps should run far enough down the back to protect the shoulder blades. Since much of the pack never touches the wearer's back directly, some of the padding is often unnecessary; too little, though, and sharp objects can poke you. Open-weave mesh over the foam helps moisture to disperse so your back doesn't get quite as sweaty as with plain nylon.

External frames need something to hold the crossbars off your back. On basic packs this is usually a wide band of tensioned nylon; mesh is better for ventilation than solid nylon. The tensioning cord or wire should be easy to tighten if it works loose. More expensive models sometimes have a pad of molded foam instead. The latter may be more comfortable, but it also reduces ventilation, lessening one of the advantages of external frames.

FITTING THE PACK

Modern packs are so complex that you can't just walk into a store, sling one on your back, and walk away. A good pack must be fitted, and it is important that this be done properly. A poorly fitted pack will prove unstable, uncomfortable, and so painful and inefficient that you may never want to go backpacking again. The best way to avoid this is to buy from a store with expert staff who can fit the pack for you. Allow plenty of time for this; it can take a while to get it right.

If you don't want to bother taking time to fit a pack—some people think having to do so means the pack is too complicated—a simple rucksack or a traditional external-frame pack would be the best choice. Even with these designs, you need to find the correct back length, though a precise fit isn't essential. A pack whose shoulder straps join the pack roughly level with your shoulders when the hipbelt, if there is one, is taking most of the weight comfortably on your hips should be fine. The first task in fitting a pack is to find the right back length. Your height is irrelevant here. The length of your legs, neck, or head makes no difference to the size of pack that will fit your back. I'm 5 feet, 8 inches tall, but I have a long torso. If I went by my height, as some pack makers still suggest, I'd end up with a pack that was too short. If a pack is too long, it will tower over your head and be very unstable; if it's too short, the hipbelt will ride above your hips and won't be able to take much weight.

The key measurement for finding the right size is the distance from the base of your neck to your upper hipbone, technically from the seventh cervical vertebra (a clearly felt knob) to the top of the iliac crest, which you can find by digging your thumbs into your sides. You can measure this yourself with a flexible tape measure, but it's much easier to get someone else to do it. Most frames come in two to five sizes. Gregory packs, for example, come in four sizes—extra small, 14 to 16 inches; small, 16 to 18 inches; medium, 18 to 20 inches; and large, 20 to 22 inches. My back measures 19.5 inches, so the medium size fits me.

Not all pack makers use the same back lengths for their sizes, though the variation is small; it partly depends on how many sizes they make. The ULA Catalyst pack comes in four sizes—small, 15 to 18 inches; medium, 18 to 21 inches; large, 21 to 23 inches; and extra large, 23 inches plus. Again I'm a medium, so that's the size of my ULA Catalyst. GoLite only offers two sizes for men and two for women in its Adventure and UltraLite pack series. The men's sizes are medium, 17.5 to 19.5 inches, and large, 19.5 to 21.5 inches. The women's sizes are medium, 15.5 to 17.5 inches, and large, 17.5 to 19.5 inches. As I'm right on the edge of the two sizes, I tried on both and decided the medium was the more comfortable and supportive fit. If you're on the edge of two sizes, try on both and see which feels better.

When you have the right back length, check that the hipbelt and the shoulder straps are the correct sizes (see The Hipbelt, earlier in this chapter). The hipbelt should ride with its upper edge about an inch above your hipbone, so that the weight is borne by the broadest, strongest part of your hips. The top of the frame, if there is one,

should then be 2 to 4 inches above your shoulders so that the load-lifter straps rise at an angle of about 45 degrees. Most pack makers tell you how to measure your back length and which of their sizes go with which back lengths. Some, like Gregory, provide stores with a fitting tool that makes finding the right size easy. All packs come with instructions for fine-tuning the fit, some more detailed than others. Instructions differ according to the specifications of the suspension system, but there are some general principles.

Once you have the right back length, it's time to fine-tune the pack for the greatest comfort. The most common way to do this is with an *adjustable*

seventh cervical vertebra

top of iliac crest

How to correctly measure the back for pack fitting.

harness, which allows you to move the shoulder straps up and down the back of the pack. On a few packs the positions of both the shoulder straps and the hipbelt are adjustable. However, hipbelt adjustments change the position of the base of the pack in relation to your body, which causes the load to press on your backside when the effective back length is shortened and to ride too high on the back when it's lengthened. Both interfere with stability and comfort, so any hipbelt position adjustments should be very fine. I've found that the best position is with the base of the hipbelt level with the base of the pack.

Lowe Alpine was first with an adjustable shoulder harness system. In its much-copied Parallux system, the shoulder straps are fitted into slots in a webbing column sewn down the center of the pack's back. Variations employ Velcro straps or a slotted plastic adjustment "ladder." Others have plastic plates that attach to each other with Velcro. These systems demand some fiddling; easier are stepless systems that use a locking slider, screw, or similar device to slide the shoulder straps up and down the central column. Even simpler are systems in which the shoulder straps are attached to a stiffened plastic yoke that slides up and down the stays; you can adjust these while wearing the pack by simply pulling on two straps attached to the base of the plate. Some adjustment systems are easy to use; others are hidden under back padding and can be hard to find, let alone use. Losing your temper doesn't help, as I know from experience. Instruction manuals aren't always much use either. Help from knowledgeable sales staff is the best bet. Whichever type you end up with, find the right position for your back and then forget about it. Obviously, any system has a limited adjustment range. At either end of this range a pack won't carry as well as it does if adjusted to

Adjustable harness systems.

a position nearer the middle. Packs that come in just one frame size will still fit only a narrow range of back lengths, however adjustable they are.

Before you try on a pack, load it with at least 25 to 30 pounds of gear. An empty or lightly loaded pack is impossible to fit properly and will of course feel fine. Most stores will fill the pack for you—sometimes with ropes—though you could take your own gear to check that it fits in the pack properly. Before putting on the pack, loosen all the adjustment straps. Then put the pack on and do up the hipbelt until it is carrying all the weight and the upper edge rides about an inch above the top of your hipbone. Next, tighten the hipbelt stabilizer straps, followed by the shoulder straps and load-lifter straps. The last should leave the shoulder straps at a point roughly level with your collarbone or just in front of it, at an angle of about 45 degrees. If the angle is smaller than that, the harness needs lengthening or the pack is too short; if it is larger, it needs shortening or the pack is too long. The aim is to have most of the pack weight riding on the hips while the pack hugs the back to provide stability. If the distance between the shoulder straps and hipbelt is too short, the load will pull back and down on the shoulders; if it's too long, although the weight will be on the hips, the top of the pack will be unstable and will sway when you walk.

Once you have the right size pack and have adjusted the harness correctly, most of your fitting problems are over. The shoulder straps themselves should curve over your shoulders a couple of inches before joining the pack. They shouldn't feel as though they are slipping off your shoulders or be so close together that they pinch your neck. The lower buckles should be several inches below the armpits so they don't touch you, but with enough webbing to allow for adjustment over different thicknesses of clothing.

Finally, make sure the sternum strap is in the correct position, above the part of your chest that expands most when you breathe but not so high that it presses on your neck. When you walk, the pack should hug your body as if it's stuck to you. If it feels awkward or uncomfortable, keep adjusting until you get it right or until you decide that this particular pack will never fit you comfortably.

Once I have the best fit I can obtain with an internal-frame pack, I usually bend over and stretch the pack on my back so the frame can start to mold to my shape, a process that is usually complete after the first day's walk. Some pack makers advise removing the stays of internal frames and bending them to the shape of your back before you start fitting the pack, but I've never been able to

do this successfully, even with help from a friend, and prebent stays are the devil to reinsert in their sleeves. Some stores have staff trained to do this for you. However, a friend suggests that "the trick is to make lots of very fine adjustments, and to make each one by bending [the stays] around gentle curves such as one's upper thigh."

You have to make minute adjustments to the harness every time you use a pack. Loosening the top stabilizer straps, tightening the shoulder straps, then retightening the stabilizers cinches the pack to the body for maximum stability but also shifts some of the load onto the shoulders. This is useful on steep descents or when skiing or crossing rough ground—anywhere balance is essential. For straightforward ascents and walking on the flat, the shoulder and stabilizer straps can be slackened off a touch so that almost all of the weight drops onto the hips, then the stabilizers should be tightened a little again until you can just slide a finger between the shoulder and the shoulder straps.

Every time you put on the pack, you have to loosen the side stabilizer straps, then tighten them after you've done up the hipbelt—otherwise the latter won't wrap around the hips properly. While you're on the move, whenever the pack doesn't feel quite right or you can feel a pressure point developing, adjust the straps to shift the balance of the load slightly until it feels right again. I do this frequently during the day, almost without noticing it.

If you want or need a custom fit, McHale, which sells through its own store in Seattle and its Web site, will make a pack to your measurements. If you always seem to be between sizes with fixed-length packs or at the ends of the adjustment systems of adjustable ones, a McHale pack might be the answer.

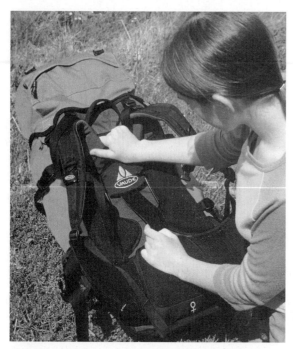

Altering the back length of an adjustable backpack (Vaude Astra 65 II).

Tightening the load-lifter straps.

Adjusting the side tension straps.

Gender-Specific Packs

Although makers don't usually say so, packs that don't come labeled as "men's" or "women's" are usually designed for the "average" man. But women often have shorter torsos, narrower shoulders, and wider hips than men do. This means men's packs may have frames that are too long (leading to an unstable carry and too much weight on the shoulders), overly wide shoulder straps that slide off and have to be held in place by a tight sternum strap, and hipbelts that dig in at the lower edge and don't touch at the top.

The past twenty years have seen a big change, with many packs now specifically designed for women. Modular packs for which you can select different hipbelts and shoulder straps are an alternative. We're all different, so being able to choose components that fit your shape or else to vary the fit of those that come with the pack means everyone should be able to find a pack that fits well.

PACKBAGS

Compared with the intricacies of frames and suspension systems, packbag design is straightforward. The choice is purely personal—the type of packbag has little effect on the comfort of your pack. How many pockets, compartments, and external attachment points you want depends on how you like to pack and the bulk of your gear. Tidy folk like packs with plenty of pockets and at least two compartments so they can organize their gear. Those who are less neat tend to go for large, single-compartment monsters so they can shove everything in quickly.

There are a couple of points to consider, however. To maintain balance and comfortable posture, the load needs to be as close as possible to your center of gravity. This means keeping it near your back and as high up as is feasible without reducing stability. While a good suspension system is the key to this, it helps if the packbag extends upward and perhaps out at the sides but not away from the back. For this reason, if your pack has large rear pockets, you should pack only light items in them. GoLite packs have large rear pockets. I find that if I pack them with light items such as hats, gloves, and windshirts they don't affect the carry, but if I put full water bottles in them I can feel the pack pulling backward. Many packs have a strap at the top running from front to back across the packbag. When tightened, this strap pulls the load in toward the back. They work well, and I look for one on a large pack.

The packbag is an integral component of an internal-frame pack. The frame may be embedded in a foam-padded back, encased in sleeves, or just attached at the top and bottom of the bag. Whatever the method, the frame and pack work together and cannot be used separately. Packbags may be attached to external frames in various ways, but the most common is with clevis pins and split rings. One frame conceivably could be used with several different packbags or with other items such as stuff sacks.

Size

How large a packbag you need depends on the bulk of your gear, the length of your trips, and how neatly you pack. I've always preferred large packs. I like to pack everything inside (including my insulating mat when possible), and I like to know I can cram everything in quickly and easily, even in the dark after the tent has just blown down in a storm. (Paranoia? Maybe, but it has happened to me.) Those who favor small packs say that a large pack is a heavy pack because you'll always fill it up. I say this applies only to the weak willed! If I had only one pack, it would be a large one. A large pack cinched down when half full is far more comfortable than an overloaded small one.

Now that there is lighter, more compact gear, I generally use a smaller pack. A pack of 4,000 cubic inches or so is now enough for most three-season trips, however long. For cold-weather trips, I now find a 5,500-cubic-inch pack ample. My 7,200-cubic-inch monster doesn't get much use anymore. I'd need to be doing a long winter trip without resupply to need that capacity.

A minor problem is that different manufacturers seem to have different ideas of what constitutes a cubic inch, so one maker's 5,000-cubic-inch pack may hold less than another's 4,500-cubic-inch model. (GoLite and some other top makers use a standard approved by the American Society for Testing Materials. If every maker used it, the problem would disappear.) When choosing a pack, think about whether your gear will all fit in with room left for food. You could even take your gear to the store and pack the sack to be sure.

Internal-frame packs usually have *compression straps* on the sides or front that you can pull in to hold the load close to the back when the pack isn't full. Traditional external-frame packs lack these, though they do appear on some new designs. Packs with compression straps and removable *extendable lids* are often specified with maximum and minimum capacities; to achieve maximum volume, you may have to raise the lid so high that the top of the pack becomes unstable, so it's wise to check this before you buy.

External-frame packbags that run the length of the frame tend to be very large. The more common three-quarter-length bags can have capacities as small as 2,500 cubic inches, though most average about 4,000 cubic inches. Extra gear (sleeping mat, tent, sleeping bag) can be strapped under the packbag without affecting how the pack carries, and if necessary, even more gear can be lashed on top. However, if you strap extra gear, other than light items like foam pads, under or above an internal-frame pack, you might ruin its balance and fit. If you need to carry a really awkward load, you can remove the packbag from an external frame and strap the load directly to the frame.

Internal Compartments

Most large packs come with zippered lower compartments, though you can get packs with one huge compartment. Compartments with long zippers that run right around the packbag or curve down to the lower edges are the easiest to use. With large packs—5,000 cubic inches or more—I prefer two compartments because they provide better access to my load. On most packs the divider separating the two compartments is held in place by a zipper or drawcord and can be removed to create a single compartment if needed. A few pack makers offer packs with more than two compartments. I suspect this might make packing difficult. I'm not that organized! With smaller packs I find a single compartment adequate. Not having the divider or zipper saves a little weight and expense, too.

Lids and Closures

Lids keep the contents of your pack in, prevent things from moving around, and protect the pack opening from rain. Most packbags have large lids, sometimes with elasticized edges for a trimmer fit, that close with two straps fastened by quick-release buckles. Ultralight packs often have no lid at all, just a rollover top that closes with buckles or a couple of drawcords and a buckle and strap.

Many packbags have a *floating lid* that attaches to the back of the pack by straps and can be extended upward over a large load or tightened down over a small one. These lids can be removed when not needed to save weight. A similar, though less effective, design is a lid that is sewn to the back of the packbag but extends when you release the straps at the back. When such a lid is fully extended, it tends to restrict head movement, interferes with easy access to the lid pocket, and fails to cover the load. Many detachable lids contain large pockets (500 or more cubic inches) and can be used as lumbar packs or even small day packs by rearranging the straps, using extras provided for that purpose or by using the pack hipbelt. They can be useful for carrying odds and ends (film, hat, gloves, binoculars) on short strolls. I've used a detachable pack lid as a day pack for daylong hikes away from camp, managing to pack in rain gear, warm clothing, and other essentials.

The lower compartments of packs are always closed by zippers. Straps that run over the zipper take some of the strain and reduce the likelihood of its bursting. Since I've had problems with lightweight zippers on day packs, I like large zippers, whether toothed or coiled; lightweight zippers, protected by straps or not, worry me. Top compartments usually close with two drawcords, one around the main body of the pack, which holds the load in, and one on the lighter-weight extension, which completely covers the load when pulled in. If the only access to the load is through the top opening, items packed at the bottom of the top compartment cannot be reached easily. Vertical or diagonal zippers in the main body are found on some large packbags. I find these useful, especially in bad weather, when I can extract the tent, including the poles, through the open zipper without unpacking other gear, opening the main lid, or letting in much rain or snow.

Zip-around front panels for suitcase-type loading, giving easy access to the whole interior of the packbag, have fallen out of popularity, probably because the pack had to be laid down to pack and unpack—not a good idea in the rain or on mud or snow. The pack couldn't be pulled tight around a partial load, either, so items would move around. Panel loading is now primarily found on travel packs.

Some large packs, however, have both top- and panel-loading main compartments. This has the advantages of both and is an alternative to the main-compartment zippers. I look for one or the other in any pack of more than 5,000-cubic-inch capacity.

Pockets

Pockets are useful for stowing small, easily mislaid items and things you may need during the day. Lid pockets are found on most packs except traditional external-frame models and some of the newer lightweight packs. The best lid pockets are large and have either curved zippers or zippers that run around the sides for easy access. Some packs also have a second flat security pocket inside the lid for storing documents, wallets, permits, and similar items.

External-frame packs normally come with one, two, or (rarely) three fixed pockets on each side. Internal-frame packs, often designed for mountaineering as well as backpacking, don't usually have fixed side pockets, since these can get in the way when climbing. Instead, optional detachable pockets can be fastened to the compression straps. These add 500 to 1,000 cubic inches per pair to the pack's capacity and 4 to 12 ounces to the weight. They can be removed to reduce the capacity of the pack or when using the pack for skiing or scrambling, when side pockets are a nuisance. Some side pockets have backs stiffened with a synthetic plate, which makes them slightly easier to pack but also heavier. A few makers also offer large pockets that can be attached to the back of a pack.

An alternative to a detachable pocket is an integral bellows side pocket with side-zipper entry, which folds flat when not used. I find bellows pockets more difficult to use than detachable pockets. They are narrow at the top and bottom, can be obstructed by compression straps, and when full can impinge on the volume of the main compartment. And you still have to carry the weight of the material when you don't need the pockets. On the other hand, they are always there when you need them—you can't forget one.

Many packs have open pockets at the base of each side. These *wand pockets* were originally designed to hold the thin wands that mountaineers use to mark routes and caches on glaciers and snowfields. They are useful for supporting the ends of long, thin items such as tent poles, trekking poles, or skis. Wand pockets are usually permanently attached, though some, like those from McHale, are detachable and can be replaced with a larger open pocket that will hold a quart or liter water bottle. Some wand pockets have elasticized edges and can be stretched to take a small water bottle. I often carry a map in the wand pocket for easy access.

With the new ultralight packs came ultralight pockets made from rugged mesh. These may have open tops with drawcord closures or else zippers. They are now my favorite pockets. You can stuff wet gear into them—tarps, flysheets, rain clothing—and it will slowly drain and dry and not soak other items. The side pockets can hold water bottles so you can reach them while wearing the pack. You can also use them for snacks, a toilet trowel, fuel bottles, and other items you want to have outside the main pack. Detachable mesh pockets are sold, so you can add them if your pack doesn't have them.

I also like pockets on the hipbelt. They are great for a compass, a whistle, snack bars, and other small items.

Many packs have internal hydration sleeves or pockets designed to hold water bladders, with an exit hole for the drinking tube. If you use a hydration system, these are useful—though you can just put the bladder in an external pocket—otherwise they can be used for storing items like maps and small items of clothing.

Straps and Patches

Side compression straps can be used to attach skis and other long items (trekking poles, tripods, tent poles, foam pads). Most packbags come with one or two sets of straps for ice axes and straps (and maybe a reinforced panel) for crampons on the lid or the front. If straps don't come with the pack, there are often patches so you can thread your own. Many packs come with far too many exterior fastenings, but you can always cut off those you'll never use.

MATERIALS

Most packs are made from a variety of coated nylons and polyesters. These fabrics are hardwearing, nonabsorbent, and flexible. *Texturized nylons*—made from a bulked filament that creates a durable, abrasion-resistant fabric—are often used for the pack base or bottom, sometimes with a layer of lighter nylon inside; some makers use this fabric for the whole packbag. The most common is Cordura, though a few companies have their own proprietary fabrics. *Packcloth* is a smoother, lighter nylon often used for the main body of the pack. All of these materials are strong and long-lasting.

One way to keep the weight of a pack down is to use lightweight fabrics. Packcloth and 500-denier Cordura are lighter than 1,000-denier Cordura, but not by enough to make a big difference in weight. (The *denier* is the weight in grams of 9,000 meters of yarn. Thus 500-denier Cordura is made from yarns that weigh 500 grams per 9,000 meters. The lower the denier, the finer the yarn.) There are some *really* lightweight fabrics, though. For ultralight packs where weight is more important than durability, ripstop nylon is sometimes used. Silicone ripstop nylon is the strongest lightweight nylon, but even so it needs care and won't last as long as heavier fabrics. DSM's Dyneema is a very light polyethylene fiber that is ten times stronger than steel, weight for weight, more durable than polyester, and very abrasion and ultraviolet resistant. There are few full Dyneema packs, however, because the material is very expensive and is only available in white or gray as it can't be dyed. One of the few full Dyneema packs is the McHale 4,000-cubic-inch internal-frame SUBPOP, which weighs 36 ounces.

Dyneema can be woven with ordinary nylon to produce a fabric with ripstop threads made from polyethylene fibers filled in with nylon. This produces a colored fabric with a white grid imposed on it that looks far less conspicuous than pure Dyneema and also costs less. It's used in many lightweight packs from companies like GoLite, McHale, and ULA and is very tough. I've used Dyneema Gridstop packs extensively, including on a five-week hike, and haven't yet damaged the fabric. Even airport baggage handlers have failed to harm it—and in the interests of testing, one pack has been through several airports unprotected. I now consider these the best fabrics for packs.

The latest material for packs is Cuben Fiber, originally developed for sails and available in a number of weights and types. Cuben Fiber is not a woven textile but a laminate of different materials with reinforcing fibers, usually Dyneema, between thin polyester films. The resulting material is very strong for the weight, stronger than most other pack materials including Dyneema Gridstop and so ideal for ultralight products. Cuben Fiber is very expensive, however, and the lightest versions aren't very abrasion resistant. ZPacks makes a range of frameless Cuben Fiber packs that weigh very little. The 2,600-cubic-inch Blast 26 weighs just 7.4 ounces. Joe Valesko, who runs ZPacks, used a Blast 26 on his Pacific Crest Trail and Con-

tinental Divide Trail hikes and says that the life span is one full through-hike, though duct tape is likely to be needed on frayed areas by the end.

While most of these fabrics are waterproof when new, the coating that makes them so is usually soon abraded. The seams will leak in heavy rain anyway. Some manufacturers advise coating the seams with sealant, but the process is too complicated and messy for me to even contemplate. I rely on liners and covers (see Pack Accessories, later in this chapter) to keep the contents of the pack dry.

Weight

For many years I used a large, heavy pack for all my backpacking on the rationale that the pack was the one item of gear whose weight wasn't significant because comfort came first. I'm less convinced about the weight now. Comfort still comes first, and for loads of 50 pounds or more, a pack with a sophisticated suspension system is certainly far more comfortable than one with a more basic design, despite the extra weight. With loads over 30 pounds, I still find a framed pack more comfortable than a frameless one, but it doesn't have to be heavy. For loads under 30 pounds, ultralight packs without frames can be perfectly comfortable. Comfort doesn't have to equal weight anymore. Indeed, a lighter pack means a lighter load, which means your legs get less tired.

Despite the increasing number of lightweight and ultralight packs, most packs are still pretty heavy, weighing at least a pound for every 1,000 cubic inches of capacity—about 62 cubic inches per ounce. Many packs are heavier, with as few as 45 cubic inches per ounce. Yet a standard 6,000-cubic-inch internal-frame pack I have that dates back to 1982 weighs less than 5 pounds, giving 77 cubic inches per ounce.

For two decades—right up until the late 1990s—the weight of packs kept increasing. More complex frames, thicker padding, heavier fabrics—which most packs are still made from—detachable pockets, detachable lids, more straps, zippers, and buckles all piled on the weight. Eventually there had to be a reaction. Other gear—tents, sleeping bags, stoves, clothing, footwear—had gotten lighter. The change came with the increased popularity of long-distance hiking and the rise of adventure racing. Fast movers and light hikers didn't want heavy packs, so lighter models began to appear on the market. The old heavyweights still dominate, but for light loads there's no longer any need to carry a heavy pack.

A good rule of thumb for estimating pack weight is that the pack shouldn't weigh more than 10 percent of the maximum total load: for a 70-pound winter load, a 7-pound pack is acceptable, but for a 30-pound summer load, a 3-pound pack would be better. Of course, if you use the same pack year-round, as many backpackers do, the 7-pound pack would carry the 30-pound load.

Acceptable weight can also be roughly determined by the volume-to-weight ratio, found by dividing the capacity by the weight in ounces. Since the average ratio for most modern packs is 60 to 65 cubic inches per ounce, any figure lower than this means the pack is heavy for its capacity (my old Dana Design Astralplane comes in at 58 cubic inches per ounce), and any higher figure means it's lightweight. Quite a few packs that should be fine with light to moderate loads come in the range of 70 to 90 cubic inches per ounce. Some are even lighter. The ULA Catalyst has 98 cubic inches per ounce, the GoLite Pinnacle 137 cubic inches per ounce, and the Gossamer Gear Murmur Hyperlight an astonishing 278 cubic inches per ounce.

I still regard comfort as the crucial factor for carrying loads. When you're lugging 60 pounds or more, a pound or two of additional pack weight is worth it if you get a more comfortable carry. But for lighter loads, especially those under 40 pounds, I now like packs with a volume-to-weight ratio of at least 100 cubic inches per ounce.

DURABILITY

Top-quality packs are very tough, but many won't last for a walk of several months. I've suffered broken internal frames, snapped shoulder straps, ripped-out hipbelts, slipping buckles, and collapsed hipbelt padding on long hikes. On my first long solo hike back in 1976, the hipbelt tore off my new external-frame pack after just 200 miles. But I've also had packs last 2,000 miles and four and a half months of continuous use with loads averaging 60 to 70 pounds. My old Gregory Cassin, a discontinued model, survived a three-month Yukon walk with a heavy load when it was five years old and had already had many months of use. The only damage was to the top of one framestay sleeve, which ripped out. (Duct tape held it in place for the rest of the walk.) This degree of use is comparable to years, if not decades, of backpacking for those who go out for several weekends a month and perhaps a couple of two- or three-week trips a year.

Of the three people I know who hiked all or most of the Pacific Crest Trail the same year I did, each broke at least one pack. After months of constant use and harsh treatment, it seems that something is almost bound to fail, considering how complex a modern pack is and how much can go wrong. The heavier the load, the more strain on the pack—another reason for keeping the weight down.

Crude repairs can, and often must, be made to equipment in the field, but I'm loath to continue backpacking in remote country with a pack that has begun to show signs of failing, at least not before it's had a factory overhaul. After replacing broken packs at great expense in both time and money on my Pacific Crest Trail and Continental Divide walks, I had a spare pack ready and waiting when I set off on a Canadian Rockies through-hike. On that walk I replaced my pack early because it wasn't able to carry the weight (the makers had changed the style of the hipbelt from earlier models). The replacement pack broke two weeks before the end of the trek, and I had to nurse it to the finish, bandaged with tape. On the Pacific Northwest Trail, my pack started to fail after four weeks when the shoulder straps began to compress and twist uncomfortably. I contacted the company, and they sent out a new pack to my next resupply point, leaving me to nurse the old pack through ten more days. Perhaps I'm unlucky or particularly hard on packs, but for future lengthy ventures I plan to have a spare pack, and I'd advise anyone else to do the same.

Reputable pack makers stand behind their products, and most will replace or repair packs quickly if you explain the situation, though that isn't much comfort if you're days away from the nearest phone when your pack fails. Even a spare pack is no good until you can pick it up. It's important to be able to effect basic repairs; in Chapter 8, I cover the items to carry in a repair kit.

PACKING

How you pack gear depends on the sort of hiking you're doing, which items you're likely to need during the day, and the type of packbag you have. For hiking on level ground on well-maintained trails, heavy, low-bulk items should be packed high and near to your back to keep the load close to your center of gravity and enable you to maintain an upright stance. This is how I pack all the time, regardless of the terrain. In theory, however, for any activity where balance is important, such as scrambling, bushwhacking, cross-country hiking on steep, rough ground, or skiing, the heavy, low-bulk items should be packed lower for better stability, though still as close to your back as possible. Women tend to have a lower center of gravity than men and may find packing like this leads to a more comfortable carry for trail hiking too. Whatever your packing method, it's important that the load is balanced so the pack doesn't pull to one side. The items you'll need during the day should be accessible, and it helps to know where everything is.

I normally use a packbag with side or rear pockets and, with heavy loads, a lid pocket, so my packing system is based on this design. I don't like anything on the outside except winter hardware (ice ax and skis) and a closed-cell sleeping mat; everything else goes inside, and I pack most items in stuff sacks to keep everything organized.

With ultralight packs with no back padding, a sleeping pad can be used to cushion your back. Standard foam pads can be placed vertically in the pack and then unrolled so you can pack gear in the middle of the pad. A Z-Rest pad (see Chapter 6) can be folded flat and put down the back of the pack, as can a self-inflating mat. All these are effective but do take up a fair amount of the capacity of the pack. If you don't use a pad, gear can be packed into two long stuff sacks that you stand vertically side by side in the pack. Make sure there are soft items next to your back. If you layer gear horizontally, the back of the pack is likely to fold at the junctions between layers.

PACKS: CHOICES AND MODELS

My ideal pack for heavy loads would have a suspension system that enabled me to carry 75 pounds as though it were 30; would be superbly stable for skiing and crossing steep, rough ground; and would allow me to walk upright on the flat. Internal or external frame? It doesn't matter. It's the performance, not the type of frame, that matters.

I would like a packbag with a capacity of at least 6,000 cubic inches; two compartments; mesh side pockets; an extendable, detachable lid with a large pocket; and straps for ice axes and skis. The total weight shouldn't be more than 4 pounds. This pack would also see me through a three-thousand-mile, six-month walk without anything breaking!

I haven't yet found my ideal large pack, but the Dana Design Astralplane comes close. It's certainly more comfortable with a heavy load than any other pack I've tried and is also very stable. It's a bit heavy, but I have no other complaints. It has a 7,000-cubic-inch capacity, two compartments, vertical zippers in the top compartment, two front pockets, a detachable lid with a large pocket, and wand pockets. The frame consists of a polyethylene framesheet with a single aluminum stay down the center plus carbon-fiber rods at the side that help transfer the weight to the hipbelt. The belt itself is massive and supportive. My medium size weighs 7 pounds, 2 ounces, and the current equivalent, the Mystery Ranch G7000, weighs 8 pounds, 4 ounces. Ultralight it's not! But I've had my Astralplane for twenty years, and it's been everywhere from the High Sierra to Greenland, Spitsbergen, Lapland, and the Yukon and it's still in good condition.

Neither of the two packs that were my choices in the previous edition are still available. Having had the opportunity to try several packs since then, I now have three favorites. For loads in the 40- to 55-pound range, I like the GoLite Odyssey. This internal-frame pack has a capacity of 5,490 cubic inches and weighs 56 ounces, just under half the weight of the Astralplane. The packbag is made from recycled nylon and has two compartments, a detachable lid with a large pocket, a big front pocket, hipbelt pockets, and a side stretch pocket. For bulky cold-weather loads, it's excellent. There is a smaller version, the 4,392-cubic-inch Quest, which weighs 49 ounces and has the same harness system but only one compartment. I used the Quest on the second half of the Pacific Northwest Trail, and it was fine with loads up to 45 pounds, which is the maximum recommended by GoLite.

The successor to the ULA P-2, a favorite for several years, is the Catalyst, a 4,600-cubic-inch internal-frame pack made from Dyneema Gridstop that weighs around 46 ounces, depending on which optional components are selected. The Catalyst has big mesh side pockets, a huge mesh front pocket, and hipbelt pockets—all of which are included in the capacity, the main body holding 2,600 cubic inches (though I reckon that's a very small 2,600 cubic inches compared with many other packs). There's no lid, just a rollover top closed by buckles. For attaching gear and tightening the pack around a small load, there are side compression straps and front shock cord. ULA's recommended maximum load is 40 pounds. I've carried 44 pounds and found it comfortable. Mostly, though, I use it for loads in the 30- to 40-pound range, when the support of a frame and a good padded hipbelt is welcome but a heavier pack isn't needed.

For lighter loads (maximum 35 pounds), I like the GoLite Pinnacle. This 32-ounce, 4,392-cubic-inch Dyneema Gridstop pack has a firm padded back and hipbelt but no frame. It has a large zipped pocket on the back, side mesh pockets, hipbelt pockets, side compression straps, and a roll top with drawcord and strap closure. It replaces the simpler Gust, which I used for loads up to 20 pounds. The Gust was lighter weight but had no padding in the hipbelt and only very thin padding in the back. I'm happy to carry the extra ounces and have the extra comfort. The Pinnacle is a big pack, roomier than needed for summer overnights with low-bulk gear, though it can be compressed around a small load easily. If the capacity isn't needed, the smaller 3,050-cubic-inch, 29-ounce GoLite Jam has the same design.

If the pack has a frame or padded back, the first thing to go into the bottom of the pack, or the lower compartment if there is one, is my self-inflating mat, folded into a square and placed against the back of the pack so it's well protected. In front of this goes the sleeping bag (in an over-sized stuff sack inside a pack liner); when I put weight on top of the sleeping bag, it fills out the corners and helps the hipbelt wrap around the hips. Next in are my spare clothes (in another oversized stuff sack). If there's space and the pack has a lower compartment, my rain gear goes in next to the zipper for quick access. If I'm carrying a bivouac bag, it too goes in the base of the pack. This means that the bottom of the pack is filled with soft items that are bulky for their weight.

I then slide tent poles down one side of the pack next to my back and if there is one, through the cutaway corner of the upper compartment floor. Next to go in are cooking pans, stove and fuel canisters, empty water containers, and small items such as candles and repair kit, with the heaviest items (such as full fuel containers) close to my back. Except for my lunch and the day's trail snacks, food bags go on top of the cooking gear, close to my back because of the weight. In front of the food bags go the tent or tarp and any camp footwear. At the top of the pack I put books, spare maps, spare camera, and the windshirt or warm top I've been wearing to ward off the early morning chill while packing. If I can't fit this in the top of the pack, I squeeze it into the lower compartment or into the front mesh pocket if there is one.

The lid pocket is filled, in no particular order, with hat, neck gaiter, gloves, mittens, sunscreen, camera accessories bag, insect repellent, camera lenses, dark glasses, and any small items that have escaped packing elsewhere. If there's no lid pocket these go in a small stuff sack at the very top of the pack. One side pocket holds a water bottle, lunch, and snacks; the other holds fuel bottles if I'm using a white-gas or alcohol stove, plus tent stakes, headlamp, and first-aid kit. Any items that didn't fit into the lid pocket or that I've overlooked also go in an outside pocket. Map, compass, mini binoculars, and writing materials go in a jacket or shirt pocket or hipbelt pocket. My camera, in its padded case, is slung across my body on a padded strap so it's both well protected and accessible. Then, once I've shouldered the pack, tightened up the straps, and picked up my poles, I'm ready for the day's walk.

Of course this system varies according to conditions. If I have a foam pad rather than a self-inflating mat, it goes on the outside of the pack. Rain gear can end up buried in the pack on days and in areas where it's unlikely to be needed. Items can move from pocket to pocket at times. The aim is convenience and comfort, not tidiness and organization for their own sake.

PUTTING ON THE PACK

Putting on the pack, repeated many times daily, requires a great deal of energy and more than a little finesse. With loads under 25 pounds, you can simply lift the pack and swing it onto your back. With most loads, though, the easiest way is to lift the pack using the shoulder strap (or the nylon "haul loop" attached to the top of the pack back on nearly all models), rest it on your hip, and put the arm on that side through the shoulder strap. You can then slowly swing the pack onto your back and slip your other arm through the shoulder strap.

With heavy loads (50 pounds or so), I swing the pack onto my bent leg rather than my hip, then from a stooped position I slowly shift, rather than swing, the load onto my back. Heavy loads make me aware of how much energy putting on a pack requires; whenever I stop on the trail, I try to find a rock or bank to rest the pack on so I can back out of the harness, and later back into it again. Such shelves are rare, though, so with really heavy loads (65 pounds or more) I usually sit down, put my arms through the shoulder straps, and then slowly stand up if I feel I haven't the energy to heave the pack onto my back. I also try to take the pack on and off less often when it's heavy; I keep items I need for the day in my pockets and rest the pack against something when I stop.

In camp I sometimes keep the pack in the tent—if I'm not in bear country and there's room—but usually I leave it outside, propped against a tree or rock or lying on the ground. I leave the items I won't need overnight in the pack, whether in or outside the tent.

During rest stops on the trail, the pack can be used as a seat if the ground is cold or wet. One advantage of an external frame is that it can be propped up with a staff and used as a backrest—its rigidity keeps it from twisting out of position and falling over, as can happen with internal-frame packs. This backrest is so comfortable that I've tried to make an internal-frame pack perform the same function. I've had some success wedging the staff into the top of the pack, but it's much easier with two trekking poles, since then you can form a tripod. Unexpected collapses still occur, however.

PACK CARE

After a trip, I empty the pack, shake out any debris that has accumulated inside, and, if it's wet, hang it up to dry. You can try to remove stains with soap or other cleansers; I regard such marks as adding to the pack's character, and I'm also wary of damaging or weakening the fabric in any way, so I don't bother.

Before a trip, I check all the zippers. I also look for signs of any stitching failure if I didn't do so the last time I used the pack.

PACK ACCESSORIES

Covers, Liners, and Stuff Sacks

Most packs aren't waterproof, whatever claims the manufacturer makes about the fabric. Water trickles in through the zippers, wicks along draw-cords, seeps through the seams, and when the waterproofing has worn off, leaks right through the fabric. There are packs made from tough waterproof fabrics with ultrasonic welded or taped seams plus watertight zippers that are waterproof or at least almost so. Makes include Vaude, Exped, Ortlieb, and Lightwave. I've tried some of these, and they do keep the rain out. However, as you still need waterproof liners and stuff sacks to separate wet and dry gear inside the pack, they're not a complete solution to rainy weather.

Water-sensitive gear (down-filled items, spare clothes, maps, books) is best stored in waterproof bags. Pack covers can be used to keep rain out of the pack, but these are easily torn and can blow off. When my last one ripped I stopped using them. You have to remove them to get into the pack, too, which can let rain in. If the items inside the pack are in waterproof bags, it doesn't matter if water enters. Some packs have built-in covers contained in the base or the lid, and a poncho can cover both you and the pack. Even if I had one of these, I'd still keep my gear in waterproof bags in wet country. The best covers are adjustable and hug the pack closely so they don't flap in the wind. Many

Putting on a heavy pack.
(1) Grab the pack by the shoulder straps. *(2)* Lift it onto your bent leg. *(3)* Swing it slowly onto your shoulder and then . . . *(4)* . . . onto your back. *(5)* Adjust the straps for a good fit.

Using a pack as a backrest in camp.

pack makers offer them, and they are also sold by companies like Outdoor Research.

I don't use a single waterproof liner that fills the pack because there are often wet items in the pack (such as the tent fly sheet and rain gear) that I want to keep separate from dry items. I used to put my sleeping bag and spare clothes in standard stuff sacks, which aren't waterproof, inside a large waterproof stuff sack or liner and use another large waterproof sack for other items. However, the advent of lightweight, waterproof stuff sacks has meant that two layers of bags isn't necessary. I now use separate waterproof stuff sacks for all water-sensitive gear. On the Pacific Northwest Trail (PNT), I used such stuff sacks, and they kept my gear dry. During the second half of the walk, it rained almost every day, sometimes heavily,

but my down sleeping bag, stored in a waterproof stuff sack in the bottom of the pack, was never damp, even though there was often water in the base of the pack, and the outside of the stuff sack was often wet. Such stuff sacks have roll tops with clip buckles and taped seams and come in various sizes. The first stuff sacks like this were fairly heavy dry bags designed for watersports. The latest ones are made from silicone nylon, usually tough Cordura, and are much lighter and more flexible. On the PNT, I used three sizes from British companies Lifeventure and PODsacs. My sleeping bag went into a 915-cubic-inch Lifeventure Dri-Store sack that weighs just 2 ounces, and my other items in 427- and 610-cubic-inch PODsacs Ultralite Drysacs weighing 1.2 and 1.5 ounces. Similar waterproof stuff sacks are the

Outdoor Research Ultralight Dry Sacks, Sea to Summit Ultra-Sil Dry Sacks, Granite Gear eVent Sil Drysacks (with eVent waterproof-breathable bases through which air can be squeezed out), and Exped Fold-Drybags. Even lighter are stuff sacks made from Cuben Fiber (see Chapter 6 for details on this material), which I've not tried yet. Mountain Laurel Designs has these in four sizes: 183 cubic inches at 0.5 ounce, 488 cubic inches at 0.7 ounce, 732 cubic inches at 1.2 ounces, and 1,220 cubic inches at 1.7 ounces. Mountainfitter and Granite Gear also make Cuben Fiber dry sacks.

Ordinary nylon stuff sacks, as provided with tents, sleeping bags, and other items, are fine for items that don't have to be kept dry. The fabric is usually coated, but the seams aren't sealed, and the closure isn't waterproof, so they do leak. I now only use them for items that don't need to be kept dry.

Inexpensive alternatives to waterproof stuff sacks include plastic shopping bags and trash bags. These are easily torn and punctured, though. I wouldn't want to rely on them to keep down gear dry unless it was wrapped in several layers. There's also the question of waste. I stopped using such bags when I became concerned at how many I was throwing away.

For some items, like books and maps, zip-closed plastic bags are convenient. Standard ones aren't that strong, however, and need replacing quite often, which is a waste of resources and can also be a problem if one splits during a trip and you haven't a spare. Aloksak bags from Loksak are much tougher. They're made from 0.6-millimeter transparent polymer film and come in a range of sizes from 4 inches by 5 inches to 12 inches by 12 inches. I use various Aloksaks for cash, documents, maps, notebook, paperback, cell phone, and other small, water-sensitive items. These bags are very light. The 4.5-by-7.5-inch one weighs 0.5 ounce. Tougher and heavier

than Aloksaks are cases like those from Aquapac. I have an Aquapac Small Waterproof Phone Case, measuring 6 inches by 6 inches, that weighs 1.1 ounces. It is possible to operate electronic devices while in both Aloksak and Aquapac bags.

I don't use waterproof stuff sacks for items that water won't harm, like cooking pots. For these, mesh stuff sacks are fine. They weigh an ounce or less, depending on size, and have the advantage of being see-through.

Lumbar Packs

For many years I wore a small lumbar pack (or fanny pack, as it's also known, though *lumbar* is more accurate, since the pack sits in the lumbar area when worn correctly) the wrong way around in order to reach small items without taking my pack off. I stopped doing this quite a few years ago for several reasons. One was the lightening of my load, which made it easier to take the pack off, but more important, I started using hipbelts with pockets attached and shirts with large chest pockets that would take all the items that I used to carry in my lumbar pack. I find this new system more efficient. However a light lumbar pack could be used with an ultralight pack with no hipbelt to take some of the weight.

Lumbar packs range from tiny models consisting of a pouch on a strip of webbing to complex models with frames and padded hipbelts. Capacities run from 50 to 1,250 cubic inches or more. The largest will hold up to 20 pounds and could conceivably be used for ultralight overnight trips. I don't like having that much weight so low on my body, however. Even with the firmest hipbelt, it feels as though it's pulling downward. I sometimes use a small basic lumbar pack for short day hikes when I want to carry binoculars, a rain jacket, and maybe a few other items, but it's been years since I took one on a backpacking trip. The lids of many packs convert to lumbar packs, and I do occasionally use those on my Dana Design Astralplane and Gregory Shasta packs for side trips from camps. They're OK for loads of 4 or 5 pounds but sag with much more.

Belt and Shoulder Pouches

Most pack makers and many other companies offer small zipped pouches and bags designed to be fitted to the pack hipbelt or shoulder straps. The most interesting such pockets are the Aarn Balance Pockets, which are designed, as the name suggests, to balance the load on your back so you can stand upright. These pockets don't hang off your shoulders but transmit the weight to the hipbelt so quite-heavy items can be carried in them. I've tried Balance Pockets, and they do work, but I found they impeded my view of my feet and made me feel clumsy. Others praise them highly, so maybe I haven't tried them for long enough. I don't find that a fairly light pack forces me to lean forward enough to be a problem, anyway. I'm not fond of belt pouches either, since they interfere with hipbelt adjustments. I prefer pockets built into the hipbelt for small items or else garment pockets. However, there are plenty of small pouches, with capacities of a few hundred cubic inches and weights from 2 to 8 ounces, and many people seem to like them.

Duffel Bags

Transporting packs by car usually isn't a problem—you just sling them in the trunk and set off. If you fly, however, your pack is at the mercy of airport baggage handlers, and it can easily be damaged. For a time some airlines made passengers sign waivers for unprotected packs, though this practice seems to have stopped.

If you fly regularly, remember that internal frames are less prone to damage than externals. (When I flew home after one hike, my external-frame pack came off the luggage carousel with a permanent bend and a couple of cracks in the frame.) You can minimize the chance of damage by tightening all straps, tucking away loose ends, and wrapping the hipbelt around the front of the pack and threading it through the ice ax loops or lower compartment compression straps to keep it in place. A long strap or a length of thick cord can be wound around the pack and then tied into a loop to give the baggage handlers something to grab. Make sure you have nothing fastened to the outside of the pack.

A duffel bag offers much more protection than these measures. But you'll need a very large duffel if you have a large pack.

You can get duffels that are fully waterproof, ideal for canoeing trips but unnecessary for getting gear from airport to airport, and ones that are padded, which is necessary only if you carry fragile items inside. (I always put items like cameras, binoculars, and headlamps in my carry-on luggage.)

A duffel needs a couple of top compression straps, a grab handle, and perhaps a shoulder strap, but that's it. Many pack makers make duffels, as do travel-focused companies like Eagle Creek.

chapter five

keeping warm and dry

dressing for the wilderness

> THERE'S NO SUCH THING AS BAD WEATHER, ONLY UNSUITABLE CLOTHING.
> —*Anonymous*

When the clouds roll in, the wind picks up, and the first raindrops fall, your clothing should protect you from the storm. If it doesn't, you may have to make camp early, crawling soggily into your tent and staying there until the skies clear. At the worst, you could find yourself in danger from hypothermia. Besides keeping you warm when it's cold and dry when it's wet, clothing should also keep you cool when the sun shines. In other words, clothing should keep you comfortable regardless of the weather. Choosing lightweight, low-bulk clothing that does all this requires care. Before looking at clothing in detail, I'll try to give some understanding of how the body works when exercising and what bearing this has on clothes.

HEAT LOSS AND HEAT PRODUCTION

The human body evolved to deal with a tropical climate, and it ceases to function if its temperature falls more than a couple of degrees below 98.4°F (37°C) or rises more than a couple of degrees above that. In cool climates, the body needs a covering to maintain that temperature, because the

Hiking in a synthetic-insulated top, fleece-lined cap, and gloves on a cold, windy fall day in the North Cascades.

heat it produces is lost to the cooler air. Ideally, clothing should allow a balance between heat loss and heat production, so that we feel neither hot nor cold. It's hard to maintain this balance when we alternate sitting still with varying degrees of activity in a range of air temperatures and conditions: when we're active, the body pumps out heat and moisture, which has to be dispersed; when we're stationary, it stops doing so.

The body loses heat in four ways, which determine how clothing has to function to keep its temperature in equilibrium:

- *Convection*, the transfer of heat from the body to the air, is the major cause of heat loss. It occurs whenever the air is cooler than the body, which is most of the time. The rate of heat loss increases in proportion to air motion—once air begins to move over the skin (and through your clothing), it can whip body warmth away at an amazing rate. To prevent this, clothing must cut out the flow of air over the skin; that is, it must be windproof.

- *Conduction* is the transfer of heat from one surface to another. All materials conduct heat, some better than others. Air conducts heat poorly, so the best protection against conduc-

tive heat loss is clothing that traps and holds air in its fibers. Indeed, the trapped air is what keeps you warm; the fabrics just hold it in place. Water, however, is a good heat conductor, so if your clothing is wet, you will cool down rapidly. This means that clothing has to keep out rain and snow, which isn't difficult —the problem is that clothing must also transmit perspiration to the outer air to keep you dry, known as breathability, or moisture vapor transmission (MVT).

- *Evaporation* occurs when body moisture is transformed into vapor—a process that requires heat. During vigorous exercise, the body can perspire as much as a quart of liquid an hour. Clothing must transport it away quickly so that it doesn't use up body heat. Wearing garments that can be ventilated easily, especially at the neck, is important, as is wearing breathable materials that water vapor can pass through.

- *Radiation* is the passing of heat directly between two objects without warming the intervening space. This is the way the sun heats the earth (and us on hot, clear days). Radiation requires a direct pathway, so wearing clothes—especially clothing that is tightly woven and smooth-surfaced—mostly blocks it. Very little heat is lost by radiation anyway. Reflective radiant barriers built into clothing really don't make any difference.

THE LAYER SYSTEM

As if keeping out rain, expelling sweat, trapping heat, and preventing the body from overheating weren't enough, clothing for walkers must also be light, durable, low in bulk, quick drying, easy to care for, and able to cope with a wide variety of weather conditions. The usual solution is to wear several light layers of clothing on the torso (legs require less protection), which can be adjusted to suit weather conditions and activity. The *layer system* is versatile and efficient if used properly, which means constantly opening and closing zippers and fastenings and removing or adding layers. In severe conditions I also use layers on my legs, hands, and head in severre conditions.

A simple layering system consists of an inner layer of thin wicking material that removes moisture from the skin, a thicker midlayer to trap air and provide insulation, and a waterproof-breathable outer shell to keep out wind and rain

WORST-CASE PLAN

Many years ago I came close to finding my own worst-case plan inadequate when I spent a week battling the high winds, lashing rain, and melting snow of an Icelandic June. I wore a wicking synthetic T-shirt; a thin wicking synthetic shirt; a thin synthetic-filled top; a thin synthetic windshirt; and a light waterproof-breathable rain jacket. I was barely warm enough when walking, because the rain jacket wasn't breathable enough and I was permanently damp. Luckily I'd taken a vapor-barrier suit as backup, so I was able to stay warm in camp, but a thicker warm layer would have been a welcome addition.

Dressed for cold, stormy weather in New Hampshire's White Mountains. Warm, waterproof hat, fleece-lined waterproof gloves, and waterproof-breathable shell jacket over windproof jacket and lightweight fleece top.

Base layer

Midlayer

long underwear top
(zipper neck)

lightweight fleece
top (zipper front)

wicking
underwear,
not cotton

wicking long
underwear
bottoms

noncotton
wicking socks

A base-layer top may be adequate on its own in warm weather. Add a thin fleece when the temperature drops. Wicking long underwear can be worn under trail pants in cold weather.

Outer layer

Rain wear

fleece hat

wind and
waterproof top

underarm
vents

pockets

Velcro cuffs

gloves with
rain shells

trail pants

side zippers

trail shoes/lightweight boots

rain jacket with hood

rain pants

Clothing for wet, windy weather.

sun hat

long-sleeved
lightweight
shirt

trail shorts

don't forget the
sunscreen!

sandals

Hot-weather wear.

while allowing perspiration to pass through. This neat three-layer system won't cope with a wide range of conditions, however. Additional layers could include one or two more midlayers such as a wind shell or soft shell and a thick, insulated garment for camp and rest stops in cold weather. I often carry six layers—a thin base layer, two thin midlayers, wind shell, rain shell, and insulated top (see the trip sidebars in Chapter 2 for lists of clothing I've carried on actual trips). Several thin layers are more versatile than one thick one, which is either on or off, often leaving you either too hot or too cold. The boundaries of the different layers have always been a little fuzzy—thick inner layers can be used as midlayers, and wind-proof midlayers are also outer shells when it's not raining—and this is getting fuzzier with garments claimed to function as all three layers. But nothing beats the versatility of having separate garments that you can combine differently according to the conditions.

How much clothing you plan to take on a particular hike depends on the conditions you expect. I take enough to keep me comfortable in the worst likely weather. If I'm in doubt as to what is enough, I sometimes take a light insulated vest just in case.

I don't carry clothing that can't all be worn together if necessary. If it's cold, I want to be able to wear everything. The only spare items I carry are underpants and socks.

The Inner Layer

Although it's sometimes described as "thermal" underwear, the main purpose of the inner layer (also known as the next-to-skin or base layer) is to keep the skin *dry* rather than *warm*—often called moisture management. If perspiration is removed quickly from the skin's surface, your outer layers keep you warm more easily. If the layer of clothing next to your skin becomes saturated and dries slowly, your other clothes, however good, have a hard time keeping you warm. No fabric, whatever the claims made for it, is warm when wet.

While you're on the move, as long as your outer layer keeps out rain and wind and your midlayer provides enough warmth, you generate heat and stay warm even if your inner layer is damp. But once you stop, wet undergarments will chill you rapidly, especially if you've been exercising hard and producing a great deal of moisture. After a climb to a pass or a summit, you often want to stop, both for a rest and to enjoy the view you've worked so hard to reach. Once you stop, however, your heat output drops rapidly, just when you need that heat to dry out your damp base layer. But that damp base layer conducts heat away from the body, producing *after-exercise chill*. The wetter and slower drying your clothing, the longer such chill lasts and the colder and more uncomfortable you'll be. Thus the inner and outer layers are important because they can minimize after-exercise chill by wicking moisture away from the skin and stopping rain from soaking your clothing; what goes on between these layers matters less, and this is where compromises can be made.

The one inner material to avoid is cotton, since it absorbs moisture quickly and in great quantities. It also takes a long time to dry, using up a massive amount of body heat. To make matters worse, damp cotton clings to the skin, preventing a layer of insulating air from forming. I haven't worn cotton next to my skin for years—not even on trips in sunny weather when some people like light cotton or cotton-blend garments because they're cooling when damp. I find thin synthetics or wool more comfortable than cotton in the heat,

and I don't need to change my top if the weather turns damp or cold.

Base-layer fabrics remove body moisture by transporting or *wicking* it away from the skin. Synthetic fibers are hydrophobic—they repel moisture—and tend to wick quickly. Natural fibers like wool and silk are hydrophilic—water loving—and absorb moisture into their fibers before passing it more slowly to the outside.

Synthetics can wick moisture by being nonabsorbent and having an open weave through which the moisture quickly passes, and having hydrophilic (water-attracting) outer surfaces that "pull" moisture through the fabric and away from the skin. In both cases, body heat pushes the moisture through the fabric.

Although synthetic wicking fabrics are very good, they can become overloaded with sweat and end up very damp on the inside. An important factor is the time they take to dry when you're not producing enough body heat to push the moisture through the fabric. The best are those with brushed or raised fluffy inner surfaces that have a minimum of material in contact with the skin, letting it dry quickly. If the inner surface is smooth and tightly woven, moisture passes through it more slowly. Oddly, both tightly woven and open-weave *outer* surfaces can speed moisture movement. In the first case moisture can spread out over the surface of the fabric and evaporate or pass into the next layer; in the second case the open weave allows moisture to pass through very quickly. Fabrics with different materials on the inside and outside are known as bicomponent fabrics. Examples include Polartec Power Stretch, Polartec Power Dry, and Páramo Parameta S.

Most fabrics come in several weights. The lightest—sometimes called silkweight—are very thin and fast wicking, ideal for aerobic pursuits such as trail running but also good for backpacking, either on their own in the heat or under other layers in cold weather. Midweight underwear is slightly heavier and thicker and usually has a tighter weave. It's warmer but often wicks more slowly, which is fine in cool weather. The heaviest and thickest fabrics are labeled *expedition* or *winter weight*. Most of these don't wick moisture or dry as fast as the lighter fabrics and are better suited for midlayers. A few, like Power Stretch and Parameta S, wick as well as or better than thin fabrics.

Designs are usually simple; most tops come with either a crewneck or a turtleneck with a zipper, buttons, or snaps at the neck. You can get short or long sleeves; I prefer short-sleeved crewneck T-shirts for warm weather and long-sleeved zippered turtlenecks for colder weather. The latter are good as midlayers too. Close-fitting garments are much more efficient than baggy ones. Some base layers come with hoods, a design that is very efficient for warmth. I prefer a separate hat, though, and the ability to vent at the neck, which hoods obstruct. My partner, hiker Denise Thorn, says she didn't realize how effective base layers could be until she wore women's styles that fitted properly rather than loose "unisex" tops. Most makers now offer women's and men's base layers, while some companies like Isis make only women's clothing. There are also bras made from wicking fabrics.

Long base-layer pants, once known as "long johns" but now more commonly called "bottoms" or "leggings," are usually body-hugging for maximum efficiency. Underpants made from a wicking synthetic material, wool, or silk are far superior to cotton. Close-fitting garments help trap air and wick moisture quickly and also fit eas-

ily under other garments. Long pants should have a particularly snug fit to avoid the discomfort of baggy long johns sagging down inside other layers; elasticized waists are essential. Long backs stop tops from riding up at the waist. Stretchy fabrics often wick fastest because of their close fit. They're generally more comfortable, too. Seams should be flat sewn to avoid rubbing and abrasion. Dark colors show dirt and stains less, but white or pale colors reflect heat better when worn alone in warm weather.

Choosing a wicking synthetic fabric can seem hard because there are so many, each with a fancy name and claiming to work better than the others. Actually there are only a few base fabrics, and they're all derived from petrochemicals. Polypropylene was the original fiber used, but most base layers are now made from polyester. Other fibers like chlorofiber, acrylic, and nylon have just about disappeared.

The Smell Factor

Synthetic base layers are notorious for smelling bad, sometimes after only brief use. Ironically, the hydrophobic properties that make them effective at wicking moisture are the main reason for this. Your body moisture contains oils that stick to the fabric as the liquid evaporates or moves into your next clothing layer. These oils attract bacteria and can also undergo oxidation, both leading to nasty smells. Like the fabric, the oils are hydrophobic. Washing in cool water doesn't remove them. Hot water does, but not all fabrics can be washed in hot water without shrinking, making it hard to get the smell out. Hanging clothes in the sun and wind can help, as can repeated washing in plenty of detergent and soaking in cold water with a little dissolved soap. It's best, though, to choose garments that can be washed and dried at hot temperatures. This is also useful for long hikes when you want to chuck all your dirty clothes into a washer and dryer at town stops without worrying about the temperature.

Many fabrics have antimicrobial treatments. Most work a little but don't stop garments from smelling for very long. Fibers such as X-Static that contain silver—a natural antimicrobial that contains no chemicals and is safe next to the skin—work best. Odor Resistant Polartec Power Dry contains silver fibers. Silver can't wear out or be washed out, so it lasts the life of the garment. It's said to remove 99 percent of bacteria in an hour and to work best in warm, humid environments. My initial experience of synthetic base layers with X-Static and other antimicrobial treatments was positive. New garments could be worn for days at a time without smelling too badly. But I've found that after many washes, the effectiveness of the antimicrobial treatment wanes, and garments smell sooner and more strongly. While I would choose synthetic base layers with antimicrobial treatments over ones without, I think that if you really want to avoid smelly base layers, then ones with a high percentage of a natural material like Cocona (derived from coconuts), bamboo, or, especially, merino wool are best.

Fabrics

POLYPROPYLENE "Polypro" is the lightest and thinnest wicking synthetic. Introduced by Helly Hansen in its Lifa line back in the 1970s, it dominated the market for a while but isn't used by many companies now. Helly Hansen and The North Face are two of the few. Polypro won't absorb moisture but quickly passes it along its fibers and into the air or the next layer. It wicks away sweat and dries so fast that after-exercise chill is negligible. However, it's the worst synthetic fabric for stinking, produc-

ing a stench that can be hard to get rid of. Apart from the odor, if you don't wash it at least every couple of days, polypro ceases to wick properly, leaving your skin clammy and cold. On long trips you have to carry several garments or rinse one out regularly and learn to live with the smell of stale sweat.

POLYESTER Polyester repels water but has a low wicking ability—not ideal for underwear, since sweat just stays on the skin. However, it can be treated with chemicals or mechanically altered so that it becomes hydrophilic, resulting in moisture being drawn through the material to the outer surface, where it spreads out and quickly dries. The drawback is that after repeated washings chemical treatments wear off, though this isn't the problem it once was. When this happens the material stops wicking.

There are many wicking polyester fabrics. Some are proprietary like Patagonia's Capilene and Lowe Alpine's DryFlow. Others, like Polartec Power Dry, CoolMax, Thermolite, and Akwatek, are used by many companies, though they may appear under names like Marmot's DriClime, which is Power Dry. Over the years I've tried many polyester base layers and concluded that they all work pretty well and there's not much difference between them.

Of the expedition-weight polyester fabrics I've used, two stand out. Polartec Power Stretch (which comes in several thicknesses) and Páramo Parameta S both wick moisture faster than any other materials of similar weight and better than many lighter-weight fabrics. Both materials have soft, brushed inner surfaces that wick moisture rapidly and smooth, tightly woven outers that spread the moisture so it evaporates quickly. Power Stretch is used by many companies; my

BASE-LAYER CHOICES

For several years now, I have been completely committed to merino wool except in hot weather. My favorite tops for cool weather (below 60°F) are lightweight zip-tops from SmartWool and Icebreaker. For the heat, I find loose-fitting synthetic shirts the most comfortable, of which my current favorite is the Páramo Katmai Light. When I wear such shirts, I carry an Icebreaker merino wool T-shirt in case of cooler weather and for camp and sleep wear. When I wear a zip-top base layer, I don't carry a spare at all.

zip-neck top and tights, made from the lightest weight Power Stretch, are made by Lowe Alpine and weigh 10 and 7 ounces, respectively—less than some expedition-weight fabrics that aren't as warm or as efficient at removing moisture. As the name suggests, the fabric is very stretchy and hugs the body. Parameta S doesn't stretch and is exclusive to Páramo. I have the Trail Shirt, a conventional design with a collar, two chest pockets, and a snap-fastened front. It weighs 14 ounces. All Parameta S and some Power Stretch garments (such as Mountain Hardwear's Zip T) can be reversed so the smooth side is on the inside. This is meant to make them cooler and thus increase the temperature range over which the garment is comfortable. It works to some extent, but I still find the Trail Shirt a bit warm in hot weather. I've had my Power Stretch and Parameta S garments for many years, and they've proved very durable. I now mostly wear them as midlayers.

Weights for base-layer tops and bottoms range from 3 ounces in light garments to 14 ounces for expedition-weight ones. Briefs start at about 2 ounces.

WOOL Wool, the traditional material for outdoor underwear, has had a remarkable revival and is now regarded by many as the best choice for base layers. I tend to agree. Though it might seem that wool wouldn't fit into a layering system with high-tech synthetics, it does. Wool is excellent at drawing moisture into its fibers and leaving a dry surface against the skin. It can absorb up to 30 percent of its weight before it feels wet and cold, so after-exercise chill is not usually a problem. I've worn wool next to my skin on many winter ski tours and have always felt warm, even in camp after an energetic day. On those tours I've also worn the same top for two weeks with no odor problem. Because wool is hydrophilic and absorbent, body oils go into the fibers rather than staying on the surface and attracting the bacteria that cause smells. Wool's limitations used to be its warmth, which made it useful only for cold weather, and the need for careful washing, often by hand. Now, however, there are very fine tops that work well in the heat and that can be machine-washed without shrinking. Wool does stretch slightly, though it usually regains its shape when washed. It is pretty durable, too.

What puts many people off wool is its reputation for being itchy. Old-style wool with coarse fibers could irritate the skin, though fine knits have always been available. When I began backpacking I wore a thin lambswool sweater I bought from a department store as my base layer in cold weather. I don't remember it's being itchy. The best wool base layers are made from fine, soft merino wool, which feels luxurious next to the skin, far more comfortable than any synthetic I've ever worn. SmartWool began the return to wool with its merino garments. Many others have followed as people learn just how wonderful wool is to wear, including Icebreaker, Terramar, Ibex, Arc'teryx, Finisterre, Sub Zero, Woolpower, and, in a mixture with synthetics, Patagonia, Helly

Hansen, and Montane. I've tried merino wool products from most of these companies and found them excellent.

Wool is also relatively light; I have an Icebreaker long-sleeved crewneck merino wool top that weighs 7 ounces and a SmartWool short-sleeved merino wool T-shirt that weighs 6 ounces, only a little more than equivalent synthetic ones. Both are light and cool enough for warm weather. Thicker, warmer garments weigh more, of course. The SmartWool Midweight Zip T and Midweight Bottoms weigh 10 and 8 ounces respectively. These are warm garments, however. I wear them only when I expect temperatures to be below freezing. The top makes a good midlayer.

SILK Silk is the other natural material used in outdoor underwear. Like wool, it can absorb up to 30 percent of its own weight before it feels damp. Silk's best attribute, however, is its luxurious texture; it's light, too—a long-sleeved top weighs 3 to 4 ounces. A silk top I wore on a two-week hike in damp, cool weather kept me warm and dry, and at the end the odor was negligible. It was badly stained with sweat and dirt, though. When I rested after strenuous exercise, the top felt clammy for a few minutes, but then it warmed up. I've never used silk since, finding merino wool easier to care for and just as effective. Among those offering silk garments are Terramar, Cabela's, and REI.

COCONUTS AND BAMBOO The latest materials to be used for base layers are plant-based and come from coconuts and bamboo. Activated carbon from coconut shells, under the brand name Cocona, is said to dry quickly and resist odors. Cocona fabrics are usually mixed with synthetics, though sometimes with wool. Makers using Cocona include GoLite, Rab, Patagonia, Haglöfs,

Vaude, Sierra Designs, Mammut, and Marmot. I've used synthetic base layers with a Cocona component and found they work fine and are more odor resistant than most synthetics.

Bamboo-fiber base layers may be 100 percent bamboo or mixed with synthetics. Bamboo base layers absorb moisture into the fibers then transmit it through to the outside, like wool. They also dry fairly quickly and don't smell badly. The fabric is very soft and comfortable to wear. Bamboo is used by the British companies Trekmates, Highlander, and BAM for base layers.

The Traditional Shirt Alternative

Cotton or cotton-synthetic shirts have always been popular for warm weather, though I find a light wool or synthetic top better because it gets less clammy and dries more quickly. And if the weather turns cold or wet, a noncotton top doesn't get cold and uncomfortable under other layers.

However, there are now a large number of synthetic shirts designed specifically for hiking in warm weather. Most are traditional in style, with collars, snap or button closures, and breast pockets. The fabrics feel nice against the skin, wick a little, though not as well as wicking base layers, and dry quickly. A loose fit is more comfortable than a close one, since it allows moisture to disperse and cool air to move inside the shirt. Unlike most base layers, these shirts resist light winds. I now wear one on any trip where I expect it to be sunny and warm much of the time. I particularly like shirts with large pockets, in which I carry maps, a notebook and pens, binoculars, a whistle, a compass, and other items. Long sleeves are more versatile: roll them up in the heat, roll them down when it's cool or you want to keep the sun off your arms. Most shirts have buttoned tabs to keep the sleeves from falling down when rolled up. If the weather is a little too chilly for the shirt alone, I wear it over a base layer.

There are many good shirts available. Basic polyester or nylon shirts are inexpensive and work quite well. However, purpose-designed hiking shirts usually have more useful pockets and ventilation features. Prices are quite high, but in my experience, these shirts are tough and will last a long time. A good example that I've used often over the years is the Mountain Hardwear Canyon, which is made from a soft and quick-drying 70/30 mix of nylon and polyester. This has one zipped pocket and one Velcro-closed pocket and mesh underarm and back panels for ventilation. The current large size weighs 9.5 ounces. I also like the Royal Robbins Coolmax Extreme Expedition, made from CoolMax polyester, which wicks quite well. This shirt has four chest pockets with Velcro closures and a mesh panel on the back. It weighs 9.6 ounces in the medium size.

However, my favorite warm-weather shirt is the Páramo Katmai Light. This is made from a very soft, silky-feeling polyester and has two big Velcro-closed pockets, a large vertical-opening zipped pocket, and wide, Velcro-closed cuffs. My medium size weighs 7.3 ounces. The Katmai shirt is very comfortable and dries extremely fast when wet. The wide sleeves are excellent for ventilation, and when the cuffs are closed, they protect against biting insects because there is no open slit as with conventional cuffs. I wore this shirt on my seventy-five-day Pacific Northwest Trail through-hike, and it was superb. Even after a week or more of wear, it looked quite smart and didn't smell, which was good for town stops. On cooler days, I wore it over a merino wool T-shirt, and it was fine as a second layer.

The Midlayer

The midlayer keeps you warm by trapping air in its fibers. It also has to deal with body moisture that has passed through the inner layer, so it needs to let that moisture through or else absorb it without losing much warmth. Some midlayer garments are windproof and will resist a fair degree of rain, but they're not a substitute for a rain jacket in a real downpour.

Midlayer clothing can be divided into two types: *trailwear* and rest wear or *campwear*. The first category includes wool tops, light- and medium-weight fleece, soft shells, and wind shells. In warm weather, one or two of these garments may be all you need for campwear as well. Mostly though, I carry a down- or synthetic-filled top or a thick fleece top to keep me warm when stationary. Of course you can wear these while hiking if necessary.

Midlayers come in every imaginable style of shirts, sweaters, smocks, vests, and jackets. Garments that open down the front at least partway are easier to ventilate than polo or crewneck styles—and ventilation is the best way to get rid of excess heat and prevent clothing from becoming damp with sweat. Far more water vapor can escape through an open neck than can wick through the fabric. Conversely, high collars keep your neck warm and hold in heat. I used to avoid pullover designs for fear I'd overheat, but as long as I can open up the top 8 or 10 inches, I've found I can cool off when necessary. Pullovers tend to weigh less than jacket styles, so I now use them regularly.

The traditional midlayer fabrics are wool and cotton, though they aren't so popular anymore. With cotton, this is for good reasons: it's heavy for the warmth provided, soaks up moisture, and is slow to dry. Many years ago I wore a thick brushed cotton (chamois) shirt on a two-week hike to remind myself how cotton shirts perform. Worn over a silk inner layer, it was comfortable and warm; worn under a waterproof-breathable shell, it never became more than slightly damp, despite wet and windy weather. I suspect that this was partly because the silk inner layer took up much of my sweat and the cotton shirt might have become damper with a synthetic inner layer. The performance then was OK, but the shirt weighed 17.5 ounces, more than twice the weight of a fleece top of equivalent warmth, and was bulky when packed. I've never hiked in a heavy cotton shirt since. Having not worn wool midlayers for many years, I started doing so again when merino wool appeared, and I now often wear a merino wool top. There are plenty now available from the companies who make wool base layers. Indeed, it's midweight wool base layers that I use as midlayers. And of course if you have some wool sweaters in your closet, they should do fine. The traditional wool shirt in check, plaid, or tartan is still around too, from traditional companies like Woolrich and Pendleton. I haven't hiked in a thick wool shirt for decades, but my friend Ed Huesers of IceBox fame (see Chapter 6 for igloos) wears them regularly instead of fleece. My ancient one, still used for outdoor work at home, weighs 15 ounces, considerably more than a fleece top of comparable warmth.

Fleece

Cotton and wool shirts and sweaters mostly disappeared from the backcountry with the advent of fleece, for many years now the standard fabric for warm garments. Fleece insulates well, moves moisture quickly, and is light, hardwearing, almost nonabsorbent, and quick drying. These properties make fleece ideal for outdoor clothing. Most fleece is made from polyester, though you may find nylon, polypropylene, and acrylic versions.

Fleece, or pile as it used to be called, was first used in clothing by Helly Hansen and tested in Norway's wet, cold climate, for which it proved ideal. In North America it became popular after Malden Mills (which changed its name to Polartec in 2007) made a smoother version called Polarfleece for Patagonia in 1979. In 1983 this was replaced by the first of the Polartec fleeces, introduced by Patagonia as Synchilla, and the takeover of outdoor warm clothing by fleece was under way. There are other manufacturers of fleece, but in my opinion Polartec still leads the way.

Fleece isn't just one fabric, of course; it comes in a wide variety of weights and finishes. The more loosely knit, thicker, furrier fabrics are sometimes called *pile*; *fleece* is often reserved for denser fabrics with a smoother finish. But makers use both terms for the same fabrics, so they are in effect interchangeable. Polartec grades its classic Polartec fleece fabrics as 100, 200, and 300 weight, and other makers have similar weights. The higher the number, the warmer and thicker the fleece. Not all fleece fits easily into this system, but it is a useful guide.

Worn over a wicking inner layer and under a waterproof-breathable shell, fleece can keep you warm in just about any weather while you are on the move and is particularly effective in wet, cold conditions. Fleece moves moisture quickly: at the end of a wet, windy day, I've often found that the outside of my fleece top is damp from condensation inside my rain jacket but the inside is dry. If you feel cold, nothing will warm you up as fast as a dry, fluffy fleece top next to your skin.

Of course, fleece has drawbacks, albeit minor ones. It's not windproof—you can easily blow through it—which means you need a windproof layer over it even in a cool breeze. Although this is a disadvantage at times, the lack of wind resistance means that garments are very breathable and comfortable over a wide temperature range—without a shell when it's warm or calm, with one when it's cold or windy. There is windproof fleece clothing, but it's heavier, bulkier, and less breathable than ordinary fleece. Another drawback is that fleece clothing doesn't compress well, so it takes up more room in the pack.

Fleece garments should be fairly close-fitting to trap warm air efficiently. They are prone to the *bellows effect*—cold air is sucked in at the bottom of the garment, replacing warm air—so the hem should be elasticized, have a drawcord, or be designed to tuck into your pants. Cuffs and collars keep warmth in best if they fit closely. A high collar helps keep your neck warm and stops warm air from escaping.

Most fleece garments are hip length, which is just about right to keep them from riding up under your pack hipbelt. Pockets are useful, especially hand-warmer pockets, for around camp and at rest stops, but they are not essential. Hoods can be nice in cold weather, though they're not found on many garments. In light fleece I like pullover tops with zippers or snaps at the neck. Fancier designs simply add more weight.

I wear fleece garments most days, since I live in a mostly damp and cool rural area in the hills and I'm outdoors almost every day. I don't like overheated houses, so I wear fleece indoors much of the year too. Over the years I've accumulated a whole wardrobe of fleece garments, from old Helly Hansen nylon-fiber pile ones—now relegated to outdoor tasks like gathering wood—

and early Patagonia Synchilla Snap Ts and Retro Cardigans to much newer Polartec Windbloc and Gore Windstopper jackets. Though fine for day-to-day wear, most are not versatile enough for backpacking; they are too warm when I'm walking and bulkier than alternatives for carrying. However, for hiking in cool weather and for campwear in warm weather, I find the lightest 100-weight fleece provides all the insulation I need. Sometimes called microfleece, this material is comfortable, soft, dense, nonstretchy, and thin. It can be worn next to the skin, though it doesn't wick very well. However it's excellent as a midlayer. When worn over a Power Stretch base layer, it's all the insulation I need while hiking in freezing weather. Garment weights run from 8 to 16 ounces. I've had several 100-weight fleece tops over the years, and they've all worn well. My favorites are two pullover designs with short neck zippers. One is a Lowe Alpine Polartec 100 top that weighs 11 ounces. (The current version is the Ecrin Zipneck, weighing 8.5 ounces.) The other is a Jack Wolfskin Gecko, made from the company's own Nanuc microfleece. This is my most used fleece because it weighs just 8 ounces. After eight years of use, I took the Gecko on the Pacific Northwest Trail, where I wore it at some point every day and used it as part of my pillow at night. It is still in excellent condition, showing just how hardwearing fleece is. Just about every maker of fleece garments has a thin microfleece top in its range, and there are plenty of choices. It takes up little room in the pack, so I carry a light fleece year-round. Expedition-weight base layers give similar warmth and make good alternatives. Besides the Power Stretch and Parameta S tops described earlier, I have a Patagonia R1 Pullover, made from a thick version of Polartec Power Dry with a smooth outer face and raised fleece pillars on the inside that trap warm air and aid wicking. It weighs 12 ounces and is more comfortable next to the skin than microfleece because it wicks well.

I used to consider midweight 200-weight fleece the most versatile, wearing it as campwear on cool summer evenings and as a midlayer while on the move in very cold weather. I rarely use it anymore, however; it's been squeezed out by better alternatives. If I want warmth when hiking I prefer to wear two lighter fleeces or, if it's really cold, a light top filled with synthetic insulation, while for camp I prefer something warmer than midweight fleece. There are plenty of midweight fleece tops, in weights from 12 to 25 ounces, with Polartec 200 being the standard fabric.

The warmest fleece, like Polartec 300, is too warm to wear while hiking except in extreme cold unless you feel the cold a great deal. It's useful as a warm layer when you're resting and in camp, especially in wet, cold weather. Most of these fabrics are quite heavy and bulky, though. There is one exception, Polartec Thermal Pro, a shaggy, furlike fleece that is very warm for the weight. It has an open weave and is very breathable and fast drying, though it has no wind resistance at all. It's also very soft and flexible and feels wonderful next to the skin. Indeed, it feels so nice and looks so soft that people often come up and stroke it—which may or may not appeal to you. Patagonia uses it in its Regulator R2 garments. I have an R2 jacket that weighs 14.5 ounces. It has Power Stretch side panels, a full-length front zipper, and two zippered hand-warmer pockets. Other companies making 6.5-ounce Thermal Pro garments include Cloudveil, Mountain Hardwear, Marmot, Lowe Alpine, and Arc'teryx.

Thermal Pro fleece is expensive but also very durable. My R2 jacket is several years old and has had much use, and it's still in good condition. I most often use it on day hikes, but I do occasionally take it backpacking when the weather may be cold and wet.

WINDPROOF FLEECE The most wind-resistant fleece is probably Polartec Wind Pro, said to have four times the wind resistance of other fleece (which is not saying much) because of its tight construction. Wind Pro will keep out cool breezes, but that's all. To make fleece fully windproof you have to add a windproof layer. This can be a thin nylon or polyester shell or lining or a membrane. Shelled and lined fleece garments are bulkier and heavier than standard fleece. They are very warm but not very versatile, since you can't separate the layers. The fabric actually called windproof fleece has a thin windproof membrane sandwiched between two layers of light fleece and looks like conventional fleece. There are two major windproof fleece fabrics: Polartec Windbloc and W. L. Gore's Windstopper fleece. Fabrics come in different weights, and garments weigh 18 ounces or more. Windproof fleece isn't as breathable as standard fleece or as fast at moving moisture. It's far warmer than standard fleece in any sort of wind but not as warm weight-for-weight in still air. It will also keep out showers, though not continuous heavy rain. If you do get it wet, it doesn't dry fast. I've tried several garments, and in all of them I've quickly overheated when walking uphill, even in cold, windy weather. For me an ordinary fleece top and a separate wind shell are far more comfortable and versatile. That said, I have a Mountain Hardwear Windstopper Vest that I sometimes pack when I want an extra warm garment just in case the weather is cooler than expected. It weighs 11 ounces and packs quite small. Slipped on over a base layer at rest stops, it's just enough to stop me from cooling down.

WATER REPELLENCY Even though fleece is non-absorbent and quick drying, moisture can be trapped between the fibers, especially in thicker and windproof garments, which slows the drying time and makes them feel damp. Some fleece fabrics have water repellency applied during manufacture; these quickly shed light rain and snow and don't hold moisture in the fibers, which speeds drying. You can improve the water repellency of any fleece by treating it with a wash-in waterproofing agent such as Nikwax PolarProof.

RECYCLED FLEECE Some fleece is made from recycled polyester and plastic soda bottles, which reduces the use of oil and natural gas (used in manufacturing polyester) and keeps plastic bottles out of landfills. Patagonia was the first company to use recycled fleece, back in 1993. Polartec now offers recycled fabrics throughout its range.

Soft Shells and Wind Shells

For many years waterproof-breathable garments were promoted as being the only shells needed, able to protect from both wind and rain. While this is true, even the best waterproof fabrics are far less breathable than those that are windproof but not waterproof. Wind shells are also softer, more flexible, more comfortable, and more durable than waterproof-breathable shells. I've always carried a wind shell as well as a rain jacket. Indeed, a wind shell is the piece of clothing I use most. It may appear as extra weight given that you still have to carry a rain shell, but it needn't be. A light rain shell is all that's needed, even in severe storms, because you can wear it with your wind shell for greater protection. It's the layering principle again. A wind shell and a light rain shell are more versatile than a standard-weight rain shell. The warmth a thin wind shell provides is surpris-

ing. Pull one over a base layer or a fleece garment and you'll notice the difference even in still air.

Wind shells—simple garments with few features, made from a single layer of untreated fabric—were too basic and low-tech to attract much attention from the marketing people until the turn of the twentieth century. Then, spurred by some new high-tech fabrics, outdoor clothing designers suddenly discovered that waterproof-breathable garments weren't suitable for all conditions and that much of the time water-resistant, windproof, highly breathable clothing was more versatile and more comfortable. The marketers called this supposedly new clothing *soft shell* and called rain gear *hard shell*. The exact meaning of soft shell is disputed. The debate seems arcane and rather unhelpful, but overall the term is applied to fairly thin windproof garments with varying degrees of water resistance.

Soft shell, then, is a new name for an old idea. Having praised wind shells for years, I'm happy to see them suddenly become the in thing, even if it took a new name to achieve it. The benefit for backpackers not concerned with the latest fashions is that there are far more garments in different styles and fabrics than there used to be. The most basic are old-style wind shells, made from a single layer of uncoated nylon or polyester. Worn over a fleece top, they keep out a surprising amount of rain. They can be extremely light. I have Montane's Featherlite Smock, made from Pertex Microlite and weighing 3 ounces. It has no features other than Lycra cuffs and hem and a short neck zipper, but it keeps out the wind and packs down small enough to hold in my fist. My favorite wind shell weighs slightly more, 5.29 ounces. This is the Montane Lite-speed, made from Pertex Microlite nylon. It's a bit longer than the lighter garments, and has a full-length front zipper, a hood, and a chest pocket. Wind resistance and breathability are both excellent, and water resistance is surprising for such a thin garment. Note that ultralight garments like these don't have great abrasion resistance and so aren't ideal for scrambling or bushwhacking. Most garments weigh a little more than these, but anything over 12 ounces is unnecessarily heavy.

The various types of Pertex are excellent for wind shells, but there are other good ones such as Supplex and Tactel. Some makers just use unbranded nylon and polyester. On the Pacific Northwest Trail, I used the GoLite King's Canyon Wind Jacket, made from recycled polyester, which has a hood and weighs 5 ounces. Many of these fabrics are made from microfibers, which have a denier less than 1: that is, each fiber weighs less than a gram per 9,000 meters, which is a hundred times finer than human hair. Microfibers are soft, supple, strong, and very comfortable. Because more fibers are packed into each thread, microfibers are very windproof and water resistant, since air spaces are fewer and smaller than in higher-denier fabrics. There are two variants on the original wind shell idea: shells treated to increase water resistance and shells with a wicking lining that increases warmth and means they can be worn next to the skin. Once you apply a coating to a fabric, however, you reduce the breathability even if it still isn't fully waterproof. Garments that don't keep out heavy rain yet aren't very breathable seem a bad compromise to me, and I've never liked them. The purpose of a wind shell is to resist wind and be highly breathable, not to be a poor imitation of a rain jacket.

While the lightest wind shells are simple pullovers with no features other than a short neck zip, I find ones with pockets and a hood more versatile. The hood in particular I find important as it can be pulled up to provide warmth and ward off the wind or light showers without needing to break stride.

Line a wind shell with a thin base-layer fabric and you have a garment that can be a base layer or a midlayer and that is windproof, fast wicking, and surprisingly warm for the weight. There are many of these garments; the classic is Marmot's DriClime Windshirt, made from nylon with a brushed DriClime wicking lining. It has a full-length zipper, a large chest pocket, and weighs just 10 ounces. I've found the DriClime Windshirt comfortable next to the skin, fast wicking, fast drying, windproof, and able to keep out brief showers and light rain. There are many similar garments from companies like Rab (Vapour-Rise) and Buffalo (Teclite). However, while these garments work well, I don't find them as versatile as two separate jackets, so I mostly use them for day hikes.

The fabrics that have stirred such interest in wind shells are stretch nylons with smooth outsides and brushed insides such as those from the Swiss company Schoeller and laminated stretch fabrics with a windproof membrane such as Gore Windstopper and Polartec Power Shield. The last two are really thin versions of windproof fleece. Although they come in different weights, all these fabrics are thicker, warmer, and heavier than simple nylon and polyester. The lightest and thinnest garments are roughly comparable to a midweight base layer plus a wind shell, the heaviest to a 100-weight fleece plus a shell. The laminated fabrics are more wind and water resistant but less breathable than the nonlaminated ones. None of them are fully waterproof, though Windstopper and Power Shield come close. Over the years, I've tested many of these garments, both with and without membranes. They've all performed reasonably well, though I've found that the most breathable are also the least windproof and water resistant and that some of the most windproof are no more breathable than many rain shells. My favorite of the fabrics is Polartec Power Shield, which I think is a good compromise between water resistance and breathability. Yet I wouldn't take any of them on a backpacking trip. They're just too heavy, with weights ranging from 14 to 32 ounces, and bulky for the warmth they provide. They're also expensive. Proponents—and there are many—say they keep you warm with fewer layers, increasing freedom of movement and comfort. Maybe so, but they're not as versatile or as warm as three separate layers: a simple wind shell, a base layer, and a 100-weight fleece. They're probably fine for cold-weather climbing and mountaineering, but they're not ideal for backpacking.

Many wind shells are pullovers, which are usually lighter than jackets and often more comfortable when worn as a shirt in camp. They're usually short, so they won't extend below a rain jacket worn over them. The size should be adequate for wearing over other midlayers. Useful though not essential features are hoods, map-sized chest pockets, and adjustable cuffs. Even unlined wind shells can be worn next to the skin, although they may feel a little clammy when you're on the move.

Insulated Clothing

While several thin layers are best when hiking, since you can add and subtract layers to suit the conditions, one thick, warm garment for camp and rest stop wear is worth carrying in all but the mildest weather. This garment could be a thick fleece such as Thermal Pro or Polartec 300, which are especially good in cold, wet weather. However, garments filled with down or synthetic insu-

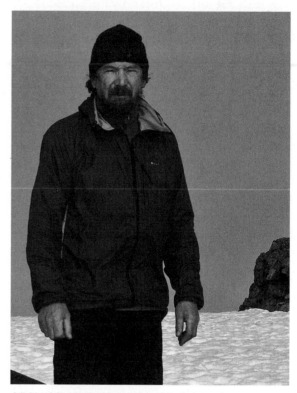

A lightweight windshirt is ideal for cold, windy weather.

lation are warmer, weigh less, and pack smaller. They are breathable and windproof, too, so you don't need a shell over them except in rain. I find they warm me psychologically as well as physically. Just knowing I have a thick, puffy garment stowed in my pack helps me feel warm on a cold day. Simple designs are best, since they weigh least. The only features I look for are insulated hand-warmer pockets. In the last edition, I wrote, "hoods are nice, but a hat does just as well." Since then, I have spent time in Yellowstone National Park in winter, with temperatures down to -35°F. In those conditions, a hood is welcome. For three-season and mild winter weather, I'm still happy with a top without a hood. In bitter cold, I now prefer one.

A down jacket and a woolly hat keep the author warm as he makes a hot drink during a rest stop on a winter trip.

Vests make good insulating garments because they keep your core warm and are light and low in bulk. On Pacific Crest Trail, Continental Divide, and Arizona Trail hikes, I carried insulated vests—down on the PCT and AZT and synthetic on the CDT. In combination with a fleece top when the temperature occasionally fell well below freezing, these were just enough to keep me warm in camp. If weight isn't critical, I often carry a jacket or a sweater, which weighs more than a vest but provides more warmth.

Whether jacket or vest, insulating garments sized to fit over your other layers are best. This means you can wear one over your hiking clothes on chilly mornings and stuff it into your pack just before you set off. And at rest stops, you can simply put it on over your other clothes so you don't lose heat by having to remove a layer. A synthetic or fleece top can be pulled on over a wet rain jacket, as it will still keep you warm when damp.

Down from ducks and geese is still the lightest, warmest insulation, despite all attempts to create a synthetic that works as well. Garments filled with down pack small and, weight-for-weight, provide much more warmth than fleece or synthetic fills. They're too hot to wear when walking unless it's extremely cold, but they're ideal at rest stops and in camp. Down is very comfortable, and its thickness is reassuring. It looks and feels warm. There's nothing like snuggling into a down garment in freezing weather. Down is expensive, but it's also very durable and will long outlast any synthetic fill. However, it *must be kept dry*: when sodden it loses its insulating ability, and it dries very slowly unless you can hang it in the hot sun or put it in a machine dryer. Down can absorb vast amounts of water, so a soaked down garment is also very heavy to carry. But keeping down dry isn't difficult if you carry it in a waterproof stuff sack and wear it only in a tent or under a tarp if it's raining. Despite this, I still carry a down top only when rain isn't likely, since I may want to wear it outside. If you really want to use a down top in wet weather, you can get down jackets with water-resistant shells like Gore Windstopper, eVent, or EPIC. They're more expensive than standard

A down jacket, fleece hat, and thick gloves keep the author warm at 18,519 feet on Kala Patthar in the Himalayas in Nepal.

shells and in my experience slightly heavier and not quite as breathable. Also, if the weather is wet it won't be freezing, so a down top isn't needed; a light synthetic one will be adequate.

The thickness of an insulated garment is the best guide to its warmth. This is known as the *loft*. Down comes in different grades, measured by how many cubic inches an ounce of down will fill. This is known as the *fill power*, and the higher the number, the more loft a given weight of down will provide. For example, 750-fill-power down is warmer weight-for-weight than 550-fill power.

For backpacking, a light down garment with sewn-through seams (where the stitching goes right through the garment—see the sleeping bag section in Chapter 6 for more on this) is all you need. Complex constructions, vast amounts of fill, and heavy waterproof-breathable shells are for Himalayan mountaineers and polar explorers. Garments suitable for backpacking need weigh no more than 25 ounces. Over the years, I've tested many down jackets. Of these, the 10.5-ounce Western Mountaineering Flight is a favorite because of the astonishingly low weight for the warmth. It's a simple garment with a down-filled baffle behind the zip, two hand-warmer pockets, and a warm, stand-up collar. The current version has a ripstop nylon shell stuffed with 850-fill-power down. There's also a Flight Vest, weighing 5.5 ounces. The Flight is excellent when sub-freezing temperatures are expected much of the time. For warmer weather with only occasional dips below freezing, lighter-weight, thinner down jackets are all that's needed. Probably the lightest of all also comes from Western Mountaineering in the form of the Flash Vest, which weighs just 3.5 ounces and is filled with 850-fill-power down. I haven't used the Flash Vest, but I did take the 7.5-ounce MontBell Ultra-Light Inner Down Jacket on the Pacific Northwest Trail, where it kept me warm in frosty camps and made a comfortable pillow. The latest version has a front zip—my original one just has studs—and 2 ounces of 800-fill-power down. MontBell now makes an even lighter down jacket, the 5.7-ounce Ex Light. Also in the same weight range is the 5.5-

ounce Patagonia Ultralight Down Shirt, an over-the-head top with a ¼-length zip and an 800-fill power down fill. These ultralight down garments do need care, but if looked after, they provide amazing warmth for the weight. They pack down into tiny bundles, too, and can be worn under a rain or wind jacket if necessary (I recommend this if using with a pack, as the very thin shell fabrics are not that abrasion resistant). Thicker down jackets won't usually fit under a shell jacket unless it's oversized.

These jackets don't have hoods. For the Yellowstone winter trips just mentioned, I took a hooded Rab Neutrino Endurance Jacket, which is filled with 800-fill-power down and has a tough weather-resistant Pertex Endurance shell. It weighs a fairly hefty 22 ounces, but with the hood up, it's very warm. The loft is no more than that of the Flight, which is about 3.5 to 4 inches (the loft of the MontBell Down Inner is 1.4 inches), but the hood makes a big difference. Western Mountaineering, MontBell, Patagonia, and Rab all make a wide range of other down tops, and there are many other good lightweight down jackets from companies like Feathered Friends, PHD, Nunatak, Crux, Mountain Hardwear, Sierra Designs, Brooks-Range, Marmot, GoLite, Cloudveil, and The North Face.

For wet-cold conditions, synthetic-filled garments are a good choice. They don't absorb much moisture, keep some of their warmth when damp, and dry quickly, so they perform better than down when wet. They're not as warm for the weight when dry, however, and they're bulkier when packed. They're warmer and lighter than heavy fleece garments, though. The best synthetic fills have good durability, but they still won't last as long as fleece or down. Although not as thick as down garments, they're soft and comfortable.

WATERPROOF FABRIC TERMS DEFINED

- *Microporous:* a material with microscopic holes that allow water vapor through but keep out liquid water (rain).
- *Hydrophilic:* a solid waterproof material with chains of water-attracting molecules built in, along which water vapor can pass through to the outside.
- *Membrane:* a very thin breathable waterproof film. *Gore-Tex* and eVent are microporous membranes; *Sympatex* is a hydrophilic membrane.
- *Laminate:* a membrane stuck to a more durable fabric, usually a form of nylon. In *two-layer laminates*, the membrane is glued to the outer fabric and the lining hangs free. In *three-layer laminates*, the membrane is glued between an outer fabric and a light inner scrim, so the finished material looks like just one layer. In *lining laminates*, the membrane is glued to the lining and the outer layer hangs free. In *drop liners*, the membrane is bonded to a light scrim and hangs free between the inner and outer layers.
- *Coating:* polyurethane applied to the inside of a fabric, usually nylon or polyester. Many makers have their own coatings, though they may come from the same source and there is often little difference between them.

You can choose from several fills. Primaloft and Polarguard, the leading synthetic fills for many years, have been joined by Climashield. Thermolite is also well regarded. All four come in several slightly different versions. In use, it's hard to tell the difference. Polarguard and Climashield are continuous filaments rather than tangles of short fibers. Primaloft is made from ultrafine short fibers. Which is best? I can't tell in actual use. Primaloft is a little softer and drapes better, but

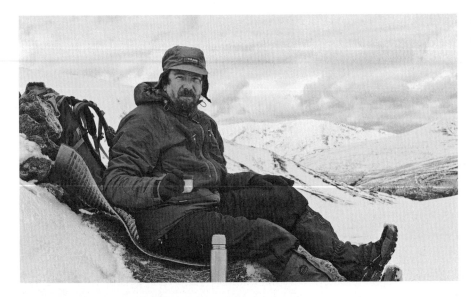

A Primaloft synthetic insulated jacket is good for warmth on damp days like this one in the Scottish Highlands in spring.

that's not really noticeable in the wilds. I would consider design and weight of a garment before the fill. There are other fills, some proprietary, like MontBell's Exceloft and Páramo's Nikwax Insulator, and some used by several makers, like Thinsulate, that are worth considering. Fills come in different thicknesses, and some garments have double layers of fill. The lightest, thinnest garments have similar warmth to a midweight fleece jacket, and the heaviest, thickest ones are as warm as a lightweight down jacket. Weights range from 5.5 ounces and 9 ounces for garments like the MontBell U.L. Thermawrap Vest and Jacket to 32 ounces and more for garments like the PHD Zeta Belay Jacket.

My favorite synthetic-fill jacket for damp subfreezing weather (this may sound like a contradiction, but in places like the Scottish Highlands, wet snow and sleet and high humidity are not uncommon in winter) is the long-discontinued GoLite Coal, which has a Polarguard fill. This hip-length jacket has a detachable hood and hand-warmer pockets and weighs 19 ounces (16.5 without

hood). It resists a fair amount of rain and has kept me warm in temperatures down to 25°F. After eight years of regular use, the Coal still looks in good condition but has lost much of its loft and isn't as warm as when new. This is to be expected with a synthetic-fill jacket. Similar hooded garments are the 18-ounce Montane Flux, 20-ounce Patagonia Micro Puff Hooded Jacket, and the 25-ounce Rab Photon Belay Jacket, all filled with Primaloft, plus the 23.5-ounce Páramo Torres Jacket, filled with Nikwax Insulator.

In milder conditions, 30 to 50°F, a lighter-weight, thinner synthetic top is fine. The Mont-Bell U.L. Thermawrap Jacket is very light at 8.8 ounces and equivalent in warmth to a 200-weight fleece plus windshirt. Although very thin, the nylon shell is windproof. The design is simple—a front zip, hand-warmer pockets, and a high, snug collar. I've hiked in it in temperatures just below freezing with a cold wind and been warm with just a base layer underneath. For three-season backpacking, it's a good choice. There are many alternatives that weigh a little more and should be a little warmer, such as the 10.2-ounce Patagonia Nano Puff Pullover, filled with Primaloft.

If it's unlikely that I'll need an insulated garment but I want something just in case, I often carry a synthetic vest or else the U.L.Thermawrap Jacket. The ultralight U.L.Thermawrap Vest would be a good choice, though I haven't tried this. There are many lightweight vests, such as the 10-ounce Patagonia Micro Puff Vest, which has a Primaloft fill. I use the similar Bise vest from U.K. company Finisterre. This also weighs 10 ounces. The fill is Primaloft Eco recycled insulation, and the shell is made from recycled polyester. The Bise is soft and comfortable and has fleece-lined hand-warmer pockets high enough to be above a pack hipbelt plus a high, warm collar.

Vests can also be used with another insulated garment to give a combination that is very warm over the core but doesn't have bulky arms, which can feel awkward in a small tent or when cooking. Each garment can be used separately as well. On trips where a wide range of temperatures is likely with rain when it's warm and frosts when it's cold, I often carry a down and a synthetic garment for versatility. The MontBell Ultra-Light Inner Down Jacket and the Finisterre Bise vest together weigh 17.5 ounces. This combination is warmer than a synthetic jacket like the Coal while weighing less.

Synthetic insulated garments don't compact as well as down garments, but they do pack down much smaller than equivalent-warmth fleece. However, compression is bad for synthetic fills, and repeated or prolonged compression can flatten the fill so it loses its loft. To get the maximum life out of my synthetic garments, I pack them at the top of the pack, using them to fill out any remaining space. I don't stuff them into the small stuff sacks usually provided with them or load heavy items on top of them.

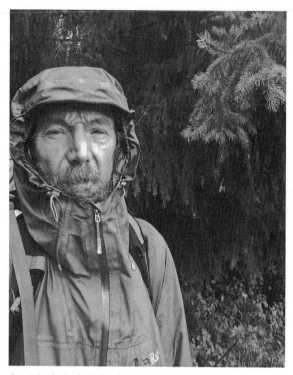

A wet day in the foothills of the Cascades on the Pacific Northwest Trail.

The Outer Layer

Keeping out wind, rain, and snow is the most important task of your outer clothing. If this layer fails in heavy rain, it doesn't matter how good your other garments are—wet clothing exposed to the wind will chill you, whatever material it's made of. In wet clothes you can go from feeling warm to shivering and being on the verge of hypothermia very rapidly, as I know from experience. Rain clothing must be waterproof; it's more comfortable if it also lets out at least some body moisture.

Don't, however, expect too much from rain gear. In heavy showers you can expect to remain pretty dry. At the end of a day of steady rain you'll probably be damp, even in the best waterproof-breathable rain gear, because the high humidity will restrict the fabric's breathability. In non-breathable rain gear you'll be wet from condensation. If rain continues nonstop for several days so that you can't dry anything out, you'll get progressively wetter, however good your rain gear. This is where wicking inner layers and fleece midlayers make a difference—they are still relatively warm when damp, and they dry quickly. A wind shell worn under your rain gear will help protect inner layers from condensation on the inside of the rainwear.

If rain keeps up for more than a few days, it's a good idea to head out to where you can dry your gear. The wettest walk I've ever done was an eighty-six-day, south-to-north trek through the mountains of Norway and Sweden. It rained most days, and on several occasions it rained nonstop for a week. The only way I could get my gear and myself dry was to spend an occasional night in a warm mountain hut or a village hotel.

Waterproof-Breathable Fabrics

When the water vapor your body gives off eventually hits your outer layer, it will condense on the inside unless it can pass through the fabric or escape through vents. Over time, this condensation can eventually soak back into your midlayers, leaving you feeling damp and chilly.

The first waterproof fabric that allowed inner moisture to escape with any success was Gore-Tex, which started the waterproof-breathable revolution back in the 1970s. Since then a host of waterproof fabrics have appeared that transmit water vapor to some degree, though Gore-Tex still leads the market. These fabrics work because of a pressure differential between the air inside the jacket and the air outside; your body heat pushes the vapor through the fabric. The warmer the air, the more water vapor it can hold. Since the air next to your skin is almost always warmer than the air outside your garments, it contains more water vapor, even in the rain. Condensation forms on the inside of shell garments when the air in your clothing becomes saturated with vapor that cannot escape. This vapor hits the inside of your shell and condenses on the cool surface. But a breathable fabric lets at least some vapor pass through as long as the outside air is cooler than the inside air. (In theory, waterproof-breathable fabrics can work both ways, but when rain clothing is needed the outside air temperature is always lower than your body temperature.) Breathable garments need to be relatively close-fitting to keep the air inside as warm as possible so the fabric can transmit moisture more effectively. However, ventilating any garment by opening the front, the cuffs, and any vents and lowering the hood is still the quickest and most efficient way to let moisture out.

Breathable fabrics aren't perfect, of course, and they won't work in all conditions. There's a limit to the amount of moisture even the best of them can transmit in a given time. When you sweat hard, you won't stay bone dry under a breathable jacket, nor will you do so in continuous heavy rain, despite makers' claims. When the outside of any garment is running with water, breathability is reduced and condensation forms. It's hard for water vapor to be pushed through a sheet of water. With the best fabrics, once your energy output slows down and you produce less moisture or once the rain stops, any dampness will dry out through the fabric. In very cold conditions, especially if it's also windy, condensation may freeze, creating a layer of ice inside the gar-

Waterproof (two- or three-ply laminate) (left) and three-layer laminate (right).

ment. The easiest way to get rid of this is to take the garment off and shake it.

In wet-cold weather, you need warm clothing between your base layer and your shell. How much depends on your level of activity. Clothing that is too thick compromises breathability. Nick Brown of Páramo has calculated that more than 1/15 inch of insulation will significantly reduce breathability. Many heavy fleece garments are thicker than this. It's best to wear only enough clothing to keep you just warm while moving rather than trying to feel toasty.

There are two main categories of breathable materials: polyurethane coatings and membranes (see Waterproof Fabric Terms Defined, earlier in this chapter). From all the fancy names, you'd think there were vast numbers of coated fabrics. Actually there are only a few, since many garment makers assign their own names to the same fabrics. Proprietary names include Triplepoint (Lowe Alpine), Helly Tech (Helly Hansen), H2NO (Patagonia), HyVent (The North Face), PreCip (Marmot), Elements (REI), Texapore (Jack Wolfskin), Omni-Tech (Columbia Sportswear), and Camp-

Tech (Campmor). Many makers use a coating called Entrant, though not always under that name. (Cloudveil calls it Cloudburst, for example.)

Coatings are as waterproof as membranes, but just as they started approaching membranes in breathability, new membranes came along that are definitely superior. I get damp more quickly in even the best coated fabrics (such as Marmot PreCip) than I do in membranes like eVent and Gore-Tex Pro Shell.

Membranes are arguably the most effective (and most expensive) waterproof-breathable fabrics. There are far fewer membranes than coated fabrics. Gore-Tex is the big name in membranes and is used by many companies including The North Face, Marmot, Cloudveil, Haglöfs, Mammut, Berghaus, Lowe Alpine, and Arc'teryx. Making inroads in to the Gore-Tex–dominated market has proven difficult for other companies. Sympatex, which works well, has all but disappeared from outdoor clothing. However, the eVent membrane has established a place for itself and is used by companies including Rab, Montane, Westcomb, Integral Designs, and Crux.

THE PICK OF THE BREATHABLES

Which breathable fabric is best? It depends on the membrane or coating and the materials used for the inner and outer layers, so there is no easy answer. There's also a big trade-off between breathability and durability. Based on my extensive use of many garments, I've found eVent the most breathable of the barrier fabrics, followed by Gore-Tex Pro Shell (I haven't tried Active Shell), though they aren't as breathable as Páramo Directional Waterproofs. Surprisingly, I've found that three-layer laminates breathe better than two-layer constructions, despite laboratory tests showing the opposite. The tests are done on a two-layer laminate without a lining, but actual garments always have a lining, which impedes breathability. There are still times, of course, when condensation will occur whatever the construction.

Early versions of Gore-Tex were not very durable, and I found Sympatex tougher (failure being defined as the garment leaking through the fabric). The latest Gore-Tex is much harder wearing, however. Pro Shell is lighter than previous Gore-Tex fabrics too.

The material eVent has proven durable too. I have eVent jackets that have had regular usage over several years that are still waterproof.

For durability Páramo is way ahead anyway, since there's no coating or membrane to puncture or peel off. If a garment starts leaking, wash it in Nikwax TX-Direct and it will keep the rain out again. If a garment is torn, you can sew a patch on and the repair won't leak. (Try that with a laminate!) Páramo fabric is also far more breathable and comfortable than coatings or laminates.

Coated fabrics have the advantages of lower cost and, in some cases, lower weight, but none compares in performance with laminates, let alone Páramo. I would choose a coated fabric only if I didn't expect to wear rain gear very often. Of the coatings I've tested, Marmot PreCip and Toray Entrant DT perform the best.

My choices are Páramo for cold weather and eVent for warmer conditions or where weight is critical.

The eVent technology is also starting to appear under other names as companies' proprietary membranes, which is confusing but does mean it's more widely available. There are a few other proprietary membranes too, like Mountain Hardwear's Conduit and MontBell's Breeze Dry-Tec. An unusual membrane is Frogg Toggs' DriPore, which is made of three layers of a nonwoven polypropylene with a layer of microporous film in the center. This fabric is very soft, and garments are lightweight and inexpensive. I haven't used any Frogg Toggs garments, but reports suggest they aren't that durable and are best for occasional use and on trails. Two new membranes are Mountain Hardwear Dry Q Elite, which is a version of eVent, and Polartec NeoShell, which claims to be

the most breathable waterproof fabric yet and is air permeable like eVent. NeoShell was not on the market at the time of writing, but I have been able to try Rab Stretch Neo and Westcomb Apoc Neoshell jackets in rain and wind, and breathability certainly seems at least on a par with eVent. Weights are 19.5 ounces for the Stretch Neo and 16 ounces for the Apoc.

Gore-Tex and eVent are microporous membranes made from expanded polytetrafluoroethylene (ePTFE). Sympatex is a hydrophilic membrane made of polyester. Gore-Tex has become a family of fabrics, and there are four versions, Paclite, Performance Shell, Pro Shell, and Active Shell. The last is said to be the most breathable. It's so new at the time of writing that

I haven't been able to test it yet. First-generation Gore-Tex was very breathable, but once contaminated with oil, whether from sweat, sunscreen, or some other source, it leaked—as I found out most unpleasantly on a cold, wet, windswept mountain pass. In second-generation Gore-Tex a thin layer of polyurethane was put over the membrane to protect it. This solved the oil problem but reduced the breathability. This solid polyurethane layer means that Gore-Tex works by vapor diffusion, that is, moisture, whether liquid or vapor, is absorbed into the PU layer and then passes through it to reach the PTFE membrane, which has holes through which it can pass directly and more quickly. So the breathability of Gore-Tex is determined by the PU layer, not the PTFE. And vapor diffusion works best when there is a high level of humidity inside the garment—after you get quite hot and sweaty, in other words. It's also slow, so condensation inside a garment is likely. However, BHA Group (part of GE Energy) claims its eVent membrane is oil repellent so that a polyurethane coating isn't needed and water vapor can pass through the pores in the membrane without having to be absorbed into the polyurethane first, a process BHA calls "direct venting." This means eVent is air permeable and works OK when humidity is low, as a buildup of dampness inside a garment isn't needed. (For an excellent detailed account of the science behind breathable fabrics, see "Waterproof Breathable Fabric Technologies: A Comprehensive Primer and State of the Market Technology Review" by Alan Dixon on Backpacking Light's Web site at http://www.backpackinglight.com/cgi-bin/backpackinglight/00316.html.) I've tried eVent garments from Rab, Montane, and Crux, and they are noticeably more breathable than any other membrane or coated fabric I've worn except Neo Shell.

Membranes can be laminated to a variety of nylon and polyester fabrics. The thicker the fabric, the more durable the garment. In three-layer laminates, the membrane is glued between two layers of fabric to produce a material that is hard-wearing but slightly stiff. Because the membrane is protected by fabric on both sides, three-layer laminates are the most durable constructions. Less durable but softer are two-layer laminates, in which the membrane is stuck to an outer layer while the inner lining hangs free, and drop liners, in which the membrane is left loose between the inner and outer layers. Finally, there are lining laminates, also described as laminated to the drop, where the membrane is stuck to a very light inner layer. This design minimizes the number of seams, which is a bonus. Drop liners and lining laminates are now rarely used in hiking clothing.

Páramo: Soft Shell or Waterproof-Breathable?

The disadvantages of coatings and membranes are that the barriers aren't very durable, can't be reproofed when they start to leak badly, and transmit only water vapor, not liquid sweat. However, Páramo Directional Waterproofs, from the company that makes Nikwax proofing products, are very durable, can be reproofed, and allow sweat through to the outside. There are no coatings or membranes. Instead, Páramo mimics the way animals stay dry—a unique waterproof-breathable system that inventor Nick Brown calls the Nikwax biological analogy. This system requires a two-layer material.

The inner layer of a Páramo Directional Waterproof is a very thin polyester fleece, called the Nikwax Analogy Pump Liner, whose fibers are tightly packed on the inside but become less dense toward the outside, like animal fur. To replicate the animal oils that keep fur water repellent, Parameta is coated with Nikwax TX.10. Like fur, Parameta pumps water in one direction only—away from the body. It does this more quickly than rain can fall, so moisture is always moving away from the body faster than it arrives, keeping you dry.

To be effective on its own, the Pump Liner would have to be very thick, however. To keep it thin (and therefore not too warm or heavy), Páramo garments have an outer layer of windproof polyester microfiber that deflects most of the rain. The combination of these two fabrics allows more moisture to get out, including condensed perspiration, than any membrane or coating. It's not dependent on humidity levels outside the garment or on the temperature inside. The whole garment, including zippers and cords, is treated with TX.10, so it won't absorb moisture or wick it inside.

I've been using Páramo waterproofs since they first appeared in the early 1990s, and I've found them very comfortable and efficient. Because there is no coating or laminate, they are very soft and comfortable, feeling more like a soft shell than a waterproof. Reproofing works, and the garments last a long time. There are two limitations. The two-layer construction makes them rather warm and fairly heavy—the lightest Páramo jacket, the Quito, weighs 17.6 ounces. Effectively, you are wearing a wind shell and a base layer. This makes them too warm for me in summer, although some people find them comfortable year-round. From fall to spring, however, I find Páramo jackets and pants comfortable and have never gotten wet or suffered condensation in them. Because the garments are very soft and the lining wicks moisture, you can wear them next to the skin, so you need only one layer instead of three. They are far more effective than any of the new and much touted soft-shell fabrics because they are fully waterproof while being just as breathable and comfortable.

Nonbreathable Rain Gear

Nonbreathable waterproof clothing is made from nylon or polyester, usually coated with polyurethane or polyvinyl chloride (PVC), though occasionally with silicone. Its greatest advantage is that it's far less expensive than waterproof-breathable fabrics. Polyurethane is much more durable than PVC, though both eventually crack and peel off the base layer. Cheap vinyl rain gear lasts about as long as it takes to put it on and isn't worth considering, despite the price. Because moisture can't escape through the fabric, condensation is copious if you wear nonbreathable garments for long. The only way to remove that moisture is to ventilate the garment, hardly practical while the rain is pouring down. One way to limit the dampness is to wear a windproof layer under the waterproof one, which traps some of the moisture between the two layers.

While you're hiking you'll still feel warm, even if you're very damp with sweat, because nonbreathable rainwear holds in heat as well as moisture. When you stop, though, you'll cool down rapidly unless you put on dry clothes. It's far better to get damp with sweat than wet from rain, however. Until the late 1970s all rain gear was nonbreathable, and people still hiked the Appalachian Trail in the rain and slogged through the wet forests of the Pacific Northwest.

Weights of nonbreathable rain tops start at 6 ounces. Few name brands offer nonbreathable rainwear. One of the few nonbreathable jackets is the Outdoor Research Ramparts Jacket, which weighs 13.4 ounces. Ponchos, for which breathability is less important, are more common, examples being the 7.4-ounce GoLite Poncho Tarp, made from silicone and PU nylon, the 11-ounce Six Moon Designs Gatewood Cape, made from silicone nylon, and the Stephenson's Warmlite Poncho (no weight or fabric information provided).

Garment Design

Material alone is not enough to ensure that a garment will perform well—design also matters. The two basic choices are jackets with full-length zippers and pullovers. I've tried both, and I much

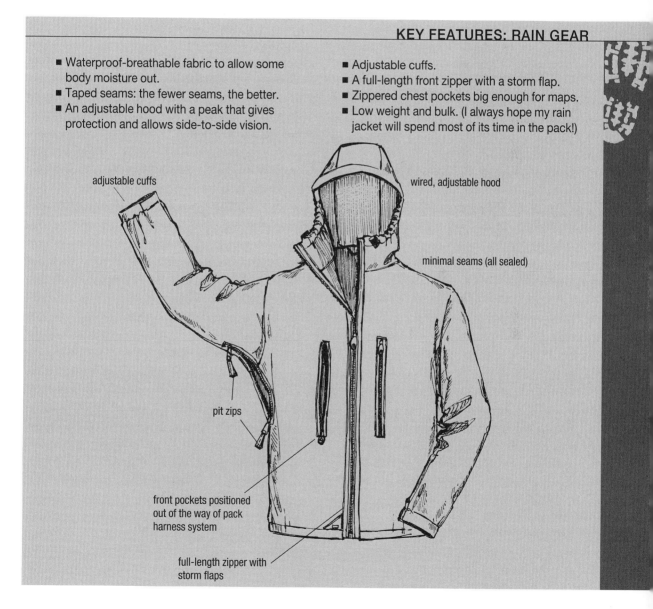

KEY FEATURES: RAIN GEAR

- Waterproof-breathable fabric to allow some body moisture out.
- Taped seams: the fewer seams, the better.
- An adjustable hood with a peak that gives protection and allows side-to-side vision.

- Adjustable cuffs.
- A full-length front zipper with a storm flap.
- Zippered chest pockets big enough for maps.
- Low weight and bulk. (I always hope my rain jacket will spend most of its time in the pack!)

adjustable cuffs

wired, adjustable hood

minimal seams (all sealed)

pit zips

front pockets positioned out of the way of pack harness system

full-length zipper with storm flaps

prefer jackets, since they are so much easier to get on and off. Pullovers are lighter weight, though, lighter enough that I took one, the Rab Demand Pull-On, on the Pacific Northwest Trail. That old standby the poncho is still popular with some backpackers. Ponchos can double as tarps or ground cloths. They have good ventilation, too, but they can act like sails in strong winds, making them unsuitable for windy places. Ponchos are usually made of nonbreathable fabrics. Hilleberg makes a curious waterproof-breathable garment called the Bivanorak (18 ounces). It's a poncho-style garment that covers you and your pack but has sleeves and can also be used as a bivouac bag or sleeping bag cover.

Length is a matter of personal choice. I like hip-length garments because they give my legs greater freedom of movement, but many people prefer longer ones so they don't need rain pants as frequently.

Seams are a potential leak point in any waterproof garment. Only Páramo garments have seams that don't leak without being sealed, because they are treated with TX.10 and are water repellent. In waterproof-breathable garments and the more expensive nonbreathables, seams are usually taped, the most effective way of making them watertight. In cheaper garments, seams may be coated with a special sealant instead. If you have a garment with uncoated seams, you can coat them yourself with urethane sealant. You also can do this when the original sealant cracks and comes off—as it will. Taped seams can peel off, though this is rare. Even so, the fewer seams, the better. The location of the seams is important, too. The best garments have seamless shoulder yokes to avoid abrasion from pack straps.

The front zipper is another possible source of leaks. Standard zippers should be covered with

a single or, preferably, double waterproof flap, closed with snaps or Velcro. The covering flap should come all the way to the top of the zipper. Many garments now have watertight zippers, first introduced by Arc'teryx, which are coated with urethane and have flaps that close over the zipper teeth. In my experience these are near enough to being waterproof, though driving rain can sometimes work its way in. I've never had much rain enter, though, and I like not having to fasten double flaps. The lack of bulk and slight weight reduction is welcome too. Most zippers open from the bottom as well as the top. These are slightly more awkward to use than single-direction zippers and have no advantages that I can see except perhaps to allow ease of movement and access to pants pockets in very long garments.

To keep rain out, hoods should fit closely around your face when the drawcords are tight-

A good hood should turn with the head and have a stiffened peak to keep rain off the face. GoLite Phantom.

RAIN JACKETS: MY CHOICES

In the last edition, I wrote that in lightweight jackets, I'd changed from the 19-ounce jacket I'd favored in the edition before that to 13- and 14-ounce jackets. Now I've changed again, to 10- and 11-ounce garments. Both are from Rab and are made from eVent. The lighter one is the Rab Demand Pull-On, a simple over-the-head smock with one chest pocket, and the heavier one the Rab Momentum jacket, which has two chest pockets. Both garments have excellent wired hoods. On trips where rain is unlikely and I'm carrying a rain jacket as much for my peace of mind as anything else, I take the Haglöfs Ozo Pullover, which weighs just 6.4 ounces. It's made of Paclite, which isn't as breathable as eVent, but the weight is the main criterion here. With a short, watertight neck zip, an adjustable hood, and a chest pocket, it's minimalist but functional.

In cold weather, I wear a Páramo Alta II jacket that weighs 29 ounces. This has a snap-closed flap inside the front zipper that you can leave fastened with the zipper undone for ventilation, a hood with a wired peak, wide cuffs you can roll up, sleeve vents, and five pockets. It deals easily with the worst winter storms and is very comfortable. Because of the weight, I use this jacket only when I expect to wear it all day every day. A wind shell or a light fleece is unnecessary with it, which saves some weight.

The Alta II is a fine jacket, but it is heavy. Páramo does have some much lighter jackets, and I've been trying the 17.6-ounce Quito Jacket, which is shorter in length and only has two internal pockets plus side zips for ventilation, and the 20.6-ounce Velez

Adventure Light Smock, again shorter in length but with a large chest pocket and side zips. Both of these garments are as protective as the Alta II, so if I think I might be carrying my jacket some of the time, I take one of them.

The Rab Demand Pull-On eVent jacket.

ened, without leaving a gap under the chin. Hoods that roll into the collar seem pointless in the backcountry. They're designed to look neat in town, but often you can't easily get them out while wearing the jacket. Detachable hoods need to have a large overlap of material to prevent rain from running down your neck; most are very difficult to attach while wearing the jackets. I've been wary

of them since I found a faded detachable hood in a gully high in the mountains. Had it been ripped off by the wind or dropped by fumbling cold fingers? Either way, someone had to function without a hood. A wired or otherwise stiffened peak or visor helps keep hail or driving rain off your face. People who wear glasses say this is essential. The best hoods move with your head so you can look to the side without staring at the lining, a problem with too many hoods. The best way to check is to try the hood on, though you can make a quick assessment by looking at the seams. A single vertical seam running back to front over the hood generally means it won't move with you; if there are two seams, or a single seam that runs across the hood from one side to the other, the hood is more likely to allow good visibility. Unfortunately, the hoods that limit vision most are the ones that give the best protection. I prefer protection to visibility, especially when the rain drives down for hours and swirling mists hide the view.

In cold weather I usually wear a fleece-lined waterproof-breathable cap with a large brim instead of a hood during light showers, and I wear it under a hood in storms and blizzards for better protection than any hood alone can give. This combination is too warm outside the snow season, though baseball caps work reasonably well. Whether or not you wear such a cap, your jacket hood must be big enough to fit warm headwear underneath, from a full balaclava to a light knitted hat. Many hoods now have a drawcord or adjustable tab at the back so they can be expanded to cover a bulky hat or shortened so the peak doesn't flop in your eyes when you take the hat off. Most of these work well. Front hood draw cords can lash your face in strong winds, so many jackets have tabs to hold them down or have cords that tuck into the jacket at each end. These can be fiddly to use but are welcome in storms.

Sleeves need to be cut full under the arms to allow for free movement. Trying on a garment is the best way to find out how well the sleeves are cut. *Articulated sleeves* with a built-in curve at the elbow may be useful for mountaineering but don't have any advantages for backpackers.

Many garments have underarm zippers or "pit zips," which are great for ventilation, though they can leak in heavy rain. However, jackets with double Velcro flaps to protect the zippers can be extremely hard to use. I wonder if designers have ever stood on a mountaintop in a blizzard with one arm in the air while the other hand gropes under pack straps trying to do up a zipper? Double flaps over pit zips are also bulky and can feel uncomfortable. Watertight zips with no flaps over them are much easier to use. I rarely use pit zips and don't regard them as essential. Wide cuffs and mesh chest pockets are easier to use for ventilation.

Cuffs need to be adjustable if they're to be any use for ventilation. I like simple external, Velcro-closed ones rather than the neater but more awkward internal storm cuffs. In the last edition, I said I abhor non-adjustable elasticized cuffs, as my arms overheated in them. However the Rab Demand Pull-On that I used on the Pacific Northwest Trail has these cuffs. As I only wore it when it was raining (which it did for most of September), I didn't find the cuffs a problem, probably mainly due to the breathability of eVent. So while I still prefer cuffs I can open, my abhorrence of closed ones has eased back quite a bit. Wide sleeves and cuffs provide the most ventilation and can even be rolled up when it's warm. They're also easy to pull over gloves or mittens.

Pockets are useful for maps, compasses, hats, gloves, and other small items as well as your cold hands. But pockets aren't always waterproof, and even if they are, water will get in when you open them in the rain or stick a wet hand inside. It's best to keep anything you want to stay dry inside a plastic bag. Páramo pockets are totally waterproof, as are some of those with watertight zippers. Pockets with standard zippers should always have covering flaps. The most water-resistant pockets hang inside the jacket, attached only at the top. My preference is for chest pockets, which are accessible when you're wearing a pack hipbelt. Hem pockets are usually inaccessible then, but I don't carry anything in them anyway, because they then flap irritatingly against my legs.

For chest pockets, the best compromise between waterproofness and accessibility is a vertical zippered entrance under the jacket's front flap but outside its zipper. (Pockets inside the jacket stay dry, but you let in wind and rain when you open the jacket front to use them.) Zippers that close upward are best because small items in the pocket are less likely to fall out when you open them. Pullover garments usually have a single large "kangaroo" pouch on the chest, which is the easiest to use and very water resistant.

Pockets don't need to be made from waterproof-breathable material. Indeed, breathability is reduced significantly if there are two or more layers of waterproof-breathable material on top of each other. Plain nylon is fine, but mesh is better, especially for chest pockets, because it adds minimum weight and you can ventilate the garment by opening the pockets. Mesh is particularly effective on a garment with two angled chest pockets on the outside, because with both pockets open but protected by their flaps, you can ventilate the whole chest and armpit area.

Mesh is also the best material for the inner lining found on most two-layer laminates and some coated garments, again because it's light and helps moisture reach the breathable layer as quickly as possible. If the mesh is made from a wicking fabric, as many now are, all the better. Mesh can get damp with condensation, but solid linings, even nylon ones, can get quite wet, however breathable the outer layer.

Drawcords are needed at the collar for tightening the hood. They are also often found at the waist, but these are unnecessary, since the pack's hipbelt closes off the jacket anyway. Self-locking toggles that grip until they are released are a boon on drawcords; trying to untangle an iced-up tiny knot with frozen fingers so you can lower your hood is not fun.

Finally, a note on shell garments with extra zippers for attaching a fleece inner layer: I hate them. The zippers add weight for no practical purpose and increase the cost. I've used such garments only briefly, but as far as I can see, they're designed purely so that the combined garment can be worn as a warm town coat. I don't find the effort of donning two garments too great to manage.

Weight and Fit

If you don't wear rain shells very often, then a light one is all you need. The lightest practical jackets start at around 5 ounces. There are plenty of good jackets between 10 and 16 ounces that should prove reasonably durable, including many made from Gore-Tex Pro Shell and a few made from eVent. Above 16 ounces you find jackets that are tough and protective for severe mountain weather and regular use but a little heavy for carrying in the pack.

Rain jackets are more comfortable if they fit properly. A jacket should be roomy enough to fit over a fleece top without feeling restrictive. A close-fitting jacket will have better breathability, but slightly large is far better than slightly small. I also like sleeves that are long enough to pull over my hands if the weather turns unexpectedly cool.

Rain Pants

Rain pants used to be uncomfortable, restrictive garments that sagged at the waist, bulged at the knees, and snagged at the ankles. Some still are. Like most hikers, I wore them only during the heaviest downpours.

The introduction of waterproof-breathable fabrics made rain pants slightly more comfortable, but it was only when designers got to work on them that they really changed. In part this is related to changes in legwear in general. Traditional rain pants needed to be big and baggy because they had to fit over heavy wool or cotton pants, which were also big and baggy. Modern legwear is made from lighter, thinner fabrics and is closer fitting—a big improvement. Softer fabrics have helped, too. The changes have been so dramatic that the best waterproof legwear is comfortable enough to be worn next to the skin.

There are two basic designs: simple pants and bibs with a high back and chest and suspenders.

RAIN PANTS: MY CHOICE

I often don't bother wearing rain pants at all in summer. Shorts are fine in warm rain—legs dry fast! If it's cool, synthetic long pants are reasonably warm when damp and dry quickly. However, I always carry an ultralight pair of waterproof-breathable rain pants like the Marmot Essence just in case it's colder than I expected. These are rather fragile and wouldn't stand up to continuous use, but because they spend most of their time in the pack, weight is my main concern. On the few occasions I've worn them, they've kept my legs adequately warm and dry. On cold-weather hiking trips, I wear Páramo Cascada trousers. These have three-quarter-length two-way side zips for ventilation and weigh 21.2 ounces.

On ski trips and ones where ice ax and crampons are likely to be used, I wear the tougher Páramo Aspira pants (30 ounces), which have full-length side zippers for ventilation, suspenders, and reinforced knees and seat. Páramo pants replace both insulating and shell layers. Mostly I wear them next to my skin, wearing base-layer pants under them only in extreme cold (below 10°F [–12°C]).

For most hiking, pants are best, since they weigh less, are less bulky, are easier to get on and off, and cost less. Bibs, however, are excellent in cold weather, especially for ski touring, since they're warmer than pants, leave no gaps at the waist when you stretch, and minimize the chance that snow will get into your clothes. Putting them on in cold and windy weather is unpleasant, to say the least, because you have to remove other layers. For that reason, and because of their weight and bulk, they're best worn all day rather than carried.

Base-layer long pants or, in really cold weather, fleece pants are the best garments to wear under rain pants, since they feel comfortable when damp. Synthetic trail pants work well too, but cotton-nylon and cotton trousers absorb moisture and tend to feel damp and cold.

Features worth having on rain pants are adjustable drawcords at the waist and knee-length zippers to allow you to get the pants on over boots. Pockets, or slits to allow access to inner pants pockets, are useful. If you wear rain pants frequently, consider full-length side zips that can be opened at the top for ventilation; they also allow you to put on rain pants over crampons or skis, though it can be hard to handle long zippers in a strong wind. Keep in mind that it's very difficult to make full-length side zippers fully waterproof. Velcro-closed flaps help, but they make it even harder to put the pants on. Watertight zippers are a better choice. I prefer full-length zippers for pants I'll wear all day; I'd rather have good ventilation and suffer the occasional leak. Gussets behind knee-length zippers help keep rain out, but they tend to catch in the zippers. For men, rain pants with flies are worth considering. I don't like elasticized hems; I find they ride up over your boot tops, letting water in. Nonelasticized hems with drawcords or Velcro-closed tabs are better. Ultralight pants omit zippers to save weight; when they'll spend most of the time on my back, I'm happy with this.

Rain pants run from 5 to 40 ounces, depending on design and fabric. As with rain jackets, heavier garments will outlast lighter ones. Rain pants suffer more hard wear than jackets, though, so if you're likely to wear them much of the time, I'd put durability above weight. But if they'll spend most of their time in your pack, the lighter the better. The heaviest garments might be a little hot in summer, while the lightest, thinnest rain pants don't give adequate protection in severe winter weather.

It's best to try rain pants on before you buy, preferably over the pants you'll wear under them so you can check that they don't bind anywhere when you move. Length is important, too. Unfortunately, few makers offer different lengths. Alterations are possible, though zipped legs make this difficult (if the zippers start a little way above the hem, pants are easier to shorten). It's better to find a pair that fits to begin with.

Rain Skirts

A more breathable alternative to rain pants is a waterproof skirt. I first came across this idea in Colin Fletcher's *The Complete Walker* back in 1984. He suggested slitting open a trash bag and wearing it over shorts when walking through wet brush. He called it "Colin's Kilt." The idea never took off back then, but now there are high-tech versions available. ULA makes one from silicon nylon called the Rain Wrap that comes in three sizes at weights of 2.9, 3.2, and 3.7 ounces. Even lighter at 1.6 ounces is ZPacks' Cuben Fiber CloudKilt. ZPacks points out that the kilt can also be used as a small ground cloth and to create a

"beak" on a tarp. I haven't tried a rain skirt, but I can see the advantages.

Umbrellas

Although they're not clothing, this seems an appropriate time to discuss umbrellas. I'd never considered carrying an umbrella or seen anyone else doing so until I met a hiker using one on a rainy day back in 1988 on the North Boundary Trail in Jasper National Park. It was much more comfortable than a rain jacket, Stu Dechka told me. His Gore-Tex jacket was draped over his pack to keep it dry. I was surprised but thought no more about it until five years later when Ray Jardine extolled the virtues of umbrellas in *The Pacific Crest Trail Hiker's Handbook*. My hiking apprenticeship took place in the windy, treeless British hills, and I'd never given umbrellas serious consideration. People on city streets seemed to have enough problems when it was windy; in the hills umbrellas would be impossible to handle. However, on reflection I could see that for hiking in forests and areas where gales are unusual, they could have advantages.

Then I had the opportunity to hike for a few days with Ray Jardine in the Oregon Cascades, and we took umbrellas. I soon discovered that in the woods they're excellent. It was wonderful to stride through the forest in heavy rain with my hood down and my jacket wide open and stay dry. The closed-off feeling of being sealed in a rain jacket was absent. At stops, the umbrella provided shelter and protected the pack. But above timberline a gusty wind was blowing. Ray showed me how to point the umbrella into the wind and close it down slightly to protect it and also keep the rain out of my face. But as we climbed higher the wind grew stronger and gusted from every direction;

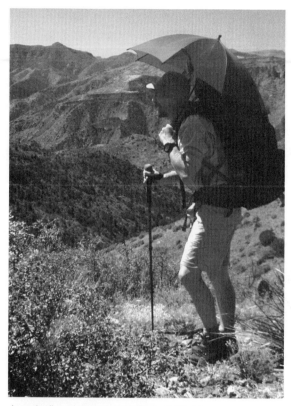

An umbrella makes a great sunshade. GoLite Dome.

eventually both our umbrellas turned inside out and ripped. (Ray thought they could be modified to prevent this.) This was late October; such severe conditions would be unusual during the summer hiking season, but I'm too cautious to hike without rain clothing even with an umbrella. (Ray and Jenny Jardine have hiked both the Appalachian and Pacific Crest Trails with umbrellas and without rain gear, but Ray does recommend carrying a light rain jacket.) When I hiked the Arizona Trail several years later, I brought a 9-ounce GoLite Dome umbrella, designed by Ray. It made a great sunshade in the desert, and I used it to fend off one heavy shower. However, while it was easy to hold on good trails and open terrain, it was awkward on rough ground and in dense vegeta-tion. You can't use two trekking poles and hold an umbrella, and overall I've decided the poles have more benefit for me, so the Dome doesn't get much use. (The Dome has been replaced by the 11-ounce GoLite Collapsible Trekking Umbrella.)

THE VAPOR-BARRIER THEORY

As always, there is a view that challenges accepted wisdom, in this case the concept of "breathability." Our skin is always slightly moist, however dry it may feel; if it really dries out it cracks and chaps, and sores appear. Our bodies constantly produce liquid—either sweat or, when we aren't exercising hard, insensible perspiration. The aim of breathable clothing is to move moisture away from the skin as quickly as possible and transport it to the outside air where it can evaporate. This inevitably causes heat loss. And as I have said, breathable shells may not work in severe weather conditions.

The vapor-barrier theory says that instead of trying to remove this moisture from the skin, you should try to keep it there so no more will be produced and the attendant evaporative heat loss will cease. You'll stay warm, and your clothing will stay dry because it won't have to deal with large amounts of liquid. To achieve this, you wear a *nonbreathable waterproof layer* either next to or close to the skin, with insulating layers over it. Because heat is trapped inside, you need less clothing.

Vapor barriers are most efficient in dry cold—in temperatures below freezing—because when humidity is high, heat loss by evaporation lessens anyway. By preventing moisture loss, vapor barriers also help stave off dehydration, a potentially serious problem in dry-cold conditions.

When I first read about vapor barriers, I thought that anyone using one would be soaked in sweat. But various reputable outdoors people said vapor barriers worked, so I decided to give the idea a try rather than reject it out of hand.

Apparently, if you have a hairy body, waterproof fabrics feel comfortable next to the skin. I haven't, and the vapor barriers I've tried make me feel instantly clammy unless I wear something under them. Thin synthetic base layers are ideal for this. Initially I tried old nonbreathable light rain gear as a vapor-barrier suit. It was not a success for hiking, since I overheated rapidly and started to sweat even when the temperature was several degrees below freezing. It was superb as campwear, however. I was as warm wearing my vapor-barrier top under a fleece jacket as I was when wearing a down jacket over it. Wearing the vapor barrier in my sleeping bag added several degrees of warmth to the bag, and since the barrier was thin and had a slippery surface, it didn't restrict me or make me uncomfortable.

I was impressed enough with these first experiments to buy a lighter, more comfortable vapor-barrier suit made from a soft-coated ripstop nylon that weighs just 7 ounces. The shirt has a zippered front and Velcro-closed cuffs; the trousers have a drawcord waist and Velcro closures at the ankles. Although the suit performs well, I haven't used it for many years, even for sleeping in. Although I know it will keep me warm, I somehow don't have real confidence in it. A down jacket looks warm, and carrying one is psychologically reassuring; two thin pieces of nylon just don't have the same effect. I used to carry the vapor-barrier suit as an emergency backup in winter, but I haven't even done that for many years.

Plastic bags, or thin plastic or rubber socks and gloves, can be worn on your feet and hands as vapor barriers. If your feet become very cold and wet, an emergency vapor barrier worn over dry thin socks with thicker socks over that does help them warm up. I used this combination near the

Páramo Quito jacket.

end of my Canadian Rockies walk, when I had to ford a half-frozen river seven times within a few hours and then walk on frozen ground in boots that were splitting and socks with holes. Dry inner socks and plastic bags made a huge difference. Today, though, I prefer waterproof-breathable socks.

Few companies make vapor-barrier gear. The two main ones are Stephenson's Warmlite and RBH Designs, which both offer complete clothing systems including gloves and socks. The fabrics used have soft, brushed, fast-wicking linings that should be far more comfortable against the skin than simple coated ones. If you want to try vapor-barrier clothing, I'd select garments from these companies.

LEGWEAR

What you wear on your legs is not as important as what you wear on your upper body, but comfort and protection from the weather still matter. Legwear needs to be either loose-fitting or stretchy, so that it doesn't restrict movement.

Shorts

Shorts are my favorite legwear. Nothing else provides the same freedom and comfort. If you keep your upper body warm, you can wear shorts in surprisingly cold conditions. Any shorts will do, as long as they have roomy legs that don't bind the thighs. Many people wear cutoff jeans, a good way to use up worn-out clothing. Some people like close-fitting Lycra shorts, which can prevent rashes caused by your thighs' rubbing together. I prefer loose-fitting shorts with wide legs, as I find these cooler and more comfortable. Running shorts are the cheapest and lightest types (my 100 percent polyester shorts weigh just 2 ounces), but they're flimsy and don't stand up well to contact with granite boulders, rough logs, and other wilderness seats. I sometimes carry them on trips when I doubt I'll wear shorts but want a pair in case the weather is gentler than expected. Shorts with liners can double as underpants.

When I'm planning to wear shorts, I prefer more substantial ones, preferably with pockets. For years I used polyester-cotton blend shorts (8 ounces) with lots of pockets and a double seat. They are very hardwearing—mine survived through-hikes of both the Pacific Crest Trail and the Continental Divide Trail. There are dozens of models; some are made from pure cotton, some from cotton and nylon, and some from 100 percent synthetics. Weights range from 4 to 16 ounces. Most shorts don't feature built-in briefs,

so you have to wear underpants or at least carry them for wearing under long pants. Most shorts also feel bulky and uncomfortable under trousers, which is further complicated by pockets and fly zippers. This is a minor point, but I like to be able to pull long pants on over my shorts when the weather changes. Having built-in briefs lets me keep my shorts on under long pants and saves the snippet of weight of underpants.

Back in 1988, at the start of my Canadian Rockies walk, I found some nearly ideal hiking shorts. Browsing in the outdoor stores in the town of Waterton, on the edge of Waterton Lakes National Park, I bought a pair of Patagonia Baggies shorts (5 ounces—current models are listed as 8.1 ounces). I wore them for most of the next three and a half months and found them comfortable and durable. The wide-cut legs made them easy to walk in, the mesh liner meant underpants weren't needed, and the nylon material dried quickly when wet. I went on to wear Baggies for a 1,000-mile Yukon walk and a 1,300-mile Scandinavian mountains walk, and over the years I've worn out several pairs. Baggies are still around and still excellent, but there are other good shorts. On a 500-mile hike in the High Sierra, I wore GoLite Terrain shorts (4 ounces), made from quick-dry nylon with a polyester crepe liner. These were just as comfortable as the Baggies. And on the Pacific Northwest Trail, I wore 4.5-ounce GoLite Sky Runner shorts, again with an inner brief, and found them fine. These GoLite shorts have been replaced by the Mesa Trail Run shorts, available in three leg lengths, which look just as good.

Long Pants

Unfortunately, the weather is not always conducive to wearing shorts. During some summers I've hardly worn them at all. I always carry long pants in case the weather changes or insects or bushwhacking make wearing shorts masochistic. Around camp and in cold weather, you can wear synthetic long underwear under shorts. It doesn't repel wind or insects, though, and I rarely wear it, since I have to remove my shorts to put it on. It's much easier to pull pants on over shorts for extra warmth—and easier to take them off when you warm up. Long underwear is best for trips so cold that you wear it all day long.

Long pants fall into two categories: those that will be worn mostly in mild conditions but occasionally in storms, and those strictly for cold, stormy weather. Many people hike in jeans, even though they're cold when wet and take ages to dry. These are potentially dangerous attributes in severe conditions, but wearing rain pants minimizes them. Other objections to cotton jeans are that they are heavy, tight, and not very durable. I find them so uncomfortable that I haven't owned a pair for years.

For three-season use, there are masses of *trail pants*. Depending on the fabric and the design, these weigh from 4 to 25 ounces. Features may include double knees, double seats, and multiple pockets, many of them zippered. Some versions, often called *wind pants*, have full-length side zippers so they can be pulled on over boots and vented in warm weather. A few, like Marmot's DriClime Side Flex Pants (9 ounces), also have wicking linings. The traditional and heaviest material for trail pants is 100 percent cotton. Cotton-polyester and cotton-nylon blends such as 65/35 are better; best are 100 percent synthetics, especially microfibers, because they are much lighter and faster drying, though just as hardwearing, windproof, and comfortable. I've worn trail pants on all my long walks, switching from polyester-cotton blends to microfibers when they became available. When I expect to wear shorts

most of the time, I carry a very basic light pair of nylon pants. Montane's Featherlite Pants, made of Pertex Microlight nylon, are probably the lightest at 4.2 ounces. Mine, the long discontinued GoLite Trunk, weigh 8 ounces. When I think I'll be wearing pants to hike in quite often, I take a more substantial pair. My favorites are the 11-ounce Montane Terra Pants, made from Tactel nylon with Cordura reinforcements on the knees and seat. I've worn them on several coast-to-coast crossings of the Scottish Highlands on the TGO Challenge, and they've proven comfortable and durable.

When buying a pair of pants, the main thing to check is the fit. Some pants are styled for fashion rather than function and can be uncomfortable to hike in, especially uphill. I like elasticized waistbands rather than conventional belt loops because I don't like wearing a belt under a pack hipbelt and I appreciate the stretchy waist when I feast in a restaurant after a long trip. I like to have at least one pocket with a snap or zipper for my wallet and money when traveling to and from the wilderness; large thigh pockets are good for carrying maps.

Trail pants with zip-off legs to convert them into shorts have become very popular. For years I viewed these as curiosities, but eventually I tried a pair and decided that, strange or not, they made sense, so I wore a pair on the Arizona Trail. I appreciated being able to simply zip on the legs when it got cool in the evening and then unzip them in the morning when it warmed up. However, if zip-offs are to be comfortable they need to be well designed and to fit properly. The big problem is that the zippers can rub. I couldn't find a comfortable pair for the Pacific Northwest Trail, despite trying fourteen different ones. The problem with all of them was that the legs zipped off just above the knee, exactly in the position where the zip presses against the leg when the knee is bent. I ended up taking separate long pants and shorts.

Light pants are generally warm enough for moderate temperatures, those times when you're just a little chilly in shorts. They're not warm enough when the mercury drops toward freezing, however. If the weather turns really cold or mornings are frosty, I wear long underwear under them. With rain pants on top, the pants-base layer combination can cope with all but the worst winter weather while I'm on the move. Three layers are more versatile than one thick pair of pants when large variations in weather can be expected. In *really* cold conditions, you can wear thicker long underwear or fleece pants under long pants.

An alternative to trail pants and long underwear is a separate single pair of warm pants. I prefer these for constant wear in reliably cold conditions, since two or more layers are more restrictive and less comfortable than one. The obvious material is fleece, which is warm, light (typically 8 to 24 ounces), nonabsorbent, and quick drying. I don't like thick fleece pants, however, because they're not windproof, aren't very light, and are bulky to pack. I've owned a pair of Helly Hansen nylon pile Polar Trousers (17 ounces) for many years but rarely use them because they require a pair of windproof pants over them in even the gentlest breeze, which then makes them too hot. Power Stretch tights are far better. My Lowe Alpine pair weighs 6.8 ounces. They're very warm, very comfortable, repel breezes and light rain or snow, and can be worn under rain pants in cold, wet weather or under trail pants in strong winds. They function well over a wider temperature range than any other fleece pants I've tried. I've worn them on spring ski tours, but mostly I carry them for campwear in winter, preferring Páramo waterproofbreathable pants when moving.

Pants made from thick stretch nylon such as Spandura (a mix of Cordura and Lycra) or the various Schoeller fabrics are a good alternative to fleece. They repel snow, rain, and wind and are extremely hardwearing. I wore these for years for winter backpacking and ski touring until Páramo came along. They disappeared for a while but have had a resurgence of popularity under the guise of soft shells. Although I think these fabrics are too heavy and bulky for tops, they are ideal for cool-weather legwear. Some are light enough to be used in all but the hottest weather—when you can wear shorts anyway. Of the various types I've tried, I like the Patagonia Simple Guide Pants, which weigh 13.6 ounces and are made from recycled polyester and spandex, and the Lowe Alpine Paradigm, which weigh 18 ounces and are made from stretch nylon. Both these pants are very breathable but not completely windproof. Pants made from Gore-Tex Windstopper and Polartec Power Shield are windproof and also very water resistant. A good example is the 18.5-ounce Rab Baltoro Alpine pants, made from Power Shield with a wicking Power Dry lining and with zipped vents on the thighs.

Wool or wool-blend pants used to be common; my first winter hiking pants were made of Derby tweed. They were warm but heavy, itchy, and very absorbent. When wet, they rubbed my inner thighs raw, and they took days to dry out. After my first weekend in stretch nylon pants, I never wore wool trousers again. Perhaps it's no wonder wool pants are now hard to find.

For severe cold, insulated pants are available. I'd never been out in conditions where I needed these—even at -30°F, my Páramo trousers worn over Power Stretch tights were warm enough while I was moving—but when I had the chance to try a couple of pairs, I realized they could be useful for campwear and for boosting the warmth of a sleeping bag. Indeed, by wearing insulated pants and top inside, a lighter-weight sleeping bag could be carried. The two pairs I tried were the 17.5-ounce Rab Photon, with a Pertex Microlight shell and Primaloft insulation, and the 18.7-ounce Páramo Torres, with Páramo's own insulation and a polyester microfiber shell. Both garments have full-length, two-way side zips, so they can be easily pulled on over boots and vented when necessary. I found them too warm when walking at 20°F but excellent for wearing at rest stops and in camp. Because they can be worn over your other legwear, they are more versatile than long base layers or fleece trousers, which you have to wear under hiking trousers, so I now carry a pair rather than either of these. The lightest with a down fill are Western Mountaineering's Flash Pants with a weight of 6.5 ounces. Slightly heavier but probably warmer are Nunatak's down-filled Kobuk Pants. Weights of the Kobuk Pants vary depending on the shell fabric; the lightest, Pertex Quantum, gives a total weight of 10 ounces. Both of these insulated pants have no features other than waist closures and so would be very comfortable for sleeping in. Feathered Friends' down-filled Helios Pants have full-length side zips and weigh 15 ounces. Other insulated pants, like Marmot's 33-ounce, down-filled 8000M Pant, are designed for mountaineering expeditions rather than backpacking.

HEADGEAR

Warm Hats

"If your feet are cold, put on a hat." This adage was one of the first pieces of outdoor lore I ever learned. It's also one of the most accurate.

When you start to get cold, your body protects its core by slowing down the blood supply

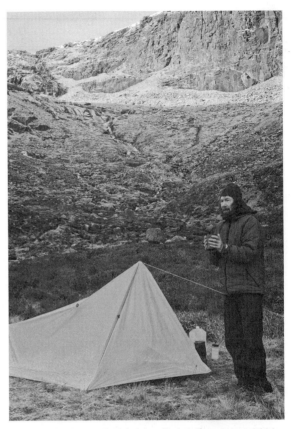

Keeping warm in a synthetic insulated jacket, fleece hat, and thick pants on a frosty morning.

to the extremities—fingers, toes, nose. However, your brain requires a constant supply of blood in order to function properly, so the circulation to your head is maintained. In cold weather, you can lose enormous amounts of heat through your bare head—up to 80 percent, according to some figures. The capillaries just below your scalp never close down to conserve heat like the ones in your hands and feet, *so you must protect your head in order to keep your body warm.*

But which hat? Long ago the choice was simple: the only material was wool, and the only styles were watch caps and balaclavas. Then came synthetic fabrics—nylon, polyester, acrylic. Designs

WARM HATS: MY CHOICES

Over the years I've collected a variety of warm hats for different weather conditions and times of year. In warm weather, I carry a SmartWool Cuffed Beanie that weighs just 1.9 ounces for campwear and in case of a cold snap. It's warm and comfortable and fits well under a hood in rainy weather. It was the only warm headwear I took on the Pacific Northwest Trail, and it was fine. I didn't need anything else. In cold weather, I carry two hats in case I lose one, which could be serious in the cold. I've twice lost hats after foolishly tucking them into my hipbelt when I couldn't be bothered to take off my pack and put them away. I try not to do this anymore, though I sometimes forget. The hat I wear most in the cold is the Outdoor Designs Windiush, made from Polartec Wind Pro fleece, which is more wind resistant than standard fleece though not fully windproof, with a thin brushed lining. The Windiush has ear flaps and a neck cord, so it can't be blown away by the wind, and so I can flip it back off my head if I start to overheat rather than be tempted to tuck it in my hipbelt. It's very warm and comfortable and fine in light winds and breezes. Strong cold winds cut through it, though. I also like to have a hat that is wind- and waterproof as well as warm so that I don't need to put up my rain jacket hood except in the worst weather. Fleece-lined waterproof-breathable caps with stiffened peaks keep rain off the face and have flaps that keep the ears warm. There are many such hats. I regularly use two: a 2.8-ounce Lowe Alpine Mountain Cap with Gore-Tex Performance Shell outer and fleece lining that is very warm and that I wear only in wintry conditions and a 2.5-ounce Páramo Cap, made from the same fabrics as the Páramo jackets, which isn't as warm and therefore gets more use. Both hats work very well.

An interesting and versatile cap is the Hat for All Seasons from Outdoor Research, which makes a large range of hats of all types. This has a removable fleece inner layer and a Gore-Tex Paclite shell with a large stiffened peak and a wicking synthetic lining. Effectively it's three hats in one: a fleece hat, a waterproof cap, and a fleece-lined waterproof cap. My original version weighs 6.5 ounces, as it has a standard Gore-Tex shell; current versions with the lighter Paclite shell are listed as 4.2 ounces. I bought one of these several years ago and took it on a couple of long winter trips and then for some reason never wore it again. To check the weight and remind myself what it's like, I just fished it out of the hat box. It looks and feels good. I must use it again. Despite the last sentence, many years have gone past without my using this hat again. I now have it to hand and really do intend using it soon.

Down hats exist, too. Many years ago I bought one, but it's too hot and the earflaps cut out sound, so I never use it while hiking, though every so often I consider taking it on cold-weather trips to sleep in. It weighs 4 ounces. Nunatak makes a Down Balaclava filled with 2 ounces of 800-fill down. It weighs 3 ounces with a Pertex Microlight shell or 4 ounces with a more water-resistant EPIC shell. I imagine it's astonishingly warm. Hats with thin layers of synthetic insulation look more practical—that is, not too hot—for most backpacking. I particularly like the look of the Montane Featherlite Mountain Cap, which has a Primaloft Eco fill and a Pertex Microlight

didn't change, though, until fleece became the main material for warm clothing and outdoor companies began employing designers to make their clothing more stylish.

Now outdoor hats come in a wild variety of colors and styles and every sort of material, including fleece, wicking synthetics, wool, and mixtures of everything. All these fabrics are warm and comfortable. I particularly like Power Stretch hats because the fabric is soft, comfortable, stretchy, very light, and quick drying. It resists light winds and rain and wicks moisture quickly.

Left: Waterproof-breathable hats with fleece linings and earflaps are excellent in storms and cold weather because they keep your head warm and protect it from wind and rain. Lowe Alpine Mountain Cap. Right: A neck gaiter such as this Buff model is very versatile. Here it's worn as a simple hat.

shell plus a stiff peak, ear flaps, and a neck cord. The weight is just 2.2 ounces.

There are many windproof fleece hats made from fabrics like Gore-Tex Windstopper available. I find these rather hot and sweaty as they're not that breathable. Headwear that covers your ears cuts out sound, too. Fleece caps with windproof shells are far more breathable and comfortable.

In cool weather I often carry one of those light fabric tubes known as neck gaiters to replace one hat. This can be pulled over the head to form a thick collar or scarf and also worn as a balaclava or rolled up to make a hat. Over the years I've collected three of these made from polypro (2.5 ounces), Power Stretch fleece (1.5 ounces), and wicking microfiber polyester (1.5 ounces). I used to have a wool one, but it was too warm, so I passed it on to someone

who felt the cold more. The stretchy microfiber neck gaiter is made by Buff. Buffs come in a huge variety of patterns and colors, and I now have several, including a U.K. Backpacker's Club one, made for the club's twenty-fifth anniversary. There are several types of Buff too, including ones made from Cool-Max and ones incorporating fleece and Gore-Tex Windstopper sections. Mine are the simple original version. I carry a Buff in winter in case I need face or neck protection and sometimes in summer instead of my wool hat—it all depends on which I find first in my box of hats.

A neck gaiter plus a hat provides almost the protection of a balaclava without the restrictiveness. I prefer this combination and haven't worn a balaclava for many years.

Whatever the style, hats can be divided into two categories: those that are windproof and those (the majority) that aren't. Windproof hats are made from windproof fleece such as Polartec Windbloc or Gore-Tex Windstopper or have an outer shell made from a waterproof-breathable or windproof fabric. In a really cold wind, any hat that isn't windproof won't keep you warm unless you put your hood up. Hats that aren't windproof are more breathable and comfortable over a wider temperature range, though, making them better for milder weather than windproof hats.

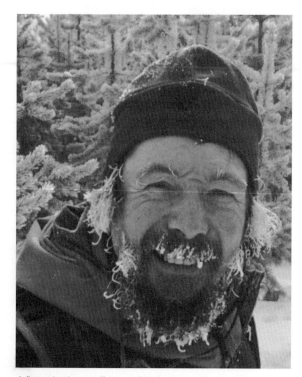

A fleece hat keeps off some of the frost on a bitterly cold winter's day.

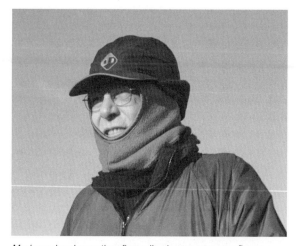

Maximum head warmth: a fleece-lined cap worn over a fleece balaclava.

The warmth of a hat is determined by both thickness and style. Whether it can be pulled down over the ears is important, since ears get cold easily. As with other clothing, the warmest hat isn't always the best; one that will keep your head warm in a blizzard may be too hot for a cool evening at a summer camp. How much you feel the cold matters, too. I know people who are happy bareheaded when I need a hat; others wear balaclavas in what feels to me like warm weather.

The basic watch cap, stocking cap, or tuque is still the standard design. Add earflaps to it and you have a Peruvian or Andean hat. Most watch caps can be pulled down over the ears anyway. Balaclavas give more protection than other designs. Some neck gaiters have a drawcord so

one end can be closed when they're worn as a hat, while others are long enough to be worn as a balaclava. The best protection against wind and rain comes from the peaked cap, with earflaps and a fleece lining, sometimes known as a bomber cap. These protect the face from rain, snow, and sun and can be used in place of a jacket hood. There are also warm headbands, useful when a full hat isn't needed but your ears feel chilly, and face masks or ski masks that cover all but the eyes and nostrils to give more protection than I've ever needed. Presumably they're good in bitter cold and severe high-mountain blizzards. If necessary, a neck gaiter can be pulled up to cover the mouth and cheeks, something I've done on occasion.

Some hat styles come in several sizes, though many don't. Because most fleece doesn't stretch the way knitted wool or acrylic does, it's important to get a good fit if you choose fleece headgear. Hats that are a bit tight are very uncomfortable after a few hours' wear, but a hat that is too loose may blow off in a breeze. Chinstraps are useful to prevent this, especially for hats with peaks or brims that can catch the wind.

Sun and Rain Hats

For many years I never wore a sun hat, even when hiking across the desert regions of Southern California and New Mexico in baking temperatures. I thought my thick head of hair shaded my head from the sun. However, though I still have the hair, I now find that a sun hat adds greatly to my comfort in hot, sunny weather. I was simply ignorant of the benefits of a hat. I used to wear a bandanna headband to keep sweat from dripping into my eyes, and I discovered that when soaked in cold water, it helped keep me cool. You can do the same with a hat, of course.

Oddly enough, it was in the Far North on a 1,000-mile Yukon walk that I learned how useful a sun hat can be. I discovered the Canadian-made Tilley Hat, a cotton duck hat with a wide brim and a fairly high crown, reminiscent of an Australian bush hat. The instructions (it comes with a detailed leaflet!) say the fit should be loose—the double cords for the chin and the back of the head hold it on in windy weather. I bought a Tilley Hat, and it not only kept off the very hot summer sun but also repelled light rain, kept leaves and twigs out of my hair when I was bushwhacking, and held my head net in place when the bugs were bad. I liked wearing the Tilley Hat so much that I wore it when I didn't really need to. The Tilley weighs 5.75 ounces and comes with a lifetime guarantee. Mine has now had more than a decade's regular use. It's faded and rather shapeless, but it's a favorite piece of equipment because it carries so many memories. Eventually, though, my first Tilley Hat did need replacing. Before my Pacific Northwest Trail hike, I took down my old battered favorite and noticed a few holes in the fabric and rather more fraying than I liked. Would it last another summerlong hike? I decided not to risk it and retired

A ball cap keeps off the sun on a spring day.

it to an honored place on a shelf. A new Tilley Hat, the same design as the original, now called the T3 Cotton Duck Hat, accompanied me on the PNT. It looked horribly new at the start but after seventy-five days was suitably trail-worn. There is now a whole army of Tilley Hats, made from a variety of materials—hemp, nylon, waxed cotton, and wool as well as cotton duck—and with different-size brims. Many other companies make good brimmed hats, including Ultimate Hats and Outdoor Research, in a variety of materials including waterproof-breathable ones. I've tried the Ultimate Gore-Tex Hat, which is quite light at 4 ounces, and found it excellent in windless conditions, when it's more comfortable and less restrictive than a hood, but poor in the wind, as rain comes in under the brim. I've only used it for day hikes, but I can see that for backpacking in wet forests where winds are unlikely, it could be worth carrying. However, my cotton Tilley Hat is reasonably water resistant anyway and more versatile than a waterproof hat that's too hot

Hot-weather clothing: sun hat, thin synthetic shirt, shorts.

in sunshine. Much as I like my Tilley Hat, wide-brimmed hats do have one disadvantage—they are not very good in strong winds. A neck cord, essential in my view, stops them being whipped away by the wind, but they still blow off your head. The sides of the Tilley Hat can be turned up and fastened to the brim with studs, which lessens the wind resistance but still doesn't stop strong gusts from flipping the hat over your head. Many hats are white or light-colored to reflect the sun. Such hats need a dark underside to the brim to absorb reflected light so it doesn't dazzle you. This is especially so when hiking on snow, sand, or pale rocks. My original Tilley Hat was dark brown, and the new one is dark green. I haven't found these colors too hot in sunny weather (and they've faded a fair bit, too—the underside of the brims are now much darker than the topside).

The alternatives to brimmed hats are caps with large visors and neck capes. Tucking a bandanna under the rim of a baseball cap gives much the same protection, though it's difficult to keep in place unless you pin it there. The advantages over wide-brimmed hats are complete protec-

tion for the neck regardless of the angle of the sun and good wind resistance, though a neck cord is still a good idea. One of the first and best of these caps was the Sequel Desert Rhat, which is made from breathable mesh lined with a reflective foil, with a cotton front and a terry sweatband. The extra large, stiffened visor has a black underside to absorb reflected light. The cape is made from cotton and attaches with Velcro. It's now my alternative to the Tilley Hat—it's lighter (at 4 ounces) and easier to pack, so I carry it when I may not need a sun hat. I take the Tilley when I expect to wear it every day. Sequel is no more, but there are several hats similar to the Desert Rhat. Good-looking ones are the Outdoor Research Sun Runner Cap at 2.8 ounces and the Ultimate Sahara Breezer Cap. Some capes are permanently attached, some are detachable. I prefer the latter; it can get warm under the cape, so I often remove it. And a cape can be awkward if you wear the cap under a hood, as I sometimes do.

For rain there are caps made from waterproof-breathable fabrics like Gore-Tex. These are useful when fleece-lined waterproof caps are too warm, though you could just wear the Hat for All Seasons (see Warm Hats: My Choices, earlier in this chapter) and remove the fleece liner. Hats with earflaps stay on best in the wind and give more protection. I tried a Marmot PreCip Cap, which has no earflaps or neck cord. It was fine when there was no wind and the rain came straight down but blew off quickly in a breeze. Of course, in heavy wind-driven rain, nothing beats a jacket hood.

GLOVES AND MITTENS

Not only are cold hands painful and unpleasant, they can make the simplest task, like opening your pack or unwrapping a granola bar, very difficult. Whether to wear gloves or mittens depends on how cold your hands get. Gloves aren't as warm as mittens because your fingers are separated, but mittens decrease dexterity, and you have to pull them off for all sorts of fine tasks. Those who suffer from cold hands usually prefer mittens. I like gloves because I can do most things with them on. (If your hands do get very cold, a good way to warm them up is to swing your arms in circles as fast as possible—this sends blood rushing to your fingertips and quickly, if a little painfully, restores feeling and warmth.)

Gloves or mittens have either gauntlet-type wrists designed to go over jacket sleeves or elasticized cuffs designed to go inside sleeves. Gauntlets are best if you use trekking or ski poles because snow and rain can't be blown up your sleeves. If you don't use poles, cuffs are better, since water running down your sleeves can't run into your gloves. Check too that gloves fit neatly over or under your jacket sleeves. Some types don't match up.

Except in reliably warm weather, I carry at least one pair of liner gloves. (On the Pacific Northwest Trail, I carried a 1.4-ounce pair of polypro liner gloves. I never wore them, but I almost did

a couple of times and was glad I had them.) These are thin enough to wear while doing things like pitching the tent or taking photographs. At 1 to 2 ounces a pair, they're hardly noticeable in the pack. They don't last long if worn regularly, though. Gloves with reinforcements on the fingers and palms are the most durable, though slightly heavier than plain ones. There are wool, silk, and synthetic versions. The natural fabrics are good for handling hot pots and stoves and putting wood on a fire because they don't melt as synthetics do. Most of these gloves aren't very water resistant and don't dry fast. If you want to wear liner gloves in the rain, SealSkinz makes thin waterproof ones (3 ounces) from the same fabric as its socks (see Chapter 3). I used to carry these in cool weather (30 to 40°F) for handling wet gear but found that they didn't stay waterproof for very long. They're not very warm either. (There is a version—the ChillBlocker Gloves—with a fleece lining, but these are thicker, of course). When my last pair wore out, I didn't replace them.

In temperatures below freezing, thicker mittens or gloves are essential. For many years I used gloves made from boiled wool. Boiling shrinks the wool fibers to make a dense fabric that increases wind and water resistance so a shell glove isn't needed. Once wet, they're slow to dry, however. Austrian-made Dachstein Mitts (6 ounces) are the classic example. Ortovox makes similar mitts plus boiled-wool gloves. There are plenty of other wool gloves and mittens, both boiled and not. I stopped wearing boiled wool gloves when my last pair wore out between the thumb and forefinger, a major wear point if you use trekking poles, ski poles, or an ice ax. Just to try a new fabric, I replaced them with windproof fleece gloves, which I found more windproof but not as warm. I could do much more with my hands while wearing them, though, because they were thinner.

Thin windproof gloves (top left), waterproof shell gloves (top right), and pile liner gloves (bottom).

However, they wore out at the base of the fingers and thumb even faster than the wool gloves did. Fleece gloves that aren't windproof are just as fragile. Fortunately, plenty of wool and windproof fleece gloves and mittens now come with reinforcements on the fingers and palms that make them much more durable. Fully windproof fleece gloves made from Gore-Tex Windstopper or Polartec Windbloc come in different thicknesses. The thinnest are very light (2 to 3 ounces) and allow excellent dexterity. They're not especially warm, though, and make a good windproof alternative to liner gloves. The thicker ones, with plush fleece or pile inside, are very warm but allow less dexterity. While windproof fleece gloves are great in blizzards and dry cold, if they get wet, they feel cold and are slow to dry. They can get a little sweaty if temperatures rise, too, as the breathability is limited. I put up with this for years until I discovered gloves made from Polartec Wind Pro, which is very breathable, quick drying, and somewhat wind resistant. My pair are Rab Phantom Grip gloves, which weigh 1.8 ounces and have a grip pattern on the palm and fingers. Wind Pro gloves are also available from Outdoor Research, Manzella, Arc'teryx, Extremities, and other companies. I think Wind Pro is the ideal compromise material for gloves. If the wind is too strong or the rain too heavy, I wear shell mittens over the gloves. Some fleece and wool mittens have a flip-back cover that lets you use your fingers without taking your mittens off.

Overmitts keep the hands warm in snowstorms.

mittens and waterproof-breathable shells. The great advantage of these is that the two layers are designed to fit together, but some soft fleece inner gloves wear out quickly if worn without the shell.

When severe cold is expected, I wear Black Diamond Shell Gloves with thick Retro Pile inner gloves. I bought them because the inner gloves are the thickest I've seen. Together, they weigh 9.5 ounces (shells 5.5 ounces, inner gloves 4 ounces) and have long, gauntlet-type wrists. They have kept my hands warm in temperatures as low as −30°F (−34°C). I use them mainly in short stints of up to an hour or so if my hands are feeling very cold, changing to lighter gloves once my hands warm up. The outers of the Black Diamonds are waterproof but not breathable, which means they can get a bit damp; however, because you can pull out the inner gloves, they dry quickly. The nearest current model is the 11.5-ounce Black Diamond Guide with a Gore-Tex insert and a removable wool/pile/Primaloft liner. There are many similar very warm gloves.

Although they're synthetic, fleece gloves don't dry very fast, so it's best to keep them dry by wearing waterproof-breathable shell mittens over them in the rain. These weigh from 1.5 to 8 ounces. You can't do much with them on, but they do keep your inner gloves dry and your hands warm. Reinforcements on the palms increase durability. For years, I've used Extremities Tuff Bags, made from Gore-Tex Paclite, which have reinforced palms and weigh 3.3 ounces. There are plenty of alternatives from companies like Outdoor Research. If you really want to save weight, Mountain Laurel Designs eVent Rain Mitts weigh just 0.99 ounce in the medium size and 1.2 ounces in the large.

While you can put together your own glove systems, many companies offer two-layer systems consisting of wool or fleece inner gloves or

Combining the shell and the insulation in one glove or mitten is the alternative to a glove system. The insulation may be down, wool, fleece, or a synthetic fill. Primaloft is probably the best of the synthetics, being very soft and comfortable and quite water resistant. The shell may be a waterproof-breathable fabric like Gore-Tex or a water-resistant windproof material. These gloves are usually very warm and great for real cold. They're not very versatile, however. A separate shell can be worn over a lighter inner glove in mild conditions, a useful advantage. Also with gloves, the lining, which may only be attached at the wrist, can come out when you remove a glove. It can be difficult to get the fingers back in place when your own fingers are cold and wet. I've tried a few pairs of gloves like this and relegated them to casual use—they could be dangerous in severe cold in the wilds. This can't happen with mitts, and as mitts are warmer anyway, I prefer them for this type of handwear. A simple pair of insulated mitts is the lightest way to keep your hands warm in temperatures well below freezing. You can't do much with them on, but if you wear thinner gloves underneath, your hands shouldn't get too cold if you have to remove them occasionally. For several years, I've carried a pair of Extremities Inferno Mitts, which have a Primaloft fill and a waterproof-breathable outer. They weigh 5.7 ounces. I only carry them on trips when below-freezing temperatures are likely most days, and even then, they usually stay in the pack. But if my hands get cold or the temperature really drops, they are a great backup.

To sum up, I carry liner gloves year-round, supplementing them with wind-resistant fleece gloves and waterproof-shell mitts in cold weather. Having the liners and the warmer fleece gloves means I can wear the ones most suited to the temperature and also means I have a spare pair if the ones I'm wearing get wet, which frequently happens due to snow melting on them and handling wet gear. The damp pair can be stored inside clothing so they can dry a little while the spares are being worn. In winter conditions, I carry a fourth pair, the Primaloft mitts if I'll just need them to warm up my hands occasionally and the shells with pile inner gloves if I'll be wearing them for long periods and handling tools such as snow shovels and ice axes, as these are much tougher than the Primaloft mitts.

Losing a mitten or a glove in bad weather can have serious consequences. Once long ago, while getting something out of my pack, I dropped a wool mitten that I'd tucked under my arm. Before I could grab it, the wind whisked it away into the gray, snow-filled sky. Luckily I was about

to descend into the warmth of a valley a short distance away. Even so, my hand, clad in just a liner glove, was very cold by the time I reached shelter. Since then I've adopted two precautions. One is to attach loops ("idiot loops") of thin elastic shock cord to my gloves so that they dangle from my wrists when I take them off. Many gloves now come with D-rings or other attachments for wrist loops; others come with the loops already attached. My second precaution is to carry a spare pair of mittens or gloves on any trip where cold weather is likely.

In an emergency, you can wear spare socks on your hands. I used this ploy at the end of my length of the Canadian Rockies walk during a bitterly cold blizzard, when my hands weren't warm enough even in wool mittens and liner gloves. With thick socks added, my hands went from achingly cold to comfortably warm, almost hot. Unfortunately, if your feet are cold, the reverse isn't possible!

BANDANNAS

Although not really clothing, a bandanna is quite useful. This 1-ounce square of cotton can be a headband, brow wiper, handkerchief, potholder, bandage, dishcloth, washcloth, towel, napkin, or cape for protecting your neck from the sun. I usually carry two, keeping one threaded through a loop on my pack shoulder strap so I can wipe sweat off my face whenever necessary. I rinse them out frequently and tie them to the back of the pack to dry.

CARRYING CLOTHES

Stuff sacks are ideal for storing clothing in the pack. They weigh from 0.5 to 8 ounces, depending on size and the thickness of the material—thin ones are fine for use inside the pack. My preference is waterproof silicone-nylon drysacks (see Covers, Liners, and Stuff Sacks in Chapter 4). I usually carry spare clothing in a stuff sack in the lower compartment of the pack. If I carry a down jacket, it has its own stuff sack for extra protection. Dry dirty clothing usually languishes in a plastic bag at the very bottom of the pack. Rain gear and clothing I may need during the day (windshirt or warm top) moves around according to how much space I have, sometimes traveling at the very top of the pack, other times at the front of the lower compartment. I don't put these garments in stuff sacks, since they can more easily fill out gaps when packed loose. Headgear and gloves go in a pack pocket, usually the top one.

FABRIC TREATMENT AND CARE

You need to be careful when washing outdoor garments. Many fabrics that are tough in the field can be damaged by detergents, softeners, and too much heat. Most fabrics function best if they're kept as clean as possible, but a few materials can be worn out by too much washing. Down in particular will lose some loft every time it's washed, and wool loses natural oils. I sometimes sponge stains and dirty marks off the shells of down garments, but I have never washed one. I'd rather send my down jacket away for professional cleaning than risk damaging it by doing it myself. Your local outdoor store should know of companies that do this. If not, ask the garment maker. If you do wash a down top yourself, you need to use a product that won't harm the down, like Nikwax Down Wash, ReviveX Down Cleaner, and Granger's 30-Degree Down Cleaner.

The other items that need special treatment are those with durable water-repellent treatments (DWR), such as all waterproof-breathable garments, most wind shells and soft shells, and some fleeces. Dirt impairs water repellency, so it's best to sponge or wipe it off as soon as possible. When water-repellent garments need washing, don't use detergents, not even mild, environmentally friendly types like Ecover, since they can damage water repellency and also leave a residue in the fabric that attracts moisture. (That's why detergent is so effective at cleaning, of course—it pulls water through fabrics.) Instead, garments should be washed with a soap-based product such as Nikwax Tech Wash, Granger's 2 in 1 30°C Cleaner/Proofer, Dri-Pak Liquid Soap, or Dr. Bronner's liquid soap. These can all be used in washing machines, though you need to remove and clean the detergent dispenser and run a rinse cycle or two to make sure there's no detergent left in the machine. If you do wash garments in detergent, rinsing them is not enough to get all the detergent out, no matter how many times you do it and no matter what the labels on the garments say. I no longer wash any garment with a water-repellent finish in detergent. Unfortunately, some garment washing instructions say detergent is OK. If you use detergent, you then need to wash the garment in liquid soap to remove detergent traces. The DWR may still be damaged and need reviving or replacing. Don't have water-repellent garments dry-cleaned either—the solvents strip off all DWR.

Even if you use soap, DWR treatments will cease to work in time—after about ten washes, according to Granger's. When this happens, dark, damp patches appear on the outside of the garment as it starts to absorb moisture, a process known as *wetting out*. Moisture absorption adds to weight and drying time and impairs breathability; condensation makes many wearers think their garments are leaking. Much work has gone into creating better DWR treatments. They certainly last much longer now than when they were first introduced, but they're not permanent.

Water repellency can be revived with heat, which melts the original DWR and spreads it over the fabric. You can put the garment in a dryer, iron it, or even run a hair dryer over it. Keep the heat settings low so you don't melt the fabric as well as the DWR. If you tumble-dry clothing, make sure all zippers are done up and flaps closed to minimize damage. One test showed that tumble-drying often damages coatings and membranes, leading to eventual leakage. Using an iron or a hair dryer is much safer. If applying heat doesn't restore the DWR, then it needs replacing, which can be done with a wash-in waterproofing treatment like Nikwax TX Direct Wash-In, Granger's 2 in 1 30°C Cleaner/Proofer, or ReviveX Wash-In Water Repellent. There are different products for different types of clothing. Nikwax makes Cotton Proof for cotton and polyester-cotton, Polar Proof for fleece, pile, and wool, and SoftShell Proof for soft-shell garments. Consult the label before treating garments. With some products that have wicking linings, such as some lined rain gear and windshirts, only the outer should be proofed, as DWR treatments can affect the wicking properties. For these garments, you need a spray such as ReviveX Spray-On Water Repellent or Nikwax TX.Direct Spray-On.

During a trip, garment care is minimal; in cold and wet weather, it's nonexistent. On walks of a week or less, I never wash anything; on longer ones, I rinse out underwear, socks, and any really grubby items every week or so, as long as it's sunny enough for them to dry quickly. I don't wash laundry in a stream or lake, of course; I fill a cooking pot (and clean it well afterward!) or even a waterproof stuff sack, using water from my large camp water container. The aim is to get rid of sweat, rather than stains and marks, so the garment functions again rather than looks smart. I don't use soap for washing, since it can pollute. If you do, biodegradable soap is best and soapy wastewater should be poured into dry ground well away from streams or lakes. You can dry garments on a length of cord strung between two bushes or on the back of the pack as you walk. On walks lasting more than a few weeks, I try to find a laundromat when I stop in a town to pick up supplies. I don't carry fabrics, like silk, that require special care, because I want to do one load and then tumble it dry on a hot setting. Because of the effect detergents can have on water-repellent treatments, I don't wash any garments with a DWR finish in a laundromat unless I can find some soap powder.

Most outdoor clothing can be stored flat in drawers, but down- and synthetic-filled garments should be kept uncompressed on hangers so they maintain their full loft; even slight prolonged compression may permanently affect the loft of synthetic fills. Check zippers and fastenings before you put garments away, and make necessary repairs. It's irritating to discover that a zipper needs replacing when you're packing hastily for a trip.

shelter
camping in the wilderness

UNDER MOST CONDITIONS, THE BEST
ROOF FOR YOUR BEDROOM IS THE
SKY. THIS COMMONSENSE ARRANGE-
MENT SAVES WEIGHT, TIME, ENERGY,
AND MONEY.

—*Colin Fletcher*, The Complete Walker

Silence. A ragged edge of pine trees, black against a starry sky. Beyond, the white slash of a snowy slope on the distant mountainside. A cocooned figure stirs, stretches. A head emerges from the warm depths, looks around in wonderment, then slumps back to sleep. Hours pass. The stars move. An animal cry, lonely and wild, slices through the quiet. A faint line of red light appears in the east as the sky lightens and a faint breeze ripples the grasses. The figure moves again and sits up, still huddled in the sleeping bag, then pulls on a shirt. A hand reaches out, and the faint crack of a match being struck rings around the clearing. A light flares, then a soft roar breaks the stillness and a pan is placed on the stove's blue flame. The figure draws back into its shelter, waiting for the first hot drink and watching the dawn as the stars slowly fade and the strengthening sun turns the black shadows into rocks and, farther away, cliffs, every detail sharp and bright in the growing light. The trees turn green again as warm shafts of golden sunlight illuminate the silent figure. Another day in the wilderness has begun.

Nights and dawns like that—and ones when the wind rattles the tent and the rain pounds down—distinguish backpacking from day walking and touring from hut to hut, hostel to hostel, or hotel to hotel. On all my walks I seek those moments when I feel part of the world around me, when I

DAWN

My campsite is near a lake backed by pale talus slopes and steep cliffs. The night sky is alive with stars and edged by the deeper blackness of surrounding forest and silhouetted mountains. I awake to the first rays of sunlight catching the highest peak. The lake shines green and gray, reflecting rocks and trees in its cool depths. How many other mornings have I waited for the sun, warm in my sleeping bag? The joy does not diminish.

merge with the trees and hills. Such times come most often and last longest when I spend several days and nights living in the wilderness.

We need shelter from cold, wind, rain, insects, and sometimes sun. It's a necessary evil. I use a shelter only when I have to, which admittedly is much of the time. But if I can sleep outside reasonably comfortably with no barrier between me and the world except a sleeping bag, I do.

The kind of shelter you need depends on the terrain, the time of year, and how spartan you're prepared to be. Some people like to sleep in a tent every night; others use one only in the worst conditions. Polar explorer Robert Peary never used a tent or a sleeping bag but slept outside in his furs, curled up beside his sled. Most mortals require a little more shelter than that. In ascending order of protection, shelters include bivouac bags, tarps, tents, and huts and lean-tos, with snow shelters as a snow country option.

BIVOUAC BAGS

Sleeping out under the stars, known as *bivouacking*, is the ideal way to spend a night in the wilderness. The last things you see before you fall asleep are the stars and the dark edges of trees and hills. At dawn you wake to the rising sun and watch color and movement return to the world. These most magical times of day are lost to those inside a tent.

Of course, since the weather can be unkind and is often changeable, instead of sunlight you may wake up to cold raindrops on your face. The simplest way to cope with weather changes is to use a waterproof *bivouac bag*, also called a *bivy bag* or a sleeping bag cover. This is a waterproof "envelope" you can slip your sleeping bag into when the weather turns wet or windy. More sophisticated (and usually heavier) designs have short poles or stiffened sections at the head to keep the bag fabric off your face. (Bags with poles at each end are

In dry places like the Grand Canyon, a shelter may not be needed.

really minitents, so I'll explore them later, in the Tents section.)

Bivy bags made from nonbreathable fabric are now rare. Sleep in one of these and you'll get damp pretty quickly. Waterproof-breathable fabrics are much better, though some condensation is still possible in humid conditions. Gore-Tex and eVent are the standard fabrics, though there are proprietary ones like Black Diamond's ToddTex. Highly breathable but not fully waterproof fabrics like Nextec's EPIC are also used. These are less prone to condensation than waterproof fabrics and will keep off dew and light rain but not heavy rain. Some ultralight backpackers use such bivy bags with small tarps that keep off most of the rain. I prefer to use a larger tarp and not bother with a bivy bag. Most bivy bags have nonbreathable, coated undersides. The idea is that your sleeping pad goes inside the bag and on top of the base, so there's no point in making the bottom breathable. Some bags have straps inside to hold your pad in place. I prefer bags made wholly from waterproof-breathable fabric, however, since I like to put my pad under the bivy bag so the bag can move with me. I don't want a nonbreathable layer above me, which can happen if I turn over with the bag while asleep or if I deliberately turn it over to put the leak-prone zipper under me, which is the best way to stay dry when it rains. Placing the pad under the bivy bag also protects the bag against abrasion and sharp stones and thorns. A bivy bag needs to be roomy enough to allow your sleeping bag to expand fully. If it compresses the sleeping bag, you're likely to feel cold and uncomfortable. If the bag is too big, however, pockets of cold air can form where it doesn't touch the sleeping bag, which is likely to lead to more condensation. All bags have hoods of some sort, closed with a zipper or drawcord and often backed by no-see-um netting—essential in bug season. The bigger bivy bags can hold some of your gear such as clothing. Weight depends on the fabric and the design but generally runs from 8 to 32 ounces. The lightest bag I know of is the

Suluk 46° CR Bivy at 2.9 ounces. This has a Cuben Fiber base and hood and an ultralight nylon top. Also very light are the 4-ounce Mountain Laurel Designs Superlight Bivy, which has a Cuben Fiber base and a nylon top; and the PHD Sleeping Bag Cover at 5.7 ounces and made of fabric described as very water resistant but not waterproof and with a simple drawcord closure. All these ultralight bivies are designed to be used under a tarp or in a tent in wet weather, and they are unlikely to be very durable.

Straight-across zippers or entrances closed by drawcords are adequate for occasional use and bags that will mostly be used as sleeping bag covers in shelters. More complex entrances with vertical, diagonal, or curved zippers that make getting in and out easier and allow you to sit up with the bag partly undone are worth considering only if you intend to bivouac regularly, since these features add weight and cost. Many models have bug netting behind the zippers so you don't have to close the bag fully against biting insects. Hooped bivies keep the fabric off your face, but I find them claustrophobic because there's so little room. I spent a night in one once, and that was enough. I prefer simple bags, which I close fully only in heavy rain, so my face is out in the air most of the time. If you need more space, a good nonclaustrophobic option is to combine a small tarp with a bivy bag. This isn't as stable as a bivy bag with integral poles, but the setup can allow you room to cook under cover and doesn't shut you into a tiny, dark space. Some people use a bivy bag under a full-sized tarp to protect their sleeping bags against any rain that might blow in.

Bivouac bags are light and convenient for places where pitching a tent might be difficult, such as in the lee of a boulder or under a spreading tree. However, while a good bivy bag will keep out rain and wind, you have to cook outside whatever the weather or the biting insects. Unless the night is calm, dry, and insect-free, I prefer to sleep in a tent or under a tarp and cook, eat, read, write, and contemplate the world in comfort. This doesn't mean I never carry or use a bivy bag; there are situations, even when tent camping, when one comes in handy.

My first bivy bag was a 19-ounce Gore-Tex model with a horizontal zippered entrance covered by a flap. It once kept me and my down sleeping bag dry during several hours of heavy rain. That was many, many years ago, and that bag long ago started to leak. Because I don't carry a bivy bag much anymore—I just sleep out in my sleeping bag and move into a shelter if the weather changes—I replaced it with a lighter-weight waterproof-breathable coated Pertex nylon bag, the Rab Survival Zone, which weighs just 8.5 ounces (though the current catalog weight is 13.7 ounces). The fabric is very thin and probably not that durable, but since I mostly carry it in winter as an emergency item and have slept in it on maybe a dozen occasions in eight years, it'll last me a long while.

Even on calm, dry nights, condensation can be a problem with bivy bags. I once tested a bivy bag high on a bare mountainside on a clear and starry summer night. There was just a slight breeze, which I avoided by sleeping in a small hollow. By dawn, a thick, damp mist covered the ground. The outside of my bivy bag was wet, and there was a lot of condensation inside and on the outside of my sleeping bag. Turning the bivy bag inside out and draping it over a boulder along with the sleeping bag soon cleared the moisture as the mist faded and the sun rose. On colder nights I've awakened to find a layer of ice inside the bivy bag. Even if it doesn't seem damp, it's advisable to air your sleeping bag as soon as possible after a night in a bivy bag to get rid of any moisture it may have absorbed. Condensation is a reason for using bivy bags only on short trips or in mostly fine weather. It's hard to keep your sleeping bag dry if the weather is damp for several days.

In winter I usually carry a bivy bag as a backup shelter and sometimes use it inside my tent or a snow shelter for extra warmth and to protect against dripping condensation. A bivy bag adds several degrees to the range of a sleeping bag.

The most interesting bivy bag I've come across is the Hilleberg Bivanorak. This 18-ounce bag is made from waterproof-breathable coated ripstop nylon and has sleeves and a hood so you can keep your arms and head protected when you sit up in it. There's a drawcord at the foot too, so you can open it up, stick your legs out, and wear it as a rain jacket. The Bivanorak is very roomy and will fit over a medium-size pack. The material does flap a little and breathability isn't that good when walking. I wouldn't want to walk far in it, but as an emergency item it's excellent. I have used it at rest stops in stormy weather and enjoyed the extra protection. As a bivy bag it's very roomy, easily big enough for a full-length mat and a bulky sleeping bag. However the fabric is quite thin and it's awkward to sit up with a mat inside, which negates one of the advantages of the design, so I prefer to keep the mat outside. I haven't used it in prolonged or heavy rain but the drawcord closures at the cuffs and foot and the hood opening mean it can't be 100 percent waterproof, though I wouldn't expect much leakage. The hood and sleeves can be tucked under the bag but the foot will always be exposed to the weather.

The Hilleberg Bivanorak, a bivy bag that becomes a rain jacket.

Carrying an emergency shelter on day hikes and side trips away from camp is a good idea, especially in winter or when you're going above timberline. An expensive waterproof-breathable bivy bag is unnecessary for this purpose, however, as well as a little heavy. Nonbreathable plastic and foil bags, sometimes called *survival bags*, are fine for emergency use. They're inexpensive and take up little room in the pack. The comfort isn't great—I once slept out in a plastic bivy bag and got extremely damp—but if you ever need one, you'll be grateful. For emergency shelter in summer I usually carry an MPI Space Brand Emergency Bag, made from polyester foil with an aluminum reflective surface. It weighs 2.5 ounces and measures 3 by 7 feet when unfolded. This is a very thin bag that will keep off the wind and rain but won't provide much warmth by itself. The MPI Extreme Pro-Tech Bag has a sealed corrugated pattern of the same fabric that traps air and is meant to be much warmer. There are elastic fibers in the construction that allow the bag to hug the body, cutting out dead air space. It weighs 12 ounces. An alternative is a plastic survival bag like one from Coghlan's that weighs 9 ounces. I've often carried one of these on day hikes.

TARPS

Tarps almost disappeared as backcountry shelters during the last third of the twentieth century as hikers turned to the seductive attractions of curving flexible poles and smooth, taut nylon tents. In the second edition I wrote that "constructing your own shelter from sheets of plastic or nylon and cord is something hardly any backpacker does these days." Since then there's been a big and somewhat astonishing resurgence in the popularity of tarps because of both the ultralight revolution and the use of trekking poles, which make good tarp supports, although most backpackers still use tents.

First, though, a definition. A *tarp* is a sheet of fabric that can be suspended from poles or trees to make a shelter. Once you add doors it becomes a tent, or at least a fly sheet. Such designs will be considered below under Tents. Here I'm talking about basic tarps only.

I first used a tarp as a cooking shelter in areas where the presence of bears made eating and cooking in or near my tent unwise and where the likelihood of rain meant that eating and cooking outside could be unpleasant. On long walks in both the Canadian Rockies and the Yukon, I carried an 8-by-9-foot silicone-coated ripstop nylon tarp, with grommets for attaching guylines along each side, to use as a kitchen shelter. On the many occasions when I made camp in cold, wet, windy weather, the protection it provided while I cooked and ate was welcome and certainly justified its 16 ounces of weight. I usually pitched it as a lean-to, slung between two trees on a length of cord. Occasionally I made more complex structures, using my staff plus fallen branches as makeshift poles. At sites with a picnic table, I found I could string the tarp above the table and create a sheltered sitting and eating area.

However, I'd never used a tarp in place of a tent on a long walk until I hiked the Arizona Trail in 2000, when the almost certain prospect of dry weather made a tent unnecessary. Since then I've used a tarp frequently, including on a 500-mile hike in the High Sierra, and it's become my favorite shelter. I now reserve tents for dependably wet, windy, or buggy places.

Another use for a tarp is as an awning for your tent, which provides a large undercover cooking, storage, and drying area that also lets you leave your tent door open in rain with no danger of leakage. I drape the tarp over the tent door, peg out the sides, then use a trekking pole or poles to support the front.

The advantages of tarps are low cost, low weight, space, views, adaptability, good ventilation, and an element of creativity in how you pitch them. Cooking under a tarp is easy because there's no sewn-in groundsheet and you can raise a corner or side for safety. With each side raised high, you have a 360-degree view yet are still protected from precipitation. With a tent you're either inside it or outside.

The disadvantages are that tarps can be difficult to erect in storms, need careful pitching to keep out wind-driven rain, and—worst of all in my view—don't keep out bugs. Condensation can occur, but it's never the problem it can be in a tent: a breeze usually prevents it. If there's no wind, then you can pitch the tarp to allow plenty of ventilation.

Lightweight tarps, weighing 5 to 32 ounces, used to be hard to find but are now widely available. Companies that make them include Hilleberg, Bozeman Mountain Works, Integral Designs, MSR, Equinox, Campmor, Oware, Lynne Whelden Gear, Moonbow Gear, Six Moon Designs, Gossamer Gear, Mountain Laurel Designs, Backpacking Light UK, and Etowah. Most tarps are made from silicone-coated nylon, some from standard polyurethane-coated nylon. The lightest (and most expensive) tarps are made from Cuben Fiber and

Tarp pitched high off the ground for good headroom and ventilation.

spinnaker cloth. Sheets of plastic from building and hardware stores can be used as tarps, but they're not very strong and can tear. Plastic is inexpensive, and some people leave torn sheets of it in the wilderness. I know; I've packed a few of them out. Disposable equipment isn't environmentally friendly whether you pack it out or not, so overall I think it's best not to use plastic for shelters.

Clockwise from top left: A lean-to tarp; an open-ended ridge using trees; an open-ended ridge using two sticks or poles; and an open-ended ridge using four sticks or poles.

Most tarps are flat sheets, though some have graceful shapes with curved sides—the two-person MSR Twing (30 ounces) has six sides, for example. The shaped tarps may be more wind-resistant, but they're also heavier and more costly. Sizes vary enormously. For solo use, 5 feet by 8 feet is probably the smallest feasible size, unless you use a bivy bag as well and accept that your tarp won't keep out all the wind and rain. I tried the 7-ounce 5-by-8-foot Integral Designs Siltarp and found it just big enough to protect me if I pitched it carefully. I prefer more space, however, and the tarp I use most measures 7 feet by 11 feet, big enough for two and

roomy for me and my gear. It's a silicone-nylon GoLite Cave 1, a Ray Jardine design. It weighs 14 ounces; stakes add another 4 to 6 ounces. The Cave has a small awning at each end, known as a "beak," that gives greater protection against rain than open ends. The beaks can be pitched down to the ground to seal off the ends in severe storms. There are plenty of stake points and guylines, including some on the sides that can be tied to poles to create more interior space and prevent sagging. GoLite no longer makes the Cave tarps. However, Ray Jardine sells kits for making your own on his Web site, Ray-Way Products, at http://www.rayjar

Left: *Tarp with bug-netting inner. GoLite Cave and Nest.* Right: *Tarp pitched as a pyramid with a single pole.*

dine.com/ray-way/Tarp-Kit/index.htm. Weights are 13.79 ounces for the solo Ray-Way Tarp and 16.76 ounces for the two-person one.

Netting

When the bugs are biting, I find a tent better than a tarp, though in warm weather, I often use one with a mesh inner, which I sometimes pitch on its own. For those who want to stick with tarps in bug season, there are netting shelters that can be hung inside. Ray Jardine sells a kit for a net tent for his Ray-Way Tarps. The solo Net-Tent weighs 9 ounces. Another example is the Six Moon Designs Serenity Net Tent, a half-pyramid design that weighs 7 ounces. Mesh inner tents designed to be used with a fly sheet but sold separately, such as those for the GoLite Shangri-La series of shelters, could be used as well. I have a GoLite Shangri-La 1 Nest that could be used with a tarp, though I've only used it with the Shangri-La 1. It weighs 16 ounces and is quite roomy for one.

Some tarps have mesh panels at the ends and mesh strips around the perimeter. These prob-ably help, but my experience is that when biting insects swarm, you need a totally closed, insect-proof shelter to keep them out. When the bugs are bad, I like a down-to-the-ground fly sheet with a zippered door and a vestibule where I can burn a mosquito coil or insect-repellent candle and an inner tent with mesh doors.

Pitching a Tarp

Tarps can be pitched in so many ways that the best advice is to experiment and practice—you don't want to be trying to figure out how to erect a stormproof shelter in the rain at the end of a long day's hike. Try different shapes and profiles. If you have a trekking pole or poles, these can be used as supports. You can easily lower the pro-file of the tarp if the weather becomes stormy by shortening the poles and then restaking the tarp from inside. You can also fit poles inside a tarp and pull the fabric over the handles without dan-ger of damaging the tarp, as can happen with a stick. Having supports inside adds to wind resis-tance and stability. If you don't have poles, you'll

Top: Tarp pitched as a low-profile ridge with a storm approaching.
*Above: Tarp pitched as a pyramid with a trekking pole. A second pole
is being used to hold the front of the tarp open.*

need to find a stout stick or two or else tie the tarp
to trees, which means camping only below timberline. You could carry tent poles, but this adds
weight. You need enough stakes to hold the tarp
down plus some cord for guylines unless your tarp
comes with guylines attached. Most tarps have
grommets or loops for attaching guylines. If yours
doesn't or you want extra stake points, you can
wrap a smooth stone in the fabric and tie a loop
of cord around the neck between the stone and
the rest of the tarp. I'd always found this method
satisfactory, but having tried the clever little
devices from Shelter Systems called Grip Clips, I
have to admit that these are easier to use and very
unlikely to tear or damage the fabric. You don't
have to hunt around for smooth pebbles, either.
Grip Clips come in various sizes; the smallest

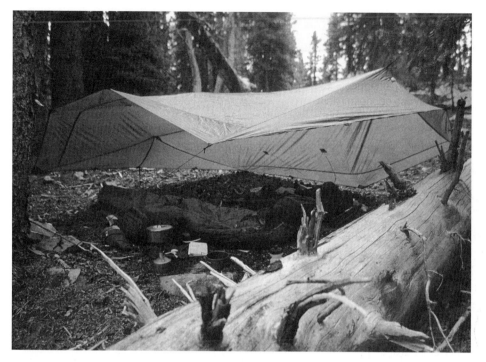

0.08-ounce Micro and the 0.2-ounce Light Fabric clips are recommended for lightweight tarps. For silicone nylon, Shelter Systems recommends fitting pieces of a balloon as gaskets because the fabric is so slippery. To use Grip Clips, you push the two open-centered halves together with the tarp fabric between them. The pieces snap together and cannot come undone. Guylines can be attached to the clips, and they come with 11 inches of cord attached.

The most common tarp shapes are the lean-to, the ridge, and the pyramid. For the first, tie the corners at each end of a long side of the tarp to trees or poles, several feet above the ground. If you use poles, they'll need guying out to keep them from falling over. The other side of the tarp can be staked to the ground or, for better ventilation if there's no wind, loops of cord can be attached to the stake points and the tarp can be pitched with an air gap between the lower edge

and the ground. Lean-tos are roomy and reasonably condensation-free, but they protect you on only one side, and they can flap in the wind.

Ridges give more protection. An open-ended ridge can be pitched by attaching lines to the centers of the short sides of the tarp and tying them to trees or trekking poles. Again, you'll need guylines to stake the poles out. If it's windy, one end of the ridge can be staked down close to the ground, which is most easily done with a tarp with a shaped end like the Ray-Way beak. This produces a sloping ridge that is more wind and rain resistant than one with both ends at the same height.

For a pyramid, stake out one side, then pull the center of the tarp over the handle of an upright trekking pole and tie it off with a bit of cord before staking out the other two corners with the tarp slack between them to leave space for a door. The center of this loose side can be pulled taut with a guyline or, more effectively, by tying it to a pole. Pyramids are quite wind resistant but are best suited to large tarps. Small tarps may not give you enough room to lie down.

These three basic shapes can be varied according to terrain and available supports. I've tied tarps to fallen trees to make unusual shapes and fitted them into awkward spots with one corner at ground level and the one diagonally opposite high in the air. Experiment. That's one of the joys of tarp camping.

With any shape, a low profile with the edges of the tarp at ground level is the most storm resistant but also the most prone to condensation.

GROUNDSHEETS

A *groundsheet*, or *ground cloth*, is useful when sleeping under the stars or under a tarp, especially if the ground is wet. I also carry a groundsheet if I'm planning on using a snow shelter or wilderness huts or lean-tos, because their floors may be wet and muddy. Unlike many people, I don't use one under my tent. I find tent groundsheets durable—I have some that have had more than a year's use and are still waterproof—and I don't want to carry the extra weight.

Cheap plastic sheets are lightweight but don't last long, and they can't be staked out, which is necessary when it's windy. Better are Polycro Ground Cloths from Gossamer Gear, made from industrial-grade, cross-linked polyolefin, which is said to be very tough for the weight. These groundsheets are still inexpensive and certainly very light. The 40-by-96-inch one weighs 1.6 ounces, and the 72-by-96-inch one 2.7 ounces. Nylon groundsheets are much better, especially those that come with grommets or stake points. Tent-footprint groundsheets, designed to be used under tents, work well and weigh 8 ounces or

more, depending on size. Many tent makers offer them. Silicone nylon makes for a very light, strong groundsheet, though it can be a little slippery. I have one that measures 54 inches by 84 inches and weighs 8 ounces. Base Designs' 2 Person Silnylon Ground Cloth measures 66 inches by 84 inches and weighs 5.4 ounces, and Equinox's silnylon Globe Skimmer Ultralite Ground Cloth measures 42 inches by 90 inches and weighs 5 ounces.

Of course, tarps can be used as groundsheets—and vice versa. I once used a groundsheet as a tarp during a thunderstorm in Yellowstone National Park. I didn't want to cook in my tent because of bears, nor did I want to sit outside in the cold storm. So I slung my groundsheet, carried for when I slept under the stars, between two trees as a lean-to and used my pack as a seat while I cooked, ate, and watched the lightning flashes illuminate the forest and the rain bounce off the sodden earth. Net tents can be used as groundsheets, too. I've done this with the GoLite Shangri-La 1 Nest when I didn't need the protection of the mesh. Indeed, any inner tent that can be unclipped and lowered could be used as a groundsheet if you want more space and don't need it.

An alternative to coated nylon is polyethylene, which comes in two forms, DuPont's Tyvek and Space Brand aluminized fabric, and is much more durable than ordinary plastic. Tyvek is used in the construction industry and can be bought in rolls and cut to size (it's also used for waterproof maps). Tyvek is very light and has become popular with ultralight hikers. AntiGravity Gear and Prolite Gear both sell Tyvek by the foot, so you can make a ground cloth the exact size you want. If you prefer a ready-made one, Six Moon Designs sells two inexpensive Tyvek Footprints. The small size measures 36 inches by 84 inches and weighs 4.5 ounces. The large size measures 48 inches by 84 inches and weighs 6.5 ounces. These don't have stake points. Equinox's 30-by-84-inch Tyvek Ground Cloth has bar-tacked loops at each corner. It's very light at 3.2 ounces, but 30 inches is a little narrow. I prefer a wider ground cloth. I haven't used Tyvek, but it's recommended by many experienced long-distance hikers. The most interesting idea for a groundsheet is the Suluk 46° Padded Ground Sheet, which is made from ⅛- or ¼-inch thick Plastazote polyethylene foam and so provides a little insulation. It comes in four sizes. The lightest ⅛-inch size weighs 1.9 ounces and measures 24 inches by 72 inches. The more practically sized ⅛-inch sheet measures 50 inches by 74 inches and weighs 4.4 ounces. I haven't used one of these, and don't know how tough the foam is, but it sounds a sensible idea and one I shall be trying out. I have used MPI Outdoors' Space Brand All Weather Blanket. Current versions are made from a four-ply laminate of clear polyethylene film, aluminum coating, reinforcing fabric, and colored polyethylene film. The blanket measures 56 inches by 84 inches and weighs 12 ounces. One side is silver, the other is blue, red, or olive. With the silver side out, these blankets make good sunshades in the desert. One drawback is that if you fold them for carrying, they tend to crack and then leak at the creases. I now roll mine, and this does seem to prolong the life. I don't use it much anymore anyway, preferring lighter-weight silicone nylon.

TENTS

A good tent provides complete protection from the weather and insects and also space to sit, cook, eat, read, make notes, sort gear, play cards, and watch the world outside. A tarp provides more space ounce-for-ounce, of course, but it doesn't give the same protection against windy weather or, especially, biting insects.

Choosing a tent can be confusing. They come in a wide variety of shapes and sizes, and few stores have the space to display many. There are limited opportunities to see tents pitched and to crawl in and out of them to assess how well they suit your needs. However, a good store should be prepared to erect a tent you're considering buying so you can have a look at it.

Condensation

A tent's primary purpose is to keep out rain and snow. Luckily that's easy to do. Ideally, a tent should also let out moisture vapor. This is not so easy. Bodies give off a fair amount of vapor, and there may be more from wet clothes, cooking, steaming drinks, wet hair, drips, and spills. Moisture from damp ground and vegetation in the vestibule and around the edges of the fly sheet can also condense on cold, impermeable tent walls. If you brush against those walls, you'll get damp too. In my experience the standard two-skin (or double-skin or double-wall) tent design with a breathable, nonwaterproof tent (nowadays sometimes called a *canopy*) and a nonbreathable, waterproof *fly sheet* or rainfly is the best solution to condensation, but it's nowhere near perfect. In theory, moisture passes through the inner fabric and is then carried away by the air circulating between the two layers. Any condensation that forms on the fly sheet can run down to the ground, with stray drips repelled by the inner wall. To prevent condensation from reaching the inner tent, the gap between the tent and the fly sheet must be large enough that wind cannot push the two together. And you need to be careful not to press the inner walls against the fly sheet.

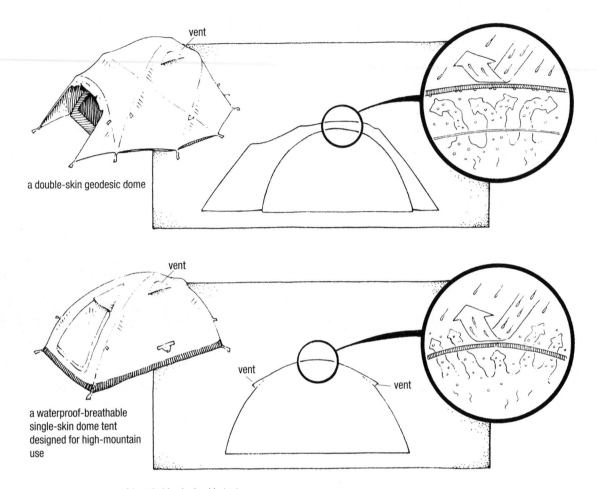

vent

a double-skin geodesic dome

vent

vent

vent

a waterproof-breathable
single-skin dome tent
designed for high-mountain
use

Double-skin and waterproof-breathable single-skin tents.

To some extent the double-layer system works. However, moist air is carried away only if there is a breeze and if it can escape. Since warm air rises and warm air holds more moisture than cold air, a vent high up on the fly sheet can create a chimney effect, drawing cool, dry air in under the bottom edge and expelling warm, damp air through the vent. Vents are more common than they used to be, but many tents still don't have them.

Two-way fly sheet door zippers are also useful for ventilation. I leave at least the top few inches open unless rain starts coming in through the gap.

Condensation is worst in calm, humid conditions. Then nothing—not even leaving all the doors open—will prevent the fly sheet from becoming very wet. One misty night I was awakened by drips falling from the tarp I was under, which was pitched as a lean-to. In a much more

KEY FEATURES: GEODESIC DOME TENTS

- Easy pitching. Check for minimum number of stakes.
- Shock-corded poles that can be quickly fitted to the tent by clips or wide sleeves.
- Waterproof, UV-resistant fly sheet.
- Uncoated inner tent to allow condensation to escape.

- Good space-to-weight ratio.
- Insect net doors. (When the mosquitoes or black flies are abundant, this is more important than any other feature.)
- A roomy vestibule.

quick-attachment clips

airspace gap between inner tent and outer fly

insect net doors

uncoated, breathable inner tent wall

vestibule

ventilation airspace gap

"bathtub" waterproof nylon

stakedown cords

A tent without a fly.

A tent with a fly and a vestibule.

enclosed tent, condensation is unavoidable. I have even left tents empty in calm, humid conditions and found the fly sheets wet with condensation in the morning.

Where bugs are a problem, I've sometimes felt my tent turning into a sauna while I cooked inside the vestibule with all the doors shut tight, producing clouds of steam that promptly condensed on the fly sheet. But being warm and damp is preferable to being eaten alive!

Condensation is a more serious problem in freezing temperatures, when the inner tent can become so cold that moisture condenses on it and then drips back on the sleeper below. If temperatures drop even more, the problem may be solved, because the moisture will freeze on the tent. But when you wake in the morning and start to move around creating heat, the ice will melt, and it can seem as though it's snowing inside the tent. Ventilation is a partial answer to this.

If you camp regularly in damp, humid climates —on the Olympic Peninsula or in the Maine woods, say—it's worth looking for a tent with plenty of ventilation options, such as hoods over door zippers and covered vents. Tents that have sloping inner doors or large mesh panels without covers are poor designs for humid areas. Condensation can drip through the open door or the mesh panels and onto the groundsheet or your sleeping bag. The best design for keeping conden-

An ultralight Cuben Fiber tent—the Terra Nova Laser Ultra 1.

WATERPROOF-BREATHABLE TENTS

I used a Gore-Tex tent on the Pacific Crest Trail, a walk that lasted more than five months, which gave me a good idea of how such tents work in different conditions. In the snowbound High Sierra, where the temperature fell below freezing most nights and the humidity was low, I had no problems with condensation, whereas my companions in two-skin tents found their fly sheets frozen solid each morning. However, in humid weather in September in the Cascades, condensation was a real problem, with moisture running down the taped seams and forming pools on the groundsheet. On too many rainy mornings I had to pack a wet tent and then pitch it, still sodden, in the evening, by which time the moisture had spread all over the groundsheet. I kept my down sleeping bag dry by sleeping in a Gore-Tex bivy bag inside the tent.

In theory, the efficiency of waterproof-breathable fabrics depends on a variation in pressure between the inside of the material and the outside, but I found that levels of condensation were related solely to the outside humidity, not to whether I closed or opened the tent doors. I also found that ventilation was the best way to minimize and clear condensation. If I were to buy another waterproof-breathable tent, I'd look for a good vent system.

But even then, I would use such a tent only where prolonged wet weather and high humidity were unlikely. On a spring ski crossing of the vast Columbia Icefield in the Canadian Rockies, our group of four had two similar-sized tunnel tents—one a two-skin model, the other Gore-Tex. Instead of four days, our crossing took eight because of blizzards, and we spent several days in the tents waiting out storms. The temperature never dropped below 24°F (–5°C); most of the time it was a degree or two either side of 32°F (0°C). This made for damp conditions with the air full of wet spindrift. The two of us in the two-skin tent stayed warm and comfortable, if bored. The condensation that formed on the fly sheet and in patches on the inner tent at night dried out during the day. The pair in the Gore-Tex tent had a rough time. Their tent was soaked inside and dripped on them constantly from the first night on, and their down sleeping bags became wet with condensation, severely reducing their warmth.

sation out of the tent has solid inner walls, a vertical door, vents at the high point of the fly sheet, and outer doors with two-way zippers. Any mesh panels should have covers.

Fabrics

Polyester and nylon are excellent fabrics for backpacking tents, being strong, light, quick drying, and durable. Canvas, the traditional tent material, is not strong enough to make lightweight tents. Polyester stretches less than nylon when wet and resists ultraviolet light better. (Whatever the fabric, it's still best not to leave tents up for long in bright sunlight.) However, nylon has a much higher tear strength weight-for-weight.

Inner tents are usually made from nonwaterproof-breathable nylon that absorbs little moisture, dries quickly, and allows moisture vapor through. Most have a light fluorocarbon finish to repel drips of condensation from the fly sheet. Tents designed for warm weather often have large mesh panels for ventilation to keep out insects and provide views of the stars when the fly sheet isn't in use. However, mesh can let in cold breezes and drips of condensation. Some tents have mesh panels with covers for cool and damp conditions. In my experience, while mesh panels do make a tent cooler, they don't decrease condensation.

The latest fabric is Cuben Fiber (see Materials in Chapter 5 for details). Cuben Fiber is extremely strong for the weight and is used to make the very lightest backpacking tents. Because Cuben Fiber is made from a composite of materials including a film, it is waterproof and doesn't need coating or treating with anything else. It is very expensive, though, and only comes in nearly transparent shades of pale gray. The use of Cuben Fiber was pioneered by small "cottage" manufacturers like Mountain Laurel Designs. The first mainstream outdoor company to use Cuben Fiber was Terra Nova. All fabrics come in different weights, with the heavier ones being more durable than the lighter-weight.

However, mesh tents are useful on nights when keeping off bugs is the main purpose of a shelter. On the Pacific Northwest Trail, I used a GoLite Shangri-La Nest, a mesh inner tent that fitted inside my Shangri-La 1 tent. On warm, dry nights with mosquitoes buzzing around, I pitched it on its own and enjoyed a cooler shelter and being able to look out at my surroundings.

Fly sheets may be coated with polyurethane or impregnated with silicone. Silicone nylon, also known as silnylon, is the lightest fabric yet has a much higher tear strength than polyurethane-coated fabrics. It also has the best resistance to ultraviolet light. Silicone encapsulates the fibers completely rather than just lying on the surface, so it can't wear or peel off, making it very durable and permanently water repellent. Even after years of use, rain still beads up on silnylon, so it dries very quickly. Polyurethane is applied to only one side of a fabric; it's put on the inside of the fly sheet to protect the coating from wear. Once the original durable water-repellent treatment (DWR) wears off, the outside can absorb moisture, making it heavy and slow to dry. Some fly sheets are coated inside and out with silicone, while others have silicone on the outside but polyurethane on the inside so the seams can be taped.

Weights for tough inner and outer nylons are about 1 to 2 ounces per square yard (usually stated in the form 1.5-ounce nylon); the lighter ones need slightly more care than the heavier materials. Deniers (see Materials, in Chapter 4) range from 30 to 75. To prevent leaks, fly sheet seams may need sealing with a seam sealant like SeamGrip unless they come with taped seams. Neither tapes nor standard sealant will stick to silnylon. You'll need McNett's special silicone sealant, SilNet. That said, I've been using silnylon tents and tarps for well over a decade, including months at a time in wet climates, and I've never sealed any seams or had any leaks.

An intriguing alternative to the breathable tent–waterproof fly sheet norm comes from Stephenson's Warmlite, whose tents have two layers made of coated fabric that are permanently linked. The inner layer also has an aluminized coating on the inside to block radiant heat. There are low and high vents to create a chimney effect. This design minimizes condensation, according to the makers, because the inner tent is warmer than in standard designs. I haven't tried a double-skin Warmlite

tent, but it makes theoretical sense and has gotten positive reviews. Friends who have one speak highly of it (see Tent Designs, later in this chapter).

Some tents now come with plastic windows in the doors or the roof so you can look out without opening the tent—at least in theory. In my experience these mist up with condensation very quickly or else are covered with rain and are actually only useful at those times when opening the door isn't a problem. These windows used to be found only in budget tents, since they were brittle and cracked easily. Now they are made from flexible and tough materials and are more widespread.

Waterproof-Breathable Tents

Tents made from waterproof-breathable fabrics are easy to pitch and quite light for their size

Left: Low-profile, single-skin bivy tent of waterproof-breathable fabric—Bibler Tripod. Below: A tent made from waterproof-breathable fabric—the Exped Polaris.

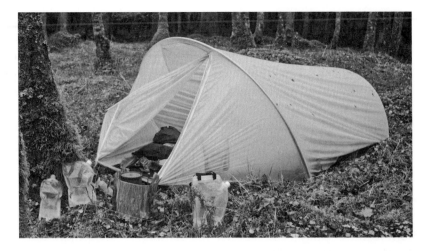

Single-skin, waterproof, nonbreathable tunnel tent—Stephenson's Warmlite 2X.

because they have a single skin. Wind can't get in under the edge of the fly sheet because there isn't one, so they can be warmer than two-layer tents. Makers of these tents include Black Diamond and Integral Designs, each using its own proprietary fabrics ToddTex and Tegraltex respectively, Terra Nova, which uses Gore-Tex, and Rab, which uses eVent. (Rab calls its eVent tents "bivis," but as you can sit up in some of them and they have crossover curved poles and zipped doors, they are actually tents.)

Waterproof-breathable tents work well in dry conditions, but they aren't breathable enough to cope with much moisture vapor in humid conditions, and then condensation is likely; moreover, the condensation can't escape by running into the ground because there is a sewn-in groundsheet. Most are designed for high-mountain alpine and Himalayan, where dry cold and snow is expected, and it's in these areas that they perform well.

Nonbreathable Single-Skin Tents

My first true backpacking tent was a single-skin (or single-wall) nonbreathable coated nylon ridge tent. It was lightweight, easy to pitch, waterproof, and low in bulk when packed. However, in wet or humid conditions, to call the condensation copious was an understatement. It ran down the walls and slowly flooded the groundsheet. I replaced that tent with a double-layer model as soon as I could and wasn't surprised when single-skin tents disappeared shortly afterward. The lightweight revolution has seen them reappear, on the basis that cutting out the inner tent and sewing the groundsheet to the fly sheet saves weight. These modern nonbreathable tents often have vents and door configurations said to reduce condensation. These might help a little, but the inside of a fly sheet in a double-layer tent can be soaked with condensation in humid weather even with vents and doors open and an air gap right around the perimeter, so there's no way a single-skin tent, without that lower air gap, will have less condensation. I'd be very wary of nonbreathable single-skin tents with sewn-in groundsheets unless I camped only in places with low humidity. And then I would probably just carry a tarp anyway. A better design has mesh panels between the groundsheet and the fly sheet so condensation can run through the mesh onto the ground. This doesn't stop condensation flicking off the fly sheet onto you when it's windy, though.

There are also single-skin tents without ground sheets, basically just fly sheets. These are still prone to condensation, but it can run into the ground rather than onto the groundsheet, so they're more practical for conditions where a tent is most needed. Most pyramid tents are floorless single-skin models, as are many of the new ridge designs. The key when using these tents is to avoid touching the walls when they're damp.

I tested seven single-skin tents for a magazine review in the damp Scottish hills. My findings were that ventilation was a key to minimizing condensation but that in calm, humid conditions, it was unavoidable. This made tents with separate groundsheets or ones attached with mesh panels far superior to ones with standard sewn-in groundsheets, as the moisture could run down the walls and into the ground rather than onto the groundsheet. Steep walls helped, too.

Some users of single-skin tents have reported light sprays of fine moisture, known as misting, during wet weather. The assumption is that some rain is coming through the fabric. While this may be so with some very fine fabrics, I think condensation being shaken off the walls is a more likely reason. I have had this happen many times. When I've checked fabrics later, they've always been watertight, so on every occasion, I think it was condensation. This isn't noticeable in a double-skin tent because any moisture coming off the inside of the fly sheet is blocked by the inner tent.

Floors

Tent floors are usually made from 2- to 4-ounce polyurethane-coated nylon or silicone-nylon on the lightest tents. Long ago nylon floors didn't stay waterproof very long and ripped easily, so people usually used a groundsheet under them, a habit that has remained even though the nylons used today are tough enough to make a groundsheet unnecessary. The tent I used on my Canadian Rockies walk back in 1988 was still waterproof after eighty nights with no protection under it, as was the groundsheet on the tent I used on the Pacific Northwest Trail in 2010 after seventy-five nights (and the last month of that hike was very wet, so I was usually camping on wet ground).

The best floors are the "bathtub" type with no ground-level seams. Short sidewalls keep out rain splashes that come under the fly sheet. Tiny punctures are the most likely damage to occur to floors. To prevent further leaks, cover them with spots of sticky nylon tape. Better yet, check the ground for sharp twigs and stones before pitching the tent to minimize the chances of puncturing the floor.

If you do use a groundsheet with your tent, make sure it doesn't extend beyond the edge of the fly sheet, or rain can collect between it and the tent floor. This can happen even when it's tucked well under the tent, though it's much less likely if you fold up the edges of the groundsheet. On the few occasions when I've used a groundsheet with a tent, I've put it inside the tent.

Poles

Most tent poles are made from flexible aluminum, though those on less expensive models may be made from fiberglass. Pyramid tents often come with rigid aluminum poles. I've never used a tent with fiberglass poles, but the general view is that they're not as strong as aluminum. Aluminum comes in different types; DAC Featherlite and Easton 7075 are regarded as the highest quality. The diameter of the tubing also affects the strength. Most backpacking tents have 8.5- to 9.5-millimeter poles. Tents designed for severe high-mountain weather may have thicker poles, such as 11.5 millimeters.

Carbon fiber is stronger, lighter, and more expensive than aluminum. Easton makes two types of carbon-fiber poles, both said to be 30 percent lighter and 300 percent stronger than aluminum poles. If you want to save a few ounces, you can—for a price—buy carbon-fiber poles for your tent from Fibraplex. These are half the weight of Easton 7075 poles. The pole on my favorite solo tent weighs 5.5 ounces. Since the shock cord linking the sections would weigh the same, I'd save maybe 2 ounces if I changed to carbon fiber. Of course, with a large geodesic dome tent with four or five long poles, the weight saving would be more significant, as would the increased cost.

Some flexible poles come prebent. If they are not prebent, they often develop a curve with use. This is not a problem as long as you don't try to straighten them, because then they may break. Pole sections are normally linked by shock cord, which makes it easy to put them together and almost impossible to lose sections (though I managed it once after a shock cord snapped).

Poles may run through nylon or mesh sleeves or attach to the tent with clips or shock cord; some have flexible hubs at pole intersections. Pole ends fit into grommets, plastic pole cups, or webbing. Clips theoretically allow better airflow between the inner layer and the fly sheet than sleeves, but I don't think they make much difference. What's more important is that poles are marked so you know where each one should go. Many poles come already marked. If not, stick different-colored tape on each one.

Poles are strong when the tent is pitched but vulnerable when lying on the ground—especially long, thin, flexible poles. Take care not to step on them. And don't use them as handholds when entering and leaving the tent. A companion once broke a flexible pole by putting all his weight on it as he left the tent during a winter gale in a remote mountain area. I had to scramble out of my sleeping bag, throw on some clothes, and repair it before the storm caused any more damage. I fixed it by slipping a short alloy sleeve over the break and binding it in place with duct tape. Such sleeves are supplied with most flexible-pole tents. I always carry one, though that's the only time I've used it.

After I'd been using trekking poles for a few years it occurred to me that carrying tent poles as well was a little superfluous, especially since trekking poles are stronger than most tent poles. However, you can't pitch a flexible-pole tent with trekking poles. Now, though, tents designed to be used with trekking poles are appearing, which makes good sense. I use mine with tarps and the GoLite Shangri-La 1 tent.

Stakes

Every tent must be staked to hold it down in wind. Fifteen to twenty stake points are plenty; more increase the weight you're carrying and the time it takes to pitch the tent. Many tents need only eight to twelve stakes. Some will stand with just three or four stakes, though more are needed if it's windy. Most stakes are made of steel or aluminum (I've found plastic too fragile for wilderness use), and they come in a variety of shapes. Thin ones work best in hard ground, wide-angled or curved ones in soft ground. For sand or soft snow, you need really wide snow pegs. I have a set of 12-inch

A selection of tent stakes. From left: plastic I-beam for soft ground, C-curve for soft ground, short pin with loop end for hard ground, Y shape for soft ground, long pin with hook end for hard ground, thick pin for hard ground, snow stake for sand and snow.

hardened aluminum stakes for snow camping. They weigh 1.8 ounces each and are drilled with holes to save weight and to attach guylines so they can be buried horizontally for maximum holding power. Hilleberg, MSR, TerraNova, Suluk 46°, and SMC make snow stakes. Hilleberg's come with a line and a hook for attaching them to guylines or stake points. Suluk 46°'s titanium stakes are the lightest at 0.41 ounces each, but they are expensive. Also very light are fabric "stakes" with short lengths of cord attached that you fill with sand or snow and then bury, such as Exped's 0.6-ounce Snow and Sand Anchors. I suspect it would be easy to make your own version of these.

Outside of snow country, I use 6- or 7-inch pins, which hold in most soils. Aluminum pins weigh around 0.4 ounce each, and titanium ones around half that. Given the high cost of titanium stakes, I didn't think they were worth buy-ing for what was only a weight-saving of about 3 ounces per shelter. However, having tried some, I found that they were stronger than aluminum stakes and hard to bend and also held better in some soils. I now prefer titanium pins. For softer ground, I usually carry two or three 6- or 7-inch V-angle or curved stakes in hardened aluminum or titanium. I don't find the difference between the two materials in weight or strength as great as with pins, so I'm not bothered which it is. These stakes weigh around 0.5 ounce each. Y-stakes are considered stronger than V-stakes, though I don't like them because they are harsh on the hands. Most tents come with adequate stakes, but a few I've tried have tiny ones that are only 4 or 5 inches long and look like toothpicks. They can weigh as little as 0.035 ounce each, but they pull out of the ground very easily and are next to useless. They are an example of taking weight-saving too far. Most tent brands sell good stakes, and they are also available from Vargo Outdoors. In hard ground stakes can be tapped in with a small rock or pushed gently with the sole of your boot. Don't hit them too hard though, or they might bend or break. If stakes are hard to pull out by hand, use another stake by hooking it into the end of the stuck stake and using it as a lever.

Stakes are easy to misplace, so I carry a couple of extras. However, on many occasions I've finished a hike with more stakes than I started with, finding ones others had lost. I keep stakes in the small nylon stuff sack supplied with most tents and carry them in a pack pocket so they're easy to find when I pitch the tent.

Guylines

Depending on the design, tents need anything from two to a dozen or more guylines to keep them taut and stable in a wind, though more than ten is too many for one- and two-person tents. Most tents come supplied with a full set of guys, but some have only the main ones plus attachment points for others. It pays to attach these extra guylines before they're needed or at least carry some cord with you. I'd rather have plenty of guylines and leave them tied back when it's calm than not have enough.

To avoid confusion and to help when sorting out tangles, different-colored guylines are useful, especially when several are attached to the tent at the same point. If the guylines are tied back in loops when you pack your tent, they're less likely to tangle. I always try to do this, though when packing in a hurry during a storm, I often forget and end up cursing myself the next night as my numb fingers undo knots. Metal locking or plas-

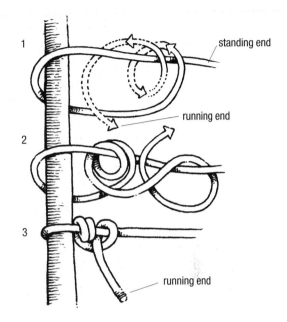

Tautline hitch. Wrap the rope around an object to create a loop. Feed the running end of the rope over the standing end and through the loop at least twice (1). Bring the running end out of the loop and over the standing end. Secure the running end as shown (2). Tighten the wraps so they lie flat and close together (3).

tic friction adjusters come with most guylines, but you can also buy them separately. It's useful to know how to tie the tautline hitch in case you need extra guylines and have no extra mechanical sliders. This knot will slide up and down the guyline when the line is slack but lock when it's tightened. Nylon stretches when wet, so guylines should be staked out tightly. If it's wet and windy, I generally retighten them before going to sleep. The lightest guyline material is Dyneema cord, which weighs around 0.018 ounce per foot. It's very tough, too. The best guyline tensioners I've used are Clamcleat's Mini Line-Loks, little plastic devices that are easy to use and weigh 0.076 ounce each.

Size and Weight

The weight of a tent depends on its size and the materials it's made from. Tents come in a wide range of sizes—from tiny bivy tents barely big enough for one person to monsters that will accommodate half a dozen Himalayan mountaineers and all their gear. At a minimum, you need enough space to lie down and stretch out without pushing against the walls or either end. This is all the space the smallest tents have. There's no room to sit out a storm in comfort (for which you need enough headroom to sit up), nor space to lay out gear inside, nor a vestibule big enough for safe cooking. They are light, though. Most of these tiny tents are designed for one occupant. The amount of space two people need depends on how cramped they're prepared to be and how friendly they are. Many tents described in catalogs as sleeping two assume very close friendships!

Most tent makers give the floor areas of their tents, as do some retailers, and they all give length and width so you can compare sizes. As a rough guide, I'd look for at least 30 square feet of floor area in a three-season tent for two (excluding the vestibule), and 35 square feet or more in a winter tent. For solo use, 18 to 20 square feet is enough. The width for two should be at least 54 inches at the widest point; for one, 36 inches will suffice. Length should be at least 7 to 8 feet. Backpackers over 6 feet tall need to consider the length of a tent carefully; in many tents, they'll find their feet pushing against the end.

In mostly dry areas where storms are unlikely and you just want a bedroom to keep out bugs or the occasional shower, the smallest, lightest tents may be fine. In wet areas or in winter, you need more room because you're likely to spend more time in your tent and in winter you'll have bulkier sleeping bags and clothing.

Being able to sit up in a tent makes a huge difference to how spacious it feels. I don't like tents, however lightweight, that don't let me sit up, because they make me feel uncomfortably confined. The key factor here is the distance between the floor and the top of your head when you're sitting cross-legged. If you measure that, you can determine from catalogs which tents will be roomy and which will give you a crick in the neck. I always look for a tent with at least 35 inches maximum inner height.

The size of vestibule you need depends on whether you intend to cook and store gear in it. For cooking, a vestibule must be high enough and wide enough to prevent the fabric from catching fire or melting. Tents for two sometimes have double vestibules, and although they're heavier, they make tent living much easier. For areas where you usually live outside and use the tent only for sleeping, vestibules don't need to be large. Indeed, it doesn't matter if there isn't one at all.

I like vestibules with large zippered door flaps that can be rolled out of the way. It's not quite the same as bivouacking, but having a wide-ranging view is far better than being encased in a nylon cocoon. I close the doors only if forced by the weather or bugs.

Many tents weigh more than they need to, as designers add excess features and "improvements." It's easy to be impressed by fancy designs. I know; I've done it. I started out using solo tents in the 4- to 4.5-pound range (weights include stakes and stuff sacks—the actual weight when carried), but a decade later my tents weighed 5 to 6 pounds. Wanting to cut that weight, I decided on 4.5 pounds as the maximum I would carry in the future. With the latest materials, that has come down to 4 pounds. Except when I'm testing heavier tents for review, I've stuck to that rule. Keeping the weight down when you share a tent is easier. I've used a 5.5-pound tent for snow camping with two and not felt cramped, and there are plenty in the 5- to 8-pound range that provide ample room.

Tent makers usually list two weights for tents. The minimum weight covers just the tent, fly sheet, and poles. The packed weight includes stakes, stuff sacks, spare parts, and instructions. The weight you'll carry is likely to be closer to the packed weight than the minimum.

Stability

The stability of your tent becomes a matter of great concern once you've struggled alone in the dark, cramming gear into a pack under a thrashing sheet of nylon after the wind has snapped one of your tent poles—which happened to me many years ago. It was pouring rain and I had to make a long night descent to the trailhead. Had it been a more remote location in winter, I could have been in serious trouble.

In the distant past, three tents collapsed on me—two because of wind and one because of a heavy, wet snowfall. On two other occasions I've camped with others whose tents have been blown down. I've also slept peacefully in a well-designed, properly pitched tent during a gale that blew down less stable tents nearby and shook others so hard that the occupants got little sleep. If you spend the night expecting your thrashing tent to collapse any minute, you'll be too exhausted to enjoy the next day.

The importance of tent stability depends on where and when you use your tent. For three-season, below-timberline forest camping, it's not a major concern. For high-level, exposed sites and winter mountain camping, it's very important.

Tent design and materials both contribute to stability. The most stable designs don't have large areas of unsupported material that can catch the wind. Many makers describe their tents as three- or four-season models. Many three-season tents are as stable as four-season ones; what they often lack is snow-shedding ability, extra space, and large vestibules. High winds can occur above timberline and in exposed areas at any time of year anyway.

Stability is relative. Hurricanes that strip roofs off buildings and blow down trees can certainly shred even the strongest four-season mountain tent. In strong winds, your experience and ability to select a sheltered site are as important as the tent you have. If pitching the tent in a storm seems impossible, it's better to go on, even after dark, in search of a more sheltered spot. You'll rarely have to camp in storm-force winds, but if you do, seek out whatever windbreaks you can—piles of stones or banks of vegetation—and consider sleeping out in a bivy bag, if you are carrying one, or even wrapped up in your tent. It may be uncomfortable, but it beats having your tent destroyed in the middle of the night.

Careful pitching is important, too. A taut tent with no loose folds of material will resist wind much better than a saggy mass of nylon. The best mountain tents will still thrash around in a storm if badly pitched. When pitched properly, a stable tent should feel fairly rigid when you push against the poles.

Inner or Outer Pitching

Traditionally the fly sheet was an extra layer thrown over the tent to protect it from rain. Originally both layers were needed to keep rain out, since neither was fully waterproof. When non-breathable coated nylon was introduced for fly sheets, it made sense for inner tents to be breathable rather than water resistant. This can present a problem when you pitch the tent in the rain.

Unless you pitch it very fast, which depends on both your skill and the design, it can get very wet. To counter this, some tent makers—mostly in wet Northern European countries—began building tents that pitched fly sheet first. Since the poles are often on the outside, these are sometimes known as exoskeleton tents. Many of them also pitch as a unit; that is, the fly sheet and inner tent go up together. If the fly sheet is damp inside with condensation, you can then detach the inner tent when packing up so it doesn't get wet from being packed with the fly. With many inner-first-pitch tents you can now pitch the fly sheet separately if you want, often with a separate groundsheet. You can't usually then add the inner tent, though.

For very wet areas where having to pitch in the rain is likely, I prefer exoskeleton tents. For drier areas either design will do, while for very dry areas inner-first pitching is probably best, since you may not need the fly at all much of the time. But in those areas, why do you need a tent at all?

Color

Dark tents can be gloomy inside in dull weather. Pale tents let in much more light. Warm colors— red, orange, yellow—give a warm light, which can be psychologically appealing in cold weather. Gray, blue, and green feel cooler; maybe too cool in dull weather but pleasant when it's hot. In most environments bright, hot colors stand out and can be an eyesore. At high latitudes where it barely gets dark during the summer, dark tents can be sooth- ing and more conducive to sleep. Overall I prefer inconspicuous greens, browns, and grays for fly sheets (and tarps) but a warm color such as yel- low for inner tents. That's except for snow camp- ing, when I like bright yellow or orange tents. Any colors other than shades of white and pale gray

look black at a distance against snow anyway, so the problem of visual pollution doesn't apply in the same way.

Tent Designs

Since the advent of curved poles in the early 1970s, designers have created a bewildering array of tent shapes, some of them bizarre. Overall, though, these developments have led to a superb range of tents that are lighter, roomier, tougher, and more durable than ever before. Some tents are hard to classify, but most fit into the categories of ridge, pyramid, dome, tunnel, and single-hoop.

Ridge Tents

Before flexible poles appeared, most tent designs were variations on the standard ridge tent, a solid structure that has had a bit of a renaissance as hikers have discovered that trekking poles make good upright tent poles. The simplest, but the least stable and most awkward to use, are those with upright poles at each end. A-poles make a far more stable tent, known as an A-frame, and leave entrances clear. It's not easy to use trekking poles as A-poles, though. Ridge tents don't have good space-to-weight ratios, and the angled walls mean a lack of headroom compared with curved pole designs. However if you use trekking poles, then ridge tents that can be erected with them are worth considering. These are usually single- skin tents, often with a bug netting inner tent as an option. Makers often refer to these designs as "shelters" or even "tarps" to distinguish them from double-wall tents. I used a GoLite Shangri- La 1 tapered ridge tent on the Pacific Northwest Trail along with the Shangri-La 1 Nest inner. The combined weight was 34 ounces with the extra stakes and guylines I added. I used the Nest as a

protected vents

Hoops and tunnels (Hilleberg Keron 3)

large vestibule

protected vent

Single-hoop tent (Hilleberg Akto)

single-skin,
floorless design

large vestibule

Pyramid tent
(Black Diamond Megamid, Mega Lite)

tapered shape

strong structure
resists snow

Semi-geodesic
(North Face Tadpole)

Geodesic dome (North Face VE 25)

Basic tent designs.

A single-skin ridge tent pitched with trekking poles—Gram-Counter Gear LiteHouse Solo.

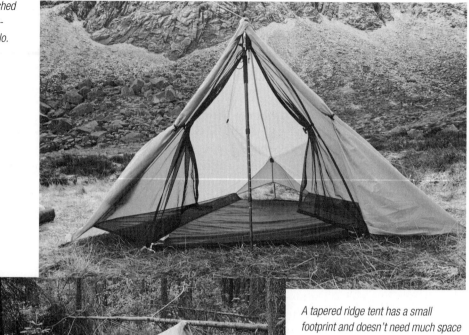

A tapered ridge tent has a small footprint and doesn't need much space to pitch—the GoLite Shangri-La 1.

ground cloth when I didn't need it as a bug shelter and so didn't carry a separate one, as I would do when using the tent without the inner. The tent is made from silicone/PU ripstop nylon and has taped seams. On its own, it weighs 17 ounces. The total area is 23 square feet. The area of the Nest is 16 square feet. I found this adequate in wet weather when I was able to store all my gear and cook undercover. The height at the front is 45 inches, so I was able to sit up. There are big covered vents front and back, so ventilation was good when it was breezy. The Shangri-La 1 was easy to pitch with trekking poles, and I grew to like it very much. On the few windy nights, it was quite stable pitched with the rear into the winds and with a guyline added to the peak to pull it taut along the ridgeline. There is a larger non-tapered version, the Shangri-La 2, that weighs 26 ounces and has an area of 45 square feet. It, too, has an optional Nest inner, which weighs 24 ounces. Similar floorless ridge tents are available from MSR (the Twin Sisters and Twin Brothers) and Black Diamond (the Betamid and Beta Light). All these can be used with separate mesh inner tents.

There are also many single-wall ridge tents with sewn-in groundsheets. Makes include Tarptent, Big Sky International, Gossamer Gear, Hilleberg, and Six Moon Designs. These tents are very light for the size, which is their main advantage. Some are astonishingly light. The Gossamer Gear Spinnshelter weighs 10.3 ounces (without stakes) and has an area of 35.4 square feet and a height at the front peak of 40 inches. It's made from ultralight spinnaker cloth. Tarptent, a leader in this field, has several interesting ridge tents that have short curved or upright poles at the rear but use a trekking pole at the front, such as the 24.5-ounce silnylon Contrail. This solo, tapered ridge tent has mesh panels between the tent and the tray ground cloth and a front vestibule. The adjustable floor area is 21 to 27 square feet, and the height at the peak is 45 inches. Many of these tents can be pitched with two trekking poles at the front to give an unobstructed doorway. Ordinary tent poles are available if you don't use trekking poles, but then of course, some of the weight advantage over tents with curved poles is lost.

There are few tents left with A-poles, though this is a stable, easy-to-pitch design that is less expensive than domes. Eureka's Timberline tents are the classic A-frames and have been around since the 1970s. These have A-poles at each end and a curved ridgepole. They're freestanding, and the lightest two-person model weighs 5 pounds, 13 ounces.

Pyramids

Long before the current lightweight revolution, Chouinard made a floorless tent called the Pyramid. Chouinard became Black Diamond, and the Pyramid became the Megamid and then the current Mega Lite. This has an area of 81 square feet and can sleep four. The Mega Lite is made of sil-

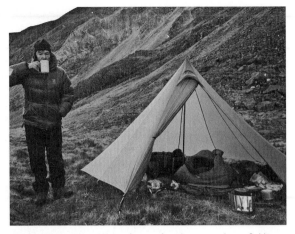

A pyramid tent gives plenty of space for winter camping—GoLite Shangri-La 3.

nylon and weighs 2 pounds, 13 ounces. There's an optional floor weighing 1 pound, 13 ounces. The tent comes with an adjustable carbon-fiber pole and a pole link converter so you can use two trekking poles instead.

The Pyramid/Megamid became popular with ski tourers, since the snow inside could be dug out for more space, something you can't do with a floored tent, and it's very light with lots of headroom. Other makers followed, and there are now several pyramid and tepee tents. I've used the 57-square-foot GoLite Shangri-La 3 (formerly the slightly bigger and heavier Hex 3), which has a body weighing 25 ounces, a 12-ounce pole, and 3 ounces of stakes, for a total weight of 2 pounds, 8 ounces for a shelter that will sleep three, is roomy for two, and feels wonderfully spacious for one. The latest Shangri-La 3 is made from PU/silicone nylon and has taped seams. A floored mesh inner tent called the Shangri-La 3 Nest weighs 1 pound, 13 ounces. The original Hex 3 proved a stable design when pitched for two nights in storms at 11,000 feet. The wind ensured that little condensation built up inside, though in calmer conditions

Geodesic dome with fly sheet.

Geodesic dome.

there has been quite a bit. I've also used the Hex 3 on a two-week spring ski tour where the space was welcome. Cooking inside is no problem, and I really like being able to stand up to get dressed. Other makes of pyramid tents include Oware and Mountain Laurel Designs. I particularly like the look of the Mountain Laurel Designs DuoMid, which comes in silnylon at 16 ounces and Cuben Fiber at 12 ounces (both without stakes). The DuoMid has 40 square feet of "usable floor space" and looks like an ideal tent for two and a luxury

for solo use. Inner net tents are available—the solo one weighing 8.5 ounces, the duo 13 ounces.

Domes

Domes have two or more flexible poles crossing each other at one or more points. Many are free-standing—they don't need staking down. This is often pushed as a huge bonus. It does indeed make pitching domes quicker and easier—if there's no wind. But I've heard stories of domes taking off like giant balloons, never to be seen again. I would always stake down a tent. I have to say that although I've owned a few over the years and tested many more, I'm not particularly fond of domes. I prefer simpler designs that give more space for the weight and are generally easier to pitch.

The two most common dome shapes are the *geodesic* and the *crossover pole*, though there are many variations. Geodesic domes are complex structures in which four or more long poles cross each other at several points to form very stable tents that are popular with mountaineers because they can withstand high winds and heavy snow loads. Crossover pole domes are simpler: two or three poles cross at the apex to make a spacious

Double-layer tunnel tent with poles on the outside—the exoskeleton design. Hilleberg Nallo 2.

tent that is lighter than a similar-sized geodesic, though nowhere near as stable—in strong winds the poles can invert, and the whole tent can wobble like a gelatin mold. To overcome this, some domes have a short pole crossing the two main ones at the apex and main poles that are offset so they cross below the apex. Weights run from 4 pounds for solo two-pole domes (sometimes called wedge tents) to 12 pounds for multipole tents that will sleep three or four.

An example of a simple two-pole crossover dome is the Kelty Gunnison 2.1, which has a packaged weight of 5 pounds, 8 ounces and sleeps two people. It has a polyurethane-coated polyester fly sheet and a breathable polyester canopy. There are two vestibules and doors with covered vents at the top of each and an area of 37 square feet. For three-season sheltered camping, this looks a fine tent. An example of a geodesic dome is the four-pole Terra Nova Quasar, which I've used for winter camping in some ferocious Scottish and Norwegian storms. There are several versions of the Quasar using different materials. The standard one weighs 8 pounds, 8 ounces. There

are vestibules and doors at both ends and room for two inside (the inner area is 32 square feet). I wouldn't use a tent like the Quasar for general backpacking, but for exposed mountain camping, especially in winter, a geodesic is a good choice.

Geodesics are very stable but not very light. Almost the same wind resistance can be obtained by adding a third pole across the front of a two-pole wedge and tapering the back of the tent to the ground to create a semigeodesic or geo-hybrid shape. On the Continental Divide Trail I used a 6-pound tent of this design (a long-gone model called the Wintergear Voyager) and found it roomy, durable, and stable in storms. For the first month of the hike I shared the tent with a companion. After that I used the tent solo, relishing the space but not the weight. One of the most popular semigeodesics for many years has been North Face's Tadpole. The latest version weighs 4 pounds, 15 ounces, and has a 27-square-foot floor and 8-square-foot vestibule. The fly sheet is coated nylon, and there are mesh panels in the sides of the inner tent. I've used the Tadpole and found it a stable

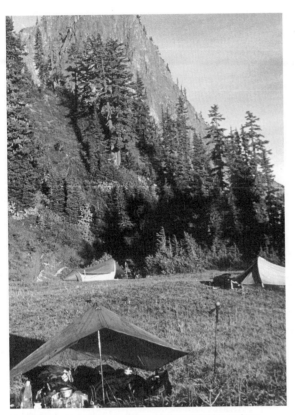

Timberline camp with tarp pitched as a tapered ridge and two tapered tunnel tents.

tent for two, though not very roomy because of the low rear and small area.

Hoops and Tunnels

Rather than crossing, in tunnel tents the poles form parallel hoops. Tunnels have a better space-to-weight ratio than any other design. They're also very easy to pitch, though they're not free-standing. This category includes the tiniest tents, weighing about 2 pounds. For years I never tried one of these because they are so low and narrow that I felt claustrophobic just looking at them. This is hardly objective, however, so I did eventually brace myself and try a 2-pound, 5-ounce

Bibler (now Black Diamond) Tripod, which appeared to have slightly more headroom than most. It is made from waterproof-breathable Toddtex and has a tiny hoop at the foot and two poles at the head, one forming the main hoop, the other running at right angles to it and holding up the fabric at the end of the tent. This does give slightly more room than in tents with just two small hoops. (It also makes it debatable whether this is a hoop tent—it fits best here in my opinion, despite the third pole. Tent classifications are often fuzzy anyway.) With the doors closed the Tripod is very dark, but it didn't prove quite as claustrophobic as I feared. Condensation was minimal—just a small amount on the groundsheet. I could prop myself up on my elbow and read inside, but there's no room for any gear other than some clothes. It's awkward getting dressed and undressed inside, too. In the conditions where I want a fully enclosed tent, I'd like more space—much more space. If I don't need an enclosed shelter, I'd prefer a tarp. These minitents are light, but in my opinion they have more disadvantages than advantages.

The simplest models that can be called real tents weigh from 3 pounds upward for double-skin (or double-wall) models and 2.25 pounds for single-skin ones. The latter can be as light as minitents, but being made from nonbreathable fabrics they're much more prone to condensation, as I found when I tried the GoLite Den 2 (now discontinued), a 3-pound, 9-ounce, two-pole model. The key to stability with tunnel tents is the distance between the poles. Large areas of material between the poles can flap and shake badly, so those with the poles close together are the most wind resistant. I used the 4.75-pound, two-pole silnylon Hilleberg Nallo 2 on a 1,300-mile Scandinavian mountains walk and found it

The Tarptent Scarp 1 with crossover poles at an exposed winter camp.

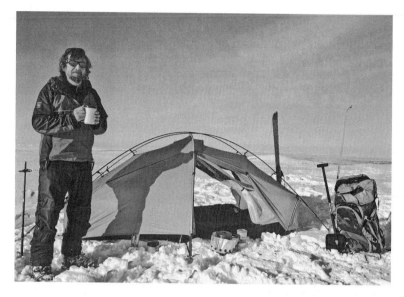

very stable as long as I pitched the rear into the wind. Crosswinds shake tunnels, though, and one night the tent was thrashing about so much I got up about midnight and dashed out into the lashing rain to turn the tent 90 degrees into the wind. The difference was astonishing. Like all Hilleberg tents, the Nallo 2 pitches as a unit or fly first. It's roomy enough for two and very spacious for one. However, lighter options such as pyramid tents like the GoLite Shangri-La 3 and single-hoop tents like the Tarptent Scarp 1 mean I haven't used the Nallo 2 for several years.

The lightest tunnel tents, indeed the lightest tents for the size of any design, are made by Stephenson's Warmlite. These are made of silnylon, and the weights are astounding—the smallest model, the single-skin 2X, weighs 2.3 pounds, yet it's 60 inches wide at the front, 48 inches wide at the rear, 134 inches long, and 40 inches high at the apex, with an area of 42 square feet. There are inside stabilizer straps for use in high winds—Warmlite tents are said to be extremely storm resistant. The lightest double-skin model,

the 2R, weighs 2.7 pounds. Both layers are made from silnylon, and they are permanently linked and pitched together.

I've used the 2X and been pleasantly surprised at how well it performed in wet and windy weather. It has a cunning and effective ventilation system consisting of a large mesh vent at the top of the door with an internal flap that can be adjusted to keep rain out, a small rear mesh vent with an external flap that can be adjusted from inside, and a zipped mesh panel along the base of the tent front. When I first saw these vents, I thought they'd be too small to be much use, but I found that they are carefully positioned so that cool, dry air is drawn in under the door and through the rear vent, pushing warm, moist air out via the top vent. The vents can also be left open in all but the worst weather, too, as they are well protected. In calm, humid weather, condensation still forms, of course, but the size of the tent means it's easy to avoid the walls, which can be wiped down with a small absorbent cloth. Stephenson's says that the 2X is not as condensation resistant as its two-skin

MAKING CAMP AFTER DARK

One day toward the end of the Canadian Rockies walk, I picked a small lake on a watershed for a camp, only to find when I reached it a half hour or so before dark that the area around it was a quagmire surrounded by steep slopes. Circling the lake, I saw there was no place to camp, so I continued down into the forest, my headlamp picking out the trail ahead. For some time I descended a steep hillside where it would have been a waste of time to even look for a campsite. Eventually the trail, which was not marked on my map, reached the valley bottom, crossed a creek, and started up the other side. There was no flat ground, but there was water—the first since the lake—so I stopped and searched for a site. I found one between two fir trees. There was barely enough room for the tent, but the ground was flat enough for me to sleep comfortably. In the morning, my site looked as makeshift as you could imagine—the sort of place no one would dream of selecting in daylight—but it had served its purpose.

tents and that it "should only be used by the 1 out of 3 intelligent enough to avoid needless sweating . . . If you usually can wear a shirt for more than 5 days without sweat odors, you can use the X tent!" The 2X is designed for two people, but I think it's better used as a solo tent because then it's easy to avoid the walls when they are damp. The 2X is very wind resistant in part due to the aerodynamic shape but also because of the large-diameter, pre-curved poles, which do not flex and which are very strong. Pitching the tent is very easy and quick and only requires seven pegs. Just insert the poles into their sleeves and peg it out. Entry into the tent is by a double-zipped flap. The inner zip is only needed if sealing the tent against insects. The flap doesn't tie back, and Stephenson's assumes that when you are in the tent, it will be zipped shut. As I like to only shut tents when the weather or bugs make it necessary, I attached a guyline to the bottom of the door so I could peg it out.

The door opens above the groundsheet, so rain will fall into the tent unless it is closed. That's because there is no separate vestibule, though Stephenson's calls the area below the door a vestibule. The assumption is that you will cook inside in stormy weather—according to Stephenson's, the "conical ends form built-in 'vestibules' for cooking and gear storage." While happy to cook in a vestibule, I am reluctant to do so inside a closed tent. When wet weather persuaded me to try, I found that it's not too difficult because of the size of the 2X. Steam goes straight out of the upper vent when the stove is placed under it, so condensation from cooking isn't a problem. I used a canister stove, probably the safest type for cooking in a tent. I'd rather have a real porch, however, and a shorter inner tent. I didn't feel comfortable having a lit stove sitting on the groundsheet, and I wouldn't recommend this. To provide a little shelter for cooking, I attached a guyline to the corner of the door so I could attach this to a trekking pole and then stake it down.

I've used the Warmlite 2X on several trips and have relished the space inside. I also like the ease of pitching and the superb wind resistance. I only now use it on trips where I should be able to cook outside, however.

There are several tunnel tents suitable for solo use, including the popular Sierra Designs Clip Flashlight at 3 pounds, 6 ounces. Larger tunnel tents often have three poles, sometimes of different sizes, with the largest placed in the middle to give more headroom. These are excellent for two or more people. I've had great success using large

*Single-hoop solo
tent, the Hilleberg
Akto—my favorite
solo tent.*

three- and four-person Hilleberg Keron three-pole tunnels (8 pounds, 9 ounces and 9 pounds, 11 ounces) for group snow camping.

Single-Hoop Tents

The problem with solo tents is that weight and size are related. Length has to remain constant, of course—one person needs the same space to stretch out as two—which means that width and height have to be reduced to cut the weight. In a slimmed-down version of a ridge, dome, or tunnel tent usually you can barely sit up. Stephenson's Warmlite tunnel tents are one of the very few exceptions to this. The solution is the single-hoop tent. As the name suggests, this design features one long, curved pole that may run across the tent or along its length. Single-hoop tents can be remarkably stable for their weight if the guying system is good. Single-hoop tents are available in solo and duo sizes at weights ranging from 1 pound, 4 ounces to 7 pounds, 6 ounces, though most are in the 2- to 4-pound range.

My favorite tent is a single-hoop model, the Hilleberg Akto, that weighs 3 pounds, 7 ounces. I've been using this little tent since the early 1990s, and it's stood up well to many nights of wild weather. Made from silnylon, it has a huge vestibule that stretches the length of one side, a protected vent above the door, and two lower vents at each end. A problem with single-hoop tents is that the fabric can be close to your face when you lie down, especially if you're tall. Hilleberg has solved this with tiny corner poles permanently attached to the fly sheet that lift the ends of the tent a little.

Following the success of the Akto, many companies have come out with similar double-wall tents. Terra Nova offers five different Laser models; Tarptent the Scarp 1, Scarp 2, and Hogback; Helsport the Ringstind Light 1 and 2; Vaude the Power Lizard UL and Power Tokee UL; Robens the Mythos Solo and Mythos Duo; GoLite the Eden 1 and 2; and Exped the Vela 1. Of these, I think the most interesting are the ultralight 20-ounce Terra Nova Laser Ultra 1 and the Tarp-

SHELTERS: MY CHOICE

Which shelter I choose depends on when and where I am backpacking. For the southwest United States and other dry areas, I use a tarp. For forest backpacking or mountains where little wind is expected, I like the GoLite Shangri-La 1 because of the low weight and the use of trekking poles to pitch it. Once more severe weather with heavy rain and strong winds is likely and I'll be using exposed sites as in the Scottish and Scandinavian mountains, a single-hoop, double-wall tent is my choice. My old favorite the Hilleberg Akto is still a great tent and probably the best compromise between weight, performance, and durability. However, the ultralight Terra Nova Laser Ultra 1 is tempting for short trips with very light loads, and the Tarptent Scarp 1 gives the room of the Akto at less weight and has the option of crossover poles for use in snow. In winter, I also like the GoLite Shangri-La 3 as it's so roomy and sheds snow well. I like all four tents, but if I only had one, it would be the Akto.

tent Scarp 1, both of which I've used. The Laser Ultra 1 is the first Cuben Fiber tent from a mainstream company rather than a cottage manufacturer and the first double-wall Cuben Fiber tent. There are short poles at each end to keep the fabric off your face and a vestibule along one side. The inner is made from breathable nylon, the floor and fly sheet from Cuben Fiber. The inner floor is 86.5 inches long, 29 inches wide at each end and 34 inches wide in the center. The center height is also 34 inches. The Akto is a little roomier but 2.75 times heavier. The weight makes the Laser Ultra 1 an astonishing tent. I've used it in rain and strong winds, and it's quite weather resistant. How durable it will prove I've yet to discover.

The Scarp 1 is the first double-wall Tarptent, the company having made its name with ultralight, single-skin shelters. The silnylon Scarp 1 is a four-season tent with two vestibules. Two pairs of short double poles and a single pole at each end support the canopy and add to stability. What really makes the Scarp 1 stand out though are the optional crossover poles, which turn it into a freestanding, three-pole dome that withstands heavy snow loads, something no single-hoop tent will do. Even buried under two feet of snow, the tent held its shape. The Scarp 1 weighs 44 ounces, which is light for a tent that is slightly bigger than the Akto. The crossover poles add another 12 ounces. The floor measures 32 inches by 86 inches, giving an area of 19 square feet. The high point is 42 inches. I've used the Scarp 1 with the crossover poles for winter snow camping and without the crossover poles for three-season backpacking and found it excellent for both. For solo use, it's palatial with good headroom and masses of storage space.

PITCHES AND PITCHING: MINIMUM-IMPACT CAMPING

One of the pleasures of backpacking is sleeping in a different place every night. This can also be one of the horrors if you're stumbling around in the rain looking for a campsite long after dark. In popular areas there are plenty of well-used sites. Take the time to look at such places and work out why they've been used so much, and you'll soon learn what to look for when selecting a site.

There are both practical and aesthetic criteria for a good campsite. A site with a good view is wonderful, as long as it's also comfortable. For a good night's rest you want as flat a site as possible. Often, however, you must make do with a slight slope;

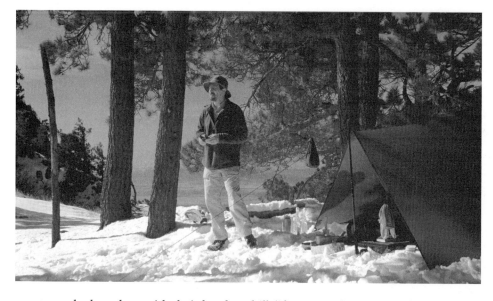

Tarp pitched in snow on a windy forested ridge.

most people then sleep with their heads uphill (if I don't, I develop a headache and can't sleep). Sometimes the slope can be so gentle that it's unnoticeable—until you lie down and try to sleep. I like to check sites by lying down before I pitch the tent. That way I also find any sharp stones or pinecones my eyes have missed. Beware of camping in hollows in wet areas, however, since rain may collect there.

If it's very windy, a sheltered spot makes for a more secure and less noisy camp, though I often head uphill and seek out a breeze if bugs are a problem. Cold air sinks, so valley bottoms are often the coldest spots. Where possible I like a site that will catch the early morning sun, making for a warm and cheerful start to the day, so I look for sites on east-facing slopes and on the west side of valleys.

Water nearby is useful, though in dry areas like deserts I often carry enough for the last few hours of a day and the next morning and have a dry camp. It's best not to camp right next to water; you could damage the bank and you may deter wildlife that

needs access to the water. In many national parks and wilderness areas, the regulations forbid camping within a few hundred feet of water or trails. Camping well away from water and trails is best.

In popular areas there are usually many regularly used campsites, so finding one isn't difficult (finding one that you don't have to share can be harder). When I'm in country where such sites are rare or nonexistent, each morning I generally work out where I'm likely to be that evening and use the map to select a possible area for a site. Usually I find a reasonable spot soon after I arrive. If an obvious one doesn't present itself within minutes, I take off my pack and explore the area. If this doesn't produce a spot I'm happy with, I shoulder the pack and move on. At times, especially when daylight hours are short, this can mean continuing into the night.

When a possible spot turns out to be unusable and I have to keep walking, sometimes tired and hungry, I remind myself that a site always turns up; it may just require a little imagination to make the most of what seems unsuitable terrain. Per-

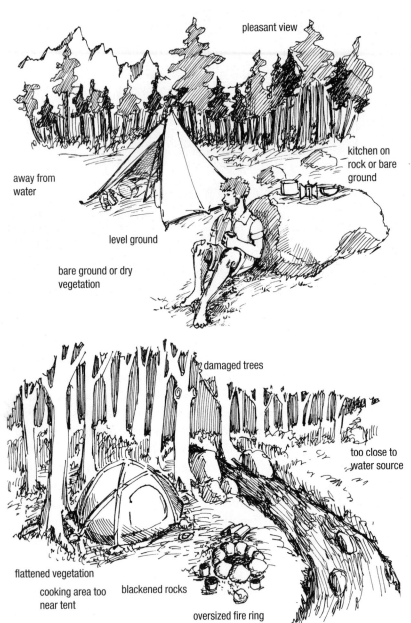

A quality campsite (top) is sited away from water sources and critical vegetation, and shows that minimum-impact methods have been used. Not-so-good campsites (above) are those near overhanging dead tree limbs, in the middle of a field during a thunderstorm, in a canyon, next to water, on soft vegetation, and near avalanche threats.

fect pitches are wonderful, yet many of those I remember best are the ones, like that in the northern Rockies, that were snatched almost out of thin air.

The most important aspect of selecting a site is to minimize your impact and leave the wilderness fresh and untouched, both for itself and for the next hikers.

All sites, whether previously used or not, should be left unmarked, which means no trenching around tents, no cutting of turf, and no preparation of the tent site. Previously unused sites should always—*always*—be left with no sign that anyone has been there. Camp on bare ground, forest duff, or dry vegetation such as grass that will be least damaged by your stay—which shouldn't be longer than one night. Avoid damp ground and soft, easily crushed vegetation. If you'll be staying more than one night on any site with vegetation, move your tent or tents each day to allow the plants to recover. Paths from tents to water, tent to tent, and tents to kitchen site are easily created if you're not careful. You can reduce the number of trips by carrying a water container big

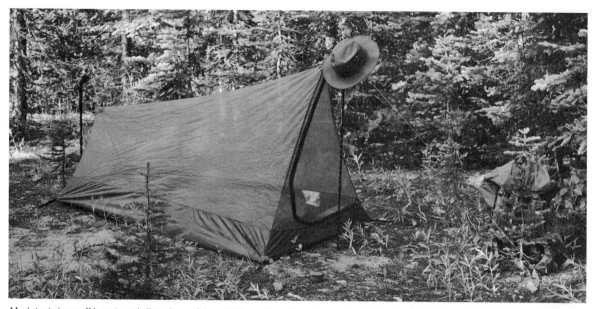

Mesh tents keep off insects and allow views of the outside world and the stars on dry nights—the GoLite Shangri-La 1 Nest.

enough to hold all the water you'll need for overnight. Siting the kitchen so there is bare ground or rocks between it and the tents also cuts down the impact. Wear light footwear, not heavy boots, or go barefoot.

Light fires only if you can do so without leaving any sign of them when you depart (see Chapter 7). If you use rocks to hold down tent stakes—rarely necessary, though often done, especially above timberline—return them to the streams or boulder fields where you got them; I've spent many hours dismantling rings of stones on regularly used sites. When you leave a wild site, make sure to obliterate all evidence that you've been there, fluffing up any flattened vegetation as a last chore.

Of course you'll often camp on sites that have been used before. If possible, I pass by a site that looks as if it's used only occasionally, perhaps stopping to further disguise the signs of its use. A well-used site, however, should be reused, because doing so limits the impact to one place in a given

area. You should still try not to add to the damage, of course. Use bare patches for tents and an existing fire ring for a fire—if there are several, dismantling all but one is a good idea. Tidying up the site may encourage others to use it rather than make new ones. As with every site, leave nothing, and don't alter the natural surroundings.

In some areas, particularly in the eastern United States, land managers have provided wooden tent platforms at many sites. Use them, since they are there to reduce impact. I first came across these in the White Mountains, New Hampshire. To stake tents down you need either very sharp, strong stakes that can be hammered into the planks or, preferably, long lengths of cord that can be attached to stake points, then run off the platforms and staked down or tied to trees. Freestanding tents would be ideal for tent platforms, but I had the Akto, which requires eight stakes. On the advice of a friend, I carried 50 feet of nylon parachute cord, and I used it all.

Camping on a tent platform in the White Mountains, New Hampshire. The Hilleberg Akto is not ideal for this! A freestanding tent would be better.

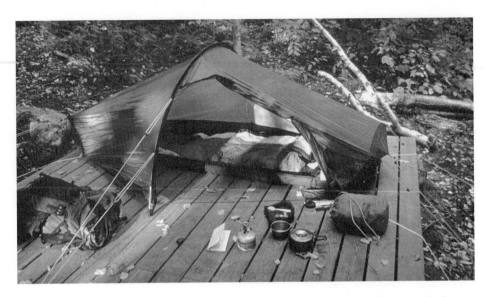

Safe Camping

Wilderness camping is generally safe as long as you have the right gear and the necessary skills. However, there are some external dangers that you need to consider.

In forests, dead trees and branches can fall on your tent; it's always wise to look up when selecting a site and not camp under dead limbs. If there are dead trees nearby, I like to be sure they're leaning away from the tent. Trees don't fall only in storms, either—the only time I've seen a tree come down was on a calm day. I heard a loud crack and looked up to see a large pine topple over and crash to the ground.

Lightning is a hazard at certain times of the year. Camping out in the middle of a large open area or above timberline isn't advisable during summer thunderstorms; you don't want to be the highest object around. On one two-week trip in the Colorado Rockies there were thunderstorms every evening, often lasting well into the night, and on several occasions I reluctantly passed up

scenic timberline campsites and descended into the security of the forest. When a deafening crack of thunder right overhead woke me up and the flashes of lightning lit up the tent, I was glad to be deep in the trees.

Big storms can cause a different and potentially serious problem in desert areas: flash floods. Heavy rainfall in mountains far away can cause walls of water to roar down desert canyons, sweeping away everything in their path. If there are signs of distant storms, I'd be very careful about camping in narrow canyons or at the bottom of drainages that are regularly swept by floods. In many desert areas, summer brings storms that sometimes make camping in any canyon bottom hazardous. I've never seen a flash flood, though I've seen the destruction these floods can cause. There is a dramatic and sobering description of a flash flood in George Steck's *Hiking Grand Canyon Loops* that is well worth reading if you're going backpacking in desert canyons. Steck narrowly escaped when his camp was overwhelmed by floodwater. He lost

It's always better to camp on clear ground than on snow. A spring camp with pyramid and geodesic dome tents.

his tarp, groundsheet, pad, sleeping bag, boots, spare clothing, eating utensils, and walking stick, though he found many items downstream the next day. This book is entertaining and informative and recommended reading for anyone venturing off the main trails in the Grand Canyon.

In mountain areas with permanent snowfields and glaciers, avalanches are a hazard. This isn't usually much of a problem except in winter and spring, but some canyons may be swept by avalanches even in summer. Signs to watch for are treeless corridors below snowfields, bent and flattened vegetation, and large areas of willows and alder—the latter often called "slide alder" because it occurs so often in avalanche zones. These shrubs are flexible enough to survive repeated avalanches.

Making Camp

Compared with finding a site, setting up camp is easy. I don't have a definite routine—it all depends on the time and the conditions. In cold or wet weather, when I'm tired or if darkness is imminent, I pitch my shelter as soon as I stop and chuck in the gear I'll need overnight. I then fill my water bottles, crawl into the shelter, change into warm or dry clothes if necessary, set up the stove, and sort out my gear in comfort while the water boils for a hot drink. (This assumes I'm not in an area where bears could be a problem, of course.) By the time the water has boiled, I'm comfortable in my sleeping bag. The whole operation from unpacking the shelter to taking the first sip can be done in less than ten minutes, though I usually like to do it in a more leisurely fifteen or twenty. The key is knowing your shelter so well that you can pitch it even when you're too tired to think. For greatest weather resistance and strength, pitch your shelter very taut and tighten guylines until you can play a tune on them. This also minimizes flapping and noise. Stakes should be at a 45-degree angle—sloping away from the tent—and pushed right into the ground. If you can't get them all the way in, make sure that the stake loop is at ground level and not around the

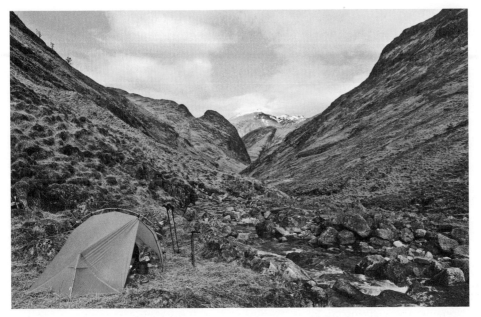

Camp on the only flat spot in a steep valley— Vaude Power Lizard UL.

top of the stake, where it might lever the stake out of the ground if the wind gets up.

When there's plenty of daylight and it's warm and sunny, I may just sit and relax for half an hour before I do anything.

In some places and at certain times, though, setting up camp is not so easy. In rocky terrain where stakes won't go in, you may have to attach loops to the staking points and tie them and the guylines to rocks to hold the tent down. I've done this only a few times, but then it's been essential— it's one reason I always carry a length of cord. In soft snow, tent stakes are nearly useless, but ice axes, crampons, skis, and ski poles can all be used to support the tent, through extra guylines tied to the stake points if necessary.

In snow, I first use skis or snowshoes to stamp out a hard platform; a snow shovel is also useful for this, especially for the final leveling of the site. If you use stakes, loop the guylines around them, then bury them lengthwise and pack the snow

down on top. Once the temperature falls below zero, they'll freeze in place. Come morning, you'll probably need an ice ax to dig them out. You could use sticks instead of stakes. An alternative, which I've never tried, is to fill stuff sacks with snow, attach guylines to them, and bury them. Don't set small items down on the snow when making camp; they could easily get buried. If snow falls during the night, bang the roof of the tent occasionally to make any buildup slide off so the tent doesn't get buried. Make sure there's ventilation high up—open the top of the fly sheet door zipper if there isn't a vent—in case snow seals the gap around the edge of the fly sheet. Brush off snow before getting into the tent, and leave any snow-encrusted garments in the vestibule.

Whatever the surface, pitching a tent is easy— except in wind. You just follow the instructions that come with it. With a new tent, do a practice run first to see how it goes up and to check that all the pieces are there. There are so many ways of putting up tents that detailed advice is impossible. If it's windy, I generally stake out the end of the inner or outer tent (whichever pitches first) that will face into the wind, then thread or clip the poles into position before raising the tent off the ground. In a strong wind, you may have to lie on the tent while you do this. The more the tent thrashes in the wind, the more vulnerable it is to damage, so speed is important. Once the basic shape is established, the rest of the staking can be done in a more relaxed manner. If the site allows, pitch rectangular or tapered tents with the tail or end into the wind; keeping the door away from the wind is a good idea for cooking, too.

Rain is not as much of a problem as wind, though you'll want to get a tent that pitches inner first up fast. If your tent is at the top of your pack you can get it out quickly without letting too much rain into the rest of your gear. You can stand packs up under a tree while you pitch the tent. Once the tent is up you can bring the pack into the vestibule and then unpack items you need for overnight straight into the dry inner tent. You can sort them out once you're inside too. Remember to fill water containers before taking off your waterproof clothing and getting into the tent. It's a pain to have to put it back on to get water. Once the tent is up you need to keep the inside as dry as possible, so leave all damp gear in the vestibule or outside. You can strip off your wet jacket while squatting in the vestibule and then sit at the front of the tent with your legs in the vestibule while you remove wet pants, socks, and boots. Once you're in the tent, put on warm clothing or slide into the sleeping bag so you don't get cold. If your sleeping bag has gotten a little damp, getting into it will help dry it out.

For various reasons—late starts, unforeseen difficulties, a planned site's being full or unsuitable or having a bear around, even by choice—you may occasionally have to make camp in the dark. For this you need a good flashlight or, preferably, a headlamp, especially on dark nights or in dense forest. To avoid losing things, try not to put any gear on the ground where it could be overlooked or kicked aside. Keep everything in the pack that isn't needed in the tent. If you're setting up a kitchen away from the tent and when going to the toilet, make sure you know the way back to your tent. I've sometimes spent rather longer than I would have liked finding the tent again. From a distance in the dark, a tent can easily look like a boulder or a tree stump. Take your flashlight with you and make sure you remember the direction back.

When striking camp, I usually pack the tent last so that it can air out and any condensation can dry. In rain, I pack everything under cover. In very heavy rain you can collapse the inner tent, leaving the fly sheet staked out, withdraw the poles, and then stuff the inner tent into its bag under the fly so it stays dry. Push the poles out of their sleeves; if you pull them, they're likely to come apart. In very cold conditions, pole sections may freeze together—don't try to force them apart or they may break. Instead, rub the joints with your hands until the ice melts. In bitter cold, I wear liner gloves for this so the metal doesn't stick to my skin. If poles are frozen together, chances are that any condensation will have frozen to the fly sheet. If the fly sheet is coated with ice on the inside and frost on the outside, shake off as much of it as you can before you pack it. If the day is sunny and you have time, you could wait for it to thaw and evaporate. Wet tents can be strapped on top of the pack or stuffed into a mesh pocket.

Once you've packed everything, check the site for anything you've overlooked, such as bits of

Airing and drying a geodesic dome tent.

trash, clothes hung over a branch to air, or small items like tent stakes or cutlery.

TENT CARE

Tents look after themselves when you're out walking. On sunny mornings, I try to dry off any condensation, spreading the tent over bushes or on dry ground or hanging it over a length of cord or branch. If the stakes are particularly dirty, I wipe them clean. Most tents come with two stuff sacks for poles and stakes but only one for the fly sheet and inner tent. I always use an extra stuff sack for the fly, because two small units are easier to pack and it keeps a dry inner tent separate from a wet fly sheet. The easiest way to pack tents is, appropriately enough, to *stuff* them into their stuff sacks rather than fold them—if you habitually fold the tent the same way, the waterproofing may crack along crease lines. I always put my tent near the top of the pack so it's accessible for quick pitching the next night. I slide the poles down one of the corners of the pack between the side and the

back. Some people strap poles to the outside of the pack, but I'm afraid they might be damaged there or even fall off and be lost. Stakes tend to work their way down to the bottom when kept in the main pack, so I put mine in a pocket.

After a trip, I hang the tent up to dry before storing it in its stuff sacks. Nylon won't rot, but a tent stored wet will mildew, which leaves stains and an unpleasant, musty smell and may damage the waterproofing. Single-skin waterproof-breathable tents need plenty of drying time; they often appear dry while still damp, since moisture can remain in the slightly absorbent inner material. If you want to wash your tent, use mild soap and warm water, never detergent, which can damage the proofing. Poles will corrode if not dried before storage. Salt corrodes poles very fast, so if you've been camping near the sea, wipe them down before you dry and store them.

WILDERNESS SHELTERS

Many wilderness areas have unlocked shelters for walkers to use. These usually provide shelter from the elements but no more, so you'll still need a sleeping bag, pad, stove, and warm clothing. On some long-distance routes, such as the Appalachian Trail, walkers can use shelters almost every night. I generally prefer the freedom and solitude of a tent or tarp, but in bad weather such shelters can be a blessing. I always like to know where they are in case I need them. It's best not to rely on them, though; they may be full.

SNOW CAVES

In deep snow you can build a shelter rather than pitch a tent. Snow is a good insulator and cuts out all wind; inside a snow shelter it's calm and

Building an igloo with the IceBox tool.

quiet even when a blizzard rages outside. To build a proper one takes a few hours. Ice axes, cooking pans, and toilet trowels can all be used as digging tools, but a proper snow shovel speeds things up considerably.

Whatever tool you use, digging snow is hot work, so it's best to strip off your warm clothing so it doesn't get soaked with sweat. There are various forms of snow shelters—caves, domes, trenches, and igloos. Which you build depends on the terrain. Caves can be dug into steep snowbanks. Start by digging a vertical slot a bit more than shoulder width that goes in at least 6 feet. Then dig out the area around the slot to form sleeping platforms with a lower area in the center that leads to the entrance to act as a sink for cold air. A curved, smooth roof will minimize drips. How big you make the cave depends on how many it must shelter, how much time you have, and how much snow there is. The entrance should slope downward out of the cave and be kept small to prevent snow and wind from blowing in. Make sure you include an air inlet to prevent carbon

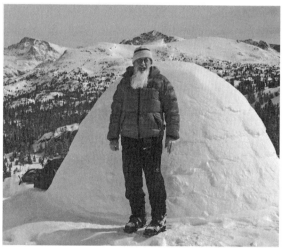

IceBox inventor Ed Huesers outside an igloo in the Wind River Range, Wyoming.

monoxide buildup when you're cooking. It's a good idea to mark the cave too. A ski pole poked through the roof does this and acts as a vent. Wiggle the pole every so often to keep the hole open.

Where there are no steep banks, you can build a snow dome. Simply pile up a huge mound of snow, leave it a short while to harden, then dig out the center, leaving walls about a foot thick. Snow domes superficially resemble igloos, but igloos are much stronger and more complex and require more skill and time to build. There is a tool that makes building igloos easy—the IceBox, a curved form into which you pack snow, and a long handle you use to determine the radius of the igloo and to ensure the snow blocks are positioned correctly. Using the form, you build a circle of snow blocks, each fitting next to the other, until the igloo is complete. The IceBox weighs a touch over 5 pounds and can easily be strapped to a pack. With the IceBox, you can build an igloo with any type of snow, even powder and "sugar" snow. Depending on the snow, it can take two people from two to four hours to build an igloo. Unlike with snow caves, you're not in the snow, either, and so stay dry. I've done two winter backpacking trips in Yellowstone National Park and one in the Wind River Range with an IceBox and also built igloos in the Cairngorm mountains in Scotland. I've had the privilege of making two of these trips with IceBox-inventor Ed Huesers and learned how to make igloos from him. Igloos are now my favorite winter shelter, being roomy and warm compared with the outside—on one night in Yellowstone, it was -9°F outside but 19°F in the igloo without the stove lit and 27°F with the stove going. Compared with other snow shelters, they are also quite light, as the walls are only 9 inches thick so daylight comes through. I wouldn't want to build an igloo every day, but for any snow trip where I stay in one place for two or more nights, they are ideal. And on out-and-back trips, the igloos can be reused. (You can read Ed's accounts of our igloo trips on his Web site under Ed's Trip Reports, "Land of Geysers: Take 2, 2007" and "Wind Rivers, 2009," at http://grandshelters.com/

eds-trip-reports.html and my account of a group Yellowstone igloo trip, "Yellowstone in Winter: An Igloo Traverse in America's Oldest National Park," on the Backpacking Light Web site – http://backpackinglight.com.)

In a storm the quickest shelter to build is a snow trench. Mountaineers high in the Himalaya have survived for several days and nights in body-size "snow coffins." A simple trench can be roofed with tilted snow blocks or with a fly sheet or tarp spread over skis or ski poles and the edges held down with snow. The aim is to get out of the storm as fast as possible. If heavy snow is falling, make sure the roof of your snow trench isn't completely buried and that there is ventilation.

SLEEPING BAGS

Keeping warm at night is essential for enjoyable backpacking. Nothing destroys the pleasure of a trip like shivering through the night in an inadequate sleeping bag. Some people just pile on extra clothes at night, but I've never met anyone who does this by choice (a forced bivouac when you aren't carrying a sleeping bag is another matter), and it sounds both uncomfortable and inefficient.

A sleeping bag traps warm air, which keeps you from feeling cold. To prevent dampness from condensation, a bag must allow the moisture vapor given off by your body to escape, so both fill and shell should be breathable. If you intend to sleep under the stars, a bag with a quick-drying or even a waterproof-breathable shell is best. Even if it's dry, dew or frost may dampen your bag.

Sleep Systems

Sleeping gear just used to mean a sleeping bag and a sleeping pad. Now we have the concept of sleep systems, which means the combination of pad, bag or quilt, clothing, and sometimes, bivy bag that you surround yourself with to keep warm at night. Finding a combination of items that is comfortable and that works well constitutes a sleep system. Although the term wasn't around back then, the first sleep system was probably the Stephenson's Warmlite Triple Bag, which combines different-weight tops with a down mattress (see Quilts and Top Bags later in this chapter).

Fill

Choosing a sleeping bag is much easier than choosing a tent. There are far fewer designs, though there are many models. The biggest decision is the kind of insulation or fill, followed by how warm a bag you need. The ideal material would be lightweight but very warm, low in packed bulk, durable, nonabsorbent, quick drying, warm when wet, and comfortable. Unfortunately, this ideal doesn't yet exist, so compromises have to be made in terms of which properties are most important—determined in part by when and where you'll camp and what shelter you'll use. The basic choice is between synthetic fibers and waterfowl down.

Synthetics

Since the mid-1970s when DuPont launched Fiberfill II, many synthetic fills have appeared; they all attempt to mimic down by being light and fluffy in order to trap warm air but low in bulk when compressed. There are two basic types of fiber. As you'd expect, *short-staple fibers* consist of short sections of fill while *continuous filaments* are endless strands of fiber. Polarguard and Climashield are the two main continuous-filament fills. There is also a continuous-filament ver-

sion of Primaloft, called Infinity. There are well-regarded proprietary versions too, like Wiggy's Lamilite. Polarguard comes in three types, 3D, HV, and X200, of which 3D is regarded as the best for sleeping bags. It has a "high void triangular cross section," which is said to prevent the fill collapsing after extended use. Climashield also comes in three varieties, Apex, CL, and HL, of which Apex is the lightest and warmest for the weight. There are "green" versions of CL and HL, the former with 40 percent recycled polyester and the latter with 100 percent. Original Polarguard and Lamilite are solid polyester. Continuous filament is generally reckoned to be the most durable fiber. I've certainly found Polarguard tough in insulated jackets (see Chapter 5). It's comfortable, too.

There are many versions of short-staple fibers, with new ones appearing frequently. The ones regarded as the best for sleeping bags are DuPont's Thermolite Extreme and Thermolite Micro and Albany International's Primaloft. Older fibers like Quallofil and Hollofil, both from DuPont, are less compressible and less durable and appear mainly in low-cost bags. Proprietary short-staple fills are mostly found in budget bags too. I've found Primaloft the most comfortable of the short-staple fibers. This microfiber is very soft and drapes around the body well. There are three types of Primaloft: Primaloft One, Sport, and Eco, of which the first is reckoned the best.

Synthetic fills cost less than down, are easy to care for, and resist moisture. But they are not "warm when wet," as some manufacturers claim—nothing is. What matters is how fast something dries, and synthetic fills dry fairly quickly, since they are virtually nonabsorbent. Because the fill doesn't collapse when saturated, it retains much of its warm-air-trapping thickness, too. A wet synthetic-filled bag will start to feel warm in a comparatively short time compared with a wet down-filled bag, as long as it's protected from rain and wind. You can't sleep outside in a downpour in a synthetic-filled bag and stay warm, however.

The disadvantages of synthetic fills compared with down are shorter life, less comfort over a wide temperature range, more packed bulk, and greater weight for the same warmth. The latest synthetics are lighter, more compressible, and more durable than earlier ones, but they still don't compare with down. In the long run, down costs less too. One company that makes both down and synthetic bags estimates that with average use, a down bag will last at least twelve years (I have bags much older than this, as do many other people), but a synthetic bag will last only four years. Because down is expensive, awkward to handle, and needs to be kept dry, if a synthetic that performs as well ever does appear it will probably replace down. That day isn't here yet, though.

Down

Down is the lightest, warmest, most comfortable and most durable sleeping bag fill. No synthetic yet comes near down for packability, low weight, and warmth. Down is the fluffy underplumage of ducks and geese and consists of thin filaments that trap air and thus provide insulation. Down recovers well from compression and goes on doing so for a long time, hence the good durability. Unlike feathers, in down there are no quills to poke through the fabric. A single piece of down is called a cluster and consists of a solid point, called a quill point, surrounded by a tangle of fine filaments. Large clusters with long tendrils fill more space and trap more air for less weight than small clusters. Large birds have large clusters, so

down from geese is generally warmer than down from ducks. The more volume a given amount of down can fill, the higher its quality, because the thickness, known as *loft*, determines the warmth. Measuring the volume filled by an ounce of down determines the *fill power*. Down of 500 to 550 fill power (500 to 550 cubic inches of down per ounce) is the least expensive but provides less warmth for the weight than down with higher fill power. The warmest, lightest, and most expensive bags are filled with down of 750 to 900 fill power. Before being tested, down is stored for five days in a large screened box and regularly mixed and blown with a warm dryer. This "conditioning" stabilizes samples for consistent results. An ounce of the down is then placed in a measuring cylinder and a 68.4-gram weight is placed on the down. (One bag maker points out that the weight is more than twice the weight of the down and that this testing procedure ignores the fact that some bag manufacturers use extremely lightweight shells—such as Pertex Quantum—and also that others unduly compress their super-high-fill down with overly beefy shells.) This process means the down is in just about perfect condition when measured. Even so, the results have a margin of error of plus or minus 5 percent. Western Mountaineering, from whose catalog I culled this information, calls the resulting fill power rating "optimistic" rather than "practical" and says that its fill power figures are the lowest its down would produce. In practice the figures can be taken as comparative rather than absolute. Down with higher fill power will be warmer for the weight than down with lower fill power, but it almost certainly won't loft as much in the wilds as under laboratory conditions.

People worry about down's lack of insulation when soaked. Down can absorb a great deal of moisture, and it takes a long time to dry. Drying a sodden down bag outside in wet weather is practically impossible; it takes dry heat. But keeping down dry need not be difficult or a chore, and it's harder to get down wet than many people think. I use down bags most of the time, including in wet places, and I haven't yet had one get more than a little damp. Packing a down bag in a waterproof stuff sack and sleeping in a tent or under a tarp when it rains are the best ways to keep it dry. It's also wise to air down bags occasionally to remove any moisture picked up from humid air or from your body.

If you want the warmth and comfort of down and the water resistance of synthetics, Norwegian bag company Nanok makes a bag with down inside and synthetic fill on the outside. The Airlock -5 has a comfort rating of 30°F and a limit of 25°F. It comes in two lengths, of which the longer 77-inch bag weighs 3.2 pounds. Such bags appear every so often but never seem to remain on the market for long. The one problem I can see is that the down is likely to long outlast the synthetic fill. Using a light synthetic bag as a cover for a light down bag is probably a better idea.

There's currently no legal standard, but sleeping bags labeled as "down" should be at least 75 percent down, the rest being small feathers, which it's impossible to totally separate from the down. Many bag makers use a higher percentage of down. The figures are often expressed in the form 85/15 or 85:15 for 85 percent down, 15 percent feathers. "Down-and-feather" fills should be at least 50 percent down, but "feather-and-down" fill is less than 50 percent down. Feather-and-down and all-feather fills have just about vanished, since they offer no advantages over synthetics, which are easier to care for. The more quills you feel in down fill, the higher the percentage of feathers.

Down is a by-product of the food industry, and most down comes from places where waterfowl are eaten in large quantities, such as China and Eastern Europe.

Owing to the cost of the fill, virtually all down bags are high quality, since it isn't worthwhile to cut costs.

Shell Materials

Sleeping bag shells need to be lightweight, hard-wearing, breathable, resistant to wind and water, nonabsorbent, quick drying, and, for down fills, downproof (so the fill doesn't leak out). Some modern synthetic fabrics have all these properties and feel comfortable next to the skin, making them suitable for the lining as well as the outer shell. Cotton and cotton-polyester shells have just about disappeared, since they're heavier, more absorbent, slower drying, and harder to keep clean. After several months of continuous use, a polyester-cotton inner lining feels sticky and unpleasant—I speak from experience—but because a synthetic liner won't absorb sweat or dirt, it stays fairly fresh as long as it's aired occasionally.

The lightest fabrics allow the fill to loft fully and mold themselves around the body, maximizing the warmth of a bag. Many nylon and polyester fabrics are used, often ripstop versions, and there really isn't much to choose between them. Some shells are made from microfibers (which weigh less than 1 gram per 9,000 meters of fiber). Although the denier is less than 1, this doesn't mean microfibers are lighter than other fabrics; it means that more fibers are packed into a thread, making a fabric that is very windproof and water resistant because air spaces are too small for wind and rain to enter easily. The thread count of a fabric—the number of threads per inch—matters too. Good fabrics have a thread count of 300 or more.

My favorite shell fabric is 20-denier Pertex Quantum nylon, which weighs just 0.9 ounce per square yard yet is hardwearing, downproof, breathable, and very soft and comfortable. It's not waterproof, but moisture quickly spreads out over its surface and dries. There are now many similar fabrics, all of which seem pretty good.

Nonwaterproof shells are highly breathable, allowing body moisture through very quickly, which keeps the fill dry and ensures good loft. They are moisture resistant and dry quickly, but they won't keep rain out for long. Waterproof-breathable shell fabrics are waterproof, but bags made from them usually aren't, since water can enter through the seams unless they are sealed, which is rare. However, new construction methods make waterproofing seams possible, and fully waterproof bags are likely to become more common. The Swiss company Exped makes down bags with high-frequency-welded seams and waterproof Pertex Endurance shells, while Crux makes down bags with sealed seams, waterproof zips, and eVent shells. And with many PHD bags, Gore-Tex shells with taped seams are an optional extra. In each case there are no stitch-holes through which water can enter, so these bags are waterproof.

There are several breathable waterproof or water-resistant shell fabrics, including Pertex Endurance, Gore Dryloft, and eVent, plus proprietary ones like Mountain Hardwear's Conduit and Sierra Designs' Dryzone. I've tried Endurance and Dryloft, and both are pretty good, keeping condensation drips from wetting the insulation of the bag. However, these shells add a little weight (they weigh from 1.7 ounces per square yard upward) and a lot of cost and don't breathe as well as nonwaterproof fabrics, as you'll quickly find out when you try to pack one into a stuff sack—starting at the foot is essential, so air can be forced out the top opening. When damp, bags with these shells take longer to dry, too—it's best to turn them inside out. In really damp conditions, I'd rather use a bivy bag over my sleeping bag. Any moisture is likely to occur between the sleeping bag and the bivy bag, leaving the insulation in the sleeping bag dry, and it's easier to dry a bivy bag. Mostly, though, I find a nonwaterproof shell fine, since when it's raining I always sleep under a tarp or in a tent. An interesting compromise would be a shell of EPIC by Nextec. This silicone-treated fabric is breathable and very water resistant but not fully waterproof. I haven't tried a sleeping bag with it, but I imagine it would work very well. EPIC is used by Feathered Friends and Nunatak. Some sleeping bags and quilts, such as those from GoLite, have waterproof-breathable panels at the foot and head end so that if these are pushed against wet tent fabric, they don't let the moisture in. I've used a GoLite quilt with Pertex Shield Eco head and foot panels and found them useful, especially at the foot end, as on sloping sites, it can be impossible not to slide down the tent and push against the back wall.

The color of your sleeping bag may seem to have no practical relevance, unless you want to sleep out unobserved. However, dark colors absorb heat and dry more quickly than light ones, and any moisture in the fill will dissipate faster. This heat absorption is noticeable to the touch. A black bag feels much warmer than a pale one when both are aired in the sun. Since light colors also show dirt more—one with a white lining looked unpleasantly grubby after a five-week trip—I prefer bags with dark linings.

A mummy-shaped sleeping bag.

Shape and Size

The most efficient sleeping bag is the one that traps warm air closest to your body. A bag with lots of room is a bag with lots of dead air space to heat. Most bags reduce this dead space by tapering from shoulder to foot. Most also have hoods to prevent heat from being lost through the head and at the neck. The resulting shape is called a *mummy bag*. It's the standard shape for high-performance, lightweight sleeping bags and is very efficient at heat retention. Some warm-weather bags dispense with the hood and have a tapered shape sometimes called semirectangular. Actual rectangular bags are fine for warm-weather camping, though heavier than tapered ones. Because they usually have a zipper that runs down one side and across the foot, they can also be used as quilts on a bed. I don't think they're really a serious choice for backpacking though. If you find a close-fitting mummy bag restrictive, a broader mummy is a much better choice than a rectangular bag.

A sleeping bag that is too wide or too long won't keep you as warm as one that fits properly, and the weight will be more than you need to carry. But a bag that is too small will be uncomfortable and won't keep you warm in spots where you press against the shell and flatten the fill.

For these reasons, bags come in different lengths and shoulder, hip, and foot girths. Many companies offer two sizes in each model. Finding a reasonable fit isn't difficult, although very tall and very broad people may find their choices limited, and short people may end up with a bag that's a little too long and slim ones with a bag that's too wide. It's worth climbing into a bag in the store to see how it fits before you buy it, even if you do feel conspicuous. A slightly roomy bag is better than a slightly small one, for both comfort and warmth. Make sure you can toss and turn and lie comfortably in the bag. Check too that the bag will accommodate any clothing you intend to wear in it, such as an insulated jacket in a cold-weather bag. All off-the-shelf bags are a bit of

KEY FEATURES: SLEEPING BAGS

- A good fit. One that is too tight will be uncomfortable, and compressed loft will reduce its insulation; too much room can lead to cold spots.
- An adjustable, shaped hood.

- A tapered shape for efficient insulation.
- A shaped foot box.
- A two-way zipper for ventilation (optional).
- A filled draft tube behind the zipper to prevent heat loss.

hood

draft collar

draft tube (behind the zipper)

foot box

Key features of sleeping bags.

a compromise. If you want a bag made to your exact specifications and requirements, Nunatak and PHD do custom ones. In fact, PHD has an excellent interactive Design Your Own Sleeping Bag program on its Web site that is easy and fun to use. You can select from masses of choices on everything from shell fabric to amount and quality of fill and design a simple ultralight summer bag or a waterproof expedition bag rated to -60°F. The Web site is well laid out, and you make the choices in a logical order and are told if any contradict earlier ones. As each choice is made, an image of the bag changes, as do panels containing the weight, temperature rating, and cost. At any time, you can go back and alter your choices to see what difference this makes. I think this is a fantastic scheme that deserves success. It's of value to

everyone but particularly those who find standard sleeping bags the wrong shape or size.

There's a theory that most sleeping bags are designed for men and may be too roomy at the shoulders and too tight at the hips for many women. An increasing number of bags are now made for women, some with narrower shoulders, wider hips, shorter lengths, and more fill at the foot and across the chest, where many women report feeling the cold. Most bag makers now make women's sleeping bags.

A problem with a close-fitting bag is that it can feel restrictive. Some people like to be able to turn over inside a bag rather than with it and bend their knees and elbows. A good solution to this problem is stretch elastic seams and baffles, as found in MontBell bags and Sierra Designs' Flex Bags.

These bags hug the body closely yet give when you move so they don't feel restrictive. Because the stretch baffles pull the fabric inward, bags with them have a somewhat strange wrinkled look, but they work really well, cutting out cold air spots and reducing air movement in the bag. I've used bags that stretch made by MontBell and the British company Mountain Equipment, and they are very warm for the weight and very comfortable.

An alternative and less effective method is to add a zippered panel to a bag so that the volume can be varied—roomy when it's not too cold, close fitting when it is. Some bags, like Mountain Hardwear's Quantum Expander Switch series, have these panels built in.

Construction

The method used to hold fill inside affects the warmth of a sleeping bag. Down fill has to be held in chambers, which give the familiar ringed or ribbed look, to keep it evenly distributed throughout the bag. To create these chambers, the inner and outer fabrics are attached in sections. The simplest and lightest way of doing this is with *straight-through* or *sewn-through* stitching (also known as quilting). This method is adequate only for bags designed for above-freezing temperatures because heat escapes through the stitch lines and cold air can blow in through them. Most of the lightest bags use sewn-through stitching.

To cut this heat loss, the inner and outer shells can be connected by short walls of fine netting, called baffles, to make rectangular boxes—hence the name *box-wall construction.* If the walls are angled (offsetting the top and bottom stitches), it is called *slant-wall construction;* if they're angled away from each other it's *trapezoidal construction.* In *V-tube* or *overlapping-tube construction* the

down-filled/polyester-filled sewn-through

box-wall

slant-wall

overlapping tubes

double-construction

shingle

Sleeping bag construction.

baffles form triangular compartments. All cold-weather down bags use some type of walled construction. Chambers should have enough down in them so they bulge slightly, creating that familiar well-padded look. If the down can move much in the chambers, it may migrate to the corners or to one side, leaving a cold spot.

Synthetic-fill bags can't use baffle construction because the fill is fixed in layers known as batts. Continuous fiber synthetics like Polarguard, Climaguard, and Wiggy's Lamlite can be used in single sheets in a bag, so no stitching is required. For cold-weather bags two or more continuous fiber sheets may be layered on top of each other. Batts of short fibers need stabilizing, usually by stitching, though Mountain Hardwear melds its Thermic Micro insulation to the shell fabric. Sewn-through construction, as in down bags, is all right for warm weather bags, but for most conditions *double-layer* or *shingle construction* is better. In the first, two or even three sewn-through layers are layered, with the seams offset to avoid cold spots—an efficient method, though it produces a rather heavy bag. In shingle construction, slanted layers of overlapping fiber are sewn to both the inner and outer shells. Some bags are made with a combination of methods—a shingle layer over a quilted one, for example. Whatever the construction method, synthetic insulation should be stitched firmly to the shell at the edges to stop it from tearing away and leaving a cold gap. Down bags also usually have baffles along the sides that prevent all the fill from ending up on the top or the bottom. Some bags dispense with these on the principle that it might sometimes be useful to shift the fill to the top or bottom of the bag to give more or less warmth. I distrust such a construction because the down could move even when I don't want it to. Another construction method I don't like, used in

both down and synthetic bags, places side baffles at ground level so that more of the fill is in the upper section. Other makers simply put more fill in the upper half of the bag. The rationale is that the fill under you is crushed anyway, so there might as well be less of it.

The problem with bags that have more fill in the top is they don't account for sleepers who don't keep their bags the "right" way up. The designers seem to assume that all users sleep on their backs and don't move during the night, although studies suggest that most people turn over many times during the night. I often wake to find the hood above me because I've turned the bag completely over during the night. Just turn on your side, and you can lift part of the base of a bag off the ground. If it has less insulation than the top, you may then feel a chilly line down your back. I prefer to have the fill equally distributed.

The outer shell on most bags is cut larger than the inner; this *differential cut* means that the inner shell has a smaller circumference than the outer shell to allow the fill to loft fully, to cut out cold spots caused by loose extra fabric on the inside, and to stop the fill from being compressed by knees or elbows pushing against the inner fabric. The idea makes sense, but I have to say I've used bags both with and without it and not noticed any difference. These days virtually all mummy bags come with differential cut whereas rectangular ones don't so they can be opened out and used as quilts.

Quilts and Top Bags

If the fill under you is useless because it's compressed, the logical thing is to do away with it altogether. Big Agnes sleeping bags, which come with both down and synthetic fills, do just that, having nothing more on the bottom than a sleeve for you to slide your sleeping pad into. I haven't used a Big Agnes bag, but Ed Huesers of IceBox fame uses a down one for winter camping and finds it warm and comfortable. Rab makes similar bags, such as the 16.6-ounce Module 100, which has down on the top and Primaloft on the lower legs with a pad sleeve on the rest of the base.

Quilts are even lighter than bags with no insulation on the base, as they don't have hoods or sleeves for a sleeping pad. Most are tapered with a drawcord at the neck and have an enclosed foot plus straps to go underneath a pad and hold the quilt in place. These can be loosened or tightened depending on the warmth required. Quilts don't usually have hoods, the idea being that you wear a hat when necessary. Quilts are very light and have become popular with ultralight backpackers. My first brief trials didn't convince me of their worth, but deciding I needed to use one for longer, I took a 25-ounce GoLite UltraLite 3-Season Quilt, rated to 20°F, on the Pacific Northwest Trail. As the coldest temperatures were only 28°F, this turned out to be a warmer quilt than I needed, and I rarely ever tightened the straps under the sleeping pad. (Overnight temperatures were warmer than expected, but I would still have been better off with a lighter quilt like the GoLite UltraLite 1-Season, which weighs 20 ounces and has a 40°F rating, and worn clothes under it on colder nights.) I did find the quilt comfortable, and I could cut out most side drafts by tightening the straps when required, but on the few chilly mornings I missed being able to sit up with it tightened around my chest as I do with a sleeping bag. When I really liked the quilt was on warm nights when I could just spread it loosely over me—as you can with a sleeping bag with a long zip—which is why I prefer a quilt to a bag with a pad sleeve on the base. Because you are not wrapped in a sleeping bag, the surface of your

sleeping mat matters, as any bare skin will be in contact with it. Some foam pads feel quite rough against the skin. Even if you normally sleep fully clad, on hot nights you might want to divest yourself of some garments, so I would still think about the feel of a pad against the skin.

Some ultralight hikers combine a quilt with a bivy bag. I can see that a bivy bag would cut out side drafts, but as the big advantage of a quilt for me is being able to drape it loosely over me, this isn't a sleep system I would use.

As well as GoLite, whose quilts are available with down and synthetic fills and recycled shells, quilts are available from Jacks 'R' Better, with fourteen down-filled quilts covering temperatures from 0 to 40°F; Nunatak, with seven down-filled models with custom options; Mountain Laurel Designs, which makes two Climashield-filled quilts; and enLIGHTened equipment, which makes six down and Climashield quilts, some with Cuben Fiber shells. The last sound particularly interesting, as the Cuben Fiber is waterproof and acts as a vapor barrier. The enLIGHTened Epiphany quilt has an 800-fill-power down fill and Cuben Fiber inside and out. The advantage of the Cuben Fiber is the low weight compared to any nylon as well as being waterproof. However, the quilt as a whole isn't waterproof, as the seams and stitch holes aren't sealed, and it is through these that air is drawn in so the down can loft. EnLIGHTened equipment is a one-man operation making innovative quilts. As the quilts are made to order, you can choose various options, including the amount of fill. There's a weight calculator, so you can see the weight of a quilt with different options. The lightest is an amazing 7.1 ounces with a 1-inch lofting down fill.

Weights of the lightest quilts from other makers are also extremely low. The Nunatak Arc

Edge weighs 11 ounces in the medium size and has a 40°F rating. The Mountain Laurel Designs 45-Degree Spirit weighs 14 ounces in the regular size, the 30-Degree Spirit 18 ounces.

For low bulk and maximum warmth for minimum weight, quilts can't be beaten. However, I like being totally enclosed in a sleeping bag in freezing temperatures and find this psychologically reassuring. I'll continue to use quilts in summer, though.

Making a quilt, especially one with a synthetic fill, shouldn't be difficult. Jake Schas, a hiker I met on the Arizona Trail, simply removed the zip from a sleeping bag. He was pleased with the result and went on to use it on the Pacific Crest Trail. Ray Jardine, who pioneered the use of quilts back in the 1990s, sells a Ray-Way Quilt Kit for making synthetic-fill quilts on his Web site, Ray Jardine's Adventure Page (http://rayjardine.com).

Bottomless bags can be used as lightweight covers to boost the performance of a sleeping bag on trips that are colder than usual. Some companies offer zip-on covers for this purpose, and some bags even come with them. They have the same problem as having more fill in the top of the bag, however—they need to be kept above you to be any use. I should mention Stephenson, which introduced this type of bag back in the 1960s. Its Warmlite Triple bags come with a down-filled air mattress and two removable down tops of 820 to 890 fill power, a thin one rated to 25°F (−4°C) and a thick one to −10°F (−23°C). Combined, they are rated to an astonishing −60°F (−51°C). The tops attach to the bottom with double zippers, so there are no cold spots. I haven't used one, but the bags look roomy, come in four sizes, and are designed so you turn over in them rather than with them. The lining is a soft vapor-barrier fabric. Weights for the total system run from 91 to 123 ounces

depending on the size and the type of pad, but you need only the thin top (16 to 20 ounces) in temperatures above 25°F and only the thick one (26 to 33 ounces) between −10 and 25°F.

Half Bags

An alternative to getting rid of the bottom of a bag is to get rid of the upper half and wear an insulated jacket. This type of bag, sometimes called an elephant's foot, was first developed by Alpine climbers for bivouacking on narrow ledges. One of the few half bags is the 14-ounce 20°F (−7°C) Akula from Nunatak, filled with 800-fill-power down and made with a variety of shells. Nunatak also offers a short quilt, the Arc A.T., that weighs a mere 8 ounces and has a rating of 40°F. I've never used one of these bags, but I imagine you'd want a thick insulated jacket with a hood and a good seal between the two items.

Design Features

Hoods

Because of the massive amount of heat you lose through an unprotected head and at the neck, a hood is very useful in all but the warmest weather. A good hood should fit closely around your head and have a drawcord with self-locking toggles that permit easy adjustment from inside the bag. Most hoods fit reasonably well, though few are easy to adjust from inside. Some have two drawcords so they can be adjusted from both sides. This seems unnecessarily complicated to me, especially when I'm trying to get out of a bag and can't find the toggles. Some toggles and drawcords dangle in your face, which is irritating. Bag makers seem to assume that sleepers will lie on their backs staring upward with their hoods neatly framing their faces. Most people don't sleep like this (I often sleep on my front), and chances are you'll end up with your face pressed into the side of the hood much of the time. If it's badly designed, this will strain the fabric and feel uncomfortable. Getting into a sleeping bag and trying the hood is the way to find out if you can live with it or if it will drive you crazy.

Bags for use in below-freezing temperatures should have large hoods in which you can bury everything but your nose. Bags for warmer conditions sometimes have smaller hoods, or even no hood at all, to save weight. In above-freezing temperatures, I often find the hood too warm and fold it under the bag.

Draft Collars

A filled, drawcord-adjusted collar or neck baffle to prevent drafts is a feature of many bags, especially those designed for cold weather. It lets you close the bag around your shoulders while leaving the hood open. The most basic, lightest bags don't have draft collars. You can drape a shirt or warm top around your shoulders if necessary. Baffles usually have a drawcord adjustment and snap fastenings on the zipper side. I find them restrictive, so I do them up only when it's really cold. Some makers—GoLite, Western Mountaineering—have a smaller filled tube in some of their bags that seals around the face rather than a large collar. This saves a bit of weight, since it requires less material than a draft collar.

Boxed Feet

To keep your feet warm, a sleeping bag should have a shaped or boxed foot section. If the two halves of the bag are simply sewn together at the foot, your feet will compress the fill when they push on it, reducing loft there. A boxed foot has an extra circular section, which could be made either in channels or as a single unit. Cold-weather bags may have an offset double layer of fill in the boxed foot. In down bags, some boxed feet have internal box walls.

Zippers

Almost all bags, except for the lightest down ones, now have zippers, usually on the side, occasionally on the top. For years I distrusted zippers—they added weight, leaked heat, and had the potential for disaster if they broke. I've now developed a grudging acceptance of them, since the latest ones are pretty tough, though I still can see no real advantages. In theory, zippers allow you to regulate temperature and make getting in and out easier. Some bags can be zipped together to make a double bag.

Most bags have full-length side coil zippers. A few curve up toward the top of the bag at the hood to make using them easier. Some bags have short central zippers, a style that used to be standard. To prevent heat loss, zippers usually have filled baffles on the inside, though these may be absent in bags for above-freezing temperatures. Unfortunately, baffles snag zippers. A stiffened, antisnag strip will lessen the number of times the zipper catches, though these are far from perfect. When the zipper does jam, as it will, don't try to yank it free—you could tear the fabric and damage the zipper. Gently ease the fabric sideways out of the zipper teeth. Two-way zippers let you open the bottom of the bag so you can stick your feet out to cool off if you overheat. You could even waddle around outside wearing your bag as a somewhat restrictive, but very warm, coat.

Sleeping Bags as Clothing

Some sleeping bags are designed to allow you to wear them as giant jackets. These have ends that can be opened up and sleeves or armholes. The

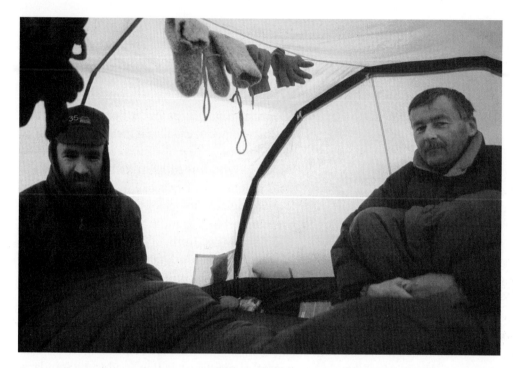

In cold weather, sit in your sleeping bag to keep warm.

down-filled, 20°F-rated Nunatak Raku has insulated sleeves and a drawcord-closed foot. Various lengths and shell fabrics are available. The weight is 32 ounces in the medium size with a Pertex Microlight shell. Feathered Friends' 35°F-rated Rock Wren and 25°F-rated Winter Wren have drawcord-closed feet and zips for your arms. Regular sizes are 27 and 34 ounces respectively. Exped has three Dreamwalker down bags with zipped armholes and zipped or drawcord feet. Weights and ratings are 25 ounces and 45°F, 31 ounces and 35°F, and 39 ounces and 20°F.

Warmth

Temperature Ratings and the New European Standard

Until the 2000s, there was no standard for measuring the warmth of sleeping bags. Makers used their own criteria, some of them very optimistic.

Synthetic-bag makers in particular were inclined to edge up the warmth of their bags to make them more comparable with down ones. Now there is a European standard, known excitingly as EN 13537, which should at least mean that bags can be compared more easily. EN 13537 isn't a legal requirement, but many companies are using it, including in North America, though not necessarily in full or for all their bags, as full compliance is very expensive because it involves many laboratory tests. Due to the cost, several companies are having independent tests done and comparing these with EN 13537. Many companies also give their own rating as well as the European.

EN 13537 gives four ratings for a sleeping bag:

■ *Upper comfort limit:* the highest temperature at which a "standard man" weighing 70 kilograms (154 pounds) should feel comfortable.

- *Comfort:* the lower limit at which a "standard woman" weighing 60 kilograms (132 pounds) in a relaxed posture, such as lying on the back, should be comfortable.
- *Lower comfort limit:* the lower limit at which the "standard man" in a rolled-up body position should be comfortable.
- *Extreme temperature:* temperature at which there is risk of health damage by hypothermia to the "standard woman." A strong sensation of cold is to be expected.

The ratings are calculated with a mannequin with fifteen heating zones to replicate body heat and temperature zones. The mannequin is dressed in a track suit and long socks (thickness not specified) and placed in the sleeping bag on a sleeping pad (again, no thickness given).

Obviously all sleeping bags tested in this way can be compared easily, which can help the buyer. The recognition that generally women sleep colder than men (though this is not true for everyone) is welcome. However, I think the ratings can be very misleading, especially "extreme temperature." Some people, especially novices, may be impressed by an "extreme" rating and think it means they will be warm at that temperature rather than very cold (not everyone reads the small print). Having looked at some EN 13537–rated bags, I would expect to feel cold in them long before the extreme temperature was reached, and I'm a warm sleeper. Overall, I think this rating is meaningless and should be ignored. Unfortunately, some makers are only quoting it for some of their bags. I'm not happy with the upper limit either, as I've been far too hot in several bags at quite a few degrees below the rated temperatures. Many makers omit this rating. The two ratings I think can be useful are the "comfort" and "lower

comfort" ones. Cold sleepers, whether male or female, should look at the former, warm sleepers the latter.

As an example, GoLite's down-filled Adrenaline 3-Season Mummy down-filled bag has a "comfort" rating of 32°F/0°C, a "lower limit" of 21°F/-6°C, and an "extreme" rating of -9°F/-23°C plus GoLite's own rating of 20°F/-7°C. Ignoring the extreme rating, what this suggests is that a warm sleeper should be warm in this bag down to the lower limit and a cold sleeper to the comfort rating.

Other Factors

As a general guide bags with comparable weights of the same type of fill should keep sleepers comfortable over roughly the same temperature range. I'd be very suspicious of any maker that rates a bag as vastly warmer than competitors' bags with a similar weight of the same quality of fill.

No rating system, however, can account for the different metabolic rates of different bodies. Warm sleepers, like me, can use lightweight bags below their rated temperatures; cold sleepers may shiver a summer night away in a bag made for polar conditions. I have a friend who sleeps buried in a four-season mummy bag while I'm comfortable in a summer bag with the hood open. Be realistic about how warm you sleep. It's easy to be tempted by a too-light bag in order to save weight. (A friend pointed out that it's just as easy to be tempted the other way and buy too heavy a bag to be sure of sleeping warm.)

Having tested dozens of sleeping bags over the years, I conclude that ratings for down bags are pretty accurate for a warm sleeper like me, while synthetic bag ratings are usually on the optimistic side. I once tested fifteen bags for a magazine review—eight synthetic, six down, and one a combination down-synthetic. I was chilly in all the synthetic bags at temperatures higher than their ratings but warm at the rated temperature in five of the down bags, the only exception being a bag with no fill on the bottom. The combination bag was also warm at the rated lowest temperature. I measured the loft of each bag. None of the synthetic bags had as much loft as the lowest-lofting down bag; mostly they had half the loft of down bags with the same temperature ratings. Adding five or ten degrees to the rating of a down bag and more to a synthetic one would be wise for many people.

Other factors also influence how warm you'll sleep. Food is fuel is heat, so however tired I am at the end of a long day, I always try to eat something before going to sleep on a cold night; if I don't, I wake up in the early hours of the morning feeling chilly. (If it's warm and I don't eat, I wake up because I'm hungry!) Putting on some clothes is an obvious thing to do when you wake up in the night feeling chilly, but a carbohydrate snack can also help warm you up. If you don't eat, fatigue can keep you shivering long after you expect to be warm. The weather is a factor, too—high humidity means a damp bag (though it may feel perfectly dry), less loft, and conductive heat loss. Thus you may feel colder when the temperature's near freezing and the humidity is high than you do when it's below freezing but dry. Wind reduces a bag's efficiency, as does sleeping under an open sky with no barrier to prevent radiant heat loss. If you regularly sleep under the stars, you'll need a warmer bag than if you always use a tent. Any barrier can make a difference. I've sometimes slept under a tree with the foot of my sleeping bag outside the tree's cover and awakened to find the foot of the bag covered with frost.

Weight

High loft requires more fill, which means more weight. Down-filled bags are much lighter than synthetics across all temperature ranges, from about 1 pound for 40°F (5°C) bags to 2.5 to 3.5 pounds for 0°F (−18°C) models. The lightest synthetic-fill bags start at about 1 pound, 12 ounces for a 40°F bag and 3.5 pounds for a 0°F bag. Based on weight alone, I'd choose a down bag, especially since my experience suggests that synthetic bag ratings are on the optimistic side.

Models and Choices

There are hundreds of sleeping bags. However, it's fairly easy to reduce the choice to a handful of models that fit your specific criteria. I look for the lightest, least bulky bag—which means one with down fill—that will keep me warm when I sleep unclothed in a tent in the average temperatures for the time and place of my trip. If temperatures are cooler than average, I wear clothes in the bag. If, like me, you camp year-round in widely different temperatures, a decision has to be made as to how many sleeping bags or quilts you need and how far you are prepared to stretch the warmth by adding clothes when necessary. A bag that will keep you warm at 40°F without clothes being worn will probably be warm enough at 25°F with the addition of warm clothing as long as there's enough room inside. To be warm in a 40°F bag at 5°F, however, would require wearing thick, insulated clothing, so it would need to be roomy. A good combination is two bags, an ultralight one for above-freezing temperatures and a heavier one with a 20 to 30°F rating, that can be used together in temperatures below 20°F. A quilt could be used over a bag to add warmth, too, with the pad straps used to keep it in position. Not all combinations are comfortable, and some can be hard to get in and out of, so it's best to ensure bags are compatible before using them in the wilds. Big Agnes suggests five of its wider bags as overbags, ranging from the 45°F-rated recycled synthetic-filled Cross Mountain to the 35°F-rated 800-fill-power down Horse Thief, both weighing 27 ounces. PHD also makes a wide down bag designed for another bag to fit inside, the 28-ounce, 23°F-rated Combi.

Some backpackers save weight by planning on always wearing clothes in their sleeping bag. I don't do this, as I want the clothes as backup for those unexpectedly cold nights. When you wear clothes in a bag, there needs to be enough room for them. Squeezing into a close-fitting sleeping bag in a high-loft down jacket will reduce the insulation of both bag and jacket. It would be better to spread the jacket over the sleeping bag.

Light shell fabrics and high-fill-power down mean that 40°F-rated bags need weigh no more than a pound. My favorite current bags of this type (the Rab Quantum 200 I described in the last edition has been replaced by the Rab Neutrino 200, and the weight has increased from 16 to 21.5 ounces) are the Western Mountaineering HighLite and the PHD Minimus, both hooded mummy bags. The HighLite weighs 16 ounces in the medium length—there are three—and has a fill of 8 ounces of 850-plus-fill-power down contained in chambers that are square rather than long and narrow and that have sewn-through horizontal seams and baffled vertical seams. There's a half-length zipper, and the lining is black. The Minimus, which contains 800-fill-power down, has different options for the shell and the zip. The most basic version, which I have, has a microfi-

ber shell and no zip and weighs 16 ounces. Both bags are fine for summer trips when I'm expecting temperatures above freezing. The HighLite is rated to 35°F, and the Minimus to 41°F, but I've found little difference between them. The Minimus is a very close-fitting bag and will fit inside the HighLite, so the two could be used together in sub-freezing temperatures. Most 35 to 40°F bags weigh in the 24- to 32-ounce range. Two of the few others weighing around a pound are the 35°F-rated Nunatak Sub Alpinist and the 40°F-rated MontBell U.L. Super Spiral Down Hugger #5, both of which look excellent.

These ultralight summer bags are fine for warm sleepers like me, but many people will find them inadequate in all but the very warmest temperatures (over 45°F/7°C). Bags in the 25 to 32°F range are only a little heavier and provide noticeably more warmth. Of the ones I've tried, the 30°F-rated MontBell U.L. Super Spiral Down Hugger #3 is wonderfully comfortable, warm, and very light at 21 ounces. It's filled with 10 ounces of 800-fill-power down and has a shell made from MontBell's very thin and ultralight Ballistic Airlight 15-denier nylon, which has a soft, silky feel. It has MontBell's "super stretch" construction consisting of elastic stitching in the baffles. There are also more boxes containing the down than in most sleeping bags, with each horizontal tube divided into six rather than two. The elastic stitching means the bag hugs the body, cutting out cold air spots and retaining maximum warmth, but also moves easily with your body so you can stretch and turn without restriction. I particularly like being able to sit up cross-legged comfortably in it. For a warm sleeper like me, the 30°F-rating is conservative. There are many other good bags in this temperature range, but few as light as the MontBell. Those that are include the 32°F-rated Western Mountaineering SummerLite at 19 ounces and the 30°F rated Feathered Friends Merlin at 23 ounces.

Three-season bags in the 15 to 25°F range are versatile, as they aren't too hot for summer for most people, and they can be extended into winter with the addition of warm clothing. The 23°F-rated PHD Minim 400 at 23.5 ounces is as light as 30- to 32°F-rated bags but noticeably warmer. It's a simple, close-fitting mummy bag with no zip (one is available as an option) that I've found warm at its rated temperature. At the same weight is the 20°F-rated Nunatak Alpinist, which I haven't used but which looks superb. Another bag I have used is the 31-ounce Rab Quantum 400. This 23°F-rated bag kept me warm at nearly 15,000 feet in the Himalaya at 19°F with no clothes on, though I did use a silk liner. The latest version is the Rab Neutrino 400, slightly lighter at 29 ounces and with a lower limit of 25°F. It looks as warm as the Quantum 400. I've used the 20°F-rated, 34-ounce GoLite Adrenaline 3-Season Mummy, filled with 800-fill-power down and with a short central zip, and found it warm and comfortable. All these bags use 800-fill-power down and very light shell fabrics to obtain this warmth at such low weights. Other three-season bags that are light and good quality are the 29-ounce, 20°F-rated Western Mountaineering UltraLite, the 27-ounce, 20°F-rated Feathered Friends Hummingbird, the 27-ounce, 16°F-rated PHD Hispar, and the 36-ounce, 15°F-rated Mont-Bell U.L. Super Spiral Down Hugger #1.

While I mostly like to sleep in little or no clothing, when temperatures are likely to be below 15°F, I prefer to use insulated clothes in a three-season bag (in those temperatures, it's nice not to take clothes off!) than carry a heavier four-season

bag. Also, I often use an igloo on these trips, and igloos are much warmer than tents, so I don't need a bag rated to 5°F or below. Most bags with such warm ratings weigh from 3 to 4 pounds and have around 25 ounces of down. Some of the lightest bags are the 32-ounce, 3°F-rated PHD Minim 600, 39-ounce, 5°F-rated Western Mountaineering Antelope MF, and the 45-ounce, 0°F-rated Feathered Friends Snowbunting plus a quilt, the 5°F-rated Nunatak Arc Expedition with weights ranging from 28 to 36 ounces depending on size and shell fabric. If you're going into sub-zero temperatures, there are bags with amazing temperature ratings at not too heavy weights, such as the -72°F-rated, 60.5-ounce PHD Hispar 1200, which should keep the coldest sleeper warm in most winter temperatures.

I use synthetic bags only when they're sent to me for tests and reviews, but they're the ones most people buy. I find down softer and more comfortable, as well as lighter and more packable. If I were buying a synthetic bag, I'd look for Polarguard, Climashield, or Primaloft, and I'd choose one rated 5 to 10° lower than the temperatures I expected to use it in. I did try a 54-ounce, 20°F (−7°C)-rated Polarguard 3D bag on a nine-day trip and found it warm and quite comfortable, though the coldest overnight temperature was only 36°F (2°C). A down bag half the weight would have been just as warm and much smaller-packing.

Some of the lighter-weight synthetic bags are the 34-ounce, 30°F-rated Integral Designs Cocoon, filled with Primaloft; the 40-ounce, 35°F-rated Big Agnes Elbert, filled with Primaloft; the 31-ounce, 32°F-rated Mountain Hardwear UltraLamina 32, filled with Mountain Hardwear's own Thermic Micro; the 35-ounce, 40°F-rated Kelty Light Year XP 40, filled with Kelty's own recycled fill; and the 42-ounce, 20°F-rated The North Face Cat's Meow, filled with Climashield.

Carrying

Sleeping bags are best carried inside the pack, where they are protected from rain, dirt, and damage. I pack my down bag at the bottom of the lower compartment, in an oversized waterproof stuff sack (see Packing, in Chapter 4). The oversized stuff sack lets the bag mold to the curve of the pack around my lower back and hips and fill the corners. A round stuff sack packed to bursting is very hard to fit in a pack without leaving lots of unfilled space. If I use a synthetic sleeping bag I pack it in an even bigger stuff sack and carry it packed as loosely as possible at the top of the pack, since compression reduces the loft of a synthetic bag. Because they are bulky when packed, many synthetic bags come with compression stuff sacks. These should never be used unless you like replacing your sleeping bag frequently.

Care

In the field, all sleeping bags benefit from being aired whenever possible to let any moisture evaporate. This is especially important with down bags, which can absorb a surprising amount of moisture overnight. It's also a good idea to remove down bags from their stuff sacks a while before you use them to let the fill expand, and to give them a shake before you climb in, which helps distribute the fill. Neither makes the slightest difference to synthetic bags.

Patch small cuts or holes in the fabric with ripstop nylon tape or duct tape to prevent fill from escaping. You can sew a patch on when you return home—just remember to coat the stitch lines with seam seal to make them downproof. If tendrils of down start to work their way through the fabric, don't pull them out, which may enlarge the hole.

ABOVE: Airing a sleeping bag on a tent on a dry morning. RIGHT: Airing sleeping bags on skis at a spring camp.

Instead, pull the down cluster back into the chamber from the other side.

At home, always make sure a bag is dry before storing it and *never* store a bag compressed; prolonged compression may damage the fill's ability to recover so it won't loft fully anymore, reducing the warmth. This affects synthetic bags the most; prolonged compression can destroy virtually all the loft. Bags should be stored so that the fill can loft—either flat, hung up, or packed loosely in a large bag. They need airflow round them, too, so don't store them in a waterproof bag; cotton, polyester-cotton, or mesh is ideal. Many manufacturers provide breathable storage sacks with sleeping bags.

Whatever the outer fabric, the shell should have a durable water-repellent (DWR) treatment. As with clothing, this treatment will wear off in time; it can be restored by low-heat tumble-drying, which also helps break up any clumps the down may have formed. Running a warm hair dryer over the bag could help revive the DWR, too. Ironing should work, but I wouldn't risk ironing a sleeping bag. When the DWR has gone completely, which does happen, you can apply a spray-on DWR treatment. Wash-in waterproofing also can be used, though drying the bag thoroughly—which is essential—is said to take a very long time.

Eventually a well-used bag will need washing. With down bags this requires great care. Down loses some of its insulating properties every time it gets cleaned, so you should do it only when the fill is so dirty that it no longer keeps you as warm as it should. If only the shell is dirty, it can be sponged clean. Synthetic fills may be damaged by washing too, so again do so only when absolutely necessary.

When washing a bag take great care. Down absorbs vast amounts of water, and a wet bag is very heavy; if it's lifted when wet, the baffles may tear under the weight of the wet down, so sliding it into a laundry basket is a good idea. Most instructions say bags should be hand washed in a large tub or else washed in a front-loading machine and dried on low heat in a large commercial tumble dryer to keep the down from forming clumps. You need a special down soap such as Nikwax Down Wash, since detergents strip the natural oils from down and shorten its life. I always send down bags out to be washed by professionals. This relieves me of the task and increases the likelihood that my bag will survive. Many experts think that improper cleaning ruins more down bags than anything else, including prolonged use.

If you decide to have someone else wash your bag, ask for recommendations from the store where you bought it or from the manufacturer. Dry cleaning isn't recommended for sleeping bags, since the solvents can remove the down's natural oils. The fumes from dry-cleaning chemicals are poisonous, too, so any bag that is dry cleaned must be aired well before being used.

Reconstruction

The shell of your down-filled bag eventually may become dirty enough that no cleaning company will touch it. This happened with the bag I used on the Continental Divide walk. It had a polyester-cotton inner shell, which was in appalling condition after 157 nights' use. Cleaners I approached wouldn't handle it, saying the inner shell was rotten and would disintegrate during cleaning. Since the expensive goose-down fill still lofted well and kept me warm, I was loath to throw the bag away, so I had it remade. This cost less than half the price of a new bag and included washing the down. The resulting bag not only was a better fit, since I could specify the length, but it weighed just 2 pounds rather than 2 pounds, 12 ounces because the new inner shell was nylon.

Liners

One way to improve the warmth of a sleeping bag is to wear clothes in it. This keeps the bag clean and extends its life too, because it needs washing less often. A liner accomplishes the same thing but adds weight. Clothes you can wear at other times; liners aren't much use for anything else. I don't really like liners because it's easy to get tangled up in them. Liners come in cotton, wicking synthetics like CoolMax, silk, fleece, and coated nylon. I'd disregard cotton entirely because of its weight, absorbency, and slow drying time. Synthetic liners make more sense—Cocoon's CoolMax Mummy Liner weighs 9 ounces. Silk is really light and low in bulk, and I have a 4.5-ounce Cocoon mummy-shaped silk liner that I sometimes use when weight isn't important. It's what I'd recommend if you really want a liner.

Coated nylon liners form a vapor barrier that keeps moisture in and stops evaporative heat loss. A vapor-barrier liner can add a surprising amount of warmth to a bag. Because drying a bag can be almost impossible in extreme cold, they're useful in such conditions just to prevent your body moisture from condensing inside the bag and dampening it. The liners weigh 4 to 8 ounces. Although I've slept in vapor-barrier clothing, I've never used a vapor-barrier liner. Makes include Integral Designs, RBH Designs, Western Mountaineering, and PHD. Because they're waterproof,

vapor-barrier liners can double as an emergency bivy bag. The converse, of course, is also true.

SLEEPING PADS

No sleeping bag provides much insulation or cushioning from the ground because the fill is compressed under your body weight. In summer weather, some hardy souls manage without a pad, putting clothing or their packs under them if it's cold, but most people, including me, use a pad year-round.

After decades of two basic types of sleeping pad, closed-cell foam and self-inflating open-cell foam, these have been joined by air mattresses, some insulated with down or synthetic fill. Neither of these is new, but modern materials and construction techniques mean they are now viable alternatives. Thickness means warmth, though how much depends on the type of pad. Self-inflating mats are not as warm for the same thickness as closed-cell foam pads and airbeds need to be much thicker than either of them to be as warm. The R-value, which measures the resistance to heat flow, tells you how much insulation a pad provides, though not all makers provide this information. The higher the R-value, the greater the insulation. The 1-inch-thick Therm-a-Rest ProLite 3 self-inflating pad has an R-value of 2.3; the 0.625-inch-thick Ridge Rest SOLite closed-cell foam pad has an R-value of 2.8. The 2.5-inch-thick Therm-a-Rest NeoAir air bed has an R-value of 2.5.

Closed-Cell Foam Pads

Closed-cell foam pads are lightweight, reasonably inexpensive, and hardwearing, but they're bulky to carry. Although they're efficient insulators, they don't provide much cushioning, and you can feel stones through them. These pads are made from foam that is either pressure blown or chemically blown; the first is warmer, more durable, and resists compression better than the second, but the two types look identical, and manufacturers rarely tell you which is which. Various materials are used to make pads—Evazote (EVA), Ensolite, and polyurethane are common ones. The big advantage of closed-cell foam is that's it's waterproof, since the air pockets in the foam are sealed inside, so it doesn't suck up water the way open-cell foam does. Closed-cell foam is pretty indestructible, too, though it can be torn apart by spiny vegetation (and duct taped back together if necessary). In time the foam compresses and doesn't provide as much insulation or cushioning, though it's still usable.

Closed-cell pads come in different lengths, widths, and thickness, and you can easily cut one down to the shape you want. I find three-quarter-length pads adequate, since I use clothes as a pillow and under my feet if necessary. This saves a little weight and bulk. Weights for short pads start at 3.7 ounces for the 18-by-29-inch NightLight pad from Gossamer Gear. The thickest, longest, widest pads can weigh 20 ounces or more.

Most foam pads have flat, smooth surfaces. But the most comfortable closed-cell foam pad I've used, Cascade Designs' very popular laminated EVA Ridge Rest, has a ridged pattern that adds softness and traps air for greater warmth. The latest version of the Ridge Rest is called the SOLite and has an aluminized reflective coating said to boost the warmth by 10 percent. Although it has more bulk than flat-surfaced pads, the 48-inch model weighs only 9 ounces, the 72-inch one 14 ounces. Cascade Designs also makes the Z-Lite, which has an egg-crate pattern

and folds up like an accordion. It comes in two lengths—51 inches at 9 ounces and 72 inches at 14 ounces—and has an R-value of 2.2. The Z-Lite is more comfortable than most closed-cell foam pads but, in my experience, not quite as comfortable or durable as the Ridge Rest. Gossamer Gear's NightLight pads also have an egg-crate pattern, but only on one side. I have the three-quarter-length one, which weighs 7.5 ounces—less than the official weight, which is 9.9 to 10.6 ounces (allowing for variation in the foam)—and is ¾-inch thick. It's slightly softer than the Ridge Rest, which makes it a little more comfortable but also not as resistant to tearing or abrasion. My mat is ragged at the edges and torn in places from being strapped on the outside of the pack. And the rolled bulk means it does have to go outside. Gossamer Gear also sells very thin closed-cell foam pads under the name Thinlight. These come in ⅛-, 3⁄16-, ⅜-, and ¼-inch thicknesses and weigh from 2 to 8 ounces. Such thin mats can be used as extra padding in the back of a pack. I used a similar British pad, the OMM Duomat, on the Pacific Northwest Trail. This pad weighs 5 ounces and is 0.2 inch thick. It measures 32 inches by 18 inches and consists of four pieces of linked foam that can be folded together to form a flat panel. I also had a three-quarter-length air bed and used the Duomat under my lower legs and feet, where I didn't need so much insulation. The Duomat also provided a seat in camp and on the trail on wet ground. While it does provide some insulation and protects against damp, it's not soft, and I wouldn't like to use it as my only pad for sleeping. Another light, thin pad is the Suluk 46⁰ Padded Ground Sheet (see Groundsheets earlier in this chapter), especially if you use a separate ground cloth with a tarp or floorless tent. Because of their bulk, closed-cell pads are normally carried on the outside of the pack, wherever there are convenient straps. In hiking through low, dense brush, however, a pad attached to the side or the bottom of a pack is likely to get ripped, as I discovered when bushwhacking down an unmaintained trail in a side canyon of the Grand Canyon. Before it was totally torn apart, I transferred it to the top of the pack, where it was above the bushes. In forests with low branches, of course, the top of the pack is not where you want to put a pad.

Self-Inflating Pads

Cascade Designs is best known for introducing the first, and in my opinion still the best, self-inflating pad, the Therm-a-Rest, back in 1973, and it has since become the nearest thing there is to a standard pad, though they now have stiff competition from Pacific Outdoor Equipment (POE). I've used a Therma-a-Rest for more than three decades. Self-inflating pads have a tough waterproof coated nylon shell bonded to an open-cell polyurethane foam core that sucks in air and inflates when you open the valve at one corner. That's the theory anyway. In reality it takes a few puffs of breath. Once the pad has reached the desired thickness, you close the valve to keep the air from escaping. Self-inflating pads combine the comfort of an air mattress with the insulation of a foam pad and are relatively luxurious to sleep on.

My first Therm-a-Rest, bought back in 1981, was a 48-inch model weighing 24 ounces. Back then the only choice was between two lengths. Now there's a whole family of Therm-a-Rests, with twelve models, many in a choice of lengths and with weights up to 8 pounds. Therm-a-Rests have become lighter over the years with new con-

Therm-a-Rest NeoAir air mattress.

struction methods and materials. My first model was replaced by the 16.5-ounce UltraLite ¾, which in turn was replaced by a 13-ounce one, and that by the current 11-ounce ProLite Small. Just the weight changed; the measurements, 47 inches long and 1 inch thick, remained the same. My original 47-inch UltraLite lasted through both the Continental Divide Trail and walks the length of the Canadian Rockies, plus many other trips, a total of well over a year's use in ten years, before finally splitting around the valve, where a repair was impossible (the valves used to be metal; now they're plastic and much better attached). The ProLite I now have has die-cut foam with holes through it, hence the reduction in weight. The warmth is reduced slightly too, but I've still found the pad warm on freezing ground. It also has a base that grips well and doesn't slide about on groundsheets. Like the UltraLite it's a great three-season pad but for cold temperatures and snow camping I'd supplement it with a foam pad.

Although slightly heavier than many closed-cell foam pads, the ProLite is much less bulky and can be folded and packed inside the pack, where it is protected from damage. I would never carry a self-inflating pad on the outside of a pack unless

PREPARING FOR BED AND COPING WITH THE NIGHT

There's no right way to prepare for bed, but this is what I do: Once I've selected a campsite and erected my shelter, if any, I lay out my sleeping mat and inflate my pad, if necessary. If the ground is cold and I want to sit on the pad, I generally blow it up rather than waiting for it to expand. Then I pull out my sleeping bag and lay it out on the pad. Depending on the temperature, I may lie on or in the bag while I cook, eat, read, make notes, study the map, watch the stars and the trees, daydream, or otherwise while away the evening until I start to feel sleepy. Then I usually strip off my clothes, get in the sleeping bag, arrange a pillow from a fleece or insulated garment, lie down, and adjust the bag until I feel warm enough. Spare clothes go in a stuff sack, which I place on or in the pack, which is either acting as a backrest, if I'm outside or under a tarp, or lying in the vestibule or just outside the tent. My footwear stays nearby too, as do my headlamp, notebook, pens, books, maps, and water bottle, all laid out where I can reach them easily. Except where bears may come around, my stove, pans, and food are on the other side of me, ready for breakfast.

Most nights don't need coping with because I sleep right through. On very, very rare occasions I've abandoned camp in the dark and fled to a more sheltered spot. Usually, though, storms mean only that I don't get quite enough sleep, and I am glad to see the first gray, distorted edges of daylight through the fly sheet.

But what do you do if you wake feeling chilly long before dawn? First, if you haven't done up the hood of the sleeping bag or have the zipper partly open, adjusting those may do the trick. Almost all nights grow colder as the hours go by, so you may need to adjust the sleeping bag a few times to stay warm. I'm so used to doing this that I barely wake at all; I just fumble with the drawcords and sink back to sleep. The next stage, if you're still cold, is to put on some clothes, especially a hat and socks, and have a snack. You could even fire up the stove and have something hot. Clothing such as an insulated jacket or a rain jacket can be spread over the sleeping bag for added warmth. Don't wear so many clothes in your sleeping bag that you compress the fill; that won't keep you warm. If your pad is only a short one and your legs or feet are chilly, put spare clothing under them to insulate them from the ground. If none of this warms you up, then either you've seriously overestimated the capabilities of your sleeping bag and clothing or the temperatures are extremely cold for the area and time of year. In that case, all you can do is shiver until dawn, with the aid of hot food and drink, then hike out and not make the same mistake again.

When temperatures drop below freezing you need to protect gear as well as yourself. Water containers can be wrapped in spare clothing or even stuff sacks and placed on top of the pack to insulate them from the ground. If you turn them upside down, any ice that forms won't be at the top, so you'll still be able to get water out. If you're sure they won't leak, you could keep water bottles in your sleeping bag; if you fill them with warm water, they'll act like hot water bottles. I also fill my pots with water. If it freezes it will soon thaw on the stove.

Rock-hard frozen boots are difficult to get on and awkward to wear. I store wet footwear inside a stuff

it was in an extremely tough stuff sack. To deflate a self-inflating pad you open the valve and slowly roll the pad up, either on a ground cloth or on your thighs, squeezing out the air as you go. Keep pressure on the rolled pad—I kneel on it—while you close the valve. The deflated pad can then be rolled or folded as you choose. Open-cell foam has a "memory." Leave it compressed for a long time and it'll stay compressed. At home, self-inflating pads should be stored uncompressed with the valve open. This also allows moisture from breath to escape. Breath doesn't harm self-sack on top of the pack or other item so they aren't on the ground and cover them with any spare clothing. If the temperatures aren't much below freezing, this is enough to keep them from turning solid. Placing them next to your sleeping bag helps stop them from freezing too. You can store them in your sleeping bag, though I've never done this—it sounds too uncomfortable. Some people use them as pillows, but when I've tried this it feels too unpleasant to persevere with for long. If boots do freeze, placing

them in the sun can thaw them out quickly. Putting a bottle of hot water in each boot is effective too. Otherwise hiking in them will thaw them out eventually, though it's not fun.

Battery-dependent gear—headlamps, flashlights, GPS, altimeters, cameras—needs protecting from cold too. I keep them off the ground, and if it's really cold in the morning I remove the batteries and store them in my pocket for a while.

extra clothing nearby or in sleeping bag if very cold

boots and cookware in vestibule

stuff sack filled with extra clothes acts as pillow

headlamp nearby

sleeping pad inflated properly

Preparing for bed and a good night's rest.

inflating pads. I always blow mine up rather than waiting for it to inflate.

Apart from Therm-a-Rest, other self-inflating mats come from Big Agnes, Exped, and Pacific Outdoor Equipment. Bozeman Mountain Works' tapered 1-inch-thick TorsoLite is only 32 inches long, but weighs just 10 ounces. I have one of these, and while the weight and low-packed bulk is welcome, I don't find it big enough to be comfortable. However, combined with a closed-cell foam mat, it's OK, and the two together can be used on snow.

Air Mattresses

Traditional air mattresses are very comfortable but also cold, since there's no fill to hold the air in place, so it moves around and conducts ground cold upward. Few traditional air mattresses are still around. But, three decades after Cascade Designs introduced the first Therm-a-Rest and killed off the air mattress for backpacking, the company came full circle and brought the air mattress back with new technology that it says gives better insulation than equivalent self-inflating mats. They are certainly lighter weight. The Neo-Air comes in four sizes: small, medium, regular, and large. The large measures 20 inches by 72 inches and weighs 14 ounces. The ProLite regular, the lightest Therm-a-Rest self-inflating mat with the same dimensions, weighs 16 ounces. The NeoAir folds flat, taking up much less room than the ProLite because, of course, there is no foam inside. The R-value is 2.5, compared with 2.2 for the ProLite. The NeoAir is not self-inflating. You do have to blow it up, and this takes a bit of effort. It takes me a minute and around 25 breaths to fully inflate it.

How has Cascade Designs managed to remove the foam from a mat and yet improve the insulation? There's only air inside, after all, and to increase insulation was why Cascade Designs added foam in the first place, as it stopped the air from circulating and cooling down. The main changes are hidden inside, where the designers have added two key features. First is a mass of airtight cells that minimize air movement, stopping it from cooling down. Second is a reflective barrier in the center of the pad to reflect heat back to your body and cold back to the ground. I was initially wary of the NeoAir, given my knowledge of air mattresses. However, once I'd slept on cold, wet ground in a temperature of 28°F and stayed warm, I was impressed. Leaning on one elbow and compressing the pad, I could feel the cold ground at that one point, but when lying on the pad, I was very warm. The internal structure makes the NeoAir more rigid than the bouncy air beds I remember from the past, and it is very comfortable. The original NeoAir and the slightly less expensive and heavier NeoAir Trekker are three-season pads not warm enough for sleeping on snow. The latest NeoAir is an all-season version, which has a more complex internal structure for added warmth. This adds weight, too, and the three sizes range from 18 to 25 ounces, as opposed to 9 to 19 ounces for the original four models.

POE also produces good air mattresses, and it was one of these, the 11-ounce tapered Ether Elite 6 ⅔ that I took on the Pacific Northwest Trail. I took this instead of the NeoAir because it had thin strips of synthetic insulation stuck on the inside of the tubes in the torso area, which make it warmer. In the mostly above-freezing night temperatures, it was fine and very comfortable. I also liked the oversized outside tubes, as these stopped me rolling off the pad. However, my joy only lasted forty-seven days, as on the forty-seventh night, it sprang a leak, just as stormy weather that would last most of the next month began. I woke in the early hours with the hard ground poking into me. Once an air mattress like this deflates, you're left lying on two thin strips of nylon with no cushioning and little insulation. I spent a chilly dawn forcing a pad that floats and is very buoyant into the cold waters of appropriately named Frosty Lake in search of bubbles that would reveal the leak. Eventually I wrestled the pad under the surface and spotted the telltale signs. The tiny pinhole was along a seam. I covered it with glue from the tiny repair kit supplied with the pad, but the next night, it

SLEEPING PADS: MY CHOICES

For more than eighteen years, I used a Therm-a-Rest most of the time and on all my long hikes. Occasionally I took a closed-cell foam pad on one- and two-night trips, which reminded me why I'd changed to a Therm-a-Rest in the first place. However, when I came to hike the Arizona Trail, I wanted a pad I could chuck on the ground without bothering about cactus spines or sharp stones, so I took a Ridge Rest. I soon found myself quite happy sleeping on stony ground on this pad, and I've gone on using it, or the Gossamer Gear NightLight, as I really like being able to throw it down where I like and not have to worry about puncturing it. It's often said that as you get older, you feel the bumps and hardness of the ground more. I seem to be the opposite. That said, I was seduced by the new amazingly comfortable air mattresses and took a POE air mattress on the Pacific Northwest Trail. When it sprang a leak, I wished I'd had the Ridge Rest and was glad I had a thin OMM Duomat as at least that gave a little insulation. I will continue using air mattresses—that comfort is hard to give up—but not on long hikes unless I have a closed-cell foam pad as well. For snow camping when insulation is essential, I do carry two pads, usually the Ridge Rest and the Therm-a-Rest ProLite, which weigh 22 ounces combined, as light as a single winter-weight pad.

went down again, though only slowly. I added more glue and then a patch, but the leak continued, spreading, I suspect, along the seam. After eighteen days of blowing up the pad every three or four hours each night, I gave up and borrowed an old Therm-a-Rest Ultralite ¾ self-inflating mat, which I used for the last ten days. This didn't feel as comfortable as the Ether Elite when lying in the tent, but I slept on it just as well. Having always carried the Ether Elite inside the pack and only used it inside the tent, I felt I had looked after it well. But it still sprang a leak. From this, I learned that finding a pinhole leak in a pad isn't a simple task and that a repair in the wilds isn't easy to do. And that air mattresses are useless when flat.

The Ether Elite 6 was updated to the Peak Elite AC, which has a radiant heat barrier as well as the insulation and a recycled nylon shell. It comes in three lengths at weights of 11, 14, and 15 ounces. The R-values are 2.5 where there is no insulation and a high 4.4 where there is—POE still only gives it a three-season rating though. I'd say this was about right, having slept on the Peak Elite AC on snow and being just warm enough at 27°F, though when I put pressure on any point, such as with an elbow, causing the mat to compress, I could feel the cold coming through. Big Agnes also makes a range of air mattresses, including ones without insulation, rated to 35°F; ones with Primaloft Eco inside, rated to 15°F; and the hefty Dual Core air mattresses (the lightest of the six sizes, the 72-inch mummy, weighs 31 ounces) with Primaloft and foam inside, rated to 0°F. The most interesting-looking air mattress, though, is the three-season Klymit Inertia X-Frame, which consists of a series of inflatable tubes with cut-out areas between, giving a skeletal look. It weighs 9.1 ounces.

One curiosity with air mattresses is that they can appear to lose some air during the night even though there is no leak. What is actually happening is that the air in the mattress is cooling down and contracting. A few breaths are usually all that's needed to restore it to the thickness you want. If it goes completely flat, then there is a leak.

The most luxurious—and expensive—air mattresses are filled with down. Pump these up (don't use your breath, as it will dampen the down), and they form a supportive and warm bed. Stephenson's Warmlite introduced down mattresses way back in 1975 with its DAM (down-filled air mattress) models. The lightest 65-inch one weighs 20 ounces. Its stuff sack doubles as a pump.

Much more recently, Exped introduced the DownMat Pump pads, which come in five sizes. The lightest is the DownMat 7 Pump Short at 22.6 ounces. This is 47 inches long and has an R-value of 5.9 and a rating of -11°F. The stuff sack, which doubles as a pump, weighs 0.6 ounce. I've tried an Exped down mattress, and it is wonderfully cozy, barely any different to a bed at home, in fact, and very warm. The weight is higher than other pads, but if you want the maximum comfort, a down mattress is the one to choose.

There are also synthetic-filled mattresses that are less expensive but a touch heavier and not as warm as down-filled ones. Exped makes five of these under the name SynMat. The lightest is the SynMat Basic 7.5, which weighs 23.3 ounces and has an R-value of 4 and a rating of 12°F. I've found this pad very comfortable and compact to pack.

Another twist in this explosion of new pad ideas is the Mammut Light Pump Mat, which looks like an air mattress but has foam inside like a self-inflating mat. There's a built-in hand pump that works well, though it takes several minutes to fully inflate the pad. It weighs 22.3 ounces and is 72 inches long. The R-value is 4.1. It's 3 inches thick and very comfortable and warm, as I found when I used it for snow camping.

Care and Repairs

No care is needed for closed-cell foam pads other than wiping off loose dirt and water. Cuts and tears don't matter. Self-inflating pads and air beds can be punctured, however. I don't throw one on bare ground even if it looks smooth and free of sharp objects. I always place an inflatable pad on a ground cloth or in a tent. Even then, a pad can spring a leak, so I always carry a repair kit consisting of nylon patches and glue. These are provided with most inflatable pads and weigh around an ounce. Sticky-backed nylon repair tape can be used too, or even duct tape as a last resort. Finding a pin-prick-sized leak can be difficult, as I found when my air bed deflated on the Pacific Northwest Trail. Immersing the pad in a creek or pool and watching for bubbles is by far the best way. You can also listen for the hiss of escaping air. Even when the leak is found, closing it effectively may be difficult, depending on where it is. I've had two leaks I couldn't repair properly, one around a valve and one on a seam. Those were two of the only four punctures I've ever had, though, and I've slept on inflatable pads on well over fifteen hundred nights in the thirty years I've been using them. Look after your pad, and punctures should be rare. Pads should also be protected against DEET-based insect repellents (see Chapter 8), as these can damage the coating, another reason for not using DEET or at least wiping it off yourself before handling or lying on a pad. Prolonged exposure to ultraviolet light can damage a pad too, as can solvents.

OTHER COMFORTS

Pillows

For a pillow, I simply use a fleece or insulated top stuffed loosely into a large stuff sack (usually the one that holds the sleeping bag). I put this make-shift pillow under my sleeping bag hood so that if I turn over with the bag in the night it stays put. For those who prefer more organized comfort than soft clothing provides, you can get lightweight pillows. Integral Designs make a delightful-sounding Primasilk pillow with Primaloft fill and a silk shell that weighs 4 ounces. Pacific Outdoor Equipment makes pillows in three sizes with brushed micro-fleece covers and foam and synthetic-fill offcuts from pad construction inside at weights of 2.8, 7, and 12 ounces; and Mammut makes some neat 5-ounce inflatable Ajungilak Air Pillows.

Chairs and Chair Kits

Carrying chairs is unusual in the wilderness, though I did once see two hikers with lawn chairs strapped to their towering packs. Rather than carry these, you can adapt a pad with a chair kit. Cascade Designs makes kits for all their Therm-a-Rests, and they'll undoubtedly work with other pads. I have a 12-ounce Lite Chair that fits shorter pads. It consists of a piece of nylon that slips over each end of the mat, with adjustable straps linking the ends. Tighten these straps and the mat folds up so you can sit in it, adjusting the tension until it feels comfortable. Many years ago my companion and I each took one of these devices on a fairly leisurely eleven-day hike in Yosemite National Park, where weight wasn't paramount. It was very pleasant sitting outside in our chairs each evening. However, we both punctured our Therm-a-Rests, despite the tough nylon base of the chairs. I figured I'd have been as comfortable sitting against a tree, a boulder, or my pack, and I've never taken the chair backpacking again, though I do occasionally use it—with the Ridge

Rest—when camping from the car. The latest version by Therm-a-Rest, the silnylon Compack Chair, weighs 6 ounces. Most chair kits weigh considerably more than this.

Some pads come designed to be used as chairs, or maybe it's the other way around. Crazy Creek was first with these and now offers a range of models. I have an Original Chair. It weighs 22 ounces and consists of a 15.5-by-33-inch closed-cell foam pad encased in ripstop nylon with carbon fiber stays in the sides and adjustable straps. It's very comfortable as a chair but a bit narrow and short for a sleeping pad. It's good for car camping, but I've never taken it backpacking.

Hammocks

Hammocks might seem to belong to tropical expeditions rather than most backpacking, but they're gathering a following, mainly owing to one design, the Hennessey Hammock, which was developed for hiking use. The original Hennessey has expanded into a range of models, of which the Ultralight Backpacker A-Sym is probably the best for hiking. (I haven't used any of them.) This hammock comes with netting and a silnylon fly sheet and so will keep out bugs and rain. There's a Velcro-closed slit in the bottom for entry, so you don't have to swing yourself in from the side (and maybe rapidly exit the other side, as I've done when trying out hammocks). The weight is 31 ounces. If there are no trees to hang it from (it has extra-wide webbing so it won't damage trees), it can be pitched as a tent using trekking poles. Oh—it can be used with a sleeping pad to make a chair, too! *A-Sym* is short for *asymmetrical,* and it's designed to make it easy to lie diagonally across the centerline, which is supposed to be more comfortable. There appear to be many happy users, and if I were looking for a hammock, this is the one I would choose. There are plenty of others. Hammocks.com stocks more than three hundred—most too heavy for backpacking, of course—while Speerhammocks.com offers hammocks more suited to backpacking along with kits so you can make your own plus a book on hammock camping. Other companies offering lightweight backpacking hammocks are Treehugger Hammocks and Clark Jungle Hammock. I've only used a basic hammock on roadside campgrounds. If I backpacked mostly in forested areas, I would certainly consider one seriously.

Relaxing in a hammock.

chapter seven

I DISCOVERED A MUSH OF OLD
RAISINS IN A POCKET AND JUST
A FEW OF THESE EACH SOON
PRODUCED THE ZOOM NEEDED
TO DO THE LAST SLOPE.
—*Hamish Brown*

the wilderness kitchen

FOOD AND DRINK

One of the joys of backpacking is taking the first sip of a hot drink at the end of a long day. Often it's the anticipation of that moment that keeps me going for the last hour or so. The tent is up, my boots are off, and I can lie back and start to unwind. I may eat and drink while lying in the tent, a gale raging outside, or while sitting outside, back against a tree or boulder, admiring the view. Either way, this period of relaxation and renewal is a crucial part of living in the wilderness, one of the aspects of backpacking that differentiates it from day hiking.

Food plays a large part in how much you enjoy the outdoors. The possibilities and permutations are endless, so you can constantly vary your diet. Wilderness dining has two extremes: gourmet eaters and survival eaters. The first like to make camp at lunchtime so they have several hours to set up field ovens; they bake cakes and bread and cook

REASONS FOR BACKPACKING

The exact route doesn't matter; we've altered our original plans several times. Time passes. We hear the scolding of squirrels, the screeching of jays, the clicking of deer hooves, the delicate whisper of breezes in the aspens, the trickle of tiny creeks, and the roar of mighty waterfalls. Yes, and the whine of mosquitoes, the buzz of rattlesnakes, and unseen animals in the night that just might be bears. But beyond these sounds—or perhaps beneath them—is a profound silence. When I leave the roaring cataracts of a river to enter a thick grove of massive, ancient conifers, it is as though I've walked under a blanket—so all-embracing, so physical, is the silence.

multicourse dinners. They walk only a few miles each day and may use the same campsite for several nights. Survival eaters breakfast on a handful of dry cereal and a swig of water and are up and walking within minutes of waking. They pound out dozens of miles every day; lunch is a series of cold snacks eaten on the move. Dinner consists of a freeze-dried meal, "cooked" by pouring hot water into the package, or more cold snacks.

Most people, of course, fall somewhere between these two extremes. I lean heavily toward being a survival eater, so you won't learn here how to bake bread or pizza. For that you'll need to turn to an outdoor cookery book, such as Dorcas Miller's *Good Food for Camp and Trail*, Claudia Axcell, Vikki Kinmont Kath, and Diana Cooke's *Simple Foods for the Pack*, June Fleming's *The Well-Fed Backpacker*, Sierra Adare's *Backcountry Cooking: Feasts for Hikers, Hoofers, and Floaters*, Teresa "Dicentra" Black's *One Pan Wonders*, Claudia Pearson and Joanne Kuntz's *NOLS Backcountry Cooking*, Mark Pallis's *Lipsmacking Backpacking*, Alan S. Kesselheim's *Camp Cook's Companion*, and the wonderfully named *Gorp, Glop and Glue Stew*, by Yvonne Prater and Ruth Dyar Mendenhall, in which 165 well-known outdoorspeople give their favorite recipes and tell some kitchen tales. And for those who don't eat meat, there's *Another Fork in the Trail: Vegetarian and Vegan Recipes for the Backcountry* by Laurie Ann March. These books are full of mouthwatering recipes and suggestions. I've been meaning to try some of them since I bought *Simple Foods for the Pack* some thirty-plus years ago.

Which foods are best for backpacking is debatable. At one hikers' gathering I attended, a speaker denounced a certain popular candy bar as "not food" and said that when they reach town hikers should head for the salad bar, not the all-you-can-eat pizza place. Others demurred, strongly. Pasta keeps me going better than rice, potatoes, or other carbohydrates, perhaps simply because I prefer it. I know other hikers who hate pasta and never eat it. What it comes down to, of course, is personal choice. If a certain food helps you enjoy backpacking, then take it with you, whatever anyone else says.

Here I describe what I eat and why. I prefer less-processed, additive-free whole foods, preferably organic, and I am mostly vegetarian. I've been known to eat candy bars at times, however, and I can't resist pizza.

Much of the information below was derived from *Food Facts*, by David Briggs and Mark Wahlqvist, a fascinating volume published in the UK and Australia in 1988 (it is long out of print, but available online at healthyeatingclub.com), and from the Dietary Guidelines published jointly by the U.S. Departments of Health and Human Services and Agriculture (http://health.gov/dietary guidelines).

Hot or Cold?

Hot food provides no more energy than cold food. Cooking food can destroy some vitamins, though some starchy food such as potatoes, beans, and lentils need to be cooked to make them more digestible and, in the case of the last two, to destroy substances that make utilizing their protein difficult. One way to cut the weight of your pack would be to eat only cold food and thus dispense with stove, fuel, and cookware. I've considered this, but I always end up taking food that needs cooking because on short trips the extra weight is so slight that it doesn't matter and on long trips the psychological boost of hot food is wonderful, especially when it's chilly or the weather turns cold and wet.

I certainly wouldn't recommend trying to survive without a stove and hot sustenance in winter, when you may have to melt snow for water and when a hot meal can send waves of welcome warmth through your cold, stiff body. If anyone becomes really cold, perhaps on the verge of hypothermia, hot food and drink are a great help.

Fats, Proteins, and Carbohydrates

Food consists of several components, and the body needs them all. The main ones are fats, proteins, and carbohydrates. All three provide energy but also serve other functions.

Fats release their energy slowly and can be stored in the body to be used when required. Because fats are digested gradually, they aren't a quick source of energy. Your body can't easily digest fats while exercising, either, so it's best to avoid eating a lot of fat during the day. Eating fats as part of your evening meal, however, enables them to release their energy during the night, which helps keep you warm. Sources of fat include dairy products, margarine, eggs, nuts, and meat. The current standard advice is that you should cut down on foods high in saturated fats (butter, animal-fat margarine, cheese, whole milk, lard, chocolate) and replace them with those high in polyunsaturated fats (vegetable-fat margarine, low-fat spreads, vegetable oil) and monounsaturated fats (olive oil). Nutritionists recommend cutting down the total amount of fat in the diet anyway, since fat can have other unwanted health effects. The body needs some fat, but nothing like the amount most people in developed countries eat. However, fats are an important part of the backpacker's diet, especially in cold weather.

Protein renews muscles and body tissue. During digestion, proteins break down into the amino acids they're made from. The body then rebuilds these into muscle and tissue protein. Complete proteins contain a full complement of amino acids; they're most commonly found in meat, eggs, and dairy products. Incomplete proteins lack one or more amino acids but can be combined to create complete proteins; they're found in grains and legumes. Thus a stew with beans and barley provides all the amino acids. The body either burns protein as fuel or stores it as fat if it isn't immediately used for muscle regeneration, so it's best to eat small amounts of protein at every meal.

The body quickly and directly turns *carbohydrates* into energy, so these are the foods most needed by the backpacker. Carbohydrates may be simple or complex. Simple ones are sugars (sucrose, dextrose, fructose, glucose, and honey); complex ones are starches (grains, vegetables, legumes). Generally you should try to rely more on complex carbohydrates, because they provide more energy over a longer period. They also provide fiber, vitamins, and minerals. Fiber is essential in your diet to prevent constipation—a potential problem for backpackers living on dehydrated food. Sugars give you a quick boost when you're tired, but it won't last and you'll feel tired again when the energy they supply is used up.

Determining what constitutes a proper proportion of these components in your diet is a nutritionist's basic reason for being. The current advice from most experts is to eat less fat and protein and more carbohydrates. Most backpackers, especially those who undertake long hikes, will have come to this conclusion, I suspect, because it's carbohydrates that speed you along the trail and that you crave when food runs low. My backpacking menu is probably 60 to 70 percent carbohydrates, the rest split equally between fats and proteins.

Vitamins and Minerals

Vitamins and minerals are also food components, but not ones you need worry about on trips of less than one month. Even if your diet is deficient in them for short periods, it's not likely to hurt you. But on long trips where you lack fresh food, adding a vitamin and mineral supplement to your diet could mean avoiding a deficiency. I've taken multivitamins on most of my long walks, though I didn't do it on the five-and-a-half-month Continental Divide Trail hike and suffered no ill effects. Now I take vitamin C (1 gram) and vitamin E tablets each day (when I remember). Whether they make any difference I can't tell, but they weigh very little, and they just might prevent a deficiency.

Calories and Weight

A *calorie* is the measure of food's energy value. The calorie measurement used in reference to food is the *kilocalorie* (kcal)—it represents the amount of heat needed to raise 1 kilogram of water one degree Celsius. (Kilocalorie, or Calorie with a capital *C*, is the proper term, but it's often referred to as "calorie" on food packages.) Sometimes kilojoules are used instead of kilocalories. There are 4.2 kilojoules to the kilocalorie.

How many kilocalories a person needs each day depends on metabolism, weight, age, gender, and level of activity. Metabolism is an extremely complex system that is not fully understood, but it defines the body processes that transform foods into usable elements and energy; any surplus is stored as fat. If you eat more kilocalories than you use, you'll put on weight; if you eat fewer, you'll lose it. Putting on weight is not usually a problem for backpackers, but losing it may be. The weight that most concerns us is the weight of the food we must carry in order to have enough energy.

People's metabolic rates differ, though generally the fitter and more active you are, the faster you'll burn up food, whether you're working or at rest. Figures are available for the kilocalories needed for "everyday life" for people of different sizes. For someone of my height (5 feet, 8 inches) and weight (154 to 161 pounds), it's about 2,500 kilocalories a day. Of that, 1,785 kilocalories make up the basal metabolism (the energy required simply to keep the body functioning), based on 1,100 kilocalories per 45 kilograms of body weight. To

KILOCALORIE DEMANDS OF VARIOUS ACTIVITIES

ACTIVITY	Kilocalories per Hour	
	128-POUND WOMAN	154-POUND MAN
sleeping, resting, fasting	30–60	60–90
sitting—reading, desk work	60–90	90–120
sitting—typing, playing piano, operating controls	90–150	120–180
light bench work, serving in store, gardening, slow walking	120–210	180–240
social sports, cycling, tennis, light factory work, light farm work	180–300	240–360
heavy physical labor, carrying, stacking, cutting wood, jogging, competitive sports	240–420	360–510
very hard physical labor, intense physical activity, heavy lifting, very vigorous sporting activity	600+	720+

be able to expend more energy without burning body stores, I need to consume more kilocalories, so it's clear that my backpacking menu must provide more than 2,500 kilocalories a day.

You can roughly calculate your kilocalorie needs based on figures that give kilocalorie demands of various activities. I did this when I wrote the first edition of this book. Before that I had just carried roughly the same weight of food on each walk, assuming it would provide the same number of kilocalories. I made the calculations because I was curious to see how closely my field-based figures compared with scientific ones and because the exercise might be useful for others in planning their food supplies.

If we include walking with a pack at the upper end of category 5 and the lower end of category 6, then men need 360 kilocalories per hour and women 240. If you walk for about seven hours a day, not including stops, as I do, that works out to 2,100 kilocalories for a woman, and 2,520 for a man (five and six per minute, respectively). Splitting up the rest of the day into nine hours of sleeping and resting (category 1), which requires 270 to 540 kilocalories an hour (women) and 540 to 810 (men), and eight hours of category 4 (setting up camp, cooking, packing, "slow walking" around the site), which requires 960 to 1,680 kilocalories (women) and 1,440 to 1,920 (men), we end up with totals of 3,330 to 4,320 kilocalories (women) and 4,500 to 5,250 (men). These figures are very rough, of course, but they seem on the high side. You could argue, however, that a lot of backpacking activity falls into categories 6 and 7 and requires more energy than given here, not less.

Those figures seem high to me, because I need only about 4,000 kilocalories a day on trips that will last no more than a few weeks. But these figures are for "average" people, and no one fits them exactly. Even so, such exercises are useful to those who would like to know how much energy they use and where it comes from.

On longer hikes, my appetite goes up dramatically after the first couple of weeks, and I now plan for more food from that time onward. I estimate that on long hikes I average at least 5,000 kilocalories a day. In bitter weather, I may need more because of the cold, and more again on ski tours, because skiing uses up energy at a far greater rate than walking.

Most foods these days have the calorie content listed on the package, which is useful for making comparisons and compiling menus. I always check labels to see if the kilocalories are listed. Unlike many who count calories, I'm searching for *high-calorie*, not low-calorie, foods. The figures in the "Nutritional Content of Some Common Foods" table are taken from a variety of sources, including the USDA National Nutrient Database (www.nal.usda.gov/fnic/foodcomp); *Food Facts*, by David Briggs and Mark Wahlqvist; and manufacturers' specifications.

Based on calories only, these figures suggest that you should live solely on margarine, vegetable oil, dried eggs, nuts, and chocolate in order to carry the least weight. But you wouldn't feel very well or find hiking easy, since these are all very high in fats (fats contain 9 kilocalories per gram, while proteins and carbohydrates have just 4).

The diet I eat of complex carbohydrates (dried skimmed milk, dried fruit, dried vegetables, pasta, rice, oat crackers, muesli, and granola bars), plus a little fat (cheese, margarine) gives about 400 kilocalories per 3.5 ounces. This works out to 2.2 pounds of food for 4,000 kilocalories per day, which is about what I carry. This diet should also provide enough protein. Only a sugar-based diet runs the risk of being insufficient in protein.

It's worth checking the caloric content of any food you intend to carry—there are significant

NUTRITIONAL CONTENT OF SOME COMMON FOODS

Food	Kilocalories per 3.5 Ounces	% Fat	% Protein	% Carbo-hydrate
DAIRY PRODUCTS, FATS, AND OILS				
margarine	720	81.0	0.6	0.4
low-fat spread	366	36.8	6.0	3.0
vegetable oil	900	100.0	—	—
instant dried skim milk	355	1.3	36.0	53.0
cheddar cheese	398	32.2	25.0	2.1
Edam cheese	305	23.0	24.0	—
Parmesan cheese	410	30.0	35.0	—
eggs, dried	592	41.2	47.0	4.1
low-fat cheese spread	175	9.0	20.0	4.0
DRIED FRUIT				
apples	275	—	1.0	78.0
apricots	261	—	5.0	66.5
dates	275	—	2.2	72.9
figs	275	—	4.3	69.1
peaches	261	—	3.1	68.3
raisins	289	—	2.5	77.4
VEGETABLES				
potatoes, dehydrated	352	—	8.3	80.4
tomato flakes	342	—	10.8	76.7
baked beans	123	2.6	6.1	19.0
NUTS				
almonds	600	57.7	18.6	19.5
Brazil nuts	652	66.9	14.3	10.9
coconut, dried	605	62.0	6.0	6.0
peanut butter	589	49.4	27.8	17.2
peanuts, roasted	582	49.8	26.0	18.8
GRAIN PRODUCTS				
oatmeal	375	7.0	11.0	62.4
muesli, sweetened	348	6.3	10.4	66.6
pasta, white	370	—	12.5	75.2
pasta, whole wheat	323	0.5	12.5	67.2
rice, brown	359	—	7.5	77.4
rice, white	363	—	6.7	80.4
flour, plain	360	2.0	11.0	75.0

Food	Kilocalories per 3.5 Ounces	% Fat	% Protein	% Carbo-hydrate
flour, wholemeal	345	3.0	12.0	72.0%
BAKED PRODUCTS				
granola bar	382	13.4	4.9	64.4
crispbread, rye	345	1.2	13.0	76.3
oat crackers	369	15.7	10.1	65.6
bread, white	271	—	8.7	50.5
bread, wholemeal	243	—	10.5	47.7
cookies, chocolate	525	28.0	6.0	67.0
fig bar	356	5.6	3.9	75.4
cake, fruit	355	13.0	5.0	58.0
MEAT AND FISH				
beef, dried	204	6.3	34.3	—
beef, corned, canned	264	18.0	23.5	—
salami	490	45.0	19.0	2.0
salmon, canned	151	7.1	20.8	—
sardines, drained	165	11.1	24.0	—
tuna, drained	165	8.2	28.8	—
SUGARS AND SWEETS				
honey	303	—	0.3	82.0
sugar, brown	373	—	—	96.4
sugar, white	384	—	—	99.5
chocolate, milk	518	32.3	7.7	56.9
custard, instant	378	10.2	2.9	72.6
DRINKS				
cocoa (mix)	391	10.6	9.4	73.9
coffee	2	—	0.2	—
tea	1	—	0.1	—
COMPLETE MEALS				
pasta and sauce	384	4.7	13.1	77.1
vegetable goulash and potato mix	375	11.9	15.9	54.4
vegetable cottage pie	391	3.0	16.3	66.5
thick pea soup	333	5.3	17.0	58.0
bean stew mix	349	2.9	17.5	67.3
fruit and nut bar	420	28.0	17.0	56.0

variations between brands, and high-calorie, carbohydrate-based foods mean less weight than low-calorie ones. For example, I'm glad I don't carry canned fish—as so many backpackers do—since according to the chart the weight per calorie (including the can) is very high. However, I really should give up my coffee in favor of cocoa!

On two- or three-day warm-weather trips, the weight of food in the pack isn't a major concern, and I sometimes take bread, fresh fruit, canned goods, and anything else I find in the cupboard. But in cold weather and on any trip when I have to carry at least a week's worth of food, weight matters a great deal. Unfortunately, you need less food for short trips and more for long ones. I've read of people who get by on a pound or so of food a day without subsisting on margarine and nuts, but I can't—at least not for more than a few days. Skimp on food and you might find yourself feeling lethargic and irritable. You might even pack in the trip without realizing that your low morale was due to a lack of food.

I need about 35 ounces of food for each day on the trail. Powdered drinks, condiments, and other odds and ends are included in this total, which roughly divides into 7 ounces for breakfast, 14 ounces for dinner, and 14 ounces eaten during the day. The main evening meal usually weighs about 7 ounces, the other 7 ounces being made up of soup, dessert, margarine, herbs and spices, milk powder, coffee, and sugar. These figures yield approximately 800, 1,600, and 1,600 kilocalories for the three meals. If the total weight of my food comes to much more than 35 ounces a day, I know I've packed too much, so I jettison some.

This 35 ounces a day equals 15 pounds a week, a considerable weight. Two weeks' food—30 pounds—is the most I ever consider carrying, and I do that only if there's no other choice. Back in 1982 on the Pacific Crest Trail I foolishly car-ried *44 pounds* of food on the twenty-three-day crossing of the snowbound High Sierra, which made for a 100-pound load, because I also car-ried snowshoes, an ice ax, crampons, and cold-weather clothing. My pack was too heavy for me to lift; I had to put it on while sitting down. The weight was ridiculous, and I attempted to carry it only because I had no idea what such a load would feel like. And I *still* ran short of food—probably because of the extra energy I needed to carry all that weight. Never again!

On long hikes and in cold conditions, I keep the weight down to 35 ounces a day by increasing the amount of fat, usually by adding more marga-rine and cheese to evening meals. Polar explorers often eat appalling amounts of fat daily, since it's the only way they can consume the 7,000 to 8,000 kilocalories they need. Eating that amount in car-bohydrates would mean huge loads and never-ending meals.

Dried Food

How bulky food is doesn't matter much on one- or two-night jaunts, but it can be a problem on longer trips. Fresh, canned, and *retort* (cooked food packed in pouches) goods are bulky and heavy, so dried foods are the backpacker's staple for long-haul hikes. Removing the moisture from food maintains its caloric value while drastically reducing its weight and bulk.

The simplest way of drying food is in the hot sun. Because this doesn't remove as much mois-ture as other methods, it's not used for many foods, though some fruits, such as bananas, may be sun-dried. Air-drying, where the food is spun in a drum or arranged on trays in a con-tainer through which hot air is blown, produces *dehydrated* foods. Reconstituted commercial dehydrated foods have a reputation for being unappetizing, because the cell structure is damaged during the process. In *spray-drying*, food is sprayed at high speed into a hot-air-filled cylinder. (This method is used to dry milk, cheese, and coffee.) The most complex and expensive method of extracting the water from foods is *freeze-drying*, where food is flash-frozen so its moisture turns to ice crystals too small to damage cell structure. The food is then placed in a low-temperature vacuum, which turns the ice directly into vapor without its passing through a liquid state (sublimation), again leaving the cells undamaged. Freeze-dried food is costly compared with dehydrated food, but it tastes better. Because the food can be cooked before being freeze-dried, you often just need boiling water to reconstitute it.

HOME DEHYDRATING Many backpackers dehydrate their own food, everything from dinners to fruit snacks. I haven't done this myself, though I've eaten home-dehydrated food and been impressed enough to plan on doing it myself "one day." Home dehydrators consist of racks of trays through which a fan blows heat from an electric motor. There are several models, or you could build your own or even use the oven on low heat (about 140°F [60°C]) with the door slightly open. I've tried dried fruits—passion fruit is particularly tasty—dried tomato sauce, and dried pasta and lentil meals. All were very palatable and quick to cook as long as they were soaked a little while first. Many outdoor cookbooks have sections on dehydrating. Alan Kesselheim's *Trail Food* has comprehensive details, as does Dorcas Miller's *Good Food for Camp and Trail.*

Cooking Times and Methods

The time food takes to cook affects the amount of stove fuel you have to carry and how long you have to wait for a meal at the end of the day. When you're crouched over a tiny stove, exhausted and hungry at the end of a long day with a storm raging all around, knowing your energy-restoring dinner will be ready in five rather than thirty minutes can be very important. Also, as you gain altitude and air pressure drops, water boils at a lower temperature, so recommended cooking times increase—times listed on food packages are for sea level. The boiling point of water drops 9°F (13°C) for every 5,000 feet in altitude; cooking time doubles for every 9°F (13°C) drop in the boiling point of water. At 5,000 feet, the cooking time is twice what it would be at sea level; at 10,000 feet, nearly four times as long; at 15,000 feet, seven times; and at 20,000 feet an agonizing thirteen times longer. These cooking times are for fresh foods, of course; precooked dried food takes only a little longer to cook at high altitude. For meals above 7,000 to 8,000 feet, you need quick-cooking and precooked foods.

These figures are important because most backpacking foods are cooked in boiling water. Since frying requires carrying oil or cooking fat and cleaning the greasy pan can be difficult, I rarely fry food. You can bake and roast if you have a fire for cooking, but I've never done so. Anglers often carry foil to wrap trout in before placing them in the embers of a campfire—the one type of roasting that makes sense to me. Baking can also be done with lightweight portable devices like the Outback Oven and the Bake-Packer. These are so easy to use that I've baked in camp very occasionally, though only with prepared mixes (see Ovens and Baking Devices, later in this chapter).

Many packaged foods—from soups to noodles—don't require any cooking. Just add boiling water and give a quick stir. They usually don't

Five days' supplies. Items in cardboard containers will be repacked in plastic bags.

taste as good as meals that require a little simmering, but I generally carry a few for those times when I want hot food quickly and I'm not too fussy. Most of my meals need five to ten minutes' simmering, a good balance between tasty and fast food.

Cooking times can be reduced by presoaking some foods in cold water. This works with dried vegetables, dried meat, soya products, and legumes, but not with pasta or rice. Some people soak food in a tightly capped bottle during the day so that it's ready for cooking when they reach camp. You can save fuel—though not time—with most foods that need simmering by bringing the water to a boil, adding the food, and then turning off the heat. As long as a tight lid is used, the food will at least partially, if not completely, cook in the hot water. If necessary you can warm it up again on the stove before eating. I often do this when I make camp with plenty of time to spare, then reheat the food when I'm ready to eat.

Making soup in a large mug.

Many freeze-dried meals are prepared by adding boiling water to the packet and waiting five or ten minutes for the food to reconstitute. This can be done with other meals by using freezer bags and saves stove fuel. The bags can be rinsed out and used again. To keep food warm while it rehydrates, the bag can be kept in an insulated bag or pot cozy (see Pot Cozies, later in this chapter).

AntiGravity Gear makes such a bag, the Enertia Pouch, with a reflective inner and a nylon outer and a weight of 1.6 ounces. I've used an earlier version of this pouch with various freeze-dried meals, and it works well. This type of cooking has become popular enough for there even to be a book on it, Sarah Svien Kirkconnell's *Freezer Bag Cooking: Trail Food Made Simple*, and a Web site, Trail Cooking, at http://trailcooking.com. A pot cozy can also be used to allow food to stay hot and to continue cooking in a pot, so again fuel can be saved.

What's Available

A list of foods suitable for backpacking would fill a separate book, so here are just a few suggestions heavily biased toward my own diet.

Suitable foods can be found in grocery stores, health-food stores, and outdoor stores. Prices are lowest in supermarkets, which actually have all the foods you need. Quite a few will be processed foods with additives, however, which may affect your decision. Check cooking times carefully; one package of soup may take five minutes to cook while one next to it on the shelf takes twenty-five. Health-food stores supply unadulterated foods and a wide variety of cereals, dried fruits, and grain bars, though the number of supermarkets selling these items is increasing. Outdoor stores are where you'll find foods specially intended for backpackers and mountaineers. Lightweight, low in bulk, often freeze-dried, and expensive, these are fine if you don't mind the cost.

The best specialty backpacking meals I've found come from AlpineAire (formerly of California but in Montana), whose foods I ate on the Continental Divide walk. Even after five and a half months on the trail, I hadn't grown tired of the food. AlpineAire foods are additive-free, made from wholemeal pasta and brown rice, and include both freeze-dried and dehydrated items. The range includes dishes for breakfast and evening meals, plus soups and light meals for lunch. Recently I've been impressed with Mary Janes Farm organic Outpost meals, which come in brown paper packages that can be burned or recycled. Other brands include Backpacker's Pantry, Natural High, Enertia Trail Food, Adventure Foods, Mountain House, Richmoor, and Harvest Foodworks.

Basic Breakfast

The only hot sustenance I normally have when I'm still bleary-eyed and trying to come to terms with being awake is a mug or two of decaffeinated coffee with sugar and dried milk (combined weight 0.3 ounce), sometimes mixed with hot chocolate. I eat 4 ounces of muesli or granola with water, dried milk (0.3 to 0.6 ounce) and a few spoonfuls of sugar (about 0.5 to 0.6 ounce) unless the brand is presweetened. I have no preference for any particular brand—there are many good ones. If it's cold enough for the water in the pan to have frozen overnight, I dump the cereal on top of the ice, then heat the lot on the stove to make a sort of muesli porridge.

For those who prefer a hot breakfast, instant oatmeal is popular (and very lightweight), and there are various dried omelet and pancake mixes. Of course, you can eat anything at any time of the day. One of my trail companions ate instant noodles for breakfast—not a food I could face at the start of the day. I traveled part of the Pacific Crest Trail with an experienced hiker who ate trail mix for breakfast, which I've tried but find too dry. Another hiker I met on the same walk ate instant freeze-dried meals three times a day for the whole six-month walk, another diet I couldn't contemplate.

Lengthy Lunch

Walking with a pack requires a steady supply of energy, so I eat several times during the day. I often eat the first mouthfuls of "lunch" soon after breakfast, before I start walking. Some people like to stop and make hot drinks during the day, or even cook soup or light meals. I don't, since I rarely stop for more than ten or twenty minutes at a time, and I'm happy to snack on cold foods and drink cold water. Also, the days when I'd most like something hot are those when the weather's so cold or wet that stopping for more than a couple of minutes is a bad idea. In such conditions I'd rather keep moving and make camp earlier. On days when long stops are pleasant, I don't feel the need for hot food.

Trail mix, or *gorp*, is a staple snack food. At its most basic, it consists of peanuts and raisins (hence gorp—"good old raisins and peanuts"), but more sophisticated and tasty mixes can include bits of dried fruit (my favorites are papaya, pineapple, and dates), a range of nuts, dried coconut, chocolate or carob chips, butterscotch chips, M&Ms, sunflower and sesame seeds, granola, and anything else you fancy. I prefer trail mix to be on the sweet side; others prefer a more savory taste. I plan on 2.5 to 3.5 ounces a day. It soon goes. On stormy days I sometimes carry a bag of trail mix in my jacket pocket so I can snack as I hike.

I used to eat several chocolate bars and other candy bars every day, but following the recommendation to cut down on fat and sugar and increase complex carbohydrates, I no longer do

so. Instead, I munch on cereal or granola bars, usually three or four a day.

I also often carry energy bars, or at least a product that has adopted that name since it became popular. Back in 1982 I discovered the California-made Bear Valley MealPack and Pemmican bars, and they've been a favorite ever since. They're filling, packed with energy, tasty, and surprisingly light, at just over 3.75 ounces a bar. They're basically a compressed mix of whole grains, dried fruit, nuts, and soy products with various natural flavorings. They contain all eight essential amino acids, which makes them a good source of protein. I ate at least one every day of the five-and-a-half-month Continental Divide Trail walk, and two or more a day on the three-month Yukon walk, and I never grew tired of them. If I ever do a trip where I eat only cold food, these bars will make up the main part of my diet. There are four varieties: Fruit 'n Nut Pemmican (420 calories), Sesame Lemon Meal-Pack (410 calories), Coconut Almond MealPack (400 calories) and Carob-Cocoa Pemmican (440 calories). Of the other energy bars, I like Clif bars and Balance bars, while Mojo bars are good for a savory rather than sweet bar.

For a contrast to bars and trail mix I usually carry some bread or crackers and cheese or vegetable spread. I like tortillas or pita bread, both of which come in resealable plastic bags. Wholemeal tortillas are best for eating unheated; white-flour tortillas taste uncooked to me. If you carry breads, beware of their going moldy. I took enough pita bread for one a day on a two-week walk in the Grand Canyon. A few days before the end of the trip I was eating one in the dark when a nasty taste filled my mouth—the next day I noticed the green patches of mold on the remaining bread.

Cheese or vegetable pâté spreads that come in squeeze tubes are, for me, a necessity on breads. Meat eaters often carry pâté or salami to go with crackers, while those with a really sweet tooth can take jam or honey, both of which come in plastic squeeze bottles or tubs. I avoid spreads that come in tubs and foil—they ooze around the edges and smear themselves on your clothes and the sides of the plastic bags they have to be kept in.

Dehydrated Dinner

A one-pot dehydrated or freeze-dried meal is the basis of my evening repast. It's possible to concoct such meals at home from basic ingredients, but I prefer to use complete meals, which I doctor to suit my taste. As I mentioned earlier, my favorites come from AlpineAire; all its meals require only boiling water and a seven-to-ten-minute wait. A typical meatless example (the company makes beef, turkey, seafood, and chicken dishes, too) is Mountain Chili (ingredients: cooked freeze-dried pinto beans, soy protein, tomato powder, cornmeal, freeze-dried corn, spices, bell peppers, onions, and salt), which has a net weight of 6 ounces. It makes two servings—maybe: if you're not hungry, haven't been walking all day, and have lots of other food to eat. I have no problem eating all 30 ounces and 680 kilocalories in one sitting. (When searching store shelves for evening meals, I look for dry weights of about 6 to 7 ounces and ignore the number of servings. If the amount is well below 7 ounces, I carry it only if I'm planning on adding extra food.)

When I don't eat freeze-dried meals, I live on pasta-based dinners. Knorr offers a host of pasta-and-sauce meals that are quick cooking and tasty; I know people who've hiked the Pacific Crest Trail using these meals as their main dinners. The staple outdoor dinner, though, is that perennial hikers' favorite—macaroni and cheese. Kraft Macaroni and Cheese Dinner, which is available in several varieties, including an organic one, is the most common brand (ingredients: pasta, cheese, dried skimmed milk, dried whey, salt, emulsifying salts, lactic acid, color). It cooks in six minutes and comes in 7.25-ounce packs, just right for a single meal (the pack says "serves 2–3"). There are several alternatives to Kraft Macaroni and Cheese Dinner. My favorites are in the Annie's Home-grown line, which is quite extensive and offers other types of pasta as well as macaroni. Some of the meals are organic, and some of the pasta is whole wheat. An example is Organic Whole Wheat Shells & White Cheddar (ingredients: organic whole wheat shell pasta, organic cheddar cheese, organic whey, salt, natural sodium phosphate). On the Pacific Northwest Trail, I ate many Annie's pasta meals, as they were available in most grocery stores, and I enjoyed every one. Makers of pasta meals often advise adding milk and margarine or butter to the dish. I add dried milk powder and extra cheese, too.

Asian noodles with flavor packets—usually sold under the name *ramen*—cook in about four minutes and are a good alternative to macaroni and cheese. Sadly, Westbrae Ramens, my favorites, have been discontinued. Ramen noodle packets usually weigh 3 to 4 ounces and make 9 ounces of cooked food. I use two packages of noodles per meal and add a packet of dehydrated soup mix, cheese, and dried milk to make a full meal.

An alternative to pasta is instant potato. I like to carry a few packets of this, as it just needs boiling water added rather than six to ten minutes simmering like pasta. At the end of very long days, I sometimes want a meal as quickly as possible. I particularly like the Idahoan brand, of which I ate quite a few on the Pacific Northwest Trail, as it was available in most grocery stores (which is hardly surprising as the PNT crosses Idaho). There are several varieties, all available in convenient pouches, of which my favorite is the Southwest Mashed Potatoes, which has jalapeño peppers in it and a good, sharp flavor. Each pouch contains four servings according to the label, but the total calorie count when reconstituted is only around 440 calories, so I add cheese and dried milk and eat the lot as one meal. The ingredients list does contain rather a lot of chemicals, but I'm prepared to eat these occasionally on the trail.

If I do make up my own meals, they're usually based on macaroni or other pasta as a base, to which I add dehydrated soup mix, such as onion or tomato, plus cheese sliced up with my pocket-knife. These are so easy to prepare that I do it in camp rather than at home. Almost every night of the eighty-six-day Scandinavian mountain hike, I dined on quick-cooking macaroni mixed with dried soup, dried milk, and cheese, plus flavorings.

There are various ways to enhance the taste of any meal. Herbs and spices, soup mix, or cheese are popular additions. I carry garlic powder (fresh cloves on short trips), curry or chili powder, black pepper, and mixed herbs (but not salt—there's usually plenty in dried food anyway). Margarine, cheese, and milk powder add kilocalories as well as taste and bulk to meals. Soup mixes can be the sauce for a meal with pasta or rice, with cheese, dried milk, and other ingredients added to increase the food value. I often mix foods on the last few evenings of a long trip, using up whatever I have left. If I'm buying pasta or rice to add to soup, I look for quick-cooking varieties.

I usually eat a bowl of soup before having my main meal, unless I'm very hungry. The mixes that require simmering for five or ten minutes taste best (I like Knorr), but instant soups require less time and fuel to prepare. The biggest problem with them is the serving size—often a meager 7 ounces when rehydrated, and only 118 kilocalories. I solve this problem by eating two packages at a time (2 ounces total dry weight). Again, adding margarine and cheese increases the energy content.

I always carry dried milk and usually cheese. I used to always carry margarine, usually Parkay or other liquid margarine in a squeeze bottles (weight about 16 ounces), since these are less messy and easier to use than tub varieties, but I stopped taking it many years ago and haven't missed it. With cheese I plan on 2 ounces a day and twice that if it's a main part of a meal. On long trips I use up any cheese in the first few days, so I eat the lowest-calorie meals I'm carrying then. Instant nonfat dry milk adds taste and calories to any dish, and is also good with breakfast cereal and tea or coffee. My one-time favorite Milkman Instant Milk is no longer available. I now prefer Organic Valley Nonfat Dry Milk, though this does need mixing with water before adding to meals or drinks to prevent it from going lumpy. Organic Valley milk comes in convenient zip-close pouches. Each pouch holds 12 ounces of milk powder, which makes around 5 to 6 pints of milk, depending on how rich you like it. Whatever the brand, I prefer dried milk powder that doesn't contain additives. A standard 7-ounce pack of instant milk will make 3.52 pints and last me at least four or five days.

Coffee with sugar, hot chocolate, and hot, spiced cider are my choices for evening drinks. A couple of mugs of coffee an evening means carrying 0.75 ounce of sugar and 0.2 ounce of instant coffee per day. I don't drink tea, but those who do seem to find a large supply of tea bags essential—though an amazing number of mugs can be wrung from just one bag when supplies run low. Hot chocolate supplies plenty of energy—unlike coffee or tea—and comes in convenient envelopes. It's particularly nice on cold evenings as a warming bedtime drink. I also like hot spiced cider drinks in mug-sized envelopes, and I now often drink one or two of these in the evening instead of coffee.

Variations

There are variations, of course, on what food can be taken on any backpacking outing. On two- or three-day trips, I sometimes pack sandwiches for each day's lunch. Retort foods are feasible then, too—they're lighter and tastier than canned goods, though heavier and bulkier than dried ones.

Cold-weather and winter hikes in northern latitudes call for a big change in my diet. Fewer daylight hours mean more time spent in camp and less on the move, while colder temperatures mean a need for more kilocalories—so I take slightly less food for daytime but more for the evening. In particular, I usually add some sort of dessert as a third course; hot instant custard with dried fruit is a favorite. A 3-ounce package provides 350 to 400 kilocalories even before you add dried fruit. Cold instant puddings are also a good way to pile on calories; preparation time can be speeded up by burying them in the snow to set.

Emergency Supplies

Many years ago I carried a foil-wrapped block of compressed emergency rations, called Turblokken, at the bottom of my pack, assuming that it would keep me going if I ran out of food. I finally ate it once when my supplies ran low and I didn't want to detour to resupply. My journal records that it was "fairly tasteless but kept me going."

In case I ran low again, I then started carrying an extra day's worth of food. However, it's many years since I did that. Now I just carry a little extra food, such as an extra Bear Valley bar or two. If you can catch fish or know which insects and plants are edible, you can, of course, try to "live off the land."

I've only once run out of food in an area so remote that I couldn't walk out to a supply point in a day or two. My situation was complicated because I was a bit unclear about where I was (notice I didn't say "lost"). I had to ration my food severely for several days and emerged from the forest extremely hungry, but without having run out of energy. I learned that, if you have to, you can get by on remarkably little food—at least for a short time. I would go to great lengths to avoid another such situation, though. Once is more than enough.

Packaging

Plastic bags are ideal for carrying food. I use them for everything that comes in a heavy container I don't want to carry or that needs extra protection, including coffee, sugar, dried milk, trail mix, muesli, cheese, herbs, spices, and meals such as macaroni and cheese that come in cardboard boxes. If I need the instructions, I tear them off and put them in the bag with the food. The only items I keep in their cardboard containers are crackers, since these break easily. Cardboard gives a surprising amount of protection, but you need to be careful not to crush them. Packages of soup, granola bars, and complete meals in sealed envelopes don't need repacking, but they can be bagged together so that it's easy to see what you have. Bagging also serves as extra protection against tears in the envelopes, which can happen. The best bags I've found are zippered ones like

By not carrying cans and by repackaging food packed in cardboard in plastic bags, I could fit all my trash from a ten-day trip into these two used food packets.

Ziplocs. I always carry a few spare bags in case one splits.

Hiking stores carry many plastic food containers, but I don't use them—they take up as much space empty as they do full and add weight; plastic bags compress to almost nothing and weigh hardly anything. I used to carry herbs and spices in empty plastic film canisters, but now these go in plastic bags too.

Unless I'm using a bear-resistant container, I keep my food together in the pack in nylon stuff sacks. When I'm carrying more than a week's food, I use two of them. I put day food, which tends to be the bulkiest of my rations, in one bag, and camp food in the other. Two smaller bags are easier to pack than one large one, and it's easier to find items.

Resupply

On trips of up to a week, resupplying isn't necessary; you can carry all you need unless your route passes through a place where you can buy food. On hikes that last more than a couple of weeks, you have to plan how to resupply. If you're prepared to live on whatever is available locally, you can shop at stores on or near your route. I did this on the Arizona Trail and the Pacific Northwest Trail and it worked quite well, though a few times there wasn't much choice. Most small stores stock dried soups, crackers, bread, cheese, candy, chocolate bars, coffee, and tea, but dried meals and even breakfast cereals can be hard to find. This can mean carrying more weight and bulk than you'd like and being prepared to adapt to what you can get.

An alternative is to send supplies to yourself to be collected along the way. This way, you know what's in each supply box and can plan accurately; items such as maps and chargers for electronic devices can also be included in the same boxes. As well as boxes sent out ahead from home a *running supply* or *bounce box* is useful. This is a box you send on to the next post office with stuff you don't need for the next section of trail. If you can only buy larger amounts of foods than you need, the surplus can go in the running supply box, as can extras of any food you really like that you might not be able to purchase again. The obvious places to send supplies are post offices. Boxes should be addressed to yourself *c/o General Delivery* (*Poste Restante* in Europe) in the town scheduled for pickup. They should be marked *Hold for Hiker* and include the intended collection date and a return address. I also write to the post offices to tell them what I'm doing. It's a good idea to phone ahead (if you can) to check that the supplies have arrived; during the Canadian Rockies walk, one box went astray, causing me a week's delay. On the Pacific Northwest Trail, I had a 300-mile section without any towns or grocery stores that I knew would take around eighteen days. I didn't want to carry food for that length of time, but to buy supplies, I would have had to travel some way off the trail, which would have added a day or two to the trip and, more important, broken the wilderness feel of such a long period between towns. However, Ross Lake Resort, a small resort in floating cabins on the lake, holds parcels for hikers, so I was able to send supplies there and only carry nine days food at a time. Such places are a boon to long-distance hikers and deserve our thanks.

Some mail-order food suppliers may drop-ship food to post offices along your route, a service I used on the Pacific Crest and Continental Divide Trails. In remote areas where there are no post offices, you could contact a park or forest ranger's office, or the nearest youth hostel, lodge, or motel, to ask if they'll hold supplies. I've done this several times and never yet been refused, though some of the latter places request a small fee (I always offer payment when I contact them). Rangers or outfitters may also be prepared to take food into wilderness cabins or camps if you're on a long trip. When I walked through the Yukon Territory, I found a commercial tour boat operator who was willing to take supplies down the Yukon River for me, which meant I was able to walk for twenty-three days without having to leave the wilderness to resupply.

You can cache food in advance if you have the time or have someone who can do it for you, though I've never done this. Obviously, cached food has to be stored in an animal-proof container, and you need to be sure you can locate it.

Another resupply alternative is to have food dropped by helicopter or brought in by bush plane. I considered this for the remote northern section of the Canadian Rockies walk but rejected it, mainly because of the high cost, but also because I wasn't happy about bringing noisy machines into the wilderness unless it was absolutely necessary. Instead, I tried to carry all my food for this three-hundred-mile section. I took seventeen days' food but spent twenty-three in the wilderness. Luckily it was hunting season, and the seasonal occupants of several remote outfitters' camps fed me as I passed through. Without them I couldn't have completed the walk. Of course, I could and should have contacted them in advance and asked if they'd take supplies in for me.

Food Storage in Camp

On trips where bears aren't likely to raid my camp, I prefer to keep my food beside me so I can cook and eat at leisure and can easily protect it against small animals and birds. Leaving food on the ground away from you, even in the pack, is a sure way to feed wildlife. Sharp teeth will quickly make holes in most materials. The Ursack stuff sack is an exception to this. Although bears are the animals people worry about most, smaller animals—mice, marmots, raccoons—probably make off with more food.

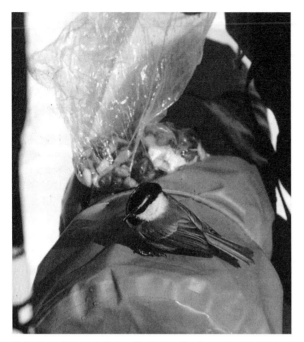

Animals and birds of all sizes like human food.

The worst problems I've had with wildlife occurred on a hike in the Grand Canyon, where deer mice abounded on most sites. One night they kept me awake for hours by running over me and my gear and rustling through the pack, whose pockets and compartments I'd left open so creatures wouldn't rip their way in. My food—inside plastic bags in a heavy-duty stuff sack and hung from a branch—was untouched, however.

Although it's inconvenient for you if animals get your food, for the animals it can be much worse. In the summer of 1995, rangers had to shoot twenty-three mule deer that were starving in the Grand Canyon; autopsies showed their stomachs were clogged with plastic bags, nylon cord, and other indigestible items. On popular backcountry sites in the Grand Canyon, posts are provided for hanging food bags and packs, and park regulations stress that all plastic bags and food must be kept packed away. In other parks there may be similar regulations in some places. When you feel like rebelling against the rules, remember those mule deer.

Hanging your food bags from a low limb may be adequate to keep small animals from getting at them. In areas where animals are likely to raid campsites, I now use an Ursack.

Bears

In bear country you need to take special precautions to keep your food safe, either by hanging it or by using a container bears can't break into. The traditional approach is to hang your food high in a tree, which isn't easy to do effectively. It needs to be at least 12 feet above the ground, 10 feet away from the trunk of a tree, and 6 feet below any branch—bears can climb and reach high. There are various ways of doing this, and all require at least 40 feet of nylon line and a tough stuff sack or two.

At times hanging food can take a long time. I've spent hours trying and wasted a lot of energy on curses as rocks whirled off into space or spun around branches, leaving a tangle of line to unwind. But whenever I've felt like giving up, I've thought about losing my food to a bear and have gone on until my food was secure. Bearbagging isn't just about protecting food, anyway, it's about protecting bears too, which is more important. A bear that finds food at a campsite may lose its fear of humans and start to raid sites regularly, becoming such a danger that it has to be killed. These are called "problem" bears. Really, though, we create the problem by taking food into the bear's territory and not protecting it adequately.

Having to hang food complicates camping, and there is a tendency to forgo it at the end of a long, hard day or in bad weather. Certainly, when mak-

Start with two stuff sacks of roughly equal weight. If you don't have enough food, put stones or gravel in one of the sacks. Tie one end of your line to one of the sacks (1). Put a small rock in another stuff sack and tie the other end of your line to the sack. Throw it over a suitable branch and haul the first stuff sack up until it's just below the branch (2). Tie the second stuff sack to the other end of the line while holding it as high as you can. Stuff any spare line into the stuff sack and then throw it up so that the two bags are at an equal height (3). When you need the food, use a trekking pole or stick to pull down one of the bags (4).

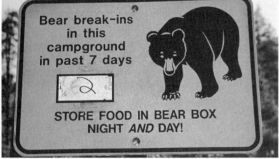

In many areas food must be secured from bears.

ing camp after dark I've sometimes suspended my food in a way I wouldn't be happy with in daylight. I've always hung it though (nowadays I use a canister or an Ursack, which makes life much easier).

The simplest bearbagging method is to tie a rock to the end of the line, throw it over a branch at least 20 feet above the ground, haul up the food until the bottom of the bag is at least 12 feet up, then tie off the line around the trunk of the tree. Even this is not that easy, since the line can become tangled around the branch. On popular sites in many areas you can see rotting strands of cord dangling from branches. Putting the rock in a small bag and tying that to the end of the line stops the rock from coming untied and shooting off into the distance, as can happen.

Up near timberline trees are usually smaller, with shorter branches. Here it's probably best to suspend food bags between two trees about 25 feet apart, which involves throwing one end of the weighted line over a branch, tying it off, and then repeating the process with the second tree. Keep the line between the two trees within reach so you can tie the food bag to it. Then haul the bag up

Put a small rock in a stuff sack. Tie the end of your line to the sack and throw it over a branch about 20 feet high. Don't let go of the other end of the rope! If you can't reach the rock, shake the line in a whipping motion to jerk the line over the branch and slowly lower the rock (1). Grab the end of the line and remove the rock (2). Attach your food stuff sack and haul it up (3). Wrap the end of the rope around the tree trunk and tie it off (4).

until it's halfway between the trees and 12 feet off the ground.

In the High Sierra, bears have learned that breaking a line rewards them with a bag of food, so standard hanging techniques don't work. The traditional way dealing with this is the counterbalance system, which involves throwing the line over a branch, tying a food bag to the end of the line, and hauling it right up to the branch; you then tie a second food bag (or bag of rocks) to the other end of the line, push any extra line into the bag,

and throw the second bag up so that both bags end up at least 12 feet above the ground and away from the tree trunk. If you leave a loop of line at the top of one of the bags, you can hook it with a stick or your staff to pull the bags down the next morning. Counterbalancing is difficult to do correctly, and bears too often get improperly hung food.

A much easier, newer method uses a keychain carabiner and a twig as well as a stuff sack for a rock and 40 feet of cord, which together weigh 4 to 8 ounces depending on the exact components (you don't need to carry the twig, of course). Less cord is needed than for the counterbalance method, and only one bag of food, though it can be used with two. This is known as the "PCT method" or "style," presumably because it was developed by Pacific Crest Trail hikers. For this method, you put a rock in the stuff sack, attach it to the line, and chuck it over a branch some 15- to 20-feet high and at least 10 feet from the trunk of the tree. Once the line is over the branch, remove the rock sack, tie the carabiner to one end, and run the other end through the carabiner. Next, attach the food sack to the carabiner by its drawcord and haul it up until it reaches the branch. Now comes the clever bit. Reach above your head with the twig and tie a clove hitch around it with the dangling line. (It's best to practice tying a clove hitch like this at home first.) Let go of the line, and the weight of the food sack will cause it to drop down. However, when the twig meets the carabiner, it can't pass through it, so the food sack will stay put some 10 feet above the ground (as long as the twig doesn't snap, so make sure it's a strong one). The loose line dangling down from the twig can be left until you need to retrieve your food.

A decreasing number of national parks provide high wires between trees or poles with pulleys for hanging food at some campsites. These make the procedure easier, though it can still be difficult

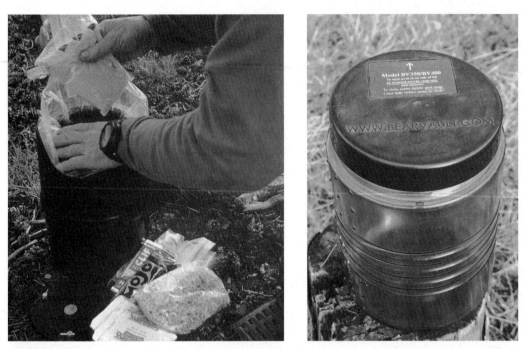

Left: Packing a bear-resistant container. The plastic liner helps reduce food smells. Right: BearVault bear-resistant container.

if you're alone and have a heavy food bag. Bear-proof boxes are provided in some areas too, such as many popular sites in the High Sierra. Always use these if you camp nearby.

When camping above timberline or where there are no large trees, as in the Far North, I used to store food well away from camp in airtight plastic bags. Now I use bear-resistant canisters or Ursack stuff sacks.

In an increasing number of areas, such as Denali and Glacier Bay National Parks in Alaska and many parts of the High Sierra where bears regularly get hung food, bear canisters are mandatory. (On the coastal section of Olympic National Park, canisters are required to protect against raccoons, which can easily get hung food, whatever the method.) They can usually be rented from park offices. It's wise to check the regulations as to which canisters are approved and where you need one before visiting a park, since they do change.

Bear-resistant canisters are wide and have a smooth surface so bears can't clamp their jaws around one or get their teeth or claws into it. Most have a round lid with recessed catches that can be opened with a quarter or a screwdriver. Canisters are great in camp but a pain on the trail; they're awkward to fit into a pack because of their hard cylindrical shape. I find the best way to pack one is to stand it up in the center of the pack with the sleeping bag below it and stuff soft gear around it. The smallest canisters will hold six days' food for one person, as long as you select low-bulk food and cram it in. Canisters are heavy, too. The original model and the one rented out by national parks is the Garcia Machine Backpackers' Cache. This weighs 2 pounds, 12 ounces (3 pounds in the first version) and has a capacity of 730 cubic inches. It's made of ABS polymer (plastic). Lighter but vastly more expensive is the Wild Ideas Bearikade, made from composite carbon fiber and aluminum alloy. The Bearikade Weekender weighs 1 pound, 15 ounces and holds 650 cubic inches; the Expedition weighs 2 pounds, 5 ounces and holds 900 cubic inches. Perhaps the most interesting canister is the Bear Vault, which is made from transparent polycarbonate and looks like a giant Nalgene bottle. It has a screw-top lid so no tools are needed to open it. The opening is much bigger than on canisters with recessed lids, which makes packing easier, and you can see what food you have left too. There are two sizes, the BV450 Solo, which holds 440 cubic inches and weighs 2 pounds, 1 ounce, and the BV500, which holds 700 cubic inches and weighs 2 pounds, 9 ounces. The latest canister, still in the prototype stage but sounding excellent, is the Camp 4 Outdoors Bearier 700, which is a large, clear polycarbonate ball that splits in the middle. This design means there is the maximum-sized opening for packing and removing food, and being transparent, you can see the contents. However, packing a large sphere in a pack probably won't be as easy as packing a cylinder. The volume is 700 cubic inches, which can be extended to 1,000 cubic inches with a ring called the Grub Hub that fits between the two halves, and the weight is "less than 2 pounds," so it's lighter for the size than other cylinders. The price should be less, too.

Despite the extra weight and the difficulty with packing, I like canisters. It's wonderful not to have to hang food and great to have easy access to it all the time. You don't have to check that there are suitable trees around before you camp, either, or sleep with half an eye open in case a bear tries to get your food and you have to leap up and try to

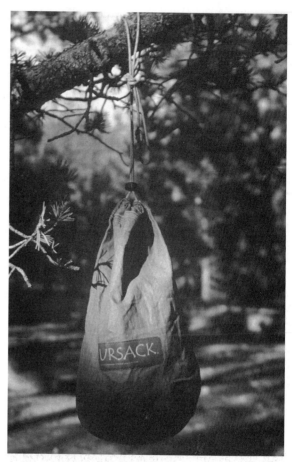

An Ursack bear-resistant stuff sack.

scare it away (without getting too close, and only try this with black bears, not grizzlies!). Canisters make good camp stools and tables, but don't use them for stoves or hot pots unless you put something heat resistant, such as foil, on them first. At night it's best to put the canister a short distance away from camp, in the middle of a flat area so a bear can't roll it down a slope.

I used a Backpackers' Cache, rented from Yosemite National Park, on a five-week hike in the High Sierra during which I met a few hikers who'd lost hung food to bears. At one of the rare popular sites I used I woke in the morning to see a bear walk past about forty feet from my camp without even pausing. A few minutes later I heard some pans clattering loudly and then some outraged and urgent yelling. Climbing onto a rock, I looked across a meadow with a small tent in the center to see a bear racing up the mountainside with something in its jaws, pursued by two half-naked campers. I presume they had hung their food with pans attached to act as a warning, but the bear had still gotten it. I'd heard people yelling and banging pots the night before too. My canister sat undisturbed twenty feet from camp.

An alternative that is lighter and easier to pack than canisters would be welcome, though, which is where the Ursack comes in. There are two models, the Ursack AllWhite, made of Spectra fabric and designed to be bear resistant, and the Ursack Minor, made of much lighter fabric and designed to protect against mice, squirrels, and other small animals—but not bears. The Minor weighs 2.7 ounces, and the AllWhite a touch under 8 ounces. Both hold 650 cubic inches. That's almost the same capacity as the Backpackers' Cache canister, which weights more than five times as much as the Ursack AllWhite. The Ursack can be squashed down when partly full like any other stuff sack, too. Does it work? Evidence from the makers and users suggests it does, though your food may get pulverized if a bear batters it around. Plastic bags inside can burst, so it's best not to pack anything liquid or sticky. It must be used properly to be effective. The mouth must be closed fully so no food is visible, and the bag then tied to a tree trunk or strong branch with a figure eight knot (so it's easy to untie). On a nine-day hike in the High Sierra I used an Ursack (an original one'equivalent to the AllWhite) and a canister (I was going into an area where canisters were a requirement). I used the Ursack for over three

days, after which all my food fit in the canister. As far as I know, nothing even touched it. I now use the Ursack anywhere that animals might try and eat my food, carrying a canister only in areas where they're required. I've had rodents chew through an ordinary stuff sack and into bags of food but fail to make any impression on the Ursack sitting next to it, so it certainly works for small animals.

Bears are attracted to food by smell as well as sight. Double-bagging smelly foods and not carrying really stinky ones in bear country is a good idea. Loksak makes bags called Opsaks that are completely odorproof. These bags come in three sizes—9 by 10 inches, 12 by 20 inches, and 28 by 20 inches—and are ideal for use with Ursacks and bear canisters. Indeed, they sound sensible for all food storage in the wilds, whatever the container.

Bears view smelly items such as toothpaste, soap, insect repellent, and sunscreen as food, so store them with your food. Food-stained clothing and dirty pots are best stored away from where you sleep, too, though the first isn't possible on hikes where you don't have spare clothing.

A good way to keep bears out of your camp is by avoiding popular backcountry sites. Bears frequent those places where there is a regular supply of food. By camping away from such sites on one eleven-day trip in Yosemite National Park, I didn't even see a bear.

If a bear does get your food *don't try to get it back*. The bear will almost certainly defend it (see Dealing with Animals, in Chapter 9).

"Wild" Food

I'm often asked why I don't "live off the land" during long wilderness hikes. The phrase conjures up the carefree image of a hiker ambling along, munching on nuts and fruits plucked from trailside bushes and scooping tasty trout from every stream.

In fact, unless you hunt or fish, finding enough to eat in the wilderness is very difficult for most people and does not allow time for walking all day. Then too, wild lands are limited and fragile; we should take no more from them than we absolutely must, which means going in with all the food we need. If every wilderness traveler relied on foraging for food, popular areas would soon be stripped bare.

Fishing, perhaps, is an exception. Mountain lakes and streams often seem full of fish (some are restocked regularly, a highly dubious practice environmentally). Anglers often carry light fishing gear (and licenses) in suitable country and thereby supplement their diets with some fresh food. For some, hiking is a means to fish remote waters.

WATER

While you can manage without food for a surprisingly long time, this isn't so for water. Dehydration can kill you in a matter of days—and long before you're in real danger, you'll cease to enjoy what you're doing as your mind dulls and your perceptions numb.

On any walk, you need to know where water sources are and what the condition of the water is likely to be. In many places water is not a problem—unless there's too much of it—but in others, especially desert or semidesert areas, the location of water sources can determine your route. Water supply is one of the first things I want to know about a region new to me.

Taking water from a hole cut through the ice of a snow-covered lake.

How much water you need per day varies from person to person and depends on the weather conditions, the amount of energy you expend, and the type of food you carry. I can walk all day without a drink in cool, damp conditions, though I don't recommend this. But I may drink a quart an hour on a very hot day in an area where there's no shade. Estimating needs for camp is easier. With the dried foods I eat, I can get by on 2 quarts a night, but I prefer to have 4 or more—and that's just for cooking and drinking, not for washing utensils or myself. It also assumes I've had enough to drink during the day and either am camping near water or expect to find a source fairly early the next day.

When you have to carry water, these calculations become important, because water weighs more than 2 pounds per quart. In desert areas of the Southwest, I've carried 3 gallons of water—a horrendous 25 pounds. Luckily, it's rare to have to carry that much, at least for a whole day. "Dry" camps (ones away from water sources) may require you to carry 3 or 4 quarts of water, but often this can be picked up late in the day so you only have to carry it for a few hours. Remember that you need enough water to get you to the next reliable source as well as for use in camp.

Snow-covered country is odd—everything is shrouded in solid water, but it's effectively a desert. Walking in snow can dehydrate you as quickly as desert walking, because the dry air sucks moisture out of your body. The thirstiest I've ever felt was when I skied all day in hot sunshine with no shade and not enough liquid. Eating snow cools your mouth but provides little real relief. The answer, easily given but not so easily carried out, is to melt enough snow in camp to keep you well supplied during the day.

Ideally, you should never allow yourself to become even slightly dehydrated. The best way to avoid this is to drink regularly, whether you feel thirsty or not. If you're not careful, though, dehydration may creep up on you, and only when your mouth starts to feel sticky and your tongue swollen do you realize how thirsty you are. Warning signs of dehydration are a reduction in urine output and a change in the color of your urine—the paler, the better. If it's dark, you need to drink a fair amount of water quickly. In order to avoid water intoxication, you should eat something as well or add fruit crystals or sports drink powder to the water to ensure that you replace essential electrolytes (sodium and potassium) that are also lost when you become dehydrated.

Sources

Streams, rivers, lakes, and ponds are obvious sources of water, easily identified on a map. In areas with plenty of these features, you won't

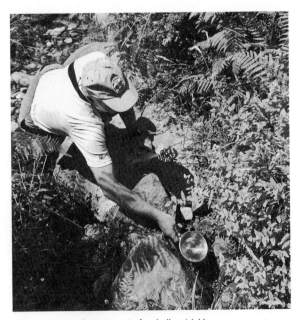

Using a mug to dip water out of a shallow trickle.

Piped springs can provide clean, fresh water if you take it from the inlet.

need to carry much or to worry about running out. Check contour lines carefully, however, to see exactly where the water is. Often the high ridges that make for superb walking are far above any water. In such places it's better to carry full bottles than to make long descents and reascents when you need a drink. Remember, too, that dotted blue lines on the map usually indicate *seasonal* water sources; the rushing stream of June, heavy with snowmelt, may have vanished completely by late September.

If water sources are scarce, you may have to hunt out tiny trickles and seeps. To find these, look for areas of richer, denser vegetation and for depressions and gullies where water may gather or run. Pause and listen, too. You can often hear water trickling even when you can't see it.

In deserts, locating water is critical to survival. "Think water" is a valuable mantra. Check guidebooks for information on water sources and, more important, ask rangers and other local people for current information. Sources can dry up quickly, so it's wise to always carry enough water to get to the next reliable source or out to a trailhead

if a source isn't guaranteed. In places it may be necessary to place water caches. I did this on the Arizona Trail where there was a 60-mile waterless section across hot Sonoran Desert. My companion and I put out two caches of 9 gallons in gallon jugs and set off with 2 gallons each for the hike of three and a bit days. We simply hid the caches under bushes near the jeep trail we drove in on to place them, then marked them on the map. All were still there when we collected them over the next few days, but plastic jugs aren't the most reliable containers, since animals can bite into them. If you place caches, it's important to carry out all the water containers. We ended that hike with our packs festooned with squashed empty water jugs.

For those who are intending more serious desert ventures and want to know about natural water sources, solar stills, and other possibilities, I recommend a look at *The Ultimate Desert Handbook* by Mark Johnson.

Safety

A real problem with water is deciding whether what you find is safe to drink. Water clarity is not necessarily an indication of either purity or contamination. Even the most sparkling, crystal-clear mountain stream may not be safe to drink from.

The invisible potential contaminants include a wide variety of microorganisms—protozoans, bacteria, and viruses—that cause intestinal disorders, some mild, some severe. The potential nasties include *Cryptosporidium*, a protozoan, that has gotten much attention recently. This causes unpleasant watery diarrhea, but once you've had the disorder you should be immune.

Viruses are the most dangerous waterborne organisms—they can cause fatal diseases like polio and hepatitis. But viruses aren't a problem in most dip a mug in a shallow puddle, then pour into your container

channeling with foil or bark; plastic or stiff paper can also be used

lower a bottle with a rope (rocks inside help the bottle sink)

Water collection methods.

of North America and Europe. If you visit some other countries, however, they're a real threat. When I went hiking in Nepal, all vegetables and fruit had to be washed in iodine-treated water, and I used iodine to purify all water. Filters, the trekking company told me, were ineffective. If you're going abroad, check with the Centers for Disease Control and Prevention about water there.

The protozoan *Giardia lamblia*, which causes a virulent gut disorder, giardiasis, is the bug that has received most attention. While *Giardia* is indeed found in some wilderness streams and lakes—though not, it seems, in the quantities people think—too many people are far too concerned about it. Giardiasis isn't fatal, and you're unlikely to be incapacitated. Although it makes some people feel quite ill, most don't even have any symptoms and become immune after being exposed to it.

Giardia lamblia lives in the intestines of humans and animals. It gets into water as cysts excreted in feces, which is one reason for always siting toilets well away from water. The symptoms of giardiasis appear a few weeks after ingestion and include diarrhea, stomachache, a bloated feeling, nausea, and foul-smelling feces. However, these symptoms occur in other stomach disorders as well, and only a stool analysis can confirm infection. The chances of catching giardiasis or other illness from water aren't high, despite media coverage to the contrary. To cover themselves, land managers generally advise people that all water needs treating, which adds to concern. People who get a gut disorder then tend to blame *Giardia* in the water because they've been warned about it, even though the cause is probably not either *Giardia* or the water.

Research published in 1995 in the journal *Wilderness and Environmental Medicine* suggests that giardiasis and other gut disorders are spread "by oral-fecal or food-borne transmission not by contaminated drinking water." Out of 34,348 cases of giardiasis reported to the study's authors, Thomas R. Welch and Timothy P. Welch, by forty-eight state health departments, a mere nineteen were associated with drinking contaminated water, and just two of them were known to be campers and backpackers. The authors compare the likelihood of catching giardiasis from drinking water to the risk of a shark attack and say that it's "an extraordinarily rare event to which the public and press have seemingly devoted inappropriate attention." In a separate study published in the online journal of the Yosemite Association, Robert L. Rockwell comes to a similar conclusion with regard to the Sierra Nevada: "You can indeed contract giardiasis on visits to the Sierra Nevada, but it won't be from the water. So drink freely and confidently." (In the summer of 2002 I did just this on a five-week hike in the High Sierra, never treating any water.)

According to both the Rockwell and Welch studies, *it's far more important to wash your hands thoroughly and keep your cooking pots clean than to treat your water.* Sharing mugs and bowls and bags of gorp is unwise too. Share food by pouring it into people's hands or their own utensils to minimize the chance of contamination.

The most recent study was done by *Backpacker* magazine in the spring and summer of 2003 (reported in the December 2003 issue). Seven backcountry water sources were tested three separate times for *Giardia* and *Cryptosporidium* by a California laboratory specializing in these protozoans. The sources ranged from the Neversink River East Branch in the Catskills in New York State to the Merced River in Yosemite National Park in California. Only one source had a high enough concentration of cysts (1.5 per liter) for *Backpacker* to advise treating it, though it was still too low to make most people ill. Two had none at all. The other four had no viable cysts. Out of the twenty-one total samples, only six tested positive for *Giardia* and only one for *Cryptosporidium*. Other research also shows such low concentrations of protozoans, when any are found at all, that infection is very unlikely. The *Backpacker* article quotes Robert W. Derlet, a hiker and a professor of medicine who is researching the water sources in the Sierra, as saying that "the warnings about backcountry water quality are vastly exaggerated. Most of them are based on rumor and hearsay, nothing more. The chances of picking up a bug are very slim, and the chances of getting sick are much, much slimmer. If you averaged every drop of water from every lake in the Sierra and put it in a reservoir, you'd have to drink 250 gallons to get enough giardia to make you sick." The evidence suggests most backcountry water is safe, and you are very unlikely to catch anything from drinking it untreated. There are far greater risks in the wilderness. If you're really worried about intestinal illness, you could ease your concerns by treating all water, but the most important thing is to take great care with hand washing and keeping your cooking utensils clean. Even if you treat all your water, it's wise to be careful about sources. No treatment method is foolproof. I treat water only if it's below habitations, including backcountry shelters and popular campsites, and popular trails; if there are cattle or signs of cattle in the area; or if it looks or smells unpleasant. When seeking drinking water I look for springs and fast-flowing streams and take the water from above trails, campsites, and bridges. With lakes I take water from the inlet or the outlet if I can. I love being able to drink deeply from a mountain stream, and I'm very reluctant to give up this wilderness pleasure.

If you do get a bad digestive upset that doesn't clear up in a few days, it's wise to see a doctor just in case it's something serious. In the meantime drink plenty, since diarrhea is dehydrating, and eat plain low-fat foods such as rice and pasta. An upset gut can be debilitating and extremely unpleasant. I once had a very severe bout of diarrhea and vomiting in Nepal (probably contracted in Katmandu) that lasted several days. The cause was undiagnosed.

Treating all water can pose its own dangers. In the Montana Rockies during my Continental Divide walk, I regularly met members of a large party doing the same hike. Most of them were very worried about giardiasis, and they filtered or boiled all water before drinking it. While restocking and resting in the town of Butte after several weeks of very hot weather, I met one of this party walking down the street looking pale and thin. He told me he'd staggered out of the mountains feeling weak and sick. He didn't have giardiasis though—he was suffering from severe dehydration. He wouldn't drink unfiltered water and hadn't filtered the amount he should have been drinking. Dehydration is a serious enough threat, far greater than giardiasis, that drinking enough water is essential whether it's been treated or not.

Treatment

Water can be treated by boiling it, adding chemicals, and filtering. Boiling and chemicals disinfect the water—that is, they kill bugs in it. Filters remove anything too large to pass through the pores, but they don't disinfect water or remove viruses unless they have a chemical component as well, in which case they're described as purifiers. Visibly dirty water can be filtered through a bandanna or a coffee filter, as can glacier meltwater, but this doesn't remove microorganisms.

BOILING Boiling is the surest way to kill dangerous organisms, but it's impractical for all water needs because it uses fuel and takes time. However, it isn't necessary to boil water for the five to fifteen minutes often advised. Just bringing it to a boil will do—harmful organisms, including *Giardia* cysts, are killed at temperatures below the boiling point even at high altitude, where it's lower than at sea level. Boiled water tastes flat. To restore the sparkle, shake it up or pour it from one container into another and back again a few times to aerate it.

CHEMICAL TREATMENT The traditional forms of chemical treatment, iodine and chlorine tablets, are lightweight and simple to use; iodine treatment is regarded as the most effective against *Giardia*, but neither is proven against *Cryptosporidium*. Both chemicals make the water taste foul. Despite what is often stated, iodine isn't highly toxic. Apparently, if you do ingest too much you'll

Water-cleaning methods.

probably vomit, getting rid of most of the iodine. Normal doses of iodine won't harm you. Wilkerson's *Medicine for Mountaineering and Other Wilderness Activities* reports that inmates of three Florida prisons have drunk water disinfected with iodine over a fifteen-year period with no ill effects. Only those with known thyroid problems or goiters need to be careful. Despite this, the European Union banned iodine for water treatment in 2009, so you can't buy iodine treatments in the twenty-seven member states anymore.

The most common brand of iodine tablets, Potable Aqua, comes in 3.5-ounce bottles containing fifty tablets that will treat twenty-five quarts. You can get neutralizing tablets that remove the aftertaste. These are made of vitamin C (ascorbic acid), so any soluble vitamin C tablets will have the same effect. But don't add them or anything else like fruit crystals until the iodine has had time to work (thirty minutes). I used chlorine tablets on the Pacific Crest Trail and Potable Aqua on the Continental Divide. I drank from filthy stock-ponds on both walks and never became ill, so presumably both treatments worked. Tablets have a limited life; you should buy a fresh supply at least annually. Once a bottle is opened, it should be used within a few weeks or else discarded.

Iodine crystals, sold in drugstores, are a long-lasting alternative to tablets. These can be held in solution and small amounts poured into water bottles when required, though you need to be sure no undissolved crystals enter the drinking water. Polar Pure (3 ounces dry weight; more, of course, when the crystals are in solution) contains iodine crystals, thermometer (to check water temperature—cold water needs more of the solution), and instructions, and will purify 2,000 quarts of water. It's safer to use than crystals alone, since there's a filter cone inside the bottle that prevents the crystals from accidentally falling into your drinking water. However, it's heavier than crystals or tablets, and you have to carry a glass container with liquid in it. I used it for a while, before I discovered chlorine dioxide.

Chlorine dioxide is meant to kill everything, including *Cryptosporidium*. It's lightweight, easy to use, and in my opinion the best chemical way of treating water. Despite the name, it doesn't kill bugs with chlorine or leave chlorine in the water. When activated, chlorine dioxide releases highly active concentrated oxygen into the water, and it's this that kills bugs. Treated water tastes fresh, with no aftertaste. Initially chlorine dioxide came in two tiny plastic bottles, one containing stabilized chlorine dioxide, the other an activator (5 percent food-grade phosphoric acid), plus a small mixing cap. The weight is 2.8 ounces, and it will purify 120 quarts. To use the treatment you put seven drops from each bottle in the mixing cap for each quart of water, wait five minutes before adding it to the water to be treated, and then wait another

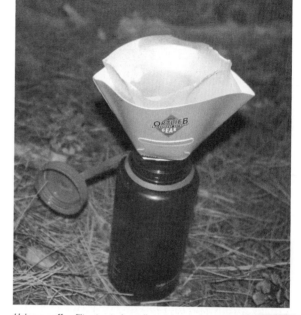

Using a coffee filter to strain sediment from pond water.

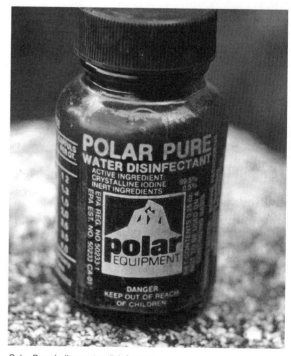

Polar Pure iodine water disinfectant.

Aquamira chlorine dioxide water purification.

The unique MIOX Purifier works by creating a cocktail of mixed oxidants that kills all bugs.

fifteen minutes before using the water. (Double the time and dose for cold or cloudy water and if *Cryptosporidium* is suspected—though how you suspect it I've no idea.) Rather than waiting fifteen or thirty minutes each time you fill up with water, you can simply wait five, add the drops to the water, and then hike on with it in your pack. Aquamira and Pristine both sell this two-bottle system. However, there are now chlorine dioxide tablets that are much easier to use: you just drop them in the water and wait. Aquamira sells these under the name Chlorine Dioxide Water Purifier Tablets in packs of twelve. Potable Aqua sells them as Chlorine Dioxide Water Purification Tablets, and Katadyn as Micropur MP1 Purification Tablets, both in packs of twenty and thirty. Each tablet treats a quart of water. If the water is clear and at 68°F (20°C), you should wait fifteen minutes before the water is safe to drink. However, if the water is dirty and the temperature 40°F (5°C), it takes four hours to kill *Cryptosporidium*. I used Aquamira on the Arizona Trail, when I drank from some really murky cattle ponds at times, and stayed healthy.

A different method of chemical treatment is the MSR MIOX Purifier, which is unlike anything else. This battery-operated Purifier is a flashlight-like tube measuring 1 inch by 7 inches. To use it you add salt to the unit followed by a tiny amount (¼ teaspoon) of water. You shake the salt and water to create a brine solution and press a button. This sends a small electrical charge through the solution creating a chemical reaction (electrolysis) that produces a "cocktail" of mixed oxidants (MIOX) that when added to untreated water kills any bugs. One dose will purify up to a gallon of water. The whole procedure only takes a few minutes but, as with other purification treatments, you then have to wait to be sure it has worked; thirty minutes for most bugs and a long four hours for *Cryptosporidium*. Purity-indicator strips show the water has been purified. Although there is a strong smell of brine when the solution is added to the water, there is no aftertaste. The MIOX runs off two CR-123 lithium camera batteries and will purify more than two hundred liters on one set. The tube weighs 2.2 ounces without batteries and the whole kit, which includes batteries, salt, purity-indicator strips, instructions, and stuff sack, 8 ounces. It's fairly easy to use, though you have to be careful to follow the sequence of actions correctly. I'd certainly rather use it than most filters, as it seems much more foolproof.

FILTERS Filtration is a high-tech way to treat water and is quite popular, though it's not my favorite. Indeed, though I've tested several pump filters over the years, including models from MSR, Sweetwater Guardian, First Need, and Katadyn, I've never taken one backpacking. In my opinion they're all too heavy, too complicated, too ineffi-

cient, and too unreliable. I'm unhappy about the need to keep them clean and use them correctly, too. I found this difficult at home; it must be much harder when you're tired, cold, and thirsty at the end of a long day on the trail, yet it's essential if filters are to be effective. I've seen people handling filters with dirty hands, letting the outlet tube dangle in the dirt, allowing water still to be filtered to splash over the filter, and storing filters unwrapped in the pack: I definitely felt safer drinking straight creek water than their filtered supply. Filters can be hard to pump and clog very easily. Carrying a replacement cartridge or a chemical disinfectant as a backup is advisable. Cleaning filters is necessary, too, which means carrying cleaning items on a long trip. Like any piece of gear, a filter isn't magic, despite what some users seem to think. Study the instructions carefully, practice at home, and make sure you know how to clean and store the filter properly.

The key with any filter is the pore size, since this determines what it will filter out. For *Giardia* and *Cryptosporidium* an absolute (maximum) pore size of 0.5 micron is the minimum needed;

Lightweight, compact water filters (from left): First Need DeLuxe, MSR MiniWorks, Katadyn Hiker, Sweetwater Guardian.

smaller pores are better, since pores may enlarge with use. Whether the filter is ceramic, carbon, or fiberglass and exactly how it works are far less important.

Filters come in three forms: bottle feed, gravity feed, and pump. The first are simple filters that substitute for the lid of a water bottle or fit inside. They're lightweight and easy to use, though you have to squeeze fairly hard to get water out. I wouldn't want to use one if I needed large amounts of water, but for drinking from on the trail they're all right. An example is the Katadyn MyBottle, which has a filter that fits inside that contains iodine, so it purifies as well. It weighs 9.7 ounces, and the bottle holds 24 fluid ounces with the filter inside. The bottle can be filled 155 times before the purifier cartridge needs replacing.

Pump and gravity-feed filters are better for camp and group use. Pumping can be slow—a quart a minute is good—and surprisingly tiring, but it can be used for any amount of water. Of the pump filters I've tried, I most liked the Katadyn Hiker, which weighs 11 ounces, has 0.3-micron pores, and has a pump rate of 1 quart per minute. The Hiker was easier to use than other models and is quite light and compact. If I carried a pump filter it would be this one.

With gravity-feed filters a bag of water is hung up with the filter unit and a hose leading into a water container below it. Most gravity filters are also bottle-feed or pump filters as well, like the first one I tried, the 15.5-ounce First Need DeLuxe (now replaced by the First Need XL), which has a pump option and is also a purifier as well as a filter. It took ten minutes to filter a quart of water. The second filter I tried, the much lighter 8.5-ounce ULA H2O Amigo, took only a minute to filter a quart, probably because it wasn't also a purifier. Sadly, the Amigo is no longer available. There are alternatives that look good, though I haven't tried any of them. The 11-ounce Katadyn Base Camp consists of a filter unit attached to a 10-quart water bag with a long hose attached. The flow rate is said to be a quart a minute. The replaceable filter unit will last for 200 gallons. Even better looking is the Aquamira Frontier Pro,

FAR LEFT: First Need DeLuxe filter/ purifier fitted to a Sigg bottle. LEFT: Putting the inlet hose in a creek before filtering water.

which weighs just 2 ounces and can be used as a bottle-feed or gravity-feed filter. As a bottle-feed filter, this tube attaches to a water bottle with a 28-millimeter opening, such as a Platypus bottle. You can then squeeze the bottle and suck water out of the bite valve at the end of the filter. It can also be attached to the tube of a hydration system. To use it as a gravity filter, you remove the bite valve, fit into the water container, and hang up. Water then drips through the filter. The Frontier Pro also has a treatment that prevents the growth of bacteria and fungi so it stays clean. If I was to use a filter, it would be the Frontier Pro, as long as there were trees around.

Filters can remove bacteria, organic chemicals, and protozoans, including *Giardia*. They can't remove viruses unless they also include chemical disinfection, in which case you might as well just use chemicals.

ULTRAVIOLET LIGHT The latest method of treating water is with UV light, and this is what I now use. It's fast, removes viruses as well as bacteria and protozoa, and requires no chemicals, no pumping, no waiting hours before water is safe to drink, and no waiting for gravity feed. SteriPEN is the name in UV treatment, and the purifier I use is the Adventurer Opti, which runs on two CR123 batteries. Disposable units will treat 50 quarts, rechargeables half that. The UV light lasts for 8,000 treatments. The Adventurer Opti consists of a long light tube and a case that is also the handle that holds the batteries and has a power button and LED light. There's a protective cap over the lamp. Even so, it needs to be looked after, as it can be broken. To use it, you press the button on the case, wait for LED to flash, and then insert the lamp into the water. You do need a container with a wide mouth for this, such as a Nalgene-type bottle or a cook pot—it won't fit into a Platypus-type container. Then you stir the water gently with

SteriPEN Adventurer Opti purifier.

the lamp until the LED light goes out, which takes 90 seconds for a quart of water.

I took the Adventurer Opti on the Pacific Northwest Trail and used it regularly for a three-week period when I was in cattle country and often taking water from horribly fouled and stinking seeps and puddles. I never got sick, so I presume it worked, which is all you can do with any treatment. A side advantage I discovered was that the device can also be used as an LED flashlight, which was useful a couple of times when I needed to change headlamp batteries in the dark.

UV treatment works regardless of the temperature of the water. However, it's not a filter, and water should be clean. On the PNT, I filtered visibly dirty water through a bandanna. However, SteriPEN has come out with a much better solution—the 2.3-ounce FitsAll Filter, which filters out suspended sediments and can be used with wide- and narrow-mouthed bottles.

Powdered Drinks

Clear, cold mountain stream water is the most refreshing drink there is, the main reason I'm reluctant to treat water unless absolutely necessary. If you like to flavor water, Kool-Aid, Wyler's, and similar fruit-flavored powdered drink mixes are the traditional choice. There are three versions: those to which you add sugar, those containing sugar, and those containing artificial sweeteners. Those presweetened with sugar are the most useful—if you're carrying the stuff, you might as well get a few extra kilocalories.

The modern alternatives to fruit-flavored sugar and chemical concoctions are powdered sports drinks like Gatorade and Hydralyte. These contain electrolytes (potassium and sodium chloride) to replace those depleted through heavy sweating, plus carbohydrates and often much other stuff, sometimes including vitamins and minerals. While such drinks may be useful for athletes, they're not needed for backpacking, even in desert regions. I've drunk them on occasion but never noticed any difference from drinking water and munching snacks, which I find more enjoyable. Such drinks have almost replaced salt tablets, which are no longer recommended because they're too high in sodium and low in potassium. Over twenty years ago on my first desert hike across the Mojave Desert, I followed the current advice and carried salt tablets, though I never used them. Oral rehydration salts, which contain potassium as well as sodium, could be carried as an emergency item, though I've never done so.

Bottles, Bags, and Hydration Systems

Even where water is plentiful, you need some form of water container. In dry, hot country several may be essential, and they need to be of good quality, since a container failure could be serious. For that reason I always carry two or more containers, never just one large one. That said, it's been many, many years since I had a container leak. Water containers used to be simple items.

There were rigid ones—bottles or canteens—for carrying water and large, soft compressible water bags for camp use. Now we have hydration systems and reservoirs with drinking hoses, all made from flexible plastic, and the distinction between trail and camp containers has vanished.

Traditional rigid bottles come in a wide variety of shapes, sizes, and makes and in both plastic and aluminum, though the latter are becoming scarce—Sigg is one of the few remaining makes. Aluminum keeps liquids cooler in warm weather than plastic. A lacquered inside stops fruit juice or sports drinks from dissolving the aluminum and tainting the drink. Plastic bottles warm up more quickly. Food-grade ones don't taint water. When you need to carry little water, pint bottles are adequate, but I prefer quarts for general use.

The classic aluminum bottles are the Swiss-made lacquered Sigg bottles. These come in six sizes, ranging from 0.3 quart to 1.5 quarts. The quart size, probably the most useful for backpacking, weighs 5 ounces. Sigg bottles are durable and have screw tops with rubber seals that don't leak—at least none of mine ever have. But they also have narrow openings, which make them hard to fill from seeps and trickles.

The big name in rigid plastic bottles is Nalgene. These come with wide and narrow mouths and in a wide variety of sizes. I find the quart wide-mouth round bottle (5 ounces) the most useful, since it's easy to fill from small trickles. Nalgene bottles are leakproof and hardwearing, unlike some cheaper bottles that leak and crack along the seams after a relatively short time. They're made from high- and low-density polyethylene and more durable but slightly heavier copolyester. The Loop-Top bottles with attached caps are useful if you're careless. (I've twice spent an hour or more searching for bottle caps I dropped in creeks—luckily I found them both times.)

Lighter and less expensive alternatives to the bottles found in outdoor stores are plastic soda bottles. Most of these are tough and long lasting. When I needed extra bottles for a two-week hike in the Grand Canyon, I bought two quart-size bottles of Gatorade, drank the contents the first day out, then used the bottles (3 ounces empty) for the rest of the trip. I am still using one of these more than twenty years later.

Many bottles have caps with valves so you can drink from them without removing the cap, often by squeezing the bottle. These are convenient if you want to drink while hiking, but I find they leak easily, so I carry them outside the pack in a mesh pocket or external bottle holder. I often carry a 3-ounce polyurethane widemouthed GoLite Biodegradable Sports Bottle rather than a heavier Nalgene bottle. It has a 21-ounce capacity. I took it on the Pacific Northwest Trail, as the SteriPEN Adventurer Opti purifier will fit in it.

Rigid bottles are heavy and bulky compared with the flexible ones that I now use for amounts larger than a quart and that can be packed flat when empty. I first tried these on the Arizona Trail; I reckoned I needed enough containers to carry three gallons, and I didn't want to rely on just one or two, both in case of failure and because very large bottles are hard to fit in the pack. I also knew that the large water bags I had previously used in camp weren't comfortable for carrying water. Wanting to keep the weight of the containers to a minimum, I chose Platypus bottles (made by Cascade Designs), the lightest I could find. The quart size weighs just under an ounce, the two-and-a-half-quart size 1.35 ounces. I carried four of the former and two of the latter for a total weight of 6.7 ounces and a capacity of 9 quarts. Because I wasn't totally convinced that such thin, flimsy-seeming containers would survive long, I also carried a quart Nalgene bottle, useful for

getting water out of tiny seeps and trickles, for which narrow-necked Platypus bottles are pretty useless, and a 4-quart flexible Ortlieb Water Bag (3 ounces). I'd used the last for years and knew it was tough. My concerns were unfounded, and the three Platypus bottles that did the whole trail survived intact and lasted for many more years. (I didn't need all these containers, and I ended up putting the Ortlieb and three of the quart Platypus bottles in my running supply box.) Platypus bottles have a triple-layer laminate with food-grade polyethylene as the inner layer plus welded seams. They will stand upright when there's water in them and are the best large flexible containers I've found for carrying water.

The standard Platypus bottles have a narrow neck that makes them awkward to fill in narrow streams or still water and hard to clean and dry. Big Zip Platypus reservoirs open fully at one end, which solves these problems. The zip closures add a fair bit of weight, however, and although they seem secure I don't have the same confidence in them as in a screw-on cap. I'd prefer not to have openings at both ends, either. The 1.8-quart Big Zip weighs 5.5 ounces, the 3-quart 5.8 ounces.

On most trips I currently carry one widemouth rigid bottle, for ease of getting water out of shallow creeks and seeps, plus two 2-quart Platypus bottles. The latter are large enough that I only need to make one trip for water for camp, which minimizes impact and means I don't have to leave camp again in stormy weather. When I started backpacking my camp water container was a collapsible water bag that held two gallons and weighed 3.5 ounces. This consisted of a double-layer flexible plastic inner bladder and a nylon cover, with a leakproof spigot and two webbing handles. All the parts were replaceable, and ripstop tape could be used for emergency repairs—and the bags did develop holes rather too frequently. Such waterbags are rare now, having been replaced by tougher single-skin bags that don't need covers or two layers, though Moonbow makes a 5-quart one called the Camp Domo (4 ounces).

I replaced that water bag with an Ortlieb Waterbag, made from a single layer of coated nylon with welded seams. My gallon-size model weighs 3 ounces and has proved much tougher than double-layer ones. Ortlieb Waterbags are available in 2-, 4-, and 10-quart sizes weighing 2.8, 4.6, and 5.6 ounces respectively. An alternative that looks good are the MSR DromLite Bags, which come in 2-, 4-, and 6-quart sizes at weights of 4.6, 5.1, and 5.7 ounces.

Other uses of a water bag are as a portable shower and, so I'm told, as a pillow. They aren't, however, very good for carrying water in the pack. The larger ones are especially awkward. I carried my two-gallon one full a number of times, usually strapped to the top or back of my pack, and the water sloshed around, altering the balance of the load in an unnerving way. For short distances I carried the bag in my hand by its strap. The Ortlieb bag isn't much better; it also feels like wobbly jelly in the pack. I find Platypus bottles far more comfortable in the pack, since they'll stand upright and behave much more like rigid bottles. Two bottles are easier to pack and to lift and pour from as well.

Hydration systems are flexible water containers (often known as bladders) with long tubes attached that dangle over your shoulder so you can drink while hiking. I've tried these, and I have to say I dislike sucking on a tube as I hike. I prefer to stop and take swigs from a water bottle. However, my stepdaughter uses one, and they are so popular that many packs come with sleeves for the containers. CamelBak was the first model to appear, but there are now plenty of others from Platypus, Nalgene, MSR, and more. Having quick access is a good idea, of course. I like to carry my water bottle in a mesh pocket or bottle holder on the side of the pack, where I can reach it easily.

In winter a thermos is very useful. By filling it with hot water in the evening, I have warm water that soon comes to a boil in the morning, speeding up breakfast. If I fill it before leaving camp, I can enjoy hot drinks (usually hot fruit juice, sometimes soup) during the day without needing to stop and fire up the stove. The best ones are unbreakable stainless steel. After smashing several glass-lined ones, I purchased a Coleman stainless steel pint thermos, which weighs 18.5 ounces. Each of its many dents shows how many glass-lined ones I would have broken. Steel ones have become lighter since I bought the Coleman, so I retired it to car use in favor of a pint Zojirushi Tuffslim Compact model with push-pour spout that weighs 11.5 ounces. This vacuum bottle has been in regular use for more than ten years and is still in good condition.

Another alternative is an insulated bottle cover. I have an Outdoor Research Water Bottle Parka that holds a 1-quart Nalgene bottle. It weighs 4 ounces, so with the bottle the weight is still half that of the stainless steel flask, yet with twice the capacity. These covers won't keep liquids hot for long, so they aren't suitable for coffee unless you like it lukewarm, but they're fine for fruit juice. It would be easy to make a similar bottle cover out of closed-cell foam and duct tape.

It's best to store water containers uncapped, so they can fully dry and not become musty. If ordinary washing doesn't clean them fully, soak them in a mild solution of bicarbonate of soda. Iodine, chlorine, or bleach can also be used for disinfecting bottles. Wash containers regularly to prevent the buildup of dirt, especially around the screw threads.

THE CAMPFIRE

Many people find sitting around a campfire the ideal way to end a day in the wilderness. But in too many places badly situated and constructed fires have left scars that will take decades to heal, and too many trees have been stripped of their lower branches, or even hacked down, to provide fuel. Even collecting fallen wood can damage the environment if not enough is left to replenish soil nutrients and provide shelter for animals and food for insects and fungi.

It is far better, and more efficient, to use a stove for cooking and clothing and shelter for warmth. But an essential element of the wilderness experience would be lost if you could never light campfires, and although I cook on a stove 99 percent of the time, I do occasionally light a fire. Fires should be treated as a luxury, however, and lit only where they have minimal impact on the environment. When the risk of forest fires is very high, fires may be banned for short periods. In areas where there has been too much damage or that are environmentally sensitive (often above the timberline), fires may be banned all the time. In national parks you may need fire permits and may be required to carry a stove. Such regulations may seem restrictive, but they prevent further degradation of popular areas.

Fires, officially permitted or not, are inappropriate in some areas, anyway. They shouldn't be lit at and above the timberline, because trees and shrubs grow slowly there and the nutrients from deadwood are needed to replenish the thin soil.

In other areas, fires can sometimes be lit even on pristine sites without significant harm to the environment, as long as you use Leave No Trace techniques. The ideal places for such fires are on

Right: The results of poorly sited, misused, and overused campfires. Notice that the ground is trampled and bare, there is an unnecessary rock ring, and firewood and log seats litter the area. A fire should leave no trace. Above: No Fires sign in the Grand Canyon.

mineral soil (sand and gravel) below the high-water mark on the coast and below the spring flood level along rivers—any traces will be washed away, and there is usually plenty of driftwood to burn.

Fires should be built on mineral soil in other pristine places, too, and never lit on organic matter, for both environmental and safety reasons. In particular, meadows and soft vegetation should never be scarred by a fire. Dry vegetation and forest duff—conifer needles—can burst into flame very easily.

Mound fires make the least impact but require the most effort. To build one you first need to find some mineral soil such as sand from a streambed that is already disturbed. Dig up enough soil to fill a large stuff sack, then heap 6 to 8 inches of it on top of a groundsheet, trash bag, or other piece of cloth. The fire can be built in a shallow depression on top of the mound and should always be much smaller than the mound so that hot coals can't fall off the mineral soil. The mound should be built in an area that will stand up to trampling, such as bare rock or earth.

Digging into the ground to create a pit for the fire is destructive and should be done only on mineral soil where there is no organic matter at all. Fires can be lit without a pit, but digging one makes it easier to disguise the site afterward.

Do not build a ring of rocks around a fire on a pristine site. Many people construct a fireplace this way, yet it really serves no purpose, although the concept is that it contains the fire. The best way to prevent a fire from spreading is to clear the area around it of flammable materials; a site 24 to 36 inches across should be big enough. Make sure there are no low branches or tree roots above or below the fire, and pitch your shelter upwind and some distance away, so that sparks can't harm it.

Other gear, especially nylon, also needs to be kept well away from fires.

Leave no sign of your fire. All wood should be burned to a fine ash, then scattered widely before you return the mineral soil to the place it came from. Spreading duff and loose vegetation over the site helps conceal it.

If you camp at a well-used site with many rock-ringed fireplaces, use one of these rather than making a new one, even a minimum-impact one. To reduce the impact it's best to dismantle the least-used fire rings, scattering any ashes and charcoal, in the hope that they won't be used again. Some backcountry sites in national parks have metal fireboxes. Obviously you should use them. Cut wood may also be supplied at such sites to prevent damage to the surrounding forest.

When collecting fuel wood, do so with care. Do not remove wood—even deadwood—from living trees. Snags are needed by wildlife and enhance the scenery and should also be left alone. A campsite surrounded by trees stripped of their lower branches and bare ground picked clean of every twig is depressing. In high-use areas, search for wood farther afield rather than close to the site. Shorelines and riverbanks are good places to scavenge for wood. Collect only what you'll use, and use only small sticks that you can break by hand, since these are easily burned to ash. You don't need axes and saws.

Lighting and Tending the Fire

There's a certain mystique to fire lighting, and survival and woodcraft books devote many pages to describing types of fires. Basically, the secret of fire lighting is simple: start small, with dry tinder. Paper makes good tinder, but I wouldn't carry it just for this purpose. I sometimes lighten my load by using pages from the books I've read; food wrappings work well, too. If you have no paper, you can use the finest twigs, tiny pinecones, dry leaves, moss, and any other dry plant material. When the weather is wet, look for kindling in dry spots under logs and at the base of large trees. Good kindling can be created by shaving slivers three-quarters of the way off a dry twig to make a feather stick. A candle stub or solid fuel tablet can be used, too. There are also commercial fire starters available, like Tinder-Quik Fire Tabs, which are waterproof and weigh a fraction of an ounce each. A candle stub or solid fuel tablet can be used, too.

Once you have a small pile of kindling, build a pyramid of small dry twigs around it, making sure there's plenty of air space. Then light the kindling. When the twigs start to catch, add slightly larger pieces of wood. Don't overdo it—it's easy to smother a new fire. At this stage the fire's shape is irrelevant; you can alter it once it's burning well. I try to arrange an area of hot coals at one end of a cooking fire—coals, not flames, provide heat. Small metal grills with short legs make balancing pans over an open fire easy. The Coghlan's Pack Grill (11 ounces) I carried on my long hike in the Yukon was worth the weight, because I often cooked over fires. Cake racks also make good lightweight grills—rest the ends on rocks.

If lighting the fire proves difficult, dismantle it and start over; don't waste kindling by pushing bits of it into the fire and lighting them. People occasionally use stove fuel to get a fire going. This is highly dangerous. *Never throw fuel onto a smoldering fire that won't light properly.* And never do something I once saw in a shelter one damp December night. Having failed to light the pile of damp wood stacked haphazardly in the fireplace, another occupant of the shelter attempted

sprinkle water on the ashes

stir the coals with a stick and sprinkle again until no more steam rises

feel the ashes to be sure they're cool

scatter the ashes over an unvegetated area

A properly doused campfire leaves no ashes at the site.

A feather stick.

to ignite it with his lit canister stove. I was busy cooking over my stove at the time, so my companion hastily decided to devote herself to getting the fire lit conventionally and took over. Luckily, she succeeded.

Never leave a fire unattended, and make sure the ashes are cold to the touch before you leave the next day—huge areas of forest have burned because of carelessness with campfires. If you're not scattering the ashes to the four winds because they're in a well-used fire ring, douse them with water to make sure they're out. Foil or silver-lined food wrappings won't burn, so don't toss them in the fire unless you're prepared to fish them out and carry them with you when you leave. This applies to hut fires as well; I've spent many hours cleaning out shelter fireplaces blocked by foil.

STOVES

Stoves have replaced wood fires for most backcountry cooking. A stove ensures that you can have hot food and drink quickly whenever you want or need it. I always carry one. In foul weather, a stove enables me to cook in the vestibule or under a tarp while I stay warm and dry inside. When you wake up to the sound of wind and rain on the fly sheet, it's wonderful to reach out, light the stove—on which you'd set a pan of water the night before—and quickly have a hot drink to brace you for the weather outside.

Perhaps it's because they're the modern version of the campfire and represent warmth, sustenance, and safety that stoves arouse such strong passions. Advocates of particular brands or models will argue fiercely that their chosen stoves are best. Some stoves are beautiful pieces of engineering, too—I have an Optimus Svea displayed on a shelf in my study—and some people collect them and like to search out old models. For those interested in this, an excellent resource is the Classic Camp Stoves Web site—spiritburner.com. This is also the site to go to if you're trying to find spare parts for a stove, particularly an old one.

There used to be few stoves to choose from, but the numbers have expanded greatly in recent years. Quality is generally good, although in some situations a malfunctioning stove is merely a nui-

sance, at other times it could be a serious problem, particularly if you're relying on it for cooking dried food or need to melt snow for water. Some stoves work well in the cold and wind, others don't. A stove that won't produce hot water when you're cold, wet, and tired is at the very least dispiriting. If you're on the verge of hypothermia it could be dangerous.

A good stove should be capable of bringing water to a boil under the most horrendous conditions you're likely to encounter, small and light enough to carry, and reasonably simple to operate. Ideally it should be field maintainable, too. Stability is also important, particularly with stoves that will be used with large pans.

Comparisons and Weights

Charts and tables that compare the weights, rates of fuel consumption, and boiling times of various stoves can be misleading. Many factors that affect a stove's performance in the field can't be duplicated in a controlled environment; moreover, individual stoves of the same model can perform very differently.

Weights aren't always easily comparable either—some models include windscreens and pan sets in the total weight. The amount of fuel you have to carry for a given period and the weight of the fuel container need to be included in the total weight as well. Often the fuel plus its container is much heavier than the stove itself.

With the advent of a wide variety of heat-exchanger stoves, wood-burning stoves, and alcohol stoves, I now feel that comparison tables are even more confusing than in the past, so I have omitted one from this edition. All the stoves I've tested are at least reasonably efficient and pretty reliable. I wouldn't use boil time as the main reason for choosing a stove anyway. Weight, type of fuel, size of pots, number of people using it, and the seasons in which it will be used all need taking into account. A tiny ultralight canister or alcohol stove is fine for a solo summer trip but totally inadequate for melting snow for a party of four in winter. Outside of freezing temperatures, any half-decent stove should bring a quart of water to boil within ten minutes as long as the burner is shielded from the wind and the pot has a lid. If the stove will be used in freezing weather, then a more careful selection is needed, as some stoves perform poorly in such conditions. As far as weight is concerned, no stove should weigh more than 25 ounces, excluding pots and windscreen—and that would be for group cooking. Stoves for solo use only weigh a few ounces.

Fuels

The availability of fuel may determine which stove you carry, especially on a long hike where you need to resupply with fuel. The choices are solid fuel, alcohol, kerosene, white gas, and butane-propane.

Different areas of the world favor different fuels, which is worth knowing if you range widely, as I do. In Scandinavia, alcohol is the common fuel; in the Alps and Pyrenees, it's butane-propane; in Africa and Asia, kerosene. This doesn't mean you won't find other fuels in those places; but you're more likely, especially in out-of-the-way places, to find the fuels that local people favor. Automotive gasoline can be found everywhere, of course, though obtaining small amounts can be difficult. Filling a quart-size aluminum fuel bottle from a high-pressure pump at a gas station isn't easy, and in my experience the fuel usually sprays everywhere. (Three of us refueled this way during my Pacific Crest Trail hike, and I'd rather not have to do it again. The gas station staff thought the whole episode was hilarious and charged us only for the amount in our bottles rather than the somewhat larger amount vaporizing off our clothes and their bays.)

How much fuel you use each day depends on the type of stove you have, the weather, and the type of cooking you do. If you cook three meals a day, bake foods, or simmer foods for a long time, you'll use more fuel than I do, since I cook just one meal a day and boil water for a hot drink at breakfast. My stove is running for approximately 30 to 45 minutes a day, and my figures for how long fuels last are based on this. If you run your stove for longer or shorter periods, you'll need to adapt my figures. Estimates should be doubled if you're melting snow, because it takes the same amount of energy to produce a given amount of water from snow as it does to bring that amount of water to a boil. The figures assume the use of a full windscreen, whether or not it comes with the stove. My figures are for solo use—but don't assume that the amount of fuel per person is the same regardless of group size. I find that larger groups are far more fuel-efficient. On ski tours I've led, groups of ten used less fuel per person—including melting snow for water—than I would expect to use on a solo summer trip. Fuel use also depends on how careful you are to conserve fuel by running the stove only when necessary, using a windscreen, and covering pots. It's also important not to have the stove turned up so high that flames reach around the sides of the pot, which wastes fuel. Adjust the stove so the flame just covers the bottom of the pot.

Models

The world of stoves has changed greatly since the last edition. Then there was just one stove system that combined burners, pots, and heat exchangers. Now there are many. The homemade alcohol stoves have become commercially available with many new models. Wood-burning stoves have had a resurgence. Many can be used with alcohol and solid fuel as well. Canister stoves have become even lighter, and some are now designed to be used in sub-freezing temperatures.

Different features are needed in different circumstances. No one stove is best for all situations. Good simmer control is essential for those who cook complex meals, but maximum heat output is more important for melting snow, and weight is crucial for ultralight hikers. Making your own alcohol, solid-fuel, or wood-burning stove is relatively easy if you don't want to buy a commercial one. There are several Web sites with instructions—see the Wings Home-Made Stoves Archives at http://wings.interfree.it and Zen Backpacking Stoves at http://zenstoves.net.

Solid-Fuel Stoves

In my opinion solid fuel isn't efficient enough for proper cooking, but it has become popular with some ultralight hikers because of the extremely low weight, ease of use, and lack of anything that can go wrong. Attracted by the very low weight, I tried solid fuel many years ago, but I soon grew tired of the long wait for water to boil, if it did at all. However, hikers have used solid fuel on through-hikes of the Appalachian and Pacific Crest Trails, so it works for some people. If your cooking needs are minimal or you usually use a campfire, solid fuel might be of interest. The Esbit Solid Fuel Stove weighs 3.25 ounces. It's really just a platform for a fuel tablet (0.5 ounce) with two fold-up pan supports. Hexamine tablets (Esbit, Coghlan's) are reckoned by aficionados to be more efficient than trioxane tablets. One advantage of solid fuel is that you can mail it.

Alcohol Stoves

Alcohol in the form of methanol (wood alcohol, methyl alcohol), ethanol (ethyl alcohol, grain alcohol), or isopropyl alcohol (rubbing alcohol, shellac thinner, solvent alcohol, alcohol stove fuel) can be found in drugstores, hardware stores, and outdoor stores, frequently under the names methylated spirits and denatured alcohol. I took an alcohol stove on the Pacific Northwest Trail and was able to buy alcohol fuel in some form or other in every little town along the way. Hardly any had butane-propane cartridges or Coleman fuel or similar. Alcohol is a good fuel to choose for long-distance hiking where you'll be buying fuel along the way. Often the three types of alcohol are mixed together. Gas-line antifreeze made from methanol can be used in alcohol stoves—HEET is a popular brand—though you should check the contents to be sure it is alcohol. On the Pacific Northwest Trail, I bought fuel in the little towns along the way and could sometimes only get one type. This turned out to be a useful experiment. I found that ethanol is by far the best fuel—usually obtained as HEET in yellow bottles, which could often be seen protruding from the mesh side pockets on my pack, and sometimes as sanitizer from a drug store. Isopropyl, labeled "rubbing alcohol" and bought when I couldn't find ethanol, was not so good. The 70 percent isopropyl was hard to light and often went out. It did work, but I wouldn't use it again by choice. The 90 percent isopropyl was odd stuff. Once lit, it burned slowly for several minutes then suddenly roared into life with a smoky flame. Once I'd tried all three types, I took care to read the small print on unfamiliar bottles and avoid 70 percent isopropyl if I had a choice and pick ethanol over 90 percent isopropyl. Pure ethanol can be used to make alcoholic drinks and so is expensive because of excise tax. It burns well, though. The type found in paint thinners and methylated spirits has methanol and other substances added to "denature" it and make it poisonous and therefore inexpensive, since it's not liable for duty. Don't drink it! And of course you can burn brandy or rum in an alcohol stove if you run out of other fuel.

Alcohol is the only liquid fuel not derived from petroleum, which makes it more environmentally friendly than other fuels. It's also the only liquid fuel that burns unpressurized, which makes it safer, and thus appealing to those who find most stoves a little scary. It's clean, too, evaporating quickly when spilled. For these reasons, it's a good fuel for cooking in a tent vestibule. It's not a hot fuel, however—it produces roughly half as much heat per fluid ounce as gasoline or kerosene. I use 4 to 5 fluid ounces a day, so a quart lasts about a week, which makes it heavier than other fuels to carry on long trips. Trangia says that a quart of alcohol will boil twenty quarts of water, which fits with my experience, since I boil 2 to 4 quarts a day. As alcohol stoves heat up the output increases, so the first pot boiled will take longer than the second, and that one will take longer than the third. That's as long as you protect the stove from the wind, of course. Strong gusts can blow out an alcohol stove.

Alcohol blackens pans, which many people don't like. This doesn't bother me; in theory, blackened pans should absorb heat faster than shiny silver ones, so I make no attempt to clean off the black. Once pans have cooled, the soot rarely comes off on your hands, unlike the soot from campfires.

One joy of alcohol stoves is that they are absolutely silent—you can hear water coming to a boil and also the wind in the trees, birdsong, the hum of insects, and other sounds that are drowned out by the roar of most stoves. Care is needed when using alcohol in daylight because the pale blue flame is invisible in bright light. Most stoves burn for only half an hour at most on one filling (depending on the wind and the use of any simmer device), so refilling while the stove is in use is sometimes necessary. However, inadvertently refilling a still-burning stove from a fuel bottle because you think it's empty could cause the fuel bottle to ignite. Sometimes there can be a small flame left even if there doesn't appear to be any heat given off. If a stove goes out during use, I refill it by pouring fuel into the burner cover or other small container, then into the burner. If this item catches fire, I simply drop it onto the stove. It is of course important to be sure there are no flammable items near any stove.

When packing an alcohol stove, I pour any unused fuel back into the fuel bottle after the burner has cooled; fuel tends to leak if carried in the burner, though Trangias come with a sealed lid that is effective as long as you don't melt the rubber O-ring by putting it on a hot burner. I also pack the burner in a plastic bag and carry it separately from the pans so that it doesn't dirty them and leave a lingering smell of fuel. Alcohol can be carried in light plastic bottles. Heavy metal ones aren't necessary, which saves a little of the extra weight of fuel needed.

TRANGIA ALCOHOL STOVES Alcohol is very popular in Scandinavia, and the Swedish-made Trangia Storm-Cookers are well made, simple, and almost indestructible.

Trangias come in several versions. Most are complete units, including burner, windscreen/pan support, pans, lid, and pot grab, that nest together for carrying. The excellent little burner itself weighs 2.5 ounces and consists of a short double-walled open brass cylinder with jets around the top, into which you pour fuel—2 fluid ounces fills it. To light it, you simply touch a match to the alcohol. In Trangia 25 and 27 units the burner rests inside a rigid aluminum windscreen, which contains foldout pan supports. With a lid over the top you have virtually a sealed unit, so heat loss is minimal. There are small holes in one side of the windscreen base, which can be turned into the wind to create a draft and make a stronger flame—these are the only stoves I know that boil water more quickly when it's windy. The flame can be controlled somewhat by dropping a simmer ring (0.75 ounce) over the jets so that only the surface of the reservoir is burning, then partially covering this with a flat metal disk, which you knock into place with a spoon or knife until you achieve the required degree of heat. It's a crude system and awkward to operate, but it does work. One filling burns for 20 to 30 minutes and will boil a couple of quarts.

Trangia 25 and 27 units come in two sizes, each with two pans, a frypan/lid, and an optional kettle. The cook kit comes in plain aluminum, nonstick aluminum, and hard-anodized aluminum versions. With the use of lighter materials, Trangia units are lighter than in the past, though I think the designation "UL" for "Ultra Light" is stretching the description a little. For solo use, the Trangia 27 UL is ideal; including two 1-quart pots, frypot/lid, and pot grab, it weighs 25.4 ounces in plain and hard-anodized aluminum and 28 ounces in nonstick aluminum. Versions including the pint-sized kettle weigh 5 ounces more. The larger Trangia 25 UL models have 1.5- and 1.75-quart pots and an optional quart kettle. The 25 UL weighs from 30.5 to 41.2 ounces depending on the pot material and whether the kettle is included or not, which isn't too heavy for two or

Trangia alcohol stove with windscreen.

three backpackers. There is also a Mini-Trangia (Trangia 28) consisting of the burner, a simplified windscreen, and a quart pan with frypan/lid that weighs 11.5 ounces. All the Trangia parts are sold separately, so you could just buy the burner, and perhaps the simmer ring and cover, and construct your own lightweight pot supports and windscreen.

A Trangia 27 was my first backpacking stove. I've had one for about thirty years. For a decade it was my regular stove and has been all over Scotland, Norway in summer and winter, Iceland, and on my 1,250-mile walk from one end of Britain to the other. Although dented, it still works perfectly. There is so little to go wrong that it's just about indestructible. Indeed, I've heard of a Trangia that was run over by a truck; the windscreen was simply beaten back into shape before being returned to use. I haven't taken mine on long trips for many years, though, because of the weight both of the unit itself and of the fuel. Despite what many people believe, the Trangia works well in cold weather, though it can be hard to get the fuel to light. I find the best method is to drop a lighted match into the burner. In my experience it takes 10–15 minutes for a pint of water to boil in a Trangia.

THE CALDERA CONE SYSYEM While efficient and durable, the Trangia system is heavy and bulky. In stormy weather, it was far more reliable than any other alcohol stove setup, however. Now there is a lightweight alternative that works just as well, Trail Designs' Caldera Cone System. This simple yet ingenious design consists of a 0.5-ounce stove made from drink cans and a cone-shaped wind-screen and pot support. The cone is made from a crescent-shaped piece of thin aluminum or titanium (the latter designed in conjunction with Titanium Goat) that can be rolled for packing. Slide the ends of the piece of metal together, and it forms a cone into which the pot is fitted and which stands over the burner, making a stable windproof unit. Because the pot has to fit into the top of the cone, the two must match. It's available for dozens of different pots at weights ranging from 1 to 2.75 ounces in aluminum and 0.4 to 1.23 ounces in tita-nium. The aluminum cone can be used with solid fuel and alcohol—an optional solid-fuel holder is available. The titanium cone can also be used with wood, which burns too hot for aluminum.

To use the stove, you simply pour fuel into the burner (maximum 1.35 fluid ounces), light it, and place the cone around it. The stove gets very hot, so it's best to place it on a piece of foil or metal to prevent it from scorching the ground. Once you place the cone around the stove and put the pot in

Caldera Cone alcohol stove with Evernew 0.9-liter pot.

place, it heats up very quickly. Because the top is blocked by the pot, it traps the heat from the stove well. One morning when the temperature was 28°F and there was a stiff wind, the aluminum Caldera Cone boiled 0.8 pint of icy water (the capacity of my mug) in a 1.5-pint pot in 5 minutes, 15 sec-onds. That's fast for an alcohol stove even in mild weather. Fuel usage is similar to other alcohol stoves, however—around 1 fluid ounce per pint of water in temperatures between 28 and 41°F with water barely above zero. It is important to only put the correct amount of fuel in the burner, as it's dif-ficult to extinguish the flame and even harder to try and pour surplus fuel out of the burner. If there's too much fuel, it's best to let it burn away. The cone gets very hot and needs to be left to cool before being handled. When it's been very windy, I've had flames coming out of the top vents, and the metal does become discolored in places.

The Caldera Cone System has become one of my favorites. I used the Sidewinder Inferno ver-sion on the Pacific Northwest Trail with both alcohol and wood, and it performed excellently the whole time. I reckon it's the best alcohol-burning stove system there is.

BRASSLITE Brasslite stoves (brasslite.com) emerged from the homemade alcohol stove scene. These stoves attracted me as soon as I saw one. They look rather like a miniature Optimus Svea 123R, both because they're made of brass and because of the shape. I found that they not only look good, they work well too. There are two Brasslite models—the 1.9-ounce Turbo I-D and the 2.5-ounce Turbo II-D. The Turbo I-D is designed for solo use with pans up to 1 quart. The fuel capacity is just 1 fluid ounce, and on full flame it burns for nine and a half minutes. It won't boil more than a quart without refueling. The Turbo II-D, the model I have, will handle pots up to 2 quarts capacity with a minimum base size of 4 inches to prevent flames from spilling around the sides, which wastes fuel. Capacity is 2 fluid ounces, and burn time is twenty minutes on full flame. Both burners have fuel chambers with a hole in the top, air ports with a simmer ring that can be closed for simmering, and wire pot supports. The simmer sleeve is closed by moving a lever, which needs to be done with a metal utensil, since it gets hot.

Brasslite recommends use of a foil heat reflector under the stove and a foil windscreen. I used ones from a multifuel stove. I also used Brasslite's 1.5 ounce, 8-ounce capacity plastic custom fuel bottle, which makes filling the stove easy and precise. The bottle has a reservoir that takes up to half an ounce of fuel. Measurement marks on it make it easy to see how much fuel you're using. I first used the stove on a two-day trip in temperatures below freezing (the lowest was 26°F [–3°C]). Once I learned to squeeze fuel on the priming pan at the base of the stove and light that, the stove lit quickly. It then boiled a pint of water in about eight minutes, about half the time of a Trangia. The simmer sleeve worked well, and by moving it carefully I could control the flame surprisingly well, certainly

The Brasslite Turbo II-D is an ultralight, hot alcohol stove with a controllable flame.

better than with a Trangia, though not as well as with a canister stove. I like the Brasslite and will be using it on future trips where I don't have to carry more than a few days' fuel at a time. It's not as sturdy as the Trangia, but it's much tougher than soda-can stoves. A windscreen is required in anything above a light breeze. Brasslite sells a 1.7-ounce aluminum windscreen.

OTHER ALCOHOL STOVES There are many other alcohol stoves available, most from cottage manufacturers. Of the ones I've tried, I particularly like the White Box Stove and the AntiGravity Gear stove. The White Box Stove (the name comes from the cardboard box in which it's packed) is one of the most powerful alcohol stoves. It's made from recycled aluminum and consists of a double-wall cylinder with the inner walls forming a cone-shaped recess at the top. A row of tiny burn holes runs around the outside of the stove about a quarter of the way below the top rim. It comes with a foil windscreen and heat reflector. The whole set weighs around an ounce. It feels tough and can't be crushed in the hand like stoves made from drink cans. There are two versions, the Original, which will hold 3 ounces of fuel and is designed for two to three people, and the Solo, which holds 1.5 ounces.

The White Box Stove has a deep well that shouldn't be filled more than half full. Lighting the fuel down in this well is most easily done by dropping a lit match into it or else using a striker like a firesteel to light the vapor. The instructions say you can hold a lighter down in the well to light it, but if you try this, you'll probably burn your fingers. Once the alcohol in the well is burning, you need to wait until flames emerge from the burn holes before placing a pot on the stove, or it will go out. This priming sequence takes about a minute. Using a priming pot speeds it up if you don't want to wait. The flames emerge forcefully from the burn holes and form a wide ring of fire. The spread of the flames is such that this stove is best used with pots with a wide diameter rather than narrow titanium mugs. Pots without handles and a pot grab are useful, too, as attached handles get very hot. On one trip, I used an Evernew 0.9-liter pot with rubber-covered handles with the White Box Stove, and the rubber started to melt. I've used this pot with gasoline stoves in the past without damaging the rubber. A large flame can shoot up from the well if the pot is removed before all the fuel is burned, so it's best to wait until the stove has gone out before taking the pot off. Just using the right amount of fuel is more efficient, anyway, as it's almost impossible to put the stove out and very difficult to pour out unused fuel if you succeed. I've used the White Box Stove under a tarp and in a tent vestibule, but care is needed and a great deal of space around

The White Box Stove is a powerful alcohol stove.

and above the stove. The heat reflector keeps the stove from scorching the ground and may add to the heating effect, though there was little difference in the boil time when I didn't use it. The windshield does make a big difference to boil time and fuel efficiency, even though the stove is powerful enough not to blow out in any but the strongest winds. Fuel efficiency overall is about average, with 1 fluid ounce needed to boil a pint. Boil times are around six minutes for a pint. I like this stove for its power, speed, and high quality. If you don't use a titanium mug and you don't want to wait too long for water to boil, it's a good choice.

The AntiGravity Gear stove is made from drink cans and weighs 0.4 ounce. It's similar to the Caldera stove in looks and is delicate compared with the White Box Stove. On its own, it's a fairly typical drink-can alcohol stove with an adequate performance—a little more than an ounce of fuel is needed to boil a pint of water, and the time taken for this is around 7.5 minutes. Like the White Box Stove, the pot sits directly on the stove, and you have to wait for flames to appear through the burn holes in the sides before putting a pot on, or it goes out. What's good is that AGG offers it in a series of cooksets with pots, pot cozies, pot grabs, fuel measuring cups, windscreens, and stuff sacks under the name Mama's Kitchen. I have the Mama's Kitchen 3 Cup Non-Stick Cook Set, which weighs 7.4 ounces. These sets are excellent value if you need all or most of the components. The pots are very light (the three-cup version is 3.8 ounces with lid), but the real gem is the pot cozy. This foil-and-bubble-wrap container keeps food hot enough to continue cooking, which saves fuel and means the lack of simmering ability isn't a problem. I've used the cozy in subzero temperatures, and it's worked well.

White-Gas and Multifuel Stoves

White gas is probably the most efficient stove fuel, lighting easily, burning very hot, and unaffected by cold temperatures. Automotive gasoline is a substitute; you can get it everywhere, and for stove use it's very cheap. But it's dirty and smoky, clogs fuel lines and jets, which need frequent cleaning when run on it, and gives off fumes you really don't want to breathe. Stoves run best and cleanest on refined white gas such as Coleman fuel, the most common one. White gas is sold in outdoor, sporting, and hardware stores and often, especially in towns near popular national parks or wilderness areas, in supermarkets. White gas is volatile fuel and ignites very easily. It requires a lot of care but it is very efficient. I use 2 to 3 fluid ounces a day, so a quart lasts at least ten days.

Kerosene is easy to get, reasonably cheap, and burns at least as hot as gasoline. MSR says its stoves boil slightly more water per amount of kerosene than of white gas. Kerosene doesn't ignite easily, so it's relatively safe—far safer than white gas. That means it's harder to light, of course. It won't burn just as a liquid as white gas will, so a wick is needed. Multifuel stoves have a pad or wick for this purpose. I find kerosene messy and hard to work with, so I use it only as a last resort. It also stains badly and takes a long time to evaporate, leaving a strong odor unless you use a deodorized version. Refined kerosene (heater or lamp fuel) is much cleaner than crude versions, which can produce dirty, smoky fumes. I became very familiar with kerosene on an eighty-six-day walk up the length of the mountains of Norway and Sweden when I used it in an MSR XGK Expedition. I've also used it on several ski tours in places like Greenland and Spitsbergen, where it has worked fine at −15°F (−26°C). Kerosene is efficient—I use 2 to 3 fluid ounces a day—but the difficulties with lighting and handling mean it's not my favorite fuel.

White-gas and multifuel stoves burn vaporized fuel, not liquid. The fuel has to be pressurized (these are sometimes called *pressure stoves*) to get it to flow to the burner. Once a stove is lit, the heat from the flames keeps the burner hot so that the fuel vaporizes as it leaves the jet. On many stoves the fuel line runs in a loop next to the burner. This preheat tube heats the fuel before it reaches the jet, speeding vaporization, which is particularly useful when using kerosene. In the simplest stoves, the fuel is transmitted from the tank to the burner by a wick that draws it up to the jet.

Originally white-gas stoves had integral fuel tanks sitting under or next to the burner. This design is still around, but most stoves now connect to a fuel bottle with a long fuel line, giving them a low profile that makes them more stable than taller models. Both types operate best when the tanks are at least half full—they should

Lighting a white-gas stove. Pump the fuel bottle until you can feel firm resistance when you push the pump in—usually after about twenty strokes when the bottle is full (1). The emptier the bottle, the more pumping is required. It's easiest to do this before you attach the fuel bottle to the stove. When the fuel bottle has been pressurized, open the valve a little until a teaspoon or so of fuel has squirted out and run down into the priming cup or onto the priming wick or pad (2). With stoves without a pump, dribble fuel into the priming cup from a fuel bottle with a pouring spout or an eyedropper filled from the fuel bottle. Light the priming fuel and wait until it has almost burned out (3). Just before it does so open the valve; the stove should roar into life, burning with a blue flame. If the priming flame goes out before you've opened the valve, use a lighter or a match; do this quickly, before the stove cools down. If the stove spurts yellow flames, turn it off; you haven't primed it enough. Wait for the yellow flames to die down, then turn it on again. If it still doesn't light properly, turn it off, wait for it to cool, and then prime it again. Once the stove is lit, let it burn for a minute or so at a low flame and then turn it on full (4). Don't turn the valve more times than recommended in the stove's instructions or you could damage the connection with the bottle. To maintain full power, pump a few strokes every so often (5). If you want a simmering flame, use the stove's simmer control (if it has one), leaving the main valve on full. If there's only one control, turn it down to simmer and don't pump the stove again as it will simmer better with low pressure in the fuel bottle. There will be a short delay between turning a valve on the pump housing and the flame changing. Controls on the burner affect the flame immediately.

never be totally filled, because then the fuel can't expand, and you won't be able to pressurize the stove properly. Built-in fuel tanks are usually small, ⅓- to ¾-pint capacity, so they may need refilling every day or two. I find it best to top up the fuel tank last thing before packing away the stove in the morning. That way I'm unlikely to run out while cooking the evening meal. If you run out of fuel while cooking, you must wait for the stove to cool down before you can refill it.

Stoves have either *roarer* or *ported* burners. In the first a stream of vaporized fuel is pushed out of the jet, ignites, and hits a burner plate that spreads it out into a ring of flame. Roarer burners, as you might guess, are noisy. In ported burners the flames come out of a ring of jets, just like a kitchen gas range. Ported burners are much quieter than roarer burners, though still pretty loud. Neither type seems more efficient than the other.

The main makers of white-gas and multifuel stoves are Primus, Optimus, MSR, Snow Peak, and Coleman.

PRIMING For fuel to flow to the burner and then vaporize, it has to be preheated, known as *priming*. Priming liquid-fuel stoves is quite easy, but it does require a little practice and should always be done with care outside, since the fuel can flare up. It's the trickiest part of using a pressure stove. Pump stoves are all primed in much the same way, though you should always follow the specific instructions. First the fuel is pressurized by pumping, usually for about twenty strokes when the bottle or tank is full. Then you open the valve a little and allow a tiny amount of fuel to dribble out into the priming cup or onto the priming pad or burner, depending on the model. Alternatively, you can use alcohol, solid-fuel tablets, or even bits of paper. These are all less likely to flare than fuel from the stove, but they're something extra to carry. Next you close the valve and light the priming fuel. If you've used too much fuel the stove can flare, so don't have your face over it. As the last flames die away, slowly open the valve again until the burner lights—have a match or lighter handy so you can light the stove if the priming fuel goes out before you open the valve. If you've primed correctly, the flame will be blue.

If the flame is yellow you need to turn the stove off and prime it again, after it has cooled down. With stoves that have a control valve on the pump and a flame adjuster at the burner, use the adjuster to control the flow of fuel, leaving the control valve open.

OPTIMUS SVEA The Optimus Svea has been around for over a century and is the classic white-gas stove. (The first Svea stoves were produced by a company called Nyberg and ran on kerosene. Production was three thousand stoves a week in the 1890s.) In the 1960s and 1970s it was one of the most popular white-gas stoves. My first white-gas stove was a Svea that I used on through-hikes of the Pacific Crest and Continental Divide Trails. It performed faultlessly.

The Svea looks like a brass can with perforations; though it doesn't sound attractive, it's aesthetically much more appealing than most stoves. It's made up of a roarer burner screwed into a ⅓-pint brass fuel tank and a circular windscreen/pan-support unit that fits around the burner. A small aluminum drinking cup fits over the top to protect the burner when it's in the pack (though I usually leave this at home—it burns your lips). The tank has a screw-on cap with a built-in safety valve designed to release pressure if the tank overheats. (If this happens, the jet of fuel that spurts out will almost certainly become a flame, so it's wise to point the tank cap away from you and anything flammable—like your tent.) The Svea's burner is operated by a key on a chain that fits onto an arm jutting out from the burner and doubles as a maintenance tool. The key is inserted through the windscreen. That and folding out the pan supports are the only setup procedure required, so this stove can be ready to use in seconds.

The Optimus Svea 123 white-gas stove is a classic that has been around for decades.

The Svea doesn't have a pump, so the tank has to be pressurized by priming it. The simplest way to do this is to fill the shallow recess at the foot of the burner tube with about a teaspoon of gasoline from the fuel bottle (you need a fuel bottle cap with a pouring spout or pouring holes) and light it. Broken solid-fuel tablets or alcohol can be used instead, though I don't find them as effective. By the time the last of the flames are dying away, the tank and burner should both be warm enough so that when you turn the key and open the jet the burner lights. If you miss this point, quickly applying a match will usually light the stove. The flame should be blue. If it's yellow, the burner hasn't been primed enough, and the stove is burning semiliquid fuel. Turn it off, let it cool, then prime it again. Once it's lit, you can use the key to control the flame, though the range of control is limited. The key also controls a built-in jet-cleaning needle, operated by turning the key beyond the "on" position. This should be done infrequently to avoid widening the jet hole. The stove will burn at full heat for up to 50 minutes on one filling, according to Optimus, which seems about right. The Svea is stable enough for small pans, but large ones demand care, because of its tall, narrow shape.

Sveas are tough and long-lived. My blackened veteran of the Continental Divide Trail, now twenty-five years old, still works fine, boiling water faster than some much newer stoves.

OPTIMUS NOVA While the Svea is a classic white-gas stove, Optimus also make a modern multi-fuel stove, the Nova, that uses a fuel bottle as the tank and is arguably the most advanced model yet made. In my tests it's certainly the quickest priming and easiest to use. It has a redesigned burner unit with conductor ribs that transfer heat to the fuel tube below the burner much more quickly than traditional designs do. This means that priming only takes 15 to 30 seconds with white gas and a little longer with kerosene, which is much faster than with other stoves. Whichever fuel you use, you don't need to change the jet, an excellent feature that saves time, the hassle of having to take the stove apart, and the risk of losing one of the tiny jets. Once lit, the flame is very powerful but can easily be turned down for simmering. The Nova comes in two versions, the standard and the plus, the main difference being the flame control, which on the Nova is a lever protruding from the burner and on the Nova+ a cylinder around the fuel line. Both work well, but I prefer the lever, which I find easier to use. One of the aspects of the Nova I like most is the self-purging pump. Instead of depressurizing the fuel bottle by unscrewing

The modern Optimus Nova multifuel stove is easy to light and powerful.

the pump slightly, which inevitably lets a spray of pressurized fuel escape, and then detaching the fuel line from the pump, with attendant drips of fuel, you just flip the fuel bottle over and wait (it says *On* and *Off* on the pump). Fuel in the tube then burns off to be replaced by air, which helps clean the jet. As this air is released, the fuel bottle is depressurized, so there's no need to unscrew the pump. Now that I've gotten used to having a clean, nondripping stove to pack I really resent models that drip fuel and leave gas on my hands. The Nova can be turned off with the control lever, so the fuel bottle stays pressurized if you're going to use it again soon. If the jet gets blocked, there's a built-in cleaning needle that you can operate by shaking the stove or by using an included magnetic tool to push the needle into the jet. With this tool you can clean the jet while the stove is lit. The magnetic tool weighs 1.5 ounces and can also be used to disassemble the stove for maintenance,

though I've never had to do this. The Nova is very ruggedly built and has a metal pump. It packs up neatly (the legs/pot supports close around the burner) and weighs 15 ounces. The Nova takes around four to six minutes to boil a pint of water and uses around 0.8 fluid ounce of fuel to do so.

COLEMAN EXPONENT FEATHER 442 Coleman is another traditional stove maker; its first stove appeared in 1923. The Feather 442 Dual-Fuel Stove is a high-tech construction bristling with levers and knobs. It has a ported burner set atop an 11-ounce fuel tank and a built-in pump. It needs priming only in very cold weather—at least in theory. It's not fully field maintainable, so I wouldn't want to rely on it on a cold-weather or remote-country trip.

The Feather 442 weighs 24 ounces and runs on white gas and unleaded gasoline. Lighting it without priming is possible, but the instructions need to be followed precisely, and flaring is likely—my success rate is about 25 percent. I find it easier to

The Coleman Exponent Feather 442 dual-fuel stove is very powerful but bulky and heavy.

light the stove by priming with a little fuel around the burner, especially in cold weather. Once lit, the Feather 442 is a powerful stove with a very fast boil time. Simmering is possible, but it doesn't allow the fine control of some stoves. The Feather 442 is on the heavy side for solo backpacking but would be all right for groups or base-camp use.

COLEMAN FYRESTORM The Fyrestorm is the best stove Coleman has produced for many years in my opinion. It can be run off unleaded petrol, Coleman and similar fuel, and also butane canisters (see Butane-Propane Cartridge Stoves later in this chapter). The Fyrestorm is a low-profile, hose-attached stove with three foldout legs and a pump that slots into a fuel bottle. There are two versions, the Ti, made from titanium and weighing 10.6 ounces, and the SS, made from stainless steel and weighing 2 ounces more. It comes with a 1-pint fuel bottle weighing 4 ounces and a windscreen and heat reflector weighing 3 ounces. It lights fairly easily with minimal priming but more pumping than other stoves. Once lit, the flame is very controllable, making simmering possible. There's a built-in jet-cleaning needle operated by the flame control that protrudes from the burner. However, if the generator becomes blocked, it has to be replaced, so the stove isn't fully field maintainable unless you carry a spare generator and the tools to fit it. Using Coleman fuel, I got times of around 4.5 minutes for boiling a pint of water, which used 0.9 ounce of fuel. As a white gas stove, the Fyrestorm is OK. Where it shines is as a canister stove, as discussed in the following section.

MSR XGK-EX MSR first came up with the idea of using a fuel bottle as a remote fuel tank back in the 1970s; its first model, the No. 9, appeared in 1973. This became the GK and then the XGK and now the XGK-EX. The MSR XGK deserves the name

multifuel, since it will run on white gas, leaded and unleaded gasoline, aviation fuel, kerosene, diesel, and more, though you may have to clean it regularly when using anything other than white gas and kerosene. The same jet can be used for white gas and kerosene, though a second one is recommended for diesel and low-grade kerosene and any other fuels that burn with a sooty yellow flame using the standard jet. For remote areas where you don't know what fuel you'll find, this stove is a good choice. I once ran one on something called white spirits for a week when that was the only fuel I could get in a remote part of Norway. The stove gave off appalling dirty fumes but otherwise worked perfectly.

The XGK has a roarer burner (and it does roar!) and a flexible fuel tube. This tube has a wide diameter and is easy to clean if it clogs. Like other MSR stoves it has a Shaker Jet, a weighted cleaning needle built into the burner that cleans the jet when you gently shake the stove. The weight

The MSR XGK-EX multifuel stove is an excellent stove for use with dirty fuel.

is 15.1 ounces including a windscreen and heat reflector, 13.3 ounces without them. The XGK is field maintainable and comes with a maintenance kit weighing half an ounce.

The XGK is easy to light, but simmering is difficult. It's great for melting snow (for which it was originally designed) and boiling water, however, and a reliable and durable well-proven expedition stove. Boiling time with Coleman fuel is around five to six minutes for a quart of water, with a fuel use of 0.8 ounce.

MSR WHISPERLITE INTERNATIONALE The MSR WhisperLite Internationale burns stove fuel, automotive fuel, and kerosene, though you need to change the jet for the kerosene. It has the same Shaker Jet as the XGK-EX. It's a small, spidery stove with a ported burner and foldaway legs/pot supports that weighs 14 ounces without windscreen and heat reflector, which add 1.8 ounces. This is a powerful stove suitable for group cooking—I've used it to cook for ten for two weeks at a time on spring ski trips with both stove fuel and kerosene, and it's worked perfectly. Flame control is limited, however, so simmering is difficult. The stove is field

maintainable and comes with a maintenance kit weighing 0.5 ounce. It's not the fastest-heating multifuel stove, taking five to seven minutes to bring a quart of water to the boil, but fuel usage is good at around 0.7 ounce per quart boiled.

For a while the WhisperLite became the nearest thing to a standard backpacking stove. I joined the throng and used a WhisperLite Internationale on my long Canadian Rockies and Yukon walks. It proved very reliable, the only maintenance needed being to the leather pump washer, which dried out. I greased it with margarine, and it worked perfectly.

MSR DRAGONFLY The big complaint with the XGK and WhisperLite stoves has always been that it's difficult to make them simmer even a little. To answer this MSR launched the DragonFly, which has a flame adjuster on the burner so the heat can be easily turned down for simmering. The burner is a roarer, and the DragonFly is one of the noisiest stoves. It has sprung-steel pan supports that fold inward and a pivoting burner and forms a neat unit for packing, though a little bulkier than a WhisperLite. The burner is also suspended above

The MSR WhisperLite Internationale stove is the multifuel version of the popular WhisperLite.

the stove base and so less affected by cold ground. The DragonFly is a multifuel stove and will burn most liquid petroleum fuels. There are different jets for white gas and kerosene. The DragonFly is powerful—I've used it for melting snow and cooking for ten on ski tours—and it does simmer well. MSR rates it the most efficient of its stoves, saying it boils more water per volume of fuel. It weighs 14 ounces without windscreen and heat reflector, and there's a 0.75-ounce maintenance kit. The boil time is five to six minutes for a quart of water. Fuel consumption is good at around 0.65 ounce per quart with stove fuel.

MSR SIMMERLITE Having made a stove that simmers with the DragonFly, MSR's designers turned their attention to weight and came up with the SimmerLite, the lightest white-gas stove at just 8.5 ounces without windscreen and heat reflector (2 ounces—there's no hole in the heat reflector, unlike those with other MSR stoves). The Simmer-Lite looks a little like the WhisperLite, with fold-out legs/pan supports and a wide ported burner. The legs are flat rather than round, however, and there's no cup around the burner. Although low in weight, the SimmerLite isn't low in power, boiling a quart in four to five minutes. Fuel usage is fine too at around 0.7 ounce per quart. Like other MSR liquid-fuel stoves, the SimmerLite has a Shaker Jet and is field maintainable. A maintenance kit weighs 0.5 ounce.

PRIMUS MULTIFUEL AND OMNIFUEL In the late 1990s Primus, once a big name in liquid-fuel stoves but that hadn't made one for many years, introduced the MultiFuel, which looks quite similar to other liquid-fuel stoves. Unlike any of them at the time (Coleman introduced the Fyrestorm many years later), however, it also runs on self-sealing butane-propane cartridges, making it extremely versatile. This is achieved by one of those simple but bril-

Top: The MSR DragonFly multifuel stove offers separate flame control, which is good for simmering. Above: The MSR SimmerLite white-gas stove is the lightest white-gas stove available.

liant devices that make you wonder why no one thought of it before; a valve on the pump that's the same as the valve on standard self-sealing cartridges and a fuel line valve that will fit either of them. The OmniFuel has the same valve plus a redesigned burner, rather along the lines of the Optimus Nova, to shorten the preheating time and make lighting the stove easier. The OmniFuel also has a flame adjuster on the burner to aid in sim-

The Primus OmniFuel multifuel stove is the only multifuel stove that works with butane-propane canisters.

mering. Both stoves have self-purging pumps. To shut the stove down, you flip the fuel bottle over and wait while the fuel line clears and the bottle depressurizes. This means no drips from the fuel line when you detach it from the pump and no need to partly unscrew the pump to release the pressure, allowing a spray of vaporized fuel to escape. The stoves are field maintainable and very ruggedly built. They come with foil windscreens and heat reflectors.

The two stoves look much the same, with three foldout legs/pan supports and a squat profile. The MultiFuel weighs 13 ounces without the pump, the OmniFuel 14.5 ounces. The solid metal pump adds five ounces to both stoves. Both burn very hot and boil water fast with cartridges, but the MultiFuel is slower than other stoves with white gas and kerosene. Both stoves also simmer well with cartridges, but again the MultiFuel is not so good with white gas and kerosene. The Omni-Fuel is better with white gas but doesn't seem to like kerosene, sputtering and flaring and burning slowly however much it's primed or pumped. I

took the OmniFuel and the Optimus Nova on a ski tour in Lapland with two friends and ended up just using the Nova, which worked so much better with the kerosene we were using. With Coleman fuel, the OmniFuel takes five to six minutes and around 0.7 ounce of fuel to boil a quart of water. The MultiFuel takes half a minute or so longer and uses 0.9 ounce of fuel.

The idea behind these stoves is excellent, and they do work well. But there are disadvantages. With the MultiFuel you have to change the jet if you switch between white gas and kerosene, so it's easier to change from one of those fuels to a cartridge. With the OmniFuel there are three jets: one for butane-propane, one for white gas, and one for kerosene and other heavy fuels. Changing the jets is only a minor hassle, but I'd rather not have it. The jets are tiny, too, and easily mislaid or lost. The stoves are quite heavy for cartridge stoves— though they support big pans better than most —but reasonable for multifuel ones. I wouldn't want to use either of them with kerosene again because of their poor performance, but if you want one stove to use with white gas and cartridges, the OmniFuel is a good choice.

PRIMUS ETAPOWER MF This stove can be used with white gas and kerosene as well as butane-propane cartridges. However, I think it performs far better with the latter, so I've included it under that heading.

SNOW PEAK GIGAPOWER WHITE GAS STOVE REGULAR The GigaPower White Gas Stove Regular is a lightweight white-gas stove that looks a little like the DragonFly. It weighs 12.5 ounces and comes with a foil windscreen. Snow Peak says that no priming is required and that there is precision flame control. *Backpacker* gave it an Editor's Choice Award, which suggests it's pretty good. I haven't used it, though, so I can offer no comment other than that it seems worth a look.

Butane-Propane Cartridge Stoves

Light, clean and simple to use, cartridge stoves are excellent for three-season use. The fuel is a blend of butane, propane, and sometimes isobutane kept under pressure as a liquid in a sealed cartridge. Open the stove valve, and the fuel rushes out as a gas, which is then ignited. Pure butane has just about vanished. It performs poorly in cool weather because it doesn't vaporize below 31°F (−1°C) at sea level and is slow to do so below 40°F (5°C). As the altitude increases the boiling point of butane drops, which is the reason butane stoves have been used successfully for Himalayan mountaineering. At 10,000 feet, butane stoves will work down to 14°F (−10°C).

Propane, however, vaporizes at −43°F (−42°C) and so works fine at all altitudes. Unfortunately it's also very volatile, so cartridges have to be strong and therefore heavy. Mix it with a larger amount of butane, and a lighter cartridge can be used, hence blended fuels. Isobutane, which boils at 11°F (−12°C), is sometimes used along with or instead of butane. Coleman cartridges are 70/30 butane/propane; Primus, 50/25/25 butane/isobutane/propane; MSR, 80/20 isobutane/propane; Snow Peak 85/15 isobutane/propane; and Campingaz CV, 80/20 butane/propane. I've used all these cartridges, and I can't say I've noticed much difference between them. All are slow in subfreezing temperatures unless the cartridges are warmed or inverted, which only works and is safe with hose-connected stoves with preheat tubes.

The problem is that butane and propane don't bond very well, and the more volatile propane burns off first, giving very fast boiling times with new cartridges. As the cartridge empties there is less propane and more butane left, and performance in the cold declines. This is made even worse because as gas is released the pressure in the cartridge falls, and as the pressure drops so does the temperature of the cartridge. You end up with less pressure to force the gas out of the car-

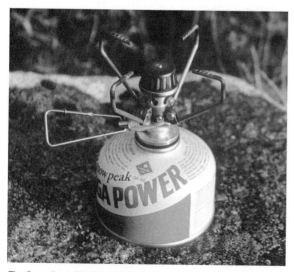
The Snow Peak GigaPower Titanium is a tiny, ultralight stove.

tridge and a colder cartridge that makes the fuel less likely to vaporize anyway. Thus in temperatures much below freezing cold cartridges don't give out much power. Once they're more than half empty, they may not produce enough energy to boil water at all. To overcome this you have to warm the cartridge, which can be done with gloved hands (bare ones can freeze to the metal) or by stuffing the cartridge inside your clothing. Keeping cartridges in your sleeping bag overnight or bringing them in as soon as you wake up can help too. Insulating cartridges against frozen ground or snow is also worth doing. A piece of foam or even a book makes a difference. Whatever you do it's a hassle, though, and I don't use standard cartridge stoves if the temperature is likely to be below 25°F (−4°C).

The longer you run a standard cartridge stove the more it cools, so running a stove for a long time—often necessary for group cooking—leads to a much more rapid drop in performance than running it in short bursts. This also makes these stoves less efficient for melting snow than stoves that run on other fuels. Overall, most cartridge stoves are best for solo or duo use when the temperature is above freezing. Under those conditions the latest stoves are very powerful, equaling or bettering white-gas boil times. Cartridge stoves are fuel efficient too. In laboratory tests with 70°F (21°C) water, MSR's figures show that its cartridge stoves are up to 25 percent more efficient than its white-gas/multifuel stoves, depending on the model. Their cartridge stoves boil on average 1.9 quarts of water per fluid ounce of fuel, the white-gas/multifuel stoves 1.5 quarts. This is a big change, white-gas stoves always used to be much more efficient than cartridge ones. The weight advantage of white-gas stoves has disappeared for long trips without resupply, when the weight of

the stove was more than canceled out by the lower weight of fuel needed.

Most stoves are vapor-feed—the fuel leaves the cartridge under pressure as a gas. To work well in the cold, stoves need to be liquid-feed, which means the fuel leaves the cartridge as a liquid. To turn it into a gas, it must then pass through a preheat tube, a part of the fuel line that runs next to or over the burner in which it vaporizes just before it reaches the burner head. The temperature of the cartridge and the pressure in the cartridge don't have much effect on vaporization, so a liquid-feed stove should work OK in below-freezing temperatures. Stove makers didn't pay much attention to this until Coleman introduced the X series stoves and Powermax cartridges, which were designed to be liquid-feed, as there was a weighted fuel line inside, whose tip was always on the bottom of the cartridge, which was used in a horizontal position. This worked really well, and the system made gas stoves easily usable in winter for the first time. However, the cartridges weren't compatible with any other stoves and were often hard to find. Coleman eventually withdrew them altogether. The company didn't abandon the liquid-feed idea, though, and introduced the Fyrestorm stove, which is designed to be used with an inverted conventional cartridge. By inverting the cartridge, the weight of the contents pushes the liquid fuel down the fuel line to the burner where there is a preheat tube. The only other stove designed to be used with inverted cartridges is the Jetboil Helios, which comes as a unit with a 2-quart pot plus heat exchanger and weighs 28 ounces. The same performance can be achieved with other hose-connected stoves with preheat tubes by inverting the cartridge and propping it up with a tent peg, boot, rock, or other object. However, as the flame control is usually on the top of the cartridge, this means you can't use it without turning the cartridge at least sideways. This isn't a major problem, but the Fyrestorm with a tripod stand for the cartridge and a flame control lever on the burner is much easier to use. Coleman also makes a Powermax Fuel Adapter that enables an X series stove to be used with an inverted standard cartridge, so if you have one of these stoves, you can still use it even though the Powermax cartridges are no more.

The industry-standard, self-sealing cartridges have a Lindahl valve that most stoves fit. A non-standard self-sealing cartridge is the Campingaz CV, commonly found in the Alps and Pyrenees, which can be used only with CV stoves or the MSR SuperFly or Primus EasyFuel. Non-self-sealing cartridges, which can't be detached from the stove until they're empty, are harder to pack, and you can't change the cartridge for a new one when the performance falls off in the cold. They can be discounted for backpacking and anyway have just about disappeared, at least in North America.

Cartridges contain from 3.5 to 21.5 fluid ounces of fuel. The tiniest, lightest ones are all right for one- or two-night trips when you don't need to carry more than one cartridge, but they're not efficient for longer trips because the ratio of metal to fuel is greater than in larger cartridges. Problems with cartridges are rare, but occasionally you get one that doesn't work. This has never happened to me, but I have hiked with people who've found their cartridges wouldn't work and had to borrow fuel. I always check every new cartridge by attaching a stove and lighting it briefly. Stove makers always say you should use only their brands of cartridges with their stoves. In fact, standard cartridges are interchangeable, and when you can't find the same brand as your stove,

which often happens to me, a different brand will work just as well.

Whatever the cartridge, I use about 1.5 to 2.5 fluid ounces a day, which means that an 8-ounce cartridge usually lasts me three or four days (though with the most fuel-efficient stoves this increases to five to six days). If you want to know how much gas is left in a cartridge, you can weigh it when new and after each trip, marking the figure on the cartridge. Alternatively, keep a record of how much empty cartridges weigh (each brand is slightly different, but 8-ounce ones weigh about 5 to 6 ounces) and then weigh any partly full cartridge and work out how much gas should be left. I do this occasionally, but mostly I rely on knowing how many days the cartridge has been used or go by the even less reliable method of hefting the cartridge in my hand and guessing.

There's one big problem with cartridges: the empties. Too many lie glinting in the sunlight at the bottom of once-pristine mountain lakes or jut out, half-buried, from piles of rocks in wilderness the world over. I have no solution to this problem. Perhaps mountain stores and cartridge makers could offer a deposit system with a refund for the return of empties. Ultimately, users must be responsible enough to carry out their trash and dispose of it properly. Cartridges can be recycled. The problem has always been getting the last fuel out of them and releasing the pressure safely. Now that Jetboil makes a tool for doing this called the CrunchIt, there's no excuse not to recycle old cartridges.

Cartridge stoves generally have ported burners, some noisier than others but quieter than white-gas/multifuel stoves. Heat output is easily adjusted, making these stoves excellent for simmering. Stoves attach to self-sealing cartridges in two ways. The most basic and lightest models simply screw into the top of the cartridge. These are often called *piggyback stoves* and are best used with low-profile cartridges. Heavier but much more stable are stoves with a flexible hose connecting the burner to the cartridge. With these stoves the burner can be safely encircled with a windscreen, something you shouldn't do with screw-in burners because the cartridge could overheat and explode, though you can use a windshield around three sides of a piggyback stove or fit a screen just around the burner (for more, see Windscreens and Heat Reflectors, later in this chapter). Screw-in cartridge stoves are good for solo use and perhaps for duos. They're not very stable with large pans, however, and so are not ideal for groups. Many cartridge stoves come with electric Piezo ignition. Turn on the gas, click the button, and a spark lights the stove. This is great when it works. Spill soup on the igniter or snap the end off, both of which I've done, and it will fail, so I always carry a fire steel, matches, or a lighter as well. Given that, I'm happy to do without Piezo ignition. Cartridge stoves are generally reliable, but if they fail they're not field maintainable. Burner heads can clog if you spill food on them, but wiping them clean usually clears them.

PIGGYBACK STOVES There are many tiny piggyback stoves in the 3.5-ounce and lighter range. Good models I've used are the MSR PocketRocket, Coleman Exponent F1 Ultralight, Snow Peak GigaPower, and Optimus Crux. Even lighter are the Soto Micro Regulator at 2.6 ounces, the Optimus Crux Lite at 2.5 ounces, the Primus Express Ti at 2.5 ounces, and the Edelrid Kiro TI at 1.9 ounces. Also ultralight is one I haven't used, the Snow Peak LiteMax Titanium at 2.4 ounces. The weight differences between these stoves are tiny and insignificant in my opinion. The differences

between these stoves have to do with how they fold up and the size of the burners and, in my opinion, are not significant either. All the ones I've used perform amazingly well, with fast boil times—two to three minutes for a pint of water—and good simmer control. Fuel consumption is pretty good, ranging from 0.25 to 0.45 ounce per pint. The packed bulk is minimal, of course, and many of them can be held in a closed fist. The flame tends to be concentrated, so hot spots in the center of pans are likely, though I've had no problems with burned food. The widest flames are those on the Optimus Crux and Crux Lite. These stoves are best used with small pans anyway, since they're unstable with large ones. While the boil times are similar, the Primus Express Ti and the Optimus Crux Lite do seem to be slightly more fuel efficient than the others. Primus says a new catalytic burning system is the reason. I took the original Micron (now replaced by the Express) on a cold fall hike in the White Mountains of New Hampshire and used it in temperatures mostly just below freezing; I was surprised and pleased when a Coleman 7.5-ounce canister lasted for six days—a fuel usage of just 1.25 fluid ounces a day, considerably less than I use with other stoves.

There are plenty of piggyback stoves from the companies named above plus Campingaz (which hasn't entered the ultralight fray) that are bigger and heavier and more suitable for larger pans, but they don't have the stability of hose-connected stoves, which I think are better when cooking for two or more. One model is worth mentioning, though—the 4.5-ounce MSR SuperFly, the only piggyback stove that fits both standard self-sealing cartridges and Campingaz's proprietary CV ones. To do this the SuperFly has an aluminum clamp with a plastic collar that slides onto the cartridge valve before the burner is screwed in place. Being

The Optimus Crux is ultralight and ultracompact and has a folding head.

able to use different types of cartridges could be useful if you travel widely, particularly to the Alps and Pyrenees, where Campingaz cartridges are all that may be available. On one two-week trip to the Queyras Alps before the SuperFly came along, I took a standard self-sealing stove and four 8-ounce cartridges (which weigh 6 ounces empty, so I had 56 ounces in total), because I knew I probably wouldn't find the cartridges locally. Sure enough I didn't, but there were plenty of CV cartridges, and I could have resupplied several times and carried only one cartridge at a time if I'd been able to use them. The SuperFly weighs an ounce and a half more than the stove I used, but it would have saved me 42 ounces in cartridge weight. Many years later, I hiked the GR20 long-distance path along the mountains of Corsica. My companion and I both took SuperFly stoves and were glad we did, as CV cartridges were the only ones we found. Even these were rare enough that we carried the big CV 470 ones, which contain 16 ounces of fuel, rather than the smaller CV 270s. The alternative to the SuperFly is the 2.6-ounce Edelrid Adapter, which can be used with any gas stove with a Lindahl valve and both types of car-

tridge. Edelrid also makes an adapter that enables puncture-style cartridges to be used with screw-in stoves.

Brunton makes a different adapter called the Stove Stand that allows a piggyback stove to be used as a low-profile one. The stove screws into the top of the three-legged stand from which the hose runs. However, it's heavy at 5.5 ounces, and while it would make a piggyback stove more stable and make it easier to warm the cartridge in cold weather, liquid-feed would still be unavailable, as piggyback stoves don't have preheat tubes.

LOW-PROFILE STOVES Hose-connected or remote-cartridge stoves are more stable because they sit on the ground and usually have larger pan supports than screw-in models, making them more suited for large pots. The Primus MultiFuel and Omni-Fuel stoves (see White-Gas and Multifuel Stoves, earlier in this chapter) fit in here and are very powerful when used with cartridges. Without the pumps needed for liquid fuels, they weigh 13 and 14.5 ounces respectively. The same model with no provision for using liquid fuel is called the Easy-Fuel and weighs 13.6 ounces. The EasyFuel also fits Campingaz CV cartridges as well as standard ones, the only low-profile stove to do so.

The weights of the stoves described above are fairly typical for hose-connected stoves, but there are some that weigh less. MSR has the 6.8-ounce WindPro, which is the same stove as the white-gas SimmerLite except that it has a cartridge connection instead of a pump. It comes with the same MSR 2-ounce windscreen and heat reflector. It's not quite as powerful as some other cartridge stoves, but it's one of the lightest hose-connected stoves. A touch heavier at 7 ounces is the Primus Spider, which has a good boil time—about three minutes for a pint—and is fuel efficient at around

0.28 ounce per pint. Also light are the Edelrid Opilio at 6 ounces and the Snow Peak Delta Pod at 9.7 ounces, neither of which have I tried.

An unusual hose-connected stove is the Edelrid Stormy EVO, which comes complete with integrated windscreen and a nonstick 1.8-quart pot at a weight of 25.5 ounces. It has folding legs but also a chain so you can hang it if required. Wind resistance should be superb—Edelrid says it's for "extreme conditions."

Trangia 25 or 27 unit owners who want to use cartridges can buy 6.4-ounce hose-connected burners made by Primus that fit inside the windscreen with the hose running through a cutout in the side. The system works very well, but the weight and bulk are high compared with a cartridge stove and foil windscreen. The most interesting hose-connected stove is the Coleman Fyrestorm, as this is designed to be a liquid-feed stove and can only be used with an inverted cartridge. Without the pump needed for gasoline fuels, the Fyrestorm Ti weighs 11 ounces. Compared with other cartridge stoves, it's not that fuel efficient, using around 0.35 ounce of gas to boil

a pint of water, nor quite as fast boiling, taking about 3.5 minutes to boil that pint. Much more importantly, though, it works fine in cold conditions without need to warm the cartridge or balance it inverted against something. To test it, I've left it outside, so that by dawn, it was covered in frost, and my fingers stuck to the metal. It lit straight away and boiled 0.68 of a pint in 2.5 minutes. It's the best gas stove running off standard cartridges that I've used in below-freezing temperatures.

HEAT-EXCHANGER STOVE At the time of the last edition, the first heat-exchanger stove, the Jetboil, had just been launched, and I'd only had time to use it a few times. Back then, I called it an "impressive innovation." Since then, that first stove has become the Classic Personal Cooking System (PCS), and the company has introduced seven more Jetboil models. Primus, who made the original Jetboil burner, now makes six heat-exchanger stoves of its own, while MSR has one very unusual and unique model. Heat-exchanger stoves come with a pot or pots with a heat exchanger welded to

The MSR WindPro butane-propane stove is the lightest low-profile, hose-attached canister stove.

the base that is designed to work with the burner. The last is important, as if they don't complement each other, the results could be more fuel usage and slower boil times (see Heat Exchangers, later in this chapter). As there are separate heat exchangers that can be attached to different pots and pots with heat exchangers attached available separately from stoves, the technology can be used with any stove. However with an integrated unit you know the two items will work together. Most heat-exchanger stoves run off butane-propane cartridges, though there is one, the Primus EtaPower MF, that can be used with white gas or kerosene as well.

Heat exchangers, which are a ring of deep corrugated fins, are claimed to speed up boil times and reduce fuel usage by greatly increasing the surface area of the base of a pot, which improves the transfer of heat to the pot. Having tested several heat-exchanger stoves, I've found that fuel consumption is certainly lower than with other stoves, but that boil times are not always faster. The last isn't that important anyway, but the first could be significant on long trips. The first heat-exchanger stoves were quite heavy compared to an ultralight stove and pot, so there was only a weight saving on long trips, especially for solo hikers. However, the latest stoves are much lighter and could save weight on a trip of only a few days. The two lightest models, both piggyback ones, are the Primus Eta Solo, which weighs 12.9 ounces and has a 0.9-quart pot, and the Jetboil Sol, which comes in titanium and aluminum versions at 9 ounces and 10.5 ounces and has a 0.8-quart pot. The Sol is new at the time of writing and I've only been able to test the titanium one briefly. These initial tests show the fuel efficiency to be as good as the original Jetboil PCS, which certainly makes it a competitor in weight terms with the lightest gas stove and small pot combinations, which

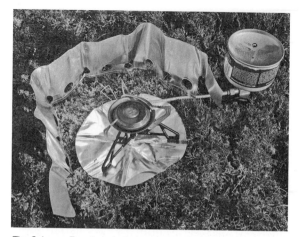

The Coleman Fyrestorm is designed to be used with an inverted canister, which means it works well in below-freezing temperatures.

weigh 5 to 8 ounces. With the Jetboil PCS, which weighs 15 ounces, I worked out that I would need to be out more than seven days before I would save any weight over an 8-ounce stove/pot set. With the 9-ounce titanium Jetboil Sol I would be around the same weight for an overnight trip (with a 6-ounce, 100 size canister for both stoves) and would save weight on a four-day trip (when I would carry a 6-ounce, 100 size canister for the Sol and a 9-ounce 250 one for the standard stove). Of course weight saving is not the only reason to use heat-exchanger stoves. Integrated stove and pot units are easy to use, especially in cold weather, as they fit together neatly. They're also more efficient in the cold, and some are wind resistant, too, though others need a separate windscreen.

JETBOIL The original Jetboil PCS consists of a small gas burner with Piezo igniter, an anodized-aluminum 1-quart pot (which Jetboil calls a cup) with lid plus a heat exchanger fitted to the base and an insulated neoprene pot cozy with webbing handle that remains on the pot while it's on the burner. The pot twists onto the burner so the two are locked together when the stove is in use. (There is a 1.2-ounce pot support that can be placed over the burner so other pots can be used, but then you lose the advantages of the heat exchanger.) The burner can be packed inside the pot along with a 100- to 110-size cartridge. A plastic cover fits over the heat exchanger to protect it from damage. The packed PCS is quite compact, though no more so than a small (quart or less) pot with an ultralight gas stove packed inside. The new Jetboil Sol is the same design but slightly more compact as the pot is smaller.

The PCS and the Sol run on standard resealable cartridges. The company says its Jetpower 100-size cartridge will boil 12 liters and that the boiling time for a pint of water is two minutes. However, I've found four minutes for a pint is usual. Fuel usage is good, a half to two thirds the amount of fuel I use with other stoves, depending on the make of cartridge (0.2 to 0.4 fluid ounce per pint boiled), so using a Jetboil stove does mean a real saving on the amount of fuel that has to be carried. A 250-gram cartridge should last at least a week with these stoves.

While the heat exchanger is the main reason for the Jetboil's fuel efficiency, the cozy also makes a difference by preventing heat loss from the sides of the pot. I boiled water with and without the cozy fitted and found that boiling times increased by almost 50 percent without it. The cozy never gets too hot to handle, showing that little heat is escaping. Although the heat exchanger keeps out breezes, a separate windscreen is needed in strong winds. In temperatures just below freezing, the Jetboil stoves work OK, even when the cartridge is sitting on frozen ground. Jetboil says that new technology means the Sol is even better than the PCS and will work fine down to 15°F. I haven't tested this yet.

There are drawbacks, of course. The main one is the shape, which is tall and narrow, making the unit somewhat unstable on rough ground. This is slightly less of a problem with the smaller Sol. There is a wide stabilizer available that fits under the pot. It weighs 0.9 ounce. The pot needs careful handling when full and is harder to clean than a wider, shallower one. You can hold the pot firmly with the webbing handle on the side of the cozy, but if boiling liquids spill or spit over the edge, likely if the pot is full, your hand can get burned. I reckon three-quarters full is best for safety. Even so, a pot grip is worth using. The pot makes a good drinking mug, but eating solid food out of it isn't as easy as with a wider pot, especially when it's almost empty—a long spoon is a good idea. The burner must be lit before you attach the pot/heat exchanger, which requires care and is best done with a low flame.

Apart from the new Sol, the most interesting Jetboil model is the hose-connected Helios, which runs off an inverted cartridge and so should be excellent in temperatures well below freezing. Jetboil says it works down to -10°F. The Helios comes with a 2-quart heat-exchanger pot with a neoprene cozy and a snap-on windscreen and weighs 28 ounces. That should be fine for two people. For three or more, there's also the Helios Guide with 2- and 3-quart pots, at a weight of 48 ounces.

PRIMUS I've used four of the six Primus heat-exchanger stoves, all of which have the designation "Eta." The two piggyback stoves, the 12.9-ounce Eta Solo, and the heavier 15-ounce EtaExpress with 0.9- and 1-quart hard-anodized aluminum pots, respectively, work OK with fast boiling times and good fuel efficiency (about 0.25 fluid ounce per pint boiled). The EtaExpress has a simple gas burner with three foldout pot supports, a tall heat-exchanger pot with foldout handles, and a frypan/lid, and a neat little windscreen that clips onto the burner. The burner and windscreen plus a 250-size cartridge can all be packed inside the pot. The burner weighs 3.5 ounces on its own. Although sold as a unit, the burner and pot could be used separately and indeed can be bought separately as the Express stove and Eta-Power Pot 1L. The pot is wider and not as deep as the Jetboil one, which I like, as it's easier to stir food, eat from, and clean. The EtaExpress is powerful, boiling a pint in about two minutes. It's also surprisingly efficient in cold weather. At one camp, I left it out overnight during freezing weather. The temperature at dawn was 25°F (-4°C), and the water in the pot had ice on top. To my surprise, the stove lit immediately and boiled a pint in three and a half minutes, which is pretty good for a piggyback stove, especially with a half-full cartridge. The Solo has much the same performance, including in the cold. It's an integrated stove and pot unit very similar to the Jetboil PCS. The pot is tall and narrow and has a wraparound pot cozy with fabric handle attached. It clips into the burner to form a secure unit. Pot supports are supplied so the stove can be used with other pots. The burner and a 100-size cartridge will fit inside the pot. Like the Jetboil PCS, the Solo works OK in breezes, but in strong winds, a windscreen is needed.

Primus's other heat-exchanger stoves are hose-connected models, and these are really excellent. The smallest is the 21-ounce EtaPackLite, which comes with a 1.2-quart nonstick aluminum pot with a plastic lid and folding, locking handle plus a circular aluminum windscreen. There's also a polypropylene bowl that fits inside the pot and protects it from the burner when stored inside and a cover for the heat exchanger. The burner weighs 8.4 ounces, which is quite light for a hose-connected burner. The pot with lid weighs 9.5 ounces, and the windscreen 3 ounces. The bowl and heat-exchanger cover add another 3.5 ounces, but these can be left behind on solo trips. A bandanna does as well.

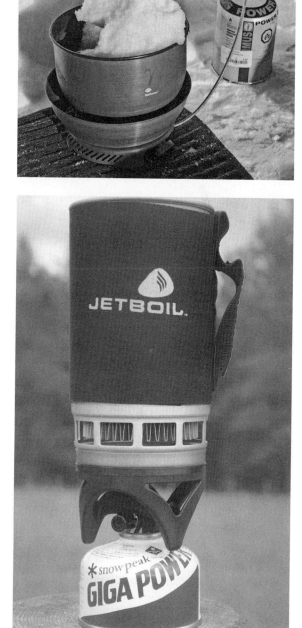

TOP: *The Primus EtaPower heat-exchanger stove is a good choice for melting masses of snow.* ABOVE: *The Jetboil stove.*

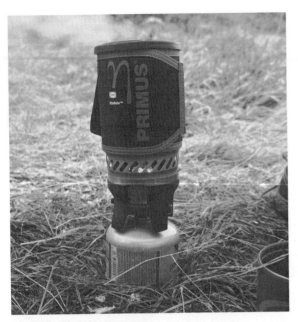

The Primus Eta Solo canister stove.

The EtaPackLite is designed for two people but is light enough for solo use, especially on cold-weather trips where snow may have to be melted, something much more easily done in a bigger, wider pot than the tall, narrow ones that come with solo heat-exchanger stoves. The Eta-PackLite boils a pint in under three minutes. Over several trips, fuel usage has ranged from 0.18 to 0.275 ounce per pint boiled depending on air and water temperature and the amount of simmering. I would expect to get 17 to 18 quarts of boiling water from one 250-size cartridge, enough for well over a week. The EtaPackLite has a preheat tube so the cartridge can be inverted in below freezing temperatures. It then works really well and is great for melting snow. I like it for solo use in winter and with two in summer.

Bigger and heavier than the EtaPackLite, the EtaPower, available in a multifuel version and a cartridge-only version, is a good stove for two or more in winter. Boil times and fuel usage are comparable with the EtaPackLite. The EtaPower weighs 29 ounces (the pump for the multifuel MF version adds 4 ounces more) and consists of the hose-connected burner, a rigid windshield that locks in place, a 2.1-quart hard-anodized nonstick aluminum pot, and a pot grip. I've used the Eta-Power for melting snow for three and more people in winter trips in the Rockies, and it's superb for this. The cartridge can be inverted in below-freezing temperatures, though I've found that it has to be extremely cold or the cartridge almost empty before this is necessary.

Other pots can be used with both the EtaPack-Lite and the EtaPower stoves, and the pots are available separately.

MSR REACTOR MSR's heat-exchanger stove is unique in having a mesh-covered radiant heat plate that glows red instead of a normal burner. A 1.7-quart pot with the heat exchanger on the base fits neatly over the burner, making a good seal against wind, so a separate windshield isn't needed, which is good because the Reactor is quite heavy at 20 ounces. The weight is all in the anodized aluminum pot and heat exchanger, the burner only weighing 6.4 ounces. There are no pot supports, and no other pots can be used. The pot has a clear plastic lid and a handle that folds over the lid. The burner plus a 250-gram cartridge fits in the pot. The size and weight make this a stove for two or three people. Its plus point is its power, as it takes barely longer than two minutes to boil a pint in above-freezing temperatures and only three minutes at 28°F with ice on the water. The Reactor also has an internal pressure regulator that means that the heat output doesn't diminish much as the cartridge empties, unlike with other vapor-feed stoves. The fuel efficiency is OK, but other heat-exchanger stoves are better. I think this is because of the lighting procedure. When the stove is lit,

The Primus EtaPackLite canister stove comes complete with windscreen and heat-exchanger pot.

blue flames flicker over the burner before it glows red. MSR says the pot must not be placed on the stove until the burner glows red. In cold or breezy weather, this can take a few minutes and uses up a little gas. The heat can be turned down a little, but simmering isn't really possible. This is a stove designed for power. The Reactor comes strewn with excessive warnings about carbon monoxide and other dangers. Research by Roger Caffin (http://backpackinglight.com/cgi-bin/backpack inglight/co_series_supplement_1_msr_reactor .html) shows CO emissions are high for this stove, so it should only be used outside. For melting masses of snow and boiling lots of water, it works well, but there are better heat-exchanger stoves. Hopefully MSR will develop this idea and produce lighter, smaller, more efficient versions.

The MSR Reactor heat-exchanger stove is powerful and unusual.

Wood-Burning Stoves

A surprising development in stoves has been the resurgence of wood-burning models. Chimney-style water boilers like the Kelly Kettle have been around for ages, but they are too heavy and bulky for backpacking. At the time of the last edition,

only the Sierra Stove and a few homemade simple fireboxes were available that weren't too heavy, and these were of little interest to most backpackers. Now there is a growing range of lightweight wood-burning stoves, including lighter versions of the chimney boilers, and an upsurge of interest. It might seem there's no point in these—if you want a fire, light one, why bother with a stove to put it in? However, open fires can't be lit every-

STOVES: MY CHOICES

In order to test them for this book and for magazine articles, I've acquired most of the stoves described here, so I sometimes have problems deciding which to take on a trip. For short ventures in mild conditions, any one will do. Longer walks and stormy weather make me choose more carefully.

For seven years the Optimus Svea 123R was my favorite stove. Then the WhisperLite Internationale replaced it as my first choice because it's easier to prime, lighter, smaller, and more stable and performs better in wind, while being just as efficient and reliable. The Internationale reigned for twelve years but was in turn supplanted in my affections by the Optimus Nova. I'm not constant when it comes to stoves! I've used the Nova on two multiweek hikes, including the Arizona Trail, and many shorter trips, and in my opinion it's the best multifuel stove yet, being easier and quicker to light and cleaner and more compact than the Internationale. In the last edition, I wrote that if I had only one stove, it would be the Nova. However, I haven't used a white gas stove except for testing purposes in several years. I now think there are lighter, easier-to-use options even for winter camping.

For most short trips, though, I use cartridge stoves because of their low weight, low bulk, and convenience, though they don't generate the same feelings as multifuel stoves. Somehow they seem characterless. Maybe it's because they're so easy to use. My current favorite is the Primus Micron Ti because it's slightly more fuel efficient than others I've tried, though there's little to choose between all the ultralight models. The Jetboil Sol has quickly become a favorite and I'll be using it often on trips where I don't expect temperatures to fall below freezing very often. I wouldn't use a cartridge stove on a long solo hike in a remote area, however, because they aren't repairable in the field. (I have had failures in the past.) On short solo cold-weather trips, I use the Coleman Fyrestorm or the Primus EtaPackLite because they work so well in below-freezing temperatures. On trips with others, I like the Primus EtaPower because it's excellent for melting masses of snow.

My interest in alcohol stoves was rekindled by the Brasslite Turbo II-D. It burst into full flame with the Caldera Cone and then became incandescent with the Caldera Ti-Tri. Being able to use wood and alcohol in one stove is marvelous. This is now my favorite stove, especially for long trips in remote places.

where without causing damage and often require time for site selection and preparation and wood gathering. Then you need to use a grill or have a method of suspending your pot over the flames. Wood-burning stoves contain the fuel and concentrate the heat. Only tiny pieces of wood are needed. Indeed, fuel has to be in little pieces to fit in the stove. Anything more than 4 or 5 inches long and too wide to easily snap with your fingers is too big. Generally enough fuel can be quickly gathered around a campsite—it can include bark, dry leaves, and cones as well as twigs. If you're camping away from trees or bushes, then fuel can be picked up during the day and stuffed into jacket or pack pockets. I carry a small stuff sack for this. It doesn't weigh much. Foraging for fuel can be enjoyable in itself. Indeed, as you become used to spotting fuel during the day, it can be hard to resist the temptation to collect far more than you need! Some types of wood light easily and burn fast. Others can be hard to light and burn slowly. Learning which types of wood are easiest to use is part of the fun of using a wood stove. Tinder is the same as with a campfire.

With a wood-burning stove, you don't need to carry heavy liquid fuel. If you want the option of a different fuel, solid-fuel and alcohol burners can be used with many wood-burning stoves. Some are designed for this. This overcomes the main disadvantage of wood-burning stoves, which is using them in wet weather. Finding dry fuel in wet weather can be difficult (though not impossible, and damp fuel can be burned in a hot fire), and the stoves should ideally be used outside, which in pouring rain is not easy or pleasant. Wood stoves can be used under a big tarp or large vestibule with the door open, but there needs to be ample ventilation so fumes and smoke can be expelled and plenty of space between open flames and flammable fabric.

Having tried a few wood-burning stoves and enjoyed cooking over a mini campfire, I decided to take one on the Pacific Northwest Trail. This was the Trail Designs Caldera Ti-Tri Sidewinder Inferno, which comes with an alcohol burner, so I had a choice of fuels. I used it with wood for most of the first forty-five days and relished doing so. It was the most fun I've had with a stove for years. I carried a small bottle of alcohol for the few wet days and those mornings when I didn't want to bother lighting wood but just wanted a quick hot drink. As it rained most of the last thirty days, I used alcohol most of the time. I missed using wood, though. Using a wood-burning stove day after day taught me much about the best way to use one. One major discovery was that my assumption that simmering would be difficult was wrong. Let the flames die down, and keep the fire just going with the occasional twig, and simmering is possible. Boiling water, usually about a pint, took from five to fifteen minutes, depending on the type and dryness of the fuel, the care taken with refueling, and the temperature. That applies to all the wood stoves I've tried as well as the Trail Designs one.

Wood-burning stoves are best suited to people like me who enjoy the camping side of backpacking, who enjoy creating a home in the wilds and tinkering with cooking. If you like the rituals of using a white gas stove, then you'll almost certainly like wood stoves. Those who regard camping as no more than an unfortunate chore on long walks and who like stoves that are fast and simple and require no thought are likely to find wood stoves too fussy and time-consuming. A wood stove is also a campfire in miniature and can be used as such. Without a pot on top, longer pieces of wood can be used. As with an open fire, many happy hours can be spent staring into the flames and poking in pieces of wood!

While having a much smaller footprint than a campfire, a wood-burning stove can still singe vegetation and leave a burn scar. Some wood stoves have a raised base on which the wood is burnt and doesn't scorch the ground below. However they may emit sparks, so they shouldn't be used near flammable materials like dry grass. Other stoves are simply walls that surround the fire, which is lit on the ground (though a separate base can be used), in which case they should only be used on bare ground. Ashes from stoves should be widely scattered or buried once they are cold.

BUSHBUDDY ULTRA This beautifully made little Canadian stove is the lightweight version (4.9 ounces/139 grams) of the original Bushbuddy (all of 1.6 ounces/45.4 grams more due to heavier materials but is otherwise identical), which was one of the first of the new wood-burning stoves. It's a double-wall stove with vent holes around the base of the outer and around the top of the inner. Bushbuddy says this is to preheat secondary combustion air so that wood burns very cleanly. It's effective, as all that's left after a fire is a small amount of fine ash. There's a grate inside the fire-box, so the fuel sits above an air space into which air enters through the lower vents, providing a draft. A pot support, also with vent holes and a cutaway section for inserting fuel, sits on top of the firebox. This can be inverted and stored in the firebox for packing. A meths burner can be used in the firebox if necessary.

The packed stove, which looks like a tin can with a ring of holes around one end, will fit inside a Snow Peak Trek 900 titanium pot and other pots the same size or larger (I stored it in an old 1-liter MSR Titan pot). The stainless steel walls of the stove are very thin and could be crushed, so it is important to store the pot carefully.

The grate and the double construction mean that the base of the stove doesn't get hot, so it can be placed on flammable surfaces and even picked up and moved if necessary. I used it on a wooden picnic table, and it didn't leave a mark. The grate means that tinder needs to be quite big. I find it easiest to light the stove without the pot support in place and then put it on before the fire grows too hot. Although the firebox provides some protection from the wind, the flames can be blown sideways out of the holes in the pot sup-port, so a sheltered site or windshield is needed. I used a Trail Designs Vari-Vent Windscreen (2.2 ounces/61 grams) with the Bushbuddy, and it worked fine. Once lit, the Bushbuddy blazes delightfully. Feeding the stove with the pot on top is quite easy as long as the wood is in very short pieces and tiny chunks.

CALDERA TI-TRI This stove system can be run on solid fuel and alcohol as well as wood. As a wood burner, it consists of a titanium cone and two tita-nium stakes. The latter are pushed through holes in the top of the cone so the pot can sit on them

The Bushbuddy Ultra wood-burning stove.

and be well above the flames. Fuel can be pushed in the cut-out in the side of the cone. The fire is lit on the ground, and the cone placed over the top. This is the simplest Ti-Tri and works reasonably well but does mean you should only use it on bare ground. This can be overcome by using a floor, such as the titanium one made by Trail Designs, and a mesh grate. The efficiency of the stove can be improved with the Inferno inset, which consists of a mesh grate and a smaller cone. The latter is inverted and placed on the grate, and the fire lit inside it. Trail Designs says this turns the Ti-Tri into a gasifier/afterburner. Using it certainly makes for a hot fire and very little ash. The cone contains the fire well, though flames can emerge through the air vents and the fuel opening. Wind resistance is good, though the unit is so light that care needs to be taken that it doesn't blow away before the pot is placed on top. To keep the fire roaring, the bottom vents can be placed into the wind so that a chimney effect is created. When a simmering heat

The Caldera Ti-Tri can burn wood, alcohol, or solid fuel. Here it's used as a wood burner with the Inferno inverted-cone inset.

is required, turn them away from the wind and let the fire die down to hot coals.

The Ti-Tri and the accessories come in different sizes to fit different-size pots—smaller pots can be used, though as they don't fill the top of the cone heating isn't as efficient. Weights range from 0.95 ounce (27 grams) to 2.4 ounces (69 grams) for the Ti-Tri Cone, 0.4 ounce (11 grams) to 1.2 ounces (35 grams) for the Inferno Cone, 0.35 ounce (10 grams) to 1.16 ounces (33 grams) for the grate and 0.32 ounce (9 grams) to 1.4 ounces (40 grams) for the floors. The whole unit comes with a plastic screw-top caddy to protect it. Trail Designs says that this can be used as a mug or bowl, but I've found that it quickly smells of burned wood or alcohol, so I only use it as a container. I've found the same with the Sidewinder version of the Ti-Tri, which is designed to fit inside your pot so you don't need the caddy. Maybe I'm messy, but I find it impossible to keep the pot free of fuel smells. The weight of the unit with caddy isn't that great anyway. I took the Ti-Tri Sidewinder Inferno, designed to fit my Evernew 0.9-quart titanium pot, on the Pacific Northwest Trail. The total weight, with alcohol burner, was 8 ounces.

SIERRA STOVE The now venerable Sierra Stove consists of a hollow-walled open chamber that sits atop a small battery-operated fan and operates like a miniature blacksmith's forge. Light a small fire in the chamber, then switch on the fan to blow air through holes in the hollow walls, and you get a roaring inferno that quickly brings water to the boil. One AA battery is said to power the fan for six hours, while an adapter with a C-cell will run it for thirty-five hours. The fan and battery unit pack inside the chamber for carrying. There are two versions, a stainless steel one weighing 16 ounces and a titanium one weighing 10 ounces. This was the first wood-burning stove I tried, long before the Bushbuddy or Ti-Tri appeared, and I was impressed. The stove goes through fuel pretty fast when the fan's on full. There are three settings:

high, low, and off. As long as the fire's hot, there's little smoke and only fine ash left afterward. If you turn the fan down or off for simmering, more smoke and ash is produced. If you want to use longer twigs, there's a 2.5-ounce Cross Grate that raises the height of the pot above the fuel box. The battery compartment isn't waterproof, and the wire between it and the stove needs care, disadvantages that don't apply to other wood-burning stoves that work just as well. These also weigh less, so good though the Sierra Stove is, I wouldn't choose it over the Bushbuddy or the Ti-Tri.

BACKCOUNTRY BOILER AND MKETTLE Chimney boiler kettles in which a double-wall sleeve containing the water fits around a tall chimney sitting atop a firebox are an old design. I've had one for many years, and it's fun for car camping. But it's too bulky and heavy for backpacking. Now there are two very similar lightweight aluminum versions, the Backcountry Boiler, which came first and is the lighter at 6 ounces, and the mKettle, which weighs 14.1 ounces on my scales. The process by which the Backcountry Boiler was designed by Devin Montgomery, who wanted a lighter chimney boiler, is fascinating (all the stages are discussed online on Backpacking Light, http://backpacking light.com). Links to its history can be found on the Boilerwerks Web site, http://theboilerwerks.com, where you can also purchase one. Both kettles have neoprene sleeves around the chimney. These devices can only be used for boiling water, which is a disadvantage, but they are efficient. I've tried both and they really do work well, boiling water very rapidly. They're designed for use with wood, which is fed in through a hole in the firebox, but can be used with alcohol burners. Not being able to cook in one is a big disadvantage for me but if you only boil water, one could be a good choice, in

which case I'd go for the Backcountry Boiler, as it's much the lighter of the two. As it is, I'll go on using these boilers for car camping and overnight trips when weight doesn't matter, and I carry another stove as well.

Safety and Maintenance

All stoves can be dangerous and should be used carefully. The most important safety point: never take a stove for granted.

Before you light a stove, always check that attachments to fuel tanks or cartridges are secure, tank caps and fuel bottle tops are tight, and controls are turned off. Study the instructions that come with all stoves, especially white-gas and multifuel models, and practice using them at home. When you're cold, wet, and tired, it's half-dark, and you desperately need a hot meal, it's important that you can safely operate your stove almost automatically. By testing stoves at home you'll also discover any faults. With one brand-new white-gas stove the pump leaked badly as soon as I started pumping. After I dismantled the pump, checked all the seals, and reassembled it, it still leaked, so I replaced it. In the backcountry I'd have had a useless stove. I also check stoves that haven't been used for a while just in case they need cleaning or maintenance.

Stoves should be refilled carefully, after making sure that there are no open flames such as campfires, burning candles, or other lit stoves nearby. This applies whether you are changing a cartridge or pouring fuel into a tank. Refueling should always be done *outside* for safety.

An overheated cartridge or fuel tank is a hazard. When the burner is directly above or alongside the fuel tank, make sure there is enough air flow around the tank or cartridge to keep it cool.

It should never become too hot to touch. Windscreens shouldn't fully surround such stoves. If you use large pans that overhang the burner, periodically check to see if the fuel tank or cartridge is getting hot because too much heat is being reflected off the pans.

Stoves, especially white-gas stoves, can flare badly when being lit. Never have your head over a stove when you light it. Also, don't light a stove that is close to any flammable material. If you need to cook in the vestibule or under a tarp, it's safest to light the stove out in the open, even if you have to stick it out into the rain and then bring it back under cover when it's burning properly. If you do light a stove in the vestibule, leave the door open so you can quickly push the stove out if anything goes wrong (but be careful where you push it if there are other tents around). I was once walking across a crowded campground on a blustery winter day when I saw a bright yellow flash inside a nearby tent. A second later, a blazing gasoline stove came hurtling through the tent fly sheet—leaving behind a neat hole—and landed near my feet. If another tent had been close by, there could have been a disaster.

A threat when using a stove inside a tent is carbon monoxide poisoning, which can be fatal. All stoves consume oxygen and give off this odorless, colorless gas. In an enclosed space they can use up all the oxygen, replacing it with carbon monoxide. There should always be good ventilation when a stove is in use. In a tent vestibule air can usually enter under the edge of the fly sheet, but this can be blocked by snow piling up around the edges of the tent or by a wet fly sheet freezing to the ground. In those cases, if there's no vent, a two-way outer door zipper is useful—the top few inches can be left open to ensure ventilation. Different types of stoves give out differ-

NEAR DISASTER

The nearest I have ever come to a serious stove accident was when I was cooking in the vestibule of a tent pitched on snow. A severe blizzard had trapped us at the same site for four nights; during the last night the wind had battered the tents so much that we'd hardly slept at all. I lit the white-gas stove in the vestibule with the door zipped shut to keep out blown snow. The burner caught, but the flame was sluggish. "Pump it some more," suggested my companion. Without thinking, I did so. There was a sudden bright surge of flame, then the whole unit was ablaze as liquid fuel shot out of the jet. Two suddenly energized bodies dived for the door zipper and yanked it open. I threw the stove out and plunged my scorched hands into the snow. Later I discovered that my eyebrows and face were also singed.

In retrospect, we were lucky. One moment's carelessness could have left us without our tent and gear or, worse, badly burned or even dead. My guess is that lack of air was the cause. I should have opened the door and tried to revive the stove outside. As it was, the fly sheet zipper partially melted and wouldn't close, so in subsequent storms we had to cook in the inner tent, which we did with great care, standing the stove on a pan lid to prevent the groundsheet from melting.

On two other occasions I've been present when a stove has caught fire, once outside a mountain hut and once inside. Each time, it was a white-gas stove. As most white-gas stove manufacturers state, these are best used outdoors, not in tents or huts. The safest fuels are solid fuel and alcohol, followed by butane-propane cartridges.

ent amounts of carbon monoxide. Roger Caffin did a detailed and fascinating analysis of this in a series of articles on Backpacking Light at http://backpackinglight.com/cgi-bin/backpackinglight/

stoves_tents_carbon_monoxide_index.html, which is updated with regular supplements.

It's best never to use a stove in the inner tent, partly because of carbon monoxide poisoning, but mainly because of fire.

Most stoves need little maintenance. Many white-gas and multifuel stoves have built-in cleaning needles. With those that don't, you may need to clean the jets occasionally with the thin jet prickers (weighing a fraction of an ounce) that usually come with stoves that need them. They should be used only when the stove's performance seems to be falling off, since too much cleaning can widen the jet and lessen the burn rate. If you lose, break, or forget your jet pricker, as I did once on a winter trip, and your soup boils over and blocks the jet, a bristle from a toothbrush makes a good substitute. (This idea was suggested by two walkers in a mountain shelter where I went in desperate search of anything that would restore my stove to working order.)

Check rubber seals and O-rings on tank caps and cartridge attachment points periodically and replace them if worn. I carry spares on long trips. You may need to carry a complete tank cap. On the Pacific Crest Trail I was glad I did so—the original one on my Svea 123R started to leak after four months of constant use.

Fuel Bottles and Tank-Filling Devices

Fuel bottles need to be leakproof and tough. They're best carried away from food, preferably in an outside pocket of the pack, just in case they leak.

Plastic bottles are fine for alcohol. Even empty soda bottles can be used. Brasslite's 8- and 16-fluid-ounce plastic bottles have pour-ing spouts and reservoirs and weigh 1.5 and 2.5 ounces. Trangia makes polyethylene fuel bottles in half-pint, pint, and quart sizes that are suitable for white gas and kerosene as well as alcohol. The Trangia bottles weigh 3.4, 4, and 5.6 ounces and have safety valves.

Metal fuel bottles double as tanks for hose-attached stoves. The standard for decades has been the Swiss-made Sigg bottle. I used the 21-fluid-ounce size, weighing 3.5 ounces, for many years for all fuels, and despite getting very battered and dented, the bottles never leaked. Sigg bottles come in sizes holding 0.4, 0.6, 0.75, 1, and 1.5 pints. Sigg doesn't sell them as fuel bottles anymore—the company stopped making stoves many years ago—but the plain aluminum bottles in the Classic series are the same as they've always been. For many years Siggs were the only round fuel bottles—the original MSR stoves were designed to use them. Now MSR, Optimus, Primus, and Snow Peak all make similar aluminum bottles with the same size threads. MSR's 11-, 20-, and 30-fluid-ounce bottles weigh 2.8, 4.9, and 7.3 ounces, Optimus's 12-, 20-, 34-, and 50-fluid-ounce ones weigh 2.6, 4.2, 5.8, and 7.5 ounces, and Primus's 18- and 30-fluid-ounce ones weigh 4.2 and 5.8 ounces. Snow Peak's 18- and 30-fluid-ounce ones weigh 6.5 and 8.5 ounces.

It's almost impossible to fill small tanks directly from standard bottles without spilling a little fuel. However, various ingenious devices help. I have a Sigg pouring cap and spout, bought many years ago for filling my Svea 123 tank. This is a standard cap with a small plastic spout inserted in one side and a tiny hole drilled in the other. By placing a finger over the hole you can control the flow from the spout. It's inconvenient to use—you have to remove the normal cap, screw in the pouring cap, fill the stove, and then change the caps again.

To avoid losing either cap, I've linked them with a piece of shock cord. The Sigg pouring spout is no longer sold. Olicamp's Ulti-Mate Pour Spout looks similar but also functions as a standard cap, which is much more convenient. The caps on Trangia fuel bottles can also be used for pouring. The Trangia cap is sold separately for use with other bottles.

For filling fuel bottles from larger containers, I use a small Coghlan's polypropylene Filter Funnel (0.75 ounce). I usually carry it on long hikes when I may have to refill with white gas from gallon cans or use fuel of dubious cleanliness. Optimus makes a similar funnel.

Accessories

Windscreens and Heat Reflectors

The one stove accessory that's essential is a windscreen. No stove will function well in a stiff breeze without one. Even if the stove stays alight, it will take a long time and a great deal of fuel to boil water, if it does so at all. In a strong wind an unprotected stove may be impossible to light. MSR's crude-looking but ultralight foil windscreen is arguably one of the greatest advances ever in backpacking stove cooking. If you don't have a windscreen, a foam pad held around the stove at a safe distance works quite well, or you could prop up your pack or boots. These are all a hassle, though, so I always carry a windscreen.

Many stoves come with windscreens, though not usually piggyback-cartridge models. Crosspieces on the burner that stop the flame from blowing out do not count as true windscreens. Aluminum and titanium foil windscreens, sold by many companies, are the best accessory you can buy for a stove that doesn't already have one. Weights run from 1 to 2.5 ounces. These windscreens can be easily trimmed to fit your stove.

Taller stoves that sit on top of fuel tanks and cartridges shouldn't be completely surrounded by a windscreen; there needs to be some airflow to the fuel container so it doesn't overheat. However, you can protect them on three sides, which is adequate. The tank or canister should always be cool enough to touch. Windscreens designed for low-profile stoves aren't tall enough for piggyback stoves. Trail Designs makes 8-inch-high aluminum foil windscreens, and Titanium Goat offers sheets of titanium foil measuring 11.75 inches by 12 inches that can be cut to size. Taller rigid aluminum windscreens are generally quite heavy. When I used the Svea 123 regularly, my windscreen was a 10-inch-tall folding Coghlan's model made of five sheets of aluminum with anchor rods at each end. This windscreen is efficient and durable and works well with screw-in cartridge stoves, but it weighs 8 ounces. Foil windscreens make these heavy types redundant. A rigid one that is worth considering for piggyback cartridge stoves is the Primus Windscreen, which fits around the burner above the cartridge. It weighs 2.1 ounces, and Primus says it should fit most stoves with a small flame ring. An alternative is a foil windscreen that wraps around the burner only, with another sheet of foil around the base of the burner as a heat reflector. For details, go to the Homemade Canister Stove Windscreen page at backpackinglight.com.

Whatever windscreen you use, it's most effective if it's close to the pan—less than half an inch away—since this traps most heat and minimizes air movement.

Heat reflectors that fit under the burner or the stove speed up cooking times only slightly in my experience. They do protect the ground and fuel

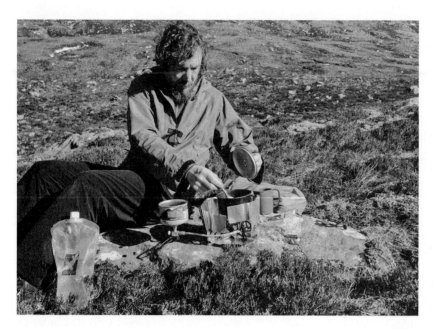

On exposed sites, windscreens are essential to protect burners from the wind as here with the Coleman Fyrestorm.

tanks and canisters from the heat, however, and can be used as stove stands, especially on snow, when one is essential.

Heat Exchangers, Pot Warmers, and Flame Diffusers

In theory heat exchangers conduct heat from the burner up the sides of a pan, speeding cooking times and reducing fuel consumption. MSR's Heat Exchanger is a corrugated aluminum collar that is compatible with MSR 1.5- and 2-quart pots. According to MSR, the Heat Exchanger increases heat efficiency by 25 percent. Since the exchanger weighs just 6 ounces, it should save weight overall on long trips. On short trips, the main advantage would be faster boiling times. Although designed for MSR pots, the Exchanger can be used with other brands. It won't work with ones less than 6 inches in diameter, though. I used the heat exchanger on several ski tours with groups and thought it did speed up boiling times, though I never quantified by how much.

I did eventually get around to doing some tests, and the results were surprising. A quart of water in an MSR Alpine pan on a Primus OmniFuel stove attached to a cartridge took 3 minutes, 55 seconds to boil. I then fitted the Heat Exchanger so it hung an inch and a half below the pot and boiled another quart. It took 4 minutes, 40 seconds. Moving the Exchanger so it was level with the base of the pot, I boiled a third quart. It took 5 minutes, 30 seconds. The Heat Exchanger was having the opposite effect from that intended. The OmniFuel has a roarer burner that spreads the flame across the bottom of the pan. To see if there was any difference, I did the test again using an MSR PocketRocket, which has a narrow flame focused on the center of the pan. With the Exchanger hanging an inch and a half below the pot the quart of water boiled in 4 minutes, 45 seconds. With it level with the pot base, it boiled in 5 minutes, 45 seconds. Without the heat exchanger, it boiled in 5 minutes, 30 seconds. These are confusing results—at least they confused me—so I

Top: Use a Scorch Buster heat-dispersion plate to spread the heat while simmering. Above: A heat exchanger welded to the base of a Primus pot.

consulted a physicist friend. He thought the heat exchanger was acting as a radiator when used with a stove with a wide flame. The flame was heating the exchanger, which then radiated the heat into the air, slowing heating of the pot. With the narrow flame he thought the exchanger trapped a cushion of hot air below the pot, which speeded up heating of the pot. This effect was lost when the exchanger was level with the base of the pot.

In that case, with both flames the heat exchanger absorbed some heat, effectively creating a pot with a larger surface area, and so slowed the heating of the water. My conclusion is that the Exchanger is best used with large pans and stoves with narrow flames. If the Exchanger gets hot, then it's probably not doing its job. With stoves with wide flames, they could be turned down to prevent the Exchanger from absorbing heat. My friend thought it wasn't worth using and that a windscreen would be much more effective. Certainly a windscreen and a lid are the two most important items for fuel conservation and fast boiling times. Heat-exchanger stoves are designed so that the burner and the heat exchanger, which fits under not around the pot, are compatible. There are now many heat-exchanger pots available to be used with other stoves. Following my tests, I'd make sure that the stove flame was contained inside the heat exchanger.

The Pot Parka is a soft, aluminized fiberglass dome that keeps pots warm. It weighs 3 ounces for the 8-inch size and 4 ounces for the 10-inch. It also forms the main part of the Outback Oven. It saves fuel because when it's in place you can melt snow or warm water with the stove on a low setting. It starts to burn if you use it with a stove on full, however, so it can't be used to speed up boil times. It can also be used to keep food warm when the stove is off.

Stoves with poor flame control can burn food that needs simmering for any length of time unless you stir constantly and lift the pot above the burner every so often. An answer to this is the Scorch Buster heat-dispersion plate, a ribbed stainless steel disk that weighs 2.8 ounces and is, in fact, the same as the diffuser plate of the Outback Oven described below. It works well and is worth carrying if you tend to burn meals.

Hanging Cook Systems

Hanging cook systems, which can be suspended from pitons or other supports, are designed for mountaineers bivouacking in tight places. Primus's Suspension Kit, a wire framework that supports pot, stove, and cartridge or fuel bottle, comes in two sizes for stoves with three or four legs at weights of 1.8 and 2.2 ounces. You could use one of these in a tent in winter to avoid cooling the fuel by placing it on the snow or suspend it from a tree if you want to cook without bending over. I've never used one.

Stands

Stoves need support on snow and, sometimes, soft ground. They also need insulating from cold ground. You can use a small square of wood, metal, or fiberglass insulation or even a book. On ski tours I usually use the blade of a snow shovel. In the snowbound High Sierra on the Pacific Crest Trail I used my natural history guide to stop my Svea stove from melting down into the snow. MSR

Outback Oven with Pot Parka, which can be used on its own to keep pots warm.

makes a flat-folding three-section base called the Trillium that weighs 3 ounces and can be adjusted to fit different MSR stoves, and UCO offers the Mightylite stove stand in two sizes at 4 and 4.3 ounces that has an elastic cord for attaching the fuel bottle to make a single unit. For piggyback stoves there is the Foot Rest from Primus. This has three folding legs and fits under the cartridge. It weighs 0.75 ounce. Mostly, though, I use a flat rock. I do like the look of the Trangia Multi-Disc, however. This circle of hard plastic with holes in one side can be used as a strainer and a cutting board as well as a stove stand. It could be used as a Frisbee, too. The weight is 3.5 ounces. For wood-burning stoves, I carry the Trail Designs' titanium Floor, which could be used with other stoves.

Stove Lighters and Fire Starters

It's best to carry more than one item for lighting your stove. Soaked matches and empty lighters won't help you. I always used to carry a box of strike-anywhere matches (half an ounce) in my food bag, another in the stove bag, and a third in a plastic bag with some toilet paper. I always kept them in Ziploc plastic bags, but waterproof metal or plastic match safes (Coghlan's makes both) provide extra protection and weigh about an ounce. Empty film canisters or other small plastic containers with secure lids can be used too. You can tear the striker off the matchbox and store it inside with the matches. I don't like book matches—the striking strip wears out quickly, and it always seems that half the matches don't work.

The chance that several boxes kept in different places in the pack all will get soaked is remote, but it could happen in a downpour or during a river ford, so carrying an emergency backup fire starter is good for peace of mind. I used to carry a canister of waterproof, windproof Lifeboat matches in my repair kit. The waterproof plastic canister contains twenty-five large matches, has strikers top and bottom, and weighs 0.75 ounce. They work when wet and burn for eleven to fifteen seconds, but beware of the hot embers after one has gone out. You can get other windproof and waterproof matches from companies like Coghlan's.

An alternative to matches is a lighter. Disposable butane lighters weigh less than an ounce, and just a spark from one will ignite white gas and butane-propane, though not kerosene or alcohol (at least not easily). If a lighter gets wet, it's easily dried; a sodden box of matches is useless. Refillable lighters like the classic Zippo (2 ounces) are an alternative. Lighters can be touchy, though, and don't always work. I wouldn't rely on one alone.

Until recently I'd never tried any fire starters other than matches or lighters, regarding other methods as rather esoteric and complicated—fun maybe, but little practical use. Then I discovered

Swedish FireSteel and Tool Logic SL3 knife with FireSteel insert. Fire starters like this one are hot and work in any weather, even rain.

the Swedish FireSteel, a modern version of the old flint and steel. This consists of an alloy magnesium rod with a plastic handle and a small flat steel bar linked by a short length of cord. Striking the rod with the bar produces extremely hot bright white sparks (5,430°F, say the makers). There are two sizes of FireSteel. The smaller Scout weighs 1 ounce and is said to produce at least 3,000 ignitions. The larger Army weighs 2 ounces and lasts for 12,000 strikes. Lighting a stove with the FireSteel is easy, and it really does work when wet. I dunked it in water and struck it while it was still dripping, and bright sparks appeared immediately. I started carrying the FireSteel as a replacement for the Lifeboat matches, but I've ended up using it as my main fire starter. Not having to protect it from damp makes it a great tool.

I also like the Fire-Lite fire starter, which consists of a plastic shaft and a tiny ridged wheel that when spun scrapes a flint and produces sparks. It's waterproof and can be used one-handed. The weight is a mere 0.32 ounce. One Fire-Lite is said to produce more than 5,000 sparks. It comes in a pack with four pieces of Tinder-Quik. The Fire-Lite is so small it could easily be lost, which is presumably why the shaft is orange in color. I now carry it as my backup fire starter.

There are several other fire starters of the flint-and-steel type. The Doan Magnesium Firestarter Tool (1.3 ounces) is perhaps the classic model. To use it you scrape flakes from a magnesium bar, then ignite them by scraping a knife across the bar to create sparks.

Survival manuals describe in detail methods of fire lighting such as bow drills that use natural materials, but these all strike me (on the basis of no experience, I should add) as unworkable in the cold and wet—when you'd need a fire most.

Transporting Stoves and Fuel

If you're planning to fly with your backpacking equipment, check the airline regulations before purchasing a ticket. Federal Aviation Administration regulations say you may carry properly purged stoves and fuel bottles—ones that are well aired and empty with no fuel smell. However, many airlines have much stricter rules of their own. Some won't carry any used stoves or used fuel bottles, some won't carry any stoves or fuel bottles at all even if new, and some won't carry used fuel bottles but will carry purged stoves.

To be sure stoves and bottles are purged, air them, preferably in sunshine, for as long as possible before the flight. Bottles can be washed out with soapy water, too.

You can send used stoves and empty fuel containers as air freight, but this is so expensive and such a hassle that you might as well buy a stove at your destination.

Some airlines will let you carry cartridge stoves but not liquid-fuel stoves. When planning a ski tour to the Yukon, I checked with the airline about stoves and was told that no used liquid-fuel stoves or fuel bottles were permitted but that cartridge stoves were fine as long as I carried no cartridges. We took cartridge stoves and discovered how difficult they are to use at 0°F (−18°C).

Fuel is obviously a hazard, and no airline will carry it. Buying fuel at your destination is the solution.

UTENSILS

Your cooking habits determine what kitchen gear you carry. One advantage of minimal cooking is that it requires minimal tools. For many years my basic kit has consisted of a 0.9-quart titanium pot with lid, a 1-pint titanium cup, a small knife, and two spoons—total weight 10 ounces. This serves my needs both on weekends and on long summer trips. When snow camping I carry an insulated 12-ounce mug instead of the titanium cup that happens to weigh exactly the same.

Pans

Pots and pans for camping are hardly the most exciting items of gear, and most people give them little thought. I used aluminum pans for well over ten years, then changed to stainless steel, followed by steel-aluminum laminate and finally, for the past two decades, titanium. To see how they performed, I've tried a wide selection over the years.

Aluminum, the standard backpacking cookware material for decades, is lightweight, heats evenly without hot spots, and conducts heat quickly, making for fast boiling times. But it pits, scratches, and dents easily, which makes it hard to clean and can give some foods a slight metallic flavor. Concerns that aluminum might contribute to Alzheimer's disease led aluminum pans to lose popularity to stainless steel. Now that these fears have turned out to be groundless, aluminum has had a revival. This has been helped by its low cost and by the introduction of hard-anodized aluminum, which is tough, scratch-proof, and hard to dent.

Many aluminum pans, however, are made of soft metal and are poorly designed, low cost being the manufacturers' only concern. Trangia aluminum pans—sold separately from the stoves—are high quality. The 1-quart size weighs 3.5 ounces, the 1.75-quart, 5.5 ounces. I have a 5-quart Trangia pot with a lock-up bail arm that weighs only 18.5 ounces; I use it when cooking for groups (when it makes a good receptacle for packing tor-

The MSR Titan Kettle in titanium (left) and the AntiGravity Gear 3 Cup Non-Stick Pot in aluminum (right). Both are good solo pots, but the AGG one is much less expensive. A typical titanium mug that can be used both as a pot and a cup—the Alpkit MytiMug (below).

tillas). Open Country, Primus, and Snow Peak are among other makers of plain aluminum pans. One pan that has become quite popular with ultralight hikers and that is very inexpensive is the Wal-Mart Grease Saver Pot, designed for straining grease. Take out the strainer and you have a 1-quart pot that weighs 2.5 ounces plus a 2-ounce lid with black plastic knob. The pot has black sides with the word "grease" imprinted and a silver base. It's very light, but the aluminum is soft and easily dented—a pot gripper made marks the first time I used it. There's a lip around the rim that could collect dirt, and the right angle between the base and sides is harder to clean than a rounded edge. For the sake of an ounce and only a small amount of cash, I'd rather have the 1-quart Trangia pan.

Hard-anodized aluminum is more expensive than standard aluminum but should last far longer. MSR, Primus, Optimus, GSI, and more all make hard-anodized aluminum cookware with nonstick coatings that are meant to be much harder wearing than those found on other metals. Primus's Litech Cook Kit has 2.1- and 1.7-quart pans, a lid, and a pot gripper and weighs 20 ounces. Primus also make the 1-quart Litech Trek Kettle, a tall pot with a pouring spout that weighs 9.4 ounces. MSR offers several hard-anodized aluminum cooksets, with pot sizes from 1.3 to 3 quarts. An example is the 1.3-quart Quick Solo Pot, which weighs 6.2 ounces and has a strainer lid and a locking, foldout handle. I've used the Primus Litech Trek Kettle and the MSR Quick Solo Pot pans, and they do heat evenly and are very easy to clean. The nonstick coating is far tougher than on other pans I've used, too. The most interesting hard-anodized pots I've come across are the GSI Halulite ones, which come in capacities from 0.6 to 1.4 quarts and which are very lightweight. I've been using the Minimalist, which consists of a plain 0.6-quart pot, a pot cozy, a plastic lid, a silicone pot gripper, and a plastic spork. The total weight is 6.1 ounces. The Minimalist doubles well as a mug and a pot. Used as a mug, it keeps drinks warm in the cold due to the pot cozy. The lid can be inverted to form a sealed lid with drinking hole when in mug mode. The silicone pot gripper is tiny but easy to use, though you do dip the top of it into the liquid if the pot is full. The spork is the only item I'm unsure about, as it's quite thin and might easily break. As the Minimalist is only marginally heavier than an insulated mug, I might well carry it instead of one in winter, as it can be used for boiling water in too.

Many standard aluminum pans come with nonstick coatings. These are fine as long as you're prepared to treat them carefully and always use plastic or wooden utensils. I prefer pots I can mistreat and scour with sand or gravel if necessary. (I know this shouldn't be required, but in my experience nonstick means "doesn't stick as badly or as often.") I have an AntiGravity Gear 3 Cup Non-Stick Pot, which weighs just 3.8 ounces with the lid. This has proved pretty tough, though I have been careful to only use plastic spoons with it. It requires a separate pot gripper, and the metal one I've been using has left marks. Overall though, for the weight, this is a good pot. AGG also makes a 2-quart version at 5.9 ounces.

Stainless steel is easy to clean, noncorroding, scratchproof, tough, and long lasting, and it doesn't taint food. Unfortunately, it's significantly heavier than aluminum and also conducts heat more slowly, leading to fractionally longer boiling times. Due to the weight, stainless steel is becoming less common for backpacking pots. Many companies no longer use it. One that still does is MSR, whose Alpine 2 Set has 1.5- and 2-quart pots, a lid/plate, and a pot handle. It weighs a hefty 1 pound, 10 ounces.

Titanium is my favorite material for pans. It doesn't pit, scratch, or affect flavor, and it cleans easily. It's much lighter than steel—45 percent lighter according to MSR—conducts heat better, and is more durable. I have a twenty-year-old 0.9-quart Evernew pan with foldout handles that weighs 5 ounces with lid. It's my most-used pot

by far and has had well over two years' worth of use in total, during which it's acquired just one small dent. It's been on several long-distance walks including the Pacific Northwest Trail and should last for many more. Evernew now makes a large range of titanium pots in sizes from 10 fluid ounces to 6 quarts and in tall mug shapes and wide pan shapes. The 0.9-quart wide pot, a size and shape that I find ideal for solo use, now comes in two versions, a 4.9-ounce nonstick one and a 4.1-ounce plain titanium one. There are other titanium pots, such as MSR's Titan 2-Pot Set with 1- and 1.5-quart pans, lid, and pot gripper at 9.6 ounces and Snow Peak's Multi Compact Titanium Cook Set with 1- and 1.5-quart pans with foldout handles and lids at 11.5 ounces. MSR also makes a 28.7-ounce-capacity Titan Kettle that weights just 4.2 ounces with lid that is excellent for solo use.

An alternative to a standard pot is a titanium mug that can be used as a pot, a style that is popular with ultralight backpackers and is typified by the Vargo T-Lite Mug, which has a 0.75-quart

Titanium pan and mug: my favorites.

capacity, foldout handles, and a lid and a weight of 4.9 ounces. There are many similar, not to say identical, mugs. If 0.75 quart isn't big enough, there are bigger ones like the popular Snow Peak Trek 900, with a 0.9-quart capacity and a weight of 6.2 ounces. The idea with these is that they replace your pot and mug. I've tried this, and while it certainly saves a little weight, I prefer having separate cooking and drinking vessels. Like any titanium product, these mugs are durable. The only downside to titanium is the very high cost. But once you have a pot, it will last a very long time.

Following the success of heat-exchanger cooking systems, pots with heat exchangers welded to the base are now available from Primus, Optimus, MSR, and Jetboil. Ones I've used work OK, but they are heavy compared with ones without heat exchangers. I'd only use them for melting snow or on very long trips when the extra weight was cancelled out by the fuel saving. They also need to be matched with a stove so that the flame isn't wider than the base of the pot (of course turning the stove down can achieve this). I've tried the Optimus Terra Weekend Heat Exchanger Cook Set, which consists of a tall, fairly narrow, 0.95-quart hard-anodized aluminum pot with foldout insulating handles and a deep lid with folding handles. I used it with an Optimus Crux Lite cartridge stove and needed to turn the flame down a little to keep it under the pot. It weighs 9.6 ounces, which is heavy for a solo pan. Of the Primus pots, the 1-quart one, which weighs 10.2 ounces, is similar to the Optimus Terra one. I prefer the wider 1.2-liter one, which weighs less at 9.5 ounces due to having a plastic strainer lid rather than a metal frypan lid. Both are made from hard-anodized aluminum.

Whatever they're made from, pans should be simple. Fairly shallow ones with rounded edges

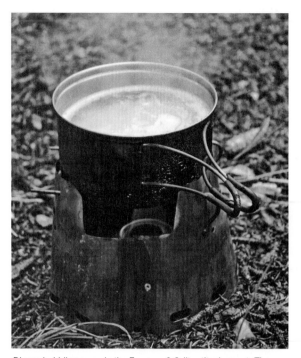

Dinner bubbling away in the Evernew 0.9-liter titanium pot. The stove unit is a Trail Designs Caldera Ti-Tri with alcohol burner.

are best, because food is less likely to burn in them and they're easy to clean. They also conduct heat more efficiently from the stove to their contents due to their large base area. Rounded bottom edges are also more efficient in theory since heat can more easily travel up the sides of the pot. Tall, narrow pots conduct heat inefficiently, though my experience with tall mugs like the Vargo Ti-Lite is that this isn't significant when boiling small quantities of water. Very shallow, wide pots, such as those found in many traditional-style mess kits, aren't very good for boiling water, though they're OK for frying. Pans that nest are standard. Often, however, cooksets don't contain the mix of pans you want. I like to make my own sets from different pans, checking to be sure that they nest together.

Although low weight is welcome, very thin pans can distort, making them hard to balance on stoves, and food tends to burn quickly in them.

Avoid attached handles on aluminum pans because they become very hot, but foldout handles on stainless steel and titanium pans stay reasonably cool unless you use the pan on an open fire. Bails that rise above the pan can get quite hot too. They're useful for suspending a pan above a fire and with large pans that can be hard to lift when full with a side handle or a pot gripper. Check the welds of handles or bails. They can fail, leaving you with a pan that has holes in it and a useless handle.

How big a pan you need depends on how many you're cooking for. I find a 1-quart size is easily large enough for solo cooking. Some minimalists can get by with a pot that holds only a pint. For two I add a 2-quart pan; when I've cooked for ten I've found a 5-quart pot just big enough for cooking pasta or rice, with a 2-quart pan adequate for the sauce.

Lids are very important for faster boil times and lower fuel use. In strong winds water may not boil at all unless the pan is covered. Good lids should fit tightly. Many are designed to double as frying pans, but people who fry foods tell me that lids don't work very well this way. They're often relatively heavy—the lid for my 1-quart titanium pan weighs 1.5 ounces—so I sometimes substitute a piece of heavy-duty foil that weighs just 0.3 ounce.

Pot Grippers

For pans without handles, you need pot grippers, or pot grabs, that clamp firmly onto the rim. I used a 2-ounce Trangia pot grab on almost every trip for nearly twenty years. MSR makes excellent pot grippers too; the 1.9-ounce PanHandler

will support up to ten pounds, and the 1-ounce LiteLifter will lift full 4-quart pots. Not all pot grippers are of this quality, though; some thin aluminum ones quickly twist out of shape. Now that I usually use the titanium pot with its foldout handles and a lid with a knob on solo trips, I carry a pot grab only when I intend to cook over an open fire, where the handles get hot.

Pot Cozies

The pot cozy is a simple but effective idea. Like a tea cozy for a teapot, it keeps a cooking pot warm. For backpacking cooking, this not only means that food can be kept warm in cold weather but that fuel can be saved by wrapping a pot in a cozy so that food can continue cooking without needing to be on the stove. Pot cozies are made from neoprene, closed-cell foam, or insulated foil. Making one is quite easy. Even I managed it with pieces cut out of an old foam pad and duct tape. Backpacking Light UK sells the material as a cozy and windshield kit. If you don't want to make your own cozy, AntiGravity Gear offers a selection at weights ranging from 0.6 ounce to 2.6 ounces depending on material and pot size. The ones made from neoprene and closed-cell foam are heavier but more durable. The foil ones do need care, as the insulation, which is mainly air, is easily crushed. A pot cozy can also be used to hold the pot while you eat out of it, keeping the food warm and meaning you don't have to hold the pot by the handle.

Ovens and Baking Devices

When I first heard about ovens for backpackers I was highly dubious, suspecting they would be heavy and difficult to use. I couldn't imagine bak-

A selection of pot grippers for pots of different sizes. You'll need the larger ones for pots that hold more than a quart.

Pot cozies like this AntiGravity Gear one keep food hot and allow it to continue cooking without being on a stove.

ing anything on a small stove in the wild. However, my assumptions started to waver with reports that the Outback Oven really did work well, so I decided I had to try it. I wasn't disappointed. (Back then the Outback Oven was made by Traveling Light; now it's under the Backpacker's Pantry umbrella—back packerspantry.com.)

If you're the sort of backpacker who hates dehydrated food and dreams of pizza, fresh bread, or apple pie, you can have them all with one of these ovens, without too much hassle.

The Outback Oven comes in two versions: the 26-ounce 10-inch for two to four people (including a nonstick baking pan) and the 9.5-ounce Ultralight for one or two. The Outback Oven consists of a foil reflector collar that fits under the burner of your stove and directs heat upward, a stainless steel riser bar and diffuser plate to spread the heat evenly and prevent scorching, a fiberglass convection dome that fits over your pan and concentrates the heat, and a simple thermometer. All the components can be packed inside a small pan.

To use the oven you need a stove with a controllable flame plus pan supports that the heat reflector can be fitted to and that will support the riser bar/diffuser plate unit. Most stoves meet these criteria, but check that the oven will fit your stove before buying one. A windscreen is essential unless it's calm. The Ultralight oven is designed to be used with pans from 6 to 8 inches in diameter and 3 to 5 inches high, which includes most 1.5- and 2-quart pans but rules out smaller ones.

Simpler and lighter than the Outback Oven is the BakePacker. The standard version weighs 8 ounces and the ultralight one weighs 4 ounces. I've tried the latter, which is designed for pots 6 to 7 inches in diameter. The BakePacker consists of an aluminum grid of heat pipes that sits in the bottom of the pan and conducts heat up through its honeycomb. You put enough water in the pot to cover the grid, then place the food to be baked on top in a plastic freezer bag or oven-roasting bag and spread it out. You then close the bag loosely and put the lid on the pot. Once the water is boiling, medium heat is enough to steam bake the mix in the bag. Because the BakePacker cooks with steam it can't produce crisp crusts, unlike the Outback Oven, and you need a supply of plastic bags. However, it's light and easy to use.

Having eaten freshly baked food on the trail, I can't go back to living on dehydrated meals all the time—or so I thought when my dalliance with baking was new and exciting. For a short while I did bake in camp occasionally. I have to admit, though, that despite my intentions it's now many years since I bothered baking in the wilds. I've discovered I can live on dried food after all.

Plates and Bowls

I usually don't bother with plates or bowls because I eat straight from the pot, but this is practical only for the solo hiker. Shallow plates spill easily and don't hold much. Deep bowls are a better choice; I carry one when I'm with a group. Plastic is the standard material, with Lexan the toughest type. GSI makes an excellent-looking bowl out of polypropylene—the Ultralight Nesting Bowl and Mug—that comes with an insulated sleeve and a lid. It's 5.1 inches in diameter and 2.7 inches deep and weighs 4.3 ounces. Plastic bowls weigh 2 to 5 ounces, depending on size. Metal bowls and plates are also available, but are cold in freezing conditions. MSR's steel Alpine Mountain Bowl holds 27 fluid ounces and weighs 3.6 ounces, the Mountain Plate has a 7.5-inch diameter and weighs 4.4 ounces, and Trangia's aluminum 8.5-inch plate weighs 3.5 ounces. Titanium plates and bowls are much lighter. Snow Peak's Trek Titanium Bowl is 5.5 inches in diameter and 3 inches deep but weighs only 1.6 ounces. Many people eat out of their mugs, but you obviously can't have a drink at the same time, which I like to do, unless you carry two mugs.

Mugs

A good mug can become a favorite item, perhaps not surprising when it provides that wake-up drink in the morning or warm-up drink after a long cold day. Synthetic materials, known generally as plastic, are light and cheap but not very durable, and they soon develop scratches and cracks. Plastic also retains tastes—last night's tomato soup will flavor the morning's cup of coffee no matter how well you wash the mug. A typical half-pint plastic mug weighs 0.75 ounce. Brand-name synthetic mugs are usually tougher than the unbranded cheap ones found in camping stores. Examples are GSI's polypropylene Cascadian Cup, which holds 12 fluid ounces and weighs 1.7 ounces, and Sea to Summit's nylon Delta Mug, which doesn't have a handle, holds 16 fluid ounces, and weighs 2.2 ounces. Collapsible plastic mugs are available, which look like a good idea because they are so compact. However, my experience has been that they can spring holes along the fold lines rather too easily. One started to leak just above the base after only two nights' use. If you like large drinks or use your mug for eating, GSI's FairShare Co-Polyester Mug is probably the largest around, with a capacity of 32 fluid ounces. It has a screw-on lid and weighs 7 ounces.

Drinks cool down fairly quickly in a single-walled mug, which is fine on a hot summer day but not so good on a frosty morning. The classic foam-insulated mug is the answer. This keeps drinks warm for a long time in the cold, even if you leave the lid off. The main brands are Aladdin and Whirley, which offer a large array of shapes and sizes and also make own-brand mugs for other companies. The nearest to a standard size is probably the 12-fluid-ounce mug. The Aladdin model weighs 5 ounces, including a half-ounce lid. If you

Selection of mugs. Clockwise from top left: Aladdin 12-ounce insulated, Aladdin 21-ounce insulated, GSI 32-ounce Fair Share, MSR double-wall stainless steel, Cascade Cup stainless steel, and polyethylene.

want a larger mug there's a 21-fluid-ounce one that weighs 7 ounces. I use the 12-fluid-ounce mug for cold-weather trips. In summer I find it keeps drinks too hot for too long. If you want your drink to stay really hot for a long time, leave the lid on the mug. This really does make a huge difference. A new twist on insulated mugs is the Sea to Summit nylon Delta-Insul Mug, which has an integrated EVA insulating sleeve. It holds 16 fluid ounces and weighs 4.4 ounces, which makes it lighter than the double-walled alternatives.

Insulated plastic mugs still hold tastes, though not as badly as polyethylene ones. Metal doesn't. But to drink hot liquids out of aluminum or enamel mugs you need asbestos lips. This means that, except for cold drinks, the cup that comes with the Svea 123R stove and doubles as a burner cover is useless. However, stainless steel and titanium mugs are fine: they don't burn your lips or

get scratched and are very durable. I have a pint mug, REI's Cascade Cup, that I bought many years ago; it can be used as a pan on any stove because it has a wide base. It weighs 4 ounces and has a clip-off handle that folds away under the cup. Because I can boil water in it for a drink while I'm eating out of my larger pan, it's my favorite of the twenty camping mugs that I'm somewhat surprised to discover I own. It nests neatly inside my 0.9-quart pan. The Cascade Cup is a larger version of the classic Sierra Cup, which holds 10 fluid ounces and weighs 3 ounces. I find the Sierra Cup a little unstable, since the top is much wider than the base. Drinks cool down in it very quickly, too, but many people like it. Snow Peak makes a titanium version of the Sierra Cup called the Ti-Backpacker's Cup that weighs 1.4 ounces, and Evernew makes the Ti Sierra Cup at 1.8 ounces. Vargo makes the larger 25-fluid-ounce Titanium

Ed Huesers enjoying drinking from his favorite porcelain mug in a backcountry igloo.

Sierra 750, which has a lid and weighs 4.5 ounces and is more like the Cascade Cup than the original Sierra Cup.

To save an ounce, I often use a 3-ounce MSR 23-fluid-ounce titanium pan with foldout handles as a mug. This model is no longer available, but there are plenty of small titanium pots and mugs with foldout handles that are similar. Evernew's Ti Ultralight Pot 1 is almost identical, with a capacity of 20.3 fluid ounces and a weight of 3.5 ounces including lid. A smaller version is the Evernew Ti Mug 400, which holds 13.5 fluid ounces and weighs 1.7 ounces, and a bigger one, the Vargo Ti-Lite Mug 900, which holds 30.4 fluid ounces and weighs 4.6 ounces. Tall, narrow titanium mugs like the Vargo Ti-Lite are quite light but won't usually nest inside wider pots, which is fine if you have plenty of space in the pack or if you're not carrying another pot anyway.

Insulated metal mugs for cold-weather use have the advantage over plastic ones that they don't hold tastes. The 6.1-ounce, 20-fluid-ounce capacity GSI Halulite Minimalist, which comes with a removable insulated sleeve, is made of aluminum, which can be hot on the lips but has a plastic lid you can drink through that overcomes this. Other cold-weather mugs are double-walled titanium or stainless steel. Examples are the GSI Glacier Stainless Bottle Cup/Pot in stainless steel, which holds 18 fluid ounces and weighs 4.9 ounces, and the Snow Peak Ti Double 220 Mug in titanium, which holds 7.4 fluid ounces and weighs 2.6 ounces. Of these, the Minimalist is the most functional because it can be used as a pot as well as a mug.

Porcelain mugs are not generally thought of as suitable for backpacking, being fragile and heavy, but some people do carry them. Ed Huesers of IceBox fame takes his favorite mug, featuring a Gary Larson cartoon about igloos, on ski tours and enjoys the luxury of drinking out of it in the igloo at night. Personally, nice though such a mug is, I shall stick to less breakable metal and plastic.

Eating Implements

Plastic cutlery is lightweight but mostly not very durable. Lexan was the toughest material, but this is hard to find now. I've broken several plastic spoons and sporks, all from reputable companies. Most haven't lasted more than a few weeks, some, particularly folding ones, only a few days. Maybe I'm tough on spoons, but the Lexan ones used to last me years. Metal spoons are far stronger. Titanium, aluminum, and stainless steel are all available. I use the Sea to Summit AlphaLight Spoon, which is made of hard-anodized aluminum and weighs 0.3 ounce, and, when I'll be eating from a deep pouch or pot, the Vargo Titanium Long-Handle Spoon, which weighs 0.6 ounce. I took both on the Pacific Northwest Trail, reckoning the combined weight wouldn't be too much of a burden, and they lasted fine. Sporks with a spoon-shaped end with fork-like tines or with a spoon at one end and a fork at the other are popular. I've tried these, but as I don't use or need a fork in the wilds anyway, I prefer a simple spoon. Everything can be eaten with that or with fingers. There are many cutlery sets that clip or link together available. If you want a knife and fork as well as a spoon, these are worth considering. Vargo's Titanium Spoon/Fork/Knife Set weighs 1.3 ounces, and Sea to Summit's AlphaLight hard-anodized aluminum 3-piece set weighs 0.8 ounce. I prefer a pocket knife anyway as it has more uses. These are discussed in the next chapter.

Washing Dishes

Stainless steel and titanium clean much more easily than aluminum. Generally a wipe with a damp cloth is enough, although for hygienic reasons you should sterilize pans and utensils thoroughly every few days. I do this with boiling water.

I don't carry detergent or dishwashing liquid—it's unnecessary and a pollutant, even if it's biode-gradable. Nor do I wash dishes directly in a water source or tip food scraps into one. Dirty dishwater should always be poured onto a bare patch of ground or into thick vegetation. To make dishwashing easier, pour cold water into a pan once it's empty to stop food residue from cementing itself to the inside. Some foods are worse than others—oatmeal is particularly bad. Hard-to-clean pans can be scoured with gravel or even snow to remove debris. Mostly I just use a soft dishcloth, which I rinse out regularly and hang on the pack to dry. Scourer sponges are an alternative but are harder to keep clean. A bandanna can be pressed into service if necessary, something I've done on trips where I've forgotten a dishcloth.

Packing

I generally pack my stove, pans, and utensils together in a small stuff sack. I don't pack the stove inside the pans, since this tends to dirty them and can make them smell of fuel, although manufacturers tout this packing "convenience" as an advantage of many small stoves. I usually carry

Forest kitchen with the stove on a rock to prevent it from scorching the ground or setting the pine needles alight.

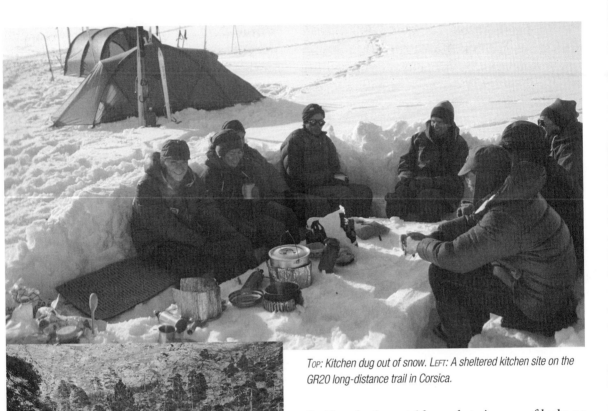

Top: *Kitchen dug out of snow.* Left: *A sheltered kitchen site on the GR20 long-distance trail in Corsica.*

fuel bottles in outside pockets in case of leaks or stand them upright at the bottom of the main compartment below my food bag, which is where I keep fuel cartridges, too. The stove and pans also end up there, since I rarely use them during the day. If you cook at lunchtime, you'll need to pack them somewhere accessible.

SITING THE KITCHEN

I like to site my kitchen next to my sleeping bag. That way I can have breakfast in bed—a good way to face a cold or wet morning, and nice any time. The stove needs to be placed on bare earth or on short, sparse vegetation so that the heat doesn't cause any damage. If the plant growth is long and luxurious, I try to find a flat rock to place the stove on, to avoid singeing the vegetation. You must, of course, return the rock to its proper place when you've finished. I set up the stove, then sort out the food I need for the evening. When all the kitchen items are arranged near the stove and I know where everything is, I start cooking.

You have to modify this pattern anywhere bears are potential visitors. In this case it's advis-able to site the kitchen at least 100 yards down-wind of where you sleep, because the smell of food might attract a bear during the night. I look for a sheltered spot with a good view, and perhaps a log or tree stump to sit on or lean against. Clean utensils can be left in place overnight. Dirty ones should be hung with the food.

chapter eight

comfort and safety

in camp and on the trail

WHEN IN THE WILDS, WE MUST NOT CARRY OUR PROBLEMS WITH US OR THE JOY IS LOST.
—*Sigurd F. Olson*

To make any walk safe and enjoyable, numerous small items (and skills) are useful. Some are essential, some are never necessary, though they may enhance your stay in the wilderness. I'm always surprised at the number of odds and ends in my pack, yet not one of them is superfluous.

LIGHT

No one goes backpacking in the Far North—Alaska, northern Canada, Greenland, Iceland—during midwinter because there's little daylight—none at all if you're north of the Arctic Circle. In midsummer, however, the Far North is light twenty-four hours a day—no artificial light is needed at "night." Most places backpackers frequent are farther south, though, and some form of light is needed regardless of the time of year. How much you need depends on where you are and when. At Lake Louise in Banff National Park in the Canadian Rockies, there are over sixteen and a half hours of daylight in mid-June, but only eight hours in mid-December; in Yosemite you'll have fourteen and three-quarters hours in June but more than nine and a half in December.

Headlamps and Flashlights

LEDs (light-emitting diodes) are now standard for backpacking headlamps and flashlights, as they are durable, lightweight, bright, and battery life is long. I haven't used an incandescent bulb light for a decade, and I can't see any reason to use one for backpacking given the fragility and rapid use of battery power. LEDs fade slowly after first use unless the power is regulated, which means a constant light output throughout most of the life of the batteries. A growing number of LED lights are now regulated. LEDs will continue to glow feebly as long as there's a smidgeon of energy left in the batteries. This isn't much use, however. Makers' maximum times are often those at

Wearing a headlamp leaves your hands free for tasks like making camp or cooking.

backpacking even though they are heavier because they free your hands for tasks such as pitching a shelter and cooking.

LEDs come in different sizes with different light outputs. Large LEDs are very bright but also use battery power more quickly than smaller, weaker LEDs. Large LEDs are good for night hiking, and the small LEDs for map reading, pitching tents, cooking, and other camp chores. Red LEDs are good for map reading without spoiling your night sight. Many lights have different sizes and colors of LEDs.

All but the simplest lights have variable light levels so you can have a very bright light for night hiking or identifying distant objects and less bright lights for close-up use and longer battery life.

Holding a flashlight in your hand when walking makes it easier to direct the light than having it on your head, and having it lower and away from your eyes gives better contrast. Unless I'm holding trekking poles or an ice ax, I prefer holding a light to having it on my head. You can of course hold a headlamp, which is what I usually do, but if you don't want a headlamp, there are many good LED flashlights.

Tiny LED flashlights may seem like toys rather than serious lights. They're not, as I discovered on my first day out on the Arizona Trail when I ended up following a narrow, snow-covered trail up steep slopes in the dark. Rather than take off my pack and dig out my headlamp, I used a single ASP Sapphire LED Light weighing half an ounce that I happened to have in a pants pocket. You have to keep the switch pressed to get a light, so I just used it every few yards or so to check where the trail went next. It was just adequate. It's guaranteed for life, including the batteries, but it's since disappeared—the only problem

which the light is just strong enough to be useful. Changing the batteries before this stage is reached is a good idea. With regulated lights, the power remains constant and then drops away suddenly. Batteries don't last quite as long, but neither do you end up with a light that is barely adequate. There is even a way of programming a headlamp for the amount of brightness or battery life you require. Developments in LED lighting have been swift and are continuing. Lights are becoming more powerful, and many lights have the option of a flood or spot beam, the first useful for lighting a wide area, such as a campsite, the second for picking out objects at a distance. The extra power means that smaller, lighter headlamps and flashlights can now be used for night hiking, saving weight in the pack. Designs have become more user-friendly, too, with battery compartments simpler to open, important in the dark with cold fingers or when wearing gloves. Headlamps and handheld flashlights both have advantages and disadvantages. I think headlamps are superior for with such small lights. I replaced it with an even smaller Princeton Tec Pulsar (it's a touch bigger than a quarter) that weighs a quarter of an ounce and mostly lives on my key ring. The two lithium cells are meant to last twelve to fourteen hours, which is a lot of squeeze time. I wouldn't rely on one of these tiny lights alone, except maybe in the Arctic in summer, but one makes a good backup. Slightly larger are ones that run off a single AAA battery, such as the Gerber Tempo, which weighs 1.1 ounces. The battery is said to last four hours, and the beam output is 27 feet. Flashlights like this would again be fine for short summer nights. For other times, a flashlight like the Mini Maglite LED, which runs off two AA batteries and weighs 4.15 ounces (with batteries), would be better. This has two power modes with battery life of 18 hours and 31 hours and throws a beam 300 feet in the high-power mode. There are flashlights like this made by many companies, including SureFire, Gerber, Photon, Streamlight, Maglite, Inova, and Fenix. When choosing a flashlight, as well as brightness and battery life, I look for an easy-to-access battery case in case I need to replace batteries in the dark and a power mode that can't be accidentally turned on in the pack (something that was a problem years ago when most lights had protruding switches). Most flashlights are now turned on by twisting part of the barrel, which is fairly foolproof.

Handheld lights are less costly than headlamps, and there's a much wider choice, but they're far less versatile, especially for camping. Many years ago I discovered that a headlamp is much more useful because it leaves both hands free. After having pitched tents and cooked while gagging on a flashlight held in my mouth, stopping every few minutes to recover, using a headlamp was a revelation. First developed

Headlamps. From left: Princeton Tec Apex, Petzl Tikka XP, Mammut Lucido T1, Petzl Tikka 2 with Core battery, Black Diamond Icon.

for predawn starts on Alpine mountaineering routes, many of the best headlamps come from mountaineering equipment manufacturers such as Petzl and Black Diamond. In early models, wires trailed from the lamp to battery packs you clipped to your belt or carried in a pocket, and they constantly caught on things. Then came headlamps with the battery case on the headband, a design far more compact, lightweight, and easy to use.

There are various webbing headbands that can adapt a small flashlight for use as a headlamp. I have a Nite Ize headband (1 ounce) that takes a Mini Maglite. It's not as comfortable as a real headlamp, and you can't adjust the direction of the beam, but it does leave your hands free.

For many, many years I've mostly used French-made Petzl headlamps, due to the superb quality and innovative designs. Before LEDs, Petzl made the best headlamps, and arguably they still do, though there is plenty of competition. In headlamps, I look for the same features as with a flashlight plus a pivoting head so the beam can be directed.

Petzl made the first LED headlamps, the Tikka and Zipka. They're still around, too, though now there are three versions of each. My favorite is the 3-ounce Tikka XP, which I used on the Pacific Northwest Trail and which I think is fine for year-round use. This has a pivoting head and two LEDs, a high output white one and a red one, each with two light levels, with output distances of 50 and 180 feet. The Tikka XP runs on three AAA batteries with a burn time of 80 to 160 hours, depending on the light level. An excellent feature is a simple dimpled plastic diffuser that slides over the lamp. Low-tech this may be, but it works well, giving the option of a spot or flood beam. The light is operated by a soft pushbutton on the top that isn't easily depressed accidentally. The battery compartment, which is situated just behind the lamp, has a simple clip opening. The XP has a soft headband and is comfortable to wear.

The Tikka and Zipka headlamps are available with a rechargeable and programmable lithium-ion battery called the Core that comes with some clever computer software. Using this, you can program the battery for different power options and battery life depending on intended usage. I've tested a Tikka 2 headlamp with this technology and found it very useful, especially for one- and two-day trips when spare batteries aren't needed. Unfortunately, you can't retrofit the Core to older lamps, so I can't use it with my more powerful Tikka XP with its flood and spot options. The Tikka 2 has four LEDs that throw what could be described as a wide spot and two light levels plus a pivoting lamp. The Core battery fits neatly between the lamp itself and the battery compartment. It makes the lamp wider by a quarter of an inch or so, but there's no weight increase over AAA batteries. With the Core battery, the Tikka 2 weighs 2.6 ounces. The battery can be removed and AAA batteries used if necessary. The Tikka links to a computer with a USB cable and brings up the program, which has a graph and two slid-

ers, one for power output and one for battery life. Any changes you make to one are instantly visible in the other. You can see if the battery is fully charged, too, and select which model of headlamp you have. Indeed, you can give personal names to the battery and headlamp if you like. All the headlamps that can use the Core battery have both maximum and economic modes, both of which can be regulated using the software. What does this mean in reality? With the Tikka 2, 100 percent light output gives a battery life of 5 hours and an 84-foot beam. Move the slider to increase the battery life, and the output is shown diminishing. If, for example, you increase the battery life to 15 hours, then the output is cut to 50 percent, giving a beam of 60 yards. You can see the difference this makes to the brightness by switching on the lamp. Economic regulated output only starts at 25 percent brightness with a battery life of 23 hours, so reducing the brightness soon results in a light that doesn't throw much of a beam. At 4 percent output, the beam only goes 12 feet, but the battery will last 115 hours. For camp use or in the tent, this may be fine, of course. You can set the output and battery life for both maximum and economic light levels and use whichever one is appropriate. And because it's regulated, the output will remain constant for the set time and not fade slowly away. The Core battery can be recharged up to 300 times. Being lithium, it works well in the cold too. The Core comes with a short USB cable, and recharging can be done by any USB device including portable solar panels and battery-powered chargers.

There are many similar headlamps to the Tikka models, such as the Princeton Tec Remix, which has four LEDs, one giving a bright spot and the others a wide flood, four light levels with output distances from 30 to 130 feet, burn times from

28 to 200 hours, and a weight of 3 ounces with three AAA batteries and the Black Diamond Spot, which has five LEDs, one very bright, two lower power, and two red, three light levels with a maximum distance of 230 feet, burn times up to 250 hours, and a weight of 3.2 ounces with three AAA batteries. Both these headlamps have the battery case as an integral part of the lamp unit, a lamp that pivots, and a simple wide headband. Other companies that make this type of headlamp include Primus and Mammut.

For the long hours of winter or when hiking in the dark in difficult terrain, an even more powerful headlamp can be an advantage, though I don't often carry one of these anymore, as the Petzl Tikka XP is perfectly adequate for my trips, and they are heavier and take heavier batteries. But if you want a really bright light, these are the ones to go for. There are many models. Here are three examples I've tried and liked, all with pivoting lamps. Mammut's Lucido TX1 has six LEDs, one very bright, one giving a narrow spot, two with lower power giving a flood beam, and three red; three light levels with a maximum distance of 345 feet; burn times up to 180 hours; and a weight with three AA batteries of 5.8 ounces. The Black Diamond Icon also has five LEDs, one giving a very bright spot beam, and four a less bright flood beam; six light levels with distances varying from 75 to 328 feet; burn times up to 164 hours; and a weight with three AA batteries of 6.8 ounces. My favorite of these brighter headlamps is the Petzl Myo RXP, which has just one bright LED with three light levels plus the same diffuser as the Tikka XP that slides over the lens to change it from spot to flood. The three light levels can be programmed so you can vary the power output, not something I've found that useful, as unlike with the Core battery, there's no way of knowing

how this affects battery life. Much more useful is the regulated power, which ensures constant lighting for half to a third of the battery life. There's also a boost mode that gives a quick burst of very bright light when needed. The Myo RXP can be run on lithium batteries too, unlike the Mammut and Black Diamond models, which is particularly useful in a headlamp that is most likely to be used in winter. The output distance runs from 75 to 252 feet, and the burn time from 50 to 95 hours depending on light level. The weight with three AA batteries is 6.1 ounces.

Whatever light you use, it needs to be handy when you need it. I usually carry mine in a pack pocket in a little stuff sack with other small items. In camp, I place it close to the head of my sleeping bag so I can find it without too much trouble if I wake in the night.

Batteries

Battery life is so good now that I don't bother carrying spares unless I'm out for several weeks (or can't remember how much use the batteries in the headlamp have had). Alkaline batteries are standard, and AA and AAA ones, as used in most small headlamps and flashlights, are easy to find in most places. I prefer lights that run on these sizes for this reason. Alternatives are lithium and rechargeable batteries. Lithium batteries are expensive, but they last much longer than alkaline and rechargeable batteries in cold weather; they also maintain a steadier beam until their power is completely drained. Lithiums are slightly lighter than alkalines as well. Two Energizer Ultimate Lithium AA batteries weigh 1.5 ounces, half an ounce less than two AA alkaline batteries. In temperatures above freezing, lithiums have no advantages other than the slight weight difference when used in low-drain items like flashlights or headlamps. I only use lithiums in these on trips where I expect bitter cold, not on summer hikes. (However, lithiums are useful year-round in high-drain items like GPS units—see Chapter 9.) Rechargeable batteries used to have limited use for backpacking because they didn't hold a charge for long. In 2005, rechargeables that will hold a charge for long periods were introduced, and there are now several brands available, all of them nickel-metal-hydride, or NiMH, batteries. Nickel-cadmium, or nicad, batteries are not as useful for backpacking because they don't hold a charge for long periods. I've used the first NiMH batteries—Sanyo Eneloop and Uniross Ultra—that will hold a charge for several years, and they have proved excellent. They are available in AA and AAA sizes. I like rechargeables because they make environmental sense, disposable batteries being toxic and requiring much energy to produce. NiMH batteries have a long life span. Sanyo says its Eneloop batteries can be recharged 1,500 times. Recharging batteries in sunny places is possible with solar chargers. This is more significant for high-power-use electronics like cell phones and GPS units than headlamps and flashlights.

Candles

Candles give out a soft, pleasant light plus a little heat. I used to often use one in camp for reading and making notes. On cold, dark winter nights, I'm always amazed at how much warmth and friendliness a single candle flame can give, especially if you put the stove windscreen behind it as a reflector and to keep off breezes. The candles designed for candle lanterns have fairly wide bases and stand up on their own. Ordinary household candles are less expensive but need to be propped up with a tent stake or small stones or dug into

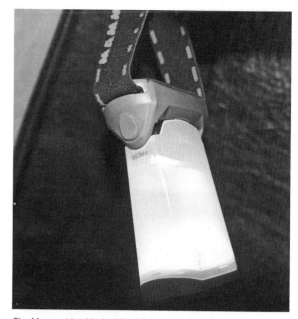

The Mammut Lucido Ambient Light turns a headlamp into a lantern that can be hung inside a tent.

the ground to stop them from falling over. I put a candle on a rock or an upturned cooking pot in a place where it won't land on anything flammable if it falls or is knocked over. I use candles in tent vestibules but never bring one into the inner tent. Used this way a lit candle is fairly safe, as long as you don't leave it unattended. After melting holes in two doors, I also make sure the candle isn't too close to the fly sheet. Because batteries last so long in LED lights, I don't often carry candles in the summer anymore. In winter the warmth is welcome.

Lanterns

While headlamps and flashlights are fine when camping and for use around camp, a lantern that throws light all around is nice to have in camp, whether outside or in the tent, especially during long, dark winter evenings. However, a really bright light means a heavy lantern, which is OK for static camps but not so good for backpacking. I'm happy with a small, light lantern that provides enough light to cook or read by and to find things in the tent. The light for a lantern can be a candle, a mantle, or an LED. The first two provide a little heat and a softer, warmer light than the latter. LEDs have the advantages of being very light and long-lasting. They can be hung anywhere, too, as there's no fire risk.

LED Lanterns

LEDs are ideal for small lightweight lanterns, and there are many on the market, some of which can double as flashlights. Ones I like the look of but haven't used include the Brunton Glorb XB, which has a bright 1-watt LED with two light levels, a run time of 50 hours on the high output, and a weight of 8 ounces with four AA batteries, and the Coleman LED Micropacker Lantern, which has two LEDs, a sliding reflector for directing the light if required, a run time of 125 hours, and a weight of 7 ounces with three AA batteries. The latter can be used as a flashlight when hiking. Probably better for this are flashlights that can be turned into lanterns by sliding a cover. Two useful-looking examples are the UCO Compact Lantern and Torch XL, which has a 0.5-watt LED, a run time of 22-plus hours, and a weight of 3.8 ounces with three AAA batteries, and the Brunton Lamplight 360, which has a single LED with two light levels that can be run off D, C, or AA batteries, a run time of 32 hours with a D cell, and a weight of 6.6 ounces with two AA batteries. Good though these lanterns sound, they duplicate an LED headlamp to some extent. Being able to use a headlamp as a lantern would be a better solution, and this is possible with some models. Mammut makes the 1-ounce Ambient light diffuser, a simple cover that clips onto Mammut Lucido TR1 and TXLite headlamps. I've used this with the TR1, which has four LEDs, two light levels that throw a flood beam 40 and 65 feet with run times of 25 hours and 60 hours, a pivoting lamp, and a weight of 2.7 ounces with three AAA batteries. The Ambient works pretty well over a small area, and I can read by it. I hope to see more such devices for use with other headlamps, especially the Petzl Tikka XP. Of course any headlamp can be hung by its strap and used as a lantern. If it has a flood beam and is hung fairly high, the result is quite effective.

Candle and Oil Lanterns

Candle lanterns protect the flame from wind and can be hung up so the light covers a wider area. One will easily light a small tent or the area around the head of your sleeping bag if you're sleeping under the stars. Most come with hanging chains, but these are rather short; I add a length of cord so I can hang the lantern from a branch. The heat from the lantern isn't enough to melt the cord—or at least it hasn't done it yet. The lanterns themselves do get hot, though, and need to be kept away from anything that might melt. If you stand the lantern on the ground there should be enough space for it to topple over without setting anything on fire.

When they work properly candle lanterns are excellent, but problems do arise. The most common design uses a glass cylinder to protect the flame and a metal or plastic candleholder. The glass slides into the candleholder to protect it when packed. The candleholder has a spring in its base that pushes the candle up as it burns. UCO is the main brand name. Candle lanterns weigh 5 to 8 ounces, depending on the model and the material (some are aluminum, some brass, some thermoplastic). A candle—they take stubby ones rather than household candles—adds 2.5 ounces. Candles can last eight to nine hours, but in practice I've found that most start to sputter and overflow before they're two-thirds used, leaving the inside of the lantern covered with wax that has to be scraped off—not an easy job, especially in camp in the dark. Part of the reason seems to be that most wicks don't run straight down the middle of the candles but curve off to the side halfway down. Although I used to use one regularly, it's now many years since I used a candle lantern, mainly because of this problem with the candles. In summer an LED light is adequate, and in winter I carry a plain candle if I want to keep the weight down or a butane-propane lantern if weight isn't so significant. There are lightweight lanterns that burn the little "tealight" tub candles. UCO makes one called the Mini that weighs 3.2 ounces. I find tub candles too dim to be useful, however.

An interesting new twist is the UCO Original Candle Lantern plus LED, which has an LED light in the base so you can use the lantern as a flashlight. You can also remove the LED and attach it to a headband. The batteries are said to last forty hours. The base doesn't add any extra weight, since it replaces the normal one. The LED base can be bought separately if you want to fit one to your lantern. The LED is powered by two CR2032 button-cell batteries and is probably fine for camp use but too weak for hiking.

White-Gas, Kerosene, and Cartridge Lanterns

Lanterns that run off butane-propane cartridges are fine for base camps and for backpacking in winter when a bright light and a little warmth can be welcome. They emit a constant hiss when lit, which can be irritating, though I soon got used to it. They use far less gas than stoves, since the heat output is much less, and will run well on almost empty cartridges that will barely power a stove.

Most lanterns have glass globes that surround and disperse the light from a glowing, lacelike *mantle*, which in turn surrounds a jet. Both the globe and the mantle are fragile, and the lantern must be protected in the pack.

Much better for backpacking are lanterns with a stainless steel mesh rather than a glass globe, as these are much tougher, though not quite as bright. I wouldn't consider a gas lantern with a glass globe for backpacking now that I've used a Primus lantern with a mesh globe. The Primus Micron weighs 4.4 ounces, has an adjustable brightness, and piezoelectric ignition. It's also available with a glass globe. Similar lanterns with mesh globes are the Brunton Lucy, which weighs 5.8 ounces and features piezoelectric ignition, and the Coleman F1 Lite, which weighs 3.2 ounces.

White-gas and kerosene lanterns are heavier; at 27.2 ounces, the Coleman Dual Fuel Lantern is one of the lightest. I wouldn't bother with one for backpacking.

Lightsticks

Lightsticks are thin plastic tubes that when bent break an internal glass capsule, allowing two nontoxic chemicals to mix and produce a pale greenish light. To me they seem no more than a curiosity (at least for backpacking). I've never carried one. If you want an emergency light a tiny LED one would be the best choice.

HEALTH AND BODY CARE

First Aid

Basic first-aid knowledge is essential for hikers, since it may be some time before help arrives if there's an accident. Taking a Red Cross, YMCA, or similar first-aid course is a good idea. Many outdoor schools also offer courses in wilderness first aid. There are many books on the subject, too. *Medicine for Mountaineering*, edited by James Wilkerson, is the standard work. It's comprehensive and good for home reference, but at 26.5 ounces it's rather heavy for carrying in the pack. More portable at 6.5 and 7 ounces are Paul Gill's *Wilderness First Aid* and William Forgey's *Basic Essentials: Wilderness First Aid*. Even lighter at 4 ounces and the only first-aid book I've ever actually carried is Fred Darvill's clear and concise *Mountaineering Medicine*. There are many other wilderness, mountaineering, and backcountry first-aid books. It seems a prolific genre. Be forewarned: a close study of these texts may convince you that you're lucky to have survived the dangers of wilderness travel and that you'd better not go back again! (The antidote to this is a glance through the statistics on accidents that occur in the home and on the road—driving *to* the wilderness is likely to be far more hazardous than anything you do *in* it.)

First-aid basics consist of knowledge, skill, and a few medical supplies. The last are only of use if you have the first two. There are many packaged first-aid kits. Some are very good, some are pretty poor. Adventure Medical and REI are among those that offer good ones. But the problem with even the best ones is that they usually contain items I don't feel are necessary, while items I consider essential are absent. Putting together a kit from the shelves of the local drugstore, as I do, means you get exactly what you want. It also means you know what you've got and are likely to know how to use it. I've been surprised at how many people with packaged kits don't know what's in them, let alone how to use everything.

Every book on wilderness medicine and backpacking features a different list of what a first-aid kit should contain. Many years ago I carried a fairly comprehensive kit (weighing a pound), but when I realized that I could substitute other gear for some of the contents and that I was carrying far more of other items than I would ever need, I drastically pruned the weight.

Now I carry a small kit weighing 4 to 5 ounces. The contents vary, but it usually contains:

- first-aid information leaflet
- 1 6-inch-wide elastic or crepe bandage for knee and ankle sprains
- 4 2nd Skin Blister Pads or other gel dressings
- roll of 1-inch tape for holding dressings in place
- 2 2-by-2-inch nonadhesive absorbent dressings for burns
- 2 butterfly closures
- 3 or 4 antiseptic wipes for cleaning wounds and blisters
- 12 assorted adhesive bandages for cuts
- 10 foil-wrapped painkillers—ibuprofen or aspirin
- 2 safety pins for fastening slings and bandages

I keep the kit in a small zippered nylon case marked with a large white cross and the words *First Aid*. Having your first-aid kit clearly identifiable is important in case someone else has to rummage through your pack for it. There are no scissors or tweezers in the kit because I have these on my knife and no large bandages because a bandanna or torn piece of clothing could be used. Other items can be used for first aid too—needles and thread, duct tape, moist wipes, even pack frames, foam pads, or tent poles for splints.

On long walks in remote country I also carry prescription antibiotics in case of illness or infection and prescription painkillers—ask your doctor about this. If you need personal medication, it will have to be added to the kit as well, of course. Such medicines don't last forever, though—be aware of expiration dates.

Groups need to carry larger, more comprehensive kits. The one I took when I led ski tours weighed 24 ounces. A plastic food storage container keeps a large first-aid kit from being crushed. Nylon pouches are lighter, however, and fine for the smaller kits. Waterproof ones are best. Otherwise, keeping the kit in a plastic bag inside the pouch is a good idea.

Tooth Care

It's wise to have a dental checkup immediately before a long trip. I can tell you from painful experience that a lost filling or an abscess is to be avoided if at all possible. If your teeth, like mine, are as much metal as enamel, I suggest carrying temporary filling materials such as Dentemp or Cavit. If you're really concerned about tooth problems, you could take an emergency repair kit such as the Adventure Medical Dental Medic kit. This comes in a waterproof case and contains five cotton pellets, five cotton rolls, dental floss, tea bag for pain relief, temporary cavity-filling mixture, three toothpicks, one wax rope, two Anbesol/ Orasol, benzocaine 20 percent medication, and an instruction sheet. It weighs 2 ounces.

Wash Kit

It's surprising how long you can go without washing your hair or body; I managed twenty-three days in the High Sierra on the Pacific Crest Trail. When every drop of water you use has to be produced laboriously by melting snow, washing—except for your hands—becomes unimportant, though I did occasionally rub my face and armpits with snow. Still, a minimum of cleanliness is necessary. In particular, you should always wash your hands after going to the toilet and before handling food. I usually manage to rinse my face most days as well. When it's cold, I save more thorough washing for when I get home or, on long trips, for a shower in a motel or campground. In hot weather I wash more often, if only to stay cool. Large water containers hung from trees make good showers—if you leave them in the sun for a few hours beforehand, the water is surprisingly warm.

Proper hand washing is essential in a group to avoid spreading stomach bugs, and it's wise for solo hikers as well. There are several phosphate-free, biodegradable soaps, including Coghlan's Plus 50 Sportsman's Soap in small squeeze tubes weighing an ounce, Sea to Summit Citronella Wilderness Wash Soap in 1.3- and 3-fluid-counce bottles, and Dr. Bronner's Soap (various scents) in 4-ounce plastic bottles. Even these soaps can pollute water sources, however, so use a minimum amount and dispose of washing water on gravel or rock at least 200 feet from any lake or stream. I prefer moist wipes, which I drop in my garbage bag after use, or hand-sanitizer gel; neither requires any water. On long trips I've carried a pack of fifty wipes. Mostly, though, I decant two or three a day into a Ziploc bag. Most recently I've been carrying antibacterial hand sanitizer, which comes in 2-ounce plastic bottles, since this leaves no residue or trash to carry out. The main ingredient is ethyl alcohol, so once you've rubbed some on your hands it evaporates very quickly, leaving your hands feeling fresh (being alcohol, hand sanitizers can also be used to star fires). Whether I carry sanitizer or wipes, they go in the plastic bag with my toilet paper to remind me to use them immediately after defecating.

If you want to do more than wash your hands or face, No-Rinse Bathing Wipes are larger than standard ones. They can be useful for removing dirt and sweat at the end of a trip so you don't smell too bad on the journey home or in that first restaurant. No-Rinse also makes 2- and 8-ounce bottles of No-Rinse Shampoo and Body Wash that could be used for the same purpose.

I don't carry a cotton washcloth or towel; both are heavy and slow to dry. A bandanna does for the former, a piece of clothing for the latter. Fleece jackets make particularly good towels. If you don't fancy using clothing to dry yourself, there are small, light pack towels. Cascade Designs' Packtowl is made from a highly absorbent viscose material and comes in several sizes. The smallest 16-by-17-inch MSR Small Nano Towel weighs 0.4 ounce, and the 25-by-54-inch extra-large XL PackTowl Personal weighs 8.5 ounces. The Packtowl works surprisingly well. I've tried the small one, which is fine for hands and face, and it soaks up masses of water—nine times its own weight, according to Cascade Designs—most of which can be wrung out so you don't have to carry it. Tie it on the back of the pack, and the Packtowl dries quickly.

My current wash kit consists of a small toothbrush (without the handle removed), a very small tube of toothpaste (I collect those often provided on long-distance flights, or you can decant some into a tiny plastic bottle), moist wipes, and a comb. The kit weighs about 2 ounces in its Ziploc bag. Like soap, toothpaste should be deposited a long way from water. You can get biodegradable toothpaste, but toothpaste isn't essential anyway; if I run out I do without. I carry a comb so I can look somewhat presentable in towns on long hikes. If I won't be passing through any towns I leave the comb in my car or with any clean clothes I've left to be picked up after the hike.

I don't shave, so I don't carry a razor. Those who do shave carry disposable razors—and usually curse them and the difficulty of shaving in the wilds—or else a tiny battery-powered shaver, such as Braun's MobileShave, which runs on two AA batteries.

Biting and Stinging Insects and Arachnids

If you're unprepared, swarms of biting insects—mosquitoes, black flies, no-see-ums—can drive you crazy in certain areas during the summer. Bites can itch maddeningly for hours, even days. I've yet to meet anyone immune to insect bites, though sensitivity varies and some people suffer much more than others. Biting insects are usually found in damp, shady areas. Camping in dry, breezy places is one way to minimize insect problems, though it's often not possible. Insects are usually less evident when you're walking, but the moment you stop anywhere sheltered they're likely to appear. The increase in West Nile virus, spread by mosquitoes, makes prevention important. West Nile virus affects the central nervous system and can be serious.

Insect repellent and clothing are your main defenses. You can cover up with tightly woven, light-colored clothing (dark colors apparently attract some insects) and fasten wrist and ankle cuffs tightly. A head net (1 to 2 ounces), worn over a hat with a brim or bill to keep it off your face, is extremely useful. It's the only defense I've found against black flies, which seem immune to repellents. If you're likely to need a head net often, Outdoor Research's 3.1-ounce Supplex nylon Bug Net Cap has a net concealed in the back of the cap. Any head net needs some form of closure at the bottom or else loops that fit under your arms to prevent it from riding up. Clothing made from no-see-um netting is available, but I've never used any. Netting clothing needs to be held away from the skin, since insects can bite through it.

Any uncovered skin needs to be protected with repellent if you don't want to be bitten. The most effective is reckoned to be DEET, short for N,N-diethyl-meta-toluamide or N,N-diethyl-3-methylbenzamide, the active ingredient in most insect repellents. Well-known brands include Muskol, Cutter, Ben's 100, Jungle Formula, Repel, Sawyer, Buggspray, and Deep Woods Off! Small bottles and tubes weigh about an ounce. Creams are the easiest to apply, but liquids go further. DEET repels most biting insects, including ticks. It also melts plastic, so it needs to be kept away from items such as watches, pocketknives, GPS units, and cameras.

DEET was developed by the U.S. Army in 1946 and first registered for public use in 1957, so it's been around a long time. It's considered safe by the EPA, which reregistered it in 1998, as long as instructions are followed. These include not applying it over cuts, wounds, or irritated skin, using just enough to cover skin or clothing and not using it under clothing. Wash skin once the repellent isn't required anymore, and wash treated clothing before using it again. The latest DEET repellents feature controlled release and contain about 20 percent DEET. Because the DEET is released slowly, one application can last all day. Sawyer says its Controlled Release Lotion works all day.

Some people react badly to DEET and feel unwell or nauseated if they use it or even smell it. My partner Denise reacts like this and never uses the stuff. Although I don't use DEET anymore, I did for many years without any adverse reactions—except that Denise wouldn't come near me! However, I was never too happy with the idea of putting something on my skin that could dissolve plastic and make some people feel ill, and since an increasing amount of gear had to be kept away from it, it seemed easier to use an alternative. If you do use DEET, you can keep it off your skin by applying it to clothing.

Oil of citronella is the traditional alternative to DEET. A more recent one is lemon eucalyptus, found in Cutter Lemon Eucalyptus Insect Repellent and Repel Lemon Eucalyptus. These generally come in 4-ounce pump bottles and 2-ounce tubes. Another non-DEET repellent is picaridin, a chemical said to be more pleasant to use than DEET and less likely to irritate the skin. It's found in Avon Skin-So-Soft Bug Guard Plus. There are also mixtures of various oils, such as Badger Anti Bug Balm, which contains castor, citronella, cedar, lemongrass, rosemary, and geranium as active ingredients, and All-Terrain Herbal Armor, which contains citronella, soybean, peppermint, cedar, lemongrass, and geranium as active ingredients. I used the latter on the Pacific Northwest Trail, and it was effective against the mosquitoes. I've also had success with Nikwax's SkitoStop spray, which contains a mix of "natural" based ingredients.

Other suggested ways of repelling insects include massive doses of vitamin B or eating lots of garlic. I can't vouch for these.

Repellents do just that. They repel, not kill. Pyrethoids are insecticides and kill insects on contact. The original pyrethrum comes from chrysanthemum flowers, though many pyrethoids are now synthetic. Permethrin is a common one. Pyrethoids can be used for backpacking in two ways: as sprays for tents and clothing and as coils for burning in camp. Sawyer Permethrin Spray and Repel Permanone Clothing and Gear Insect Repellent spray are two types of pyrethoid sprays. I've sprayed tents

Adult dog tick (Dermacentor variabilis).

with permethrin and found that it stops insects from landing on the tent so you don't wake up with the fly sheet black with them. You should use these sprays at home and let the tent dry before use. Applications are said to last up to two weeks of exposure to light. When sprayed items are stored in the dark the permethrin doesn't degrade, so items don't need retreating before use if they've had less than two weeks' use. There's no point in putting permethrin on your skin, since it will last only fifteen minutes. It can be used on clothing though, including head nets.

In an enclosed space such as a tent vestibule or under a tarp, burning a mosquito coil can keep insects away. On my walk through the Yukon, I often lit a coil at rest stops and found that even in the open it kept mosquitoes away. You can also buy citronella candles, but these are much heavier than coils. Coils come in packs of ten or twelve weighing about 7 ounces. Coghlan's is a well-known brand. Its pack of ten coils comes with a metal stand. Each coil lasts five to ten hours. When lit, they smolder like an incense stick, sending wreaths of insect-repelling smoke into the air. Remember that the end of a burning coil is hot and can burn you and melt holes in synthetic gear. Coils come wrapped in thin bubble wrap in a cardboard box. I keep the packing to protect coils against breakage (they still snap occasionally—the broken pieces are still usable) and store them in a plastic bag to protect them from moisture.

Making camp when bugs are biting requires speed and a fair bit of teeth gritting. I pitch the tent as fast as possible, fill my water containers, get in the tent, close the fly sheet door, light a mosquito coil in the vestibule, and stay there until dawn. No-see-ums (midges in Scotland—the worst biting insects I've encountered) will enter by the thousands under a fly sheet if no coil is burning, so I set up a coil last thing at night, then sleep with the insect-netting inner door shut. By dawn the inner door is often black with hungry no-see-ums and the vestibule is swarming with them. I unzip a corner of the netting, stick my hand out, strike a match, and light the coil. Then I retreat and close the netting again. Within five minutes most of the insects will be gone or dead, and I can open the inner door and have breakfast in peace. I keep the coil burning until I leave the tent. The tent often becomes hot and stuffy and stinks of burnt coil, but it's better than being bitten or having to eat breakfast while running around in circles, as I've seen others do. Even if you douse yourself with repellent, no-see-ums will make your skin and scalp itch maddeningly

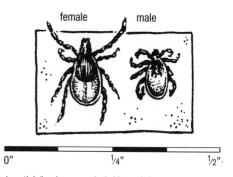

Adult deer tick (Ixodes scapularis/dammini).

by crawling in your hair and over any exposed flesh, even though they won't bite. In bear country where you are cooking away from your tent, a breezy kitchen site is a good idea, or else you just have to be as quick as possible, perhaps making do with cold food and drink.

Ticks, which are arachnids, not insects, are usually no more than an unpleasant irritant, but they can transmit Rocky Mountain spotted fever (found mainly in the East, despite the name—60 percent of cases come from North Carolina, Oklahoma, Arkansas, Tennessee, and Missouri; the disease also occurs in Canada and through Central America into South America; similar spotted fever diseases occur in other continents) and Lyme disease (found throughout much of the world—in the United States, it's most common in the Northeast, Minnesota, Wisconsin, the mid-Atlantic states, and along the Pacific coast). Luckily, both can be cured with timely treatment. Symptoms of Rocky Mountain spotted fever, which include the sudden onset of fever, chills, severe headache and muscle ache, general fatigue, and a loss of appetite, begin to appear two to fourteen days after a bite. A rash will develop within two to five days, beginning first on wrists, hands, ankles, and feet. If untreated, the disease lasts for a couple of weeks and is fatal in 20 to 30 percent of cases, depending on one's age.

Lyme disease also appears a few days to a few weeks after a bite and usually involves a circular red rash, though not always. It isn't fatal, but if not treated it can recur years later and lead to bizarre symptoms and severe, crippling arthritis.

A more common, though less serious, tick-borne illness is Colorado tick fever, found in the western United States and Canada, which appears four to six days after the tick bite. Symptoms are fever, headache, chills, and aching. Your eyes may

To remove a tick, grasp it at the mouth end with fine tweezers or a tick removal tool. Tug gently outward until the tick lets go. A tick removal kit containing magnifier, curved tweezers, antiseptic swabs, and instructions can be handy.

feel extra sensitive to light. The illness lasts, on and off, for about a week. There is no specific cure, but most victims recover completely.

If you are bitten by a tick and feel ill in the next three or four weeks, consult a doctor.

A sensible precaution is to check for ticks when you're in areas where they occur (local knowledge is useful here) and when you're walking in tick season, usually late spring and early summer. Ticks crawling on your body can be detached with tweezers (found on most Swiss Army Knives)—apply these to the skin around the tick not the tick itself so the head isn't left in the flesh. Pull ticks straight out, along with a tiny bit of skin. *Don't twist or burn embedded ticks*, because the mouthparts could remain in the wound and cause infection. Body searches usually locate most unattached ticks, though some ticks are no bigger than a pinhead. (Searches work better when two people "groom" each other.) Tick kits weighing a couple of ounces consist of a magnifier, curved tweezers, antiseptic swabs, and instructions. The Tick Nipper Tick Remover looks like a pair of plastic pliers and includes a 20x magnifier, while the Pro-Tick Remedy is made from steel. Both items weigh 0.5 ounce.

Ticks live in long grass and vegetation and attach themselves to you as you brush past. A tick then crawls about for a while, possibly for several hours, before biting and starting to suck blood. The bite is painless and doesn't itch, which is why body searches are necessary. Long pants tucked into your socks or worn with gaiters protect against ticks. If your clothing is light colored it's easier to spot the dark ticks crawling around on it.

Bee and wasp stings can be very painful. There are various remedies. Sting Eze is benzocaine-based and comes with a sponge applicator. Each pen holds 0.5 fluid ounce. People who have adverse reactions to stings should carry an EpiPen containing epinephrine (a prescription medication) and inject this as soon as symptoms appear. Bees leave their stingers behind in the wound. A Sawyer Extractor suction pump (4 ounces) can be used to suck the stinger out of the skin, or you can scrape it out with a knife blade. A moist aspirin taped over the sting site is said to stop pain.

Sunscreen

Protecting your skin against sunburn is a *necessity*—sunburned shoulders are agony under a pack, and a peeling nose also can be very painful. In the long run, overexposure may increase the risk of skin cancer. To minimize burning, use sunscreen on exposed skin whenever you're in sunlight, especially between 10 a.m. and 4 p.m. when the sun is strongest. Don't forget your feet if you're wearing sandals without socks. Brimmed and peaked hats help shade your face and cut the need for sunscreen, as does long, tightly woven clothing.

All sunscreens have a sun protection factor (SPF); the higher the SPF, the more protection. SPFs of 15 and above are recommended, especially for high altitudes, where ultraviolet light (the part of the spectrum that burns) is stronger. UV light increases in intensity 4 percent for every 1,000 feet of altitude. I burn easily, so I apply a sunscreen of SPF 15 or higher several times a day. Snow reflects sunlight, so when crossing snowfields protect all exposed skin, including that under your chin and around your nostrils. The best sunscreens are creamy rather than greasy and don't wash off when you sweat—at least not quickly. They should protect against both UVA and UVB rays; both can damage the skin, though it's the latter that cause sunburn. The skin is damaged long before it starts burning. Surveys suggest that most people don't use enough sunscreen (independent surveys, not those sponsored by sunscreen makers). Apply it lavishly and often, starting a half-hour before you venture into the sun. Large bottles are the least expensive. Small amounts can be decanted into smaller containers with secure lids for carrying in the pack. Sunscreen has a shelf life of three to four years, so you don't need to use it up quickly.

If you get sunburned, various creams and lotions will help reduce the suffering, but it's best to avoid the problem in the first place. I don't carry any sunburn treatment.

Lip Balm

Lips can suffer from the drying effects of the wind as well as from sunburn, and they can crack badly in very cold conditions. A tube of lip balm weighs less than an ounce yet can save days of pain.

Sunglasses

Most of the time I don't wear sunglasses, except during snow travel, when they are essential to prevent corneal burning, a very painful condition known as *snow blindness*. This can occur even when the sun isn't bright, as I learned on a day of thin mist in the Norwegian mountains. Because visibility was so poor and wearing sunglasses made it worse, I didn't wear them but skied all day straining to see ahead. Although I didn't suffer complete snow blindness, my eyes became sore and itchy; by evening I was seeing double, and my eyes were painful except when closed. Luckily it was the last day of my trip; otherwise I would have had to rest for at least a couple of days to let my eyes recover. It's my guess that sunlight filtered through the fine mist and reflected off the snow. I should have worn sunglasses with amber or yellow lenses, since these improve definition in poor light, and I now always carry a pair.

The main requirement of sunglasses is that they cut out all ultraviolet light, which cheap ones may not do. Those designed for snow and high-altitude use should also cut out infrared light. Glass lenses are scratch resistant; polycarbonate lenses weigh less. Large lenses that curve around the eyes are best, since they give the most protection. Quality glasses include Bollé, Vuarnet, Ray-Ban, Cébé, Julbo, Smith, Native Eyewear, and Oakley. For snow use, glacier-type glasses with side shields are best. They are essential at high altitudes. I have two pairs of glacier glasses, Julbo Sherpas (1 ounce) with gray lenses for bright light, and Bollé Crevasses (1.5 ounces) with amber lenses for hazy conditions. I always carry both pairs on trips in snow, both to deal with different conditions and because losing or breaking a pair could be serious. On summer hikes where I might encounter snow, pale sand, or rock, I carry the Sherpas with the side shields removed. I rarely wear them, however; I prefer a hat to shade my eyes.

If fogging is a problem there are antifogging products such as the Smith No Fog Cloth. I've never used these, but people who wear glasses all the time tell me they're quite effective.

Keeping glasses on can be a problem, especially when skiing. The answer is a loop that goes around your head or neck. Glacier glasses usually come with these, but many sunglasses don't. Various straps, such Croakies and Chums, slip over the earpieces. I've used Croakies, and they work well.

In severe blizzards and driving snow, goggles give more protection than glasses. For well over a decade I've had a pair of Scott ski goggles with amber double lenses, which improve visibility in haze. They weigh 4 ounces. The foam mesh vents above and below the lenses reduce fogging, though the goggles suffer this more than glacier glasses. A wide elasticized, adjustable headband plus thick, soft foam around the rim makes them comfortable to wear. For a few years I stopped carrying them, since I rarely used them. Then I had a horrendous descent down a steep ridge in strong winds and driving, stinging snow that kept blowing behind my glacier glasses so I couldn't see. Every few minutes I had to stop and clear the glasses. Goggles would have made the descent quicker, safer, and more pleasant. Goggles can be worn over a hat or hood and pushed down around your neck when not needed, which is less risky than pushing them up on your forehead and having them fall off. Bollé, Jones, Cébé, Smith, and Scott all make good goggles.

Sanitation

All too often, every rock within a few hundred yards of a popular campsite sprouts ragged pink and white toilet paper around its edges. Aside from turning beautiful places into sordid outdoor privies, unthinking toilet siting and waste disposal create a health hazard—feces can pollute water

Outhouse sign. Where there are outhouses you should always use them.

sources. As a result, land-management agencies sometimes provide outhouses and deep toilet pits at popular destinations. Mount Whitney, the highest peak in the lower forty-eight states, has one on its summit.

Outhouses are obtrusive and detract from the feeling of wilderness. Careful sanitation techniques can ensure that no more need be built. Good methods prevent water contamination, speed decomposition, and shield humans and animals from contact with waste.

To prevent water contamination, always site toilets at least 200 feet (70 paces) from any water. Heading uphill is usually a good way to achieve this. Look for somewhere comfortable to squat that is out of sight of trails, campsites, and anywhere people might see you. The best way to achieve rapid decomposition is to leave waste on the surface, where the sun and air soon break it down. But this isn't a good idea in popular areas and is now not recommended anywhere. As well as being unsightly, it attracts insects and animals. Instead, dig small individual catholes 6 to 8 inches deep, in dark organic soil if possible, since this is rich in the bacteria that break down feces. After you've finished, break feces up with a stick and mix them with the soil—they decompose more quickly— then fill in the hole and camouflage it. Feces don't decompose very rapidly in catholes, so where they are sited is important. Ideally they should be on a rise where water won't flow and wash the feces downstream. A site that catches the sun is good too, since heat speeds up decomposition.

You need some sort of small digging implement for making catholes. Small trowels have been popular for this for years, the standard being the 2-ounce orange plastic Coghlan's Backpacker's Trowel, which I carried for years. An alternative is the 3.1-ounce recycled polycarbonate GSI Cathole Sanitation Trowel. These plastic trowels make digging catholes easy in soft ground, but they aren't so good in stony terrain, when they can break as well as fail to make much impact on the ground. A metal trowel is more effective and durable here. Very tough-looking is the U-Dig-It Stainless Steel Hand Shovel, which has a folding handle. It's quite weighty at 6.5 ounces, however. Much lighter is the Sea to Summit Pocket Trowel at 3.5 ounces, with an aluminum handle and a hard-anodized aluminum blade. I no longer use any of these though since discovering that a tent stake can be used to dig catholes, especially V-angle or curved stakes. If you prefer something larger, a 1.8-ounce snow or sand stake works very well. A bandanna can be used to pad the handle, or you could tape on a piece of foam or cork as some backpackers have done—see http://andyhowell.info/Colin -Ibbotson/Peg-trowel.pdf for examples.

Large groups should not dig big latrines unless there are limited cathole sites or the group is stay-

A pit toilet with a view.

ing at a site for more than one night. The idea is to *disperse* rather than concentrate waste. If you do dig a latrine, it should be sited as for a cathole.

There remains the problem of toilet paper. I use a standard white roll with the cardboard tube removed—3.5 ounces. (Avoid colored paper because the dyes can pollute.) Although toilet paper seems fragile, it is amazingly resilient and shouldn't be left to decorate the wilderness. You have two options—burning it or packing it out. The first should never be used when there is any fire risk, however minute. If you have a campfire, though, it makes sense to burn used toilet paper in it. Mostly you should pack it out in doubled plastic bags. In some areas where campfires are banned, such as Grand Canyon National Park, this is required. As long as the bags are kept sealed, used paper doesn't smell. The paper should be disposed of in a toilet, the plastic bags in a garbage can. Women also should pack out used tampons unless they can be burned, which requires a very hot fire. If tampons are buried, animals will dig them up. More specific advice for women, plus a lot of good general advice on backcountry toilet practices, can be found in Kathleen Meyer's humorous *How to Shit in the Woods.*

For those prepared to try them, natural alternatives to toilet paper include sand, grass, large leaves, and even snow. The last, I can assure you, is less unpleasant than it sounds. I've not had much success with plants or stones, however, and I'm happy to bag and carry out toilet paper. If you like the idea of natural substitutes, there's a good article by Mike Clelland! on Backpacking Light complete with illustrations at http://backpacking light.com/cgi-bin/backpackinglight/toilet_paper _free.html.

Deep snow presents a problem. Digging a cathole just means the contents will appear on the surface when the snow melts. This is still the best method in little visited areas, however. It's even more important to be sure catholes are sited where no one is likely to find them and in places where no one will camp, such as narrow ridge tops and thick bushes or stands of trees. In really remote areas feces can be left on the surface, since then they'll start to decompose straightaway. In both cases check where water flows in the summer— by observation and from the map—and try to site your toilet well away from any creeks. In popular areas consider packing feces out. If they're frozen, this is less unpleasant than it sounds. The 2-ounce Cleanwaste Wag Bag Toilet in a Bag, designed for

WOLVES

The river is a half mile or so away. I set off toward it to collect water as dusk falls. In the middle of an expansive meadow I suddenly sense that I am watched. Looking toward the forest, I freeze with a mixture of awe, excitement, and fear. A few hundred yards away, on the fringe of the timber, a pack of wolves is watching me. I count six, some of them pale gray, others almost black. After a few seconds they begin to move off slowly in single file, one of them always stationary, watching. When that one falls to the rear another stops, and the pack continues. Eventually they disappear. I do not know how long I have been holding my breath.

the removal of feces, could make it more acceptable. This consists of a waste bag, a zip-closed storage bag, toilet paper, and hand sanitizer. The biodegradable waste bag is puncture proof and contains an environmentally friendly gelling agent with the wonderful name of Pooh-Powder that turns feces into a stable gel.

Urination is a matter of less concern. Urine is sterile, so it doesn't matter too much where you pee. However, the salts in urine may attract animals, so it's best to pee on bare ground rather than vegetation that could be damaged by animals' licking the salt off the leaves. In snow urine leaves unsightly yellow stains that should be covered up.

The only time urination becomes a problem is when you wake in the middle of a cold, stormy night and are faced with crawling out of your sleeping bag, donning clothes, and venturing out into the wet and wind. The answer is to pee into a wide-mouthed plastic bottle. With practice, men can do this easily. I use a cheap plastic pint bottle (2 ounces) with a green screw top that clearly distinguishes it from my water bottles. I've marked

it with a large letter *P* as well. I carry it mainly in winter and spring. A pee bottle could also be useful in summer when biting insects are around, since otherwise you'd have to get dressed before leaving the tent. (Not to do so is to invite disaster. On a course I led, a student left his tent one night clad in just a T-shirt, despite warnings. He was out less than a minute, but in the morning he emerged covered with no-see-um bites from the waist down.)

For women pee bottles clearly present problems. Two devices may help. The Lady J Adapter fits into the mouth of a shaped bottle called the Little John Portable Urinal and can be used in a tent. An alternative is Sani-fem's Freshette, a close-fitting plastic funnel with attached tube that can be used with any bottle.

EQUIPMENT MAINTENANCE AND REPAIR

It's an unusual trip when something doesn't need repairing, or at least tinkering with, so I always carry a small repair kit in a stuff sack. Although the contents vary from trip to trip, the weight hovers around 4 ounces. Repair kits for specific items such as the stove and the inflatable pad travel in this bag.

The most-used item in the kit is the waterproof, adhesive-backed ripstop nylon tape, which patches everything from clothing to fly sheets. You can buy this in rolls, but I prefer the strips that come stapled to a card. Most types have four to six different colored strips of nylon, measure 3 by 9 inches, and weigh about an ounce. There are several brands, including Kenyon K-Tape and Coghlan's. When applying a patch, round the edges so it won't peel off, and patch both sides of the hole if possible. Patches can be reinforced with adhesive around the edges. I carry a small tube of seam sealant or epoxy for this purpose, or I use the glue that comes with the inflatable pad repair kit.

An alternative to sticky ripstop tape is duct tape, the mainstay of many repair kits. I carry strips of duct tape wrapped around a small piece of wood, and have used it to hold together cracked pack frames, split ski tips, broken tent poles, and other items. On clothing, sleeping bags, and tent fabrics, however, I find sticky nylon tape better because it is more flexible and stays on longer. Duct tape leaves a sticky residue too. Professional repairers and cleaners hate it. Duct tape is usually silver. Coghlan's offers colored duct tape with peel-off backing.

Large pieces of nylon are useful for patching bigger tears and holes. Since repair swatches often come with tents and packs, I've built up a collection from which I usually take two or three sheets of different weights, including a noncoated one for inner tent repair; the biggest swatch measures 12 by 18 inches. They have a combined weight of half an ounce.

Also in the repair kit goes a selection of rubber bands. These have many obvious uses, and some not so obvious. A length of shock cord tied in a loop makes an extra-strong rubber band. Any detachable pack straps not in use also end up in the repair bag—perhaps "oddities kit" would be a better name.

My sewing kit consists of a sewing awl, two heavy-duty sewing machine needles, two buttons, two safety pins, a cotter pin (for rethreading drawcords), two ordinary sewing needles, and several weights of strong thread packed in a small zippered nylon bag. The total weight is only 1.5 ounces, yet with this kit I can repair everything from packs to pants.

For details of how to repair outdoor gear see Annie and Dave Getchell's excellent book *The Essential Outdoor Gear Manual*.

Nylon Cord

The final item in the repair bag—nylon cord—deserves a section of its own because it's so useful. I use *parachute cord* (paracord), which comes in 50-foot lengths with a breaking strength of 350 pounds at a weight of 4 ounces per hank. Over the years I've used it for pitching a tarp, making extra tent guylines, bearbagging food, replacing boot laces, hanging out wet gear, tying items to my pack (wet socks, crampons, ice ax), fashioning a swami belt (made by wrapping the cord around and around your waist) for use with a carabiner and rope for river crossings, lashing a broken pack frame, lowering a pack down and pulling it up short steep cliffs or slopes (with the cord fed around my back, a tree, or a rock—not hand over hand), and anchoring gaiters and hats. The ends of cut nylon cord must be fused with heat or they'll fray.

Paracord has been around for decades. Now there are lighter and stronger alternatives in Spectra and Dyneema cord. Dyneema cord comes in 1.5- and 2-millimeter thicknesses. The first weighs 2.25 ounces per 50 feet and has a breaking strain of 242 pounds, and the second weighs 5.25 ounces per 50 feet and has a breaking strain of 617 pounds. I've used the 1.5-millimeter Dyneema cord (purchased online from Backpacking Light UK), and it's surprisingly easy to knot given how thin it is. I think it'll do all the duties of paracord.

Knife

A small knife is useful for backpacking, but you don't need a large, heavy sheath knife or "survival" knife for most purposes. I mostly use a blade for opening food packets and slicing cheese, as well as cutting cord and other items. Scissors are the other tool I use frequently, and it's convenient and lighter to have these on a knife.

Small pocketknives, especially the classic Swiss Army Knife (SAK), are the standard backpacking tools. Beware of inferior imitations—the only genuine brands are Wenger and Victorinox. There's a huge range of models with just about every blade or tool you could want.

For years I've used the Victorinox Climber, which weighs 2.5 ounces and has two blades, scissors, can opener/screwdriver, bottle opener/ screwdriver, corkscrew, tweezers, and toothpick, plus a couple of those slightly strange tools whose usefulness is unclear—a reamer/punch and a multipurpose hook. If I'm really trying to keep the weight down I carry a tiny Victorinox Classic, which weighs 0.7 ounce and has a small blade, a file/screwdriver, scissors, tweezers, and a toothpick. I was dubious about such a tiny knife at first but was pleasantly surprised to discover that it did everything I wanted from a knife. I have found though that the Classics are not as tough as the larger SAKs, and after a while, the

Victorinox Classic Swiss Army Knife.

blades don't go back into the handle fully, and the spring clip on the scissors slips to the side. When this happened to my last Classic, I decided to replace it with a different mini-knife. This was the Leatherman Style CS, which folds open to reveal much stronger scissors than the Classic's and also has a knife blade, nail file and cleaner, flat Phillips screwdriver, tweezers, and a carabiner clip. It weighs 1.5 ounces. I took it on the Pacific Northwest Trail, and it worked fine and will, I think, prove more durable than the SAK Classic.

Recently I've been fascinated by the Traveller model (3.25 ounces). Just when it seemed that Victorinox really couldn't add anything more to an SAK, up pops one with an altimeter and thermometer built into the handle, displayed on a tiny digital screen. (See Chapter 9 for information on altimeters.) It has the same blades as the Climber.

I have sometimes carried other knives such as the 7.5-inch French Opinel folding knife with wooden handle and single locking carbon steel blade. It weighs just 1.75 ounces, and the blade holds an edge better than the stainless steel Swiss Army ones. Recently I've been tempted by the Tool Logic SL3, which has a 3-inch blade and weighs 2.75 ounces, because it has a FireSteel in the handle and a notch on the blade for drawing it across (see Stoves, in Chapter 7). There are many other small knives and folding multitools around: Gerber, Schrade, Kershaw, SOG, and Buck are some of the other quality ones. Most of the multitools have pliers, which I rarely need, but not scissors, which I use regularly.

Keeping your knife blades sharp is important. I don't carry a sharpener, however, because the best place to sharpen them is at home.

IN CASE OF EMERGENCY

Signaling

If you are injured or become seriously ill in the wilderness, you need to alert other people and rescuers to your whereabouts. Displaying a bright item of clothing or gear is one way to do this. Your headlamp or flashlight can be used for sending signals, in daylight as well as at night. Noise can attract attention, of course, and I always carry a plastic whistle. For years this was a Storm Whistle (0.8 ounce), from the All-Weather Safety Whistle Company of St. Louis, which is said to be one of the loudest, reaching almost 95 decibels. I've passed this whistle on to my stepdaughter and replaced it with a Fox 40 Classic (0.5 ounce with lanyard). I've never used it, but it's always there just in case. Whether you use light or sound, the recognized distress signal is six regular flashes or blasts, pause, then six more.

In most remote areas, initial searches are likely to be made by aircraft, so you need to be seen from above and from afar. A fire, especially with wet vegetation added, should create enough smoke to be easily seen. Ideally, you should light three fires in the form of a triangle, an internationally recognized distress signal. Flares are quicker and simpler to use, and various packs are sold. I've never carried flares, but they would have been reassuring at times during the Canadian Rockies and Yukon walks. Carrying several small flares seems to make more sense than one big one; larger flares last longer, but unless you carry several, you have only one chance to draw attention to your plight. Packs of six to eight waterproof miniflares with a projector pen for one-handed operation weigh only 8 ounces or so. The flares reach a height of about 250 feet and last six seconds.

Flares need to be handled and used carefully. A much safer alternative is a strobe light. Some LED lights can be set to flash regularly.

Using an ordinary mirror as a signal mirror. Capture the sun's reflection in your palm, then flick the mirror up and down to send a signal to approaching aircraft.

Signaling mirror with sighting hole.

PLBs should be used for emergencies only. They send out a signal via satellites that gives your position and triggers a search-and-rescue effort.

satellites

receiving station

control center (search and rescue)

Mirrors can be used for signaling, though obviously only in sunlight. Plastic ones are cheap and light (0.5 ounce upward). I have an MPI Safe Signal mirror weighing 1.25 ounces. It's made from polycarbonate and is silver on one side and red on the other, for use with a flashlight at night (the effect is very bright). I sometimes carry it in my "office" pouch. Any shiny reflective object, such as aluminum foil (stove windscreen), a polished pan base, a watch face, a camera lens, or even a knife blade could be used instead.

If you are in open terrain and have no other signal devices, spreading light- and bright-colored clothing and gear out on the ground could help rescuers locate you.

Personal Locator Beacons and Satellite GPS Messengers

Personal locator beacons (PLBs) have been around for decades and are standard safety items on boats and planes. They were illegal for land use in the United States until July 2003, however. PLBs send out a signal via satellites that gives your position and triggers a search-and-rescue (SAR) effort. I've carried PLBs twice. The first time was on my 1,000-mile solo hike in the Yukon where I was loaned one, unofficially, by local people concerned for my safety in remote wilderness. "If it goes off by accident, jump over a cliff before the rescue teams arrive," I was told, only half jokingly. It lay mostly forgotten in a pack pocket for the next three and a half months. The second occasion was when I led a skiing expedition in Greenland. In this case the PLB was not only official but also a legal requirement. Both these trips were into very remote, little visited country where an accident or illness could have been fatal. Whether PLBs are needed in most backcountry areas, which are much more accessible, is debatable. They will undoubtedly save lives and make the work of SAR teams easier and safer. However, as with cell phones, there is a danger that some people will regard PLBs as substitutes for skill. They could easily be misused too, with people using them for minor inconveniences or concerns that don't warrant calling out a rescue. At present the very high cost will probably limit the number of people who carry them but as with all electronics prices are likely to fall. Whether or not to carry one is a personal decision but they should only be used when absolutely necessary.

The PLBs I carried were designed for carrying on aircraft, and were large and heavy. The one I carried in the Yukon weighed 16 ounces and was the size of a paperback book. There are now many much lighter and smaller PLBs, and some have other functions than just sending an emergency signal. Most also use GPS (see Chapter 9) as well as sending signals to search-and-rescue satellites. Two of the leading companies are McMurdo and ACR Electronics. McMurdo's 5.3-ounce FastFind 210 is a basic PLB that just sends your location to rescue services. Once activated, it will continue to do this for twenty-four hours. No subscription is required for the FastFind. The ACR Electronics SARLink PLB has a few more features than the FastFind, including a bright LED strobe light, but weighs more at 8.9 ounces. Slightly heavier at 9.1 ounces is the SARLink View, which has an LED digital display that gives your GPS position in latitude and longitude and lets you see what the beacon is doing. It can also be linked to a subscription satellite service that lets you send nonemergency messages via text or e-mail to friends and family to let them know you are OK.

An alternative to PLBs is the SPOT Satellite Messenger Service using GPS signals. This subscription-based service sends your location and a custom message via text or e-mail, plus a Web link so your position or track can be seen on Google Maps, to prearranged contacts (and Facebook and Twitter) and, if necessary, an emergency signal to the GEOS Rescue Coordination Center. This enables messages to be sent when there is no cell phone signal. The only thing it won't do is tell you your location or confirm that signals have been sent, as there is no display screen. I tried one of the first SPOT devices and wasn't convinced it was reliable enough, but the latest SPOT Messenger has proved far better. It weighs 4.2 ounces with three AAA lithium batteries. If the SOS function is activated, the batteries will last six days with a clear view of the sky and three days if half the sky is obstructed. If you're recording your track, the batteries will last seven days with a clear view and again half that if half-obstructed. And 700 messages can be sent on one set of batteries when the sky is clear and 350 when half-obstructed. As well as the stand-alone SPOT Messenger, there is a SPOT Connect that turns your smartphone into a satellite communicator

Smartphone inside a SealLine waterproof case.

via Bluetooth so it then has all the functions of the Messenger plus the advantage of being able to type out messages rather than just send predetermined ones. The Connect unit weighs 4.9 ounces with two AA lithium batteries. And there's a SPOT device called the Communicator that works with the DeLorme Earthmate PN-60w GPS and allows text messages to be sent as well as your track, prearranged messages, and emergency messages. A big advantage of both the Connect and the Communicator is that they link to devices that tell you your location. All the SPOT devices are rugged and designed for backcountry use.

Which of these devices to choose, if any, depends on how much contact with the outside world you like. If it's minimal, as it is for many backpackers, and you just want to be able to send a

signal if there's an emergency, then the McMurdo FastFind is all that's needed. If you want to be able to send messages and your track, then I'd choose one of the SPOT devices, as these are lighter weight than the SARLink PLBs. The SPOT Messenger works fine, but if you carry a smartphone anyway, the Connect gives you more options. In future, I will carry a SPOT Connect on long walks in remote places where cell phone signals are unavailable. Whichever you choose, remember that the emergency signal function should never be used except in life-or-death situations.

Cell Phones

An increasing number of hikers carry cell phones, though many backpackers feel they have no place in the wilderness and detract from the reasons for being there. Their usefulness in an emergency is undeniable, and many people have been rescued quickly because they had phones. However, too many people use their phones for what can only be regarded as frivolous reasons, such as asking for advice on routes and where to find water to drink. Some people seem to think a phone is a substitute for wilderness skills—if you get lost, you can just make a call. This is irresponsible and puts great pressure on rangers and rescue services. Phones should be used only in real emergencies where you need outside help. Relying on a phone is unwise anyway: they can break, and batteries can fade. Also, they're unlikely to get a signal in remote areas, deep canyons, and dense forests. I couldn't get a connection much of the time on the Pacific Northwest Trail, especially the eastern half. Only in the inhabited section around Puget Sound was a signal obtainable most of the time. If you do bring one and want to use it other than in an emergency, do so away from others. It can be very irritating to reach a summit or a pass and hear someone talking on a phone. Think, too, about how much a phone detaches you from the wilderness you've come to experience.

The many other functions now available on cell phones means that they may be carried mainly for purposes other than actually making phone calls. A smartphone can be a GPS, camera, radio, Internet connection, e-book reader, and music player. I carried a smartphone on the Pacific Northwest Trail (the HTC Desire, which weighs 5.5 ounces with battery) mainly for use as a GPS. As a safety device, a smartphone can be used to send text messages or e-mails updating friends and family on your progress and assuring them you are OK. And in conjunction with a SPOT Connect, this can be done even when there is no cell phone connection. The other functions of a smartphone are discussed under Cameras and Entertainment, later in this chapter, and GPS, in Chapter 9.

Battery Chargers

Electronic devices like cell phones, music players, cameras, and GPS units use a great deal of battery power, so if you use them regularly, you either need to carry many spare batteries or have some means of recharging them. There are many solar panels and chargers around. The best for backpacking looks to be the water-resistant, rubberized Powermonkey eXplorer, which consists of a charger unit and separate foldout solar panels with a Velcro strap for attaching them to the top of a pack. Each weighs 3 ounces. There are adapters for a wide range of electronic gadgets and for AA and AAA rechargeable batteries, so this could power headlamps, too. Powermonkey says it will provide power for 96 hours of standby time for cell phones, 40 hours for iPods, 6 hours for MP3/MP4 players, and 1,600 photos on a digital

MAPPING APPS FOR PHONES

Among the thousands of apps available for cell phones, the most useful for hikers are ones that turn your phone into a mapping GPS. These apps have all the functions of a stand-alone GPS, so you can plot and record routes and waymarks and access data on position, elevation, speed, direction, time taken, time to destination, and more. Most useful is being able to see your position on a topographic map on the screen so you know exactly where you are. Apps are available for the different operating systems—iPhone, Android, Symbian, Windows Mobile—and usually come with a selection of maps. Apart from my choice, ViewRanger, which runs on Android, iPhone, and Symbian phones, other useful-looking topo map apps include BackCountry Navigator (http://backcountrynavigator.com) for Android and Windows Mobile, and Topo Maps (http://topomapsapp.com), iTopo Maps (http://itopomaps.com), and Fugawi iMap (http://fugawi.com) for iPhones. There is also an app, My Tracks (http://mytracks.appspot.com), for Android that works with Google Maps. This isn't as useful, but it is free.

camera. The charger unit can itself be charged from the mains as well as from the solar panels, so the latter could be left at home on short trips or when enough sunshine to charge it is unlikely. The Powermonkey eXplorer has been widely praised. I intend trying it. I have tried the tiny Freeloader AA/AAA Charger, which weighs a mere 1.9 ounces including two AA rechargeable batteries. The Charger can be recharged from Freeloader solar panels or by USB from a PC or other device. It's fine for supplying some power to a cell phone or iPod. I used the Freeloader charger with the Freeloader Pico Solar Charger, a tiny solar panel weighing 1.7 ounces. On the Pacific Northwest Trail, I carried this strapped to the top of my pack. In sunny weather, it took three days to gather enough power to provide half a charge for my smartphone. This wasn't an ideal trail for a solar charger, however, as I was often under tree cover, and there often wasn't much sun at all. In open alpine country or the desert, I would expect it to perform much better. When fully charged, the Pico is said to power a cell phone for 35 hours, an iPod for 14 hours, and a GPS for 1½ hours.

Much the most fascinating battery charger is the nPower PEG (Personal Energy Generator), which is charged by your kinetic energy. The case is made from titanium, and there's a lithium battery inside to store the energy. It weighs 11 ounces and is compatible with more than 3,000 handheld devices. The company says that one minute of walking provides approximately one minute of listening time on an iPod Nano and twenty-six minutes of walking provides approximately one minute of talk time on a 3G phone call. It won't power your phone for long then even after a ten-hour day, but it looks a good choice for music players.

Rescue Procedures

If you're alone and suffer an immobilizing injury or illness, all you can do is make yourself as comfortable as possible, send out signals, and hope someone will respond. In popular areas and on trails, attracting attention shouldn't be too difficult, but in less-frequented places and when traveling cross-country you may be totally dependent on those who have details of your route to report you missing when you don't check in as arranged.

Groups should send for help if they can't handle the situation themselves. It's important that whoever goes has all the necessary information: the location of the injured person(s), compass bearings, details of local features that may help rescuers find the place, the nature of the terrain, the time of the accident, a description of any injuries, and the size and experience of the group. All this should be written down so that important details aren't forgotten or distorted. Once out of the wilderness, the messenger should contact the local law enforcement, park, or forest service office.

Most mountain rescue teams are made up of local volunteers. These people give up their time to help those in need, often at great personal risk and cost. If you need their services, make a generous donation to the organization afterward; they are not government funded in many countries.

Rope

Roped climbing is for mountaineers. However, there are rare times when backpackers need a short length of rope for protection on steep terrain. Full-weight climbing rope isn't necessary; I've found quarter-inch line with a breaking strain of 2,200 to 3,400 pounds perfectly adequate. A 60- to 65-foot length (the shortest that's much use) weighs 20 ounces or so. For a rope to be useful, you need to know how to set up belays, how to tie on, and how to handle it safely. This is best learned from an experienced climbing friend or by taking a course. Ropes need proper care. They should be stored out of direct sunlight and away from chemicals. A car seat or trunk is not a good place to keep ropes. Even with minimum use and careful storage, ropes deteriorate and should be replaced every four or five years. I've mostly carried ropes for glacier crossings during ski tours. These have been full-weight, full-length climbing ropes. I haven't carried a rope when hiking for nearly twenty years.

Snow Shovel

In deep snow, a shovel is both an emergency tool and a functional item. The emergency uses range from digging a shelter to digging out avalanche victims. More mundane uses are for leveling tent platforms, digging out buried tents, clearing snow from doorways, digging through snow to running water, collecting snow to melt for water, supporting the stove, and many other purposes. I find a snow shovel essential in snowbound terrain. They come with either plastic or metal blades. I prefer metal; plastic blades won't cut through hard-packed snow or ice. There are many models, usually with detachable blades. Voilé, Life-Link, Backcountry Access (BCA), Black Diamond, G3, Ortovox, and Safety on Snow (SOS) make good snow shovels. I have a BCA Tour Shovel with a large aluminum blade that weighs 18 ounces.

Fishing Tackle

I once carried a length of fishing line and a few hooks and weights on a long wilderness trip, in case I ran out of food. I duly ran short of food, and on several nights I put out a line with baited hooks. On each successive morning I pulled it in empty. Experienced anglers probably would have more success, and if you're one, I'm sure it's worthwhile to take some lightweight fishing tackle, depending on where you're headed. Fishing rods need not be heavy or long. The carbon-fiber Tenkara Hane, which was codesigned by Ryan Jordan of Backpacking Light, weighs 2.7 ounces and has a packed length of 16 inches yet extends to 9 feet, 10 inches.

Navigation

Route finding as a skill is discussed in Chapter 9, and it therefore makes sense to leave any detailed discussion of equipment until then. Here I will mention the effect navigation can have on your load. On any trip a compass and a map, weigh-ing between 1 and 4 ounces, will be the minimum gear you'll need. On most trips you'll need more than one map, and you may carry a trail guide as well. On trips of two weeks and longer, I usually end up with 25 to 35 ounces of maps and guides. A GPS receiver will add at least another 3 ounces. Chapter 9 contains details of these.

OFFICE

I carry a notebook, pen, and pencil on every trip. Along with a paperback book, maps, and various papers, they live in a small pouch or stuff sack. There are many suitable pouches, mostly containing several compartments and designed to be fastened to pack hipbelts or shoulder straps. Weights range from a few ounces to a pound or more. I use a simple single-compartment waterproof nylon pouch with a Velcro closure that weighs an ounce. If I have books and maps that won't fit in this flat pouch, I carry them in a small waterproof stuff sack. My office lives in a pack pocket where it is easily accessible. I could use my smartphone for taking notes, but having tried this, I find the tiny virtual keyboard quite hard to use for very long and also when my fingers are cold. It uses battery life, too. And back at home, I like to have my journals—my memories—in physical form as a row of notebooks on a shelf rather than as bytes on a computer hard disk. Also, I sit in front of a computer too long at home working. Out in the backcountry, I prefer not to and find it more relaxing to write with a pen.

Writing Paper and Notebooks

Keeping a journal on a walk is perhaps the best way of making a record for the future. I've always kept journals, long before I began writing for anyone other than myself, and by reading them I can spend hours reliving a trip I'd almost forgotten. In order to record as much as possible, I try to write in my journal every day, often making a few notes over breakfast and at stops during the day, then more extensive ones during the evening. This is difficult enough to do on solo trips; when I'm with companions, I'm lucky if I write in it every other day. I use single journals for long trips (over two weeks) and an annual journal for other trips.

There are masses of suitable notebooks. Those with tear-out pages are very light, but I prefer bound ones. I mostly use oilskin notebooks with water-resistant black covers. The leading brand is Moleskine (http://www.moleskineus.com; the final *e* is correct—it's the French spelling). A 3.5-by-5.5-inch notebook with 192 pages weighs about 4 ounces. If you want to make notes when the weather's wet, waterproof notebooks are available from Rite in the Rain. The 4-by-6-inch All-Weather Outdoor Journal has 50 detachable sheets and weighs 3 ounces. The bound 4-¼-by-6-¾-inch, 8.1-ounce Travel Journal has 78 sheets plus 15 pages of reference material. To write on the waterproof paper, you need a pencil, Space Pen, Inka Pen, or Rite in the Rain's All-Weather Pen. These notebooks are waterproof, but they're also expensive. I have an Outdoor Journal, which I use only in really wet weather.

In my notebook I keep route plans, addresses of people at home and people I meet along the way, lists of how far I go each day and where I camp, and any other information I may need or collect along the way. Looking at my Canadian Rockies journal, I see I kept records of my resting pulse rate (which ranged between 44 and 56) and how much fuel my stove used (ten to fourteen days per quart). I also made shopping lists and, toward the end, a calendar on which I crossed off the days.

(There was a reason for this—buses at the finish ran only three times a week.) Such trivia may not seem worth recording, but for me they bring back the reality of a trip very strongly.

I usually carry at least two Inka or Space Pens, which have waterproof ink in case my notebook gets wet, and usually a refillable pencil as well. Inka and Space Pens will write at any angle and aren't affected by the altitude, temperature, or humidity, which can affect ordinary pens (I've seen other pens refuse to work in the cold and burst at high altitude, oozing ink over clothes). They weigh half an ounce each.

Documents and Papers

The documents you need to carry on a trip can amount to quite a collection, though they never weigh much. On trips close to home, you may need none. On any trip abroad you'll need your passport, perhaps a visa and hiking permit, and insurance documents. It's wise to carry airline or other travel tickets too. It's useful to have some form of identification such as a driver's license in case of emergency. While walking I keep my papers sealed in a plastic bag in the recesses of my "office." Trail permits, if required, also go in a plastic bag, but I often carry them in a pocket or my fanny pack so they're quickly accessible if I meet a ranger.

In case your documents are lost or stolen or you have an accident or become ill, it's a good idea to carry a list of important information, including who to contact in an emergency, separate from other paperwork. Leave a copy of this at home, too. You should also leave as detailed an itinerary as possible, including dates when you expect to phone home, or send a card, letter, e-mail, or text message.

Wallet and Money

In the wilderness, money serves no purpose, and on short trips close to home I carry very little. On long trips money is essential at town stops. I try not to carry loose coins, which are relatively heavy. It's best to carry small-denomination notes, since in remote places there may be no place that will accept large bills. I also carry a credit card, in case of unexpected larger expenses. I used to carry my wallet—nylon, 1.5 ounces—with me, after removing the extra clutter it somehow generates. But it's not waterproof and it's easier not to remove the clutter. Zippered plastic bags will do, but they don't last long and I hate throwing them away, so now I use an Aloksak from Loksak. Aloksaks are tough, reusable transparent waterproof bags with zip closures. Mine is the 4.5 by 7 inches size. It weighs a quarter of an ounce.

Watch

I'm often tempted to leave my watch at home, but a watch has its uses, even in the wilderness. It's helpful to know how many daylight hours are left when deciding whether to stop at a good campsite or push on. When the sun's visible, you can estimate time fairly accurately, but on dull, overcast days it's almost impossible. A watch with a built-in calendar also helps keep track of the days, something that can be confusing on long trips. Checking your watch when you stop for a break may also help get you moving again, especially when you realize that the intended "couple of minutes" has somehow become half an hour. If your watch has an alarm, you can set it to wake you for morning starts. These days I wear a wrist altimeter, the Suunto Altimax or the Highgear Alterra, that tells the time and date and has an alarm as well as being a barometer, altimeter, and thermometer. Of course other electronic instruments such as GPS receivers and smartphones also have clocks, so a watch is no longer essential. Even so, I prefer a watch on my wrist for quick reference, partly, I guess, just out of habit.

BINOCULARS AND MONOCULARS

Few walkers carry binoculars, which surprises me. They're practical for scouting the trail or the country ahead and for checking out whether that dark lump under the tree you're approaching is a mossy boulder or a bear (I once changed my route when a dark object in a distant berry patch turned out to be a grizzly). I use mine regularly, and they've often saved me from taking a route that would have led to a dead end or an obstacle when hiking cross-country. I also use them to survey rivers from a high point for possible fords.

Aside from functional uses, binoculars open up the world of birds and wildlife to the walker. Whether it's otters playing in a lake, a grizzly rooting through a meadow, or an eagle soaring overhead, binoculars allow you to watch wild creatures from a safe distance (both for you and for them).

There are a wealth of ultralight minibinoculars. Mine are 8x21—at 5.5 ounces the lightest pair I could find. I've had them more than twenty years, and the make—Sirius—has disappeared, but there are many similar ones. They're so small I carry them in a shirt or jacket pocket. When selecting binoculars, note the relationship between the first number, which is the magnification, and the second, which is the diameter in millimeters of the front lens, known as the aperture. The size of the aperture determines how much light the lenses admit. Large figures mean plenty of light but also more weight owing to the bigger pieces of glass. Divide the aperture by the magnification and you can get a figure called the exit pupil. The bigger this is the better the image in poor light. My minibinoculars have an exit pupil of 2.6, which is low so they aren't much use when it's very dull. Again, though, a bigger exit pupil means heavier binoculars.

A monocular is a lighter alternative to a pair of binoculars, of course. I find monoculars harder to hold steady and focus than binoculars and gave up on mine many years ago. However, a reader suggests they are easier to use than binoculars if you wear glasses. There are many models, the lightest weighing just 3 ounces.

PHOTOGRAPHY

Taking photographs is probably the most popular nonessential backpacking activity. Everyone likes to have a visual record of trips. But if you simply point the camera at every scene regardless of the light or viewpoint, you may end up with pictures that aren't very satisfactory. Those who take the time and care to study the details of a place in order to make the best picture, the one that most reflects how they see it, may share my feeling that this gives them a deeper appreciation of the wilderness. Photography can also record all the other aspects of a trip, too—campsites, hooded figures in the rain, exhausted faces, elated faces, details of rocks and plants, everything in fact that makes up backpacking.

Anyone wanting to pursue the subject of wilderness photography further can learn a great deal from the late Galen Rowell's books and from *Outdoor Photographer* magazine.

Photography is about seeing, not about equipment. No amount of expensive gear will make someone a good photographer. That said, the more ambitious you become, the more gear you end up carrying. I used to carry around 10 pounds of cameras and accessories, which seems an enormous amount to the nonphotographer. But I've become something of a professional over the years, and I go on most walks knowing I have to come back with a set of pictures. Recently I've cut the weight by half, though, and my photos don't seem to have suffered.

Choosing a good camera for the outdoors can be even more difficult than selecting a tent or rucksack. Due to the vast number of models available and the rapid speed of developments, most cameras only have a life of a few years. Here I'm going to look at types of cameras and the features relevant for backpacking use.

Cameras

Film still has aficionados, but for the vast majority of people, photography now means digital images. For backpacking, I think digital cameras are particularly good because you don't have to carry film, which is sensitive to moisture, heat, and cold. Not needing to carry film is also an advantage on long trips as a bag of film is quite heavy and bulky (about an ounce a roll), while a memory card that will hold hundreds of images is tiny and only weighs a fraction of an ounce. Digital images can be uploaded to the Internet and e-mailed home during a trip. You can see the results, too, and retake pictures if necessary.

There are four types of camera to consider for backpacking: smartphones, compacts, DSLRs with interchangeable lenses and optical viewfinders that show the image as seen through the lens, and an intermediate type known as "micro system," "hybrid," "interchangeable lens," or "compact system" cameras. This last type are cameras that are compact-like in size but which have interchangeable lenses and sensors the same size as many DSLRs but not through-the-lens viewing (I'll refer to them as "MSCs" for convenience). All will take adequate pictures in good light for use on the Internet and for small prints. For difficult light—dusk, dawn, heavy shade, storms, snow—only the best smartphone cameras and compacts can produce even reasonable results.

Megapixels and Sensors

Advertisements promote the idea that the more megapixels a camera has, the better pictures it will take, and digital cameras are often judged purely by how many megapixels they have. However, sensor size is actually more important. Tiny compact cameras have tiny sensors that can't record the detail that larger sensors can, even if they have more megapixels. A 12-megapixel DSLR will take higher-quality images than a 12-megapixel compact, especially at high ISOs (which measures the sensitivity of the sensor to light—the higher the ISO the more sensitive the sensor). Indeed if more megapixels are crammed onto a small sensor, more "noise" (a grainy, blotchy appearance, sometimes with distorted color) can result at high ISOs than on cameras with fewer megapixels. These differences only matter for large prints and crops of parts of the image. For most computer viewing and small prints, they aren't significant, and compact cameras are perfectly adequate. With the best compact cameras (Canon G series, Panasonic LX series, and Ricoh GR and GX series), images shot at low ISOs (100, 200) can make good large prints. The optimum number of megapixels for a compact-camera sensor seems to be around 10; anymore than that, and noise becomes a problem, so much so that some makers have cut the limit back to 10. If you want the best-quality images, then a camera with a larger sensor is needed. The very best quality comes from medium-format and full-frame DSLRs, but these are too heavy for backpacking unless your main aim is photography. For most people—including myself, taking pictures for publication in books and magazines—the sensors found in MSCs and the lightest, smallest DSLRs, known as APS-C-size sensors (from a long-forgotten film size), will produce excellent results. As MSCs weigh less and are more compact than the smallest DSLR, I think they are the ideal cameras for backpackers wanting good-quality results. Having carried DSLRs for many years (and film SLRs before that), I am making the transition to an MSC system (Sony NEX). I usually carry two cameras, as images are important. At present, these are the MSC and my old DSLR. Soon it will be two MSCs.

Lens

Most compact cameras come with a zoom lens that is 35 to 38 millimeters at the widest end (this is the 35-millimeter film equivalent, as there are many different compact sensor sizes, and as this determines the focal length a single compact focal-length system doesn't exist, so the old 35 mm one is still used), which is not very wide for landscape photography. I think at least 28 mm is needed. Happily, there are some compacts with 28 mm and even 24 mm. Cutting out compacts whose lenses aren't at least 28 mm at the widest end reduces the choice greatly. The long end of the zoom isn't as important in my opinion, unless you are interested in wildlife photography, when a long telephoto is needed. Most compacts have a 100- to 200-mm long end to the zoom, which should be ample for most uses. If you want a long lens, then there are "super zoom" compacts with lenses that run from 300 mm to 500 mm. These are heavier and bulkier than compacts with shorter zooms but still much lighter than DSLRs, especially ones fitted with a long zoom, though sometimes heavier than MSCs.

MSCs and DSLRs have the advantage that you can use whatever lens you like—as long as you don't mind carrying it. With my DSLR, I sometimes carry three zoom lenses—11- to 18-mm wide angle, 18- to 55-mm mid-range, and 55- to 250-mm telephoto (these are the digital focal lengths, with most MSCs and non-full-frame DSLRs, you multiply the focal length by 1.5 or 1.6 to get the 35 mm equivalent). When weight matters, I just carry the mid-range zoom, as I did on the Pacific Northwest Trail. Because the sensor size is much the same, lenses for MSCs aren't much lighter or smaller than the one for DSLRs. It's the camera bodies that are much smaller. The smallest interchangeable lenses are those for the micro four-thirds Olympus and Panasonic cameras, as these have smaller sensors than most MSCs though still much bigger than those found in compact cameras.

Weight

Even the lightest DSLRs are heavy and bulky compared with most compacts, which can be carried in a pocket. Except for super-zoom or super-tough models, there's no need for a compact to weigh more than 12 to 14 ounces, and many weigh much less—the lightest is 3.5 ounces. The lightest DSLR weighs 13 ounces, and that's without a lens or a battery, which usually weighs at least 2 ounces. Add a mid-range zoom and a battery, and the lightest DSLR setup is 22 ounces. MSCs sit between compacts and DSLRs. My Sony NEX-5 body weighs 10 ounces with battery and 17 ounces with an 18- to 55-mm zoom. While bigger than a compact, it's noticeably smaller than a DSLR and so fits in a smaller and lighter camera pouch.

Anti-Shake

An increasing number of cameras and DSLR lenses come with an anti-shake mechanism that counters the involuntary movement of the hands when taking a picture. This is useful for low-light photography and with cameras with no viewfinder, as holding a camera out in front of you isn't a very stable position. Also, when you have been exercising hard and are a little out of breath, it can be hard to hold the camera still! I have lenses with an anti-shake function, and I can get sharper pictures at lower shutter speeds than without it, so I do think it's worth having.

Viewfinder or LCD Screen

All digital cameras come with LCD screens on which you can view your images straight after taking them. All compacts and some DSLRs have a "live view" LCD screen on which you can compose the picture before taking it. The advantage is that you can see exactly what you are capturing, including how altering the exposure settings changes the lighting, which you can't see through an optical viewfinder. Even more important than the actual image is the histogram, a graph that shows the brightness levels of the image. I use the histogram to adjust the exposure regularly. If the graph goes off the histogram at the right edge, then the brightest parts of the image will be overexposed. If the histogram goes off the left edge, then the darkest parts of the image will be underexposed. Ideally, the histogram should be toward the right edge without going off it for a well-exposed picture in most light conditions. Screens have two disadvantages. One, mentioned previously, is that it's harder to hold a camera steady away from the body. The other is that LCD screens can be hard to see in bright sunlight. The first disadvantage is countered by tilting screens. I can flip up the screen on my NEX-5 and look down on it while I hold the camera against my body. Screen visibility in bright sunshine has improved too, though it can still be hard to see much detail. DSLRs always have an optical viewfinder, but on the lighter-weight amateur models, these don't show 100 percent of the picture, which means objects like twigs can intrude on the edges of the image. Some compacts and MSCs have optical viewfinders (sometimes as optional extras), but the problem is that they don't show the view through the lens, and so the view doesn't change when you zoom the lens. Better are electronic viewfinders that show the same image as the screen but which aren't affected by bright light and allow the camera to be held to the eye. Overall, I prefer traditional optical viewfinders as these are clearer than electronic ones. I have, however, become used to the screen on the NEX-5 and no longer feel it's not real photography if I don't put the camera to my eye.

The Tough Ones

Electronic cameras aren't designed for backcountry use. Most are vulnerable to damp, dust, and knocks. I always carry mine in padded cases, which of course adds bulk and weight. There are a couple of cameras designed for use on construction sites that don't need careful protection and which should be excellent for the roughest outdoor activities. Cameras like the 13.6-ounce, 6-megapixel Fuji FinePix Big Job HD-3W with a 28- to 84-mm lens and the 14-ounce, 8-megapixel Ricoh Caplio 500G Wide with a 28- to 85-mm lens are waterproof and dustproof and designed to survive drops onto concrete. Both are quite a

bit heavier and bulkier than other compacts and don't have a huge zoom range, though the lenses do start at 28 mm. I wouldn't choose one of these, but if you want a camera you don't have to take too much care of and can use without concern for scrambling or taking photos in the rain or a blizzard, they sound a good choice.

Camera Phones

An increasing number of phones have cameras built in. These have tiny sensors and limited features and controls, but they are by no means useless, and if your main use of images is for the Internet, they could be all you need. And if you carry a phone anyway, that saves the weight of a separate camera, though you will need several batteries or a portable charger if you take many photos, as the camera does use quite a bit of power. The HTC Desire phone I used on the Pacific Northwest Trail has a 5-megapixel camera, and I took pictures with this that I uploaded to my blog and my Facebook page whenever I had a connection, so friends and family could see pictures of the walk as I went along. I also e-mailed images back to *TGO* magazine in the U.K., where they were published with reports on the walk. At 3 inches by 6 inches, the printed images looked OK.

Batteries

All digital cameras are dependent on batteries. Many have proprietary ones, and others use AAs. I always carry spare batteries and, on any trip longer than week, a portable charger (see Battery Chargers, earlier in this chapter). On a multiweek trip, I send the plug-in charger ahead in my running supply box so I can recharge all batteries at town stops. I generally find I can get 250 to 400 images per battery. Using the flash and reviewing images on the screen uses battery power, so I avoid these most of the time.

Filters

Filters are often overused, and I carry very few of them. I want the light and colors in my pictures to look natural. For protection and to cut out ultraviolet light, I keep a skylight filter on every lens. I also use a polarizer to cut glare and to darken blue skies. If the sky is bright and the land dark (or vice versa), I use a graduated neutral-density filter in a filter holder. Each filter weighs about 0.75 ounce with case.

Memory Cards and Image Storage

Memory cards will hold hundreds of images, so on a short trip, only one or two may be needed. On longer trips, I carry enough cards for the whole trip. They are very light, around 0.3 ounce including plastic case depending on the type. I don't carry any other storage device, as cards are the lightest option and also one of the toughest. Although rare, faults can develop on cards though, so I don't use huge-capacity ones. I'd rather carry four 4 GB cards than one 16 GB card, as all four are unlikely to fail.

Supports

In low light, you need something to steady the camera, especially at low ISO speeds (100 and 200). (As a rough guide for handheld shooting, the shutter speed should approximate or be faster than the focal length of the lens. For example, a 28 mm lens shouldn't be handheld at slower than $\frac{1}{30}$ second; a 200 mm lens no slower than $\frac{1}{250}$—with lenses and

cameras with anti-shake mechanisms, you may be able to handhold those lenses at $\frac{1}{15}$ and $\frac{1}{125}$ or even slower.) A camera support can be as simple as propping your arms on a rock, bracing yourself against a tree, or even lying down.

If you carry a monopod, minitripod or clamp, or tripod, you don't need to rely on natural supports, which may not be in convenient places. One of my Pacerpoles has a slot into the handle for a Pacerpole Camera Mount onto which I can screw the camera or a tripod head. I use this for wildlife photography when I don't have time to remove my pack and set up the tripod. There are many small tabletop tripods and clamps. The best I've come across is the Joby GorillaPod, which has flexible legs so it can be twisted around a branch or a post as well as being used as a mini tripod. There are four sizes of GorillaPod for different weights of camera. The lightest is the Original, which weighs 1.6 ounces and will support cameras up to 11.5 ounces in weight, making it ideal for all but the heaviest compacts. I have the SLR GorillaPod, which weighs 5.8 ounces and will support cameras up to 28 ounces and so is fine for MSCs and the lightest DSLRs. I like this odd-looking device because it is very versatile. It can be attached to a trekking pole or ice ax, and these can be rammed into the ground firmly if there is no other option.

I use a tripod most of the time, both for self-portraits and for low-light photography. The problem is finding a lightweight one that doesn't develop the shakes after minimal use. I have several; the one I use most is an old Cullman Backpack tripod that weighs 21.5 ounces and has been held together with duct tape for the best part of two decades. Not having found any other light tripod that looked as good, I used it again on the Pacific Northwest Trail, and it survived OK. Now that I have a smaller MSC camera, I am looking for a lighter tripod. Of those I've examined, the Tamrac ZipShot—which has shock-cord-linked leg sections, stands 44 inches high, and will support up to 48 ounces—is very light at 11 ounces, but the height isn't adjustable. Most lightweight tripods are most stable when not fully extended. More conventional is the Velbon V-Pod, which is even lighter at 9.7 ounces and will support up to 70 ounces. It has adjustable legs but only extends to 40 inches. I usually strap my tripod to the side of the pack so I can get to it easily.

Protection and Carrying

You can protect your camera by carrying it in your pack, but you won't take many pictures that way. I like to sling a camera across my body so that I can get at it quickly. But it's vulnerable there, so I keep it in a foam-padded, waterproof case. There are many such cases sold by Tamrac, Lowepro, Crumpler, Tenba, Kinesis, and others. Padded cases come in shapes and sizes to fit every camera. Weights range from a few ounces for cases for tiny compacts to 32 ounces and more for cases for DSLRs with long telephoto lenses. Zing pouches are slightly different, being made of stretch neoprene. They don't provide as much protection as a padded case, but they are lighter and more compact. I use them to carry lenses and spare camera in the pack, where less protection is needed. The Zing Medium Pouch, which is 4 inches in diameter and 7 inches long, weighs 4 ounces. The Standard SLR Case, which fits small DSLRs, weighs 4.5 ounces. I attach my camera pouch (a long discontinued model—they do last) to a wide shoulder strap and carry it across my body bandolier style with the pouch resting just above my hip. That way, my camera is quickly accessible—cameras

stored in packs don't take many pictures. A spare battery and memory card live in a small pocket in the pouch so I can change these without having to take off my pack. Other memory cards and batteries in a plastic bag plus spare lenses and spare camera, if carried, in pouches, live in the pack.

Cleaning

I carry lens-cleaning cloths for removing marks from lenses and a blower brush for puffing out the inside. But the danger of damaging equipment in field conditions makes me keep cleaning and tinkering to an absolute minimum.

Recording

Digital cameras record the date and time of the image, which helps in identifying the location. Some also have GPS built in, or else you can buy a GPS module that will let you tag your images. I haven't used GPS with a camera like this. The date and time information plus my notes on the route and the day's walk are usually enough for me to work out where a photo was taken. Consulting the map may then be needed to work out what the mountain or lake in the image is called. If you want to be certain, you could write down the details when you take the photo or record it if your camera or phone has that facility. I used to make notes when I used film but don't do so with digital.

ENTERTAINMENT

Reading Matter

Because I'm a book addict, I always carry at least one paperback on every walk. Too often I end up with several. There are three kinds of books that might find their way into your pack: trail guides, natural history guides, and books for pure entertainment. On my 124-day Canadian Rockies walk, I read thirty-six books, an average of one every three and a half days—twenty-four were fiction and twelve were nonfiction. This doesn't include a field guide that I carried all the way, parts of which I read several times, and a trail guide I carried on the first half of the walk.

Natural history guides are a problem because you usually need several if you want to identify trees, flowers, mammals, birds, and insects. In a group, each member can carry a different volume, but the solo walker has to be selective. I usually carry the smallest bird and tree guides I can find, sometimes adding a flower guide if the weight can be kept down. The lightest guides are the little Finder books published by the Nature Study Guild. The ones for trees are particularly good. I always look for a guide that covers everything, but sadly these are few. The best I've found is Ben Gadd's *Handbook of the Canadian Rockies*, which is a complete natural history field guide and also covers geology, history, weather, and much more. I carried it when I hiked the length of the Canadian Rockies. It weighs a hefty 2 pounds in the latest full-color edition, though. On the Arizona Trail I carried the National Audubon Society's *Field Guide to the Southwestern States* (16.5 ounces) and *Field Guide to the Pacific Northwest* (15.8 ounces) on the Pacific Northwest Trail.

I may not be carrying paper books much longer, however, as e-book readers can hold hundreds of titles and weigh no more than small paperbacks. On the Pacific Northwest Trail, I used the Kindle app on my smartphone to read occasionally, sometimes in camp and sometimes during boring road walking. In dull light, the little screen was quite pleasant to use, but in sunlight, the words just disappeared. As the phone was also my GPS, I couldn't afford the battery life to use it as an e-book reader often, but it did show me the advantage of such gadgets. Amazon's stand-alone Kindle has a nonglare screen and only weighs 8.7 ounces. It can hold up to 3,500 books, and the battery lasts a month with the wi-fi connection turned off. It sounds ideal for backpacking. The only disadvantage I can see is that it would take away the excitement of browsing secondhand bookshelves in stores in little towns and hoping to find something worth reading.

A planisphere showing the stars in position for each month is well worth carrying if you're interested in identifying constellations and planets. Small ones weigh less than 0.25 ounce and take up no space. I don't use mine often, but when I do, I'm very glad I remembered to bring it.

Radios, Music Players, Etc.

Many phones now come with radios, and smartphones come with music players as well. Although I carry a smartphone, I rarely listen to the radio or music when backpacking because, even in the tent, it cuts me off from the world I'd come to experience. Proponents of radios point out that books do the same, but to my mind they don't have the same effect; you can still hear the sounds of nature when reading. Modern devices have many uses. My friend John Manning hiked the Pacific Crest Trail with an iPod that contained his favorite Beach Boys tracks and was used to download and store the images from his camera. If you use a radio or play music, please use headphones. Sound carries in the quietness of the wilderness. I remember coming off a high Pyrenean peak, my eyes set on a necklace of mountain tarns far below surrounded by green sward ideal for camping, only to be greeted, while still a half mile away, by the tinkling sounds of music coming from the only tent I could see. Once down there, I found the sound permeated the whole basin, so I pushed on into the next valley bottom to camp—much later than I'd planned, but in quiet. An advantage of smartphones and tiny music players is that they are usually used with headphones.

Cards and Games

There are various games that groups can take along for entertainment, and, of course, you can make up your own, but a deck of cards is the most obvious lightweight entertainment to carry. You can buy miniature decks, though a standard one weighs just 3.5 ounces. I've never carried cards, but a companion did on a ski crossing of the Columbia Icefield in the Canadian Rockies, and we played many games during the four days we spent stormbound in the tents. You could carry cards on solo trips for playing solitaire, though I can't imagine wanting to. A hiking book I read many years ago did recommend carrying a deck in case you became lost. Don't panic, the author recommended; just sit down and start playing solitaire, because some damn fool is then bound to pop up behind you and tell you which card to play next!

Thermometer

Few people carry thermometers, but I'm fascinated by the temperature data I've collected over the years. My immediate finding, reinforced whenever I camp with others, was that it's never as cold as people think. Also, I've noted that you really do feel warmer when the temperature drops a few degrees below freezing and the humidity falls than when it's a few degrees above. On the Canadian Rockies walk, I recorded no temperatures below freezing during July and August and only three freezing nights in September; yet by the middle of October it was freezing hard every night. During four days I spent stormbound on the Columbia Icefield, the temperature in the tent ranged, astonishingly, from 28 to 75°F (−2 to 24°C), depending on whether we were cooking and whether the doors were open. Having such data gives me a reference for what temperatures to expect when I revisit an area, which helps with planning.

I used to carry a separate thermometer but haven't done so for many years as various electronic instruments have them built in, including my altimeter watch and Kestrel 4500 Weather Station (see next chapter).

There are also tiny thermometers, with windchill charts on the back, attached to split rings for hanging on jacket and pack zippers. These come under a variety of labels, and their weight is negligible. They provide only a rough idea of temperature.

chapter nine

on the move

skills and hazards

MAY YOUR TRAILS BE CROOKED,
WINDING, LONESOME, DANGEROUS,
LEADING TO THE MOST AMAZING VIEW.
MAY YOUR MOUNTAINS RISE INTO AND
ABOVE THE CLOUDS.

—*Edward Abbey*

Walking is very easy. Walking in the wilderness with a pack isn't quite so simple. You have to find your way, perhaps in dense mist or thick forest; you need to cope with terrain, which may mean negotiating steep cliffs, loose scree, and snow; and you must deal with hazards ranging from extremes of weather to wild animals. Most wilderness walking, however, is relatively straightforward as long as you're reasonably fit, have a few basic skills, and know a little about weather and terrain.

FINDING THE WAY

Maps

Knowing how to read a map is a key wilderness skill, yet many hikers can barely do so. There are trails that are so well signposted and the trail guides so accurate that you don't really need a map. Even in such areas, though, you may find unmarked trail junctions where it's impossible to work out which way to go without a map.

With a map you plan walks, follow your route on the ground, and locate water sources and possible campsites. But maps also can open an inspiring world—I can spend hours poring over a map, tracing possible routes, wondering how to connect a mountain tarn with a narrow notch, specu-

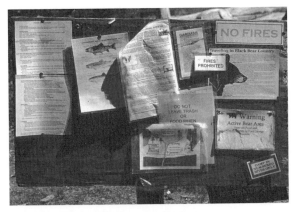

A plethora of signs, indicating a popular place.

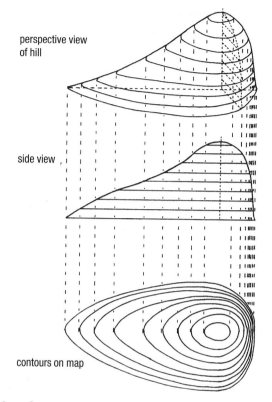

perspective view of hill

side view

contours on map

ABOVE: Contour lines join together points of equal elevation. The patterns they form represent the three-dimensional shapes of features. Once you can interpret them, you can tell what the hills, valleys, and ridges of an area are like (right).

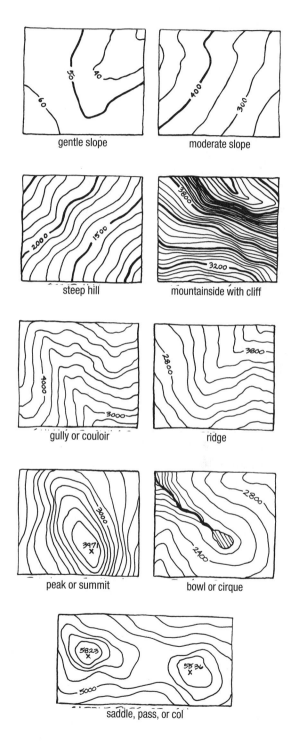

gentle slope

moderate slope

steep hill

mountainside with cliff

gully or couloir

ridge

peak or summit

bowl or cirque

saddle, pass, or col

lating whether it's possible to follow a mountain ridge or if it will turn out to be a rocky edge that forces me to take another route.

Every map has a key. Using this key to interpret the symbols, you can build a picture of what the terrain will be like. There are two types of maps: *planimetric* and *topographic.* The first represents features on the ground; the second shows the topography, or the shape of the ground itself. Topographic ("topo") maps use *contour lines,* which join points of equal elevation starting from sea level. Contour lines occur at given intervals, usually from 15 to 500 feet. U.S. Geological Sur-

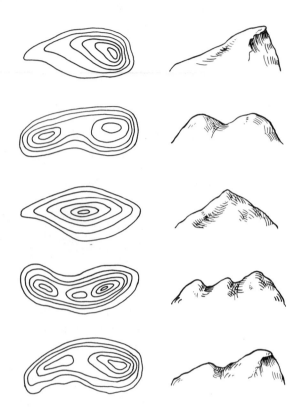

The topo views (left) match the appropriate profiles (right).

vey (USGS) 1:24,000 maps have a contour interval of 40 feet. On most maps, every fifth contour line is thicker and has the elevation indicated, though you may have to trace it for some distance to find this marker. The closer together the contour lines, the steeper the slope. If they're touching, expect a cliff (though cliffs of less height than the contour interval won't show on the map). Some maps mark cliffs, others don't; check the key to see if you might encounter cliffs not shown on the map.

The patterns that contour lines form represent the three-dimensional shapes of features. Once you can interpret them, you can tell what the hills, valleys, and ridges of an area are like and plan accordingly.

The *scale* tells you how much ground is represented by a given distance on the map. The standard scale for USGS topo maps outside Alaska is 1:24,000. These are known as *7.5-minute maps* because of the area of latitude and longitude they cover. On a 1:24,000 map, 1 inch equals 24,000 inches on the ground, which is roughly 2.5 inches

USGS topo map with scale and declination information. These maps cover the whole country but often don't contain up-to-date trail information.

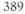

per mile. In Alaska, 1:63,360 maps—about 1 inch to the mile—are the norm. These *15-minute maps* are still available for some other areas but are being replaced by 1:24,000 ones—a pity, since the scale is adequate for backpacking and each sheet covers a larger area. USGS topo maps, sometimes known as *quads* (from *quadrangle*), are the standard in the United States.

For most of the world, metric scales are standard, with 1:25,000 and 1:50,000 the most useful for walkers. Smaller-scale maps covering larger areas, such as 1:100,000 and 1:250,000, are helpful for planning. Although the greater detail of large-scale maps is best for walking, it's possible to use smaller-scale ones in the wilderness. In remote areas they may be all that's available. I've used 1:250,000 maps in Greenland and even 1:600,000 in the northern Canadian Rockies.

Most Forest Service maps are planimetric, but there are some topographic ones covering designated wilderness areas, such as the 1:63,360 maps covering the Ansel Adams and John Muir Wildernesses in the Sierra. The Bureau of Land Management also makes an increasing number

A MOUNTAIN STORM

The wind whipping along the rocky ridge drives sheets of rain into my face. Clouds swirl all around, ripped apart at times to reveal sharp pinnacles soaring above me or the dark outline of a lake far below in the valley. I scramble along the narrow crest, exhilarated by the storm's fury and reveling in the rough rock under my hands. I am at the heart of the world. There is no sense of time; it's a shock when I come to the top of the talus slope that leads safely down into the valley. I hesitate to leave the storm, but the thought of dry clothes and the warmth of camp spurs me into the long descent.

of metric topo maps at different scales, such as 1:100,000, with contour intervals of 50 meters.

Several companies produce maps for wilderness use that are more up to date and have more trail information than USGS topo maps. Those from National Geographic Trails Illustrated are excellent. Printed on a paperlike recyclable plastic called Polyart, they are tear-proof and waterproof. The maps are also attractively designed,

Tom Harrison Trail Map with trails clearly marked, along with distances. Maps like this are excellent for trail hiking but are available only for popular areas.

A map printout showing route and comments. I used a set of these maps, made for me by Li Brannfors, on the Pacific Northwest Trail.

clear, and easy to read. The scale varies from map to map. Each map is based on USGS data, but this is customized for outdoor recreation and updated every year or two to keep the maps accurate. Trails Illustrated maps are topographic, but they also contain information needed for planning trips, such as the location of trailheads, ranger stations, and campsites, plus the precise route of trails, advice on bearbagging, *Giardia*, park and wilderness area regulations, and outlines of topics like wildlife, history, geology, and archaeology. Tom Harrison's 1:63,360 trail maps to the High Sierra and Green Trails' 1:69,500 maps of the Pacific Northwest are also superb. Earthwalk Press's maps are worth looking out for, too; I found the 1:48,000 map covering part of the Grand Canyon very good. For the northeast Appalachians, Map Adventures' waterproof topo map of the White Mountains of New Hampshire and Maine is excellent as are the Appalachian Mountain Club's maps.

Maps based on USGS quads are now available on DVD or can be downloaded from the Internet to your computer, smartphone, or GPS, from companies like National Geographic Topo!, Delorme Topo North America, ViewRanger, and Trails.com. You can draw routes on the map and calculate distances and ascents, then print out the results so you have a complete route plan or even download them to some GPS units. Maps can be printed too, though with an A4 printer you'll need several sheets to cover much of an area. You can get waterproof tear-resistant paper such as National Geographic's Adventure Paper for this. Maps can be bought at outdoor stores, bookstores, agency offices, and direct from the publishers. Web sites such as Map Link and the USGS are very useful. (See Appendix 3.)

The first long walk I did using printed-out and downloaded maps was the Pacific Northwest Trail. Long-distance hiker Li Brannfors, who I'd met in the High Sierra many years ago, had hiked the PNT the year before me and recorded his route on his GPS unit (which meant carrying loads of batteries—I'm glad someone else did this!). Li kindly sent me A4 printouts of topographic maps with his route and alternatives marked. These maps were my main ones and were carried, folded, in an Aloksak bag (they were on plain paper) in a shirt pocket for quick access. I also had ViewRanger software with topo maps on my HTC Desire smartphone, which has GPS function (see GPS, later in this chapter). If I needed to locate my exact position, I could do so quickly with ViewRanger. I also carried larger-scale national park and Forest Service maps so I had an overview of areas and could place myself in the landscape and identify surrounding features.

For general planning, the state atlases and gazetteers published by DeLorme are useful. The maps are topographic (mostly 1:250,000 or 1:300,000, though national parks may be shown at 1:70,000). They also give a great deal of other information. I've used the Arizona and Utah atlases for planning a thousand-mile walk in the Southwest canyons. I haven't done the walk yet, but the planning has been fun!

Many topographic maps have a grid superimposed on them; each line in the grid may be numbered. If it is, you can record the grid reference for precise location. Also, counting the number of squares a route crosses is a quick way to estimate the distance.

To work out distances on maps without grids, a map measurer is useful. You set this calibrated wheel to the scale of the map and run it along your route. You can then read the distance off a scale on the device. It weighs only a fraction of an ounce, but I've never carried one. You could draw a grid on a map, but I've never done this, either.

Laying a piece of string along the route and measuring it is another way of determining distance.

While large-scale topographic maps are the best for accurate navigation, other maps offer useful information. Land-management agencies, such as the National Park Service, often issue their own maps showing trails and wilderness facilities. These maps are more up to date than the topographic maps for the same area. Forest Service and Bureau of Land Management planimetric maps (usually half an inch to the mile) often show roads and trails that don't appear on topo maps. These planimetric maps don't have contour lines, so they don't tell you how much ascent and descent there is over a particular distance. (The 1:600,000 map I used in the northern Canadian Rockies was planimetric; I worked out when I would be going uphill and downhill by studying the drainage patterns of streams, but I had no way of knowing whether I was headed for a 300- or a 3,000-foot climb.) Some planimetric maps are shaded to show where the higher ground lies, but this gives only a rough idea of what to expect.

Maps normally have the date of publication listed with the key, along with the dates of any revisions. Remote areas are rarely remapped, and you may find that some maps are decades old. Obviously, the older the map, the less accurate the information may be, especially with regard to man-made features like roads. The maps I used in the northern Yukon in the 1990s didn't show the Dempster Highway, built in the 1960s and 1970s. I added it myself from highway maps, which are updated regularly. On one section of the Arizona Trail, which I hiked in 2000, the USGS map I used had last been field-checked thirty-six years earlier in 1964. Features can disappear as well, of course, and trails on maps may be hard or impossible to follow if they haven't been maintained. It's wise to consult current guidebooks and ranger stations if you don't want to risk a nasty surprise.

I am a firm believer in doing virtually all navigating with only a map. As long as you can see features around you and relate them to the map, you know where you are. The easiest way to do this is by *setting*, or *orienting*, the map, which involves turning it until the features you can see are in their correct positions relative to where you are. If you walk with the map set, it is easier to relate visible features to it.

Many people automatically use a compass for navigating, ignoring what they can see around them, yet even at night you can navigate solely with a map. Many years ago I completed a night-navigation exercise on a mountain leadership-training course and was the only person to travel the route without relying on a compass. It was a clear night, and the distinctive peaks above the valley were easily identifiable on the map, while the location of streams showed me where I was on the valley floor. The others in the group navigated as though we were in total darkness, relying on compass bearings and pace counting. If you always depend on such methods, you cut yourself off from the world around you, substituting figures and measurements for a close understanding of the nature of the terrain. I don't like my walking to be reduced to mathematical calculations.

When you're following a trail, an occasional map check is enough to let you see how far along you are. When you're going cross-country, however, study the map carefully, both beforehand and while on the move. Apart from working out a rough route, note features such as rivers, cliffs, lakes, and, in particular, contour lines. Be prepared not to always find what you expect, though. The lack of contour lines around a lake may mean you'll find a nice flat, dry area for a camp when

you arrive, or it may mean acres of marsh (as happened to me a few times in the Canadian Rockies). Close-grouped contour lines at the head of a valley may mean an impassable cliff or a steep but climbable slope. You have to accept that sometimes you'll have to turn back and find another route, that sometimes you'll have to walk twice as far as planned to reach your destination and it will take you twice as long. No map will tell you everything. Flexibility in adapting your plans to the terrain is important.

Always keep your map handy, even if the route seems easy or you're on a clear trail. A garment pocket is the obvious storage place. Unless the maps are made of waterproof plastic, it's essential to protect them from weather. Unfortunately, most map cases are bulky, awkward to fold, and hard to fit into a pocket or fanny pack. Those from Ortlieb (a fraction over 2 ounces) are quite flexible and very tough. Plastic bags work well, but they don't last long. An Aloksak bag is a good, durable alternative. You can cover maps with special clear plastic film, and some hikers use waterproofing products, such as wipe-on Nikwax Map Proof, which I'm told are effective. I don't bother with waterproofing maps. Although some of mine look disreputable, I've never had one disintegrate.

The Compass

Although I prefer to navigate with just a map, I always carry a compass. For trail travel I hardly need it, except perhaps when at an unsigned junction in thick mist or dense forest. For cross-country walking, though, a compass may prove essential, especially when visibility is poor.

The standard compass for backpacking is the *orienteering* type, with a liquid-damped needle and a transparent plastic baseplate. Silva is the best-known brand; Suunto and Brunton are others. Corporate changes have led to some confusion, however. Johnson Outdoors holds the rights to the brand name Silva in the United States and used to distribute the Swedish-made Silva compasses. In 1996 Silva bought Brunton and ended its link with Johnson, but Johnson still had the rights to the name Silva. This has led to the strange situation where the original Swedish Silva compasses are sold in the United States and Canada under the Brunton label (though as Silva elsewhere in the world), while compasses sold under the name Silva by Johnson Outdoors are now made in Finland by Silva's big rival Suunto. (And, ironically, Silva and Brunton were taken over in 2006 by Finnish company Fiskars, who are selling Brunton but not Silva to Swedish company Fenix Outdoor.) So there are three brands but only two makers. Luckily both make top-quality compasses.

I mostly use the smallest, lightest model—the Brunton 7DNL (Silva Field 7 outside North America), which weighs 0.8 ounce. This is just 0.2 ounce lighter than the Silva Ranger 3 I used to use. But that's still a 20 percent weight saving. For backpacking, models with sighting mirrors and other refinements are unnecessary.

The heart of the compass is the magnetic needle, which is housed in a rotating fluid-filled, transparent, circular mount marked with north, south, east, and west, plus degrees. The base of the dial is marked with an orienting arrow, fixed toward north on the dial, and a series of parallel lines. The rest of the compass consists of the baseplate, with a large direction-of-travel arrow, roamers for taking grid references, and a set of scales for measuring distances on a map. Some baseplates also have a small magnifying glass built in to help you read map detail.

The main features of an orienteering compass, including a magnifying lens. The compass housing is a rotating ring, also known as the azimuth.

A compass helps you walk toward your destination, even if you can't see it, without reference to the surrounding terrain. Without a compass, you might veer away from the correct line. The direction you walk is called a *bearing*. Bearings are given as degrees, or the angle between north and your direction, reading clockwise. To set a bearing, you use the compass baseplate as a protractor. Point the direction-of-travel arrow toward your destination, then turn the compass housing until the red end of the magnetic needle aligns with the orienting arrow. As long as you keep these two arrows pointing to the north and follow the direction-of-travel arrow, you'll reach your destination, even if it's hidden. However,

Taking a compass bearing from a map. Align the compass with your objective on the map (left), then rotate the housing to line up the orienting arrow with the north-south grid lines (right).

you can rarely take a bearing on something several hours away and walk straight to it (although it's possible in desert and wide-open tundra). It's better to locate a visible, stationary feature (a *checkpoint*) that lies along your line of travel, such as a boulder or a tree, and walk to that. You may have to leave your bearing to circumvent an obstruction, such as a bog or a cliff, but that's all right as long as you keep the chosen feature in sight. Once you reach a checkpoint, you can check your bearing and find another object to head for.

Taking a map bearing with an orienteering compass from the trail to Tomahawk Lake. Place an edge of the baseplate on the point on the trail at your location and line up the edge with Tomahawk Lake. Rotate the compass housing until the orienting arrow is aligned with north on the map. Remove the compass from the map and turn it—without rotating the housing—until the magnetic needle and orienting arrow are aligned. The direction-of-travel arrow now points to Tomahawk Lake.

In poor visibility, solo walkers may have to walk on their bearings by holding the compass and literally following the arrow. Two or more walkers can send one person ahead to the limit of visibility. The scout stops so another walker can check the position with the compass and direct the scout to move left or right until in line with the bearing. Then everyone else joins the scout and the process is repeated. It's a slow but very accurate method of navigation, particularly useful in whiteout conditions. I've used it many times when skiing.

If you know where you are but not which way you need to go to reach your destination, then you need to take a bearing off the map. To do this, place an edge of the baseplate on the spot where you are, then line up the edge with your destination. Rotate the compass housing until the orienting arrow is aligned with north on the map. Remove the compass from the map and turn it, without rotating the housing, until the magnetic needle and orienting arrow are aligned. The direction-of-travel arrow now points in the direction you want to go. The number on the compass housing at this point is your bearing.

This process is straightforward, but you must account for magnetic variation. Most topographic maps have three arrows somewhere in the margin showing three norths. *Grid north* can be ignored for compass navigation (though not for GPS navigation—see UTM sidebar, pages 368–70); the other two are very important. One is *magnetic north*, the direction the compass needle points. The other is *true north*. The top of the map is always true north, so if your map has no grid marked on it, you can use the margins. Because compasses point to magnetic north and maps are aligned to true north, the difference between them should be taken into account when using the two in conjunction. This angle is measured in degrees and minutes (60 minutes equal 1 degree) and is called the *magnetic variation* or *declination*.

Since magnetic north lies in the Far North of Canada, true north can be either east or west of magnetic north. In parts of Michigan, Indiana, Ohio, Kentucky, Tennessee, and North and South Carolina, however, magnetic north and true north coincide. In areas of North America to the east of those states, true north is west of magnetic north, but to the west of them, true

Aiming off.

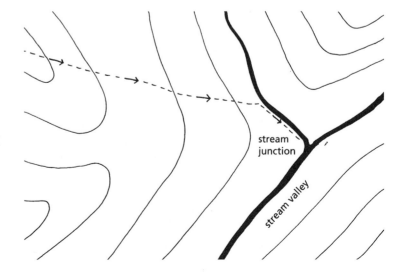

stream
junction

stream valley

north is east of magnetic north. The declination is usually marked on topo maps. For example, the the National Geographic TOPO maps for Olympic National Park give the declination in 2010 as 17 degrees east. Just to confuse matters further, magnetic north isn't stationary but moves in a (luckily) predictable pattern. The declination on an old map will not reflect the current position of magnetic north. When you buy a map, it's wise to check the date as well as the declination. In 2010, I bought Forest Service topo maps of the Pasayten and Salmo-Priest Wilderness Areas dated 1991 and 1993 respectively. The declinations were given as 19 and 20 degrees east. In fact, in 2010, they were 16 and 17 degrees east. Some maps list the rate of change so you can work out the current figure. If your map isn't new and doesn't show the rate of change, you may be able to find it in a trail guide. You also can calculate the magnetic variation yourself by taking a bearing from one known feature to another, recording the bearing (without taking any declination into account) and then taking the same bearing from the map. The difference between the two is the current declination. If you stick a piece of tape on the compass as a declination mark, you won't have to recompute it every time you use the compass. You will have to remember to move it if you visit different areas, though. Some compasses come with adjustable declination marks.

In the eastern United States, because magnetic north lies west of true north, when you take a bearing from the map you add the declination figure. However, if your bearing is taken from the ground and transferred to the map (not something you're likely to do often), you subtract the declination. A mnemonic for remembering this is "empty sea, add water"—MTC (map to compass), add. Of course, in western states the oppo-

site applies; you subtract declination when taking a bearing from the map and add it when taking one from the ground.

There's always an element of error in any compass work. If your bearing is 5 degrees off, then you'll be 335 feet off the correct line of travel after walking 0.6 mile, 650 feet after 1.2 miles, and more than half a mile after 6.2 miles. This makes it difficult to find a precise spot that lies some distance from your starting point unless you can take a bearing on some intermediate feature. One of the few compass techniques I use, other than straightforward bearings, is *aiming off*, which is especially handy in poor visibility. If your destination lies on or near an easy-to-find line such as a stream, you can make a deliberate error and aim to hit a line on one side or the other of your destination. When you reach the line, you know which way to turn to reach your destination. I used aiming off on a large scale in the Canadian Rockies. I knew that hundreds of miles somewhere to the northwest was the little town of Tumbler Ridge, which I wanted to reach, and that a road ran roughly east-west to the town. By heading north rather than northwest, I knew I'd hit the road east of Tumbler Ridge, and after a week's walking I did—and found myself 46 miles away. But I knew where the town was, and, more important, where I was.

The compass has other, more complex uses; you'll find instructions for them in good navigation books. Don't rely on your compass blindly, though. There are areas high in iron ore where a compass won't work.

Keep your compass where you can reach it easily; otherwise you might be tempted to skip checking it when you're unsure of your direction. As I've learned, this can mean retracing your steps a considerable distance. Like most people,

I have a loop of cord attached to my compass (most come with small holes in the baseplate for this purpose), though I don't often hang it around my neck. I may tie the loop to a zipper pull on a garment pocket so that I don't lose the compass and can refer to it quickly whenever I want to.

GPS

GPS (global positioning system) is a government-operated system that consists of twenty-eight satellites 12,000 miles up, four of them used for backup. Each satellite orbits earth twice a day and sends out a continuous signal, giving its position and the time. By locking onto a minimum of four satellites, a GPS receiver on the ground can *triangulate* its position. An accurate fix may not be obtainable if the satellites aren't in the right align-

ment, however. Also, there must be a line of sight between the receiver and the satellites; it can be impossible to get a fix in dense forest or below steep cliffs.

Using electronic gadgets like GPS in the wilderness is frowned on by some. Whatever you think about the place of electronics in the wilds, one thing is clear: they won't go away. Indeed, their use will increase as more devices designed for wilderness use are developed. It is futile to debate whether the wilds are an appropriate place for such technology. The point is to look at electronic devices exactly as we would any other new gear: to consider what purpose they serve and just how useful they are. After all, they're only tools, like packs or stoves.

I've tried a number of GPS units, but this is an area of rapid development, so before buying a unit I'd recommend getting up-to-date expert advice. GPSinformation.net is the Web site for such information.

GPS receivers have become increasingly user-friendly and practical, so much so that the most advanced ones can be used as stand-alone navigation devices (though a map and compass are

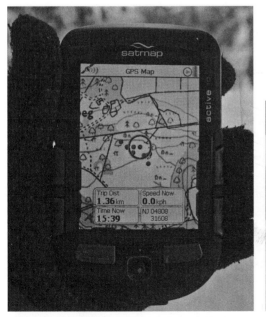

The Satmap Active 10 GPS is waterproof and shockproof, so no case or cover is needed.

Smartphone used as a GPS with ViewRanger software showing topo map and user's position.

GPS: MY CHOICE

Of the stand-alone GPS receivers I've tried, my favorite is the Satmap Active 10 because it's waterproof and shockproof and has a large screen—2.7 inches by 2 inches. It runs off either three AAs or a proprietary lithium polymer battery. Battery life depends on the type of batteries with lithium AAs, and the lithium polymer battery having the longest life—fifteen to eighteen hours. The weight with the lithium polymer battery is 8.1 ounces. There's no touch screen, just large controls that are fairly easy to operate with cold fingers or when wearing gloves. Instead of downloading maps, they are supplied on SD cards. There are six main screens and many options, making this quite a complex device. Even so, it's fairly intuitive, and the basics can be picked up quickly.

However, as I carry a smartphone anyway, I now mostly use this as a GPS with ViewRanger software (app). This can be used with most smartphones, including iPhones. Maps can be downloaded from the ViewRanger Web site. On the Pacific Northwest Trail, I found that ViewRanger does everything I require from GPS mapping. In fact, it was a delight to use. The control icons are small and unobtrusive and only need to be visible when required, so the map can fill the whole screen. Tracks can be recorded, and routes created, and there's a trip menu that gives details of distance, speed, time taken, altitude, direction, and more. ViewRanger also works with the phone's camera so you can see where you took them on the map. The HTC Desire GPS picked up signals quickly and was as good as any stand-alone GPS I've used.

show your location. Lines of waypoints could be put into the receiver and followed, or you could record your route and follow it back, but there was no actual map and so no information on the topography or any important features. Paralleling the development of GPS was the growth of computer mapping, and the two were soon linked, so you could plan routes on a map on the computer then download them to a GPS unit and also download routes back onto the computer map after a day out. Then technology was introduced so that maps could be viewed on the GPS receiver's screen in full color. This was a breakthrough and has made GPS far easier to use. Instead of struggling to transfer the grid reference from the GPS unit to a paper map, which can be difficult in a storm, you just glance at the screen, and there is your position on the map. There are now many mapping GPS units available. These mostly use proprietary software so you can't use other companies' mapping even though the maps are often identical.

While all this was going on in the outdoor, GPS and computer-mapping world GPS receivers began appearing in mobile phones, especially smartphones, and were quickly followed by mapping applications. At first these were just road maps, but then topographical maps appeared; so now, with the right software, you don't need a separate GPS receiver if you have a smartphone (or an iPad, and undoubtedly other tablet devices in the future). All the functions found on GPS receivers are present. With any phone, what matters is that it has an in-built GPS receiver and doesn't rely on signals from phone masts to show your location, so that it will work where there is no phone signal. This is becoming more common, but you do need to check to be sure this feature is included.

still very useful, and I wouldn't recommend going without these). Not so many years ago, GPS receivers all had black-and-white screens and just provided latitude and longitude or UTM coordinates that had to be plotted on a map to

This convergence of GPS receivers, mobile phones, and computer mapping is exciting and innovative. It really feels as though satellite navigation for the outdoors has finally come of age. The process isn't complete (and I'm sure there will be new so-far-unthought-of developments to come).

One argument against using a smartphone as a GPS is that smartphones aren't designed for outdoor use. Outdoor GPS receivers are usually shock resistant, weather resistant, and overall very tough. Most mobile phones aren't, being designed for urban life rather than the hills, and so need more care and protection. That said, I took my HTC Desire on the Pacific Northwest Trail, stored in an Aloksak bag in a small padded pouch, and it survived fine. In rain, I used the phone inside the Aloksak bag, so it never got wet. Since I bought the Desire, the first smartphone designed for outdoor use has appeared—the Motorola Defy, which is dust, shock, water, and scratch resistant. As well as a GPS, it has a 5-megapixel camera and all the other smartphone features. It weighs 4.1 ounces. I'm sure there will be other similar phones.

While I am enthusiastic about these new navigation options as they make navigation so much easier, I am also realistic. There are disadvantages, and they don't totally replace map and compass. Operating tiny buttons and delicate touch screens when it's cold is difficult. (Touch screens can't be used with ordinary gloves. However, gloves with special electroconductive material on the finger and thumb tips are appearing, such as the Manzella Sprint TouchTip Glove and PowerStretch TouchTip Glove, which are made from thin stretch fleece and have a grip pattern on the palm.) Although phone screens have grown larger, they can still only show a small area. (One reason I chose the HTC Desire was for the larger

than average screen—3.7-inch diagonal.) You can zoom out, but then detail is lost. I find that using a GPS map in conjunction with a larger paper map is the best approach. Battery life is also a potential problem. If you just switch the device on occasionally to find your position, batteries can last a very long time. If you keep it switched on for navigating or to record your route, batteries may barely last a day's walk. And if you use other features such as camera, radio, music player, Internet access, and more, batteries can fade quickly. This is a particular temptation with a GPS phone that can also be your entertainment in the evening. The next day, you might find the batteries dead. One answer is to ensure you have spare batteries if you have a device whose batteries can be changed. Some have built-in rechargeable batteries that can't be removed. I chose the HTC Desire in part because the battery can be replaced with a fresh one when you can't charge it. This can't be done with the iPhone. I took three batteries (weighing 3 ounces in total) on the Pacific Northwest Trail and found that one would last a week if I switched the wi-fi off and only used the GPS for short periods of time and the camera very occasionally. Leaving the GPS on to record a track, the battery lasts seven to eight hours. It's also worth turning off any applications not needed and turning down the screen brightness, which uses a great deal of power. Sounds and vibrating alerts can be turned off, too—I always do this, anyway, as I find beeps and tremors irritating. Most devices have power-saving options too. Just check that the low power options will allow track recording or other applications to function.

As well as showing your position, GPS receivers can tell you a host of information: trip distance, speed (current and average), trip time (which can be split into time moving and stationary), altitude, direction headed, direction to next location, time to next location, GPS accuracy, and much more. They also function as clocks with not just the time but also the date and the time of sunset and sunrise. In conjunction with PLBs and satellite communicators like SPOT, GPS can be used for emergency signaling.

A route can be made by linking together a series of locations, usually known as *waypoints*. The GPS will guide you along this route. And if you record your track and need to retrace your steps, this track can be turned into a route so you can follow it back. The whole time you can see exactly where you are on the map. Using GPS like this means walking with the receiver in hand and consulting it regularly. This uses battery power and is unnecessary most of the time. I mostly use the GPS to verify my position or when I need to know exactly where I am. I've used it like this in whiteouts and blizzards in featureless, snow-covered terrain, and it is reassuring to have the GPS confirm you are where you think you are. On the Pacific Northwest Trail, I used the GPS whenever I found locating the correct route with map and compass difficult, as it made route-finding much easier and quicker. A few times I used it to find junctions with disused trails hidden in dense vegetation. To find these junctions, I would switch on the GPS and the ViewRanger mapping software and follow the route on the screen map until I had reached the right point. Usually there was no sign of the trail, but after I had followed its line a short distance, signs of it would appear. A few times I followed the GPS map for an hour or so, but mostly it was for less than half an hour.

Outdoor-mapping GPS units are available from Garmin, Magellan, Lowrance, Satmap, and Delorme. All these companies can also supply maps for different countries.

Altimeters

Knowing the altitude can be useful in mountainous terrain, and glancing at a wrist altimeter is a quick way to do this. Although I don't regard it as essential, I use an altimeter regularly, especially when hiking cross-country.

On an ascent, knowing the height and the time means you can monitor progress and work out how long it will take to reach the top. If you know the height at which you need to leave a ridge or start an ascent from a wooded valley, an altimeter will tell you when you reach that point. During a long traverse on steep, difficult terrain during a ski tour in the High Sierra, I could see from the map that the only safe descent to the valley was through a tiny notch that led into a wide, shallow gully. By using the altimeter I was able to ski through trees in growing darkness directly into the notch. It would have been much harder to find by map and compass alone.

A wrist altimeter for navigation. The Suunto Altimax.

Altimeters come in two types, ones that work by barometric pressure and ones that work from GPS. Barometric altimeters work by translating changes in air pressure into vertical height. To maintain accuracy, they must be reset at known heights. Temperature changes can cause inaccurate altimeter readings. The best altimeters are temperature compensated, but the least expensive ones usually aren't. The best way to minimize inaccuracies is to avoid temperature variations by keeping the altimeter at the same temperature as the outside air. For quick reference, you can wear a wrist altimeter on the outside of your jacket. GPS altimeters can only be relied on to give a rough estimate of altitude. They may be spot-on, but they could be hundreds of feet out. For this reason, some GPS receivers have a barometric altimeter as well and use the two together to produce a more accurate result. The reason for the lack of guaranteed accuracy with GPS altimeters is quite technical and has to do with the geometry of the satellites. For a detailed explanation, see GPS Information, http://gpsinformation.net/main/altitude.htm. In my experience of regularly using both types of altimeter, barometric ones are more reliable as long as they are reset often at known heights.

I have two wrist-altimeters, the 1.9-ounce Suunto Altimax and the smaller but slightly heavier 2.6-ounce Highgear Alterra (the weight difference is because the Altimax has a plastic case, the Alterra a metal one). Both will measure the altitude from deep in the ocean to above the summit of Everest, which should cover all eventualities. They'll also record data, such as the amount of ascent and the time taken, which is useful for planning future trips, and tell you the rate of ascent and descent, which is useful for timing your progress (though it can be depress-ing when you calculate just how long it will take to reach the next pass—sometimes it's better not to know). I also have altimeters on my GPS and my Kestrel 4500 Weather Meter, so I don't really need an altimeter watch as well. However, as I like to have a watch on my wrist I can quickly refer to for both time and altitude, I still use one. On the Pacific Northwest Trail, I carried all three and used the Alterra most, followed by the Kestrel, which I checked at rest stops and in camp. When I checked all three, they rarely disagreed by more than 20 feet. When they did, it was because the weather was changing rapidly.

Navigating by Natural Phenomena

There are many ways to navigate without a map or compass, but I habitually use only two—the sun and the wind, and then only as backups. Knowing where they should be in relation to my route means I'm quick to notice if their position has shifted. If I've veered off my intended line of travel—easy to do in rolling grassland or continuous forest—I stop and check my location. I also check that the wind hasn't shifted and see what the time is so that I know where the sun should be.

Learning More

There are many helpful books for those who want to learn more about navigational techniques. The classic is *Be Expert with Map and Compass* by Björn Kjellström; a good modern one is David Seidman's *Essential Wilderness Navigator*. And on GPS, Stephen W. Hinch's *Outdoor Navigation with GPS* is up to date. To learn more than these books can teach, you'll need to take a course at an outdoor center or join an orienteering club.

Right: Trail markers. Know what they mean, but please refrain from making your own—you might confuse future hikers. Below: A cairn or duck marks the line of a trail. Bottom: Tree blazes also show the line of a trail.

| cairn | paint | metal badge | signs | blaze |

Waymarks and Signposts

Paint splashes, piles of stones (called cairns, or ducks), blazes on trees, posts, and other devices mark trails and routes throughout the world. (In Norway, wilderness ski routes are marked out with lines of birch sticks.) These *waymarks*, combined with signposts at trail junctions, make finding many routes easy, but I have mixed feelings about them—part of me dislikes them intensely as unnecessary intrusions into the wilderness; another part of me follows them gladly when they loom up on a misty day. But waymarking of routes doesn't mean you can do without map and compass or the skills to use them. Useful though it is, I would not like to see waymarking increase. I'd rather find my own way through the wilderness, and I don't build cairns or cut blazes, let alone paint rocks. In fact, I often knock down cairns that have appeared where there were none before, knowing that if they are left, a trail will soon follow. Painting waymarks in hitherto unspoiled terrain is vandalism. On a weeklong hike in the Western Highlands of Scotland, I was horrified to discover a series of large red paint splashes daubed on boulders all the way down a 3,300-foot

Trail sign at a junction with distances to trailheads and other trails. Mazatzal Mountains, Arizona.

mountain spur that is narrow enough for the way to be clear. There wasn't even a trail on this ridge before. Now it has been defiled with paint that leaps out from the subtle colors of heather, mist, and lichen-covered rock. May the culprit wander forever lost in a howling Highland wind, never able to locate a single spot of paint!

Guidebooks

There are two kinds of wilderness guidebooks: area guides and trail guides. The first give a general overview, providing information on possible routes, weather, seasons, hazards, natural history, and so on. Often lavishly illustrated, they are usually far too heavy to carry in your pack. I find such books interesting when I return from an area and want to find out more about some of the places I've visited and things I've seen. They're also nice to daydream over. An example is my own *Scotland* in Cicerone Press's World Mountain Ranges series.

Trail guides are designed as adjuncts to maps. Indeed, some of them include the topographic maps you need for a specific location. If you want to follow a trail precisely, they're very useful, though your sense of discovery is diminished when you know in advance about everything you'll see along the way. Some cover only specific trails; others are miniature area guides, with route suggestions and general information. Most popular destinations or routes have a trail guide, and many have several. Since trail guides frequently contain up-to-date information not found on maps, I often carry one, especially if I'm visiting an area for the first time. An increasing number of guidebooks are available as e-books that you can download and use on your smartphone or e-book reader, reducing the weight greatly.

There are a vast number of guidebooks. Good trail guides include the *100 Classic Hikes* series from Mountaineers (mountaineersbooks.com); the *50 Hikes* series from Countryman (countryman press.com); the Sierra Nevada guides from Wilderness Press (wildernesspress.com); the Sierra Club's guides (sierraclub.org/books), which cover areas from the Smoky Mountains to the Grand Canyon; and the hiking guides from Falcon which cover a selection of states and wild areas. The Appalachian Mountain Club's *White Mountain Guide*, now in its twenty-eighth edition, is a classic for this region. Lonely Planet (lonelyplanet.com) has an increasing number of good hiking guides, including excellent ones to the High Sierra and Yellowstone and Grand Teton National Parks, as well as a good overseas travel guide series. Cicerone Press has a worldwide selection of useful hiking guides covering everything from day hikes to long backpacking routes such as the Pacific Crest Trail, the Arctic Circle Trail in Greenland, and many in the Alps and Pyrenees. I used Cicerone's *GR20: Corsica* by

SORT OF LOST

On the Pacific Crest Trail, two of us mislaid the trail in the northern Sierra Nevada after a "short-cut" took us off the map. The evening this happened we "camped above a river we think may lead to Blue Lake" (journal entry, June 22, 1982), the lake being the next feature we expected to recognize. My rather confused journal entry for June 23 describes what happened next: "Took three hours before we were back on the trail and even then we weren't sure where. We must have been farther north and east than we thought. The hill we thought was the Nipple wasn't and when we'd finally given up trying to reach it we found ourselves traversing the real Nipple just after I'd been talking about Alice in *Through the Looking Glass* only reaching the hilltop by walking away from it."

We didn't know we were back on the Pacific Crest Trail until we found a trail marker telling us so. Once we knew exactly where on the trail we were, all the other features fell into place, and the terrain we'd been crossing suddenly made sense. That's when we realized we couldn't reach the peak we were seeking because we were already on it!

On Being "Lost"

What constitutes being lost is a moot point. Some people feel lost if they don't know to the yard exactly where they are, even if they know which side of which mountain they're on, or which valley they're in. It's possible to "lose" a trail you're following, but that doesn't mean you're lost.

I think it's very hard to become totally lost when traveling on foot; I've never managed it. I was "unsure of my whereabouts" during the week I spent in thick forest in the foothills of the Canadian Rockies, but I knew my general position, and I knew which direction to walk to get to where I wanted to go. Although I couldn't pinpoint my position on a map (indeed, I couldn't locate myself to within twenty-five miles in any direction, and I've never been able to retrace my route on a map), I wasn't lost, because I didn't allow myself to think I was. Being lost is a state of mind.

The state of mind to avoid is panic. Terrified hikers have been known to abandon their packs in order to run in search of a place they recognize, only to die from a fall or of hypothermia. As long as you have your pack, you have food and shelter and can survive, so you needn't worry. I've spent many nights out when I didn't know precisely where I was. But I had the equipment to survive comfortably, so it didn't matter. A camp in the wilderness is a camp in the wilderness, whether it's at a well-used, well-posted site or on the banks of a river you can't identify.

The first thing to do if you suspect you're off course is to *stop and think*. Where might you have gone wrong? Check the map. Then, if you think you can, try to retrace your steps to a point you recognize or can identify. If you don't think you can do that, use the map to figure out how to get from where you are (you always know the area

Paddy Dillon when I hiked that route and found it excellent (I also met the author along the way, researching a new edition). Bradt (bradt-travelguides.com) publishes a series of invaluable trekking guides to remote places, from South America to Spitsbergen.

The big three long-distance trails all have detailed guidebooks. Those on the Appalachian Trail are published by the Appalachian Trail Conservancy, those on the Continental Divide Trail by the Continental Divide Trail Society and the Continental Divide Trail Alliance, those on the Pacific Crest Trail by Wilderness Press, which also publishes a guide to the John Muir Trail.

Ed Huesers checking his GPS unit on a ski tour in the Wind River Range, Wyoming. Before the trip, Ed downloaded waypoints and possible igloo sites to the GPS device.

you're in, even if it's a huge area) to where you want to be. It may be easiest to head directly for a major destination, such as a road or town, as I did in the foothills of the Canadian Rockies, rather than trying to find trails or smaller features. Often it's a matter of heading in the right direction, knowing that eventually you'll reach somewhere you want to be.

I don't mind not knowing exactly where I am—sometimes I enjoy it. There's a sense of freedom in not being able to predict what lies over the next ridge, where the next lake is, and where the next valley leads. I enjoy the release of wandering through what is, from my perspective, uncharted territory. I never intend to lose myself, but when it happens I view it as an opportunity rather than a problem.

COPING WITH TERRAIN

On and Off Trail

As long as you stick to good, regularly used trails, you should have no problems with terrain except for the occasional badly eroded section. Don't assume that because a trail is marked boldly on a map it will be clear and well maintained. Sometimes the trail won't be visible at all; other times it may start off clearly, then fade away, becoming harder to follow the deeper into the wilderness you go. Trail guides and ranger stations are the best places to find out about specific trail conditions, but even their information can be inaccurate.

Many people never leave well-marked trails, feeling that cross-country travel is simply too difficult and too slow. They're missing a great deal. Going cross-country differs from trail walking and requires a different approach. The joys of off-trail travel lie in the contact it gives you with the country you pass through. The 15-to-20-inch dirt strip that constitutes a trail holds the raw, untouched wilderness a little at bay. Once you step off it, the difficulties you will encounter should be accepted as belonging to that experience. You can't expect to cover the same distance you would on a trail or to always find a campsite before dark. Uncertainty is one of the joys of off-trail travel, part of the escape from straight lines and the prison of the known.

Learning the nature of the country you're in is very important. Once you've spent a little time in an area—maybe no more than a few hours—you should be able to start interpreting the terrain and modifying your plans accordingly. In the northern Canadian Rockies, I learned that black spruce forest meant muskeg swamps so difficult to cross that it was worth a detour of any length to avoid them; if the map showed a narrow valley, I knew it would be swampy, so I would climb the hillside and contour above the swamps; if it showed a wide valley, I would head for the creek because there probably would be shingle banks I

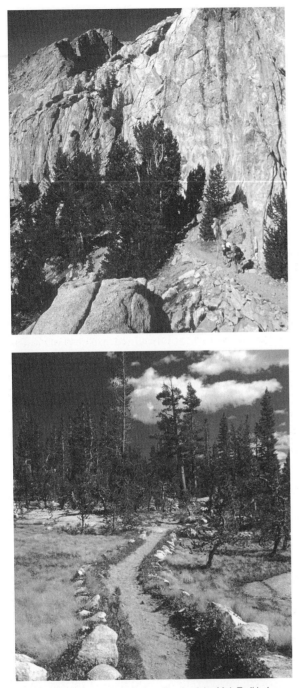

Top: A well-constructed mountain trail—the John Muir Trail below Selden Pass. Note the rocks lining the trail to keep it in place and the smooth tread. Above: A trail through a meadow edged with stones.

could walk on by the forest edge. It's useful to be able to survey the land ahead from a hillside or ridge—for which binoculars are well worth their weight—and I often plan the next few hours' route from a hilltop.

Compared with walking on trails, cross-country travel is real exploration, both of the world around and of yourself. To appreciate it fully you need to be open to whatever may happen. Distances and time matter far less once you've shrugged off the trail network. What matters is being there.

The Steep and the Rough

Steep slopes can be unnerving, especially on descents. If you're not comfortable going straight down and there's no trail, take a switchback route across the slopes. Look for small flatter areas where you can rest and work out the next leg of the descent. Making a careful survey of the slope before you start down is always wise. Work out routes between small cliffs and drop-offs.

Slopes of stones and boulders, known as *talus*, occur on mountainsides the world over, usually between timberline and the cliffs above. Trails across them are usually cleared and flattened, though you may still find the going tricky. Balance is the key to crossing rough terrain, and trekking poles are a great help, though you need to be sure they don't get caught between two rocks. Cross large boulder fields slowly and carefully, testing each step and trying not to slip. Unstable boulders, which may move as you put your weight on them, can easily tip you over. The key to good balance is to keep your weight over your feet, which means not leaning back when descending and not leaning into the slope when traversing.

You may go crazy trying not to slip on the smallest stones, known as *scree*, though, so you

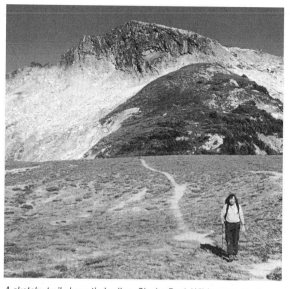

A sketchy trail above timberline. Glacier Peak Wilderness, North Cascades. Keep an eye on the map in areas where trails vanish.

for any distance. You may think that traversing around minor summits and bumps on mountain-ridge walks will require less effort than going up or down, but in my experience it won't. (Still, I'm frequently drawn to traversing. Heed my words, not my practice!)

In general, treat steep slopes with caution. If you feel uncomfortable with the angle or the ground under your feet, retreat and find a safer way. Backpacking isn't rock climbing, though it's surprising what you can get up and down with a heavy pack if you have a good head for heights and a little skill. *Don't climb what you can't descend* unless you can see that your way is clear beyond the obstacle. And remember that you can use a length of cord to pull up or lower your pack if necessary.

However, it's unwise to drop packs down a slope; they may go farther than you intend. Bad route finding once left two of us at the top of a steep, loose, and broken limestone cliff in Glacier National Park in Montana; foolishly, we decided to descend rather than turn back, and it took us several hours of heart-stopping scrambling to reach the base. At one point my companion

just have to let your feet slide. Some people like to run down scree—a fast way to descend—but the practice damages scree slopes so quickly that it should no longer be indulged—too much scree running turns slopes into slippery, dangerous ribbons of dirt embedded with rocks. Be very careful if you can't see the bottom of a scree slope—it may end at the edge of a cliff. Because climbing, descending, or crossing a scree slope without dislodging stones is impossible, a group should move at an angle or in an arrowhead formation so that no one is directly under anyone else. Because other groups may be crossing below you, if a stone does start rolling you should shout a warning—"*Rock!*" is the standard call. If you hear this, *do not look up*, even though you'll be tempted to. Instead, cover your head with your pack or your hands.

Traversing steep, trailless slopes is tiring and puts great strain on the feet, ankles, and hips. It's preferable to climb to a ridge or flat terrace, or descend to a valley, rather than to traverse a slope

Watch your footing on narrow trails on steep, rocky mountainsides like this one in the Ochil Hills, Scotland.

Left: A ladder takes a trail over a rock slab in the White Mountains, New Hampshire. Middle: A line of rocks marking where a trail crosses a large rock slab. Right: When descending a steep, rocky ridge—like this one on King's Peak, Uinta Mountains, Utah—take short steps and watch for loose rocks.

Right: A narrow trail on a steep, vegetated mountainside. Glacier Peak Wilderness, North Cascades. Above: Scrambling requires good balance and a good head for heights.

decided he could safely lower his pack to the next ledge, even though he would have to drop it the last few feet. The pack bounced off that ledge and a few more before being halted by a tree two hundred feet or so below. Amazingly, nothing broke—not even the skis strapped to the pack. If we'd lost the pack or the contents had been destroyed, we would have had serious problems.

Snow

Much of what I just said about traversing rock slopes applies to crossing snow. However, you may come upon small but steep and icy snow-fields in summer when you aren't carrying an ice ax or crampons. Having a staff or trekking poles makes it easier to balance across snow on small holds kicked with the edge of your boots, though you shouldn't attempt this if there is dangerous ground below the snow slope, since you can't stop a slide with a staff. Without a support, take great care and, if possible, look for a way around a snow slope, even if it involves descending or climbing.

The trail may be buried in snow, but trail signs can still point the way.

Bushwhacking

"Bushwhacking" is the apt word for thrashing through thick brush and scrambling over fallen trees while thorny bushes tear at your clothes and pack. It's the hardest form of "walking" I know, and it's to be avoided whenever possible—though sometimes you have no choice. On the Pacific Northwest Trail, there are some cross-country sections where the bushwhacking is desperate—

Left: A slightly overgrown forest trail. Glacier Peak Wilderness.
Above: Trekking poles are useful for balance in thick, rough vegetation, especially on sloping terrain.

endless-seeming thrashes through tangled, twisted bushes on steep slopes on which I came to hate the otherwise pretty and delicate-looking vine maples, whose long, flexible, but tough branches tripped me regularly. Ron Strickland, the man behind the PNT, calls it "bucking the brush."

Bushwhacking takes a long time and a lot of energy, with very little distance to show for it; half a mile per hour can be good progress. Climbing high above dense vegetation and wading up rivers are both preferable to prolonged bushwhacking. But if you like to strike out across country, bushwhacking eventually will be essential.

Bushwhacking can be necessary even during ski tours. On one occasion in the Algäu Alps, four of us descended from a high pass into a valley. The snow wasn't deep enough to fully cover the dense willow scrub that spread over the lower slopes and rose a yard or two high. Luckily the scrub didn't spread very far, but skiing through it was a desperate struggle, since the springy branches constantly knocked us over and caught at our poles and bindings.

Unmaintained trails can quickly become overgrown, too. I made the mistake of wearing shorts while descending one in the Grand Canyon; the upper part of the trail ran through dense thickets of thorny bushes and small trees, and my legs were soon bloody. It was quite a relief to reach the desert farther down, where at least the cacti and yuccas were widely spaced.

MINIMIZING IMPACT

A trail is a scar on the landscape, albeit a minor one. But where there is a trail, walk on it. Cross-country travel is for areas where there are no trails. Don't parallel a trail in order to experience off-trail walking. Most damage is caused when

A multichannel trail in need of restoration.

A steep switchbacking trail, High Sierra.

A boardwalk built to allow ground damaged by too many hooves and boots to recover.

walkers walk along the edges or just off a trail, widening it and destroying the vegetation alongside. Always stick to the trail, even if it means walking in mud.

On slopes, you should always use the switchbacks. Too many hillsides have been badly damaged by people shortcutting switchbacks, creating new, steeper routes that quickly become water channels. In meadows and alpine terrain, where it's easy to walk anywhere, multiple trails often appear where people have walked several abreast. In such terrain, you should follow the main trail, if you can figure out which it is, and walk single file. When snow blocks part of a trail, try to follow the line where the trail would be; don't create a new trail by walking around the edge of a snow patch unless you need to do so for safety.

When you walk cross-country, your aim must be to leave no sign of your passing—that means no marking with blazes, cairns, or subtle signs like broken twigs unless they're removed later. It also means avoiding fragile surfaces where possible, walking around damp meadows, and staying off soft vegetation. Rock, snow, and nonvegetated surfaces suffer the least damage; gravel banks of rivers and streams are regularly washed clean by floods and snowmelt, so walking on them causes no harm.

It would take a skilled tracker to follow a good solo walker's cross-country route. Groups have a more difficult time leaving no sign of their passage. The answer is to keep groups small and to spread out, taking care not to step in each other's boot prints. As few as four sets of boots can leave

Left: Boardwalks to protect soft, wet ground on a trail in the White Mountains, New Hampshire. Right: Hiking along the smooth slabs beside a creek when going cross-country in rocky mountain terrain.

the beginnings of a trail that others may follow in fragile meadows and tundra. Where these new trails have started to appear, walk well away from them so you don't help in their creation. The aim should be to use obvious trails but not make new ones or expand signs of faint ones.

In many areas, land-management agencies maintain and repair trails, often using controversial methods. However, wide, eroded scars made by thousands of boots (and sometimes hooves) hardly create a feeling of wilderness either. Unfortunately, some popular trails may be saved only by employing drastic regulations. Walkers can help by following trail-management instructions, staying off closed sections, and accepting artificial surfaces as necessary in places.

Generally, when walking cross-country you should always consider your impact on the terrain and pick the route that will cause least damage.

WILDERNESS HAZARDS

Weather

Most outdoor hazards are caused by the weather. Wind, rain, snow, thunderstorms, freezing temperatures, thaws, and heat waves all introduce difficulties or dangers. Coping with weather is the reason backpackers need tents, sleeping bags, and other equipment.

With a little knowledge you can often predict the weather at least a few hours ahead, though you can't compete with expert meteorologists using satellite images and computers. For any given trip, knowing in general what weather to expect should be part of your trip planning. Area guides, local information offices, and ranger stations are the places to get details of regional weather patterns.

For a specific day, check Internet, radio, television, and newspaper forecasts if you can; park and forest service ranger stations often post daily weather forecasts. If you don't see one, inquire. If you monitor forecasts for an area you visit regularly, you'll soon be able to develop an annual weather overview. If you're going to an unfamiliar area, checking weather patterns for some time in advance can give you an idea of what to expect. Before I hiked the Arizona Trail I followed Web weather reports for several months so I knew that it had been dry even by Arizona standards. I also knew that the first real storm for months was due about the time I reached Arizona, so I wasn't too surprised (though delighted) to land in Phoenix in pouring rain.

Even the most detailed recent forecast can be wrong. Regional patterns can mean rain in one valley and sun in another just over the hill. Mountains are particularly notorious for creating their own weather. Weather has less impact on travel over low-level and below-timberline routes—if it rains, you don rain gear; if it's windy, you keep an eye out for falling trees.

High up, however, a strong wind can make walking impossible, and rain may turn to snow. On any mountain walk you should be prepared to descend early or take a lower route if the weather worsens. Struggling on into the teeth of a blizzard when you don't have to is foolish and risky. It even may be necessary to sit out bad weather for a day or more. I've done so on a few occasions and have been surprised at how fast the time passes.

Weather Forecasting

Observation is the key to short-term weather forecasting. Watch out for slight changes. Which way are the clouds moving? What type of clouds are they? Thickening clouds can mean rain, thinning ones sun. Fast-approaching clouds may mean a storm soon. What direction is the wind blowing? Has it shifted, and if so which way? How strong is it? Any big change in the direction or strength of the wind suggests a change in the weather. Knowing the air pressure can greatly increase the accuracy of your forecasts. If the pressure is rising, dry weather is likely; if it's falling, wet weather is probably on the way. The faster the rate of change, the quicker the weather will change. All altimeters are barometers and so can be used for forecasting. They have to be kept at the same altitude, however, so camp is the best place to do this. I set the altitude when I reach camp, then note the barometer reading. Next morning I check the barometer again and look at the overnight pattern. It's heartening to see that the pressure is rising after several days of bad weather. Unfortunately, the opposite also is true.

For many years, I have carried a small weather data recorder. My current one, which I expect to last for many years, is the Kestrel 4000 Weather Meter, which weighs 3.75 ounces with two AA batteries (which last an astonishing amount of time—400 hours according to Kestrel). The Kestrel 4000 is a sophisticated instrument that measures and records current, average, and maximum wind speeds; temperature; wind chill; barometric pressure; the pressure trend; altitude; relative humidity; dew point; temperature; and wet-bulb temperature. With it you can keep a record of the wind speed and also discover just what various wind speeds mean when hiking and when camping. I now know that wind speeds above 30 mph are uncomfortable to walk in, so if the forecast is for speeds above that I plan on sticking to sheltered ground. I also know that a gusty 20 mph wind can

rattle most tents. The humidity and temperature readings are useful, too. (I now know there can be a huge difference in humidity between the floor and peak of a tent, showing that vents should be high up.) By recording data from the Kestrel 4000 I can build up a picture of the weather in areas I visit often and know what to expect at different times of year. Of course, notes can be used for the same purpose, but knowing that the average nighttime temperature was 25°F (−4°C) with a low of 20°F (−7°C) and the average wind speed was 35 mph with gusts to 45 tells me much more than notes that say "frosty" for each morning and "windy" or even "very windy" for each day.

An excellent book on weather in the backcountry is *Weathering the Wilderness*, by William E. Reifsnyder. It's long out of print but well worth seeking out, as nothing anywhere near as good has been published since. It describes the weather you can expect in the Sierra, Cascades, Rockies, Appa-

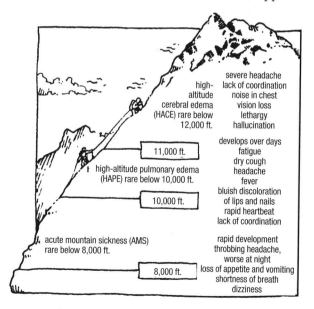

The possible effects of altitude.

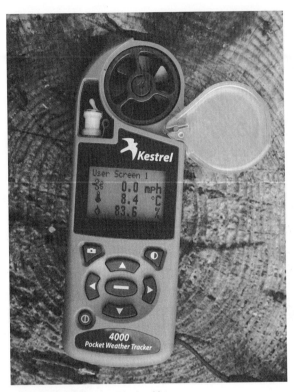

The Kestrel 4000 Pocket Weather Meter.

lachians, Olympics, and the Great Lakes Basin at different times of year and includes tables covering temperature, rainfall, and hours of sunshine. It also explains weather patterns and has photographs of cloud types.

Altitude

As you go higher, atmospheric pressure lessens, making it harder for your body to extract oxygen from the air. This may result in *acute mountain sickness* (AMS), typified by headaches, fatigue, loss of appetite, dizziness, and a generally awful feeling. AMS rarely occurs at altitudes below 8,000 feet, so many backpackers never need worry

about it. But if you do ascend high enough and experience AMS, the only immediate remedy is to descend. If you don't, the effects usually pass in a few days.

To minimize the chances of AMS, acclimatize slowly by gaining altitude gradually. If you're starting out from a high point, you can aid acclimatization by spending a night there before setting off. It's also important to drink plenty of fluids—dehydration is reckoned to worsen altitude sickness. Most backpackers won't get higher than the 14,000 feet of the Sierra or the Rockies; spending three or four days hiking at 6,000 to 8,000 feet should minimize altitude effects, but it's not always easy to do this. The altitude where you sleep is important too; if you sleep below 8,000 feet you can ascend to 14,000 feet without much likelihood of altitude sickness.

The only time I've suffered from mountain sickness was when I took a cable car up to 10,600 feet on the Aiguille du Midi in the French Alps. The moment I stepped out of the cable car I felt dizzy and a little sick and had a bad headache. But we'd gone up in order to ski down, so I was soon feeling fine again.

Much more serious than AMS are *high-altitude cerebral edema* and *high-altitude pulmonary edema* (fluid buildup in the brain or lungs), which can be fatal. Cerebral edema rarely occurs below 12,000 feet; pulmonary rarely below 10,000 feet. Lack of coordination and chest noises are among the symptoms, but you may not be able to differentiate between AMS and edema. Your only course is to descend—quickly.

Medicine for Mountaineering, edited by James Wilkerson, includes a detailed discussion of high-altitude illness that is worth studying by those planning treks in high mountains.

Avalanche debris, High Sierra.

Avalanches

Avalanches are a threat to every snow traveler who ventures into mountainous terrain, more so for the skier than for the walker. In spring, great blocks of snow and gouged terrain stripped of trees mark avalanche paths and show the power of these snow slides. Avalanches can be predicted to some extent, and many mountain areas, especially those with ski resorts, post avalanche warnings. Heed them. Anyone heading into snow-covered mountains should study one of the many books on the subject. *Avalanche Safety for Skiers and Climbers*, by Tony Daffern, is one of the best for home study, while *The ABCs of Avalanche Safety*, by Sue Ferguson and E. R. LaChappelle, is light enough at 2 ounces to carry in the pack.

Lightning

Lightning is both spectacular and frightening. Thunderstorms can come in so fast that you can't reach shelter before they break (although I've learned that I can run very fast with a heavy pack when I'm scared enough). If you see thunderclouds building up or a distant storm approaching, head for safety immediately—don't wait until the thunder starts. In thunderstorms, avoid summits, ridge crests, tall trees, small stands of trees, shallow caves, lakeshores, and open meadows. Places to run to include low points in deep forests, near but not next to the bases of high cliffs, depressions in flat areas, and mountain huts (these are grounded with metal lightning cables). Remember that, statistically, being hit by lightning is very unlikely, though this may fail to comfort you when you're out in the open and the flashes seem to be bouncing all around.

During a storm, there's danger from ground currents radiating from a lightning strike; the closer to the strike you are, the greater the current. Wet surfaces can provide pathways for the current, which may also jump across short gaps rather than go through the ground. If part of your body bridges such a gap, some of the current will probably pass

In a lightning storm, beware of ground currents. Don't lie or sit on the ground. Instead, squat on an insulating mat, with your hands and arms off the ground. Put metal gear, such as framed packs and hiking poles, some distance away so they don't burn you if there's a nearby strike.

through it. Your heart, and therefore your torso, is the part of your body you most need to protect from electric shocks, so it's advisable to crouch with just your feet on your foam pad so that any ground current passes through your limbs only. I'd also keep away from damp patches of ground and wet gullies and rock cracks. Groups should spread out.

Metal can burn you after a nearby strike—if you're caught in a storm, move away from pack frames and tent poles. The most frightening storm I've encountered woke me in the middle of the night at a high and exposed camp in the Scottish Highlands; all I could do was huddle on my foam pad and wait for it to pass, while lightning flashed all around me.

Anyone who is hit by lightning and knocked unconscious should be given immediate mouth-to-mouth resuscitation if breathing or the heart have stopped.

Hypothermia

Hypothermia occurs when the body loses heat faster than it produces it. It can be a killer. The causes are wet and cold, abetted by hunger, fatigue, alcohol, and low morale. The initial symptoms are shivering, lethargy, and irritability, which develop into lack of coordination, collapse, coma, and death, sometimes very quickly.

Because wind whips away heat, especially from wet clothing, hypothermia can occur in temperatures well above freezing. Indeed, it is often in summer that unwary dayhikers get caught, venturing high into the mountains on a day that starts sunny but becomes cold and rainy. Too many people die or have to be rescued because they weren't equipped to deal with stormy weather.

If you start to notice any of the symptoms of hypothermia in yourself or any of your party, take immediate action. The best remedy is to stop, set up camp, get into dry clothes and a sleeping bag, start up the stove, and have plenty of hot drinks and hot food. Pushing on is foolish unless you've first donned extra clothes and had something to eat. After you're clothed and fed, exercise will help warm you up, since it creates heat. Even then you should stop and camp as soon as possible.

If you're properly equipped and stay warm, dry, well fed, and rested, you should be in no danger of becoming hypothermic.

RIGHT: A temperature inversion with the valleys full of cloud (cold air) and the summits bathed in sunshine (warm air). BELOW: Cloud hanging on one side of a ridge in the White Mountains, New Hampshire.

returned. Deep frostbite is a serious condition and can be properly treated only in a secure shelter with a reliable source of heat. *Frostbitten areas should not be rubbed; this can damage the frozen tissue.*

Heat Exhaustion

Most walkers are afraid of the cold, but heat can be dangerous too. The opposite of hypothermia, heat exhaustion occurs when the body cannot cool itself sufficiently. Typical symptoms are muscle cramps, nausea, and vomiting. Because the body uses perspiration for cooling, the main cause of heat exhaustion is dehydration and electrolyte depletion—if you are severely dehydrated, you cannot sweat.

The main way to prevent heat exhaustion is to drink plenty of water, *more than you think you need* on hot days. Don't neglect eating as well; water alone won't replace the salts lost when you sweat, so you could still become ill. If you start showing symptoms, stop and rest somewhere shady— exercise produces heat. If you feel dizzy or weak, lie down out of direct sunlight and drink water

Frostbite

When body tissue freezes, that's frostbite. It can be avoided by covering up and by keeping warm. Minor frostbite is most likely to occur on the extremities—the nose, ears, fingertips, and toes. If any of these areas feels numb and looks colorless, it may be frostbitten. Rewarming can be done with extra clothing, by putting a warm hand over the affected area, or in the case of fingers or toes, holding them against someone's armpit, groin, or stomach. I've come across mild frostbite only once, to a companion's nose on a windy mountaintop in February with a temperature about 0°F (−18°C); she pulled a woolen balaclava over her face, and within half an hour the color had

LEFT: Suspension bridges are often found in mountain regions. It's always worth detouring to a bridge rather than risking a ford. BELOW: A simple pole bridge. Edge across slowly and watch for wet, slippery sections. BOTTOM: A wire cable strung across a logjam as a handhold. The crossing above raging whitewater was still tricky, as the logs were wet from rain and spray.

copiously. In very hot weather, travel in the early morning and the late afternoon and take a midday siesta in the shade to minimize the chance of heat exhaustion. A sun hat or umbrella also helps.

Fording Rivers and Streams

Unbridged rivers and streams can present major hazards. Water is more powerful than many people think, and hikers are drowned every year fording what may look like relatively placid streams. If you don't think you can cross safely, don't try.

If no logs or boulders present a crossing, wading a stream or river may be the only option. Whether you prospect upstream or downstream for a potential ford depends on the terrain. If you can view the river from a high point, you may be able to see a suitable ford. Otherwise, check the map for wide areas where the river channels may be braided. Several shallow channels are easier to cross than one deep one, and wide sections are usually shallower than narrow ones. Check the map for bridges, too—many years ago, after torrential rain had turned even the smallest streams into raging torrents, two companions and I walked many extra miles upstream and camped far from where we'd intended because we didn't

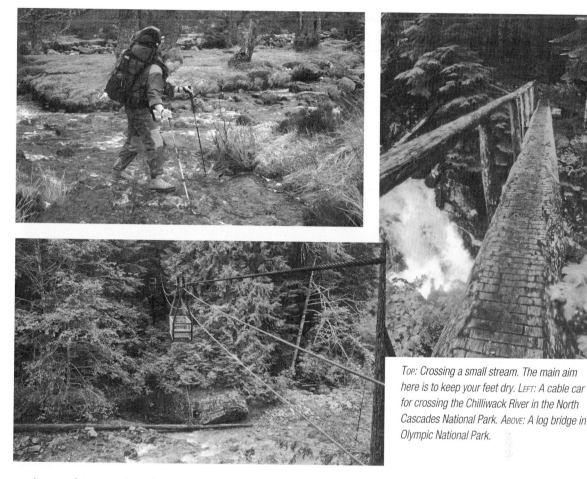

Top: Crossing a small stream. The main aim here is to keep your feet dry. Left: A cable car for crossing the Chilliwack River in the North Cascades National Park. Above: A log bridge in Olympic National Park.

notice on the map that there was a bridge not far downstream of where we were.

On a weeklong trip during the height of the spring snowmelt in Iceland, my route was almost totally determined by which rivers I could cross and which I couldn't (which was most of them). During my walk through the northern Canadian Rockies, I spent many hours searching for safe fords across the many big rivers there.

In the end, only experience can tell you whether it's possible to cross. If you decide fording is feasible, study your crossing point carefully before plunging in. In particular, check that the far side

isn't deeper or the bank undercut. Then cross carefully and slowly with your hipbelt undone so that you can jettison your pack if you're washed away. If this does happen, try to hang on to the pack by a shoulder strap—it will give extra buoyancy, and you'll need it and its contents later. You should cross at an angle facing upstream so the current won't make your knees buckle. Feel ahead with your leading foot, but don't commit your weight to it until the riverbed beneath it feels secure. One of your trekking poles or a stout stick is essential in rough water. If the water is fast flowing and starts to boil up much above your knees, face upstream so the force of the water doesn't buckle your knees

undo your pack hipbelt and sternum strap so you can jettison the pack if you fall in

if you don't have a hiking staff, find a stout stick to use for support

take off or roll up long pants so they don't drag in the current

don't hurry: security is important, not speed

shuffle across, taking short steps and feeling ahead with your leading foot for secure placements

if the water is stronger and deeper than you expected and starts to boil up much above your knees, turn back before it knocks you over

Good fording technique.

turn back—it could easily knock you over, and being swept down a boulder-littered stream is not good for your health.

If I'm wearing sandals, wet feet are no problem. For shallow crossings, I don't even break my stride. If I'm wearing shoes or boots and carrying sandals, I change into the sandals unless my footwear is already wet. If there are lots of fords, I keep the sandals on, even in cold weather, so I have dry shoes for campwear. If I can see that the river bottom is flat and sandy or gravely rather than rocky, I sometimes cross wearing just a pair of dirty socks.

Mountain water is very cold, and you'll often reach the far side feeling shivery. I've found that the best way to warm up is by gulping down some carbohydrates like trail mix or candy and then hiking hard and fast. The best clothes for fording are shorts and a warm top. Long pants can drag in

the water and aren't very warm when they become soaked.

Groups can use various techniques to make fords safer. Three people can cross in a stable tripod formation, or a group can line up along a pole held at chest level. In the past, I've used a rope to belay forders, but the newer thinking is that roped crossings are dangerous—there's too great a chance of someone's slipping and being trapped underwater by the rope.

I have never swum across a river—the water in the areas I frequent is generally too cold, too fast, and too boulder strewn for this to be practical. Bigger, warmer, slower rivers can be swum, however.

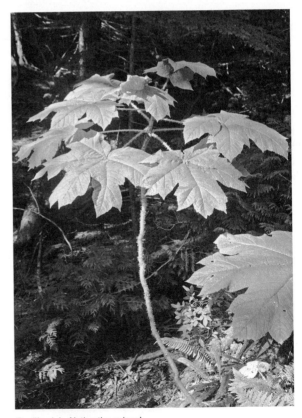

Devil's club. Notice the spines!

Clockwise from top left: Stinging nettle (Urtica dioica)*, devil's club* (Oplopanax horridus)*, poison ivy, poison sumac, and poison oak.*

If you can't find a safe crossing, you have one final option before you turn back—wait. In areas where mountain streams are rain fed, they recede quickly once the rain stops; a raging torrent can turn into a docile trickle in a matter of hours. (And placid streams can swell just as quickly, so you should camp *after* you've crossed a river, or you may wake to a nasty shock.) Glacier- and snow-fed rivers are at their lowest at dawn. If you camp on the near side, you may be able to cross in the morning. Meltwater streams are the worst to ford because you can't see the bottom through the swirling silt.

Poisonous Plants

There are a few poisonous plants that can harm you by external contact. One is the *stinging nettle*, which has a sharp but transitory sting. Although painful, it's nothing to worry about unless you dive naked into a clump. At low elevations you may find the nastier *poison oak*, *poison ivy*, and *poison sumac*. These closely related shrubs can cause severe allergic reactions, raising rashes and blisters in many people. They have leaves in groups of three that often hang across trails at knee height. If you brush against this stuff, high socks and boots are good protection from snakes and scorpions

don't place your hands behind rocks

When hiking in rattlesnake or scorpion country, be wary around bushes and rock piles.

immediately wash the affected area well with water (soap isn't required), if you have any, since the oil that causes the problems is inactivated by water. The oil is also tenacious and long-lived, so also wash any clothing or equipment that has come into contact with the plants. If you still start to itch after washing the affected area, calamine lotion and cool saltwater compresses can help. Some cortisone creams can help with red and itchy rashes where no blisters have yet developed, as well as later when the rash has healed and is scaly yet still itchy.

A final plant to watch out for is *devil's club*, whose stems are covered with razor-sharp spines that can break off and remain in the wound, causing inflammation. It's found in montane forests in the Cascades and British Columbia. I came across large stands of this head-high, large-leafed shrub mixed in with equally tall stinging nettles in the Canadian Rockies, just south of the Peace River. I normally try to avoid any unnecessary damage to plants, but on this occasion I used my staff to beat my way through the overhanging foliage.

Many agencies, park offices, Web sites, and guidebooks provide identification information; you may also find warning notices at trailheads. If you rely on plants for food, you need to be very sure you know what you're eating, especially with fungi. There are numerous guides.

DEALING WITH ANIMALS

Encountering animals in the wilderness, even potentially hazardous ones, is not in itself a cause for alarm, though some walkers act as if it were. Observing wildlife at close quarters is one of the joys and privileges of wilderness wandering, something to be wished for and remembered long afterward.

You are the intruder in the animals' world, so don't approach closely or disturb them, for their sake and for your safety. When you do come across animals unexpectedly and at close quarters, move away slowly and quietly and cause as little disturbance as possible. With most animals you need fear attack only if you startle a mother with young, and even then, as long as you back off quickly, the chances are good that nothing will happen.

Some animals pose more of a threat and need special attention, however. (Insects, of course, are also animals, and are the ones most likely to be a threat—to your sanity if not your physical health. The items and techniques needed for keeping them at bay were discussed in Chapter 8.)

Snakes

The serpent is probably more feared than any other animal, yet most species are harmless, and the chances of being bitten by one are remote. In the major North American wilderness areas there are four species of poisonous snakes—the *coral snake, rattlesnake, copperhead,* and *water moccasin* (also called a *cottonmouth*). Not all areas have them. They are rarely found above timberline or in Alaska and Maine. Their venom is unlikely to seriously harm fit, healthy persons. In many parts of South America, Asia, Africa, and Australia, much more deadly species exist, and anyone intending to hike there should obtain relevant advice.

Snakebites rarely occur above the ankle, so wearing boots and thick socks in snake country minimizes the chances of being bitten. Snakes will do everything possible to stay out of your way; the vibrations from your feet are usually enough to send them slithering off before you even see them. However, it's wise to be cautious around bushes and rock piles in snake country—there may be a snake sheltering there. At a campsite in snake country, do not pad around at night barefoot or in sandals or light shoes without checking the ground first.

Rattlesnakes seem to strike more fear into people than other snakes do, though I don't understand why. By rattling, at least they warn you of their presence so you can avoid them.

While walking in the cool of the night can be a way to avoid the heat in deserts, it's not a good way to avoid snakes. On the Pacific Crest Trail, I hiked through the Mojave Desert with three other backpackers. Battered by the heat of the day, we decided to take advantage of a full moon and hike at night. However, we quickly found that rattlesnakes, which abound in the Mojave, come out at night, and we couldn't distinguish them from sticks and other debris. Several times we stopped and cast around anxiously with our flashlights for the source of a loud rattle. Once we found a snake, a tiny sidewinder, between someone's feet. We didn't hike at night again.

On that trip, I carried in my shorts pocket a snakebite kit with implements for cutting and sucking the wound. Such kits are frowned on now as being dangerous. Using them could easily cause more harm than the bite itself. The Sawyer Extractor, a suction device that doesn't require cutting the wound, can be used. Otherwise wash the bite with soap and water, then bandage it and

Be alert for signs of bears, which may appear on the ground as prints, droppings, or diggings, and on tree trunks as parallel scratches as high as 6 feet above the ground.

black bear tracks

bear scat

black bear claw marks on tree

keep the limb hanging down to minimize the chance that venom will enter the bloodstream. The victim should stay still and rest while someone goes for assistance. If you're on your own, you may have to sit out two days of feeling unbelievably awful unless you're close enough to habitation or a road to walk to aid quickly. That's if the bite contained any venom anyway—about 25 percent don't.

For those who want to know more about snakebite treatment, I recommend *Medicine for Mountaineering,* edited by James Wilkerson.

Bears

In many mountain and wilderness areas, black bears and grizzly bears roam, powerful and independent. Knowing they're out there gives an edge to your walking; you know you're in real wilderness if bears are around. In many areas though, bears no longer roam. Grizzlies in particular have been exterminated in most of the lower states; there are now just tiny numbers in small parts of Montana, Idaho, and Wyoming (mainly in Glacier and Yellowstone National Parks). They're found in any numbers only in Alaska and western Canada (the Yukon, Northwest Territories, British Columbia, and western Alberta). I like knowing they're there, lords of the forests and mountains, as they have been for millennia.

The chances of seeing a bear, let alone being attacked or injured by one, are remote. In Yellowstone National Park, home to both grizzly and black bears, there were 47 million visitors between 1980 and 1997. Just twenty-three of them were injured by bears. That makes the odds on being injured by a bear in Yellowstone about 1 in 2.1 million. You are at far greater risk from drowning, falling, or vehicle accidents. In more than ten thousand miles of walking in bear coun-

try, most of it alone, I've seen only twenty-four black bears and three grizzlies, and none has threatened me—most have run away.

However, you should minimize your chances of encountering a bear. Dave Smith's *Backcountry Bear Basics* is recommended reading for anyone venturing into bear country. I also recommend Doug Peacock's *Grizzly Years,* an excellent personal account of two decades of studying grizzlies while living among them.

When you're on the move, you want bears to know you're there so they'll give you a wide berth. Most of the time, their acute senses of smell and hearing will alert them to your presence long before you're aware of them. However, a wind blowing in your face, a noisy stream, or thick brush can all mask your signals. In these circumstances, make a noise to let any bears know you're around. Many people wear small bells on their packs for this purpose, but these aren't really loud enough, and they tinkle annoyingly even when you don't need them, scaring away other wildlife. It's better to shout or sing and clap your hands in thick brush or when you can't see far and the wind is in your face. Don't forget to use your eyes—I once came across a hiker sitting on a log eating his lunch, all the while calling out to warn bears he was there. I walked toward him for several minutes without his seeing me and finally startled him by calling out a greeting when I was a few steps away.

In open terrain and on trails, scan ahead for bears. A pair of binoculars helps greatly with this. They'll help you determine if that tree stump ahead is actually a grizzly sitting by the trail. Look for evidence of bears, too—paw prints and scat (dung) are obvious signs, but also look for scratch marks on trees and mounds of freshly dug earth in alpine meadows where grizzlies have been digging for rodents.

If you see a bear before it sees you, detour away from it quietly and quickly. Be particularly wary of female grizzlies with cubs—70 percent of known attacks are by mothers defending their young. If the bear is aware of you, move away from it, perhaps waving your arms or talking to help it identify what you are. Don't stare at it or act aggressively; you don't want to be seen as a threat. The only grizzly I've met at fairly close quarters moved slowly away from me once I'd made a noise and let it know I was there. The nearest it came was about fifty yards.

Many people suggest climbing a tree if a bear charges you. Dave Smith thinks this is a bad idea, since the bear will usually catch you and pull you down. (One bear-country saying is that the way to tell the difference between black bears and grizzly bears is to climb a tree—black bears will climb up after you, grizzlies will knock the tree down.)

Very occasionally, a bear will charge. Advice is mixed regarding what to do if one does. Don't run—bears are much faster than you are. Dropping an object, such as a camera or an item of clothing, may distract it and allow you to escape. Don't drop your pack—if the bear eats your food, it may learn to regard future walkers as food sources. Your pack will also help protect your body if the bear does attack. If dropping something doesn't work, your choices are trying to frighten the bear by yelling, banging objects together (metal on metal may be effective), backing away slowly, or standing your ground while acting nonthreatening by talking quietly to the bear (the option Dave Smith advises). If the bear actually attacks you (many charges don't result in physical contact), you can play dead or fight back. The best position for the first is lying on your front with your legs slightly apart, your elbows tucked in, and your hands protecting your neck so the bear can't easily roll you over. Keep your pack on to protect your back and neck. If the bear doesn't leave you alone fairly quickly when you play dead, fight back instead, since it may view you as prey.

You could also use one of the powerful pepper sprays such as Counter Assault. This is a strong version of cayenne pepper–based antidog sprays that has been shown to repel bears both in the wild and in controlled tests. In one case a grizzly that had already knocked a man down and was biting him ran off when sprayed in the face. The manufacturer stresses that it isn't a substitute for knowing about bear behavior and taking the usual precautions, but—the advertising says—"it's better than no protection at all." It doesn't guarantee protection, however, and isn't a reason to take risks or feel overconfident. Pepper spray is nontoxic (the bears aren't harmed) and comes in an 8-ounce canister. There's also a holster for carrying it on your belt. I've never carried it, though I might if I went hiking in Alaska again.

Bear-country ranger stations and information offices have up-to-date reports on areas that bears are using and whether any have caused trouble. Trails and backcountry campsites may be closed if necessary. For your own safety and that of the bears, obey any regulations that are in force.

HUNTERS

In many areas the late summer and autumn see the backcountry fill up with hunters carrying high-powered rifles. Try to make sure they don't shoot you by wearing something bright, like an orange hat or jacket. In some areas, officials recommend wearing two or more pieces of blaze orange. Hunting season is not the time to be wearing camouflage in the wilderness.

ADVENTURE TRAVEL

The opportunities for backpacking worldwide increase every year with new trails and hiker facilities appearing. Different countries have different hiking traditions and local cultures, and one of the joys is discovering and adapting to these. In Western Europe, there are many lodges along long-distance paths, and many hikers use these rather than camp. In Himalayan countries, it's usual to hike with a guide and porters.

Of the many wonderful trails and wild places worldwide, here are my picks of the ones I've hiked, followed by those I would like to hike. First, there's the Everest Trek in Nepal, which climbs to base camp below the world's highest mountain. This isn't a remote wilderness trail—there are many lodges, and you'll meet many hikers along the way—but it is spectacular, and the culture is fascinating, and the local people very friendly. For a wilder, remoter experience, the Himalayan trek to Makalu Base Camp is tremendous, a hike that takes you deep into the mountains. In Europe, the Pyrenees are a lovely area, more suited to backpacking than the Alps in my opinion, with many trails, of which the Pyrenean High Level Route, which is more than 600 miles long, is the finest. Out in the Mediterranean on the island of Corsica is the magnificent GR20, which runs along the rocky spine of the island. This is a challenging route with many sections of rock scrambling. Much farther north in the Arctic is the 280-mile Kungsleden in Swedish Lapland, a remote trail through forest, tundra, and mountain with reindeer for company. And out in the Atlantic is my home country, where there is much excellent hiking, especially in the Scottish Highlands, where the elevation may be quite low, but the open terrain and wild weather can still make hiking a challenge.

South of the equator lie many wild areas and trails I have yet to hike. New Zealand and Australia both have exciting-looking trails in magnificent mountains. In the former, the Fiordland and Mount Aspiring National Parks both look spectacular (most people know them from the *Lord of the Rings* films) and have many trails, while in Australia, the 139-mile Larapinta Trail in the arid West MacDonnell Ranges in the Northern Territories sounds challenging and starkly beautiful. Across the Pacific Ocean in South America is the long chain of the Andes Mountains where there are many superb wild areas and trails. I like the look of the 52-mile Torres del Paine Circuit in Chile, which goes right round the wildly dramatic spires of the Torres del Paine mountains, and the popular 26-mile Inca Trail in Peru, which leads through fantastic scenery to the ruins of Machu Picchu.

HIRING A GUIDE

In some parts of the world, such as the Himalaya, hiking without a local guide can be difficult, especially in remote areas, unless you can speak the local language. If you are going to be out for several weeks you may need porters to carry food and equipment too. Joining an organized trek is one way to deal with this but it is possible to hire guides and porters yourself. In cities like Katmandu there are many guiding and trekking companies offering this service. National tourist bureaus, adventure travel and outdoor magazine advertisements, trekking Web sites, and hiking guidebooks are sources of information. To check the reputation of a guide or trekking organization you could put a query on an Internet hiking newsgroup or message board. Nothing beats a personal recommendation.

When hiring guides and porters all the details of their employment should be established clearly at the time. As well as their duties and payment this should include food and equipment, both of which you may be expected to provide (and which can usually be bought or hired locally). Procedures for cooking, sanitation, water treatment, and trash disposal should be established before the hike begins, too. Tipping after the trek is the norm. The booking agency should be able to tell you the standard rate.

POLITICAL INSTABILITY AND TERRORISM

The political situation is very volatile in many countries with violent demonstrations and uprisings always possible. Getting caught up in these can be frightening and dangerous, even when visitors are not targeted. Sometimes, though, kidnapping rich Westerners (and even a threadbare hiker living on minimum means is rich in many countries) for ransom or political leverage is a deliberate tactic. Even worse some terrorist organizations target and murder visitors from countries they see as enemies. It is important when planning trips abroad to find out the up-to-date position regarding security in the places you intend visiting. This information is available on the State Department's Bureau of Consular Affairs Web site at http://travel.state.gov/travel/travel_1744.html.

VACCINATIONS

Vaccinations against various diseases—everything from yellow fever to hepatitis—are necessary when visiting many countries. Courses of vaccination can take four to six weeks to complete so you need to contact your doctor well in advance of your trip. Information on what vaccinations are needed plus other health information can be found in the Centers for Disease Control (CDC) biennial Yellow Book, Health Information for International Travel, and on the CDC website (www.cdc.gov/travel).

MONEY

When traveling it's best to carry some coins and low denomination notes in the local currency for small value purchases. In some remote areas where only cash is accepted you may need a fair amount, in which case it's best to carry it in small sums in different places on your person and in your pack. It's best to obtain foreign currency in advance of your trip too so you can get the best exchange rate and not end up trying to find an exchange bureau after a long tiring flight. For anything other than small expenses credit cards are ideal, being safer and more convenient than cash. The main brands are usable in a surprising number of places (in Norway, for example, you can pay for accommodation and food in remote unstaffed mountain huts by filling in a credit card slip). In towns credit cards can be used to withdraw more cash from banks or ATMs. Bankcards can be used for this too but only if your bank is part of the same international network. Traveler's checks, the traditional means of dealing with foreign currency, aren't as convenient as credit cards or ATMs but might still be useful at times, though I haven't carried any for many years. If you do use traveler's checks ones from widely recognized brands such as American Express or Visa are best. Dollar checks are welcome in many developing countries, ones in the local currency or Euros are more likely to be accepted in Western Europe.

WEB PLANNING SOURCES

Finding information for foreign travel used to be difficult and time-consuming. The Internet changed all that. The problem now is the vast amount of information available. Say you are interested in Nepal, a prime destination for overseas hiking. Enter "Nepal" on Google and you get an astonishing 255,000,000 results. Refine the search to "Nepal Hiking" and you still get 5,680,000 results. Even if you then search for just one popular hike in Nepal, the Annapurna Trek, there are 1,280,000 results. This overwhelming volume of information can be reduced by using sites that have done the searching for you and which provide links to selected relevant sites. One of the best of these is a site called Traildino .com (www.traildino.com), which claims to be the world's largest such site. Click on "Nepal" and then "Annapurna Circuit" on Traildino and you will find a route description with photographs and just twenty-six links, a manageable number.Most countries' tourist boards have Web sites too. Nepal's can be found at welcomenepal.com.

a final word

Thank you for reading my words. I hope you've found them interesting, entertaining, and useful. I enjoyed writing them. As always, comments and suggestions are welcome. I can be found on the Internet at http://christownsendoutdoors.com.

As I write these last words, I am preparing for a late-winter, two-week hike. My study floor is scattered with gear, my head full of possibilities and plans. After weeks sitting at my desk writing, it's time to head out on the trail again. Maybe we'll meet out there.

Happy trails.

equipment checklist

This is a list of every item you might take on a backpacking trip. No one would ever carry everything listed below; I select items from this master list to create smaller, specific lists of what I need for each particular trip.

PACKS

- Backpack
- Fanny pack
- Day pack

FOOTWEAR AND WALKING AIDS

- Boots
- Trail shoes
- Sandals
- Footbeds
- Wax (for cleaning and waterproofing boots)
- Socks
- Liner socks
- Fleece socks
- Insulated booties
- Gaiters
- Staff/trekking poles
- Ice ax
- Crampons

- Snowshoes
- Skis
- Ski poles
- Ski boots
- Climbing skins
- Ski wax

SHELTER

- Tent with poles and stakes
- Tarp
- Bivouac bag
- Groundsheet
- Sleeping bag
- Sleeping bag liner
- Sleeping pad
- Pillow

KITCHEN

- Stove
- Fuel
- Fuel bottles
- Pouring spout
- Windscreen
- Pan(s)
- Mug
- Plate/bowl
- Spoon(s)
- Pot grab
- Baking accessory

- Pot scrubber
- Water containers
- Thermos bottle
- Insulating water bottle cover
- Water purification tablets
- Water filter
- Matches/lighter/fire starter
- Plastic bags
- Bear bag and cord
- Bear-resistant container
- Food

CLOTHING

INNER LAYER

- T-shirt
- Shirt
- Long underwear
- Underpants

MIDLAYER

- Synthetic shirt
- Wool shirt
- Cotton shirt
- Wool sweater
- Fleece top
- Insulated top
- Vapor-barrier suit

OUTER LAYER

- Windproof top
- Rain jacket
- Rain pants

LEGWEAR

- Shorts
- Trail pants
- Fleece pants

HEADGEAR

- Sun hat
- Watch cap
- Balaclava
- Neck gaiter
- Fleece-lined cap
- Bandanna

HANDS

- Liner gloves
- Thick wool/fleece mittens
- Shell mittens
- Insulated gloves/mittens

MISCELLANEOUS: ESSENTIAL

- Flashlight/headlamp and spare bulb and battery
- Candles
- Candle lantern
- Oil lantern

- Butane-propane lantern
- First-aid kit
- Compass
- Whistle
- Map
- Map case
- Altimeter
- Map measurer
- Guidebook
- GPS receiver
- Repair kit:
  - Ripstop nylon patches
  - Duct tape
  - Needles and thread
  - Glue
  - Stove maintenance kit/pricker
  - Rubber bands
- Waterproof matches
- Wash kit
- Sunglasses
- Goggles
- Sunscreen
- Lip balm
- Insect repellent
- Mosquito coils
- Head net
- Pepper spray
- Flares
- Strobe light

- Fishing tackle
- Cord
- Knife
- Notebook, pen, and documents
- Watch
- Toilet trowel
- Toilet paper
- Rope
- Plastic bags

MISCELLANEOUS: OPTIONAL

- Binoculars
- Photography equipment:
  - Cameras
  - Lenses
  - Flash
  - Spare batteries
  - Tripod
  - Minitripod/clamp
  - Filters
  - Cable release
  - Lens tissue
  - Film
  - Padded camera cases
- Books
- Cards
- Games
- Radio
- Portable CD player/Ipod/MP3 player
- Thermometer

further reading

This is a list of books I've found inspirational, helpful, or at least interesting. It's by no means comprehensive, and some may be out of print. Check your library or used book stores and Web sites. Many are not backpacking books as such, but all of them are about, or relevant to, wilderness travel. I've also included my other books.

Obviously I hope this book will serve as a guide and inspiration for your wilderness hiking. But it's only one person's view. Many of the books that have influenced me and that I feel are the most useful and enlightening are gathered here.

Colin Fletcher's classic *The Complete Walker* first appeared in 1968. The fourth edition, cowritten with Chip Rawlins, was published in 2002. Two authors mean that it's almost two books with different approaches and opinions, sometimes contradictory, usually entertaining. Fletcher takes what might be called a standard approach to backpacking; Rawlins is much more on the lightweight side. The ultralight manual is Ray Jardine's *Trail Life*, a provocative, entertaining, inspiring, and sometimes infuriating book. A much lighter and amusing though still informative read is *Allen and Mike's Really Cool Backpackin' Book* by Allen O'Bannon, which contains some excellent cartoon-style illustrations by Mike Clelland. *Allen and Mike's Really Cool Backcountry Ski Book: Traveling and Camping Skills for a Winter Environment* is similarly entertaining about winter camping and ski touring.

Karen Berger is the author of a growing number of backpacking books, all worth consulting. If you're interested in long-distance trails, her *Hiking the Triple Crown* is a great resource. Also useful for long-distance hiking and full of interesting statistics is Roland Mueser's *Long-Distance Hiking*.

For equipment repair and maintenance Annie Getchell and Dave Getchell Jr.'s *The Essential Outdoor Gear Manual* is comprehensive. For people repair and maintenance, otherwise known as first aid, *Medicine for Mountaineering and Other Wilderness Activities*, edited by James A. Wilkerson and now in its fifth edition, is one for the bookshelf, while Fred T. Darvill Jr.'s *Mountaineering Medicine and Backcountry Medical Guide* and Paul G. Gill Jr.'s *Wilderness First Aid* are light enough for the pack. Sanitation is a key health issue, and here Kathleen Meyer's uncompromisingly titled *How to Shit in the Woods* is a key text. More general minimum impact information is contained in Bruce Hampton and David Cole's *Soft Paths* and Annette McGivney's *Leave No Trace*.

Bears are a particular concern for many hikers, and there are several books on this subject. I think the most useful and sensible is Dave Smith's *Backcountry Bear Basics*. A more personal book about bears and about hiking and camping in their country is Doug Peacock's *Grizzly Years*.

Except for the last one, the works above are basically instructional books. Many of them are inspirational as well, but this is not their main purpose. Hiking stories and adventures can inspire and also, by example, give much information about what it's like to hike in a particular area or for months at a time. In my opinion there are two classic hiking books, both by the late Colin Fletcher: *The Thousand-Mile Summer* and *The Man Who Walked Through Time*. The first tells the story of the author's hike the length of California, the second his hike the length of the Grand Canyon. The other great wilderness writer of the past fifty or so years is the late Edward Abbey. His books aren't specifically about backpacking, though many feature hiking stories, such as the excellent "A

Walk in the Desert Hills" in *Beyond the Wall*, but they are celebrations of wild places and nature and the freedom found there plus a call to defend them from exploitation. His classic work is *Desert Solitaire*, a series of essays based on the time he spent as a ranger in Arches National Park, but all his books are worth reading.

Going further back than Abbey and Fletcher, we come to John Muir, a prodigious hiker as well as a mountaineer, naturalist, and conservationist. There are many collections of his work available. Of the individual books, I recommend *My First Summer in the Sierra* and *The Mountains of California*. There are also many books about Muir and his wilderness philosophy: I think *The Pathless Way* by Michael P. Cohen is the best. A more general and pretty definitive study of the development of wilderness philosophy and conservation is Roderick Frazier Nash's *Wilderness and the American Mind*.

Abbey, Edward. *Abbey's Road*. New York: Plume, 1991.

———. *Beyond the Wall: Essays from the Outside*. New York: Holt, Rinehart and Winston, 1984.

———. *Desert Solitaire: A Season in the Wilderness*. New York: Simon & Schuster, 1990.

———. *Down the River*. New York: Plume, 1991.

———. *The Journey Home: Some Words in Defense of the American West*. New York: Perennial Classics, 2000.

———. *The Monkey Wrench Gang*. New York: Perennial Classics, 2000.

Adkins, Jan, ed. *The Ragged Mountain Portable Wilderness Anthology*. Camden ME: Ragged Mountain Press, 1993.

Alden, Peter, et al. *National Aubudon Society Field Guide to the Southwestern States*. New York: Knopf, 1999.

Alden, Peter, and Dennis Paulson. *National Audubon Society Field Guide to the Pacific Northwest*. New York: Knopf, 2008.

Annerino, John. *Hiking the Grand Canyon*. Rev. and expanded. San Francisco: Sierra Club Books, 1993.

———. *Running Wild: An Extraordinary Adventure of the Human Spirit*. New York: Thunder's Mouth Press, 1997.

Appalachian Long Distance Hikers Association. *Appalachian Trail Thru-Hiker's Companion*. 11th ed. Harpers Ferry WV: Appalachian Trail Conference, 2004.

Appalachian Trail Guidebooks. Harpers Ferry WV: Appalachian Trail Conference.

Axcell, Claudia, Vikki Kinmont Kath, and Diana Cooke. *Simple Foods for the Pack*. 3rd ed. San Francisco: Sierra Club Books, 2004.

Berger, Karen. *Hiking the Triple Crown: How to Hike America's Longest Trails: Appalachian Trail, Pacific Crest Trail, Continental Divide Trail*. Seattle: Mountaineers, 2001.

Berger, Karen, and Daniel R. Smith. *Along the Pacific Crest Trail*. Englewood CO: Westcliffe, 1999.

———. *The Pacific Crest Trail: A Hiker's Companion*. Woodstock VT: Countryman, 2000.

———. *Where the Waters Divide: A 3,000-Mile Trek along America's Continental Divide*. Woodstock VT: Countryman, 1997.

Bezruchka, Stephen. *Trekking in Nepal: A Traveler's Guide*. 8th ed. Seattle: Mountaineers, 2011.

Birkett, Bill, ed. *Classic Treks: The 30 Most Spectacular Hikes in the World*. Boston: Little, Brown, 2000.

Brower, David R., with Steve Chapple. *Let the Mountains Talk, Let the Rivers Run: A Call to Those Who Would Save the Earth*. San Francisco: HarperCollins West, 1995.

Brown, Hamish. *Hamish's Mountain Walk*. Dingwall, Scotland: Sandstone Press, 2010.

Brown, Tom, Jr., with Brandt Morgan. *Tom Brown's Field Guide to Wilderness Survival*. New York: Berkley, 1983.

Butler, Elias, and Tom Myers. *Grand Obsession: Harvey Butchart and the Exploration of the Grand Canyon*. Flagstaff: Puma Press, 2007.

Cahalan, James M. *Edward Abbey A Life*. Tucson: University of Arizona Press, 2001.

Clelland!, Mike. *Ultralight Backpackin' Tips*. Guilford CT: FalconGuides, 2011.

Cohen, Michael P. *The Pathless Way: John Muir and American Wilderness*. Madison: University of Wisconsin Press, 1984.

Colorado Trail Foundation. *The Colorado Trail: The Official Guidebook*. 6th ed. Golden CO: Colorado Mountain Club Press, 2002.

Connally, Craig. *The Mountaineering Handbook*. Camden, ME: Ragged Mountain Press, 2005.

Continental Divide Trail Society. *Guide to the Continental Divide Trail.* 7 vols. Baltimore: Continental Divide Trail Society.

Copeland, Kathy, and Craig Copeland. *Don't Waste Your Time in the Canadian Rockies: The Opinionated Hiking Guide.* 6th ed. Canmore AB: hikingcamping .com, 2009.

———. *Don't Waste Your Time in the North Cascades: An Opinionated Hiking Guide to Help You Get the Most from This Magnificent Wilderness.* Berkeley: Wilderness Press, 1996.

Crane, Nicholas. *Clear Waters Rising: A Mountain Walk Across Europe.* New York: Penguin, 1997.

Cudahy, Michael. *Wild Trails to Far Horizons.* London: Unwin Hyman, 1989.

Daffern, Tony. *Backcountry Avalanche Safety: Skiers, Climbers, Boarders and Snowshoers.* 3rd edition. Surrey, BC: Rocky Mountain Books, 2009.

Daniell, Gene, and Steven D. Smith, eds. *AMC White Mountain Guide: Hiking Trails in the White Mountain National Forest.* 28th ed. Boston: Appalachian Mountain Club Books, 2007.

Darvill, Fred T., Jr. *Mountaineering Medicine and Backcountry Medical Guide.* 14th ed. Berkeley: Wilderness Press, 1998.

Dempster, Andrew. *The Munro Phenomenon.* Edinburgh: Mainstream, 1995.

Dudley, Ellen. *The Savvy Adventure Traveler: What to Know Before You Go.* Camden ME: Ragged Mountain Press, 1999.

Eng, Ronald C., ed. *Mountaineering: The Freedom of the Hills.* 8th ed. Seattle: Mountaineers, 2010.

Fayhee, M. John. *Along the Arizona Trail.* Englewood CO: Westcliffe, 1998.

Ferguson, Sue, and E. R. LaChapelle. *The ABCs of Avalanche Safety.* 3rd ed. Seattle: Mountaineers, 2003.

Fleming, June. *The Well-Fed Backpacker.* 3rd ed. New York: Vintage, 1986.

Fletcher, Colin. *The Man Who Walked Through Time.* New York: Vintage, 1989.

———. *River: One Man's Journey Down the Colorado, Source to Sea.* New York: Knopf, 1997.

———. *The Secret Worlds of Colin Fletcher.* New York: Vintage, 1990.

———. *The Thousand-Mile Summer.* New York: Vintage, 1987.

Fletcher, Colin, and Chip Rawlins. *The Complete Walker IV.* 4th rev. ed. New York: Knopf, 2002.

Forgey, William. *Basic Essentials: Wilderness First Aid.* 2nd ed. Old Saybrook CT: Globe Pequot, 1999.

Frazine, Richard Keith. *The Barefoot Hiker: A Book about Bare Feet.* Berkeley: Ten Speed, 1993.

Gadd, Ben. *Handbook of the Canadian Rockies.* 2nd ed. Jasper AB: Corax, 1995.

Getchell, Annie, and Dave Getchell Jr. *The Essential Outdoor Gear Manual: Equipment Care, Repair, and Selection.* 2nd ed. Camden ME: Ragged Mountain Press, 2000.

Gill, Paul G., Jr. *Wilderness First Aid: A Pocket Guide.* Camden ME: Ragged Mountain Press, 2002.

Gorman, Stephen. *Winter Camping: Wilderness Travel and Adventure in the Cold-Weather Months.* 2nd ed. Boston: Applachian Mountain Club Books, 1999.

Hampton, Bruce, and David Cole. *Soft Paths: How to Enjoy the Wilderness without Harming It.* Rev. ed. Molly Absolon and Tom Reed, ed. Mechanicsburg PA: Stackpole, 1995.

Herrero, Stephen. *Bear Attacks: Their Causes and Avoidance.* New York: Nick Lyons Books, 1988.

Heuer, Karsten. *Walking the Big Wild: From Yellowstone to the Yukon on the Grizzly Bears' Trail.* Toronto: McClelland & Stewart, 2002.

Hillaby, John. *Journey Through Britain.* London: Paladin, 1970.

Howe, Nicholas S. *Not Without Peril: One Hundred and Fifty Years of Misadventure on the Presidential Range of New Hampshire.* Boston: Appalachian Mountain Club, 2000.

Jackson, Jack, ed. *The World's Great Adventure Treks.* London: New Holland, 2004.

Jardine, Ray. *Trail Life.* LaPine, OR: AdventureLore Press, 2009.

Johansson, Jörgen. *Smarter Backpacking.* Sweden: NUI Publishing, 2010.

Johnson, Mark. *The Ultimate Desert Handbook: A Manual for Desert Hikers, Campers, and Travelers.* Camden ME: Ragged Mountain Press, 2003.

Jones, Tom Lorang, and Jerry Sieve. *Arizona Trail: The Official Guide.* Englewood, CO: Westcliffe, 2005.

Jones, Tom Lorang. *Colorado's Continental Divide Trail: The Official Guide*. Englewood CO: Westcliffe, 1997.

Kephart, Horace. *Camping and Woodcraft: A Handbook for Vacation Campers and for Travelers in the Wilderness*. Knoxville: University of Tennessee Press, 1988.

Kesselheim, Alan S. *Trail Food: Drying and Cooking Food for Backpackers and Paddlers*. Camden ME: Ragged Mountain Press, 1998.

Kjellström, Björn. *Be Expert with Map and Compass: The Complete Orienteering Handbook*. Rev. and updated ed. New York: Collier Books, 1994.

Krakauer, Jon. *Eiger Dreams: Ventures among Men and Mountains*. New York: Anchor, 1997.

———. *Into the Wild*. New York: Anchor, 1997.

———. *Into Thin Air: A Personal Account of the Mount Everest Disaster*. New York: Anchor, 1998.

Leopold, Aldo. *A Sand County Almanac: With Essays on Conservation*. New York: Oxford University Press, 2001.

Lopez, Barry. *Arctic Dreams: Imagination and Desire in a Northern Landscape*. New York: Vintage, 2001.

Lynx, Dustin. *Hiking Canada's Great Divide Trail*. Calgary AB: Rocky Mountain Books, 2000.

Macfarlane, Robert. *Mountains of the Mind*. New York: Pantheon, 2003.

Macfarlane, Robert. *The Wild Places*. New York: Penguin, 2008.

Manning, Harvey. *Backpacking, One Step at a Time*. 4th ed. New York: Vintage, 1985.

Matthiesen, Peter. *The Snow Leopard*. New York: Penguin, 1996.

McGivney, Annette. *Leave No Trace: A Guide to the New Wilderness Ethic*. 2nd ed. Seattle: Mountaineers, 2003.

McNeish, Cameron. *The Wilderness World of Cameron McNeish: Essays from Beyond the Black Stump*. Glasgow: In Pinn, 2001.

McPhee, John. *Encounters with the Archdruid*. New York: Farrar, Straus & Giroux, 1971.

Meyer, Kathleen. *How to Shit in the Woods: An Environmentally Sound Approach to a Lost Art*. 2nd ed. rev. Berkeley: Ten Speed, 1994.

Miller, Arthur P., and Marjorie L. Miller. *Trails Across America: Traveler's Guide to Our National Scenic and Historic Trails*. Golden CO: Fulcrum, 1996.

Miller, Dorcas. *Backcountry Cooking: From Pack to Plate in 10 Minutes*. Seattle: Mountaineers, 1998.

———. *Good Food for Camp and Trail: All-Natural Recipes for Delicious Meals Outdoors*. Boulder CO: Pruett, 1993.

———. *More Backcountry Cooking: Moveable Feasts from the Experts*. Seattle: Mountaineers, 2002.

Molvar, Erik. *Alaska on Foot: Wilderness Techniques for the Far North*. Woodstock VT: Countryman, 1996.

Mortlock, Colin. *Beyond Adventure*. Milnthorpe UK: Cicerone, 2001.

Morton, Keith. *Planning a Wilderness Trip in Canada and Alaska*. Calgary AB: Rocky Mountain Books, 1997.

Mueser, Roland. *Long-Distance Hiking: Lessons from the Appalachian Trail*. Camden ME: Ragged Mountain Press, 1998.

Muir, John. *John Muir: The Eight Wilderness Discovery Books*. Seattle: Mountaineers, 1992.

———. *The Mountains of California*. New York: Modern Library, 2001.

———. *My First Summer in the Sierra*. New York: Modern Library, 2003.

———. *Sacred Summits: John Muir's Greatest Climbs*. Graham White, ed. Edinburgh: Canongate, 1999.

Nash, Roderick Frazier. *Wilderness and the American Mind*. 4th ed. New Haven: Yale University Press, 2001.

Newby, Eric. *A Short Walk in the Hindu Kush*. Oakland: Lonely Planet, 1999.

O'Bannon, Allen. *Allen and Mike's Really Cool Backcountry Ski Book: Traveling and Camping Skills for a Winter Environment*. Helena MT: Falcon, 1996.

———. *Allen and Mike's Really Cool Backpackin' Book*. Helena MT: Falcon, 2001.

O'Bannon, Allen, and Mike Clelland. *Allen and Mike's Really Cool Telemark Tips: 109 Amazing Tips to Improve Your Tele-Skiing*. Helena MT: Falcon, 1998.

Parker, Paul. *Free-Heel Skiing: Telemark and Parallel Techniques for All Conditions*. 3rd ed. Seattle: Mountaineers, 2001.

Parsons, Mike, and Mary B. Rose, *Invisible on Everest: Innovation and the Gear Makers*. Philadelphia: Northern Liberties Press, 2003.

Peacock, Doug. *Grizzly Years: In Search of the American Wilderness.* New York: Henry Holt, 1990.

Powell, John Wesley. *The Exploration of the Colorado River and Its Canyons.* New York: Penguin, 2003.

Prater, Gene. *Snowshoeing.* 5th ed. Dave Felkley, ed. Seattle: Mountaineers, 2002.

Prater, Yvonne, and Ruth Dyar Mendenhall. *Gorp, Glop and Glue Stew: Favorite Foods from 165 Outdoor Experts.* Seattle: Mountaineers, 1982.

Reifsnyder, William E. *Weathering the Wilderness: The Sierra Club Guide to Practical Meteorology.* San Francisco: Sierra Club Books, 1980.

Reynolds, Kev. *Walking in the Alps.* New York: Interlink Books, 2000.

Rockwell, Robert L. "*Giardia Lamblia* and Giardiasis, with Particular Attention to the Sierra Nevada." *Sierra Nature Notes*, 2 (2002) (rev. 5/2002): www .yosemite.org/naturenotes/giardia.htm.

Roper, Steve. *The Sierra High Route: Traversing Timberline Country.* Seattle: Mountaineers, 1997.

Ross, Cindy. *Journey on the Crest: Walking 2,600 Miles from Mexico to Canada.* Seattle: Mountaineers, 1987.

Rowell, Galen. *The Art of Adventure.* San Francisco: Sierra Club Books, 1996.

———. *Galen Rowell's Vision: The Art of Adventure Photography.* San Francisco: Sierra Club Books, 1993.

———. *High and Wild: Essays and Photographs on Wilderness Adventure.* Special expanded ed. Bishop CA: Spotted Dog Press, 2002.

———. *In the Throne Room of the Mountain Gods.* San Francisco: Sierra Club Books, 1986.

———. *Mountain Light: In Search of the Dynamic Landscape.* San Francisco: Sierra Club Books, 1986.

Russell, Terry, and Renny Russell. *On the Loose.* Salt Lake City: Gibbs-Smith, 2001.

Schaffer, Jeffrey P. *Yosemite National Park: A Natural-History Guide to Yosemite and Its Trails.* 4th ed. Berkeley: Wilderness Press, 1999.

Schaffer, Jeffrey P., and Andy Selters. *The Pacific Crest Trail.* 5th ed., 2 vols. Berkeley: Wilderness Press, 1990–95.

Schmidt, Jeremy. *Adventuring in the Rockies: The Sierra Club Travel Guide to the Rocky Mountain Regions of Canada and the U.S.A.* Rev. ed. San Francisco: Sierra Club Books, 1993.

Secor, R. J. *The High Sierra: Peaks, Passes, and Trails.* 2nd ed. Seattle: Mountaineers, 1999.

Seidman, David, with Paul Cleveland. *The Essential Wilderness Navigator: How to Find Your Way in the Great Outdoors.* 2nd ed. Camden ME: Ragged Mountain Press, 2001.

Selters, Andy. *Glacier Travel and Crevasse Rescue.* 2nd ed. Seattle: Mountaineers, 1999.

Simpson, Joe. *Touching the Void.* New York: HarperPerennial, 2004.

Skurka, Andrew, *A Walker's Complete Guide to Backpacking & Hiking Gear,* Andrew Skurka, 2011

Slack, Nancy G., and Allison W. Bell. *AMC Field Guide to the New England Alpine Summits.* Boston: Appalachian Mountain Club Books, 1995.

Smith, Dave. *Backcountry Bear Basics: The Definitive Guide to Avoiding Unpleasant Encounters.* Seattle: Mountaineers, 1997.

Smith, Steven D., and Mike Dickerman. *The 4,000-Footers of the White Mountains: A Guide and History.* Littleton NH: Bondcliff Books, 2001.

Snyder, Gary. *The Practice of the Wild: Essays.* Washington DC: Shoemaker & Hoard, 2003.

Soles, Clyde. *Rock and Ice Gear: Equipment for the Vertical World.* Seattle: Mountaineers, 2000.

Starr, Walter A., Jr. *Starr's Guide to the John Muir Trail and the High Sierra Region.* 12th ed. rev. San Francisco: Sierra Club Books, 1977.

Steck, George. *Hiking Grand Canyon Loops: Adventures in the Backcountry.* Guilford CT: Falcon, 2002.

Steele, Frederic L. *At Timberline: A Nature Guide to the Mountains of the Northeast.* Boston: Appalachian Mountain Club, 1982.

Stegner, Wallace. *Beyond the Hundredth Meridian: John Wesley Powell and the Second Opening of the West.* Lincoln: University of Nebraska Press, 1982.

Stevenson, Robert Louis. *Travels with a Donkey; An Inland Voyage; The Silverado Squatters.* London: Dent, 1984.

Strickland, Ron. *The Pacific Northwest Trail Guide: The Official Guidebook for Long Distance and Day Hikers.* Seattle: Sasquatch, 2001.

———. *Pathfinder: Blazing a New Wilderness Trail in Modern America.* Corvallis, OR: Oregon State University Press, 2011.

Thoreau, Henry David. *A Week on the Concord and Merrimack Rivers/Walden, or Life in the Woods/The Maine Woods/Cape Cod*. New York: Viking, 1985.

Tilman, H. W. *The Seven-Mountain Travel Books*. Seattle: Mountaineers, 2003.

Townsend, Chris. *The Advanced Backpacker: A Handbook for Year-Round, Long-Distance Hiking*. Camden ME: Ragged Mountain Press, 2001.

———. *Adventure Treks: Western North America*. Seattle: Cloudcap, 1990.

———. *Backpacker's Pocket Guide*. Camden ME: Ragged Mountain Press, 2002.

———. *Crossing Arizona: A Solo Hike Through the Sky Islands and Deserts of the Arizona Trail*. Woodstock VT: Countryman, 2002.

———. *The Great Backpacking Adventure*. Sparkford UK: Oxford Illustrated, 1987.

———. *High Summer: Backpacking the Canadian Rockies*. Seattle: Cloudcap, 1989.

———. *Long Distance Walks in the Pyrenees*. Swindon UK: Crowood, 1991.

———. *The Munros and Tops: A Record-Setting Walk in the Scottish Highlands*. Edinburgh: Mainstream, 2003.

———. *Walking the Yukon: A Solo Trek Through the Land of Beyond*. Camden ME: Ragged Mountain Press, 1993.

———. *World Mountain Ranges: Scotland*. Milnthorpe, UK: Cicerone Press, 2010.

Townsend, Chris, and Annie Aggens. *Encyclopedia of Outdoor and Wilderness Skills*. Camden ME: Ragged Mountain Press, 2003.

Turner, Frederick. *John Muir: Rediscovering America*. Cambridge MA: Perseus, 2000.

U.S. Department of Agriculture, Agricultural Research Service. *USDA National Nutrient Database for Standard Reference, Release 16-1*. www.nal.usda.gov/fnic/foodcomp. 2004.

Vickery, Jim Dale. *Wilderness Visionaries: Leopold, Thoreau, Muir, Olson, Murie, Service, Marshall, Rutstrum*. Minocqua WI: NorthWord Press, 1994.

Waterman, Laura, and Guy Waterman. *Backwoods Ethics: Environmental Issues for Hikers and Campers*. 2nd ed. rev. Woodstock VT: Countryman, 1993.

———. *Forest and Crag: A History of Hiking, Trail Blazing and Adventure in the Northeast Mountains*. Boston: Appalachian Mountain Club, 2003.

———. *Wilderness Ethics: Preserving the Spirit of Wildness*. Woodstock VT: Countryman, 1993.

Welch, Thomas R., and Timothy P. Welch. "Giardiasis as a Threat to Backpackers in the United States: A Survey of State Health Departments." *Wilderness and Environmental Medicine* 6 (1995): 162–66.

Wilkerson, James A., ed. *Medicine for Mountaineering and Other Wilderness Activities*. 5th ed. Seattle: Mountaineers, 2001.

Wright, Peter. *Ribbon of Wildness: Discovering the Watershed of Scotland*. Edinburgh: Luath Press, 2010.

resources

PERIODICALS

Backcountry Magazine, 802-644-6606, http://www.backcountrymagazine.com

Backpacker, 800-666-3434, http://www.backpacker.com

Explore: Canada's Outdoor Magazine, 416-599-2000, http://www.explore-mag.com

Outdoor Photographer, 800-283-4410, 310-820-1500, http://www.outdoorphotographer.com

Outside, 800-678-1131, 515-246-6917, http://www.outsideonline.com

TGO The Great Outdoors, 44-0141-302-7736, http://www.tgomagazine.co.uk

ORGANIZATIONS

American Avalanche Association, 970-946-0822, http://www.americanavalancheassociation.org

American Hiking Society, 800-972-8608, http://www.americanhiking.org

American Long Distance Hiking Association–West, http://www.aldhawest.org

American Mountain Guide Association, 303-271-0984, http://www.amga.com

Appalachian Long Distance Hikers Association, http://www.aldha.org

Appalachian Mountain Club, 800-372-1758, http://www.outdoors.org

Appalachian Trail Conservancy, 304-535-6331, http://www.appalachiantrail.org

Arizona Trail Association, 602-252-4794, http://www.aztrail.org

The Backpackers Club, http://www.backpackersclub.co.uk

Bureau of Land Management, 202-208-3801, http://www.blm.gov

Canadian Avalanche Center/Canadian Avalanche Association, 250-837-2141, http://www.avalanche.ca

Canadian Parks and Wilderness Society, 800-333-WILD (800-333-9453), http://www.cpaws.org

Centers for Disease Control and Prevention, Travelers' Health Hotline, 800-CDC-INFO (800-232-4636), http://wwwnc.cdc.gov/travel

The Colorado Trail Foundation, 303-278-3177, http://www.coloradotrail.org

Continental Divide Trail Alliance, 303-838-3760, http://www.cdtrail.org

Continental Divide Trail Society, http://www.cdtsociety.org

Green Mountain Club (The Long Trail), 802-244-7037, http://www.greenmountainclub.org

Highpointers Club, http://www.highpointers.org

Leave No Trace, 800-332-4100, 303-442-8222, http://www.lnt.org

National Park Foundation, 202-354-6460, http://www.nationalparks.org

National Park Service, http://www.nps.gov

NOLS—National Outdoor Leadership School, 800-710-NOLS (800-710-6657), http://www.nols.edu

Outward Bound, 866-467-7651, 720-497-2340, http://www.outwardbound.org

Pacific Crest Trail Association, 916-285-1846, http://www.pcta.org

Pacific Northwest Trail Association, 877-854-9415, http://www.pnt.org

Sierra Club, 415-977-5500, http://www.sierraclub.org

Tom Brown's Tracker School, 609-242-0350, http://www.trackerschool.com

USDA Forest Service, 800-832-1355, http://www.fs.fed.us

Wilderness Medical Associates, 888-WILD-MED, http://www.wildmed.com

Wilderness Medicine Institute, 866-831-9001, http://www.nols.edu/wmi

Wilderness Society, 800-THE-WILD (800-843-9453), http://www.wilderness.org

Wildlands Network, 877-554-5234 x 702, http://www.twp.org

Yellowstone to Yukon Conservation Initiative, 403-609-2666 (Canada), http://www.y2y.net

MAPS

Appalachian Mountain Club, 800-262-4455, http://www.amcstore.outdoors.org

Backcountry Navigator, 360-216-1017, http://www.backcountrynavigator.com

DeLorme, 800-561-5105, http://www.delorme.com

Earthwalk Press (available at http://www.boredfeet.com, http://www.omnimap.com, and other outlets)

East View Maplink, 800-962-1394, http://www.maplink.com

Fresh Tracks Maps, http://www.freshtracksmaps.com

Fugawi, 416-920-9300, http://www.fugawi.com

Green Trails Maps, http://www.greentrails.com

Map Adventures, 207-879-4777, http://www.mapadventures.com

Map Tech, 877-587-9004, http://maptech.mytopo.com

MapTools, 650-529-9410, http://www.maptools.com

Nat Geo Maps (Topo!, Trails Illustrated), 800-962-1643, http://www.natgeomaps.com

Sylvan TopoPhone, 505-758-7712, http://www.sylvanascent.com

Tom Harrison Maps, 415-456-7940, http://www.tomharrisonmaps.com

Trails.com, http://www.trails.com

US Topo Maps, http://nationalmap.gov/ustopo/index.html

ViewRanger, 44-1223-421-356, http://www.viewranger.com

WEB SITES

Adventure Alan's Ultralight Backpacking, http://www.adventurealan.com

American Trails, http://www.americantrails.org

America's Roof, http://www.americasroof.com

TheBackpacker.com, http://www.thebackpacker.com

BackpackGearTest.org, http://www.backpackgeartest.org

Backpacking Light, http://www.backpackinglight.com

Backpacking Lightweight, http://www.backpacking.net

Classic Camp Stoves, http://www.spiritburner.com

Gpsinformation.net, http://www.gpsinformation.net

GORP—Great Outdoor Recreation Pages, http://www.gorp.com

Peakbaggers, http://www.peakbaggers.com

Ryan Jordan, http://www.ryanjordan.com

TrailQuest, http://www.trailquest.net

Ultimate Backpacking Gear Weight Calculator, http://www.chrisibbeson.com/U/index.php

Wings, The Homemade Stove Archives, http://wings.interfree.it/html/main.html

Zen Backpacking Stoves, http://www.zenstoves.net

BLOGS

There are hundreds of outdoor blogs, far more than any one person can follow. Here I've listed my favorites of those I've read, plus my own.

Alan Sloman's Big Walk, http://alansloman.blogspot.com

Canoe in the Mist, http://canoeinthemist.blogspot.com

Chris Townsend Outdoors, http://www.christownsendoutdoors.com

Helen's Wondering Wanderings, http://helenswonderings.blogspot.com

Hiking in Finland, http://www.hikinginfinland.com

Mungo Says Bah!, http://www.mungosaysbah.com

Must Be This Way, http://www.andyhowell.info/trek-blog

The New Nomads, http://www.thenewnomads.com

The Pain Cave, http://desertpaincave.blogspot.com

PTC*, http://www.petesy.co.uk

Ryan Jordan, http://www.ryanjordan.com/blog

Section Hiker, http://www.sectionhiker.com

Self Powered, http://selfpowered.blogspot.com

Thunder in the Night, http://thunderinthenight.blogspot.com

The Wilderness World of Cameron McNeish, http://www.cameronmcneish.co.uk

EQUIPMENT COMPANIES

Outdoor companies mentioned in the book are listed here, along with some others that offer interesting products. Companies move, get taken over, and go out of business, of course, so this list is only a guide. Some companies sell products from other brands. Here I've listed their own label gear.

1000 Mile, 44-01923-242-233, sales@1000mile.co.uk, http://www.1000mile.co.uk
Socks

Aarn Design, 64-3-388-1979, aarndesign@paradise.net.nz, http://www.aarnpacks.com
Packs, tents

Acorn, 877-412-7467, http://www.acornearth.com
Fleece socks

ACR Electronics, 954-981-3333, http://www.acrelectronics.com
PLBs (personal locator beacons)

Adidas USA, 800-448-1796, consumer.relations@adidas.com, http://www.adidas.com/us
Footwear

Advance Chemicals, 877-533-3901, http://www.advancechemicals.ca
Pristine water treatment

Adventure Medical Kits, 510-261-7414, questions@adventuremedicalkits.com, http://www.adventuremedicalkits.com
Medical kits and more

Alico Sport, 39-0423-688-556, info@alicosport.it, http://www.alicosport.it
Footwear

All-Weather Safety Whistle Co., 314-436-3332, stormwhistles@stormwhistles.com, http://www.stormwhistles.com
Whistles

Alpina Sports Corp., info@alpinasports.com, http://www.alpinasports.com
Ski touring equipment, Rottefella bindings, Crispi boots

ALPS Mountaineering, 800-344-2577, sales@alpsmountaineering.com, http://www.alpsmountaineering.com
Packs, tents, sleeping bags, sleeping pads

Alt-Berg, 44(0)-1748-826922, info@altberg.co.uk, http://www.altberg.co.uk
Boots

Annie's, 800-288-1089, http://www.annies.com
Pasta meals and other food

AntiGravity Gear, 910-794-3308, customerservice@antigravitygear.com, http://www.antigravitygear.com
Ultralight gear, especially stoves, cozies, and cookware

Aquamira, 360-306-5586, sales@aquamira.com, http://www.aquamira.com
Water treatment

Aquapac, 866-929-0639, info@aquapac.net, http://www.aquapac.net
Waterproof pouches

Aquaseal, 360-794-8250, staydry@aquaseal.com, http://www.aquaseal.com
Waterproofing products

Arc'teryx Equipment, 866-458-BIRD (866-458-2473), http://www.arcteryx.com
Packs, clothing

Asolo USA, 603-448-8827, asolousa@gmail.com, http://www.asolo.com
Footwear

Atlas Snow-Shoe Co., 800-985-8012, http://www.atlassnowshoe.com
Snowshoes

Atwater Carey, c/o Wisconsin Pharmacal, 800-558-6614, info@pharmacalway.com, http://www.pharmacalway.com
First-aid kits, hand sanitizer, insect repellent, water treatment

Avon, http://shop.avon.com
Skin-So-Soft insect repellent

Backpackers' Cache, 559-732-3785, http://www.backpackerscache.com
Bear-resistant containers

Backpacker's Pantry, 800-641-0500, info@backpackerspantry.com, http://www.backpackerspantry.com
Food, Outback Ovens

Backpacking Light, http://www.backpackinglight.com
Clothing, tarp and accessories, cookware

Backpacking Light UK, 44(0)-01684-576423, http//www.backpackinglight.co.uk
Tarps, lightweight equipment

Badger Balm, 603-357-2958, custserv@badgerbalm.com, http://www.badgerbalm.com
Anti-bug balm

Baffin, 800-387-5858, http://www.baffin.com
Insulated boots

BakePacker, 866-576-0642, info@bakepacker.com, http://www.bakepacker.com
Baking accessory

Baldas, info@caribou.ca, http://www.baldas.caribou.ca
Snowshoes

Bear Valley, Intermountain Trading Co., 800-323-0042, customerservice@mealpack.com, http://www.mealpack.com
Energy bars

BearVault, 866-301-3442, sales@bearvault.com, http://www.bearvault.com
Bear canisters

Berghaus, 44-1254-277247, http://www.berghaus.com
Packs, clothing, footwear

Beyond, 800-741-3369, connect@beyondclothing.com, http://www.beyondclothing.com
Clothing

Big Agnes, 877-554-8975, http://www.bigagnes.com
Sleeping bags, tents, self-inflating pads, trekking poles

Big Sky International, 888-535-7085, 307-224-4500, info@bigskyinternational.com, http://www.bigskyproducts.com
Shelters

Black Diamond Equipment, 801-278-5533, climb@bdel.com, ski@bdel.com, mountain@bdel.com, http://www.blackdiamondequipment.com
Tents, trekking poles, packs, LED headlamps, ski touring and climbing gear, accessories

The Boilerwerks, devin@theboilerwerks.com, http://www.theboilerwerks.com
Backcountry Boiler lightweight chimney kettle

Bollé, 800-423-3537, http://www.bolle.com
Sunglasses, goggles

Boreal, 34-965-800-589, info@e-boreal.com, http://www.e-boreal.com/us
Footwear

Bozeman Mountain Works, http://www.bozemanmountainworks.com
Quilts, bivy bags, self-inflating pads, tarps, clothing, accessories

Brasher, 44(0)-191-516-5780, info@brasher.co.uk, http://www.brasher.co.uk
Footwear, socks

Brasslite, 267-307-4585, aaron@brasslite.com, http://www.brasslite.com
Alcohol stoves

Brooks-Range Mountaineering, 510-797-7980, info@brooks-range.com, http://www.brooks-range.com
Clothing, shelters, sleeping bags, snow shovels, accessories

Brunton, 800-443-4871, 307-857-4700, info@bruntongroup.com, http://www.bruntonoutdoor.com
Compasses, solar chargers, binoculars, lighting, altimeters, weather stations

Buck Knives, 800-326-2825, pfstore@buckknives.com, http://www.buckknives.com
Knives

Buff, 707-569-9009, buff@buff.us, http://www .buff.us
Headgear

Buffalo Systems, 44-0114-258-0611, info@ buffalosystems.co.uk, http://www.buffalo systems.co.uk
Clothing

Bushbuddy, 250-234-3919, traveler@ bushbuddy.ca, http:// www.bushbuddy.ca
Wood-burning stoves

CamelBak, 800-767-8725, 707-792-9700, product@camelbak.com, http://www.camelbak.com
Hydration systems

Campingaz, 44-(0)1275-845-024, consumerservices@ colemanuk.co.uk, http:// www.campingaz.com
Canister stoves, lanterns, fuel

Campmor, 888-226-7667, http://www.campmor.com
Outdoor equipment and clothing

C.A.M.P USA, 303-465-9429, climbing@camp-usa .com, http://www.camp-usa.com
Ice axes, crampons, trekking poles, packs, clothing, climbing gear

Caribou Mountaineering, 800-824-4153, 361-668-3766, caribou@granderiver.net, http://www.caribou.com
Packs, sleeping bags

Cascade Designs, 206-505-9500, consumer@ cascadedesigns.com, http://www.cascade designs.com
Therm-a-Rest sleeping pads, sleeping bags, MSR stoves and equipment, Platypus bottles and hydration systems, SealLine sacks, Tracks staffs

Casio, 800-836-8580, http://www.casio.com
Altimeter watches

Chaco, 888-211-1908, http://www.chacousa.com
Sandals and shoes

Chuck Roast Equipment, custserv@chuckroast.com, http://www.chuckroast .com
Fleece clothing

CiloGear, 503-305-3858, ciloinfo@gmail.com, http://www.cilogear.com
Packs

Clamcleat, 44-(0)1707-330101, http://www .clamcleat.com
Line-Loks

Cleanwaste, 877-520-0999, http://www.thepett .com
Human waste disposal products

Clikstand, 530-386-7873, info@clikstand.com, http://www.clikstand.com
Stove stands, windscreens

Cloudveil, 877-255-8345, cloud@cloudveil.com, http://www.cloudveil.com
Clothing

Cocoon by Design Salt, 800-254-7258, cocoon@ cocoonusa.com, http:// www.designsalt.com
Cotton and silk sleeping bag liners

Coghlan's, 877-264-4526, coghlans@coghlans.mb .ca, http://www.coghlans .com
Accessories

Coleman, 800-835-3278, http://www.coleman.com
Stoves, packs, sleeping bags, tents, footwear, accessories

Columbia Sportswear, 800-MA-BOYLE (800-622-6953), http://www .columbia.com
Clothing, footwear

Conform'able, http:// www.conform-able.com
Footbeds

Crazy Creek Products, 406-446-3446, http:// www.crazycreek.com
Camping chairs, sleeping pads

Crispi, http://www.crispi usa.com
Footwear

Crumpler, 718-384-3020, us_enquiries@crumpler .com, http://www .crumpler.com/us
Camera bags

Crux, 33-(0)965-27-48-58, carol@odl.uk.com, http://www.crux.uk.com
Tents, packs, sleeping bags, shell clothing, down clothing

Cutter, http://www.cutter insectrepellents.com
Insect repellents

Dahlgren, 888-870-1156, info@dahlgrenfootwear .com, http://www.dahl grenfootwear.com
Socks

Danner, 877-4DANNER (877-432-6637), info@ danner.com, http://www .danner.com
Footwear

Dave Page, Cobbler, 800-252-1229, http:// www.davepagecobbler .com
Footwear resoling and repairs

Devold, 800-433-8653, sales@devoldusa.com, http://www.devold.com Wool base layers, sweaters, and socks

DMM Climbing, 801-942-8471, xcalibur@mindspring.com, http://www.dmmclimbing.com Ice axes, crampons, climbing equipment

Doan Firestarter, 216-932-6243, http://www.doanfirestarter.com Magnesium fire-starting tool

Dr. Bronner's Magic All-One, 877-786-3649, info@drbronner.com, http://www.drbronner.com Liquid soap

Duofold, 800-994-4348, http://www.duofold.com Base layers

Duracell, 800-551-2355, http://www.duracell.com Flashlights, batteries

Eagle Creek, 800-874-1048, http://www.eaglecreek.com Travel packs, duffel bags, accessory pouches

Eastern Mountain Sports, 888-463-6367, http://www.ems.com Outdoor gear retailer

Easton Technical Products, 801-539-1400, tubeinfo@eastontp.com, http://www.eastonpoles.com Tent poles and stakes

Ecover, 800-449-4925, http://www.ecover.com Ecological washing and cleaning products

Energizer, 800-383-7323, http://www.energizer.com Lithium AA and AAA batteries, flashlights

Enertia Trail Foods, 877-ENERTIA (877-363-7842), sales@trailfoods.com, http://www.trailfoods.com Food

EnLIGHTened equipment, enlightenedequipment@charter.net, http://www.enlightenedequipment.webs.com Quilts

Equinox, 877-322-5909, explore@equinoxltd.com, http://www.equinoxltd.com Ultralight packs, pouches, tarps, bivies, ground cloths, more

Esatto, 866-372-8861, http://www.esatto.biz Custom hiking boots

Etowah Outfitters, http://www.etowahoutfitters ultralightbackpackinggear.com Tarps, solid fuel, alcohol stoves, accessories

Eureka!, 262-631-6600, http://www.eurekatent.com Tents, sleeping bags, lighting

eVent, 800-391-0696, info@eventfabrics.com, http://www.eventfabrics.com eVent fabrics

Evernew, 323-266-6212, sales@evernewamerica.com, http://www.evernewamerica.com Cookwear, stove, utensils

EWS, 320-253-4573, skipulk@yahoo.com, http://www.skipulk.com Ski pulks

Exped, 866-326-4586, service@exped.com, http://www.exped.com Tents, sleeping bags, sleeping mats, bivy bags, packs, trekking poles

Feathered Friends, 888-308-9365, customerservice@featheredfriends.com, www.featheredfriends.com Down sleeping bags, clothing, and accessories

Fenix, www.fenixlight.com LED flashlights and headlamps

Ferrino, info@caribou.ca, www.ferrino.caribou.ca Packs, tents, sleeping bags, clothing

Finisterre, 44-(0)1872-554481, info@finisterreuk.com, http://www.finisterreuk.com Clothing

Fischer Skis US, 603-314-7110, http://www.fischerskis.com Ski touring equipment

Fisher Space Pen, 702-293-3011, weborders@spacepen.com, http://www.spacepen.com Pens

Five Ten, 909-798-4222, http://www.fiveten.com Footwear

Forty Below, 253-846-2081, support@40below.com, http://www.40below.com Overboots, insulated booties, clothing, accessories

Four Seasons Survival, 814-234-0698, http://fourseasonssurvival.3dcartstores.com Spark-Lite fire starters

Fox River, http://www
.foxsox.com
Socks

Freeloader, 44-(0)1684-
774000, http://www
.solartechnology.com
Solar chargers

Freshette, 800-542-5580,
sanifem@aol.com, http://
www.freshette.com
Female urinary director

Frogg Toggs, 800-349-
1835, info@froggtoggs
.com, http://www.frogg
toggs.com
Rain clothing

G3 Genuine Guide Gear,
service@genuineguide
gear.com, http://www
.genuineguidegear.com
Snow shovels, ski touring
gear

Gabel USA, 450-263-8813,
info@gabelsport.com,
http://www.gabel.it
Trekking poles

Garmin International,
913-397-8200, http://www
.garmin.com
GPS

Garmont USA, info@
garmontusa.com, http://
www.garmontusa.com
Footwear, Bridgedale
socks, Life-Link poles

General Ecology, 800-441-
8166; info@generalecology
.com, http://www.general
ecology.com
Water purifiers, including
First Need

Gerber, 866-348-5661,
http://www.gerberuk.com
Knives, multitools,
flashlights

GoLite, 888-546-5483,
http://www.golite.com
Shelters, packs, sleeping
bags, clothing

GoLite Footwear, 877-
610-8870, http://www
.golite-footwear.com
Footwear

Gore, 800-GORE-TEX
(800-467-3839), http://
www.gore.com
Gore-Tex fabrics

Gossamer Gear, 512-374-
0133, info@gossamegear
.com, http://www
.gossamergear.com
Shelters, packs, sleeping
pads, trekking poles

Joby, 888-569-JOBY (888-
569-5629), info@joby
.com, http://www.joby
.com
Flexible tripods
(GorillaPods)

Granger's, 44-1773-521-
521, info@grangers.co.uk,
http://www.grangers.co.uk
Waterproofing and
cleaning products

Granite Gear, http://www
.granitegear.com
Packs, tarps

Gregory Packs, 877-477-
4292, customerservice@
gregorypacks.com, http://
www.gregorypacks.com
Packs

Grivel, 800-366-
2666, http://www.
libertymountain.com,
http://www.grivel.com
Ice axes, crampons

GSI Outdoors, 800-
704-4474, contact@
gsioutdoors.com, http://
www.gsioutdoors.com
Cookware and accessories

Hagan Skis, www.hagan-
ski.com
Backcountry ski
equipment

Haglöfs, 46-(0)226-67-
000, haglofs@hglofs.se,
http://www.haglofs.com/
en-US
Packs, sleeping bags,
clothing, footwear

Harvest Foodworks,
800-268-4268, thefolks@
harvestfoodworks.com,
http://www.harvestfood
works.com
Food

Helly Hansen, 800-435-
5901, http://www.helly
hansen.com
Clothing

Helsport, http://www
.helsport.no
Tents, sleeping bags,
packs, clothing

Hennessey Hammock,
888-539-2930, info@
hennessyhammock
.com, http://www
.hennessyhammock.com
Hammocks and
accessories

Highgear, help@4implus
.com, http://www.high
gear.com
Electronic altimeters

Hikelight.com, 800-933-
4453, hikelight@yahoo
.com, http://www.hike
light.com
Ultralight equipment,
backpacking videos

Hilleberg USA, 866-
848-8368, tentmaker@
hilleberg.com, http://www
.hilleberg.com
Tents

Hillsound, 604-876-2555,
kris@hillsound.ca, http://
www.hillsound.com
Lightweight crampons

Hi-Tec Sports USA, 800-
521-1698, http://www
.hi-tec.com
Footwear

Hyperlite Mountain Gear, 800-HMG-9208 (800-464-9208), info@ hyperlitemountaingear .com, http://www.hyper litemountaingear.com Shelters, packs, accessories

Ibex Outdoor Clothing, 800-773-9647, info@ ibexwear.com, http:// www.ibexwear.com Wool clothing

IceBox, 866-772-2107, iglooinfo@grandshelters .com, http://www.grand shelters.com Igloo-building tool

Icebreaker, 866-363-7466, cs@icebreaker.com, http:// www.icebreaker.com Merino wool clothing

Idahoan, 800-746-7999, http://www.idahoan.com Instant potato meals

Industrial Revolution, 888-297-6062, info@ industrialrev.com, http:// www.industrialrev.com/ uco UCO candle lanterns, accessories

Inka Pen, 800-678-6483, info@niteize.com, http:// www.writeanywhere.com Write anywhere pen

Inova, 800-678-6483, info@niteize.com, http:// www.inovalight.com LED flashlights

Inov-8, 508-480-8856, sales@inov8.us, http:// www.inov8.com Ultralight footwear

Integral Designs, 303-926-7228, info@ integraldesigns.com, http://www.integral designs.com Shelters, accessories

Isis, 866-875-8689, info@ isisforwomen.com, http:// www.isisforwomen.com Women's clothing

Jacks 'R' Better, 800-595-0413, 757-643-8908, thejacks@jacksrbetter .com, http://www.jacksr better.com Quilts, hammock accessories

Jack Wolfskin, 49-6126-954-0, http://www .jack-wolfskin.com Packs, tents, sleeping bags, clothing, footwear

Jandd Mountaineering, 760-597-9030, custsrv@ jandd.com, http://www .jandd.com Packs

JanSport, 510-614-4000, http://www.jansport.com Packs

Jetboil, 888-611-9905, customerservice@jetboil .com, http://www.jetboil .com Cooking systems and accessories

Julbo, 802-651-0833, info@julbousa.com, http:// www.julbousa.com Sunglasses, goggles

K2 Skis, 800-985-2189, http://www.k2skis.com Backcountry ski equipment

Kahtoola, 866-330-8030, info@kahtoola.com, http://www.kahtoola.com Lightweight crampons, Microspikes, snowshoes

Katadyn, 800-755-6701, http://www.katadyn.com Water treatment, Optimus stoves, Trek'n'Eat food

Kayland, 603-758-6486, info@kaylandusa.com, http://us.kayland.com Footwear

Keen, 866-676-KEEN (866-676-5336), http:// www.keenfootwear.com Footwear, socks

Kelty, 800-535-3589, http://www.kelty.com Packs, shelters, sleeping bag, sleeping pads

Kenyon, 401-792-3704, kcp@kenyonconsumer .com, http://www.kenyon consumer.com Camping accessories, thermal underwear

Kershaw Knives, 503-682-1966, http://www.kershaw knives.com Knives

Kestrel Meters, 800-891-8493, info@kestrelmeters .com, http://www.kestrel meters.com Weather meters

Kick Ass Quilts, http:// www.arrowhead equipment.webs.com/ kickassquilts.htm Quilts

Kifaru International, 800-222-6139, angie@kifaru .net, http://www.kifaru.net Shelters, packs, sleeping bags

Kinesis Photo Gear, 888-716-5550, http://www .kgear.com Camera bags and accessories

Lafuma USA, http://www .lafumausa.com Clothing, footwear, packs, sleeping bags

La Sportiva North America, 303-443-8710, custserv@sportiva.com, http://www.lasportiva usa.com
Footwear

Lawson Outdoor Equipment (Mountainfitter), info@ mountainfitter.com, http://www.lawson equipment.com
Cuben Fiber tarps and dry bags, accessories

LazerDesigns.com, 877-365-2737, info@ lazerdesigns.com, http:// www.asplights.com
Micro flashlights, ASP Lights

Leki, 800-291-2161, http:// www.leki.com
Hiking poles

Lifeventure, 44-(0)118-981-1433, customer .services@lifeventure .co.uk, http://www .lifeventure.co.uk
Dry sacks, accessories

Light My Fire, 888-297-6062, http://www.lightmy fireusa.com
Swedish FireSteel, sporks, kitchen items

Lightwave, 33-(0)965-27-48-58, carol@odl.uk.com, http://www.lightwave .uk.com
Lightweight packs, tents

Limmer Boot, 603-694-BOOT (603-694-2668), http://www.limmerboot .com
Boots, including custom-made

L.L. Bean, 800-441-5713, http://www.llbean.com
Outdoor gear, clothing

Loksak, 800-355-1126, customerservice@loksak .com, http://www.loksak .com
Water-, odor-, dust-, and humidity-proof bags

Lowa, http://www.lowa boots.com
Footwear

Lowe Alpine, 877-888-8533, lowecs@lowealpine .com, http://www .lowealpine-usa.com
Packs

Lowepro, 707-827-4000, http://www.lowepro.com
Camera bags

Lowrance, http://www .lowrance.com
GPS

LuxuryLite, 979-798-2248, sales@luxurylite .com, http://www .luxurylite.com
Packs, sleeping bags, stove system, hiking poles

Lynne Whelden Gear, lwgear@juno.com, http:// www.lwgear.com
Lightweight packs and shelters

Madshus, http://www .madshus.com
Backcountry ski equipment

Magellan, http://www .magellangps.com
GPS systems

Maglite, 909-947-1006, http://www.maglite.com
Flashlights

Mammut Sports Group USA, 802-985-5056, http:// www.mammut.ch
Packs, sleeping bags, clothing, footwear, headlamps

Mango, 845-258-9903, info@mangoenergy.com, http://www.mangoenergy .com
Power Traveller's Powermonkey electronic chargers

Manzella, 800-645-6837, info@manzella.com, http://www.manzella.com
Gloves

Marmot, 888-357-3262, http://www.marmot.com
Sleeping bags, tents, packs, clothing

Mary Janes Farm, 888-750-6004, iris@ maryjanesfarm.org, http:// www.maryjanesfarm.org
Dried meals, organic food

McHale Packs, 206-533-1479, http://www .mchalepacks.com
Custom-made packs

McNett, 360-671-2227, http://www.mcnett-out door.com
Water treatment, waterproofing, repair kits, seam seal

Merrell, 800-288-3124, http://www.merrell.com
Footwear

MKettle, 503-468-4160, info@mkettle.com, http:// www.mkettle.com
Lightweight chimney kettle

Moleskine, 888-822-1036, http://www.moleskineus .com
Notebooks

Montane, 44(0)-1670-522-300, http://www .montane.co.uk
Clothing

MontBell, http://www .montbell.us
Packs, tents, sleeping bags, clothing

Montrail, 855-MY-TRAIL (855-698-7245), http://www.montrail.com Footwear

Moonbow Gear, 603-744-2264, info@moonbowgear.com, http://www.moonbowgear.com Packs, tents, tarps, bivy bags, clothing, accessories

Mountain Equipment UK, 44-161-366-5020, http://www.mountain-equipment.co.uk Sleeping bags, tents, clothing

Mountain Hardwear, http://www.mountainhardwear.com Tents, sleeping bags, packs, clothing

Mountain House, 800-547-0244, http://www.mountainhouse.com Food

Mountain Laurel Designs, 540-588-1721, http://www.mountainlaureldesigns.com Shelters, packs, bivy bags, cookware, accessories

Mountainsmith, 800-551-5889, http://www.mountainsmith.com Packs, tents, sleeping bags, trekking poles

Mountain Tools, 831-620-0911, http://www.mountaintools.com Super gaiters, climbing equipment

MSR (see Cascade Designs) Stoves, tents, snowshoes, cooksets, water treatment

Mystery Ranch, 406-585-1428, http://www.mysteryranch.com Packs

Nalgene, 800-NALGE-CS, (800-625-4327), customer_service@nalgene.com, http://www.nalgene.com Water bottles

Nanok, 47-23-38-09-10, mail@nanok.no, http://www.nanok.no Sleeping bags, tents, clothing

NEOS Overshoe, 800-777-9021, http://www.overshoe.com Overshoes

New Balance, 800-253-7463, customerhelp@newbalance.com, http://www.newbalance.com Footwear

Nextec, 203-422-0590, http://www.nextec.com EPIC fabric

Nike, 800-344-6453, http://www.nike.com Footwear, clothing

Nikwax North America, 800-563-3057, inquiries@nikwax.com, http://www.nikwax-usa.com Waterproofing and cleaning products, insect repellent

No-Rinse, 800-223-9348, http://www.norinse.com Washing products

Northern Lites, 800-360-LITE (800-360-5483), snowshoe@northernlites.com, http://www.northernlites.com Snowshoes

The North Face, 866-715-3223, http://www.thenorthface.com Tents, sleeping bags, packs, clothing, footwear

NPower PEG, 888-214-3137, http://www.npowerpeg.com Personal energy generator

Nunatak, 866-NUNATAK (866-686-2825), info@nunatakusa.com, http://www.nunatakusa.com Down quilts and clothing

Omega Pacific, 800-360-3990, info@omegapac.com, http://www.omegapac.com Ice axes

The OMM, http://www.theomm.com Packs, clothing, accessories

One Source Network, 888-381-2390, 770-381-2390, sales@osnusa.com, http://www.osnusa.net Velbon tripods

Open Country, http://www.opencountrycampware.com Cookware

Opinel USA, 860-451-9010, sales@opinel-usa.com, http://www.opinel-usa.com Knives

Optimus Stoves, http://www.optimusstoves.com Stoves, cookware

Organic Valley, 888-444-6455, organic@organicvalley.coop, http://www.organicvalley.coop Organic food

The Original Bug Shirt Co., 800-998-9096, 705-729-5620, mail@bugshirt.com, http://www.bugshirt.com Insect-proof clothing

Ortlieb USA, 800-649-1763, 253-833-3939, info@ortliebusa.com, http://www.ortliebusa.com Dry bags, waterbags

Ortovox USA, 801-886-8050, infousa@ortovox.com, http://www.ortovox.com
Wool clothing, packs, snow safety equipment

Osprey Packs, 866-284-7830, 970-564-5900, http://www.ospreypacks.com
Packs

Outdoor Designs, 800-366-2666, info@equipuk.com, http://www.libertymountain.com, http://www.outdoordesigns.co.uk
Shelters, gloves, gaiters, hats, accessories

Outdoor Equipment Supplier, brian@outdoorequipmentsupplier.com
MacCat Tarps, accessories

Outdoor Research, 888-467-4327, 206-467-8197, http://www.outdoorresearch.com
Bivy bags, clothing, accessories

Oware, 888-292-4534, http://www.owareusa.com
Tarps, bivy bags, clothing, accessories

Pacerpoles, 44-(0)7726-409992, http://www.pacerpoles.com
Pacerpoles

Pacific Outdoor Equipment, 406-586-5258, http://www.pacoutdoor.com
Sleeping pads, dry bags

The Packa, 276-780-2354, packa@thepacka.com, http://www.thepacka.com
Full-coverage backpacking rain parka

Páramo Directional Clothing Systems, 44-01892-786444, info@paramo.co.uk, http://www.paramo.co.uk
Clothing

Patagonia, 800-638-6464, customer_service@patagonia.com, http://www.patagonia.com
Clothing

Pelican Products, 800-473-5422, 310-326-4700, sales@pelican.com, http://www.pelican.com
Flashlights

Pertex, http://www.pertex.com
Fabrics

Petzl America, 801-926-1500, info@petzl.com, http://www.petzl.com/us
Headlamps, ice axes, crampons

PHD Mountain Software, 44-1423 781133, office@phdesigns.co.uk, http://www.phdesigns.co.uk
Down sleeping bags, clothing

Photon Light, 877-584-6898, custservice@photonlight.com, http://www.photonlight.com
LED flashlights

PODsacs, 44-(0)1773-601870, info@podsacs.com, http://www.podsacs.com
Packs, dry sacks

Polar Equipment, 408-867-4576, questions@polarequipment.com, http://www.polarequipment.com
Polar Pure water treatment

Polarmax, 800-552-8585, info@polarmax.com, http://www.polarmax.com
Base layers

Polartec, http://www.polartec.com
Clothing fabrics

Primus, 307-857-4700, info@bruntongroup.com, http://www.primuscamping.com
Stoves, cookware, lanterns, headlamps, tents, sleeping pads

Princeton Tec, 800-257-9080, 609-298-9331, info@princetontec.com, http://www.princetontec.com
Flashlights, headlamps

Prolite Gear, 406-582-0508, service@prolitegear.com, http://www.prolitegear.com
Tyvek, comprehensive range of lightweight equipment

Rab, 44 (0) 1773 601870, rabinfo@equipuk.com, http://www.rab.uk.com
Down sleeping bags, clothing, bivy bags

Rainy Pass Repair, 888-RIP-STOP (888-747-7867), 206-523-8135, repair@rainypass.com, http://www.rainypass.com
Equipment and clothing repairs

Ray Jardine's Adventure Page, http://www.rayjardine.com
Kits for quilts, tarps, packs, sleeping pads, books, videos

Rayovac, 800-237-7000, http://www.rayovac.com
Flashlights

RBH Designs, 860-231-7334, info@rbhdesigns.com, http://www.rbhdesigns.com
Vapor-barrier clothing and accessories

Redfeather Snowshoes, 800-525-0081, redfeather@ orcind.com, http://www .redfeather.com
Snowshoes

Reebok, 866-870-1743, http://www.reebok.com
Footwear, clothing

REI, 800-426-4840, 253-891-2500, http://www.rei .com
Outdoor retailer

Reliance Products, 800-665-0258, 204-633-4403, http://www.reliance products.com
Water treatment

Rite in the Rain, 253-922-5000, sales@riteintherain .com, http://www .riteintherain.com
All-weather notebooks, paper, and pens

Robens, http://www .robens.de
Tents, tarps, sleeping bags, sleeping pads

Rocky Boots, 877-795-2410, http://www.rocky boots.com
Boots, socks

Rohner, 41-(0)71-727-86-86, info@rohner-socks .com, http://www.rohner -socks.com
Socks

Royal Robbins, 800-587-9044, http:// www.royal robbins.com
Clothing

Salewa, 303-444-0446, info@salewa.us, http:// www.salewa.us
Footwear, clothing

Salomon, http://www .salomon.com
Footwear, packs, clothing, ski touring gear

Sanyo, http://www .us.sanyo.com
Eneloop rechargeable batteries

Satmap, 888-226-5430, info@satmap.com, http:// www.satmap.com
GPS

Sawyer Products, 800-356-7811, feedback@ sawyerproducts.com, http://www.sawyerprod ucts.com
Water treatment, insect protection, sun care, first aid

Scarpa North America, 303-998-2895, http:// www.scarpa.com
Boots

Sea to Summit, 303-440-8977, info@seatosummit .com, http://www .seatosummit.com
Sleeping bags, dry sacks, cooking utensils, hats, accessories

SealSkinz, 800-868-2629, sales@danalco.com, http:// www.danalco.com
Waterproof-breathable socks and gloves

Seventh Generation, 800-456-1191, http://www .seventhgeneration.com
Laundry products

Shelter Systems, 866-777-1066, 831-464-2002, eleanor@shelter-systems .com, http://www.shelter -systems.com
Grip clips

Sierra Designs, 800-736-8592, http://www.sierra designs.com
Tents, sleeping bags, packs, clothing

Sigg, 888-507-SIGG (888-507-7444), http://www .mysigg.com
Water bottles

Silva, 800-572-8822, http://www.silvacompass .com
Compasses

Six Moon Designs, 503-430-2303, http://www .sixmoondesigns.com
Ultralight packs, tents, tarps, bivy bags, rain gear

Slumberjack, 800-233-6283, slumberjack@ slumberjack.com, http:// www.slumberjack.com
Sleeping bags, sleeping pads, tents

SmartWool, customerservice@ smartwool.com, http:// www.smartwool.com
Wool socks and clothing

SMC, 800-426-6251, 360-366-5534, http:// www.smcgear.com
Ice axes, crampons, mountaineering gear

Snow Peak, 503-697-3330, http://www.snowpeak.com
Stoves, cookware, shelters, lanterns

SOG Knives, 425-771-6230, http://www.sog knives.com
Knives

Soto, info@sotooutdoors .com, http://www .sotooutdoors.com
Stoves, lanterns, cookware, accessories

Speer Hammocks, 252-619-8292, tttgear@gmail. com, http://www.speer hammocks.com
Hammocks

SportHill, 800-622-8444, http://www.sporthill.com
Clothing

SPOT, 866-OKI-SPOT (866-654-7768), marketing@findmespot .com, http://www .findmespot.com
Tracking and locating GPS satellite beacons

Stephenson's Warmlite, 603-293-7016, info@ warmlite.com, http:// www.warmlite.com Tents, down sleeping bags, down-filled sleeping pads, vapor-barrier clothing

Streamlight, 800-523-7488, 610-631-0600, cs@ streamlight.com, http:// www.streamlight.com Flashlights, headlamps

Stubai, 507-339-0336, cj@ stubaidirect.com, http:// www.stubaiusa.com Ice axes, crampons, mountaineering gear

Sub Zero, 44 (0)116-2402634, sales@subzero .co.uk, http://www .subzero.co.uk Base layer and midlayer clothing

Suluk 46°, 416-561-4733, info@suluk46.com, http:// www.suluk46.com Titanium equipment, bivy bags

SunDog, 800-672-9342, http://www.sundog.com Pouches, bags

Sun Precautions, 800-882-7860, http://www .sunprecautions.com Sun-protection clothing

Superfeet, 800-634-6618, customercare@superfeet. com, http://www. superfeet.com Footbeds

SureFire, 800-828-8809, helpyou@surefire.com, http://www.surefire.com Flashlights

Survitec, 904-562-5900, sales-sspi@survitecgroup .com, http://www .survitec-spi.com McMurdo PLBs (personal locator beacons)

Suunto, 800-543-9124, http://www.suunto.com Compasses, altimeter watches

Tamrac, 800-662-0717, info@zipshottripod.com, http://www.zipshottripod .com Camera bags, tripod

Tarptent, 650-587-1548, info@tarptent.com, http:// www.tarptent.com Shelters

Teko, 800-450-5784, info@tekosocks.com, http://www.tekosocks.com Socks

Tektite, 800-540-2814, http://www.tek-tite.com Flashlights

Tenba, 914-347-3300, info@tenba.com, http:// www.tenba.com Camera bags

Tenkara, 888-483-6527, info@tenkarausa.com, http://www.tenkarausa .com Fishing tackle

Terramar Sports, 914-934-8000, info@ terramarsports.com, http://www.terramar sports.com Base layers

Terra Nova, 44-(0)1773-833300, info@terra-nova .co.uk, http://www. terra-nova.co.uk Tents, bivy bags, extremities headwear, handwear, gaiters, accessories

Teva, 800-367-8382, http://www.teva.com Sandals, shoes

ThermoJet Stove, info@ thermojetstove.com, http://www.thermo jetstove.com Alcohol stove

Thorlo, 888-846-7567, http://www.thorlo.com Socks

Thru-Hiker, 415-462-1745, information@thru -hiker.com, http://www .thru-hiker.com Quilt kits, clothing kits, materials

Tiffen, 800-645-2522, techsupport@tiffen.com, http://www.tiffen.com Zing Designs neoprene camera bags

Tilley Endurables, 800-ENDURES (800-363-8737), tilley@tilley.com, http://www.tilley.com Hats, clothing

Timberland, 888-802-9947, http://www .timberland.com Footwear, clothing

Timberline Filters, 800-777-5996, aew@t-line .com, http://www.timber linefilters.com Water filters

Titanium Goat, info@ titaniumgoat.com, http:// www.titaniumgoat.com Ti-Tri Caldera stove system, bivy bags, trekking poles, packs, cookware, accessories

Toko, 41-(0)71-757- 73-73, info@toko.ch, http:// www.toko.ch Footwear care, ski wax

Tool Logic, 425-771-6230, 888-405-6433, toollogicsales@sogknives.com, http://www.sogshopping.com Knives, multitools

Tough Traveler, 800-GO-TOUGH (800-468-6844), service@toughtraveler.com, http://www.toughtraveler.com Child carriers, luggage

Trail Designs, info@traildesigns.com, http://www.traildesigns.com Caldera Cone stove systems, cookware, accessories

Tramplite, http://www.tramplite.com Ultralight packs

Trangia, 800-366-2666, info@trangia.se, http://www.trangia.se Stoves, cookware

Trekmates, 44-115-9409-176, sales@trekmates.co.uk, http://www.trekmates.co.uk Gore-Tex socks, clothing, sleeping pads, accessories

Tubbs Snowshoes, 800-987-1051, http://www.tubbssnowshoes.com Snowshoes

TyRy, 800-322-6325, info@tyry.com, http://www.tyry.com AlpineAire, Richmoor, and Natural High foods

U-Dig-It Enterprises, 208-939-8656 U-Dig-It trowel

Ultimate Direction, 866-Drink-Me (866-374-6563), http://www.ultimatedirection.com Hydration equipment

Ultimate Hats, 800-477-4287, info@ultimatehat.com, http://www.ultimatehat.com Hats

Ultralight Adventure Equipment (ULA), 435-753-5191, http://www.ula-equipment.com Packs, rain skirt

Uniross, 905-286-0648, http://www.uniross.com Ultra rechargeable batteries

Ursack, info@ursack.com, http://www.ursack.com Bear-resistant sacks and accessories

Ushba, 800-366-2666, http://www.ushba.com Ultralight ice ax, climbing equipment

Van Gorkom Custom Boots, 250-847-0412, vangorkomboots@gmail.com, http://www.hikingbootshandcrafted.com Custom-made hiking boots

Vargo, 877-932-8546, info@vargooutdoors.com, http://www.vargooutdoors.com Titanium stoves, cookware, stakes, utensils

Vasque, 800-224-HIKE (800-224-4453), customer.service@vasque.com, http://www.vasque.com Footwear

Vaude USA, 800-366-2666, http://www.vaudeusa.com Tents, sleeping bags, sleeping mats, packs, clothing

Vibram FiveFingers, 978-318-0000, http://www.vibramfivefingers.com Vibram FiveFingers footwear

Victorinox, 800-442-2706, http://www.swissarmy.com Swiss Army knives

ViewRanger, http://www.viewranger.com Mapping app for cell phones

Vitalyte, 800-283-6505, http://www.vitalyte.com Sports drink

Voile USA, 801-973-8622, info@voile-usa.com, http://www.voile-usa.com Backcountry ski equipment, snow shovels

Wenger, 800-267-3577, custsvc@wengerna.com, http://www.wengerna.com Swiss Army knives, Swiss watches, footwear, tents, packs, sleeping bags, water bottles

Western Mountaineering, http://www.westernmountaineering.com Down sleeping bags, clothing

Whirley Drink Works, 800-825-5575, http://www.whirleydrinkworks.com Insulated mugs

White Box Stoves, 406-551-4085, billinmt@yahoo.com, http://www.whiteboxstoves.com Alcohol stoves

Wiggy's, 866-411-6465, wiggys@wiggys.com, http://www.wiggys.com Sleeping bags, sleeping pads, packs, tents, clothing

Wigwam Mills, 920-783-1000, http://www.wigwam.com
Socks

Wild Ideas, 805-693-0550, info@wild-ideas.net, http://www.wild-ideas.net
Bearikade bear-resistant containers

Wild Things, 877-WTHINGS, sales@wildthingsgear.com, http://www.wildthingsgear.com
Packs

Wisconsin Pharmacal, 800-558-6614, info@pharmacalway.com, http://www.pharmacalway.com
Potable Aqua water treatment, Atwater Carey first-aid kits, Sting Eze

Wolverine Worldwide, 800-789-8586, http://www.wolverineworldwide.com
Footwear

Woolpower, 843-875-0240, info@gransfors.us, http://www.woolpower.se
Wool clothing

Woolrich, 800-966-5372, service@woolrich.com, http://www.woolrich.com
Clothing

X-Socks, 39-(0)37-67-18-611, customercare-it@x-bionic.com, http://www.x-socks.com
Socks

ZPacks, valesko@gmail.com, http://www.zpacks.com
Packs, shelters, accessories

ZZ Manufacturing, 800-594-9046, contact@wisementrading.com, http://www.zzstove.com
Sierra wood-burning stoves

metric conversions

LENGTH

1 mile = 5,280 feet = 1.61 kilometers
1 yard = 3 feet = 0.914 meter
1 foot = 12 inches = 30.48 centimeters
1 inch = 2.54 centimeters = 25.4 millimeters
0.5 inch = 12.7 millimeters
0.25 inch = 6.35 millimeters

WEIGHT

1 ounce = 28.35 grams
1 pound = 16 ounces = 453.6 grams
2.2 pounds = 1 kilogram

CAPACITY

(U.S. liquid measure)
1 fluid ounce = 2 tablespoons = 29.56 milliliters
1 gill = 4 ounces = 1 cup = 0.1 liter
1 cup = 16 tablespoons = 8 fluid ounces
   = 236 milliliters

1 pint = 16 fluid ounces = 2 cups = 0.5 liter
1 quart = 32 fluid ounces = 2 pints = 0.9 liter
1 gallon = 128 fluid ounces = 4 quarts = 3.8 liters

CAPACITY

(British imperial liquid and dry measure)
1 gill = 5 ounces = 142 cubic centimeters = 0.142 liter
1 pint = 4 gills = 568 cubic centimeters = 0.568 liter
1 quart = 2 pints = 4.5 liters
1 gallon = 4 quarts = 4.5 liters

TEMPERATURE

$°F = (°C \times 1.8) + 32$
$°C = (°F - 32) \times 0.555$

index